Praise for Th

"*The Angelical Languag*
written on the subject of the Enochian magical system and language of Elizabethan luminary, Dr. John Dee. This two-volume magnum opus demonstrates Aaron Leitch's familiarity with practical magic as well as his skill as a meticulous researcher. A must-have book."
—**CHIC CICERO AND SANDRA TABATHA CICERO,** Chief Adepts of the Hermetic Order of the Golden Dawn

"This extensive tome, ten years in the making, is a profound step in the evolution of magickal understanding. Though debate continues to surround the 'legitimacy' of Dee and Kelley's Enochian system, its influence on modern magick is undeniable. Aaron Leitch has taken it upon himself to deeply explore the ins and outs of the Angelical Language, examining its linguistics and origins with accuracy and an eye for detail. For serious practitioners interested in an approach to Enochia that is both scholarly and mystical, I can't suggest this book highly enough."
—**RAVEN DIGITALIS,** author of *Shadow Magick Compendium* and *Planetary Spells and Rituals*

"The most in-depth analysis of the Enochian alphabet and the Enochian language that has appeared to date."
—**DONALD TYSON,** author of *Necronomicon*

"Aaron Leitch is to be congratulated on producing what is surely by far the most lucid, thorough, practical, and coherent study of the apparently diverse workings of Dr. John Dee and Edward Kelley to date."
—**DAVID RANKINE AND SORITA D'ESTE,** authors of *Practical Elementary Magick*

"A tremendous amount of original research and creative effort have gone into this work, and it represents a fascinating—if difficult—study of the Angelic language from a specific individual's understanding of it, and is worthy of its competition. It is a deep, learned, and intense work, an Enochian scholar's tour de force of his subject."
—**OSBORNE PHILLIPS,** coauthor of *Planetary Magick* and *Mysteria Magica*

The

ANGELICAL LANGUAGE

About the Author

Aaron Leitch has been a scholar and spiritual seeker for over three decades. He is an ordained Gnostic Priest and a member of the Hermetic Order of the Golden Dawn, the Societas Rosicruciana in America, and the academic Societas Magica. His writings cover such varied fields as religion and mythology (from ancient Middle Eastern to Renaissance European), Solomonic mysticism, shamanism, Neoplatonism, Hermeticism and alchemy, traditional Wicca and Neopaganism, and more. He is the author of *Secrets of the Magickal Grimoires*, *The Angelical Language*, Volumes I and II, and the *Essential Enochian Grimoire*. He also has edited and/or contributed to various projects concerning the Western occult mysteries. Leitch and his wife cofounded Doc Solomon's Occult Curios, which caters to those exploring the old magick.

Visit his blog at AaronLeitch.wordpress.com, his Facebook @Kheph777, and Doc Solomon's at DocSolomons.com/wp/shop.

The *ANGELICAL LANGUAGE*

VOLUME II

An Encyclopedic Lexicon of the Tongue of Angels

BASED ON THE JOURNALS OF
DR. JOHN DEE AND EDWARD KELLEY

AARON LEITCH

LLEWELLYN
WOODBURY, MINNESOTA

Second Edition
First Printing, 2025

Cover design by Kevin R. Brown
Cover illustration © from Albrecht Dürer / SuperStock
Editing by Brett Fechheimer

Library of Congress Cataloging-in-Publication Data (Pending)
ISBN: 978-0-7387-8135-8

Llewellyn Publications
A Division of Llewellyn Worldwide, Ltd.
2143 Wooddale Drive
Woodbury, Minnesota 55125-2989, U.S.A.
www.llewellyn.com

Printed in China

FSC
www.fsc.org
MIX
Paper | Supporting responsible forestry
FSC™ C007683

Other books by Aaron Leitch

The Essential Enochian Grimoire:
An Introduction to Angel Magick from Dr. John Dee to the Golden Dawn
(Llewellyn)

Llewellyn's Complete Book of Ceremonial Magick:
A Comprehensive Guide to the Western Mystery Tradition (contributor)
(Llewellyn)

Secrets of the Magickal Grimoires:
The Classical Texts of Magick Deciphered
(Llewellyn)

Ritual Offerings (editor and contributor)
(self-published)

The Spirit-Magick of Abramelin
(self-published)

The Enochian Saga: Exploring the Angelic Journals of Dr. John Dee
(self-published)

A Course in the Tongue of Angels
(self-published)

Codex Septemgenius
(self-published)

Doc Solomon's Occult Calendar
(self-published)

Contents

Introduction to Volume II

The work you hold in your hands is the second volume of a massive study of the Angelical language as recorded by Dr. John Dee and Edward Kelley—two magicians who lived during the Elizabethan era in England. In the introduction to the first volume, I explained who these men were, so I will not go into such detail here. Suffice it to say they were two extremely important figures in Western mysticism and occultism, and their recorded journals have had a profound impact on nearly every Western esoteric tradition that has followed them.

What concerns us most in this work are the records of their encounters with various Angels. Dee was a meticulous journalist, and he recorded his Angelic séances in every detail, along with the details of his daily life with Kelley during the years they were most active in speaking with the Angels. Not only did these celestial beings relate hundreds of sermons on religious and mystical philosophy, but they transmitted an entire system of Angel magick along with details about their own native language.

This book is not about that system of magick (although some obscure details about it can be found in volume I of this work). Instead, this volume focuses entirely upon the Angelical language itself. As I described in the previous volume, this is the aspect of Dee's work that fascinated me the most as I delved ever deeper in my own studies of so-called "Enochian" magick. That is, as a mystic, I was excited by the prospect of being able to pray to and evoke the Angels via their own native tongue.

To this end, I gathered Dee's original journals—published as *Five Books of Mystery, A True and Faithful Relation of What Passed for Many Years Between Dr. John Dee . . . and Some Spirits*, and Dee's own personal grimoire including the *48 Claves Angelicae*—a collection of the forty-eight Angelical invocations Dee was supposed to use to open the Gates of Heaven and call out the Angels therefrom. I also gathered the best texts available about Dee's magickal system—such as Donald Laycock's *Complete Enochian Dictionary*, Geoffery James' *The Enochian Magick of Dr. John Dee*, and Donald Tyson's *Enochian Magic for Beginners*.

However, when I was fortunate enough to become involved with a group of accomplished Enochian scholars, I soon learned that all of the texts *about* Dee's system left much to be desired when it came to understanding the Angelical language. Most of them had been written by authors who had not studied Dee's original journals page by page, and thus did not entirely understand the context surrounding the language.

For example, both James and Laycock focused upon the Keys outlined in Dee's *48 Claves Angelicae*, with limited reference to Causabon's *A True and Faithful Relation*. However, neither author had studied *A True and Faithful Relation* exhaustively, and were thus unaware of several corrections to the Keys made by the Angels later in Dee's records. (And the *48 Claves* does not always preserve these corrections.)

Another shortcoming is found in the breakdown of the Angelical words themselves. Both Laycock (who happened to be a linguist) and James attempted to analyze the words based upon their understanding of modern linguistics—which led to some conflicts with Dee's journals. Most of these conflicts arose from their sometimes unsuccessful attempts to recognize compound words and separate them into their base elements. Laycock, for instance, has broken the word *Cnoqod* (unto his servants) into *C Noqod*. In his dictionary section, one can find an entry for *Noqod*, but none for the actual Angelical word *Cnoqod*. Meanwhile, there is no indication in Dee's records that *Cnoqod* is a compound at all.

Once these words were broken down in such a fashion, the next step made by both Laycock and James was to correct the base words. For an example, we might look at James' work on Key Four. Toward the end of this Key—in the original diaries—we find the word *Zirenaiad* (I am the Lord God). James has this listed as three distinct words: *Zir* (I am), *Enay* (the Lord), and *Iad* (God). While the base words are correct, you will notice that breaking them apart caused James to add a letter *y* to complete the word *Enay*. Neither James nor Laycock had yet discovered that letters are dropped in Angelical compounds when two base words end and begin with the same letter. Thus, the phrase *Zir Enay Iad* is combined by dropping the *y*[1] and forming the compound *Zirenaiad*. Such compound words must be preserved if we want to understand how Angelical works.

There are even several cases in which the authors have added words into the Keys where they seemed necessary. This mostly involved parts of speech or grammatical elements such as articles, adjectives, and pronouns—all of which are rare or absent from Angelical. Thus, the language tends to work like ancient tongues (such as Egyptian or biblical Hebrew), which played no part in James' and Laycock's studies of Angelical.

Most of the shortcomings of previous Angelical scholarship related to pronunciation. The Hermetic Order of the Golden Dawn made up their own system based loosely on modern Hebrew pronunciation—and Aleister Crowley followed suit. (Some today consider this "Golden Dawn Liturgical" Angelical.) Geoffrey James left the subject alone entirely, and simply included Dee's phonetic cues as they appear in the *48 Claves Angelicae*. (However, without a key to those notations, they are of little help to most students.)

Laycock went so far as to offer a guide to pronunciation. However, I found it less than useful because it gives "probable" pronunciations for the *letters of the alphabet* rather than for the phonetic elements that actually make up the words when spoken—such as letter combinations, digraphs, diphthongs, and syllables. Not only this, but the given pronunciations were based upon modern English, with some inclusions from modern Italian and other languages. Laycock does not appear to have drawn from Early Modern (or "Shakespearean") English and Middle

English—both of which have much more to do with Dee's Angelical pronunciation than modern languages.

The available work on Angelical has also ignored Dee's pronunciation notes in *A True and Faithful Relation*. I will explain these notes later in this work—however, at the time James and Laycock were writing, Dee's notes were still an enigma. No one had cracked the phonetic system Dee was using in those notes, and thus they were simply ignored.[2] This has led to the modern misconception that "correct pronunciations" do not exist for Angelical at all—yet Dee's notes make it fairly clear that they do, in fact, exist.

Finally, I could find no source for the comprehensive information necessary to learn the language in a practical sense. I needed every word along with its meaning, all of its spelling variations, its use of root words, the sentence from the Keys in which it is found, its numbered location in the Keys, and commentary about the mystical meanings behind the word. Therefore, I had no choice but to begin work on my own Angelical Lexicon.

Some may object to granting such attention to what might be a constructed language. From a non-mystical point of view, it is just as possible that Angelical is a cypher of some sort (akin to Trithemius' famous *Steganographia*), or even a complete hoax generated to cover politically sensitive information. Personally, I feel it is immaterial if the language is "real" or constructed. If it is real, then it is nothing short of miraculous that we have access to it. If it is not real, then its creation is a work of genius comparable to—or even surpassing—Tolkien's creation of Elvish. We might study Angelical as we would Orwell's Newspeak or Heinlein's Martian—although we are fortunate to have a much larger sample of Angelical than we do of these latter sources.

In fact, from both a mystical *and* an historical point of view, I believe that Dee's Angelical language is the true mystery language of the West. An Angel named Nalvage informed Dee that Angelical was preferred before Hebrew, which had long been considered the mystery language of the West. Then, Dee's grimoire—containing the *48 Claves Angelicae* (said to be invocations composed of the native tongue of the Angels)—became foundational to the Western Hermetic and esoteric traditions.

It influenced the Golden Dawn and all who followed. From the rediscovery of Dee's documents to today, the deeper mysteries of the language have been slowly opening to the light of day.

Many students have encountered "Enochian" magick (in some form) previously, only to find pages full of invocations and names in an alien language. Rumors of its power (or even danger) surround the subject matter, but straightforward explanations of *what it is* and *how it works* are lacking. The student may ultimately put the material away and simply leave others to specialize in the subject. However, the willing seeker no longer has to feel intimidated. The understanding of the Angelic material has expanded greatly, and new resources are now being made available for all students who might take an interest. This work is one of those resources.

Since beginning my in-depth study of the Angelical language, I have found it extremely useful in practical areas. Reciting the Keys with full comprehension of every word is a wonderful and powerful experience. Not to mention the fact that it makes the actual voicing of the Keys more precise, and much less labored or forced. When working with spirits and the art of summoning, it is amazing what can be accomplished when one issues commands in Angelical. Even more impressive are the results of addressing an Angel in his or her own language!

I believe it is important to discover the real nature of the language, exactly as first received by Dr. John Dee and Sir Edward Kelley. We should not try to force the language into preconceived molds before attempting to observe it upon its own terms. Therefore, the words in this Lexicon are presented as they are recorded in Dee's journals—with all later corrections, and no omissions, additions, or (most importantly) alterations based on modern languages.

I have always felt that a grassroots study of Dee's Angelical (rather than later half-understood recensions) would lead to further expansions of the language. This is why I have taken the time to illustrate each word with all of its variations, to break down the elements of compounds, and discover the root words at their hearts. From these, along with a better understanding of Angelical grammar, we might go far in expanding the Lexicon.

With that in mind, know that this work is *not* offered as definitive of the Angelical language, but merely as a study aid for further research. This leaves a great amount of work and experience to be achieved by every individual student. I have presented the material as the Celestial Language of power that I have found it to be. The student of Angelic magick will find a comprehension of the language to be invaluable—and the deeper that comprehension, the more powerful the utterance of the Keys.

In order to create this Lexicon, it was first necessary to return to Dee's journals and generate a "corrected version" of the forty-eight Angelical Keys. Thankfully, I was not alone in this undertaking. As a member of the *Enochian-l* mailing list, I communicated with folks who had also done work toward analyzing and correcting the Keys.[3] Their results do not always agree with my own, as there are several places in the text that are obscure or incomplete in *A True and Faithful Relation*, and we (and even Dee himself) came to various opinions on what should be the correct wording.[4]

Once I had the corrected version of the Keys, I used that to create the *Angelical Keys Cross-Reference*—which adopts the numbering style used by Geoffrey James in his work. (You will find that my numbers do not match his, due to the fact that my corrected Keys have a different wording.) With that in hand, I was finally able to compile my *Encyclopedic Lexicon of the Tongue of Angels*. From there, I was able to analyze the language's grammar and linguistics. All of these together, plus an exhaustive study of Dee's journals, form the basis of the work you are now reading.

This second volume of my work is an exhaustive analysis of the Celestial Speech as recorded by Dee. This is where I have preserved all of the linguistic information concerning the language. I outline its basic principles, root words, affixes, parts of speech, and phonology. This is also where I explore the subjects of Middle English and Early Modern English, and the influence these stages of the language had on Dee's conception of Angelical.

This volume culminates in the Angelical Lexicon itself. This new work is not just another "Enochian dictionary." The Lexicon includes every word from the forty-eight Keys, all defined or related words from the *Book of Loagaeth*, and every random Angelical word or phrase found throughout Dee's lengthy journals. All of the words have been analyzed and cross-referenced to discover hidden word elements and root words. Every entry in the Lexicon includes:

- The Angelical word in English and Angelical characters.
- Its "English sense" (definition).
- Its location (cross-reference numbers for words from the Keys, page-references to Dee's published journals for all other words).
- Comparisons to every related Angelical word.
- Notes about the word's definition, history, or usage—both Dee's original marginal notations and new commentary.
- Dee also left phonetic notations for most of the words he recorded. For centuries these notes have been a source of confusion for scholars. In this new work, Dee's notations are deciphered at last! All of his pronunciation notes are included and fully explained. (A new pronunciation key has been invented to make reading the words much easier for the modern reader.)

As added features, this volume includes the Angelical Keys cross-reference (containing a fully corrected version of the forty-eight Keys, cross-referenced by number), and a lengthy English-to-Angelical section (including tips for translating English texts into proper Angelical).

Methodology

You will likely notice that my Lexicon does not resemble existing "Enochian dictionaries." Such dictionaries do not often illustrate the compounds, roots, affixes, and other linguistic intricacies of the Angelical words. Nor do they demonstrate how each word is used in the Keys, for *every* occurrence and version of the word (conjugations, compounds, etc). Nor do they provide commentary about the words, their origins, or the way they were used in Dee's journals and the Keys.

Thus, in order to unlock these mysteries, I set out to perform a deep analysis of the words of the Keys. I began my project with the first word of Key One (or word 1.1), and compared it with *each and every* individual word in the Keys. That way, I could discover if word 1.1 appeared again with alternate spellings, as part of compound words, or even if similar words shared a common root.

Then, I moved to the second word of Key One (or word 1.2) and repeated the procedure. I continued this tedious process through all the Keys until the very last word of the Key of the Aethyrs (word 30.157) had been compared and cross-referenced with *every* word in the forty-eight Keys (including both the spelling of the words *and* their English definitions). This arduous word-by-word comparison revealed several fascinating aspects of Angelical grammar—most of which I had never seen published. (Until now, of course!)

Besides the words of the forty-eight Keys, I have also included all words from the *Book of Loagaeth* for which Dee recorded definitions, or which appear similar to other defined words. I have also exhaustively scoured both Dee's *Five Books of Mystery* and his *A True and Faithful Relation* for each and every instance where the Angels spoke to Dee (or one another) in their native tongue. These words are all included in the Lexicon in this volume, even if they have no definitions.

This Lexicon does not include any Enochian material developed by those who followed Dee—such as the Golden Dawn and Aleister Crowley. I do not mean to negate their work or suggest that it has no merit—however, I again stress the importance of learning the language as Dee received it before moving on to these sources. Some of their material may be of little use, and some of it may be worthwhile.

The material in both volumes of *The Angelical Language* is based strictly upon Dee's journals and personal grimoire. All references to Dee's *Five Books of Mystery* ("Five Books") are drawn from Joseph Peterson's outstanding work *John Dee's Five Books of Mystery*. All references to *A True and Faithful Relation* ("TFR") are drawn from *The Magickal Review*'s edition of Meric Casaubaon's *A True and Faithful Relation of What Passed for Many Years Between Dr. John Dee . . . and Some Spirits*. Finally, any reference to Dee's personal grimoire (Sloane MS 3191) will point to Geoffery James' *The Enochian Magick of Dr. John Dee*. See the bibliography in this volume for further information on sources and manuscripts.

I sincerely hope that you will find this text to be an invaluable resource. I encourage you to use this book as a study tool, so that you can experience the mysteries behind the Angelical tongue.

Zorge,
Aaron Leitch
March 2009

Endnotes

1. Both *i* and *y* are the same letter in Angelical.
2. I even saw it suggested that these were not phonetic notes at all, but alternate spellings of the words!
3. As of this date (2010), some of this work can be found on Callisto Radiant's *Enochian Linguistics* website, at http://www.madimi.com/enochmnu.htm.
4. I used the *48 Claves Angelicae* as my secondary reference in these cases.

Chapter 1

Angelical Linguistics

There are two primary sources available for the Celestial Speech: The Holy *Book of Loagaeth* and the forty-eight Angelical Keys. The First ("hidden") Table of *Loagaeth* (sides A and B) contains approximately 4802 words compiled into ninety-eight lines of text. It is a wonderful sample of the language, which could be used to analyze the letters of the remaining forty-eight Tables.

Unfortunately, no translation of the Holy Book was ever recorded in Dee's surviving journals. We know only what the Angels claimed is in the text, and a few precious words translated here and there. In many ways, modern scholars have to approach the *Book of Loagaeth* as archaeologists once approached Egyptian hieroglyphics. We can examine the words and make a lot of educated guesses about linguistic patterns, but without an "Angelical Rosetta Stone," we are ultimately flying blind.

Perhaps this Rosetta Stone already exists in the forty-eight Angelical Keys. The Keys represent a much smaller sample of the language—totaling only 1070 words, and much fewer if we exclude words that repeat. However, unlike the Holy Book, the text of the Angelical Keys came with English translations. This grants us a wonderful opportunity to analyze the Angelical words closely—looking for syntax and grammar, root words, compounds, affixes, and so forth. (Then, with any luck, we can apply what we learn to the text of *Loagaeth*—beginning with the first Table.)[1]

When comparing the Holy Book with the forty-eight Keys, it can be easy to assume one is reading two different languages.[2] However, my own analysis of the text of *Loagaeth* leads me to believe that its language is one and the same with that of the Keys. I have found several words from the Keys within *Loagaeth* as well—some of them intact and some of them in modified forms. I have also found the names of several Angelical letters in the text, and a couple of direct references to *Heptarchic* Angels.[3] While the words of the forty-nine Tables do seem alien to those familiar with the Keys, I think this is merely because *Loagaeth* represents a much larger sample of the language.

Having said that, I will also concede that the language used in the Keys does seem to have a slightly different "feel" and flow than the text in the Holy Book. (Donald Laycock illustrates this adequately in the introduction to his *Complete Enochian Dictionary*.) Remember chapter 2 of volume I, where I quoted Raphael, who said of the forty-nine parts of *Loagaeth*:

> Every Element hath 49 manner of understandings. Therein is comprehended so many languages. They are all spoken at once, and severally, by themselves, by distinction may be spoken. [*Five Books of Mystery*, p. 297]

I assume that the "elements" of *Loagaeth* are the forty-nine individual Tables—forty-eight of which may be opened by human effort via the Keys. If each of these Tables contain forty-nine interpretations and languages (or, perhaps, *dialects* of Angelical), it makes for a total of 2401 interpretations/dialects. It is probable that the language of the forty-eight Keys represents a sample of one of these Angelical dialects.

Angelical "English Senses" and Fluid Definitions

Throughout Dee's journals, the Angels, when translating Angelical words, referred to the English equivalents as "senses" or "significations" rather than definitions or translations. This was because the given English elaborations are filled with glosses, poetic license, and implied adjectives. The Angelical words merely "signify a concept," and we are somewhat free to apply any English words that properly (and poetically) illustrate the concept. (If you refer to the third and fourth columns of the Angelical cross-reference, you will see how the "essential concepts" of the Angelical words differ from the English elaborations given by Nalvage.)

As an example, we can look at the various interpretations of the word *Malpurg* (Fiery Darts):

Malpurg (Fiery Darts)
Malprg (Through-thrusting Fire)
Malpirgi (Fires of Life and Increase)

An even better example of fluid definition is found in the word *Cocasb* (Time):

Acocasb (Time)
"Cacocasb" (Another While)
Cocasb (Time)
Cocasg (Times)
Qcocasb (Contents of Time)

Furthermore, *Cocasb* likely shares a root with:

Cacacom (Flourish)
Cacrg (Until)
Casasam (Abiding)
Capimali (Successively)
"Capimao" (While)
Capimaon (Number of Time)
Capmiali (Successively)

Angelical shares this trait of "fluid definitions" with ancient human languages such as Sumerian, Egyptian, and Hebrew. Modern English tends to possess more specific definitions, which are necessary in order to create and utilize our sophisticated technology. However, in previous ages it was possible to use a single word to represent any number of related concepts. (For instance, consider the ancient Egyptian word *Khepher*—which might indicate creation, formation, transformation, mutation, and so on.) The precise meaning intended by the author was indicated by context.

Root Words

Several Angelical words with dissimilar spellings turn out to have similar definitions—revealing many previously unknown root words. Compare the following words:

Londoh (Kingdom)

Adohi (Kingdom)

Both of these words translate as "Kingdom"—but they would not have appeared near one another in a simple alphabetical listing. We can see, however, that they share the letters *doh*—and this is likely an Angelical root word.

Conversely, I found that many words with similar spellings had *dissimilar* definitions. This often highlighted relationships between concepts within the language that were not apparent at first glance. For instance, compare the spelling similarities between these words:

Ors (Darkness)

Orsba (Drunken)

Orscor (Dryness)

Orscatbl (Buildings)

All of these seem to share a common linguistic root (*Or* or *Ors*), but they have definitions that are considered unrelated in English. By contemplating how these concepts might relate to one another, it can tell us something about how Angels "think."

These root words also support the idea that Angelical works similarly to ancient languages such as Hebrew. Such early tongues are based upon a series of simple root words—usually of two or three letters, each of which may or may not stand on its own as a proper word. Affixes can then be added to the roots to alter inflection or tense.

For example, consider the Angelical word *I* (Is)—which is the likely root of the word *Ip* (Not). By adding affixes, we obtain:

Ipam (Is Not)

Ipamis (Can Not Be)

An even more important root is *Ia*, which does not stand as a word on its own in the Keys.[4] However, it is possibly the root of several existing words—just a few of which are listed here as an example:

Iad (God)

Iaiadix (Honor)

Iaida (The Highest)

Iaidon (All Powerful)

Further, the first word in the above list, *Iad* (God), appears to be the root element of several additional words:

Geiad (Lord and Master)

Iadnah (Knowledge)

Iadpil (To Him)

Ioiad (Him the Liveth Forever)

Laiad (Secrets of Truth)

At the front of the Lexicon, I have included a list of all of the root words (or letter combinations) that I have discovered to date. (The list includes mostly those root words that do not already stand as words on their own.)

Compounds

Also akin to early (and, of course, many modern) languages, Angelical roots/words may be compounded in order to convey more sophisticated concepts. For instance, the three words *Zir* (Am), *Enay* (Lord), and *Iad* (God) are combined to form *Zirenaiad* (I am the Lord Your God).

I have found that, most often, compounds are made between nouns or verbs and the words that modify or indicate them. The following examples are an extremely small sample of such modifier-compounds found throughout the forty-eight Keys. (Note that I have placed the modifiers within each word in bold.) There are possessive adjective (*his, her*) compounds:

*Busdir**tilb*** (Glory [of] Her)

*Elzap**tilb*** (Her Course)

*Lonshi**tox*** (His Power)

Here are some demonstrative pronoun (*this, those*) and relative pronoun (*which/that*) compounds:

__Ar__coazior (That Increase)	*__Ds__abramg* (Which Prepared)
__Ar__tabas (That Govern)	*__Ds__chis* (Which Are)
__Unal__chis (These Are)	*__Ds__i* (Which Is)
__Oi__salman (This House)	*__Ds__om* (That Understand)

Conjunction (*and, or, but, as*) compounds are very common:

Cors__ta__ (Such As)	*__Od__chis* (And Are)
__Crp__l (But One)	*__Od__miam* (And Continuance)
__Ta__blior (As Comforters)	*__Od__zamran* (And Appear)
__Ta__viv (As the Second)	*__Q__mospleh* (Or the Horns)

Compounds are regularly created from forms of the verb *to be* (*is, are, were*, and—apparently—*is not*):

__Chis__holq (Are Measured)	*Page__ip__* (Rest Not)
Unal__chis__ (These Are)	*Od__ip__uran* (And Shall Not See)
__I__noas (Are Become)	*__Zir__enaiad* (I Am the Lord God)
__I__dlugam (Is Given)	*Gchis__ge__* (Are Not)

There are fewer (although no less significant) examples of nouns compounded with adjectives or verbs other than *to be*.

I have also found that compounding Angelical words often results in changes to their spelling. For example, the word *Dsonf* (Which Reign) is a combination of *Ds* (Which) and *Sonf* (Reign). However, notice that there is only one *s* found in *Dsonf*. That is because Angelical combines duplicate letters when forming compounds. Therefore, the final *s* of *Ds* and the first *S* of *Sonf* combine into one *s* in *Dsonf*.

Another example is the word *Gmicalzoma* (Power of Understanding). This is a combination of *Gmicalzo* (Power) and *Oma* (Understanding). However, we can see that the final *o* of *Gmicalzo* and the first *O* of *Oma* have been combined into a single letter in the compound.

There are also several examples of completely inexplicable spelling changes when compounds are formed. For instance, the word for *Day* in

Angelical is *Basgim*, while the compound word for "Midday the First" is *Bazemlo* (*Bazem* + *"Lo"*). The change of the *s* to a *z* is not surprising, because these letters represent a similar sound. However, note how the *gi* of *Basgim* has disappeared entirely from the compound *Bazemlo*. We can therefore guess that *Bas*/*Baz* is an Angelical root indicating "daytime." However, we cannot guess what rules apply to the spelling change between *Basgim* and the *Bazem* element in *Bazemlo*.

It might be helpful to provide another example, so we will look at the word *Soba* (Whose). In the compound *Sobhaath* (Whose Works), the spelling has altered to *Sobha*. In the compound *Sobolzar* (Whose Courses), the spelling becomes *Sobo*. Even more inexplicable, in the compound *Solamian* (Whose Continuence), the spelling is altered to *Sola*.

Conjugation

Further spelling changes may come from conjugation instead of compounding. These changes appear so random, even professional linguists can find no rhyme or reason behind them.[5] Several examples follow:

Goho (Sayeth)	*Naoln* (May Be)	*Zir* or *Zirdo* (Am)
Gohia (We Say)	*Noan* (To Become)	*Zirom* (Were)
Gohol (Saying)	*Noar* (Has Become)	*Zirop* (Was)
Gohon (Have Spoken)	*Noas* (Have Become)	
Gohus (I Say)	*Noasmi* (Let Become)	
Gohulim (Is Said)		

Unfortunately, I cannot report that I have discovered anything useful in this regard. Given the apparently haphazard manner in which the spellings are altered, I can't even state with surety that conjugations, as we would recognize them, even exist in Angelical. Many Angelical words (verbs and nouns) alter their spelling even when they do not conjugate or compound with other words. Just a few examples are:

Aai, Aao (Amongst)

Acocasb, Cocasb (Time)

Butmon, Butmona (Mouth)

Efafafe, Ofafafe (Vials)

Netaab, Netaaib (Government)

Affixes

Having learned somewhat about Angelical roots and compounds, I was able to isolate what *appear* to be several Angelical affixes. For example, there are some instances where the addition of *-o* to a word seems to add the connotation of *of*:

Caosg (Earth)	-	*Caosgo* (Of the Earth)
Vonph (Wrath)	-	*Vonpho* (Of Wrath)
Iad (God)	-	*Oiad* (Of God)

However, this does not appear to be a set rule. First, an equivalent to the word *of* is *extremely* rare in Angelical. (Usually, it is simply implied by context.) Second, some words appear with additional *-o* affixes without gaining an *of* connotation. Examples are:

Zol (Hands)	-	*Ozol* (Hands)
Zien (Hands)	-	*Ozien* ([My Own] Hand)
Micalz (Mighty)	-	*Micalzo* (Mighty / Power)

Another likely affix is *-ax*, which may be an indicator of action similar to our own suffix *-ing*, which can turn verbs into active participles (e.g., "The running water is very deep") or present progressives (e.g., "He is running very fast."):

Blior (Comfort)	-	*Bliorax* (To Comfort)
Om (Know)	-	*Omax* (Knowest)

There are other verbs that end with the *-ax* suffix, but we have no examples of the same words without the affix: *Camliax* (Spake), *Tastax* (Going Before). We might possibly add *Gizyax* (Earthquakes) and *Coraxo* (Thunders of Judgment and Wrath) to this list—they may be nouns by English standards, but they still indicate violently active forces. Meanwhile, there are some "*-ing* clause" verbs in the Keys that do not appear with the *-ax* suffix—such as *Dluga* (Giving unto) or *Panpir* (Raining Down).

Rarities: Pronouns, Prepositions, Adjectives, Articles, Case

There are several aspects of grammar that are rare or even nonexistent in the Angelical tongue. For instance, personal pronouns are used very infrequently in the Keys—and it is difficult to say why they are used in the places we do find them. However, while these pronouns are used less frequently than is the case in modern English, they are used more frequently than the other rarities we will discuss in this section. The existing personal pronouns are:

Ol (I)
Tox (Him / His)
Nonca (You, plural)
"T" (It)
Tiobl (Her)
Yls (Thou, singular)
"Pi" (She)
"Ip" (Her)
Par (Them)

Relative pronouns like the following seem to be a bit more common, as they are not as easily implied by context:

Sobam (Whom)
Ds, Dst (That, Which)
Casarm, Casarma (Whom)
Soba, Sobca, Sobra (Whose)

Plus, we find these possessive adjectives:

Tilb (Her)
Tox (His / Him)
Aqlo (Thy)

However, they are used sparingly, and—as we saw previously—they are often found in compound with their nouns. In such cases, I note that they often follow the noun—such as in *Lonshitox* (His Power) and *Elzap-tilb* (Her Course).

Non-possessive adjectives are even more uncommon in the Angelical text of the Keys. When they *are* used, they typically follow the rule of English—falling immediately before the noun they indicate, and not usually compounded with it. Some examples are *Vohim Gizyax* (Mighty Earthquakes) and *Adphaht Damploz* (Unspeakable Variety).

On the other hand, most of the poetic adjectives we see in the English translations are not implied in the essential definitions of the Angelical words—such as *Orri* (Barren Stone), *Grosb* (Bitter Sting), or *Sapah* (Mighty Sounds), all of which are nouns that show no linguistic indication of their adjectives. It would appear that adjectives in such cases are left entirely up to the author, or reader, of the text.

Another rarity in Angelical is the use of prepositions (*at, on, in, for*). We already know that there *may* be an affix to indicate "of" (*-o*). There is also one instance of the word *De* (of) that stands alone in the Keys. Plus the following prepositions are found here and there throughout the Keys:

Aai, Aaf, Aaiom, Aao (Amongst)
Aspt (Before)
"Azia" (Like unto)
Oq (Except/But)
Bagle (For)[6]
De (Of)
Pugo (As Unto)
Vors, Vorsg (Over)
Mirc (Upon)
Nothoa (Amidst)
Oroch (Under)
Pambt (Unto)
Tia (Unto)
Zomdux (Amidst)
Zylna (Within)

All of this indicates that prepositions exist to some extent in Angelical, but they are not often used unless context makes them unavoidable.

Meanwhile, I have discovered that articles (*a, an, the*) are not used in Angelical at all. Articles are implied entirely by the context of the sentence. This trait is also common to many historical languages, such as Latin.

I have also found that grammatical case does not often apply to Angelical. In modern English, the case of a noun or pronoun can be subjective (*he*), objective (*him*), or possessive (*his*). In Angelical, much as with conjugation, there do *appear* to be some examples of spelling changes from one case to another. (See the list of pronouns at the beginning of this section.) However, there is no indication these changes have anything at all to do with case.

Meanwhile, there are several examples of *vocative* case in the Angelical tongue. A noun takes the vocative case when it indicates someone being *addressed*. For example, in the phrase "Open the door, John," the word *John* is vocative. The sentence does not need the addition of *John* in order to be complete, but we include it to specify that John is being addressed. Of course, there is no vocative *case* in English—so we do not see any spelling change to the word *John* when used vocatively.

However, some older languages such as Latin do utilize a vocative case. The most famous example comes from Shakespeare's play *Julius Caesar*, during the scene in which Caesar's best friend Brutus stabs him in the back. After the assault, Caesar turns to Brutus and says, "*Et tu, Brute?*"[7] *Brute* is the vocative case of the name *Brutus*.

The first example of the vocative case in Angelical is found within the First Table of *Loagaeth*, where we find the word *Befas*.[8] It would appear this word aroused the curiosity of Dee and/or Kelley, because it is similar to the name of a Heptarchic Angel the men had already met: *Befafes*—the Angelic Prince of Tuesday. In the margin, Dee makes the following notation:

> Befes the vocative case of Befafes. [*Five Books of Mystery*, p. 310]

Therefore, we know that someone in the text of the First Table of *Loagaeth* (presumably the Creator) is directly addressing Befafes for some reason—and the vocative case alters *Befafes* to *Befes*.

The second example of vocative case appears in *A True and Faithful Relation*, while Dee and Kelley are having a conversation with the Heptarchic Angel Madimi. The Angel suddenly halts the discussion to say:

> *Carma geta, Barman.* [*A True and Faithful Relation*, p. 32]

When Dee asked Madimi what this phrase meant, she translated it as "Come out of there, Barma." *Barma* turned out to be the name of a spirit inhabiting Kelley, which Madimi proceeded to exorcise. The form *Barman*, then, is a vocative case of *Barma*.

Finally, there *may* be a third example of vocative case—also found in the First Table of *Loagaeth*—in the word *Bobogelzod*. This word certainly appears to have some relationship with the Heptarchic King of Sunday *Bobogel*—and could very well represent a vocative case of his name.

Thus, we know that Angelical makes use of the vocative case. We do not know, however, what rules govern the spelling changes.

Phonetic Glosses

Note: Throughout the remainder of this chapter, I will illustrate some pronunciations according to a key found on page 95 of this volume as well as with the Angelical Psalter in volume I. You can also find a chart illustrating the Angelical characters on page 106 of this volume.

It is vital to remember that Dee was *not* recording the words in Angelical characters. Kelley spoke the language fluently while in his trance state, and Dee merely wrote down in English letters what he heard. I have no doubt that many of the words recorded by Dee are exact in their Angelical spelling—meaning we could take the English letters and transliterate them directly into Angelical. However, there are many examples of words that have "phonetic glosses." This is what I call spelling "peculiarities" that appear in different instances of the same word—which are apparently intended to give us pronunciation cues.

Take, for example, the word *Crip* (But), which appears without the *i* in the compound *Crpl* (But One). Therefore, the *i* likely does not represent an Angelical character in this word—leaving only *Crp* (But). The shortest and most radical[9] version of the word should be the "correct" spelling. What we have in *Crip* is a phonetic gloss—letting us know that *Crp* is pronounced "krip" rather than "kurp."

There is also the element *Purg* (Flames), which appears in such words as *Ialpurg* (Burning Flames) and *Malpurg* (Fiery Darts). Yet these same words appear elsewhere as *Ialprg* (Burning Flame) and *Malprg* (Through-thrusting Fire). Therefore, *Prg* and *Purg* are likely the same word with the same Angelical spelling. The extra *u* is merely a phonetic gloss, telling us where to place the vowel sound. Elsewhere, we even see the word *Prge* (Fire)—yet another phonetic gloss, adding the *e* to tell us the *g* is a soft "juh" sound. All of these clues suggest the true pronunciation of the Angelical word *Prg* is identical to the English word *purge*. However, the word is probably spelled *Prg*.

Compounds are not the only places we can look for phonetic glosses. Several words that stand alone in the Keys appear more than once with different spellings. For example, consider the word *Abramig* (Prepared). This word appears only once in this form. Meanwhile, it appears in three other places in the Keys in the form of *Abramg*—twice standing alone and once in a compound. Therefore, we might suspect that *Abramg* is the radical spelling of this word. The extra *i* in *Abramig* merely tells us where to place the vowel sound ("ay-bray-mig" rather than "ay-bram-jee").

Another good example is the word *NA*—which appears in the *Five Books* and the *Book of Loagaeth* as a Name of God. We might assume this word is pronounced "nah" or "nay." However, in the Keys we can find the same word written phonetically as *Enay* (Lord). Thus, we know the proper pronunciation of *NA* is "en-ay," and it should be spelled with only two letters.

As further examples, we can compare the following words:

F (Visit)	-	*Ef* (Visit)
L (First)	-	*El* (First)
S (Fourth)	-	*"Es"* (Fourth)

The added *E* in each case is apparently a phonetic gloss—once again showing us where to place the vowel sound in the pronunciation of the words.

Further phonetic glosses seem to be associated with the Angelical digraphs—although the subject is fairly uncertain. In ancient languages (at least, those that possessed an alphabet), digraphs are usually indicated by a single character. For example, the Hebrew letter *Peh* represents the sounds of both "P" and "Ph." The letter *Tau* represents both "T" and "Th." Likewise, there are several examples of this in Angelical:

Cnoqod is pronounced "see-noh-kwod" (Q = Qu)
(Also see: *Cnoquod*)
Cormp is pronounced "kormf" (P = Ph)
(Also see: *Cormf*)
Lonsa is pronounced "lon-sha" (S = Sh)
(Also see: *Lansh*)
Noncp is pronounced "non-sef" (P = Ph)
(Also see: *Noncf*)
Sapa is pronounced "say-fa" (P = Ph)
Telocvovim is pronounced "tee-loch-voh-vee-im" (C = Ch)
(Also see: *Teloch*)
Vonpo is pronounced "von-foh" (P = Ph)
(Also see: *Vonpho*)

The above is fairly convincing evidence that Angelical digraphs are indeed represented by single letters. That would mean that the secondary letters in these digraphs (the *h* in *Ph* and *Ch*, the *u* in *Qu*, etc.) are merely phonetic glosses, and should not be included when the words are spelled in Angelical characters.

However, there also exist *counter*examples in Dee's journals. The very first word of the Holy *Book of Loagaeth* (Table One, side A) was originally recorded by Dee as *Zuresk*. Later, Raphael corrected this by telling Dee the word must contain seven letters—*Zuresch*. (The *ch* taking its hard sound, as in the English words *ache* or *chrome*.) Because of this correction, we know the *Ch* digraph is—in this case—actually written with two letters instead of just one.

If we continue to look through the first few lines of *Loagaeth* (which Raphael spelled out in Angelical character by character)[10], we find several further examples of two-character digraphs as well.

Another good counterexample is the word *Hoath* at the end of the first Angelical Key. I included the transmission of this word in volume I, chapter 3 (in the section "Dee Suspected of Cryptography?"), where Nalvage was still associating numbers with each letter of the words.

There we can see undeniably that Nalvage transmitted both a *t* and an *h* for *Hoath*, and gave a number to each letter. Therefore, once again we can see an Angelical digraph represented with two letters as in modern English.

Thus, we are left with several examples of one-character digraphs and several examples of two-character digraphs. That leaves us with a large number of two-character digraphs in Dee's records that give no clue to their proper Angelical-character spelling. Was Dee writing these words in transliteration (letter for letter) or phonetically? Where no such clues exist, I have recorded the digraphs in the Lexicon in Angelical characters just as Dee recorded them in English. Yet there remains some room for debate on the issue.

As a final entry in this section, I would like to mention a short phonetic note that Dee recorded in his journal for a word in the *Book of Loagaeth*. For Table One, side A, line 23, Dee recorded the word *Au*. In the margin, he noted "*au* sounds *af*." It might seem that Dee was indicating that the *u* could sound like an *f*. However, it is more likely that he was indicating a "v" sound for this word—so that *Au* is actually *Av*. In the written English of Dee's time, *u* and *v* were essentially the same letter. So Dee would have had to utilize the *f* as a kind of phonetic gloss, to approximate the phonetic sound of *v*.

Early Modern English and Angelical

Before we continue discussing the pronunciation of Angelical, we must first consider a few points about the English used by Dee to record the words. As mentioned previously, Kelley spoke the Angelical words aloud while Dee recorded them in English characters. (He also added marginal notes with phonetic pronunciation clues.) These words and notes are all recorded in—and represent sounds familiar to—Elizabethan English. A little study into this vernacular will make sense of many of Dee's seemingly inexplicable phonetic notes.

Dee lived from 1527 until 1608 CE, making him a contemporary of people such as William Shakespeare (1564–1616), Edmund Spenser

(1552–99), and Francis Bacon (1561–1626). These men all spoke "Elizabethan" English, albeit with different regional dialects. (Queen Elizabeth I reigned from 1558 until 1603.) As any Enochian scholar can tell you, reading Dee's journals is a challenge similar to reading Shakespeare's plays or King James' (1566–1625) authorized Bible. (Remember that the quotes you read throughout this book have had their spelling modernized.) Therefore, a study of Shakespeare's English is necessary if one wishes to estimate the sound of the Angelical language recorded by Dee.

Contrary to what some people may believe, the English spoken by Dee and Shakespeare was *not* Old English or Middle English. It was, in fact, a form of English called *Early Modern English*. This stage of the language existed roughly between the late 1400s and the late 1600s.[11] In other words, it was the standard version of the language during the Renaissance era in England. It was *not* spoken with the "Queen's English" accent we currently associate with the British upper class and royalty. Nor was it the Cockney dialect we associate with the working class in London's East End.[12] These accents did not originate (as we know them) until the eighteenth and nineteenth centuries.

Those who study Shakespearean phonetics commonly suggest that spoken Early Modern English sounded more like the "hillbilly" accent found in the Appalachian regions of the eastern United States. That is because the ancestors of so many of the people who live in Appalachia migrated from England when Early Modern English was prevalent, and then settled into isolated communities. Their language therefore remained unchanged for hundreds of years, and it currently contains the most similarities with Early Modern English. Of course I am not suggesting that we read the Angelical Keys in the voice of Jed Clampett. It is important, however, to place the phonetic sounds we are going to explore in their proper context.

Early Modern English is a transitional stage of the language between Middle English and what we speak today (present-day English). It retained some of the spelling conventions of Middle English, but had shifted to a pronunciation more familiar to the present day. That, in fact, is why Early Modern English so often confuses modern students. We can listen to plays by Shakespeare and—for the most part—understand what we are hearing. There may be puns or catchphrases we don't recognize, and there are a few words that have changed in meaning, but the words still sound basically like present-day English.

However, when we try to *read* the same material, there are some glaring departures from what we learned about English in school. These departures are partially thanks to the Middle English spelling conventions that had not yet passed out of the system by the time of Shakespeare and Dee.

Further departures and confusion arise from the fact that English had not been standardized during the Early Modern English phase.[13] The "educated" languages such as Latin had reached a standard, but English had not. Just as the definitions of the words were somewhat fluid, so were the spellings. Most words were spelled according to how they sounded to the author (a factor that could vary widely from region to region), or according to how the author believed they "should" be spelled. The rules were so fluid that the same word might be spelled in different ways within the *same text*. (Of course, we have already discovered this within Dee's record of the forty-eight Keys.)

Thankfully, there is a brighter side to Early Modern English as well. *Most* of the grammatical rules you learned in school—and take for granted to this very day—apply to Dee's English. (That is why the language sounds similar to our own when spoken.)

For the most part, the consonants in Early Modern English sounded pretty much the way we use them today. A *g* before an *e* or *i* generally had the soft "juh" sound (as in *general*, *budge*, and *giant*), but otherwise a *g* took the hard sound (as in *grand*, *glad*, and *haggard*). The letter *r* probably sounded longer and more drawn out than present-day English. For example, the name *Henry* has three syllables in Early Modern English. So does the word *angry*.[14] The letter *z*[15] was rare, but was used by Dee and Kelley as we use it today (as in *zest*, *zip*,and *sizzle*). The letter *x* took the sound of "ks" in the middle or at the end of a word (as in *excite*, *taxes*, and *fox*), but the sound of "zee" or "tz" at the beginning (as in *xylophone* and *xenophobe*).

Most of the digraphs are familiar: *Th* (as in *this*, *that*), *Sh* (as in *sheet*, *dish*), *Ph* (as in *phantasm*, *phone*), and so on. The digraph *Ch* also existed—sometimes representing the "tch" sound (as in *church*, *chain*), and other times a guttural "kh" sound (as in *ache*, *chrome*, and *chronicle*). *Kn* had finally developed the "nh" sound we know today (as in *knight*, *knife*). Early Modern English also recognized the rare *Gn* digraph as a throaty "nh" sound (as in *gnat*, *gnaw*, and *gnarl*).

Therefore, if you are a native English speaker, you can read the Angelical Keys pretty much as they appear. You can most often go with your gut reaction on how the letter combinations of the words should sound.

Most of the differences between Early Modern and present-day English appear where vowel sounds are concerned. Of course, most of the grammatical rules are still the same as we know them. For instance, an *e* following a consonant at the end of a word will become silent, and make the preceding vowel long (as in *bake*, *precede*, *pipe*, *hope*, and *duke*).

However, as we shall see, the written form of Early Modern English used many peculiar letter combinations to represent the vowel sounds—many of them left over from the more archaic spellings of Middle English. I would like to highlight a couple of points that most often result in confusion for students:

First, written Early Modern English used the letters *i*, *y*, and *j* interchangeably. The basic rule was that *i*/*y* represented the vowel sounds, while *j* (actually an elongated *i*) represented the consonant sound.

I/*y* could be used at the beginning or end of a word—making the sounds of "yuh" at the beginning (as in *yard*, *your*, and *yellow*) and "ee" at the end (as in *lady*, *windy*). Sometimes, an *i*/*y* at the end of a word could have the long "eye" sound (as in *sty*, *ply*, and *sky*). If it follows an *a*, it makes that vowel long (as in *day*, *stay*, and *dais*). In the middle of a word, *i* possessed its typical short sounds (as in *bit*, *sit*, and *whither*) or long sounds (as in *bite*, *kite*, *blight*, and *sight*).

Meanwhile, either the letter *i or* its elongated *j* version could appear in a word with the consonant "juh" sound.[16] It might appear at the start of a word (as in *justice*, *jump*, and *John*)[17] or in the middle (as in *adjust*, *object*, and *majestic*). Finally, as if to confuse matters further, the "juh" sound could also be represented by a *g* (as in *danger*, *sage*, and *range*).

The next common point of confusion, for modern students, is between the letters *u* and *v*. These letters were also interchangeable in Early Modern English, and might indicate either a vowel or a consonant sound.

If the letter was used at the beginning of a word, it was always written as *v*. It might take the consonant "vuh" sound if preceding a vowel (as in *very*, *visit*, and *vast*). Or, it might take the vowel sound if preceding a consonant: either the long "yew" sound (as in *vtopia*, *vtilize*, and *vseful*),[18] or the short "uh" sound (as in *vp*, *vtmost*, and *vsher*).[19]

The *u* form of the letter could be used anywhere else in the word. Whether it took the vowel or consonant sound was the same as for the letter *v*. It could take the consonant sound if it preceded a vowel (as in *sauage*, *saue*, and *Dauid*).[20] Or, it could take the vowel sound if it preceded a consonant (as in *mud*, *scrub*, and *button*.)[21]

I should also point out that the letter *w* was fairly rare. It was more often written like a literal double *u* (or *v*)—*uu* or *vv*.

On the following pages, you will find reference charts for Early Modern English phonetics, which can be applied to Angelical words, as well as the pronunciation notes Dee left in his records. It is not an ultimate guide to proper Angelical pronunciation (as we shall see later, there are also several Middle English influences upon Angelical), but it gives us a much clearer picture than systems based upon Hebrew or other phonologies.

When you encounter an Angelical word with an obscure spelling—*or* one of Dee's seemingly inexplicable phonetic notes—simply look for that word's letter combinations in the right-hand column of these charts. The left-hand column will indicate the sound likely made by those letters in Angelical (and Early Modern English):

Early Modern English Phonetics Chart[22]

(for Angelical Pronunciation)

Consonant Sounds	
Phonetic Sound (as in)	Letter Combinations in Early Modern English
B (*boat, clobber*)	b, bb
D (*dive, ladder*)	d, dd
F (*fan, rough, phone*)	f, ff, gh, ph
G (*guard, giggle*)	g, gg
H (*house, hover, who*)	h, wh
J (*budge, jump, adjust, magic*)	dg, dge, j, i, d, di, dj, g
K (*cake, back, chrome*)	k, kk, c, cc, ck, ch
L (*land, spill, will*)	l, ll
M (*metal, mammal*)	m, mm
N (*name, manner, knight, gnome*)	n, nn, kn, gn
P (*pine, speck, puppet*)	p, pp
R (*road, serrate, write*)	r, rr, wr
S (*save, bless, cereal*)	s, ss, c
T (*Table, little, lottery*)	t, tt
W (*water, work, what*)	uu, vv, w, wh
X (*except, flax, excite*)	x
Y (*yes, yellow, your*)	y, i
Z (*zoo, haze, blizzard, xylophone*)	s, z, zz, (very rarely: x)

Vowel Sounds	
Phonetic Sound (as in)	**Letter Combinations in Early Modern English**
A – long (*date, day, eight, whey*)	a, aa, ai, ay, ei, ey, (maybe: eh)
A – short (*bat, cat, apple*)	a, æ[23]
E – long (*beet, heat, believe, only*)	e, ee, ea, ie, y, æ[24]
E – short (*fed, bed, head, dead*)	e, ea
E – silent (*taste, hope, wage*)	e
I – long (*I, bite, blight, style, height*)	i, igh, ai, y, ei, ye
I – short (*bit, cliff, miss, pen*)	i, j, e
O – long (*oar, bone, although*)	o, oo, ou, ov, ow, oa, ough, ovgh
O – short (*hot, tall, father, auburn*)	o, a, au, av, aw, augh, avgh, ough, ovgh
U – long (*root, through, brute*)	o, u, v, ou, ov, oo, ough, ovgh, eu, ew
U – short (*cup, of*)	u, v, o

Digraphs	
Phonetic Sound (as in)	**Letter Combinations in Early Modern English**
"Kwuh" (*queen, quick*)	qu
"Ow" (*out, drought, house, town*)	ou, ov, ow, ough, ovgh
"Oy" (*oil, boy*)	oi, oy
"Shuh" (*shine, shower, wish*)	sh
"Tch" (*chase, church, witch*)	ch, t, c, cch, tch
"Thuh" (*that, whither, thorn*)	th, (very rarely: y)[25]

Take note that several of the above letter combinations appear more than once. For example, the combination *ough* appears under four different headings, because it might indicate any of the following sounds:

Long *o* (as in *although, dough*)

Short *o* (as in *thought, cough*)

Long *u* (as in *enough, rough, tough*)

digraph *ow* (as in *drought, bough*)

This means that—just as with Early Modern English itself—there will always be some ambiguity in the pronunciation of Angelical words. However, at the very least, this information will allow us to make educated guesses rather than engaging in blind speculation based upon present-day English, Hebrew, or other languages.

Middle English and Angelical

Having said the above about Early Modern English, I feel it is necessary to add a few words about Middle English and its influence on the Angelical language.

Dee may have been writing his notes in his own contemporary English; however, we must keep in mind that he was receiving a sacred magickal language from the Angels, which they claimed was an ancient proto-tongue. This is not uncommon for magickal languages, most of which are archaic in some form. For example, the priests of ancient Babylon made use of the older Sumerian language in their rites. In Dee's time, dead languages like Latin and Hebrew (the latter was solely a liturgical language in Dee's time) were the standard mystery languages. Therefore, it is no surprise that Angelical would have also had an archaic sound to the ears of Dee and Kelley. That is where Middle English comes into the picture.

Middle English was the language used by Chaucer to write his *Canterbury Tales*. One of the best-known traits of Middle English was the manner in which it tended to pronounce most of the letters in each word—so the vowels were clearly pronounced. As the English language drifted toward its Early Modern phase, the syllables began to blend together into the sounds we are familiar with today.

By taking Dee's phonetic clues into account, I have discovered a general "Middle English" trait throughout Angelical. This is especially applicable to vowels or groups of consonants. For example, all the vowels in the word *Aai* are sounded ("ay-ay-ii"). In the word *Balye*, the *a*, *y*, and *e* are all sounded distinctly ("bay-lii-ee"). The word *Momao* follows the same rule—with the *a* and both *o*'s sounded distinctly ("moh-may-oh").

For consonants, we can look at the final *m* in *Mapm*, which sounds alone ("map-em"). Or the initial *L* in *Lring*, which also makes its own sound ("el-ring"). Another example is the word *Zlida*, where the initial Z stands alone ("zohd-lida").

I could give dozens of examples of this convention, but I think these should suffice as an illustration. This in no way means that *every* letter in every Angelical word should be pronounced! However, the convention appears often enough to give the language a slightly "Middle English" flavor. In this way, the Angelical tongue would have sounded archaic to Dee and Kelley—thus fulfilling the "requirement" for a magickal language.

General Notes on Angelical Phonology

This section is where I have gathered all of my notes on the phonology of the Angelical language. They are taken from everything we have seen in this chapter so far, as well as Dee's own pronunciation notes. (See the Lexicon for more on Dee's notes.) What you see below can be applied directly to the Angelical words, as Dee recorded them, and which you will find in the Lexicon.

Vowels

Pronouncing the vowels in the Angelical tongue does not present much of a problem. As we shall see in the Lexicon, a vowel will usually take its short sound when it is followed by a consonant in its syllable. For some examples, see *Lap*, *Iad*, and *Zir*. However, when a vowel is attached to the *preceding* consonant (i.e., it stands at the end of its syllable), or when it stands alone in a syllable, it takes its long sound. For examples of this, see *Momao*, *Napeai*, and *Paradial*. Dee's phonetic notes—which we shall see in the Lexicon—usually divide the words by syllables, thus indicating to which consonant (if any) each vowel is attached.

Consonants

Of course, it is the consonants that cause most students (and adepts!) to stumble with Angelical pronunciation. While the consonants generally make the sounds we are familiar with, there are several words that contain peculiar groupings of consonants that make little or no phonetic sense to modern English-speaking readers. There are certain grammatical rules one must learn to make sense of it all:

When two consonants are placed together, they can:

1) Make a digraph as they would in present-day English (*Ph*, *Ch*, *Th*, *Qu*, etc.), as in *Dorpha*, *Ethamz*, *Chis*, *Teloch*, and *Norquasahi*. Or they can:

2) Make a new consonant sound as they would in present-day English (*Gr*, *Tr*, *Gn*, etc.), as in *Grosb*, *Trian*, *Gnay*, etc.

However, if neither of the above apply (as in *Nazpsad*, *Farzm, Zchis*), then:

3) The "peculiar" consonant letter is pronounced as a syllable unto itself, after the manner of Middle English. By "peculiar," I mean the consonant in the cluster that stands as the "odd man out." For instance, in the cluster *gsp*, we find that the letters *sp* naturally form a sound together (as in *spot* or *speak*). Meanwhile, the letters *gs* do not make a natural sound in English. Therefore, that *g* is the peculiar one in the group—and it is pronounced by itself, in its own syllable.

In Angelical, a letter standing alone in a syllable is not pronounced phonetically. To continue our *gsp* example, the *g* would take neither its hard sound ("guh"—as in *game* or *good*) nor its soft sound ("juh"—as in *giant* or *huge*). Instead, one would actually pronounce the letter's *name*—sounding like "gee."

Let's take a look at some examples in Angelical: the word *Nazpsad* is pronounced "nayz-pee-sad." The central *p* stands out in this case as the peculiar consonant, and is therefore pronounced as "pee." The word *Farzm* is pronounced "farz-em." The final *zm* does not combine naturally in English, and the *m* is pronounced by itself as "em." As a final example, the word *Zchis* is pronounced "zohd-kiis." The initial letters *Zch* do not combine, therefore the Z is pronounced as "zohd." In each case, the peculiar consonant stands alone as its own syllable.

I admit it seems odd that Angelical consonants should sound like the *names* of English letters. (After all, they have their own Angelical names!) However, notice that long vowels also sound like their English names (long *a* = "ay," long *e* = "ee," long *o* = "oh," etc.)—and any Angelical vowel that stands alone in a syllable takes the long sound. It would appear, then, that the same principle is applied to Angelical consonants when they stand alone. That is to say, Angelical recognizes "long consonants." Just as a long *Un* (A) sounds like "ay," so a long (or extended) *Tal* (M) sounds like "em."

While we are still on the subject of "long consonants," I should mention that the letter *Ceph* (Z) sometimes takes its long sound ("zohd") for no apparent reason. For example, when the Angel Nalvage transmitted the *Corpus Omnium* to Dee and Kelley, he informed them that the word *Moz* could be pronounced "moz" or "moz-ohd." The shorter pronunciation indicates "Joy," while the pronunciation with the extended Z ("zohd") indicates "Joy of God."

As we can see, there is no grammatical reason why the *z* in *Moz* should be extended. The same is true for the word *Zacar* (zay-kayr)—which appears in the forty-eight Keys several times with the extended Z (zohd-ay-kayr). My best guess is that this is not based upon a grammatical rule at all. Perhaps, instead, it is merely a poetic (or lyrical) gloss—after the manner in which a singer will elongate or add syllables to a word in a song to fill metre or emphasize emotion. This is suggested by the difference between "moz" as "Joy" and "moz-ohd" as "Joy of God."

Special Cases

Another quirk of the letter *Ceph* (Z) is that it is sometimes interchangeable with *Pal* (X). This is perhaps because *z* was somewhat rare in the Elizabethan era, and *x* more often served for the "z" sound (as in *xenophile* or *xylophone*). We see evidence of this in the *Book of Loagaeth*, where the Angelical letter-name *Drux* (N) is given the alternate spelling of *Druz* in the margin.[26]

The letter *Don* (R) is another Angelical character of interest. When the letter *r* becomes the peculiar consonant in a cluster, it is neither pronounced "ar" (the long consonant sound) nor given its own syllable. Instead, it is merely pronounced "ur" (as in the English words *turn* or *spur*)—so that it combines with the consonant before it. For example, see *Prdzar* ("purd-zar"), *Prge* ("purj"), and *Dialprt* ("dii-al-purt").

There is one final special case I want to record here. In his journals, Dee established that the word *Baltle* was pronounced "bal-tayl" (the first syllable rhyming with *ball* and the second with *tail*).[27] I found the pronunciation of the three-letter cluster in the second syllable—*tle*—very odd. I decided to investigate further by searching for other words ending in *le*, and found *Bagle* and *Cicle*. As you will see in the Lexicon, Dee's notes on these words are less than helpful. I find it likely that each of these words should end with the sound of "ayl" (as in the English words *bail* or *tail*). In fact, I suspect that any time we see *le* as the final two letters of a three-consonant cluster, they will have the "ayl" sound.

Endnotes

1. The Archangel Raphael says of the first Table: "Let this lesson instruct thee to read all that shall be gathered out of this book hereafter. [. . .] It shall be sufficient to instruct thee." [*Five Books of Mystery*, p. 291]
2. See the introduction to Laycock's *The Complete Enochian Dictionary*.
3. All of these are included in the Lexicon.
4. It does, however, appear in *Loagaeth*—although without definition. I note it is very similar to the Hebrew word *Iah* or *Yah* (God).
5. See the introduction to Laycock's *The Complete Enochian Dictionary*.
6. *Bagle* appears elsewhere as a form of *because*.
7. "And you, Brutus?"
8. Table One, side A, line 21.
9. *Radical*, used in this sense, means "root" or "smallest unit."
10. See *John Dee's Five Books of Mystery*, pp. 288–95.
11. After what linguists refer to as the "Great Vowel Shift." The main difference between Middle English and Modern English is the pronunciation of the vowels.
12. Think of Eliza Doolittle in the play *My Fair Lady*: "The rine in spine styes minely on th' pline!"
13. The first English dictionary was not published in London until 1604.
14. Based on Shakespearean phonetics.
15. Called *Zed*, *Ezod*, *Zod*, and sometimes *Izzard*.
16. Present-day English entirely dropped the use of *i* for the consonant sound.
17. Or: *iustice*, *iump*, *Iohann*.
18. Which we write today as *utopia*, *utilize*, *useful*.
19. That is, *up*, *utmost*, *usher*.
20. That is, *savage*, *save*, *David*.

21. In the Lexicon, I have sometimes modernized the usage of *u* and *v* in order to make the words more comprehensible to the modern eye. For instance, the word *Zomdux* (Amidst) appears in Dee's journals as *Zomdvx*.
22. Do not confuse this chart with my own phonetic Angelical pronunciation guide and notes found in the Lexicon and Angelical Psalter.
23. This character—which appears as a combination of *a* and *e* (or *Æ*)—is called an "ash." Sometimes it has the short "a" sound (as in *ash*, *apple*, *ask*), and sometimes it has a long "e" sound (*ether*, *eon*)
24. See the previous footnote.
25. In Old and Middle English, the letter *y* could often indicate the *Th* digraph. This is where we get words like *ye* that are pronounced "thee." This convention was formally dropped from Early Modern English, although some authors in Shakespeare's time still used it. I doubt, however, that it applies to any Angelical words, as Dee seems to have regularly used *y* to indicate the "yuh" sound.
26. See the *Five Books of Mystery*, p. 291, footnote 136, and *Loagaeth*, Table One, side A, line 1.
27. See the entry for *Baltle* in the Lexicon.

Chapter 2

The Forty-Eight Angelical Keys: A Cross-Reference

In order to create the Angelical Lexicon, it was first necessary to create this cross-reference, which contains the entire text of the forty-eight Keys—with the words arranged into columns and categorized by cross-reference numbers. The numbers are then used throughout the Lexicon to indicate in which Key, and where in the Key, any Angelical word can be found.

Dee left two manuscripts containing the forty-eight Keys: The first is his personal Angelical journal, where he recorded Nalvage's transmission of the Keys.[1] The other is a text called the *48 Claves Angelicae*—which is part of a grimoire Dee created separately from his journals, containing the major points of his Angelic magick.[2] The words of the Keys in the *48 Claves* have some differences from those in Dee's private records. I assume the differences are corrections Dee made between recording the words in his journal and recopying them into his grimoire.

Students might notice that the Keys in my cross-reference do not match the same Keys in *The Enochian Magick of Dr. John Dee* by Geoffrey James, in *The Complete Enochian Dictionary* by Donald Laycock, and in other sources. While these books are legendary, and were instrumental in my own study of the Angelical language, I ultimately discovered conflicts between their work and Dee's journals.[3]

Therefore, the text in my cross-reference represents my own analysis of the Keys and their grammatical structure—drawn first from *A True and Faithful Relation*, and secondarily from Dee's *48 Claves Angelicae*. I have striven to preserve the text as received by Dee and Kelley, rather than force it to match my own ideas of what it "should" look like. Where I have encountered ambiguities in Dee's journals or doubt in my own work, I have used the *48 Claves Angelicae* as Dee's final say on the matter.

The following presentation of the Angelical Keys is divided into four columns:

First Column: Cross-Reference Numbers

In *The Enochian Magic of Dr. John Dee*, Geoffrey James introduced a cross-reference numbering system for the Angelical Keys, which seems to have become somewhat traditional among "Enochian" scholars. Although my presentation of the Keys differs from James', I have chosen to retain the same style of cross-referencing. (Note: The Call of the Aethyrs is really the nineteenth in the series. However, again following tradition, I have used "30" for its reference number because the Call actually represents thirty Keys.)

Every word of the Keys has been assigned a number to designate its location. For instance, the fifth word of the twelfth Key is numbered 12.5. We can, then, easily reference the Keys in this cross-reference to see that word 12.5 is *Chis* (Are). These numbers are then used throughout the Lexicon to indicate the locations of the words in the Keys. Therefore, if we look up the word *Chis* in the Lexicon, we can easily discover the locations of *every* appearance (or version) of that word in the Keys.

Second Column: Angelical Words

These are the actual Angelical words as recorded by Dee in his journals, or in his *48 Claves Angelicae*.

Any corrections I have made to this text are indicated with footnotes. Also, you will note some instances of a hyphenated *z-* in this column.

This indicates places where the Angels appear to have given the full "zohd" (or "zed") pronunciation of the letter *z*. For example, the word *Zchis* (They Are) is pronounced "zohd-kiis," and is written in column 2 as "Z-chis."

Third Column: "English Senses"

This column contains the poetic translations of the Angelical words from column 2. These are also found in Dee's journals or the *48 Claves Angelicae*.

Because the poetry of the Calls was written during the time of King James and Shakespeare, I have found it necessary to modernize the text in some places. (See my analysis of the poetry of the Keys in volume I, chapter 3.) Any additions I have included in the text are contained in parentheses. Footnotes will indicate other thoughts, changes, corrections, and so forth.

Fourth Column: Literal Translations

This column is entirely new to the study of the Angelical Keys. As we have seen in the last chapter, many aspects of grammar (such as pronouns and articles) are rare or absent from Angelical. In order to illustrate this, column 4 presents the forty-eight Keys in their *literal* translation. This will show us these missing aspects of grammar at a glance, and can teach us much about how Angelical actually works from a linguistic point of view.

Note that some words appear in this column within quotation marks. These are words that appear strikingly different from the "English senses," and are fully explained in the Lexicon.

Key One			
1.1	Ol	I	*I*
1.2	sonf	reign	*"to reign"*
1.3	vorsg	over you	*over (you)*
1.4	goho	sayeth	*"to say"*
1.5	Iad	the God of	*God*
1.6	Balt	Justice	*justice*
1.7	lansh	in power exalted above	*"exalted power"*
1.8	calz	the firmaments	*firmaments (heavens)*
1.9	vonpho	of wrath:	*of wrath*
1.10	sobra	in whose	*whose*
1.11	z-ol	hands	*hands*
1.12	ror	the Sun	*Sun*
1.13	i	is	*is*
1.14	ta	as	*as*
1.15	nazpsad	a sword	*sword*
1.16	graa	and the Moon	*Moon*
1.17	ta	as	*as*
1.18	malprg	a through-thrusting fire:	*"Fiery Arrow"*
1.19	ds	which	*which*
1.20	holq	measureth	*"to measure"*
1.21	qaa	your garments	*"created form"*
1.22	nothoa	in the midst of	*amidst*
1.23	zimz	my vestures	*vestures*
1.24	od	and	*and*
1.25	commah	trussed you together	*"to truss together"*
1.26	ta	as	*as*
1.27	nobloh	the palms of	*palms*
1.28	zien	my hands:	*hands*
1.29	soba	Whose	*whose*
1.30	thil	seats	*seats*
1.31	gnonp	I garnished with	*garnished*
1.32	prge	the fire of	*fire*

1.33	aldi	gathering	*gathering*
1.34	ds	and (which)	*which*
1.35	urbs	beautified	*"to beautify"*
1.36	oboleh	your garments	*garments*
1.37	grsam	with admiration,	*admiration*
1.38	casarm	to whom	*whom*
1.39	ohorela	I made a law	*"legislate"*
1.40	caba	to govern	*to govern*
1.41	pir	the holy ones,	*holy ones*
1.42	ds	and (which)	*which*
1.43	zonrensg	delivered you	*"to deliver"*
1.44	cab	a rod	*rod*
1.45	erm	(along with) the ark of	*ark*
1.46	iadnah	knowledge.	*knowledge*
1.47	pilah	Moreover,	*moreover*
1.48	farzm	you lifted up your voices	*"to speak up"*
1.49	znrza	and swore	*"to swear"*
1.50	adna	obedience	*obedience*
1.51	gono	and faith	*faith*
1.52	iadpil	to Him	*(unto) Him*
1.53	ds	that	*that*
1.54	hom	liveth	*"to live"*
1.55	toh	and triumpheth	*"to triumph"*
1.56	soba	whose	*whose*
1.57	ipam	beginning is not	*"is not"*[4]
1.58	ul	nor end	*end*
1.59	ipamis	cannot be,	*cannot be*
1.60	ds	which	*which*
1.61	loholo	shineth as	*"to shine"*
1.62	vep	a flame	*flame*

1.63	zomdux	in the midst of	*"amidst"*
1.64	poamal	your palace	*palace*
1.65	od	and	*and*
1.66	bogpa	reigneth	*"to reign"*
1.67	aai	amongst you	*amongst (you)*
1.68	ta	as	*as*
1.69	piap	the balance of	*balance*
1.70	baltle	righteousness	*righteousness*
1.71	od	and	*and*
1.72	vaoan/vooan	truth.	*truth*
1.73	zacar	Move,	*move*
1.74	ca	therefore,	*therefore*
1.75	od	and	*and*
1.76	zamran	show yourselves:	*"to appear"*
1.77	odo	open	*"to open"*
1.78	cicle	the mysteries of	*mysteries*
1.79	qaa	your creation:	*creation*
1.80	zorge	Be friendly unto me:	*be friendly unto me*
1.81	lap	For	*for*
1.82	zirdo	I am	*(I) am*
1.83	noco	a servant of	*servant*
1.84	mad	the same your God:	*god*
1.85	hoath	the true worshipper of	*true worshiper*
1.86	iaida	the Highest.	*The Highest*

Key Two			
2.1	Adgt	Can	*Can*
2.2	upaah	the wings of	*wings*
2.3	zong	the winds	*winds*
2.4	om	understand	*"to understand"*
2.5	faaip	your voices of	*"voicings" (songs)*
2.6	sald	wonder	*wonder*
2.7	viiv	o you the second of	*second*
2.8	L	the First,	*First*
2.9	sobam	whom	*whom*
2.10	ialpurg	the burning flames	*burning flames*
2.11	izazaz	have framed within	*"to frame"*
2.12	piadph	the depths of my jaws	*"my gut"*
2.13	casarma	whom	*whom*
2.14	abramg	I have prepared	*"to prepare"*
2.15	ta	as	*as*
2.16	talho	cups	*cups*
2.17	paracleda	for a wedding	*wedding*
2.18	qta	or as	*or as*
2.19	lorslq	the flowers	*flowers*
2.20	turbs	in their beauty	*(in) beauty*
2.21	ooge	for the chamber	*chamber*
2.22	baltoh	of righteousness.	*righteousness*
2.23	givi	Stronger	*stronger*
2.24	chis	are	*are*
2.25	lusd	your feet	*feet*
2.26	orri	than the barren stone:	*(barren) stone*
2.27	od	And	*and*
2.28	micalp	mightier	*mightier*
2.29	chis	are	*are*
2.30	bia	your voices	*voices*
2.31	ozongon	than the manifold winds.	*manifold winds*

2.32	lap	For	*for*
2.33	noan	you are become	*"have become"*
2.34	trof	a building	*a building*
2.35	cors	such	*such*
2.36	tage	as is not	*as (is) not*
2.37	oq	but	*but*
2.38	manin	in the mind of	*mind*
2.39	iaidon	the All Powerful.	*the All Powerful*
2.40	torzu	Arise	*arise*
2.41	gohel	sayeth the First.	*sayeth the First*
2.42	zacar	Move	*move*
2.43	ca	therefore	*therefore*
2.44	cnoqod	unto His servants.	*(unto) servants*
2.45	zamran	Show yourselves	*"to appear"*
2.46	micalzo	in power	*power*
2.47	od	and	*and*
2.48	ozazm	make (for) me	*make (me)*
2.49	urelp	a strong seething	*seething*
2.50	lap	for	*for*
2.51	zir	I am of	*am*
2.52	Ioiad	Him that liveth forever.	*Him That Liveth Forever*

Key Three			
3.1	Micma	Behold	*behold*
3.2	goho	sayeth	*"to say"*
3.3	piad	your God	*(your) God*
3.4	zir	I am	*(I) am*
3.5	comselh	a Circle	*circle*
3.6	azien	on whose hands	*hands*
3.7	biab	stand	*"to stand"*
3.8	oslondoh	12 Kingdoms.	*12 kingdoms*
3.9	norz	Six	*six*
3.10	chis	are	*are*
3.11	othil	the seats of	*seats of*
3.12	gigipah	living breath	*living breath*
3.13	undl	the rest	*the rest*
3.14	chis	are	*are*
3.15	tapuin	as sharp sickles:	*as (sharp) sickles*
3.16	qmospleh	or the horns of	*or the horns*
3.17	teloch	death	*death*
3.18	quiin	wherein	*wherein*
3.19	toltorg	the creatures of the earth	*creatures*
3.20	chis	are	*are*
3.21	ichisge	[and][5] are not	*are not*
3.22	m	except (by)	*except*
3.23	ozien	mine own hand,	*hand*
3.24	dst	which (also)	*which*
3.25	brgda	sleep	*"to sleep"*
3.26	od	and	*and*
3.27	torzul	shall rise.	*"arise"*
3.28	ili	In the first	*the first*
3.29	eol	I made you	*made*
3.30	balzarg	stewards	*stewards*

3.31	od	and	*and*
3.32	aala	placed you	*"to place"*
3.33	thilnos	in seats 12 of	*12 seats (of)*
3.34	netaab	government,	*government*
3.35	dluga	giving unto	*"to give"*
3.36	vomzarg	every one of you	*every one*
3.37	lonsa	power	*power*
3.38	capmiali	successively	*successively*
3.39	vors	over	*over*
3.40	cla	456,	*456*
3.41	homil	the true ages of	*(true) ages*
3.42	cocasb	time,	*time*
3.43	fafen	to the intent that	*intent*
3.44	izizop	from your highest vessels	*vessels*
3.45	od	and	*and*
3.46	miinoag	the corners	*corners*
3.47	de	of	*of*
3.48	gnetaab	your governments	*(your) governments*
3.49	vaun	you might work	*"to work"*
3.50	nanaeel	my power:	*(my) power*
3.51	panpir	pouring down	*"to pour down"*
3.52	malpirgi	the fires of life and increase	*fires of life and increase*
3.53	caosg	upon the earth	*earth*
3.54	pild	continually.	*continually*
3.55	noan	Thus, you are become	*"have become"*
3.56	unalah	the skirts of	*skirts*
3.57	balt	justice	*justice*
3.58	odvooan	and truth	*and truth*
3.59	dooiap	In the Name of	*(in the) name*
3.60	mad	the same your God,	*god*
3.61	goholor	lift up,	*lift up*

3.62	gohus	I say,	*(I) say*
3.63	amiran	yourselves.	*yourselves*
3.64	micma	Behold,	*behold*
3.65	iehusoz	His mercies	*(God's) mercies*
3.66	cacacom	flourish	*"to flourish"*
3.67	od	and	*and*
3.68	dooain	Name	*name*
3.69	noar	has become	*(has) become*
3.70	micaolz	mighty	*mighty*
3.71	aaiom	amongst us.	*amongst (us)*
3.72	casarmg	In whom	*in whom*
3.73	gohia	we say,	*(we) say*
3.74	z-acar	move	*move*
3.75	uniglag	descend	*"to descend"*
3.76	od	and	*and*
3.77	imuamar	apply yourselves unto us	*"to apply unto"*
3.78	pugo	as unto	*as unto*
3.79	plapli	partakers of	*partakers*
3.80	ananael	the secret wisdom of	*secret wisdom*
3.81	qaan	your creation.	*creation*

Key Four			
4.1	Othil	I have set	*"to set"*
4.2	lasdi	my feet	*feet*
4.3	babage	in the south	*south*
4.4	od	and	*and*
4.5	dorpha	have looked about me	*"to look about"*
4.6	gohol	saying	*"to say"*
4.7	gchisge	are not	*are not*
4.8	avavago	the Thunders of Increase	*Thunders of Increase*
4.9	cormp	numbered	*"to number"*
4.10	pd	33	*33*
4.11	dsonf	which reign in	*which reign*
4.12	viudiv	the second Angle	*second angle*
4.13	casarmi	under whom	*whom*
4.14	oali	I have placed	*"to place"*
4.15	mapm	9639	*9639*
4.16	sobam	whom	*whom*
4.17	ag	none	*none*
4.18	cormpo	hath yet numbered	*hath (yet) numbered*
4.19	crpl	but One,	*but one*
4.20	casarmg	in whom	*(in) whom*
4.21	croodzi	the second beginning of things	*beginning*[6]
4.22	chis	are	*are*
4.23	odugeg	and wax strong	*and wax strong*
4.24	dst	which also	*which (also)*
4.25	capimali	successively	*successively*
4.26	chis	are	*are*
4.27	capimaon	the number of time:	*number of time*
4.28	odlonshin	And their powers	*and powers*
4.29	chis	are	*are*
4.30	talo	as the first	*as the first*
4.31	cla	456:	*456*

4.32	torgu	Arise	*arise*
4.33	norqrasahi	you sons of pleasure	*sons of pleasure*
4.34	od	and	*and*
4.35	fcaosga	visit the earth,	*visit the earth*
4.36	bagle	for	*for*
4.37	zirenaiad	I am the Lord your God	*I am Lord God*
4.38	dsi	which is	*which is*
4.39	odapila	and liveth.	*and live*
4.40	dooaip	In the Name of	*(in the) Name*
4.41	qaal	the Creator,	*Creator*
4.42	z-acar	move	*move*
4.43	odzamran	and show yourselves	*and "appear"*
4.44	obelisong	as pleasant deliverers	*pleasant deliverers*
4.45	restil	that you may praise Him	*to praise (Him?)*
4.46	aaf	amongst	*amongst*
4.47	normolap	the sons of men.	*sons of men*

Key Five			
5.1	Sapah	The Mighty Sounds	*Mighty Sounds*
5.2	zimii	have entered into	*"to enter"*
5.3	duiv	the third angle	*third angle*
5.4	od	and	*and*
5.5	noas	are become	*(have) become*
5.6	taqanis	as olives	*as olives*
5.7	adroch	in the olive mount	*olive mount*
5.8	dorphal	looking with gladness upon	*"looking upon"*
5.9	caosg	the earth	*earth*
5.10	od	and	*and*
5.11	faonts	dwelling within	*dwelling*
5.12	piripsol	the brightness of the heavens	*heavens*
5.13	tablior	as continual comforters,	*as comforters*
5.14	casarm	unto whom	*whom*
5.15	amipzi	I have fastened	*"to fasten"*
5.16	nazarth	pillars of gladness	*pillars (of gladness)*
5.17	af	19	*19*
5.18	od	and	*and*
5.19	dlugar	gave them	*"to give"*
5.20	zizop	vessels	*vessels*
5.21	z-lida	to water	*"to water"*
5.22	caosgi	the earth	*earth*
5.23	toltorgi	with her creatures	*(with) creatures*
5.24	od	and	*and*
5.25	z-chis	they are	*they are*
5.26	esiasch	the brothers of	*brothers*
5.27	L	the First	*The First*
5.28	taviv	and second	*and second*
5.29	od	and	*and*
5.30	iaod	the beginning of	*beginning*
5.31	thild	their own seats	*seats*

5.32	ds	which	*which*
5.33	hubar	are garnished with[7] continually burning lamps	*lamps*
5.34	peral	69636	*69636*
5.35	soba	whose	*whose*
5.36	cormfa	numbers	*numbers*
5.37	chista	are as	*are as*
5.38	la	the first,	*the first*
5.39	uls	the ends,	*ends*
5.40	od	and	*and*
5.41	qcocasb	the contents of time.	*contents of time*
5.42	ca	Therefore,	*therefore*
5.43	niis	come you	*come*
5.44	od	and	*and*
5.45	darbs	obey	*obey*
5.46	qaas	your creation.	*creation*
5.47	fetharzi	Visit us in peace	*visit (in) peace*
5.48	od	and	*and*
5.49	bliora	comfort.	*comfort*
5.50	iaial	Conclude us as	*"to conclude"*
5.51	ednas	receivers of	*receivers*
5.52	cicles	your mysteries:	*mysteries*
5.53	bagle	For why?	*for*
5.54	geiad	Our Lord and Master	*Lord and Master*
5.55	il	is all one.	*is one*

Key Six			
6.1	Gah	The spirits of	*spirits*
6.2	sdiv	the fourth Angle	*fourth angle*
6.3	chis	are	*are*
6.4	em	nine,	*nine*
6.5	micalzo	mighty in	*mighty*
6.6	pilzin	the firmaments of waters	*firmaments of waters*
6.7	sobam	whom	*whom*
6.8	el	the First	*the First*
6.9	harg	hath planted	*"to plant"*
6.10	mir	a torment to	*torment*
6.11	babalon	the wicked	*wicked*
6.12	od	and	*and*
6.13	obloc	a garland to	*garland*
6.14	samvelg	the righteous:	*the righteous*
6.15	dlugar	giving unto them	*"to give"*
6.16	malpurg	fiery darts	*"Fiery Arrows"*
6.17	arcaosgi	to van the earth	*(to van?) the earth*
6.18	od	and	*and*
6.19	acam	7699	*7699*
6.20	canal	continual workmen	*workmen*
6.21	sobolzar	whose courses	*whose courses*
6.22	fbliard	visit with comfort	*visit (with) comfort*
6.23	caosgi	the earth	*earth*
6.24	odchis	and are	*and are*
6.25	anetab	in government	*(in) government*
6.26	od	and	*and*
6.27	miam	continuance	*continuance*
6.28	taviv	as the second	*as second*
6.29	od	and	*and*
6.30	d	the third.	*third*
6.31	darsar	Wherefore	*wherefore*

6.32	solpeth	harken unto	*hearken (unto)*
6.33	bien	my voice.	*(my) voice*
6.34	brita	I have talked of you	*"to speak of"*
6.35	od	and	*and*
6.36	zacam	I move you	*move*
6.37	gmicalzo	in power and presence	*in power*
6.38	sobhaath	whose works	*whose works*
6.39	trian	shall be	*shall be*
6.40	luiahe	a song of honour	*song of honor*
6.41	odecrin	and the praise of	*and praise*
6.42	mad	your God	*god*
6.43	qaaon	in your creation.	*creation*

Key Seven			
7.1	Raas	The east	*east*
7.2	isalman	is a house of	*is a house*
7.3	paradiz-	virgins	*virgins*
7.4	oecrimi	singing praises	*"to sing praises"*
7.5	aao	amongst	*amongst*
7.6	ialpirgah	the flames of the first glory	*flames of the first glory*
7.7	quiin	wherein	*wherein*
7.8	enay	the Lord	*the Lord*
7.9	butmon	hath opened His mouth	*mouth*
7.10	od	and	*and*
7.11	inoas	they are become	*(have) become*
7.12	ni	28	*28*
7.13	paradial	living dwellings	*living dwellings*
7.14	casarmg	in whom	*in whom*
7.15	ugear	the strength of men	*strength*
7.16	chirlan	rejoiceth	*"to rejoice"*
7.17	od	and	*and*
7.18	zonac	they are appareled with	*appareled*
7.19	luciftian	ornaments of brightness	*(ornaments of) brightness*
7.20	corsta	such as	*such as*
7.21	vaulzirn	work wonders	*work wonders*
7.22	tolhami	on all creatures.	*(upon) all creatures*
7.23	soba	Whose	*whose*
7.24	londoh	kingdoms	*kingdoms*
7.25	odmiam	and continuance	*and continuance*
7.26	chistad	are as the third	*are as the third*
7.27	odes	and fourth	*and fourth*
7.28	umadea	strong towers	*strong towers*
7.29	od	and	*and*
7.30	pibliar	places of comfort,	*places of comfort*
7.31	othilrit	the seats of mercy	*seats of mercy*

7.32	odmiam	and continuance.	*and continuance*
7.33	cnoquol	O you servents of	*servants*
7.34	rit	mercy,	*mercy*
7.35	z-acar	move,	*move*
7.36	zamran	appear,	*appear*
7.37	oecrimi	sing praises unto	*"to sing praises"*
7.38	qadah	the creator,	*Creator*
7.39	od	and	*and*
7.40	omicaolz-	be mighty	*(be) mighty*
7.41	aaiom	amongst us.	*amongst (us)*
7.42	bagle	For	*for*
7.43	papnor	to this remembrance	*remembrance*
7.44	idlugam	is given	*is given*
7.45	lonshi	power	*power*
7.46	od	and	*and*
7.47	umplif	our strength	*strength*
7.48	ugegi	waxeth strong	*"to wax strong"*
7.49	bigliad	in our Comforter.	*(in our) comforter*

Key Eight			
8.1	Bazemlo	The midday the first	*midday the first*
8.2	ita	is as	*is as*
8.3	piripson	the third heaven	*(third?) heaven*
8.4	oln	made of	*made (of)*
8.5	nazavabh	hyacinth pillars	*(hyacinth) pillars*
8.6	ox	26	*26*
8.7	casarmg	in whom	*in whom*
8.8	uran	the Elders	*elders*
8.9	chis	are	*are*
8.10	ugeg	become strong	*become strong*
8.11	dsabramg	which I have prepared for	*which prepared*
8.12	baltoha	my own righteousness,	*righteousness*
8.13	gohoiad	sayeth the Lord,	*sayeth God*
8.14	solamian	whose long continuance	*whose (long) continuance*
8.15	trian	shall be	*shall be*
8.16	talolcis	as bucklers to	*as bucklers*
8.17	abaivonin	the stooping dragons	*stooping dragons*
8.18	od	and	*and*
8.19	aziagiar	like unto the harvest of	*like unto the harvest*
8.20	rior	a widow.	*widow*
8.21	irgilchisda	How many are there	*how many are there*
8.22	dspaaox	which remain in	*which remain*
8.23	busd	the glory	*glory*
8.24	caosgo	of the earth	*of the earth*
8.25	dschis	which are	*which are*
8.26	odipuran	and shall not see	*and shall not see*
8.27	teloah	death	*death*
8.28	cacrg	until	*until*
8.29	oisalman	this house	*this house*
8.30	loncho	fall	*fall*
8.31	od	and	*and*

8.32	vovina	the dragon	*dragon*
8.33	carbaf	sink.	*sink (i.e., stoop)*
8.34	niiso	Come away,	*come away*
8.35	bagle	for	*for*
8.36	avavago	the Thunders	*Thunders*
8.37	gohon	have spoken.	*spoken*
8.38	niiso	Come away,	*come away*
8.39	bagle	for	*for*
8.40	momao	the crowns of	*crowns*
8.41	siaion	the temple	*temple*
8.42	od	and	*and*
8.43	mabza	the coat of	*coat*
8.44	iadoiasmomar	Him that is, was, and shall be crowned	*"God eternally crowned"*
8.45	poilp	are divided.	*"to divide"*
8.46	niis	Come,	*come*
8.47	zamran	appear	*appear*
8.48	ciaofi	to the terror	*terror*
8.49	caosgo	of the earth	*of earth*
8.50	od	and	*and*
8.51	bliors	to our comfort	*comfort*
8.52	od	and of	*and*
8.53	corsi	such	*such*
8.54	ta	as	*as*
8.55	abramig	are prepared.	*prepared*

Key Nine			
9.1	Micaoli	A mighty	*mighty*
9.2	bransg	guard of	*guard*
9.3	prgel	fire	*fire*
9.4	napta	with two edged swords	*swords*
9.5	ialpor	flaming	*flaming*
9.6	dsbrin	(which have	*which have*
9.7	efafafe	vials	*vials*
9.8	p	8	*8*
9.9	vonpho	of wrath	*(of) wrath*
9.10	olani	for two times	*twice*
9.11	od	and	*and*
9.12	obza	a half:	*half*
9.13	sobca	whose	*whose*
9.14	upaah	wings	*wings*
9.15	chis	are of	*are*
9.16	tatan	wormwood	*wormwood*
9.17	od	and of	*and*
9.18	tranan	the marrow of	*marrow*
9.19	balye	salt),[8]	*salt*
9.20	alar	have settled	*"to settle"*
9.21	lusda	their feet	*(their) feet*
9.22	soboln	in the west	*west*
9.23	od	and	*and*
9.24	chisholq	are measured	*are "to measure"*
9.25	cnoquodi	with their ministers	*(with) ministers*
9.26	cial	9996.	*9996*
9.27	unal	These	*these*
9.28	aldon	gather up	*"to gather"*
9.29	mom	the moss	*moss*
9.30	caosgo	of the earth	*of earth*
9.31	ta	as	*as*
9.32	lasollor	the rich man	*rich man*

9.33	gnay	doth	*doth*
9.34	limlal	his treasure:	*treasure*
9.35	amma	Cursed	*cursed*
9.36	chiis	are they	*are (they)*
9.37	sobca	whose	*whose*
9.38	madrid	iniquities	*iniquities*
9.39	z-chis	they are.	*(they) are*
9.40	ooanoan	In their eyes	*eyes*
9.41	chis	are	*are*
9.42	aviny	millstones	*millstones*
9.43	drilpi	greater than	*greater than*
9.44	caosgin	the earth	*earth*
9.45	od	and	*and*
9.46	butmoni	from their mouths	*mouths*
9.47	parm	run	*run*
9.48	zumvi	seas of	*seas*
9.49	cnila	blood:	*blood*
9.50	dazis	Their heads	*heads*
9.51	ethamz-	are covered with	*"to cover"*
9.52	achildao	diamond	*diamond*
9.53	od	and	*and*
9.54	mirc	upon	*upon*
9.55	ozol	their [hands][9]	*hands*
9.56	chis	are	*are*
9.57	pidiai	marble	*marble*
9.58	collal	sleeves.	*sleeves*
9.59	ulcinin	Happy is he	*happy*
9.60	asobam	on whom	*(on) whom*
9.61	ucim	they frown not.	*frown not (i.e., smile)*
9.62	bagle	For why?	*for*
9.63	iadbaltoh	The God of Righteousness	*God of Righteousness*
9.64	chirlan	rejoiceth	*"to rejoice"*

9.65	par	in them.	*(in) them*
9.66	niiso	Come away,	*come away*
9.67	od	and	*and*
9.68	ip	not	*not*
9.69	ofafafe	your vials.	*vials*
9.70	bagle	For	*for*
9.71	acocasb	the time	*time*
9.72	icorsca	is such as	*is such as*
9.73	unig	requireth	*"to require"*
9.74	blior	comfort.	*comfort*

Key Ten

There were many difficulties in the reception of Key Ten. The original reception of the Key on pages 130–33 of *A True and Faithful Relation* was flawed, and corrected somewhat on page 192 during the transmission of the English. However, Dee's final result in his *48 Claves Angelicae* does not match the English given in the journal. Both James and Laycock took stabs at fixing it, and Patricia Shaffer has worked on it from her unique standpoint.

The following is my own work on Key Ten. Readers who reference the *48 Claves Angelicae* will see that Dee had "Eors" listed as the word for "thousand."[10] However, this was corrected to *Matb* on page 192 of *A True and Faithful Relation* (10.45 below).

No word was originally given for "hundred," but this was also corrected on page 192 of *A True and Faithful Relation*, where the word for "hundred" was given as *Torb*. "Eors" itself does not seem to have a place in the Calls (see the Lexicon).

There is one final problem with Key Ten, and this is an odd placement of the word *Ol*. It appears in the *48 Claves Angelicae* between *Vohim gizyax*—"Mighty Earthquakes" (10.42–43 below[11]). Of course *Ol* is given as "I" in Key One, and is also given as "24" in Keys Ten and Fourteen. Neither of these translations fit within this part of Key Ten. What struck me as significant is that *Ol* as "24" is given only a few words before the "Mighty Earthquakes" portion of the Key. My current theory is that this recurrence of the word is merely a mistake (perhaps on the part of Kelley), and I have thus removed it from the Call below.

Key Ten			
10.1	Coraxo	The Thunders of Judgment and Wrath	*Thunders of Judgment and Wrath*
10.2	chis	are	*are*
10.3	cormp	numbered	*"to number"*
10.4	od	and	*and*
10.5	blans	are harboured	*"to harbor"*
10.6	lucal	in the north	*north*

10.7	aziazor	in the likeness of	*likeness of*
10.8	paeb	an oak	*oak*
10.9	soba	whose	*whose*
10.10	lilonon	branches	*branches*
10.11	chis	are	*are*
10.12	op	22	*22*
10.13	virq	nests of	*nests*
10.14	eophan	lamentation	*lamentation*
10.15	od	and	*and*
10.16	raclir	weeping	*weeping*
10.17	maasi	laid up	*stored*
10.18	bagle	for	*for*
10.19	caosgi	the earth	*earth*
10.20	ds	which	*which*
10.21	ialpon	burn	*burn*
10.22	dosig	night	*night*
10.23	od	and	*and*
10.24	basgim	day:	*day*
10.25	od	and	*and*
10.26	oxex	vomit out	*"to vomit"*
10.27	dazis	the heads of	*heads*
10.28	siatris	scorpions	*scorpions*
10.29	od	and	*and*
10.30	salbrox	live sulphur	*live sulfur*
10.31	cinxir	myngled with	*"to mingle"*
10.32	faboan	poison.	*poison*
10.33	unalchis	These be	*these are*
10.34	const	the thunders	*thunders*
10.35	ds	that	*that*
10.36	daox	5678	*5678*
10.37	cocasg	times	*times*
10.38	ol	in the 24th part of	*24th*
10.39	oanio	a moment	*moment*

10.40	yor	roar	*roar*
10.41	torb	with a hundred	*hundred*
10.42	vohim	mighty	*mighty*
10.43	gizyax	earthquakes	*earthquakes*
10.44	od	and	*and*
10.45	matb	a thousand	*thousand*
10.46	cocasg	times	*times*
10.47	plosi	as many	*as many*
10.48	molui	surges	*surges*
10.49	ds	which	*which*
10.50	pageip	rest not	*rest not*
10.51	larag	neither	*neither*
10.52	om	know	*know*
10.53	droln	any	*any*
10.54	matorb	(long)	*long*
10.55	cocasb	time	*time*
10.56	emna	here.	*here*
10.57	lpatralx	One rock	*one rock*
10.58	yolci	bringeth forth	*"to bring forth"*
10.59	matb	1000	*a thousand*
10.60	nomig	even as	*even (as)*
10.61	monons	the heart of	*heart*
10.62	olora	man	*man*
10.63	gnay	doth	*doth*
10.64	angelard	his thoughts.	*thoughts*
10.65	ohio	Woe	*woe*
10.66	ohio	woe	*woe*
10.67	ohio	woe	*woe*
10.68	ohio	woe	*woe*
10.69	ohio	woe	*woe*
10.70	ohio	woe	*woe*
10.71	noib	yea	*yes*
10.72	ohio	woe	*woe*

10.73	caosgon	be to the earth,	*unto the earth*
10.74	bagle	for	*for*
10.75	madrid	her iniquity	*iniquity*
10.76	i	is	*is*
10.77	zirop	was	*was*
10.78	chiso	and shall be	*shall be*
10:79	drilpa	great.	*great*
10.80	niiso	Come away,	*come away*
10.81	crip	but	*but*
10.82	ip	not	*not*
10.83	nidali	your noises.	*noises*

Key Eleven			
11.1	Oxiayal	The Mighty Seat	*The Mighty Seat*
11.2	holdo	groaned	*groaned*
11.3	od	and	*and*
11.4	zirom	they were	*(they) were*
11.5	o	5	*5*
11.6	coraxo	Thunders	*Thunders*
11.7	ds	which	*which*
11.8	zildar	flew into	*fly into*
11.9	raasy	the east	*east*
11.10	od	and	*and*
11.11	vabzir	the Eagle	*eagle*
11.12	camliax	spake	*spake*
11.13	od	and	*and*
11.14	bahal	cried with a loud voice,	*"to cry loudly"*
11.15	niiso	Come away!	*come away*
11.16	od	And	*and*
11.17	aldon	they gathered themselves together	*"to gather together"*
11.18	od	and	*and*
11.19	noas	became	*"to become"*
11.20	salman	the house of	*house*
11.21	teloch	death[12]	*death*
11.22	casarman	of whom	*whom*
11.23	holq	it is measured	*"to measure"*
11.24	od	and	*and*
11.25	ti	it is	*it is*
11.26	ta	as	*as*
11.27	z-chis	they are	*(they) are*
11.28	soba	whose	*whose*
11.29	cormf	number	*number*
11.30	iga	is 31.	*is 31*
11.31	niisa	Come away,	*come away*

11.32	bagle	for	*for*
11.33	abramg	I have prepared for	*"to prepare"*
11.34	noncp	you.	*you*
11.35	zacar	Move,	*move*
11.36	ca	therefore,	*therefore*
11.37	od	and	*and*
11.38	zamran	show yourselves:	*"to appear"*
11.39	odo	open	*"to open"*
11.40	cicle	the mysteries of	*mysteries*
11.41	qaa	your creation:	*creation*
11.42	zorge	Be friendly unto me:	*be friendly unto me*
11.43	lap	For	*for*
11.44	zirdo	I am	*(I) am*
11.45	noco	a servant of	*servant*
11.46	mad	the same your God:	*god*
11.47	hoath	the true worshipper of	*true worshiper*
11.48	iaida	the Highest.	*the Highest*

Key Twelve			
12.1	Nonci	O you	*you*
12.2	dsonf	that reign	*that reign*
12.3	babage	in the south	*south*
12.4	od	and	*and*
12.5	chis	are	*are*
12.6	ob	28	*28*
12.7	hubaio	the lanterns of	*lanterns*
12.8	tibibp	sorrow	*sorrow*
12.9	allar	bind up	*"to bind up"*
12.10	atraah	your girdles	*girdles*
12.11	od	and	*and*
12.12	ef	visit us.	*"to visit"*
12.13	drix	Bring down	*"to bring down"*
12.14	fafen	your train	*train*
12.15	mian	3663	*3663*
12.16	ar	that	*that*
12.17	enay	the Lord	*the Lord*
12.18	ovof	may be magnified	*"to magnify"*
12.19	soba	whose	*whose*
12.20	dooain	name	*name*
12.21	aai	amongst you	*amongst*
12.22	ivonph	is wrath.	*is wrath*
12.23	zacar	Move,	*move*
12.24	gohus	I say,[13]	*I say*
12.25	od	and	*and*
12.26	zamran	show yourselves:	*"to appear"*
12.27	odo	open	*"to open"*
12.28	cicle	the mysteries of	*mysteries*
12.29	qaa	your creation:	*creation*
12.30	zorge	Be friendly unto me:	*be friendly unto me*
12.31	lap	For	*for*
12.32	zirdo	I am	*(I) am*

12.33	noco	a servant of	*servant*
12.34	mad	the same your God:	*god*
12.35	hoath	the true worshipper of	*true worshiper*
12.36	iaida	the Highest.	*the Highest*

Key Thirteen			
13.1	Napeai	O you swords of	*swords*
13.2	babagen	the south	*south*
13.3	dsbrin	which have	*which have*
13.4	ux	42	*42*
13.5	ooaona	eyes	*eyes*
13.6	lring	to stir up	*to stir up*
13.7	vonph	wrath of	*wrath*
13.8	doalim	sin,	*sin*
13.9	eolis	making	*"to make"*
13.10	ollog	men	*men*
13.11	orsba	drunken	*drunken*
13.12	dschis	which are	*which are*
13.13	affa	empty:	*empty*
13.14	micma	Behold	*behold*
13.15	isro	the promise of	*promise of*
13.16	mad	God	*god*
13.17	od	and	*and*
13.18	lonshitox	His power	*his power*
13.19	ds	which	*which*
13.20	iumd	is called	*(is) called*
13.21	aai[14]	amongst you	*amongst*
13.22	grosb	a bitter sting.	*(bitter) sting*
13.23	zacar	Move	*move*
13.24	od	and	*and*
13.25	zamran	show yourselves:	*"to appear"*
13.26	odo	open	*"to open"*
13.27	cicle	the mysteries of	*mysteries*
13.28	qaa	your creation:	*creation*
13.29	zorge	Be friendly unto me:	*be friendly unto me*
13.30	lap	For	*for*
13.31	zirdo	I am	*(I) am*
13.32	noco	a servant of	*servant*

13.33	mad	the same your God:	*god*
13.34	hoath	the true worshipper of	*true worshiper*
13.35	iaida	the Highest.	*the Highest*

The transmission of Key Fourteen is missing from Dee's journals. We only have the English for this Key given later (see *TFR*, page 193), and the Angelical provided in Dee's *48 Claves Angelicae*.

Key Fourteen			
14.1	Noromi	O you sons	*sons*
14.2	bagie	of fury,	*fury*
14.3	pasbs	the daughters	*daughters*
14.4	oiad	of the just,	*of God*
14.5	ds	which	*which*
14.6	trint	sit	*"to sit"*
14.7	mirc	upon	*upon*
14.8	ol	24	*24*
14.9	thil	seats	*seats*
14.10	dods	vexing	*"to vex"*
14.11	tolham	all creatures	*all creatures*
14.12	caosgo	of the earth	*of earth*
14.13	homin	with age,	*age*
14.14	dsbrin	which have	*which have*
14.15	oroch	under you	*under*
14.16	quar	1636.	*1636*
14.17	micma	Behold	*behold*
14.18	bial	the voice	*voice*
14.19	oiad	of God	*of God*
14.20	aisro	promise of	*"to promise"*
14.21	tox	him	*him*
14.22	dsium	which is called	*which (is) called*
14.23	aai	amongst you	*amongst*
14.24	baltim	fury, or extreme justice.	*extreme justice (fury)*
14.25	zacar	Move	*move*
14.26	od	and	*and*
14.27	zamran	show yourselves:	*"to appear"*
14.28	odo	open	*"to open"*

14.29	cicle	the mysteries of	*mysteries*
14.30	qaa	your creation:	*creation*
14.31	zorge	Be friendly unto me:	*be friendly unto me*
14.32	lap	For	*for*
14.33	zirdo	I am	*(I) am*
14.34	noco	a servant of	*servant*
14.35	mad	the same your God:	*god*
14.36	hoath	the true worshipper of	*true worshiper*
14.37	iaida	the Highest.	*the Highest*

The transmission of Key Fifteen is missing from Dee's journals. We only have the English for this Key given later (see *TFR*, page 193), and the Angelical provided in Dee's *48 Claves Angelicae*.

Key Fifteen			
15.1	Yls	O thou	*thou*
15.2	tabaan	the governor of	*governor*
15.3	lialprt	the first flame	*first flame*
15.4	casarman	under whose	*(under) whose*
15.5	upaahi	wings	*wings*
15.6	chis	are	*are*
15.7	darg	6739	*6739*
15.8	dsoado	which weave	*which weave*
15.9	caosgi	the earth	*earth*
15.10	orscor	with dryness	*dryness*
15.11	ds	which	*which*
15.12	omax	knowest	*knowest*
15.13	monasci	the great name	*great name*
15.14	baeovib	righteousness	*righteousness*
15.15	od	and	*and*
15.16	emetgis	the seal of	*seal*
15.17	iaiadix	honour.	*honor*
15.18	zacar	Move,	*move*
15.19	od	and	*and*
15.20	zamran	show yourselves:	*"to appear"*
15.21	odo	open	*"to open"*
15.22	cicle	the mysteries of	*mysteries*
15.23	qaa	your creation:	*creation*
15.24	zorge	Be friendly unto me:	*be friendly unto me*
15.25	lap	For	*for*
15.26	zirdo	I am	*(I) am*
15.27	noco	a servant of	*servant*
15.28	mad	the same your God:	*god*
15.29	hoath	the true worshipper of	*true worshiper*
15.30	iaida	the Highest.	*the Highest*

Key Sixteen			
16.1	Yls[15]	O thou	*thou*
16.2	vivialprt	of the second flame[16]	*second flame*
16.3	salman	the house of	*house*
16.4	balt	justice	*justice*
16.5	ds	which	*which*
16.6	acroodzi	hast thy beginning	*beginning*
16.7	busd	in glory	*glory*
16.8	od	and	*and*
16.9	bliorax	shalt comfort	*"to comfort"*
16.10	balit	the just:	*the just*
16.11	dsinsi	which walkest upon	*which walk*
16.12	caosg	the earth	*earth*
16.13	lusdan	with feet	*feet*
16.14	emod	8763	*8763*
16.15	dsom	that understand	*that understand*
16.16	od	and	*and*
16.17	tliob	separate creatures:	*"to classify creatures"*
16.18	drilpa	Great	*great*
16.19	geh	art	*are*
16.20	yls	thou	*thou*
16.21	madzilodarp	in the God of stretch forth and conquer.	*God of conquest*
16.22	zacar	Move	*move*
16.23	od	and	*and*
16.24	zamran	show yourselves:	*"to appear"*
16.25	odo	open	*"to open"*
16.26	cicle	the mysteries of	*mysteries*
16.27	qaa	your creation:	*creation*
16.28	zorge	Be friendly unto me:	*be friendly unto me*
16.29	lap	For	*for*
16.30	zirdo	I am	*(I) am*
16.31	noco	a servant of	*servant*

16.32	mad	the same your God:	*god*
16.33	hoath	the true worshipper of	*true worshiper*
16.34	iaida	the Highest.	*the Highest*

Key Seventeen			
17.1	Yls	O thou	*thou*
17.2	dialprt	third flame	*third flame*
17.3	soba	whose	*whose*
17.4	upaah	wings	*wings*
17.5	chis	are	*are*
17.6	nanba	thorns	*thorns*
17.7	zixlay	to stir up	*to stir up*
17.8	dodsih	vexation	*vexation*
17.9	odbrint	and hast	*and has*
17.10	taxs	7336	*7336*
17.11	hubaro	lamps living	*(burning) lamps*
17.12	tastax	going before	*"to precede"*
17.13	ylsi	thee.	*thee*
17.14	sobaiad	Whose God	*whose God*
17.15	ivonpovnph	is wrath in anger.	*is "wrath of wrath"*
17.16	aldon	Gird up	*"to gather"*
17.17	daxil	thy loins	*your loins*
17.18	od	and	*and*
17.19	toatar	harken.	*"to listen"*
17.20	zacar	Move,	*move*
17.21	od	and	*and*
17.22	zamran	show yourselves:	*"to appear"*
17.23	odo	open	*"to open"*
17.24	cicle	the mysteries of	*mysteries*
17.25	qaa	your creation:	*creation*
17.26	zorge	Be friendly unto me:	*be friendly unto me*
17.27	lap	For	*for*
17.28	zirdo	I am	*(I) am*
17.29	noco	a servant of	*servant*
17.30	mad	the same your God:	*god*
17.31	hoath	the true worshipper of	*true worshiper*
17.32	iaida	the Highest.	*the Highest*

Key Eighteen			
18.1	Yls	O thou	*thou*
18.2	micalzo	mighty	*mighty*
18.3	ialpirt	light and	*light*
18.4	ialprg	burning flame of	*burning flame*
18.5	bliors	comfort	*comfort*
18.6	ds	which	*which*
18.7	odo	openest	*"to open"*
18.8	busdir	the glory	*glory*
18.9	oiad	of God	*of God*
18.10	ovoars	to the center	*center*
18.11	caosgo	of the earth.	*of the earth*
18.12	casarmg	In whom	*in whom*
18.13	laiad	the secrets of truth	*secrets of truth*
18.14	eran	6332	*6332*
18.15	brints	have	*have*
18.16	casasam	their abiding	*abiding*
18.17	ds	which	*which*
18.18	iumd	is called	*(is) called*
18.19	aqlo	in thy	*thy*
18.20	adohi	kingdom	*kingdom*
18.21	moz	joy,	*joy*
18.22	od	and	*and*
18.23	maoffas	not to be measured.	*"measureless"*
18.24	bolp	Be thou	*(be) thou*
18.25	comobliort	a window of comfort	*window of comfort*
18.26	pambt	unto me.	*unto (me)*
18.27	zacar	Move	*move*
18.28	od	and	*and*
18.29	zamran	show yourselves:	*"to appear"*
18.30	odo	open	*"to open"*
18.31	cicle	the mysteries of	*mysteries*
18.32	qaa	your creation:	*creation*

18.33	zorge	Be friendly unto me:	*be friendly unto me*
18.34	lap	For	*for*
18.35	zirdo	I am	*(I) am*
18.36	noco	a servant of	*servant*
18.37	mad	the same your God:	*god*
18.38	hoath	the true worshipper of	*true worshiper*
18.39	iaida	the Highest.	*the Highest*

The Key of the Aethyrs			
30.1	Madriiax	O you heavens	*heavens*
30.2	dspraf	which dwell in	*which dwell*
30.3	[Lil]	[the First Aethyr]	*[the First Aethyr]*
30.4	chismicaolz	are mighty in	*are mighty*
30.5	saanir	the parts	*parts*
30.6	caosgo	of the earth,	*of the earth*
30.7	od	and	*and*
30.8	fisis	execute	*"to execute"*
30.9	balzizras	the judgment of	*judgment*
30.10	iaida	the Highest.	*the Highest*
30.11	nonca	To you	*(to) you*
30.12	gohulim	it is said,	*(it is) said*
30.13	micma	Behold	*behold*
30.14	adoian	the face of	*face*
30.15	mad	your God,	*god*
30.16	iaod	the beginning of	*beginning*
30.17	bliorb	comfort:	*comfort*
30.18	sabaooaona	whose eyes	*whose eyes*
30.19	chis	are	*are*
30.20	luciftias	the brightness of	*brightness*
30.21	piripsol	the heavens:	*heavens*
30.22	ds	which	*which*
30.23	abraassa	provided	*"to provide"*
30.24	noncf	you	*you*
30.25	netaaib	for the government of	*government*
30.26	caosgi	the earth,	*earth*
30.27	od	and	*and*
30.28	tilb	her	*her*
30.29	adphaht	unspeakable	*unspeakable*
30.30	damploz	variety	*variety*
30.31	tooat	furnishing	*"to furnish"*

30.32	noncf	you	*you*
30.33	gmicalzoma	with a power (of) understanding	*power of understanding*
30.34	lrasd	to dispose	*to dispose*
30.35	tofglo	all things	*all (things)*
30.36	marb	according to	*according to*
30.37	yarry	the providence of	*providence*
30.38	Idoigo	Him that sitteth upon the Holy Throne	*Him who sits upon the Holy Throne*
30.39	od	and	*and*
30.40	torzulp	rose up	*"to rise"*
30.41	iaodaf	in the beginning	*(in the) beginning*
30.42	gohol	saying,	*"to say"*
30.43	caosga	The earth	*earth*
30.44	tabaord	let her be governed by	*be governed*
30.45	saanir	her parts	*parts*
30.46	od	and	*and*
30.47	christeos	let there be	*let there be*
30.48	yrpoil	division	*division*
30.49	tiobl	in her,	*(within) her*
30.50	busdirtilb	that the glory of her	*glory (of) her*
30.51	noaln	may be	*may be*
30.52	paid	always	*always*
30.53	orsba	drunken	*drunken*
30.54	od	and	*and*
30.55	dodrmni	vexed	*vexed*
30.56	zilna	in itself:	*(within) itself*
30.57	elzaptilb	Her course	*her course*
30.58	parmgi	let it run with	*(let) run*
30.59	piripsax	the heavens	*heavens*
30.60	od	and	*and*

30.61	ta	as	*as*
30.62	qurlst	a handmaid	*handmaid*
30.63	booapis	let her serve them:	*"to serve"*
30.64	lnibm	One season	*one season*
30.65	oucho	let it confound	*"to confound"*
30.66	symp	another:	*another*
30.67	od	and	*and*
30.68	christeos	let there be	*let there be*
30.69	agtoltorn	no creature	*no creature*
30.70	mirc	upon	*upon*
30.71	q	or	*or*
30.72	tiobl	within her	*(within) her*
30.73	lel	the same:	*same*
30.74	ton	All	*all*
30.75	paombd	her members	*members*
30.76	dilzmo	let them differ in	*"to differ"*
30.77	aspian	their qualities:	*qualties*
30.78	od	And	*and*
30.79	christeos	let there be	*let there be*
30.80	agltoltorn	no one creature	*no one creature*
30.81	parach	equal with	*equal*
30.82	asymp	another.	*another*
30.83	cordziz	The reasonable creatures of earth, or men	*"mankind"*
30.84	dodpal	let them vex	*"to vex"*
30.85	od	and	*and*
30.86	fifalz	weed out	*weed out*
30.87	lsmnad	one another:	*one another*
30.88	od	And	*and*
30.89	fargt	the dwelling places,	*dwelling places*
30.90	bams	let them forget	*"to forget"*
30.91	omaoas	their names.	*names*

30.92	conisbra	The work of man	*work of man*
30.93	od	and	*and*
30.94	avavox	his pomp,	*his pomp*
30.95	tonug	let them be defaced:	*"to deface"*
30.96	orscatbl	His buildings,	*buildings*
30.97	noasmi	let them become	*(let) become*
30.98	tabges	caves for	*caves*
30.99	levithmong	the beasts of the field:	*beasts of the field*
30.100	unchi	Confound	*"to confound"*
30.101	omptilb	her understanding with	*her understanding*
30.102	ors	darkness	*darkness*
30.103	bagle	For why?	*for*
30.104	moooah	It repenteth me	*"to repent"*
30.105	olcordziz	I made man.	*made mankind*
30.106	lcapimao	One while	*one while*
30.107	ixomaxip	let her be known,	*let her be known*
30.108	odcacocasb	and another while	*and another while*
30.109	gosaa	a stranger:	*stranger*
30.110	baglen	Because	*because*
30.111	pii	she is	*she is*
30.112	tianta	the bed of	*bed*
30.113	ababalond	an harlot,	*harlot*
30.114	odfaorgt	and the dwelling place of	*and the dwelling place*
30.115	telocvovim	him that is fallen:	*"death dragon"*
30.116	madriiax	O you heavens	*heavens*
30.117	torzu	arise,	*arise*
30.118	oadriax	the lower heavens	*lower heavens*
30.119	orocha	beneath you,	*beneath*
30.120	aboapri	let them serve you:	*"to serve"*
30.121	tabaori	govern	*"to govern"*

30.122	priaz	those	*those*
30.123	artabas	that govern:	*that govern*
30.124	adrpan	Cast down	*cast down*
30.125	corsta	such as	*such as*
30.126	dobix	fall.	*"to fall"*
30.127	yolcam	Bring forth with	*"to bring forth"*
30.128	priazi	those	*those*
30.129	arcoazior	that increase:	*that increase*
30.130	odquasb	And destroy	*and destroy*
30.131	qting	the rotten:	*rotten*
30.132	ripir	No place	*no place*
30.133	paaoxt	let it remain	*"to remain"*
30.134	sagacor	in one number:	*in one number*
30.135	uml	Add	*"to add"*
30.136	od	and	*and*
30.137	prdzar	diminish	*"to diminish"*
30.138	cacrg	until	*until*
30.139	aoiveae	the stars	*stars*
30.140	cormpt	be numbered:	*(are) numbered*
30.141	torzu	Arise,	*arise*
30.142	zacar	move,	*move*
30.143	odzamran	and appear	*"to appear"*
30.144	aspt	before	*before*
30.145	sibsi	the covenant of	*covenant*
30.146	butmona	his mouth	*mouth*
30.147	ds	which	*which*
30.148	surzas	he hath sworn	*"to swear"*
30.149	tia	unto us	*unto (us)*
30.150	baltan	in his justice:	*justice*
30.151	odo	Open	*"to open"*
30.152	cicle	the mysteries of	*mysteries*
30.153	qaa	your creation:	*creation*
30.154	od	and	*and*

30.155	ozazma	make us	*"to make"*
30.156	plapli	partakers of	*partakers*
30.157	iadnamad	undefiled knowl-edge.	*pure knowledge*

Endnotes

1. *A True and Faithful Relation*, p. 79ff.
2. See Sloane MS 3191. James' *Enochian Magick of Dr. John Dee* is derived from this same grimoire.
3. See the Introduction to volume I of this work.
4. There is no indication of the word *beginning* in the Angelical here.
5. Dee had the word *to* in this place. However, the word *and* makes more sense. Remember, however, that neither *to* nor *and* (*Od*) are indicated in the Angelical. They are implied only by context.
6. There is no indication of the word *second* in this Angelical.
7. The word *garnish* (*Gnonp*) does not appear in this place.
8. Parentheses are Dee's.
9. Dee had *heads* in this place. However, the Angelical indicates *hands* instead, and that makes more sense in the Call.
10. *The Enochian Magic of Dr. John Dee*, by Geoffrey James, p. 85.
11. And James p. 85.
12. The English for words 11.16–18 is found in *A True and Faithful Relation*, p. 193. Dee noted that no Angelical had been given in the Key for (all of) those words, so he went back and added words 11.16 and 18 (*Od*) and 11.19 (*Noas*).
13. Note this departure from the Repetitive Formula Pattern (see the Lexicon). This addition of *Gohus* ("I Say!") is found in *A True and Faithful Relation*, p. 136.
14. Words 13.21–22 are missing from *TFR*. We have only the English given for them later (see *TFR*, p. 193), and we find the Angelical in Dee's *48 Claves*.
15. The first twelve words of this Key are missing from *TFR*. We have only the English given for them later (see *TFR*, p. 193), and we find the Angelical in Dee's *48 Claves*.
16. The Angel Illemese gives this English in *A True and Faithful Relation*, p. 200, adding *of the*.

Chapter Three

An Encyclopedic Lexicon of the Tongue of Angels

How to Use This Lexicon

I will illustrate here how to use this Lexicon with a few examples. First, a standard entry looks like this:

> **Busdir** (buz-der) *n.* Glory
>
> 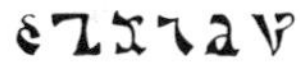
>
> 18.8 . . . openest *the glory* of God.

As we can see, the main entry appears in bold type. Immediately following that, in parentheses, is the word's pronunciation—given in a special key included in this chapter.

Following that is the grammatical function or part of speech (noun, verb, conjunction, and so on). Note that these designations are somewhat loose in Angelical. There are cases where a word might appear as different parts of speech depending on how it is used—such as the English word *promise*, which could be a noun (as in *a promise*) or a verb (*to promise*), although the Angelical does not indicate the difference by anything more than the context of the sentence. In such cases, I have generally applied the part of speech that matches its usage in the sentence in question. In several cases, I have suggested more than one part of speech for a given word.

Next is the definition—or "English sense"—of the word. See the "Angelical Linguistics" chapter for discussion about English senses and fluid definitions.

Then, to the extreme right of the page, we see the word spelled in Angelical characters (running right to left). Note that these characters will not always match the English letters given for the same word. This is due to what I call "phonetic glosses" utilized by Dee as he recorded the words. (Also see the "Angelical Linguistics" chapter for a full discussion of Dee's phonetic glosses.)

Finally, we have the cross-reference number indicating in which Key the word appears and the position of that word within the Key, followed by a sample of the sentence in which the word is used. (The English words indicated by the Angelical are in italics.) This allows one to see at a glance exactly how the word is used in the Keys, which is how we know its proper part of speech.

Following is an example of a compound word entry:

Busdirtilb (buz-der-tilb) [*Busdir* + *Tilb*] *comp.* Glory (of) Her

30.50 . . . that *the glory of her* may be . . .

This entry is the same as a standard entry, with one addition: the word elements that make up the compound are included in brackets directly after the pronunciation. These word elements will each have their own entries in the Lexicon, pointing back to the compound word itself.

There are three further types of entries to cover here. First, the main entry may appear in italics:

Iusmach (jus-mak) *v.* To Beget

The italics indicate that the word comes from a source other than the forty-eight Angelical Keys—such as words from *Loagaeth*, words from the *Corpus Omnium* (see chapter 3 in volume I), the names of the Angelical letters, words from the Alchemical Cipher the Angels gave to Dee, random words spoken by the Angels, and so on. These entries will always include a reference note explaining where the word comes from. (Also see the "Sources for All Words Found in This Lexicon" section of this chapter for a list of sources used to compile this Lexicon.)

Second, the main entry may appear in ALL CAPS:

PERAL (pee-AR-al) 69636

30.50 . . . lamps *6936* whose numbers are. . .

These entries indicate an apparent word in the forty-eight Angelical Keys that, in translation, is defined as a grouping of numbers. Because of this ambiguity, I have indicated these words with ALL CAPS.

Third, the main entry may appear in quotation marks:

"Azia" (ay-ZII-ay) *prep.* Like (unto)

Compounds:

Aziagiar (ay-zii-AY-jii-er)
[*"Azia" + "Giar"*] Like unto the Harvest

This indicates a "word element." Most often, this is an element of a compound word, and the entry will point back to the compound itself. Such entries are in quotation marks because compounding often changes the spelling of the words (see the "Angelical Linguistics" chapter). Therefore, when they stand alone, both the spelling and the pronunciation of such word elements are suspect.

Searching out these "word elements" from the mass of known Angelical words represents a significant expansion of our previous understanding of the language. Although we can't be sure of their spelling and forms of proper usage, it offers us a solid foundation from which to explore the language deeper. At the very least, it definitely expands the available data in hunting for the root forms of the words.

Of course, sometimes compounds are made from words that appear elsewhere in the Keys on their own. In such cases, we know how such words are spelled and pronounced, so their entries do not appear in quotation marks. Their entries will, however, point to the compound as well.

Finally, here are the explanations of the various sections you will find within each main entry:

Pronunciation Notes

The pronunciation notes are perhaps the most unique and useful aspect of this Lexicon. While Dee included small phonetic notes with most of the words he recorded, modern students have found them less than useful. (Remember John Dee was writing in Early Modern English, which often confuses modern students.) Because of this, most existing "Enochian dictionaries" pay little attention to Dee's notations, and the authors have provided pronunciations based loosely upon their own understanding of present-day English.

On the other hand, I have spent some time deciphering Dee's notes on their own terms. His notations seem to be rather haphazard for the first two Keys, but he settles into a fairly standard format by the end of Key Two. My analysis of this format has led me to the following assumptions:

1) Dee generally divided his phonetic notes by placing spaces between the syllables.
2) A letter that stands alone in a syllable takes its long sound. For instance, an *a* standing alone will sound like "ay," an *l* standing alone will sound like "el," etc. Otherwise:
3) Vowels take their long or short sounds depending on their position within a syllable. If a vowel appears at the end of the syllable, it usually takes the long sound. If it appears in the middle of a syllable (i.e., it is directly followed by a consonant within the same syllable), it will most often take the short sound. Finally:
4) The general rules of Early Modern English apply overall, although there are some Middle English inclusions as well. (Again, see the "Angelical Linguistics" chapter for more information.)

I have arrived at the above assumptions primarily with the aid of marginal notations left by Dee along with his phonetic notes—which often gave examples of other words that rhymed with a given Angelical word or syllable. He also used several useful phonetic notations in the *48 Claves Angelicae* that further backed up my research.

In this Lexicon, I have included *all* of Dee's phonetic notes from his journals. If he left such a note (or notes) for a word, I have indicated it by adding an asterisk (*) to the word's pronunciation. Then, within the "Pronunciation Notes" section of the entry, I have recorded Dee's note (*in italics*) and followed it with my own explanation.

The bulk of these notes are found in *A True and Faithful Relation*, recorded as Dee received the forty-eight Angelical Keys. (Much thanks goes to Patricia Shaffer, who tirelessly gathered all of Dee's *TFR* notes into one document, entitled *DeesPronunciationNotes.RTF*.) Therefore, I do not include references with these notes, as the word is already cross-referenced by Key.

However, Dee also left pronunciation notes in the *Five Books of Mystery* and the *48 Claves Angelicae*. If such secondary notes exist, I have also included them and referenced their sources.

If Dee did not include any notes for a word, I have given a pronunciation based upon my overall study of the language. If I include a pronunciation note in such an entry, it is only to explain my own work, and there will be no asterisk or reference to Dee's journals.

"Also" and Shared Root

Angelical words are formed primarily of small root words that undergo (often inexplicable) metamorphosis when used in different ways. Therefore, most of the entries in the Lexicon include notes that compare the main word with other words from Dee's journals. This helps us discover the Angelical roots at the hearts of the words.

First and foremost is the "Also" section found in most entries, which points out all of the differing "versions" of the same word in the Lexicon.

Some entries also have a "Shared root" section, to indicate differing words that may share a linguistic root. (This is based upon both similar spellings and similar definitions.) In these cases, I will likely include a notation highlighting the probable root.

Other Notes

Sometimes Dee also left notes about the definition of a word. If so, the definition in this Lexicon will include an asterisk (*), and the word's entry will include a "Note" section with Dee's comment (*in italics*). I then include my own comments directly thereafter.

In many cases, I have comments to make on a word where Dee was silent. At such times, there will be no asterisk or italics, but my own notes will appear in the "Note" section. There may be more than one "Note" section for any given entry.

Compare from *Loagaeth*

Finally, some entires include a "Compare from *Loagaeth*" section. This is drawn from my work on the first Table of the Holy Book—which is the only Table containing entire words in each cell, rather than single letters. I believe this was intended primarily to help us decipher the words in the remaining forty-eight Tables.

My work on this first Table was similar to my earlier work on the Angelical Keys. I simply began with the first word on the first side of the Table (which happens to be *Zuresch*), and compared it with every other word in the Table. (Remember there are nearly 4802 words in total! See the chapter on the *Book of Loagaeth* in volume I.) I then moved to the second word in the Table and repeated the same process, and so on.

In fact, my work on the first Table is still ongoing, and I will present my results at a future date. Meanwhile, I have discovered several words in *Loagaeth* that also appear in the Keys, as well as many words that appear linguistically related to words from the Keys. I have also found the names of several Angelical letters and one or two known "Enochian" Angels. These *Loagaeth* words that are recognizably similar or identical to those in this *Lexicon* are included in the "Compare from *Loagaeth*" section. (This helps to illustrate that the language of the Holy Book is not separate from the language of the forty-eight Keys.)

Abbreviations Used in This Lexicon

1 Enoch	= The Ethiopic Book of Enoch
Five Books	= *John Dee's Five Books of Mystery*
48 Claves	= *48 Claves Angelicae* (from Sloane 3191)

RFP	= Repetitive Formula Pattern (*See note)
TFR	= *A True and Faithful Relation . . .*
adj.	= adjective
adv.	= adverb
comp.	= compound
conj.	= conjunction
n.	= noun
pl.	= plural
prep.	= preposition
pron.	= pronoun
prop. n.	= proper noun
sing.	= singular
v.	= verb

*Note on *RFP*: From Keys Eleven to Eighteen, Dee was instructed to append the last fourteen words of Key One—*Zacar, ca, od zamran. Odo cicle qaa. Zorge, lap zirdo noco mad, hoath Iaida.* This was dubbed the "Repetitive Formula Pattern" by Patricia Shaffer. In the Lexicon, each word that appears in the Repetitive Formula Pattern is simply marked *RFP*, instead of listing out all references for the word in Keys One and Eleven to Eighteen. *RFP* words will always be found within the last fourteen words of each of these nine Keys.

Note, however, that the final words of these Keys do differ in some minor details in Dee's *48 Claves Angelicae*. (For example, see the *RFP* at the end of Key Twelve.) When this occurs, I have stuck with the *48 Claves* as Dee's final say.

Sources for All Words Found in This Lexicon

The Angelical Keys are found in *TFR* on pages 79–138, 190–194, and 199–208. They are also found in Dee's *48 Claves Angelicae*, part of Sloane MS 3191. The words from the *48 Claves* are shown in the third column of Geoffrey James' section on the Keys in *The Enochian Magick of Dr. John Dee*, p. 65ff.

The names of the thirty Aethyrs are all found on page 209 of *TFR*. The names of the ninety-one Parts of the Earth are found on pages 140–152 of *TFR*. However, they are also found in Dee's Angelical grimoire (which he compiled from his raw journals), known as Sloane MS 3191 (specifically, part II: *The Book of Earthly Knowledge, Aid, and Victory*). Dee did some corrective editing of the Parts' names as he transferred them from his journals to the grimoire. I have opted to stick with his corrected versions. (See James' *The Enochian Magick of Dr. John Dee*, pages 103–116.)

The words of the *Corpus Omnium* are all found on pages 74–76 of *TFR*.

The names of the twenty-one Angelical letters are found on pages 269–271 of the *Five Books*. Their perfected forms are found in Kelley's handwriting at the end of *Loagaeth* (Sloane 3189)—see the *Five Books*, page 405.

The words of the Alchemical Cipher are found on pages 387–389 of *TFR*.

Words from the first ("hidden") leaf of *Loagaeth* are found on pages 288–343 of the *Five Books*. Those from the final leaf are found on page 19 of *TFR*. I have only taken words from the first and final Tables, the only two that contain entire words in each cell.

Exclusions from This Lexicon

I have been selective with the proper nouns I have included in the Lexicon. There are, by necessity, entries for names of God and Angels that appear in the forty-eight Angelical Keys. I have also included any names that appear in *Loagaeth*, as well as those Angels who are found only in Dee's journals (such as *Galvah, Murifri, Nalvage, Vasedg*, and so on).

However, you will not find entries for most of the proper names—of God, Angels, and spirits—found in the magickal squares Dee received in his advanced Angelic magick (namely, The *Heptarchia*, Parts of the Earth, and Great Table of the Earth—or Watchtower systems). I have used the Lexicon to analyze these proper names, and I have included references where I find similarities. (For example, see the entry for *Laiad*, which seems to be the root for the name of the Elder *Laidrom* from the Southern Watchtower.)

The ninety-one Parts of the Earth are not given their own entries, but you can find them included within the entries of their associated

Aethyrs. (The Aethyrs are included because they are named successively in the last thirty Keys.)

Finally, I have also excluded the thousands of undefined words in the Tables of *Loagaeth*. However, I have included the few words that were given definitions, that are identical to words already found in the Keys, or that appear linguistically similar to words from the Keys. (See the "Compare from *Loagaeth*" section above.) As stated previously, I will present my work with the undefined words of *Loagaeth* in a later work.

Pronunciation Key (Fully Explained)

Based on my studies of Dee's records (see the "Pronunciation Notes" section), I have offered pronunciations for almost every word in the Lexicon. You may notice that this key is very different from the pronunciation guides we normally see for the "Enochian" language. Most often, such guides are alphabetical—meaning that they present the Angelical (or English-equivalent) letters, and then suggest what sounds these letters might make *individually*. While it is good to know what sound each letter makes, it tells us little about what sounds are made when the letters are combined into actual syllables and words.

My pronunciation guide, on the other hand, is entirely phonetic. It begins with the sounds that make up the *syllables*. Then, it presents the phonetic notations I have created to represent those sounds. These notations are intended to be simple and intuitive to the modern reader.

Vowels

Short vowels are mostly represented by single letters, while I have extended the long vowels to two letters:

Phonetic Sound	-	*Notation*
a –long (*cake, day*)	-	ay
a –short (*bat, cat*)	-	a
e –long (*beet, seat*)	-	ee
e –short (*bed, wed*)	-	e
i –long (*bite, kite*)	-	ii
i –short (*bit, sit*)	-	i
o –long (*boat, slope*)	-	oh

o –short (*bot, stop, father*)	-	o, ah
u –long (*boot, blue*)	-	oo
u –short (*but, cup*)	-	u

Note: There are some cases where an *a* falls at the end of a word. I feel this likely indicates something between a long and short *a*—or a *schwa*. In such cases, I have simply left a single *a* in my pronunciation. It can be treated as a short *a*, but it is more akin to a schwa sound. (I assume Dee, had he intended the long "a" sound, would have ended the words with *ay* or *eh*.) For example, the word *Amma* (Cursed) likely ends with a sound somewhere in between the long and short *a* (schwa)—"am-a."

Consonants

If consonants are written together (as in *br*, *cr*, *gr*, *st*, *th*, and *tr*), simply pronounce the combined sound as you would in present-day English (*break*, *crate*, *grab*, *start*, and so forth). Otherwise, standard consonant sounds are indicated by the following:

Phonetic Sound	-	*Notation*
b (*branch, blurb*)	-	b
d (*dog, during*)	-	d
f (*far, fork*)	-	f
g (*gap, gourd*)	-	g
h (*half, heavy*)	-	h
j (*jump, giant, bludgeon*)	-	j
k (*kind, can*)	-	k
l (*large, loud*)	-	l
m (*many, move*)	-	m
n (*north, never*)	-	n
p (*pace, pardon*)	-	p
r (*rain, banner*)	-	r, er
s (*serve, circle*)	-	s
t (*test, tax*)	-	t
w (*water, wind*)	-	w
x (*exit, except*)	-	ks
y (*yellow, your*)	-	y
z (*zoom, zebra*)	-	z

"Long Consonants"

There are many cases where Dee indicated a consonant standing alone in a syllable. At these times, the letter does not make its usual consonant sound. Instead, the syllable is pronounced the same as the English name of the consonant. I have dubbed these "long consonants" (see the "General Notes on Angelical Phonology" section of the "Angelical Linguistics" chapter), and I represent their sounds as follows:

Phonetic Sound	-	*Notation*
d	-	dee
f	-	ef
g	-	jee
j	-	jay
l	-	el
m	-	em
n	-	en
p	-	pee
q	-	kwah
r	-	ur
s	-	es
t	-	tee
y	-	wii
z	-	zohd, zed

Digraphs and Diphthongs

The digraphs and diphthongs are fairly standard in modern English:

Phonetic Sound	-	*Notation*
ch (church, witch)	-	ch
ch (ache, chrome)	-	kh
ou, ow (out, town)	-	ow
oi, oy (oil, boy)	-	oy
qu (queen, quick)	-	kw
sh (shine, wish)	-	sh
ph (phone, philosophy)	-	f
th (that, whither, thorn)	-	th

Also Note

There are a few instances when the letters *sg* occur in Angelical words—such as *Caosg* or *Vorsg*. In these cases, Dee does not indicate that the "g" sound should stand alone as its own syllable. Thus, I find it likely it is intended to combine with the *s* to make a kind of "zh" (or hard "sh") sound—as we hear in English words like *measure*, *pleasure*, and *treasure*. I have indicated this sound in the Psalter and Lexicon with the digraph *zh*.

Accented Syllables

Dee included accent marks throughout the *48 Claves Angelicae* and *A True and Faithful Relation*. I have indicated these accents in my pronunciations by writing the related syllable in ALL CAPS. For instance, the word *Cacacom* (To Flourish) is recorded in the *48 Claves* as *ca-cá-com*. In the Lexicon, I have given the pronunciation of "kay-SAY-som"—showing an accent on the second syllable.

Dee did not record accents for all of the Angelical words. Yet many of the unaccented words are closely related to accented versions, so we can make educated guesses. For example, Dee left no accent marks for the word *Bliorax* (To Comfort). However, he did indicate—in both the *48 Claves* and *TFR*—that *Bliora* (Comfort) should be accented on the second syllable. Therefore, we can make an educated guess that *Bloriax* should also be accented on the second syllable.

I have included these speculative accents where I could, and noted my reasoning for each. In cases where no clues at all were left by Dee, I have avoided making uneducated guesses. Plus, only in rare cases have I adopted an accent from an uncompounded word into a compounded word, or vice versa. As discussed in the chapter on Angelical linguistics, compounding often drastically changes the pronunciation of the word —and Dee's notes indicate that this includes accented syllables as well.

Angelical Root Words

I have discussed the nature of Angelical root words in the chapter on Angelical linguistics. For the most part, these simple letter combinations are three to four letters in length, although there are some rare examples of one-letter or two-letter root words.

Below, I have included a list of root words I have found through analysis of the Lexicon. This list is not intended as concrete or exhaustive. Some of the entries are tentative at best, and I admit there could be any number of roots that I have missed or failed to recognize.

Moreover, I have included in this section mostly those roots that do not stand as words on their own. There are other Angelical words that appear to be in their root form (such as *Mal* or *Ror*) that do stand as words on their own. Such words have their own Lexicon entries, and do not appear in this brief list.

Thus, we can see the work on Angelical root words has only begun—the tip of the proverbial iceberg. However, I feel that learning these root concepts is essential to understanding, and eventually expanding, the Angelical tongue.

Aba: Stooping, Sinking
("Abai," Carbaf)

Abra: Prepair, Provide
(Abramig, Abramg, Abrassa)

Al: Gather, Bind, Settle, Place
(Aala, Alar, Allar, Aldi, Aldon, Oali)

Asb/Osb: Sting, Destroy
(Grosb, "Quasb")

Asch: [definition uncertain]
(Ascha, Masch)

Asp: Quality
(Asp, Aspiann Aspiaon)

Ava Avav: Thunder, Pomp
("Avav," Avavox, Avavago)

Azia: Alike, Likeness
("Azia," Aziazor)

Bab: Dominion, Wicked, Harlot
(Ababalond, Bab, Babalon, Babalel, Babage, Babagen, Bablibo, Bobogel)

Bag: Fury?
(Bag, Bagie, Bagenol, Bagnole)

Bal/Balt: Justice, Righteousness, Judgment
(Baligon, Balit, Balt, Baltan, Baltim, Baltle, Balzarg, Balzizras)

Bas/Baz: Day, Daytime
(Basgim, Basmelo, Basledf, Baspalo, Bazchim, "Bazem," Bazpama)

Bia/Bie: Voice
(Bahal, Bia, Bial, Bien)

Bli/Bil: Comfort
("Bigl," "Bliard," Blior, Bliora, Bliorax, Bliorb, Bliors, "Bliort," Pibliar)

Boap: Service
(Aboapri, Booapis)

Brin: Have, Has
("Brin," "Brint," Brints)

Chr: Let There Be, Be It (i.e., To Exist)
(Chr, Chramsa, Christeos)

Coa: Increase
("Coazior," Hecoa)

Coc/Cac/Cap: Time, Duration, Succession
(Acocasb, "Cacocasb," Cocasb, Cocasg, Qcocasb, Cacacom, Cacrg, Casasam, Capimali, "Capimao," Capimaon, Capmiali)

Com: Connect, Truss, Encircle
(Commah, Comselh)

Con/Cor: Man, Manmade and Number
(Conisbra, Cordziz)
(Cormf, Cormfa, Cormp, Cormpo, Cormpt, Sagacor, Coronzom)

Dod: Vexation
(Dodpal, Dodmni, Dods, Dodsih)

Doh: Kingdom
(Adohi, Londoh)

Ecr/Ecri: Praise
("Ecrin," Oecrimi)

Fa: Song, Singing
(Faaip, Farzem)

Fao/Far: Dwelling
(Faonts, Fargt, "Faorgt")

Gah: Pure Spirit
(Gah, Gahoachma, Gahire)

Goh: Speak, Say
(Goho, Gohia, Gohol, Gohon, Gohulim, Gohus)

Hom: Live, Age
(Hom, Homil, Homin)

Huba: Lamps, Lanterns
(Hubaio, Hubar, Hubaro)

I/Ip: The Verb *To Be*
(I, Ip, Ipam, Ipamis, Ripir)

Ia/Iad: God, The Highest, Divine
(Iad, Geiad, "Iadoias," Iadpil, Iadnah, Iaiadix, Laiad, Iaida, Iaidon, Iaisg, Ioiad, Oiad, Piad)

Ialp: Light, Fire
(Yalpamb, Ialpirt, Ialpon, "Ialpor," "Ialprt")

Isr: Promise
(Aisro, Isro, Isr)

L/Lo: One, First, You (sing.)
(Aqlo, Bolp, Yls, Ylsi, "Lo," El, L, La, Lu, Ol, Ili, Lil, Ul, Uls, "Yl")

Lans/Lons: Power
(Lansh, Lonsa, Lonshi, "Lonshin")

Lusd/Lasd: Feet, Base
(Lasdi, Lusd, Lusda, Lusdan)

Lza: Course
("Elzap," "Lzar")

Mad: Godly, Pure, Heavenly
(Mad, "Madriax," Madriiax, Madrid, Oadriax)

Mica/Mical: Might, Power
(Gmicalzo, Micalp, Micalzo, Micaoli, Micaolz, Miketh, Omicaolz)

Nan/Nana: Wisdom, Power
(Ananael, Nanaeel)

Nap: Sharpness
(Napeai, Napta, Nazpsad)

Naz: Straightness
(Nazpsad, Nazarth, Nazavabh)

Noa: Become
(Noaln, Noan, Noar, Noas, Noasmi)

Nonc: You (pl.)
(Nonca, Noncf, Nonci, Noncp)

Noqo: Servant
(Cnoqod, Cnoquodi, Cnoquol, Noco)

Nor: Son
("Nor," "Norm," Noromi)

Oan/Aon: Small Unit (as in Moment, Eye)
(Oanio, Ooanamb, Ooaona, Ooanoan, "Qanis")

Obl/Obo: Dressing, Garland, Garment
(Obloc, Oboleh)

Oia: Eternal/Forever
("Iadoias," Ioiad)

Ol: To Make
(Eol, Eolis, Oln)

Ola/Ala: Two, Twice
(Olani, Pala, Pola)

Olo/Ollo: Man, Men
("Olap," Ollog, "Ollor," Olora)

Om: Wisdom, Understanding
(Om, "Oma," Omax, "Omp")

Ooa/Oa: Name
(Dooain, Dooaip, Dooiap, Omaoas)

Or/Ors: Darkness, Dryness, Beneath, Barren, etc.
(Oroch, Orocha, Orri, Ors, Orsba, Orscatbl, Orscor)

Ox: masculine, active?
(Oxex, Oxiayal, Tox)

Paca/Pacad: ?
(Pacaduasam, Pacaph)

Pam: Not
(Ipam, Ipamis, "Pam," "Pamis")

Parac: Equate, Join, Wed
(Parach, Paracleda)

Pir/Pr: Holy, Celestial
(Pir, Piripsax, Piripsol, Piripson, "Pirgah," "Pirgi," "Prg," Prge, Prgel, "Purg")

Poil: Division
(Yrpoil, Poilp)

Qa/Qaa: Create
(Qaa, Qaal, Qaan, Qaaon, Qaas, Qadah)

Racl/Rocl: Weep?
(Raclir, Rocle)

Rza: To Swear
(Surzas, Znrza)

Sem/Sam: ?
(Samhampors, Sem, Semhaham)

Sm/Sym: Another
(Asymp, Symp, "Smnad")

Sob/Sol: Whose, Whom
(Asobam, Soba, Sobam, Sobca, "Sobha," "Sobo," Sobra, "Sola")

Tab/Cab: Govern
(Anetab, Gnetaab, Netaab, Netaaib, Tabaam, Tabaord, Tabaori, "Tabas," Tabitom, Cab, Caba)

Uch: Confuse, Confound
(Oucho, Unchi, Urch)

Von/Voh/Vov: Anger, Wrath, Might
(Vohim, "Vnph," "Vonin," Vonph, Vonpho, "Vonpo," "Vovim," Vovina)

Zie/Zo: Hands
(Azien, Ozien, Zien, Ozol, Zol)

Zil/Zyl: Go within, Fly into, Stretch forth
(Zildar, Zildron, "Zilodarp,", Zylna)

Zim: Enter, Territory
(Zim, Zimii, Zimz)

Zir: Am, Was, Were
(Zir, Zirdo, Zirom, Zirop, Zirzird)

Zli, Ilz: Water
(Pilzin, Zlida)

Zom: Amidst
(Zom, Zomdux)

Zong: Wind
(Zong, Ozongon)

Zur: Pray?
(Zuraah, Zurah, Zure)

The Angelical Alphabet

Graph	*Un*	*Or*	*Gal*	*Ged*	*Veh*	*Pa*
E	A	F	D	G/J	C/Ch/K	B

Drux	*Ger*	*Mals*	*Ur*	*Na*	*Gon*	*Tal*
N	Q/Qu	P/Ph	L	H	I/Y	M

Gisg	*Fam*	*Van*	*Ceph*	*Don*	*Med*	*Pal*
T	S	U/V	Z	R	O	X

An Angelical to English Dictionary

Un (A)

Aai (ay-AY-ii)* *prep.* Amongst (You)

1.67 . . . reigneth *amongst you* . . .
12.21 . . . whose name *amongst you* is wrath.
**13.21 . . . is called *amongst you* a bitter sting.
**14.23 . . . which is called *amongst you* fury.

Pronunciation notes:

(*Dee 1.67—AAI*)

(*Dee 12.21—A a i*) Three syllables. Each letter appears to stand alone.

(*Dee 1.67—aäl*) See the *48 Claves*. Here, Dee seems to have mistakenly written an *l* in place of the final *i*. However, he does include a dieresis over the second *a*, to indicate that it does not combine its sound with the preceding vowel.

I have adopted the accent from *Aaiom* (amongst).

Note:

**Words 13.21–22 are missing from Dee's journals. We are likewise missing the entirety of Key Fourteen. We have only the English given for these Keys on *TFR*, p. 193. However, this word does appear in these locations in Dee's *48 Claves*.

Also:

Aaf (ay-AF)	Amongst
Aaiom (ay-AY-om)	Amongst (Us?)
Aao (ay-ay-OH)	Amongst
Eai (ee-AY-ii)	Amongst
Oai (oh-AY-ii)	Amongst

Aaiom (ay-AY-om)* *prep.* Amongst (Us)

3.71 . . . is become mighty *amongst us*.
7.41 . . . be mighty *amongst us* . . .

Pronunciation notes:

(**Dee 3.71—A ai om*)

(**Dee 7.41—A AI om*) Three syllables. The first *a* stands alone in the first syllable. In the second syllable, the *ai* (or *ay*) makes essentially the same sound as the first syllable (as in the English words *dais* and *say*).

(**Dee 3.71—a-aí-om*) See the *48 Claves*. Note the accent on the second syllable.

(**Dee 7.41—aaîom*) See the *48 Claves*. I am unsure why Dee placed a circumflex over the *i* in this case.

Note:

This might appear to be a compound of *Aai* (amongst) and *Om* (understand). However, see below for *Aao*, another variant of this word that utilizes the letter *o* without the letter *m*.

Also:

Aaf (ay-AF)	Amongst
Aai (ay-AY-ii)	Amongst (You)
Aao (ay-ay-OH)	Amongst
Eai (ee-AY-ii)	Amongst
Oai (oh-AY-ii)	Amongst

Aaf (ay-AF)* *prep.* Amongst

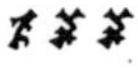

4.46 . . . praise him *amongst* the sons of man.

Pronunciation notes:

(**Dee—A af*) Two syllables, with the first *a* standing alone. I have adopted the syllable from other versions of this word.

Also:

Aai (ay-AY-ii)	Amongst (You)
Aaiom (ay-AY-om)	Amongst (Us?)
Aao (ay-ay-OH)	Amongst
Eai (ee-AY-ii)	Amongst
Oai (oh-AY-ii)	Amongst

Aala (AY-ay-la)* *v.* To Place

3.32 . . . I made you stewards and *placed you* in seats . . .

Pronunciation notes:

(**Dee—A ala*) Dee originally wrote this word as *haala*. However, he excluded the *h* in his phonetic note. Three syllables, with the initial *a* standing alone.

(**Dee—áâla)* See the *48 Claves*. Here, Dee confirms that the *h* is unnecessary. He places the accent on the first syllable. He also placed a circumflex over the second *a*, indicating a long sound.

Also:

Oali (OH-ay-lii) — To Place

Probable shared root:

Alar (AY-lar) — To Settle / Place
Aldi (AL-dii) — Gathering
Aldon (AL-don) — Gird up
Allar (AL-lar) — To Bind up

Aao (ay-ay-OH)* *prep.* — Amongst

7.5 . . . singing praises *amongst* the flames . . .

Pronunciation notes:

(**Dee—A a ó*) Like the word *Aai*, this version is also divided into three syllables. (There is no *ao* letter combination in Early Modern English—these letters make two separate sounds, as in the English word *chaos*.) Dee places the accent on the last syllable.

Also:

Aaf (ay-AF) — Amongst
Aai (ay-AY-ii) — Amongst (You)
Aaiom (ay-AY-om) — Amongst (Us?)
Eai (ee-AY-ii) — Amongst
Oai (oh-AY-ii) — Amongst

"Aath" (or "Ath") (ath) *n.* — Works (or Deeds)

Compounds:

Sobhaath (sob-HAY-ath) [*Sobha* + *"Aath"*] Whose Works

Note:

See also *Vaun* (to work)—which appears to be a verb, rather than the noun intended by "Aath."

Ababalond (ay-BAY-bay-lond)* *n.* Harlot

30.113 . . . she is the bed of *an harlot* . . .

Pronunciation notes:

(**Dee—A bá ba lond*) Four syllables, with an accent on the second syllable. The initial *a* stands alone.

(**Dee—abábâlond*) See the *48 Claves*. Here, Dee again placed an accent over the second syllable. He also placed a circumflex over the third *a* to indicate its long sound.

Note:

The similarity between this word and the name of the ancient empire of Babylon. Beginning with *1 Enoch* (likely written during the Judaic captivity in Babylon), the kingdom of Babylon has been a biblical symbol of iniquity. See Revelation 17, where the iniquities of the world of man are symbolized by a woman whose forehead is inscribed with the words *Mystery, Babylon the Great, the Mother of Harlots and Abominations of the Earth*. Also see note at *Babalon* (Wicked).

Also:

Babalon (bay-BAY-lon) Wicked

Possible shared root:

Bab (bab) Dominion
Babage (bay-BAY-jee) South
Babagen (bay-BAY-jen) South

"Abai" (ay-bay-ii) *v.* To Stoop

Compounds:

Abaivonin (ay-bay-II-voh-nin) [*"Abai"* + *Vonin*] Stooping Dragons

Note:

Stooping here means "diving," as in an eagle stooping after its prey. Note that *stooping* is a verb, but is used in the compound (*Abaivonin*) as an adjective.

Probable shared root:

Carbaf (kar-baf) — Sink (or Stoop)

Abaivonin (ay-bay-II-voh-nin)* [*"Abai"* + *Vonin*] *comp.*

Stooping Dragons

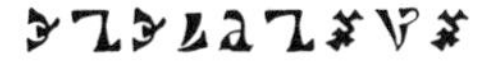

8.17 . . . as bucklers to *the stooping dragons* . . .

Pronunciation notes:

(**Dee—A ba í uo nin*) Five syllables, with an accent on the third syllable. Dee originally wrote this word with a *u* in the fourth syllable. However, when *u*/*v* is written before a vowel, it should take the consonant sound of *v*.

(**Dee—Abaíuônin*) See the *48 Claves*. Dee again places the accent on the third syllable. He further places a circumflex over the *o* to indicate its long sound.

Aboapri (ay-BOH-ay-prii)* *v.* — To Serve

30.120 . . . the lower heavens beneath you, *let them serve you.*

Pronunciation notes:

(**Dee—A bo a pri*) Appears to be four syllables. While Dee shows the second *a* standing alone, I have opted to give it the short sound in my pronunciation (as in the English word *boa*).

(**Dee—abóâpri*) See the *48 Claves*. Here, Dee placed an accent on the second syllable. He also placed a circumflex over the second *a* to indicate its long sound.

Also:

Booapis (boh-OH-ay-pis) — To Serve

Note:

It would appear that *Boap/Booap* serves as the common root between these two words.

Abramig (ay-BRAY-mig)* *v.* To Prepare

8.55 . . . of such as *are prepared.*

Pronunciation notes:

(**Dee—A bra mig*) Three syllables. The initial *A* stands alone. The second *a* also appears to be long. See the pronunciation notes for *Abramg*—where we learn that the final *g* has a hard sound. Also, we can see from *Abramg* that the *i* in *Abramig* is likely a phonetic gloss.

(**Dee—a-brâmig*) See the *48 Claves*. Dee placed a circumflex over the second *a*, confirming the long sound.

I have adopted the accent from *Abraassa* (to provide).

Also:

Abramg (ay-BRAY-mig) To Prepare

Possible shared root:

Abraassa (ab-RAY-sa) To Provide

Compare from *Loagaeth*: *Abra, Abrimanadg*

Abramg (ay-BRAY-mig)* *v.* To Prepare

2.14 . . . whom *I have prepared* as cups for a wedding . . .

11.33 . . . *I have prepared* for you . . .

Pronunciation notes:

(**Dee 2.14—Abramg*)

(**Dee 11.33—Ab ramg. g not as dg*) Both *a*'s appear short in this note—however, the pronunciation notes for *Abramig* (to prepare) indicate both are long. In this note, Dee lets us know that the final *g* has a hard sound rather than the soft "dg" sound. Finally, Dee's note seems to indicate only two syllables. However, if the final *g* is hard, there should be a vowel sound between the *m* and the *g*—making three syllables. Again see *Abramig* (to prepare), where this vowel sound is shown as a short *i*.

I have adopted the accent from *Abraassa* (to provide).

Compounds:

Dsabramg (dee-say-bray-mig) [*Ds* + *Abramg*] — Which Prepared

Also:

Abramig (ay-BRAY-mig) — To Prepare

Possible shared root:

Abraassa (ab-RAY-sa) — To Provide

Compare from *Loagaeth*:

Abra, *Abrimanadg*

Abraassa (ab-RAY-sa)* *v.* — To Provide

30.23 . . . which *provided* you for the government . . .

Pronunciation note:

(**Dee—Abraássa*) Three syllables, with the accent likely on the second syllable. In Early Modern English, the double *a* makes a long "a" sound, and the double *s* makes a regular "s" sound.

(**Dee—abraássa*) See the *48 Claves*. This note essentially matches that from *TFR*.

Possible shared root:

Abramig (ay-BRAY-mig) — To Prepare

Abramg (ay-BRAY-mig) — To Prepare

ACAM (ay-KAM)* — 7699

6.19 . . . and *7699* continual workmen . . .

Pronunciation notes:

(**Dee—A cám*) Two syllables, with the accent on the second syllable.

(**Dee—Acám*) See the *48 Claves*. Note the accent again on the second syllable.

Note:

This word was not originally given with Key Six. It was added later when Nalvage transmitted the English for the Key (see *TFR*, p. 190). This seems to have been the case with many of the numbers mentioned in the Keys.

Achildao (ay-KIL-day-oh)* *n.* Diamond

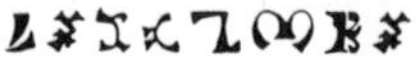

9.52 Their heads are covered with *diamond* . . .

Pronunciation notes:

(**Dee—A chil da o kil*) Four syllables. Dee indicates that the *ch* should take the harder "k" (or "kh") sound. The first *a* stands alone. Both the second *a* and the final *o* should take their long sounds.

(**Dee—a-chíldao*) See the *48 Claves*. Dee again indicates the initial *A* stands alone. He also placed an accent over the *i* in the second syllable.

Acocasb (ay-KOH-kasb)* *n.* Time

9.71 . . . for *the time* is such . . .

Pronunciation notes:

(**Dee—A co casb*) Three syllables. The initial *A* stands alone. The *o* of the second syllable should take a long sound.

(**Dee—acócasb*) See the *48 Claves*. Dee placed an accent over the second syllable.

Also:

"Cacocasb" (kay-KOH-kasb) Another While
Cocasb (KOH-kasb) Time
Cocasg (KOH-kazh) Times
Qcocasb (kwah-KOH-kasb) Contents of Time

Possible shared root:

Cacacom (kay-SAY-som) Flourish
Cacrg (KAY-kurg) Until
Casasam (kay-SAY-sam) Abiding
Capimali (kay-pii-MAY-lii) Successively

"Capimao" (kay-pii-MAY-oh) While
Capimaon (kap-ii-MAY-on) Number of Time
Capmiali (kap-mii-AY-lii) Successively

Note:
Also see *Pild* (continually).

Acroodzi (ak-roh-OD-zii)* *n.* Beginning

16.6 . . . which hast thy beginning in glory . . .

Note:
The transmission of the first twelve words of Key Sixteen is missing from Dee's journals. We only have the English given for it on *TFR*, p. 194. However, they do appear in Dee's *48 Claves*.

Pronunciation notes:
(**Dee—acroódzi*) See the *48 Claves*. Dee places an accent over the second *o*—which should be part of the third syllable. See pronunciation notes for *Croodzi* (beginning of things).

Also:
Croodzi (kroh-OD-zii) Beginning (of things)

Note:
Also see *Iaod* (beginning), *Iaodaf* (in the beginning), *Amgedpha* (I will begin anew), and *Nostoah* (it was in the beginning).

Adgmach (aj-mak) *n.* Glory (i.e., Adoration, Praise)*

Note:
(**Dee—Adgmach adgmach adgmach* [= much glory].) See the *Five Books* pp. 309–10. This seems to be a kind of *Trisagion* (like the "Holy Holy Holy . . . " songs sung by Angels in biblical literature.). The *Adgmach* phrase is spoken during a longer prayer offered by "many voices": "It is good, O God, for you are goodness itself. And great because of the size of greatness itself. *Adgmach, adgmach, adgmach*! I am, and this pace

is, holy. *Adgmach, adgmach, adgmach hucacha.*" *Adgmach* must therefore indicate "glory."

Also see:

Busd (glory), which seems to indicate "wondrous."

Prigah (glory), which relates to light and fire (possibly the light of the Sun).

Adgt (ajt)* *aux. v.* Can

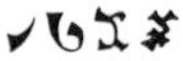

2.1 *Can* the wings of the winds understand . . .

Pronunciation notes:

(**Dee—Adgt*) This appears to be only one syllable.

Adna (ad-nah) *n.* Obedience

1.50 . . . and swore *obedience* and faith to him . . .

Pronunciation notes:

Dee left no specific note, so this word likely sounds as it appears. I suggest two syllables, and both *a*'s should be short.

Compare from *Loagaeth*:

Adna, Adnay, Adney, Adnah, Adnih, Adnava, Adnab, Adnor

Adohi (ay-DOH-hii)* *n.* Kingdom

18.20 . . . which is called in thy *kingdom* Joy . . .

Pronunciation notes:

(**Dee—A do hi*) Three syllables. The initial *A* stands alone. The *o* likely takes the long sound, as does the final *i*.

(**Dee—adóhi*) See the *48 Claves*. Here, Dee placed an accent over the second syllable.

Also:

Londoh (lon-DOH) Kingdom

Note:

It would appear that "doh" is the root here.

Compare from *Loagaeth*:

Aldoh, Ardoh, Doh, Dohoh

Adoian (ay-doh-II-an)* *n.* Face

30.14 . . . behold *the face of* your God.

Pronunciation notes:

(**Dee—A do í an*) Four syllables, with an accent on the third syllable. (**Dee—adoían*) See the *48 Claves*. Here, Dee again placed an accent over the *i* in the third syllable.

Adphaht (ad-fot)* *adj.* Unspeakable

30.29 . . . and her *unspeakable* variety . . .

Pronunciation notes:

(**Dee—Ad phaht*) Two syllables. The *ah* in the second syllable should indicate a short "o" sound ("ah")—as in the English word *father*.

Compare from *Loagaeth*:

Adepd, Adepoad, Adeph, Adaph, Adapagemoh, Adphamagel

Adroch (ad-roch)* *n.* Olive Mount

5.7 . . . and are become as olives *in the olive mount* . . .

Pronunciation notes:

(**Dee—Ad roch as otch*) Two syllables. The *ch* at the end of the word has the "tch" sound—as in the English words *church* and *churn*.

Note:

The "Mount of Olives"—to the east of Jerusalem—is an important location in biblical literature. (See 2 Samuel 15, Zechariah 14, Matthew 21, 24–26, 39.) It is supposed to be the place where God will begin to redeem the dead in the End Times—and is thus a major burial site for Jewish people to this very day. It does *not* appear to be the mountain from Jesus' Sermon on the Mount.

Also see:

Qanis (olives).

Compare from *Loagaeth*:

Adroh, Adroth

Adrpan (ay-dir-pan)* *v.* To Cast Down

30.124 *Cast down* such as fall.

Pronunciation notes:

(**Dee—A dr pan dir*) Three syllables. Dee shows us that the second syllable is pronounced "dir." The initial *A* stands alone.

AF (af)* 19

5.17 . . . pillars of gladness *19* and gave them . . .

Pronunciation notes:

(**Dee—Af*) One syllable.

Affa (af-fa)* *adj.* Empty

13.13 . . . making men drunken which are *empty*.

Pronunciation notes:

(**Dee—Af fa*) Two syllables. When this word is spoken fluently, the two *f*s combine into one sound.

Note:

This word is a palindrome. It is spelled the same forward as it is spelled backward.

Ag (ag)* *adj.* or *pron.* No/None (No One)

4.17 . . . whom *none* hath yet numbered . . .

Pronunciation notes:

(**Dee—Ag as agg in nag*) One syllable. Dee shows a double *g* in his phonetic note, which (in Early Modern English) indicates a hard sound instead of a soft sound (as in *stagger* or *bigger*). *Ag* sounds like the English words *nag* and *bag*.

Note:

The words *Ag* and "Agl" are pronouns ("none = no one"). However, the word *Ag* becomes an adjective in *Agtoltorn* (no creature).

Compounds:

"Agl" (ag-el) [Ag + L] No One Creature
Agltoltorn (ag-el-tol-torn) [Ag + L + "Toltorn"] No One Creature
Agtoltorn (ay-jee-tol-torn) [Ag + "Toltorn"] No Creature

Note:

Also see *Ge* (Not), *Ip* (Not), and *Pam* (Not).

"Agl" (ag-el) [Ag + L] *comp., pron.* No One

Compounds:

Agltoltorn (ag-el-tol-torn) [Ag + L + "Toltorn"] No One Creature

Agltoltorn (ag-el-tol-torn)* [Ag + L + "Toltorn"] No One Creature

30.80 . . . let there be *no one creature* equal with another . . .

Pronunciation notes:

(**Dee—Ag l ter torn*) Four syllables. The first *l* stands alone, leaving the *A* and *g* to combine together. Also note that Dee seems to have made a mistake in his phonetic note—giving the sound of "ter" for the letters *tol*. (**Dee—ag L tortorn*) See the *48 Claves*. The *l* again stands alone. I also note that Dee once again indicates a "tor" sound where the letters *tol* should be. I have settled upon the *tol* version in my pronunciation.

Note:

The words *Ag* and "*Agl*" are pronouns (none = no one). However, the word *Ag* becomes an adjective in *Agtoltorn* (no creature).

Also:

"Agl" (ag-el) [Ag + L] — No One Creature
Agtoltorn (ay-jee-tol-torn) [Ag + "Toltorn"] — No Creature

Agtoltorn (ay-jee-tol-torn)* [Ag + "Toltorn"] *comp.* — No Creature

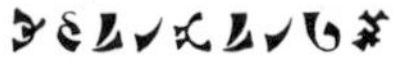

30.69 . . . let there be *no creature* upon or within her . . .

Pronunciation notes:

(**Dee—A g tol torn*) Four syllables. The *g* does not combine with the *t*, and therefore must stand alone. Because of this, the *a* is also forced to stand alone.

Note:

The words *Ag* and "Agl" are pronouns (none = no one). However, the word *Ag* becomes an adjective in *Agtoltorn* (no creature).

Also:

"Agl" (ag-el) [Ag + L] — No One Creature
Agltoltorn (ag-el-tol-torn) [Ag + L + "Toltorn"] — No One Creature

Aisro (ay-ii-sroh)* *v.* — To Promise

14.20 Behold the voice of God *promise of* him which is called . . .

Pronunciation notes:

(**Dee—aîsro*) See the *48 Claves*. Dee placed a circumflex over the *i* to indicate its long sound. This likely means the *A* must stand alone, so the word contains three syllables.

Note:

The transmission of Key Fourteen is missing from Dee's journals. We only have the English for this Key given later (see *TFR*, p. 193). Plus, the word *Aisro* appears in this location in Dee's *48 Claves*.

I believe this word is intended as a verb. "Promise of him which is called . . . " is likely an adjuration to make a promise *by* him who is called.

Also:

Isro (iz-roh) — Promise of

Note:

It is possible that the -*o* suffix (of) is in use here.

Also see:

Sibsi (covenant), Surzas (sworn), and Znrza (swore).

Alar (AY-lar)* *v.* — To Settle / To Place

9.20 . . . *have settled* their feet in the west . . .

Pronunciation notes:

(**Dee—A lar*) Two syllables. The *A* stands alone in the first syllable. I have adopted the accent from *Aala* (settle / place).

Also:

Allar (AL-lar) — To Bind Up

Probable shared root:

Aala (AY-ay-la) — To Place
Aldi (AL-dii) — Gathering
Aldon (AL-don) — Gird Up
Oali (OH-ay-lii) — To Place

Note:

See Note at *Allar*.

Alca (al-ka) *v.?* — To Signify(?)

Note:

See the *Five Books*, p. 354. Here, the Angel Illemese says of the *Book of Soyga*, "Soyga signifieth not Agyos. *Soyga alca miketh.*" (*Agyos* is Greek for "holiness," and is "Soyga" when spelled backward.) When Dee asked what these words meant, he was told, "The True Measure of the

Will of God in Judgment, Which Is by Wisdom." Based on context, I feel that the word *Alca* probably means "to signify"—while *Miketh* (related, perhaps by root, to *Micaolz*—mighty) is translated as the "True Measure of the Will of God . . . " etc.

Aldi (AL-dii) *v.* — To Gather

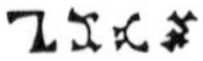

1.33 . . . garnished with the fire of *gathering* . . .

Pronunciation note:

I have adopted the accent from *Aala* (settle/place).

Note:

This word should be a verb, but in Key 1.33, it is actually used in a prepositional phrase, indicating the noun *fire*. Taken all together, the words *fire of gathering* make a noun phrase.

Also:

Aldon (AL-don) — Gird-up, Gather Together

Probable shared root:

Aala (AY-ay-la) — To Place
Alar (AY-lar) — To Settle/Place
Allar (AL-lar) — To Bind Up
Oali (OH-ay-lii) — To Place

Aldon (AL-don)* *v.* — Gird Up, To Gather Together

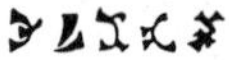

9.28 These *gather up* the moss of the earth . . .
**11.17 And *they gathered themselves together in* the house of death . . .
17.16 *Gird up* thy loins and hearken.

Pronunciation notes:

(**Dee 9.28; 17.16—Al don*) Two syllables. Both vowels seem to take their short sounds. I have adopted the accent from *Aala* (settle/place).

Note:

**This word was not given during the transmission of Key Eleven. Nor does it appear in Dee's 48 *Claves*. We have only the English for the Key given on *TFR*, p. 193. Patricia Shaffer suggests this word here, and I have to agree.

Also:

Aldi (AL-dii) — Gathering

Probable shared root:

Aala (AY-ay-la) — To Place
Alar (AY-lar) — To Settle / Place
Allar (AL-lar) — To Bind Up
Oali (OH-ay-lii) — To Place

Compare from *Loagaeth*:

Aldex

Allar (AL-lar)* *v.* — To Bind Up

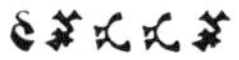

12.9 . . . *bind up* your girdles and visit us.

Pronunciation notes:

(**Dee—Al lar*) Two syllables. Both *a*'s are likely short. When spoken, the double *l* should combine into one sound (as in Early Modern English). I have adopted the accent from *Aala* (settle / place).

Also:

Alar (AY-lar) — Settled

Probable shared root:

Aala (AY-ay-la) — To Place
Aldi (AL-dii) — Gathering
Aldon (AL-don) — Gird Up
Oali (OH-ay-lii) — To Place

Note:

The concept of *Alar/Allar* seems to be of "setting" or "establishing." The phrase *gird up your loins* is an old one meaning to get ready or to set oneself firmly on a course, and this is likely the meaning of *bind up your girdles* in Key Twelve.

Compare from *Loagaeth*:

Alla

Amgedpha (am-JED-fa)* *v.* I Will Begin Anew

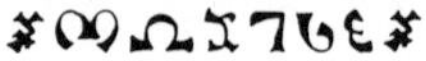

Pronunciation note:

(**Dee—Amgédpha*) See the *Five Books*, p. 324. Dee places an accent over the *e*.

From *Loagaeth*:

(***Dee—Amgedpha = I will begin anew.*) See the *Five Books*, p. 324.

Note:

Also see *Acroodzi* (beginning), *Croodzi* (beginning of things), *Iaod* (beginning), *Iaodaf* (in the beginning), and *Nostoah* (it was in the beginning).

Amipzi (ay-mip-zii)* *v.* To Fasten

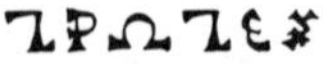

5.15 . . . unto whom *I have fastened* pillars of gladness . . .

Pronunciation notes:

(**Dee—A mip zi*) Three syllables. The *A* stands alone.

Amiran (am-ir-an)* *pron.* Yourselves

3.63 Lift up, I say, *yourselves*.

Pronunciation notes:

(**Dee—Amiran*) I suggest three syllables.

Amma (am-a)* *adj.* Cursed

9.35 *Cursed* are they whose iniquities they are.

Pronunciation notes:

(**Dee—Am ma*) Two syllables. The two *m*'s combine into a single sound, as in the English word *summer*.

Note:

This word is a palindrome. It is spelled the same forward as it is spelled backward.

Amzes (am-zes) *n.?* Those That Fear God(?)

Note:

See the *Five Books*, pp. 324–25. Here Kelley sees what the *Book of Loagaeth* looks like from the outside. It is covered in blue silk, and has the title *Amzes naghezes Hardeh* painted upon it in gold. Kelley says this signifies "the universal name of Him that created universally be praised and extolled forever."

However, also see *TFR*, p. 174, where the Angel Ave reveals that the title of Enoch's book was "Let Those That Fear God, and Are Worthy, Read." (Dee, at that point, notes, "The title of Enoch's books expounded into English.") If this happens to be the real translation, then perhaps *Amzes* indicates "Those That Fear God." (Also see *Hoxmarch*—Fear of God.)

Pronunciation notes:

(*Dee—Amzes naghezes Hardeh—Note this to be pronounced roundly together.*) Perhaps this means the three words should be pronounced as if they were one?

Ananael (an-AN-ee-el)* *n.* Secret Wisdom

3.80 . . . partakers of *the secret wisdom of* your creation.

Pronunciation notes:

(**Dee—Ananael*) Dee gives us little clue here. The word is likely four syllables.

(**Dee—anánæl*) See the *48 Claves*. Dee shows an accent over the second syllable. Also, note that the final *ae* is written as *æ* (called an *ash*)—indicating that the two letters combine to form one sound. I believe, in this case, the ash indicates a long "e" sound (as in the English spelling of the word *encyclopædia*).

Note:

The similarity between this word and the name of the Archangel of Venus, *Anael* (or *Annael*). Annael was the first Angel contacted by Dee and Kelley (see the *Five Books*), which initiated the transmission of the entire Angelic system of magick.

Possible shared root:

Nanaeel (nay-NAY-ee-el) — (My) Power

Anetab (ay-NEE-tayb)* *n.* — (In) Government

6.25 . . . and are *in government* and continuance as . . .

Pronunciation notes:

(**Dee—A né tab*) Three syllables, with an accent on the second. Based on the other versions of this word (see below), I have given the *a* in the final syllable a long sound.

(**Dee—anétab*) See the *48 Claves*. The accent is again shown on the second syllable.

Also:

Gnetaab (nee-TAY-ab) — (Your) Governments
Netaab (nee-TAY-ab) — Governments
Netaaib (nee-TAY-ay-ib) — Government
Tabaam (tay-BAY-an) — Governor
Tabaord (tay-BAY-ord) — (Let) Be Governed
Tabaori (tay-BAY-oh-rii) — Govern
"Tabas" (tay-BAS) — Govern
Cab (kab) — Rod/Scepter
Caba (ka-BA) — To Govern

Angelard (an-jee-lard)* *n.* Thoughts

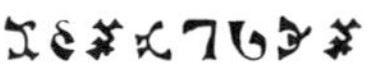

10.64 . . . even as the heart of man doth *his thoughts* . . .

Pronunciation notes:

(*Dee—An ge lard*) Three syllables. The *e* should take its long sound.

(*Dee—angêlard*) See the 48 *Claves*. Here, Dee placed a circumflex over the *e*—confirming its long sound.

Aoiveae (ay-oy-VEE-ay)* *n.* Stars

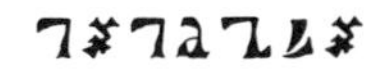

30.139 . . . until *the stars* be numbered.

Pronunciation notes:

(*Dee—A oi vé ae*) This appears to be four syllables, with an accent on the third. The initial *A* stands alone. The Early Modern English letter combination *oi* (or *oy*) makes an "oy" sound—as in the words *boil* or *toy*. The *e* in the third syllable likely takes a long sound.

(*Dee—Aoivéâe*) See the 48 *Claves*. Here, Dee again placed the accent over the *e* in the third syllable. He also placed a circumflex over the second *a* to indicate its long sound.

Apachana (ap-AY-kay-na)* *n.* The Slimy Things Made of Dust**

Pronunciation note:

(*Dee—ap-á-cha-na*) See the *Five Books*, p. 320. Four syllables, with an accent on the second. The second and third *a*'s seem to take the long sound.

From *Loagaeth*:

(***Dee—The slimy things made of dust.*) See the *Five Books*, p. 320.

"Apila" (ap-ii-la) *v.* — To Live

Compounds:

Odapila (ohd-ap-ii-la) [Od + "Apila"] — And Liveth

Note:

Also see *Hom* (To Live).

Aqlo (AY-kwah-loh)* *pron.* — Thy (Your)

18.19 . . . is called *in thy* kingdom Joy.

Pronunciation notes:

(**Dee—A q lo quu*) Three syllables. The initial *A* and the *q* stand alone. Dee shows that the *q* should sound like "quu" (or "qw")—making the sound of "kwah." The final *o* should likely take a long sound.
(**Dee—á-q-lo*) See the *48 Claves*. This note is essentially the same as that in *TFR*. However, Dee here placed an accent over the first syllable.

Possible shared root:

Bolp (bohlp) — Be Thou
Yls (yils) — Thou
Ylsi (yil-sii) — Thee
L (el) — First
"Lo" (loh) — First

Ar (ar)* *pron.* — That

12.16 Bring down your train 3363 *that* the Lord may be magnified . . .

Pronunciation notes:

(**Dee—Ar*) One syllable.

Compounds:

Arcaosgi (ar-kay-OZH-ii) [Ar + Caosgi] — To(?) the Earth
Arcoazior (ar-koh-ay-zhor) [Ar + "Coazior"] — That Increase
Artabas (ar-tay-bas) [Ar + "Tabas"] — That Govern

Note:

The word *Ar* (That) is a conjunction, while the word *Ds* (Which/That) is a pronoun.

Compare from *Loagaeth*:

Ar, Arh

"Ar" (ar) *v.?* To Van?

Compounds:

Arcaosgi (ar-kay-OZH-ii) ["Ar" + Caosgi] (To Van?) the Earth

Note:

The English word *van* is—by one definition—a shortened form of the word *vanguard*, the front part of an advancing army. Its use here in the Keys—as part of the phrase *to van the earth*—appears to treat it as a verb. A more proper definition of "Ar" may be "to advance upon (especially with hostile intent)."

Arcaosgi (ar-kay-OZH-ii)* ["Ar" + Caosgi] *comp.* (To Van?) the Earth

6.17 . . . fiery darts *to van the earth* . . .

Pronunciation notes:

(*Dee—Ar ca ós gi*) Four syllables, with an accent on the third syllable. See pronunciation notes at *Caosgi* (Earth) for more information.

(*Dee—arcaósgi*) See the *48 Claves*. Note the accent again on the third syllable.

Note:

Literally, this compound should translate: "That (the) Earth." There is no indication of the word for *to van* in the Key, and *Ar* is properly defined as "that." Could it be that an identical Angelical word *Ar* might translate as "to van"? Also see note at "Ar."

Arcoazior (ar-koh-ay-zhor)* [Ar + "Coazior"] *comp.* That Increase

30.129 . . . Bring forth with those *that increase* . . .

Pronunciation notes:

(**Dee—Ar co a zior*) Likely four syllables. The *a* in the third syllable stands alone. The *zi* in the fourth syllable likely sounds similar to the *ti* and *si* in the English word endings *-tion* and *-sion* (as in the English words *aggression*, *tradition*, etc.). I have represented this sound in my pronunciation with "zh."

Argedco (ar-JED-koh)* *v.* With Humility We Call Thee, with Adoration of the Trinity.**

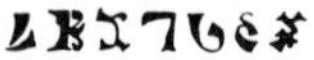

Pronunciation note:

(**Dee—argédco*) See the *Five Books*, p. 310. Dee places an accent over the *e*.

From *Loagaeth*:

(***Dee—With humility we call thee, with adoration of the Trinity.*) See the *Five Books*, p. 310.

Compare from *Loagaeth*:

Argednon

Arn (arn) *prop. n.* "The Second Aethyr"

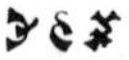

30.3 . . . which dwell in *the second aethyr* . . .

Note:

This (word 30.3) is the single space in the Key of the Aethyrs, which must be changed for each invocation—replacing word 30.3 with the name of the appropriate Aethyr. No established definitions were given for these names.

Arn contains the three Parts of the Earth *Doagnis*, *Pacasna*, and *Dialioa*.

Arphe (ar-fay) *v.* I Desire Thee, O God*

From *Loagaeth*:

(**Dee—I desire thee, O God.*) See the *Five Books*, p. 320.

Artabas (ar-tay-bas)* [Ar + "Tabas"] *comp.* That Govern

30.123 . . . govern those *that govern* . . .

Pronunciation notes:

(**Dee—Ar ta bas*) Three syllables. The *a* in the second syllable appears to be long.

Arzulgh (ar-zulj) *prop. n.* Spirit Opposing *Befafes**

From *Loagaeth*:

(**Dee—This is the name of the spirit contrary to Befafes*) See the *Five Books*, p. 310. *Befafes* is an Angel of the *Heptarchia*.

Compare from *Loagaeth*:

Arzusen

Ascha (ask-a) n/a?*

From *Loagaeth*:

(**Dee—Gohed, pronounced as Iohed, signifieth One Everlasting and all things Descending upon One, and Gohed Ascha is as much to say as One God.*) See the *Five Books*, p. 304. The word *Gohed* means "One Everlasting . . ." (referring to God), so it is not clear exactly what *Ascha* adds in the phrase *Gohed Ascha* ("One God" or "One Everlasting God").

Pronunciation note:

The *sch* letter combination should sound like "sk" (as in *school*). Note, also, that in the *Book of Loagaeth*, Dee gives the pronunciation for the word *Zuresch* as "zuresk"—further indicating the "sk" sound for *sch*.

Also see:

Masch

Compare from *Loagaeth*:

Asch, Ascha, Aschah, Aschal, Ascham, Asche, Aschedh, Aschem, Ascheph, Aschi, Aschin, Aschma, Aschol, *and probably* Dasch, Gascheth, Hasche, Pasch, Pascha, Pascheph, *and maybe* Iemasch, Surascha, Vascheth

Asobam (ay-SOH-bam)* *pron.* (On) Whom

9.60 . . . *on whom* they frown not . . .

Pronunciation notes:

(**Dee—A so bam*) Dee originally wrote this word as *Asobama*—but he dropped the final *a* in his phonetic note *and* in the *48 Claves*. So the word is only three syllables long. The initial *A* stands alone. The *o* should take its long sound.

(**Dee—a-sóbam*) See the *48 Claves*. Here, Dee placed an accent over the second syllable.

Also:

"Saba" (SAY-bay)	Whose
Soba (SOH-bay)	Whose
Sobam (SOH-bam)	Whom
Sobca (SOB-kay)	Whose
"Sobha" (SOB-hay)	Whose
"Sobo" (SOH-boh)	Whose
Sobra (SOB-ray)	Whose
"Sola" (SOH-lay)	Whose

Asp (asp) *prop. n.* "The Twenty-First Aethyr" (Quality?)

30.3 . . . which dwell in *the twenty-first aethyr* . . .

Note:

This (word 30.3) is the single space in the Key of the Aethyrs, which must be changed for each invocation—replacing word 30.3 with the name of the appropriate Aethyr. No established definitions were given for these names.

Asp contains the three Parts of the Earth *Chirzpa*, *Toantom*, and *Vixpalg*.

Possible shared root:

Aspian (as-pii-an) Qualities (i.e., "Characteristics")

Aspian (as-pii-an)* *n.* Qualities (Characteristics)

30.77 . . . let them differ in *their qualities.*

Pronunciation notes:

(**Dee—As pi an*) Three syllables. The *i* should take its long sound.

Possible shared root:

Asp (asp) "The Twenty-First Aethyr"

Note:

Compare to the name of the Part of Earth (and its Angelic Governor), *Aspiaon.*

Aspt (aspt)* *prep.* Before, In Front

30.144 . . . and appear *before* the covenant of his mouth . . .

Pronunciation notes:

(**Dee—Aspt*) One syllable.

Note:

Could there be a relationship between this word and the name of the *Apst*, an Angel of medicine of the Northern Watchtower?

Astel (as-tel) n/a

Note:

See *Five Books*, p. 366. The Angel Illemese appears to Dee and Kelley with a bundle of empty boxes that he calls virtuous. When Dee asks for an explanation, Illemese says, "Will you have my bill? [. . .] I will show it. Serve it, where you list. *Iudra galgol astel.*" Dee states that he and Kelley do not understand, and wish to know how it can be served. But Illemese never offers definitions for these Angelical words.

Also see:

Garnastel (gar-nas-tel) n/a

Asymp (ay-simp)* *pron.* or *adj.* Another

30.82 . . . no one creature equal with *another.*

Pronunciation notes:

(**Dee—A symp*) Two syllables. The *A* stands alone.

Also:

Symp (simp) Another

Probable shared root:

"Smnad" (sem-en-ad) Another

Note:

The root here may be "sm" or "sym."

Atraah (ay-tray-a)* *n.* Girdles

12.10 . . . bind up *your girdles* and visit us.

Pronunciation notes:

(**Dee—A tra ah*) Three syllables. The first *a* stands alone. In Early Modern English, a double *a* indicates a long sound—which Dee indicates for the second syllable in his phonetic note.

(**Dee—atraâh*) See the *48 Claves*. Here Dee placed a circumflex over the *third a*. Dee seems to have used *âh* to indicate a vowel sound similar to what we hear in the English words *father* and *fall*.

Audcal (od-kal) *n.* Gold (the Mercury of the Philosopher's Stone)*

From the *Alchemical Cipher*:

See *TFR*, pp. 387–89. The Angel Levanael says of Audcal, "It is Gold. [. . .] *Audcal* is his Mercury. *Darr*, (in the Angelical tongue), is the true name of the Stone." Therefore *Audcal* (Gold) is here described as the alchemical Mercury (or essence) of the Philosopher's Stone.

Note:

(**Dee—We know that the Philosopher's Stone being left by metal, with metal, and upon metal, etc . . .*) Dee is here speaking of touching base metals with the Philosopher's Stone, which would turn them into gold.

Pronunciation note:

The *au* letter combination should make a short "o" sound (as in *auburn* or *autumn*).

"Avav" (ay-vav) *n.* Pomp

Compounds:

Avavox (ay-vay-voks) ["Avav" + Tox] His Pomp

Possible shared root:

Avavago (av-AY-vay-go) Thunders (of Increase)

Note:

Perhaps there is something of the concept of "pomp," in the "Thunders of Increase"—as in a mighty king or god preceded by thunderous sounds and trumpets. This is, after all, the nature of the Thunders and Voices described in *Merkavah* (and related) literature such as St. John's Revelation.

Avavago (av-AY-vay-go)* *prop. n.* Thunders (of Increase)

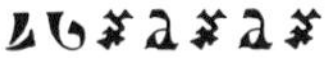

4.8 . . . are not *the Thunders of Increase* numbered . . .?
8.36 . . . *The Thunders* have spoken . . .

Pronunciation notes:

(**Dee 4.8—Ava va go*) Four syllables. The second and third *a*'s are long.

(**Dee 8.36—A uá ua go*) Four syllables, accent on the second syllable. The first *a* seems to stand alone in word 8.36—but such is not indicated in other notes for this word. Next, Dee shows in word 4.8 that the *u*'s should actually sound like *v*'s. Finally, the *g* should take a hard sound when preceding an *o*.

(**Dee 4.8—avávâgo*) See the *48 Claves*. Accent on the second syllable. The third *a* carries a circumflex—indicating its long sound.

(**Dee 8.36—auávâgo*) See the *48 Claves*. This note matches the previous note.

Note:

The generic Angelical word for "thunder" is likely *Const*. The Thunders mentioned here and elsewhere in the Keys are groups of Angels. See *Coraxo* (Thunders) and *Sapah* (Mighty Sounds). Also note the Thunders, Lightnings, and Voices which proceeded from the Divine Throne in the vision of St. John (Book of Revelation). The Avavago are mentioned only in Keys Four and Eight—both of which seem to relate to the Southern Quarter of the Universe.

Possible shared root:

Avavox (ay-VAY-voks) ["Avav" + Tox] His Pomp

Avavox (ay-VAY-voks)* ["Avav" + Tox] *comp.* His Pomp

30.94 The work of man and *his pomp* . . .

Pronunciation notes:

(**Dee—A ua vox*) Dee spelled this word *Auavox*. However, the *u*/*v* preceding a vowel should take the "v" sound—which I have used in the spelling *Avavox*. The initial *A* stands alone. I have taken the accent from *Avavago* (Thunders of Increase).

(**Dee—auâuox*) See the *48 Claves*. Here, Dee placed a circumflex over the second *a* to indicate its long sound.

Possible shared root:

Avavago (av-AY-vay-go) Thunders (of Increase)

Note:

See note at "Avav."

Aviny (ay-VII-nee)* *n.* Millstones

9.42 . . .are *millstones* greater than the earth . . .

Pronunciation notes:

(**Dee—A vi ny*) Three syllables. The *i* should take its long sound. The *y* at the end of a word should take the long "e" sound.

(**Dee—auíny*) See the *48 Claves*. Here, Dee placed an accent over the second syllable.

"Azia" (ay-ZII-ay) *prep.* Like (unto)

Compounds:

Aziagiar (ay-zii-AY-jii-er) ["Azia" + "Giar"] Like unto the Harvest

Also:

Aziazor (ay-ZII-ay-zor) Likeness of

Note:

Also see Pugo (as unto).

Aziagiar (ay-zii-AY-jii-er)* ["Azia" + "Giar"] *comp.* Like unto the Harvest

8.19 . . .and *like unto the harvest of* a widow.

Pronunciation notes:

(**Dee—A zi á gi er*) Five syllables, with an accent on the third syllable. Both *a*'s stand alone. Both *i*'s likely take the long sound. The *g* should take a soft sound before an *i*.

(**Dee—aziágîer*) See the *48 Claves*. Dee again placed an accent on the third syllable. He also added a circumflex over the second *i* to indicate its long sound.

Also:

Aziazor (ay-ZII-ay-zor) Likeness of

Aziazor (ay-ZII-ay-zor)* *n.* Likeness of

10.7 . . . *in the likeness of* an oak . . .

Pronunciation notes:

(**Dee—A zí a zor*) Four syllables, with an accent on the second syllable. Both *a*'s stand alone, and the *i* likely takes its long sound.

(**Dee—aziâzor*) See the *48 Claves*. Here, Dee again placed an accent over the *i* in the second syllable. He also placed a circumflex over the second *a* to indicate its long sound.

Note:

It appears that "azia" is the root here. Note that an *o* is suffixed onto the root word, which sometimes indicates "of." (The further addition of an *r* is an anomaly.) "Azia" appears in what might be a compound word below.

Possible Root or Compound:

Aziagiar (ay-zii-AY-jii-er) ["Azia" + "Giar"] — Like unto the Harvest

Azien (az-EEN)* *n.* — Hands

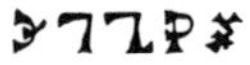

3.6 . . . *on whose hands* stand 12 . . .

Pronunciation notes:

(**Dee—Azien*) I assume there should be two syllables here. The Early Modern English letter combination *ie* can make a long "e" sound. (It can also make a long "i" sound—but usually in combination with *ght*. So I have settled on the long "e" sound instead.)

I have adopted the accent from *Ozien* (hand).

Also:

Ozien (oh-ZEEN) — (Mine Own) Hand

Zien (zeen) — Hands

Probable shared root:

Ozol (oh-ZOHL) — Hands

Zol (zohd-OL) — Hands

Note:

There is no indication at this time that *Azien* (hands) and *Azia* (likeness) are related concepts.

Pa (B)

Bab (bab) *n.* — Dominion

From *Corpus Omnium*:
Found in the post-Deluge portion of the Table, in the phrase *Zna Bab Iad* (Moving Dominion of God).

Note:
This word is a palindrome. It is spelled the same forward as it is spelled backward.

Possible shared root:

Ababalond (ay-BAY-bay-lond)	Harlot
Babage (bay-BAY-jee)	South
Babagen (bay-BAY-jen)	South
Babalon (bay-BAY-lon)	Wicked

Note:
Perhaps the Heptarchic Angels *Babalel* (king of Tuesday), *Bobogel* (king of Sunday), and *Bablibo* (lunar Governor of Sunday) share *Bab/Bob* as a root. (See *Babalon* for more on King Babalel, and *Babagen* for more on King Bobagel.)

Compare from *Loagaeth*:
Babalad, Babna

Babage (bay-BAY-jee)* *n.* — South

4.3 I have set my feet *in the south* . . .
12.3 O you that reign *in the south* . . .

Pronunciation notes:
(**Dee 4.3—Ba bage*) Two syllables. The final *e* should make the second *a* long and the *g* soft. The first *a* also seems to be long.
(**Dee 12.3—Ba ba ge*) Seems to be three syllables. Both *a*'s long.

(**Dee 4.3—babâge*) See the *48 Claves*. Here, Dee placed a circumflex over the second *a* to indicate its long sound. There is no such indication for the first *a*.
I have adopted the accent from *Bablon* (wicked).

Also:

Babagen (bay-BAY-jen) South

Possible shared root:

Bab (bab) Dominion
Babalon (bay-BAY-lon) Wicked
Ababalond (ay-BAY-bay-lond) Harlot

Note:

If baba or *bab* is a shared root between these words, then I am unsure of the reason for this apparent bias against the southern angle of the Heavens/compass in the Angelical language. The poetry of the Keys also tends to lean toward an anti-northern angle bias.

Compare from *Loagaeth*:

Babalad, Babna

Babagen (bay-BAY-jen)* *n.* South

13.2 O you swords of *the south* . . .

Pronunciation notes:

(**Dee—B ba gen jen*) Three syllables. For some reason, Dee forgets the *a* in the first syllable in his phonetic note. (Or, this could be a minor error in *TFR*.) However, other versions of this word suggest it should be a long "a" sound. Dee does indicate that the *g* in the third syllable should take the softer "j" sound.
(**Dee—Babâgen*) See the *48 Claves*. Dee placed a circumflex over the second *a* to indicate its long sound.
I have adopted the accent from *Bablon* (wicked).

Also:

Babage (bay-BAY-jee) South

Possible shared root:

Bab (bab) — Dominion
Babalon (bay-BAY-lon) — Wicked
Ababalond (ay-BAY-bay-lond) — Harlot

Note:

See the "Compare from *Loagaeth*" section for the word *Bobagen*, which may be related to *Babagen*. If this is the case, then also compare to the name of the Angel *Bobogel*, the Heptarchic King of Sunday. Perhaps *Bobogel* is related to the South because the Sun at midday (its zenith) is associated with the South in astrology.

Compare from *Loagaeth*:

Babalad, Babna, Bobagen

Babalon (bay-BAY-lon)* *n.* or *adj.* — Wicked

6.11 . . . a torment to *the wicked* . . .

Pronunciation notes:

(**Dee—Babálon*) Likely three syllables, with an accent on the second syllable. Both *a*'s likely take their long sound—which is supported by the pronunciation of Ababalond (harlot).
(**Dee—babálon*) See the *48 Claves*. This note matches that from *TFR*.

Note:

Wicked is usually an adjective, but it is used here as a noun.

Also:

Ababalond (ay-BAY-bay-lond) — Harlot

Note:

Notice the similarity between this word and the name of the ancient empire of Babylon. (The famous Temple to Marduk even appears in the Genesis 11 as the "Tower of Babel"—where the confusion of tongues took place.) Beginning with *1 Enoch* (likely written during the Judaic captivity in Babylon), the kingdom of Babylon has been a biblical symbol of iniquity. Also see note at *Ababalond* (harlot).

Also compare to the name of the Angel *Babalel*, the Heptarchic King of Tuesday. As the King of Tuesday and Mars, perhaps "The Wicked" (or even "The Wicked of God") is a fitting title for this Angel.

Possible shared root:

Bab (bab)	Dominion
Babage (bay-BAY-jee)	South
Babagen (bay-BAY-jen)	South

Compare from *Loagaeth*:

Babalad, Babna

Baeovib (bee-oh-vib) *prop. n.* Righteousness

15.14 . . . knowest the great name *righteousness* . . .

Pronunciation notes:

(**Dee—Bæôuib*) See the *48 Claves*. The ash (*æ*) in Dee's phonetic notation can indicate a short *a* or a long "e" sound. (I assume the long *e* in this case.) Dee placed a circumflex over the *o* to indicate its long sound. The *u* is somewhat unsure, although I have assumed it should make the sound of *v* when preceding a vowel. (I have also spelled the word with a *v*.) This should be a word of three syllables.

Note:

The transmission of Key Fifteen is missing from Dee's journals. We only have the English for this Key given later (see *TFR*, p. 193). Plus, the word appears in this location in Dee's *48 Claves*.

It appears this is a proper noun—likely a Name of God. See also *Baltoh*, *Baltle*, and *Samvelg* (all forms of "righteous").

Bag (bag) *prop. n.* "The Twenty-Eighth Aethyr" (Fury?)

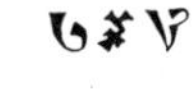

30.3 . . . which dwell in *the twenty-eighth aethyr* . . .

Note:

This (word 30.3) is the single space in the Key of the Aethyrs, which must be changed for each invocation—replacing word 30.3 with the name of the appropriate Aethyr. No established definitions were given for these names.

Bag contains the three Parts of the Earth *Labnixp*, *Pocisni*, and *Oxlopar*.

Possible shared root:

Bagie (bag-EE) — Fury

Note:

The names of the Heptarchic Angels *Bagenol* (prince of Friday) and *Bagnole* (solar Governor of Friday). If the word *Bag* is a root indicating "fury," this could indicate an etymology for these Angels.

Bagie (bag-EE)* *n.* — Fury

14.2 O you sons of *fury* . . .

Pronunciation notes:

(**Dee—bagíe*) See the *48 Claves*. The only phonetic clue Dee gives us is the accent mark. I am assuming two syllables here. The *a* might take the short sound in the first syllable. In Early Modern English, the *ie* letter combination should make a long "e" sound (as in the English word *believe*).

Note:

The transmission of Key Fourteen is missing from Dee's journals. We only have the English for this Key given later (see *TFR*, p. 193). Plus, the word appears in this location in Dee's *48 Claves*.

See also Baltim (extreme justice, or fury).

Possible shared root:

Bag (bag) — "The Twenty-Eighth Aethyr"

Bagle (BAY-gayl)* *conj.* For (Wherefore, Because)

4.36 . . . *For* I am the Lord . . .
5.53 . . . *For why?* Our Lord and Master is One.
7.42 . . . *For*, to this remembrance . . .
8.35 . . . *For* the Thunders have spoken . . .
8.39 . . . Come away, *for* the crowns of the temple . . .
9.62 . . . *For why?* The God if Righteousness . . .
9.70 . . . *For* the time is such . . .
10.18 . . . Laid up *for* the earth . . .**
10.74 . . . *For* her iniquity is great . . .
11.32 . . . *For* I have prepared for you . . .
30.103 . . . *For why?* It repenteth me . . .

Note:
***Bagle* at 10.18 is the only instance where the word is not synonymous with "because" or the older "wherefore" (or "for why?").

Pronunciation notes:
(*Dee 4.36; 7.42; 8.35, 39; 9.62, 70; 10.18—Ba gle*) Two syllables. Long *a*. Also note that the final letters *le* following a consonant usually make an "ayl" sound in Angelical. (See *Baltle* and *Cicle* for examples.)
(*Dee 5.53—Ba' gle*) Accent on the first syllable.
(*Dee 10.74; 11.32; 30.103—Bagle*)
(*Dee 5.53—Bágle*) See the *48 Claves*. The accent is again shown on the first syllable.

Also:
Baglen (BAY-gayl-en) Because

Note:
Aso see Lap (for) and Darsar (wherefore).

Compare from *Loagaeth*:
Baged

Baglen (BAY-gayl-en)* *conj.* Because

30.110 . . . *Because* she is the bed of an harlot . . .

Pronunciation notes:

(**Dee—Baglen*) Dee does not leave us much of a clue. However, I suggest three syllables, accent on the first syllable, based on the pronunciation notes for Bagle.

Also:

Bagle (BAY-gayl) For (Wherefore, Because)

Note:

Also see Lap (for) and Darsar (wherefore).

Bahal (BAY-hal)* *v.* To Cry Loudly (i.e., To Yell)

11.14 . . . the Eagle spake and *cried with a loud voice* . . .

Pronunciation notes:

(**Dee—Ba hal*) Two syllables. The first *a* appears to take its long sound.
(**Dee—báhal*) See the *48 Claves*. Here, Dee placed an accent upon the first syllable.

Note:

See also Faaip (voices).

Shared root:

Bia (bii-a) Voices
Bial (bii-al) Voice
Bien (bii-en) (My) Voice

Balit (bal-it) *n.* The Just

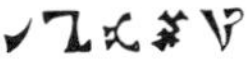

**16.10 . . . shall comfort *the just* . . .

Note:

**The transmission of the first twelve words of Key Sixteen is missing from Dee's journals. We only have the English given for it on *TFR*, p. 194. However, they do appear in Dee's *48 Claves*.

The phrase *the just* has an implied noun: *people*. In the complete phrase *the just people*, the word *just* is an adjective.

Also:

Balt (balt)	Justice
Baltan (bal-tan)	Justice
Baltim (bal-tim)	Extreme Justice (or Fury)

Note:

See also Baltoh (*righteousness*).

Also compare to the name of the Angel *Baligon*, the Heptarchic King of Friday. The Just may be a root for his name. If his name is a compound, perhaps it is (Balit + Gono), "Faith (of) the Just."

Possible shared root:

Baltle (bal-tayl)	Righteousness
Balzarg (bal-zarj)	Stewards
Balzizras (bal-zii-sras)	Judgment

Balt (balt)* *n.* Justice

1.6 . . . sayeth the God of *Justice* . . .

3.57 . . . become the skirts of *justice* . . .

**16.4 . . . the house of *Justice* . . .

Pronunciation notes:

(**Dee 1.6; 3.57—Balt*)

Note:

**The transmission of the first twelve words of Key Sixteen is missing from Dee's journals. We only have the English given for it on *TFR*, p. 194. However, they do appear in Dee's *48 Claves*.

Also:

Balit (bal-it)	The Just
Baltan (bal-tan)	Justice
Baltim (bal-tim)	Extreme Justice (or Fury)

Compounds:

Baltoh (bal-toh) [Balt + Toh]	Righteousness

Baltoha (bal-toh-ha) [Balt + "Toha"] (My) Righteousness
Iadbaloth (ii-ad-BAL-toh) [Iad + Balt + Toh] God of Righteousness

Possible shared root:

Baltle (bal-tayl) Righteousness
Balzarg (bal-zarj) Stewards
Balzizras (bal-zii-sras) Judgment

Baltan (bal-tan)* *n.* Justice

30.150 . . . sworn to us *in his justice* . . .

Pronunciation notes:

(**Dee—Baltan*) Likely two syllables.

Also:

Balit (bal-it) The Just
Balt (balt) Justice
Baltim (bal-tim) Extreme Justice (or Fury)

Note:

See also Baltoh (*righteous*).

Possible shared root:

Baltle (bal-tayl) Righteousness
Balzarg (bal-zarj) Stewards
Balzizras (bal-zii-sras) Judgment

Baltim (bal-tim) *n.* Extreme Justice (or Fury)

14.24 . . . called amongst you *fury* (or *extreme justice*) . . .

Note:

The transmission of Key Fourteen is missing from Dee's journals. We only have the English for this Key given later (see *TFR*, p. 193). Plus, the word appears in this location in Dee's 48 *Claves*.

Also:

Balit (bal-it)	The Just
Balt (balt)	Justice
Baltan (bal-tan)	Justice

Note:

Bagie (fury).

Possible shared root:

Baltle (bal-tayl)	Righteousness
Baltoh (bal-toh)	Righteous
Balzarg (bal-zarj)	Stewards
Balzizras (bal-zii-sras)	Judgment

Baltle (bal-tayl)* *n.* Righteousness

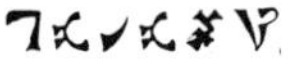

1.70 . . . balance of *righteousness* and truth . . .

Pronunciation notes:

(**Dee—Baltale to be sounded*) Should be two syllables. The letters *le*, following a consonant, combine to form the "ayl" sound at the end of the word. (See *Cicle* and *Bagle*.)

Also:

Baltoh (bal-toh)	Righteousness

Possible shared root:

Balit (bal-it)	The Just
Balt (balt)	Justice
Baltan (bal-tan)	Justice
Baltim (bal-tim)	Extreme Justice (or Fury)
Balzarg (bal-zarj)	Stewards
Balzizras (bal-zii-sras)	Judgment

Note:

See also "Piamol." See also *Baeouib* and *Samvelg* (both are forms of "righteous").

Baltoh (bal-toh)* [Balt + Toh] *comp.* Righteousness

2.22 . . . the chamber of *righteousness* . . .

Pronunciation notes:

(**Dee—Baltoh*) Likely two syllables.

Also:

Baltle (bal-tayl) Righteousness

Compounds:

Baltoha (bal-toh-ha) [Balt + "Toha"] (My) Righteousness
Iadbaloth (ii-ad-BAL-toh) [Iad + Balt + Toh] God of Righteousness

Note:

Also see Baeouib (righteousness) and Samvelg (the righteous).

Possible shared root:

Balit (bal-it) The Just
Balt (balt) Justice
Baltan (bal-tan) Justice
Baltim (bal-tim) Extreme Justice (or Fury)
Balzarg (bal-zarj) Stewards
Balzizras (bal-zii-sras) Judgment

Baltoha (bal-toh-ha)* [Balt + "Toha"] *comp.* (My) Righteousness

8.12 . . . which I have prepared for *my own righteousness* . . .

Pronunciation notes:

(**Dee—Bal to ha*) Three syllables. The *o* takes a long sound (likely due to the *oh* letter combination).

(**Dee—baltôha*) See the *48 Claves*. Here Dee placed a circumflex over the *o* to indicate its long sound.

Also:

Baltle (bal-tayl) Righteousness

Compounds:

Baltoh (bal-toh) [Balt + Toh] — Righteousness

Iadbaloth (ii-ad-BAL-toh) [Iad + Balt + Toh] — God of Righteousness

Note:

Also see *Baeouib* (righteousness) and *Samvelg* (the righteous).

Balye (bay-lii-ee)* *n.* — Salt

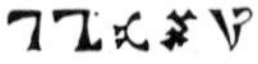

9.19 . . . and of the marrow of *salt* . . .

Pronunciation notes:

(**Dee—Ba ly e*) Three syllables. I suggest a long *a* in the first syllable. I have given the *y* a long "i" sound in the second syllable. Finally, the *e* stands alone in the third syllable.

Balzarg (bal-zarj)* *n.* — Stewards

3.30 . . . I made you *stewards* and placed you . . .

Pronunciation notes:

(**Dee—BALZARG arg as in barge*) I suggest two syllables. Dee indicates a soft *g* at the end.

Note:

Saying *steward* is another manner of saying *caretaker*. It could indicate a "Governor."

Possible shared root:

Balit (bal-it) — The Just

Balt (balt) — Justice

Baltan (bal-tan) — Justice

Baltim (bal-tim) — Extreme Justice (or Fury)

Baltoh (bal-toh) — Righteousness

Balzizras (bal-zii-sras) — Judgment

Balzizras (bal-zii-sras)* *n.* Judgment

30.9 . . . execute *the Judgment* of the Highest.

Pronunciation notes:

(**Dee—Bal zi zras*) Three syllables. I assume a long *i* at the end of the second syllable.

Possible shared root:

Balit (bal-it)	The Just
Balt (balt)	Justice
Baltan (bal-tan)	Justice
Baltim (bal-tim)	Extreme Justice (or Fury)
Baltoh (bal-toh)	Righteousness
Balzarg (bal-zarj)	Stewards

Bams (bams)* *v.* To Forget

30.90 . . . let them *forget* their names . . .

Pronunciation notes:

(**Dee—Bams*) One syllable.

Barees (bar-ees) *n.*? n/a

Note:

See the *Five Books*, p. 188. The Ruling Prince of the *Heptarchia*, Hagonel (not to be confused with the Son of the Sons of Light with the same name) presents his Seal—which is identical to the common symbol of the Sun (a circle with a dot in the center)—and calls it *Barees*. No definition is given.

Basgim (bas-jim)* *n.* Day

10.24 . . . which burn night and *day* . . .

Pronunciation notes:

(**Dee—Bas gim*) Two syllables. The vowels are all short. The *g* should take its soft sound when preceding an *i*.

Shared root:

Bazemlo (bas-em-loh) Midday the First
"Bazem" (bas-em) Midday

Note:

These words apparently share "bas/baz" as a root.

"Bazem" (bas-em) *n.* Midday

Compounds:

Bazemlo (bas-em-loh) ["Bazem" + "Lo"] Midday the First

Shared root:

Basgim (bas-jim) Day

Note:

These words apparently share "bas/baz" as a root.

Also:

Compare the names of the Heptarchic Angels *Baspalo* (Mercury Governor of Monday), *Basledf* (Venus Governor of Monday), and *Bazpama* (Mars Governor of Wednesday). Also compare the name of the Part of the Earth (and its Angelic Governor) *Bazchim*.

Bazemlo (bas-em-loh)* ["Bazem" + "Lo"] *comp.* Midday the First

8.1 *The midday the first* is as the third heaven . . .

Pronunciation notes:

(**Dee—Baz me lo*) Dee originally wrote this word as *Bazmelo*. However, see *TFR*, p. 200, where Illemese corrects this:

(*Illemese—Basem lo, or Basemlo*) Three syllables.

(**Dee—Bazmêlo*) See the *48Keys*. Dee preserved the *Bazmelo* spelling of the word here. He even placed a circumflex over the *e* to indicate a long sound. However, I have settled upon the correction made by Illemese.

Shared root:

Basgim (bas-jim) — Day

Note:

These words apparently share *bas/baz* as a root.

Also:

Compare the name of the Heptarchic Angel *Basmelo*, the solar Governor of Thursday. See the pronunciation note—as this might explain why Dee originally wrote Bazemlo as "Basmelo" instead. I suggest the Governor's name should be pronounced as Dee describes above—with a long "e" sound (bas-mee-loh).

Befafes (bef-ay-fes) *prop. n.* — Light From Light,* *Heptarchic* Prince of Tuesday, Mars

Note:

(**Dee—Befafes his etymology is as much to say "Light from the Light."*) See the *Five Books*, p. 310. However, see *Ialpirt* (light)—which I assume refers to a different kind of Light than expressed in Befafes' name.

I have not included most of the Heptarchic names and those derived from tablets and magick squares elsewhere in the Angelical system in this Lexicon. However, the name of the Prince of Tuesday, *Befafes*, plays an important role between *Loagaeth* and the forty-eight Keys.
Also see *Obelison* (Pleasant Deliverer), a name of Befafes.

Also:

Befes (bef-es) — Heptarchic Prince of Tuesday (vocative)

Compare from *Loagaeth*:

Bef, Befas

Befes (BEF-es)* *n.* — Heptarchic Prince of Tuesday (vocative)**

Pronunciation note:

(**Dee—Béfes*) See the *Five Books*, p. 310. Dee places an accent over the first *e*.

From *Loagaeth*:

(***Dee—Befes the vocative case of Befafes. Befafes O, is to call upon him as on God. Befafes O, is as much to say, "Come Befafes and bear witness." Befafes his etymology is as much to say "Light from the Light."*) See the *Five Books*, p. 310. *Befafes* is the Heptarchic Prince of Tuesday.

Also:

Befafes (bef-ay-fes) — Heptarchic Prince of Tuesday, Mars

Compare from *Loagaeth*:

Bef

Bia (bii-a)* *n.* — Voices

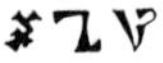

2.30 . . . mightier are *your voices* than the manifold winds . . .

Pronunciation notes:

(**Dee—Bia*) Likely two syllables with a long *i*. See pronunciation note for *Bien* (my voice). I believe the final *a* should take the short sound, as Dee did not write it by itself.

Also:

Bial (bii-al) — Voice
Bien (bii-en) — (My) Voice

Shared root:

Bahal (BAY-hal) — Cry with a Loud Voice

Note:

The *Bia* family of words seem to indicate the physical speaking voice. See also *Faaip* (voices/psalms) and *Farzem* (uplifted voices)—both of which seem to indicate the action of speaking or singing.

Biab (bii-ab)* *v.* To Stand

3.7 . . . on whose hands *stand* 12 kingdoms.

Pronunciation notes:

(**Dee—Biab*) Likely two syllables with a long *i*, as in the English word *dial*.

Note:

Why would this word seem to share a root with the words for "voice" (*Bial*, *Bien*, etc.)?

Bial (bii-al) *n.* Voice

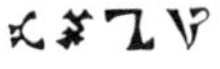

14.18 Behold *the voice* of God . . .

Pronunciation notes:

Likely two syllables with a long *i*. See pronunciation note for *Bien* (my voice).

Note:

The transmission of Key Fourteen is missing from Dee's journals. We only have the English for this Key given later (see *TFR*, p. 193). Plus, the word appears in this location in Dee's *48 Claves*.

Also:

Bia (bii-a) Voices

Bien (bii-en) (My) Voice

Note:

See also Faaip (voices/psalms) and Farzem (uplifted voices).

Shared root:

Bahal (BAY-hal) Cry with a Loud Voice

Bien (bii-en)* *n.* (My) Voice

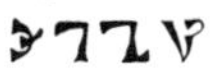

6.33 . . . hearken unto *my voice*.

Pronunciation notes:

(**Dee—Bi en*) Two syllables. The *i* is likely a long vowel.

Also:

Bia (bii-a) — Voices
Bial (bii-al) — Voice

Note:

See also *Faaip* (voices/psalms) and *Farzem* (uplifted voices).

"Bigl" (big-el) *n.* — Comforter?

Compounds:

Bigliad (big-lii-ad) ["Bigl" + Iad?] — (In Our) Comforter

Note:

It is not certain that *Bigliad* should be a compound, or if *Iad* is merely a root in this word.

Pronunciation notes:

See *Crpl* (but one) for a similar pronunciation.

Possible shared root:

"Bliard" (blii-ARD) — Comfort
Blior (blii-OR) — Comfort
Bliora (blii-OH-ra) — Comfort
Bliorax (blii-OH-raks) — To Comfort
Bliorb (blii-ORB) — Comfort
Bliors (blii-ORS) — Comfort
"Bliort" (blii-ORT) — Comfort
Pibliar (pib-lii-AR) — Places of Comfort

Bigliad (big-lii-ad)* ["Bigl" + Iad?] *comp.* — (In Our) Comforter

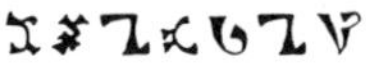

7.49 . . . our strength waxeth strong *in our comforter* . . .

Pronunciation notes:

(**Dee—Big li ad*) Three syllables. The *i* at the end of the second syllable takes a long sound.

(**Dee—Biglîad*) See the *48 Claves*. Here, Dee adds a circumflex over the *i* to indicate its long sound.

Note:
Bigliad is a direct reference to God. It would seem to be a compound of *Iad* (God) and *Blior* (comfort)—though note the radical change from *Blior* to *"Bigl."* I'm not sure what the root would be in this case.

Blans (blanz)* *v.* To Harbor

10.5 . . . and *are harboured* in the north . . .

Pronunciation notes:
(**Dee—Blans*) One syllable. The *a* is likely short.

"Bliard" (blii-ARD) *n.* Comfort

Pronunciation note:
I have adopted the accent from *Bliora* (comfort).

Compounds:
Fbliard (ef-blii-ard) [F + "Bliard"] Visit (with) Comfort

Also:

"Bigl" (big-el)	Comforter
Blior (blii-OR)	Comfort
Bliora (blii-OH-ra)	Comfort
Bliorax (blii-OH-raks)	To Comfort
Bliorb (blii-ORB)	Comfort
Bliors (blii-ORS)	Comfort
"Bliort" (blii-ORT)	Comfort
Pibliar (pib-lii-AR)	Places of Comfort

Blior (blii-OR)* *n.* Comfort

9.74 . . . as requireth *comfort* . . .

Pronunciation notes:

(**Dee—Bli or*) Two syllables. I have adopted the accent from *Bliora* (comfort).

Also:

"Bigl" (big-el)	Comforter
"Bliard" (blii-ARD)	Comfort
Bliora (blii-OH-ra)	Comfort
Bliorax (blii-OH-raks)	To Comfort
Bliorb (blii-ORB)	Comfort
Bliors (blii-ORS)	Comfort
"Bliort" (blii-ORT)	Comfort
Pibliar (pib-lii-AR)	Places of Comfort

Compounds:

Tablior (TAY-blii-or) [Ta + Blior]	As Comforters

Possible compounds:

Bigliad (big-lii-ad) ["Bigl" + Iad?]	(In Our) Comforter

Bliora (blii-OH-ra)* *n.* Comfort

5.49 . . . visit us in peace and *comfort* . . .

Pronunciation notes:

(**Dee—Bli ó ra*) Three syllables, with the accent on the second syllable. The *o* stands alone.

(**Dee—blíora*) See the *48 Claves*. Again the accent is shown on the second syllable.

Also:

"Bigl" (big-el)	Comforter
"Bliard" (blii-ARD)	Comfort
Blior (blii-OR)	Comfort
Bliorax (blii-OH-raks)	To Comfort
Bliorb (blii-ORB)	Comfort
Bliors (blii-ORS)	Comfort
"Bliort" (blii-ORT)	Comfort
Pibliar (pib-lii-AR)	Places of Comfort

Bliorax (blii-OH-raks)* *v.* Shalt Comfort (or To Comfort)

16.9 . . . and *shalt comfort* the just . . .

Note:

The transmission of the first twelve words of Key Sixteen is missing from Dee's journals. We only have the English given for it on *TFR*, p. 194. However, they do appear in Dee's *48 Claves*.

Also:

Note this could be an example of the *-ax* affix, indicating action.

Pronunciation notes:

(**Dee—bliôrax*) See the *48 Claves*. Dee placed a circumflex over the *o* to indicate a long sound. The accent is taken from *Bliora* (comfort). See other versions of this word for further pronunciation notes.

Also:

"Bigl" (big-el)	Comforter
"Bliard" (blii-ARD)	Comfort
Blior (blii-OR)	Comfort
Bliora (blii-OH-ra)	Comfort
Bliorb (blii-ORB)	Comfort
Bliors (blii-ORS)	Comfort
"Bliort" (blii-ORT)	Comfort
Pibliar (pib-lii-AR)	Places of Comfort

Compounds:

Tablior (TAY-blii-or) [Ta + Blior] As Comforters

Bliorb (blii-ORB)* *n.* Comfort

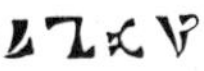

30.17 . . . God, the beginning of *comfort* . . .

Pronunciation notes:

(**Dee—Bliórb*) Likely two syllables, with an accent on the second syllable.

Also:

"Bigl" (big-el)	Comforter
"Bliard" (blii-ARD)	Comfort
Blior (blii-OR)	Comfort
Bliora (blii-OH-ra)	Comfort
Bliorax (blii-OH-raks)	(Shalt) Comfort
Bliors (blii-ORS)	Comfort
"Bliort" (blii-ORT)	Comfort
Pibliar (pib-lii-AR)	Places of Comfort

Bliors (blii-ORS)* *n.* Comfort

8.51 . . . to the terror of the earth, and *to our comfort* . . .

18.5 . . . burning flame of *comfort* . . .

Pronunciation notes:

(**Dee 8.51—Bli ors*)

(**Dee 18.5—B liors*) Two syllables. Based on other versions of this word, I suspect that Dee's note at word 18.5 is a misprint. I have taken my pronunciation from the note at 8.51. The *i* at the end of the first syllable should likely take a long sound.

I have adopted the accent from *Bliora* (comfort).

Also:

"Bigl" (big-el)	Comforter
"Bliard" (blii-ARD)	Comfort
Blior (blii-OR)	Comfort
Bliora (blii-OH-ra)	Comfort
Bliorax (blii-OH-raks)	To Comfort
Bliorb (blii-ORB)	Comfort
"Bliort" (blii-ORT)	Comfort
Pibliar (pib-lii-AR)	Places of Comfort

"Bliort" (blii-ORT) *n.* Comfort

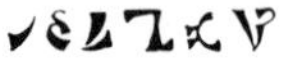

Pronunciation note:

I have adopted the accent from *Bliora* (comfort).

Compounds:

Comobliort (koh-moh-blii-ort) ["Como" + "Bliort"] — Window of Comfort

Also:

"Bigl" (big-el) — Comforter

"Bliard" (blii-ARD) — Comfort

Blior (blii-OR) — Comfort

Bliora (blii-OH-ra) — Comfort

Bliorax (blii-OH-raks) — To Comfort

Bliorb (blii-ORB) — Comfort

Bliors (blii-ORS) — Comfort

Pibliar (pib-lii-AR) — Places of Comfort

Bobagelzod (boh-bay-JEL-zohd)* *n.?* — Heptarchic King of Sunday, Sol?

From *Loagaeth*:

See the *Five Books*, p. 313. This would appear to be the name of the Heptarchic King of Sunday and Sol, *Bobagel*. Perhaps this is a formal vocative case of his name? (See the "Angelical Linguistics" chapter.)

Pronunciation note:

(**Dee—Bobagélzod*) See the *Five Books*, p. 313. Dee places an accent over the *e*. I have given the first *a* and *o* their long sounds based on similar words (see *Babagen*, *Babalon*, etc.).

Compare from *Loagaeth*:

Bobagen

Bogpa (bog-pa)* *v.* — To Reign

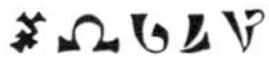

1.66 . . . and *reigneth* amongst you . . .

Pronunciation notes:

(**Dee—Call it Bogpa*) I assume two syllables.

Note:

See also *Sonf* (reign).

Bolp (bulp)* *v.?* or *pron.* (Be) Thou

18.24 *Be thou* a window of comfort unto me.

Pronunciation notes:

(**Dee—Bolp*) One syllable. I assume this word sounds similar to the English word *gulp*.

Probable shared root:

Aqlo (AY-kwah-loh)	Thy
Yls (yils)	Thou
Ylsi (yil-sii)	Thee
L (el)	First
Ol (ohl)	I, Myself

Note:

If *Ol* (myself) is the root here, then the pre- and suffixed letters (*B* and *p*) alter it to its antonym (thou). Also see the word *I* (is/are), which goes through a similar antonymic change into *Ip* (not).

I also note that this word seems to indicate action, even though *thou* is technically a personal pronoun.

Booapis (boh-OH-ay-pis)* *v.* To Serve

30.63 . . . as a handmaid *let her serve them.*

Pronunciation notes:

(**Dee—B o o a p i S*) This is a very confusing note, and I doubt that Dee intended every one of these letters to stand alone. (To make sense of this, I have taken the pronunciation notes for *Aboapri* into account.) I have combined the initial *B* and the first *o*, and left the second *o* to stand alone. This makes a word of four syllables.

I have applied the accent to the second syllable based on *Aboapri* (to serve).

Also:

Aboapri (ay-BOH-ay-prii) — To Serve

Note:

It would appear that *boap/booap* serves as the common root between these two words.

Bornogo (bor-noh-goh) *prop. n.* — Heptarchic Prince of Sunday, Sol

From *Loagaeth*:

This name appears in a star pattern on the ninth Table of *Loagaeth*. *Bornogo* is the Heptarchic Prince of Sunday and Sol. Interestingly, it would seem a version of the name *Bobgel* (the King of Sunday) also appears in *Loagaeth*. (See *Bobogelzod*.)

Bransg (branzh)* *n.* — Guard

9.2 A mighty *guard of* fire with two-edged swords . . .

Pronunciation notes:

(**Dee—Bransg*) This word is likely one syllable. All of these letters fit naturally together in English. The *a* should take its short sound. The *sg* should make the sound of "sj" (a kind of "zhuh" sound)—which I have represented as *zh*. (See *Vorsg* for another example.)

Note:

A *guard*, as the word is used in Key Nine, refers to troops who have been assigned to something specific—such as an honor guard assigned to carry a flag. The *mighty guard* in Key Nine is like a defensive platoon.

Brgda (burj-da)* *v.* — To Sleep

3.25 . . .which *sleep* and shall rise.

Pronunciation notes:

(**Dee—as Burgda as burgen to bud*) Apparently two syllables, with a soft "g" (or "j") sound followed immediately by a *d*. (Almost like a hard "j" or "dg" sound—as in *fudge* and *budge*.) As is often the case, the *r* nested between two incompatible consonants adopts an "ur" sound.

"Brin" (brin) *v.* Have

Compounds:

Dsbrin (dee-es-brin) [Ds + "Brin"] Which Have

Also:

"Brint" (brint) Has

Brints (brints) To Have

Note:

"Brin" is likely the root word for *Brints* and its related words.

"Brint" (brint) *v.* Has

Compounds:

Odbrint (ohd-brint) [Od + "Brint"] And Has

Also:

"Brin" (brin) Have

Brints (brints) To Have

Note:

"Brin" may represent the root word here.

Brints (brints)* *v.* To Have

18.15 . . . 6332 *have* their abiding . . .

Pronunciation notes:

(**Dee—Brints*) All one syllable. The *i* is likely short.

Also:

"Brin" (brin) Have

"Brint" (brint) — Has

Note:

"Brin" may represent the root word here.

Compare from *Loagaeth*:

Brtnc

Brita (brit-a)* *v.* — To Speak of

6.34 *I have talked of you* and I move you . . .

Pronunciation notes:

(**Dee—Brita*) Likely two syllables.

Note:

Also see *Camliax* (Spake).

Busd (buzd)* *n., adj.* — Glory, Glorious

8.23 . . . in *the glory* of the earth . . .

**16.7 . . . thy beginning *in glory* . . .

Pronunciation notes:

(**Dee 8.23—Bufd*) One syllable. I notice "Bufd" is spelled with an *f* while every other version of the word (*Busdir, Busdirtilb*) is spelled with an *s*. In Dee's English, elongated *s*'s were often used that highly resemble *f*'s. Therefore, it is likely that this word should read *Busd*. (See *Casasam* / "-Cafafam" for a similar example.)

(**Dee 8.23—busd*) See the *48 Claves*. Here, Dee confirms that the *f* in *TFR* should actually be an *s*.

Note:

**The transmission of the first twelve words of Key Sixteen is missing from Dee's journals. We only have the English given for it on *TFR*, p. 194. However, they do appear in Dee's *48 Claves*.

Also:

Busdir (buz-der) — Glory

Note:

Busd would seem to indicate *glory* in the sense of "wondrous." See also *Ialpirgah* (flames of the first glory), which properly relates to light and fire—and possibly the light (glory) of the rising Sun. And *Adgmach* (glory), which appears to indicate "adoration, praise." Also see "Lzirn" (wonders) and *Sald* (wonder).

Also compare *Busd* to the Heptarchic Angel *Busduna*, the lunar Governor of Tuesday. Apparently, *Busduna* contains an etymology of "glorious."

Busdir (buz-der)* *n.* — Glory

18.8 . . . openest *the glory* of God.

Pronunciation notes:

(**Dee—Bus dir*) Two syllables.

Also:

Busd (buzd) — Glory

Compounds:

Busdirtilb (buz-der-tilb) [Busdir + Tilb] — Glory (of) Her

Note:

See note at *Busd*.

Busdirtilb (buz-der-tilb)* [Busdir + Tilb] *comp.* — Glory (of) Her

30.50 . . . that *the glory of her* may be . . .

Pronunciation notes:

(**Dee—Bus dir tilb*) Three syllables.

Butmon (but-mon)* *n.* — Mouth

7.9 . . . the Lord *hath opened his mouth* . . .

Pronunciation notes:

(*Dee—But mon*) Two syllables. Both vowels are probably short.

Also:

Butmona (but-moh-na) Mouth
Butmoni (but-moh-nii) Mouths

Note:

Compare to the name of the Angel *Butmono*, the Heptarchic Prince of Thursday. If the *-o* affix (of) applies here, Butmono's name means "of the mouth"—like the mouth of God.

Butmona (but-moh-na)* *n.* Mouth

30.146 . . . the covenant of *his mouth* which he hath sworn . . .

Pronunciation notes:

(*Dee—But mo na*) Three syllables. The *o* likely takes a long sound.
(*Dee—butmôna*) See the *48 Claves*. Here, Dee placed a circumflex over the *o*—thus confirming its long sound.

Also:

Butmon (but-mon) Mouth
Butmoni (but-moh-nii) Mouths

Note:

See note at *Butmon*.

Butmoni (but-moh-nii)* *n.* Mouths

9.46 . . . and *from their mouths* run seas of blood.

Pronunciation notes:

(*Dee—BUT MO NI*) Three syllables. It is unclear why Dee wrote this word in all caps. The *o* in the second syllable should take its long sound. Likewise for the *i* in the final syllable.

(**Dee—butmôni*) See the *48 Claves*. Here, Dee placed a circumflex over the *o* to indicate its long sound.

Also:

Butmon (but-mon)	Mouth
Butmona (but-moh-na)	Mouth

Note:

See note at *Butmon*.

Veh (C/K)

Ca (see-ay)* *adv.* Therefore

1.74 Move, *therefore* . . .
2.43 Move, *therefore* . . .
5.42 *Therefore*, come you and obey . . .
11.36 Move, *therefore* . . .

Pronunciation notes:
(*Dee 1.74—Call it C A [two syllables]*) Each letter here stands alone.
(*Dee 2.43—Ca*)
(*Dee 5.42—Ca Sa*) This note suggests one syllable, with the *C* taking the sound of "S."
(*Dee 1.74—c-a*) See *48 Claves*. Two syllables are again indicated.

Note:
See also "Ca" (*as*).

Compare from *Loagaeth*:
Ca

"Ca" (kay) *prep.* As?

Compounds:
Icorsca (ii-KORS-kay) [I + Cors + "Ca"] Is Such as

Also:
Ta (tay) As

Note:
The English word *as* is generally translated as *Ta*. However, there is precedent elsewhere in the Keys for this switch from *T* to *C*. See *Cab* (scepter) and *Caba* (govern).

Cab (kab) *n.* Rod/Scepter

1.44 . . . delivered you *a rod* with the arc of knowledge . . .

Note:

This word obviously means *scepter*—such as a ruling king would carry. It is intimately connected with the word *Caba* (govern), which precedes *Cab* in the Key by a few words.

Also:

Caba (ka-BA) — Govern

Shared root:

Tabaam (tay-BAY-an) — Governor
"Tabas" (tay-BAS) — Govern

Note:

Note that the *T* (of the Taba root) becomes a *C* here. Note also the word Icorsca (*is such as*)—which uses *Ca* for *as* rather than the normal *Ta*. There does seem to be some relationship between the letters *T* and *C* in the Angelical.

Caba (ka-BA)* *v.* — To Govern

1.40 . . . a law *to govern* the holy ones . . .

Pronunciation notes:

(**Dee—call it Caba*) Should be two syllables.
(**Dee—cabá*) See *48 Claves*. The accent is on the second syllable.

Also:

Cab (kab) — Govern

Shared root:

Tabaam (tay-BAY-an) — Governor
"Tabas" (tay-BAS) — Govern

Note:

See note with Cab (scepter) and "Ca" (as?). Also see *Tabaam*.

Cabanladan (kab-an-lad-an) n/a

Note:

See *TFR*, pp. 34–35. This session is recorded entirely in Latin. Here we find this Angelical phrase spoken by "a Voice": *Garil zed masch, ich na gel galaht gemp gal noch Cabanladan.* No translation or context is offered.

Cacacom (kay-SAY-som)* *v.* To Flourish

3.66 . . . his mercies *flourish* . . .

Pronunciation notes:

(**Dee—Ca ca com*) Three syllables. See *Casasam* (abiding)—indicating the *c*'s in Cacacom (except for the initial *C*) should also take the soft "s" sound.

(**Dee—ca-cá-com*) See the *48 Claves*. Here, Dee indicates the accent on the second syllable.

Also:

"Cacocasb" (kay-KOH-kasb)	Another While
Cacrg (KAY-kurg)	Until
Casasam (kay-SAY-sam)	Abiding

Possible shared root:

Acocasb (ay-KOH-kasb)	Time
Capimali (kay-pii-MAY-lii)	Successively
"Capimao" (kay-pii-MAY-oh)	While
Capimaon (kap-ii-MAY-on)	Number of Time
Capmiali (kap-mii-AY-lii)	Successively
Cocasb (KOH-kasb)	Time
Cocasg (KOH-kazh)	Times
Qcocasb (kwah-KOH-kasb)	Contents of Time

Note:

Also see *Pild* (continually).

"Cacocasb" (kay-KOH-kasb) *n.* Another While

Pronunciation note:

I have adopted the accent from other versions of this word.

Compounds:

Odcacocasb (ohd-kay-KOH-kazb) [Od + "Cacocasb"] And Another While

Also:

Acocasb (ay-KOH-kasb)	Time
Cacacom (kay-SAY-som)	Flourish
Cacrg (KAY-kurg)	Until
Cocasb (KOH-kasb)	Time
Cocasg (KOH-kazh)	Times
Qcocasb (kwah-KOH-kasb)	Contents of Time

Probable shared root:

Casasam (kay-SAY-sam)	Abiding
Capimali (kay-pii-MAY-lii)	Successively
"Capimao" (kay-pii-MAY-oh)	While
Capimaon (kap-ii-MAY-on)	Number of Time
Capmiali (kap-mii-AY-lii)	Successively

Note:

Also see *Pild* (continually).

Cacrg (KAY-kurg)* *prep.* or *conj.* Until

8.28 . . . shall not see death *until* this house fall . . .
30.138 . . . add and diminish *until* the stars be numbered . . .

Pronunciation notes:

(**Dee 8.28—Ca curg*)

(**Dee 30.138—Ca crg cúrg*) Two syllables. The *r* takes the "ur" sound. With word 30.138, Dee seems to indicate the second syllable carries the accent (over the *úr*).

(**Dee 8.28—cacarg*) See the *48 Claves*. Here, Dee uses an *a* in the second syllable instead of a *u* to indicate the implied vowel sound. (This *a* and the corresponding *u* are strictly phonetic glosses.)
(**Dee 30.138—cácrg*) See the *48 Claves*. Here, Dee placed the accent upon the first syllable. (I have adopted this in my own pronunciation.)

Also:

Cacacom (kay-SAY-som)	Flourish
"Cacocasb" (kay-KOH-kasb)	Another While

Probable shared root:

Acocasb (ay-KOH-kasb)	Time
Casasam (kay-SAY-sam)	Abiding
Capimali (kay-pii-MAY-lii)	Successively
"Capimao" (kay-pii-MAY-oh)	While
Capimaon (kap-ii-MAY-on)	Number of Time
Capmiali (kap-mii-AY-lii)	Successively
Cocasb (KOH-kasb)	Time
Cocasg (KOH-kazh)	Times
Qcocasb (kwah-KOH-kasb)	Contents of Time

Note:
Also see *Pild* (continually).

"Cafafam" n/a

Note:
See *Casasam* (abiding).

Calz (kalz)* *n.* Firmaments (i.e., Heavens)

1.8 . . . above *the firmaments* of wrath . . .

Pronunciation notes:
(**Dee—Calz*) One syllable.

Note:
See also *Piripsol* (Heavens).

Camascheth (kam-ask-eth) n/a

Note:

See *TFR*, p. 22. Here, the guardian Angel of Lord Lasky of Poland says a prayer on Lasky's behalf, which ends with, "Grant this *Camascheth galsuagath garnastel zurah logaah luseroth*." No translation is offered.

Compare from *Loagaeth*:

Vascheth

Camikas (kam-ii-kas) n/a

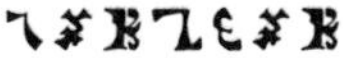

Note:

See the *Five Books*, p. 276. Here, Kelley is once again convinced the Angels are evil devils sent to lead humans astray. The Archangel Raphael holds his hands to Heaven (in what appears to be exasperation) and exclaims, "*Camikas Zure!*" No translation is suggested.

Camliax (kam-lii-aks)* *v.* Spake (i.e., Spoke)

11.12 . . . the Eagle *spake* and cried . . .

Pronunciation notes:

(**Dee—Cam li ax*) Three syllables. The *i* likely takes its long sound.

(**Dee—camlîax*) See the *48 Claves*. Here, Dee placed a circumflex over the *i* to indicate its long sound.

Note:

This could be an example of the suffix *-ax* indicating action.

Also see:

Brita (To Speak of).

Canal (san-al)* *n.* (Continual) Workmen

6.20 . . . and 7699 *continual workmen* whose courses . . .

Pronunciation notes:

(**Dee—Canal Sanal*) Two syllables. The initial *C* takes a soft sound (as in *circle* or *cereal*).

Canse (kan-say) *adj.* Mighty*

Note:

(**Dee—Canse signifieth mighty, and Cruscanse more mighty.*) See *Five Books*, p. 304. *Cruscanse* (more mighty) is found in *Loagaeth*, but *Canse* (mighty) was mentioned only in a marginal note.

See also *Micaolz* (mighty), *Micalp* (mightier)

Also:

Cruscanse (krooz-kan-say) Very Mighty

Compare from *Loagaeth*:

Can, Cans

Caosg (kay-OZH)* *n.* Earth

3.53 . . . on *the earth* continually . . .

5.9 . . . looking with gladness upon *the earth* . . .

**16.12 . . . walkest upon *the earth* with feet . . .

Pronunciation notes:

(**Dee 3.53—Caosg*)

(**Dee 5.9—Ca ósg*) Two syllables, accent on the second syllable. Also note that an *a* followed by an *o* usually appears to take its long sound (as in the English word *chaos*).

I assume that the final *sg* letter combination makes a soft "j" or "zhuh" sound. I have represented this sound with the letters *zh*. (See *Vorsg* and *Cocasg* for this same sound.)

(**Dee 3.53—caósg*) See the *48 Claves*. The *o* again carries the accent.

(**Dee 5.9—ca-ósg*) See the *48 Claves*. This note matches the one in *TFR*.

Note:

**The transmission of the first twelve words of Key Sixteen is missing from Dee's journals. We only have the English given for it on *TFR*, p. 194. However, it does appear in Dee's *48 Claves*.

Also:

Caosga (kay-OS-ga)	Earth
Caosgi (kay-OZH-ii)	Earth
Caosgin (kay-OS-jin)	Earth
Caosgo (kay-OS-go)	Of the Earth
Caosgon (kay-OS-gon)	Unto the Earth

Caosga (kay-OS-ga)* *n.* Earth

30.43 . . . *the earth*, let her be governed . . .

Pronunciation notes:

(**Dee—Ca ós ga*) Likely three syllables—with the accent on the second syllable. The *g* should take the hard sound before an *a*—as in the English words *gave* and *gantry*. Finally, the *a* in the first syllable should be long, because it precedes an *o*.

(**Dee—Caósga*) See the *48 Claves*. Here, Dee again placed an accent upon the second syllable.

Also:

Caosg (kay-OZH)	Earth
Caosgi (kay-OZH-ii)	Earth
Caosgin (kay-OS-jin)	Earth
Caosgo (kay-OS-go)	Of the Earth
Caosgon (kay-OS-gon)	Unto the Earth

Compounds:

Fcaosga (ef-kay-OS-ga) [F + Caosga]	Visit the Earth

Caosgi (kay-OZH-ii)* *n.* Earth

5.22 . . . vessels to water *the earth* . . .

6.23 . . . visit with comfort *the earth* . . .

10.19 . . . laid up for *the earth* . . .
**15.9 . . . weave *the earth* with dryness . . .
30.26 . . . for the government of *the earth* . . .

Note:
**The transmission of Key Fifteen is missing from Dee's journals. We only have the English for this Key given later (see *TFR*, p. 193). Plus, the word appears in this location in Dee's *48 Claves*.

Pronunciation notes:
(**Dee 5.22—Ca ós gi*)
(**Dee 6.23—Ca os gi kaosgi*)
(**Dee 10.19; 30.26—Ca os gi*) In these notes, Dee indicates three syllables, with an accent on the second syllable. He also gives the initial *C* its hard ("K") sound. The *a* preceding an *o* should take the long sound (as in the English word *chaos*), and the *g* preceding an *i* likely takes its soft sound. Finally, because the *g* is soft, it likely combines with the *s* to make a kind of "zhuh" sound—which I have indicated in my pronunciation as *zh*.
(**Dee 5.22; 30.26—caósgi*) See the *48 Claves*. Note the accent again on the second syllable.
(**Dee 15.9—caôsgi*) See the *48 Claves*. Note the circumflex over the *o*, indicating its long sound.

Compounds:

Arcaosgi (ar-kay-OZH-ii) ["Ar" + Caosgi]	To(?) the Earth

Also:

Caosg (kay-OZH)	Earth
Caosga (kay-OS-ga)	Earth
Caosgin (kay-OS-jin)	Earth
Caosgo (kay-OS-go)	Of the Earth
Caosgon (kay-OS-gon)	Unto the Earth

Caosgin (kay-OS-jin)* *n.* Earth

9.44 . . . millstones greater than *the earth* . . .

Pronunciation notes:

(**Dee—Ca os gin*) Three syllables. The *a* in the first syllable should be long. The *g* should take a soft sound when preceding an *i*.

(**Dee—caósgin*) See the *48 Claves*. Here, Dee placed an accent over the second syllable.

Also:

Caosg (kay-OZH)	Earth
Caosga (kay-OS-ga)	Earth
Caosgi (kay-OZH-ii)	Earth
Caosgo (kay-OS-go)	Of the Earth
Caosgon (kay-OS-gon)	Unto the Earth

Caosgo (kay-OS-go)* *prep. phrase* — Of the Earth

8.24 . . . in the glory *of the earth* . . .
8.49 . . . to the terror *of the earth* . . .
9.30 . . . the moss *of the earth* . . .
**14.12 . . . all creatures *of the earth* . . .
18.11 . . . to the center *of the earth* . . .
30.6 . . . mighty in the parts *of the earth* . . .

Pronunciation notes:

(**Dee 8.24—Ca, or Ka os go*)

(**Dee 8.49—Ca as go Ka*)

(**Dee 9.30; 18.11—Ca os go*)

(**Dee 30.6—Ca ós go*) These notes indicate three syllables, an accent on the second syllable. The *C* takes a hard sound, and so does the *g*. (The *g* took a soft sound in *Caosg*, but the final *o* changes the sound.) Finally, I assume a long sound for the *a* because it precedes an *o*.

(**Dee 8.24, 49; 9.30; 14.12; 18.11; 30.6—caósgo*) See the *48 Claves*. Here, Dee indicates an accent on the second syllable.

Note:

**The transmission of Key Fourteen is missing from Dee's journals. We only have the English for this Key given later (see *TFR*, p. 193). Plus, the word appears in this location in Dee's *48 Claves*.

Also:

Caosg (kay-OZH)	Earth
Caosga (kay-OS-ga)	Earth
Caosgi (kay-OZH-ii)	Earth
Caosgin (kay-OS-jin)	Earth
Caosgon (kay-OS-gon)	Unto the Earth

Caosgon (kay-OS-gon)* *prep. phrase* Unto the Earth

10.73 . . . woe *be to the earth* . . .

Pronunciation notes:

(**Dee—Ca ós gon*) Three syllables. The accent mark is placed in the middle of the second syllable. The *a* should be long, followed by a short *o* (as in the English word *chaos*). The *g* preceding an *o* should take the hard sound.

(**Dee—Caósgon*) See the *48 Claves*. Again, Dee shows an accent over the second syllable.

Also:

Caosg (kay-OZH)	Earth
Caosga (kay-OS-ga)	Earth
Caosgi (kay-OZH-ii)	Earth
Caosgin (kay-OS-jin)	Earth
Caosgo (kay-OS-go)	Of the Earth

Capimali (kay-pii-MAY-lii)* *adv.* Successively

4.25 . . . also *successively* are the number of time . . .

Pronunciation notes:

(**Dee—Ca pi ma li*) Four syllables.

(**Dee—Capimáli*) See the *48 Claves*. Accent on the third syllable.

Also:

"Capimao" (kay-pii-MAY-oh)	While (period of time)
Capimaon (kap-ii-MAY-on)	Number of Time
Capmiali (kap-mii-AY-lii)	Successively

Possible shared root:

Acocasb (ay-KOH-kasb)	Time
Cacacom (kay-SAY-som)	Flourish
"Cacocasb" (kay-KOH-kasb)	Another While
Cacrg (KAY-kurg)	Until
Casasam (kay-SAY-sam)	Abiding
Cocasb (KOH-kasb)	Time
Cocasg (KOH-kazh)	Times
Qcocasb (kwah-KOH-kasb)	Contents of Time

Compare from *Loagaeth*:

Cap

Note:

Also see *Pild* (continually).

"Capimao" (kay-pii-MAY-oh) *n.* — While (period of time)

Pronunciation note:

I have adopted the accent from *Capimali* (successively).

Compounds:

Lcapimao (el-ka-PII-may-oh) [L + "Capimao"]	One While

Also:

Capimaon (kap-ii-MAY-on)	Number of Time
Capimali (kay-pii-MAY-lii)	Successively
Capmiali (kap-mii-AY-lii)	Successively

Possible shared root:

Acocasb (ay-KOH-kasb)	Time
Cacacom (kay-SAY-som)	Flourish
"Cacocasb" (kay-KOH-kasb)	Another While
Cacrg (KAY-kurg)	Until
Casasam (kay-SAY-sam)	Abiding
Cocasb (KOH-kasb)	Time
Cocasg (KOH-kazh)	Times
Qcocasb (kwah-KOH-kasb)	Contents of Time

Compare from *Loagaeth*:
Cap

Note:
Also see *Pild* (continually).

Capimaon (kap-ii-MAY-on)* *n.* — Number of Time

4.27 . . . also successively are the *number of time* . . .

Pronunciation notes:
(**Dee—Capi ma on*) Four syllables. The first *a* seems to be short in this case. I have adopted the accent from *Capimali* (successively).

Also:

Capimali (kay-pii-MAY-lii)	Successively
"Capimao" (kay-pii-MAY-oh)	While (period of time)
Capmiali (kap-mii-AY-lii)	Successively

Possible shared root:

Acocasb (ay-KOH-kasb)	Time
Cacacom (kay-SAY-som)	Flourish
"Cacocasb" (kay-KOH-kasb)	Another While
Cacrg (KAY-kurg)	Until
Casasam (kay-SAY-sam)	Abiding
Cocasb (KOH-kasb)	Time
Cocasg (KOH-kazh)	Times
Qcocasb (kwah-KOH-kasb)	Contents of Time

Compare from *Loagaeth*:
Cap

Note:
Also see *Pild* (continually).

Capmiali (kap-mii-AY-lii)* *adv.* — Successively

3.38 . . . power *successively* over 456 . . .

Pronunciation notes:

(**Dee—Capmiali*) Likely four syllables. See pronunciation notes for *Capimaon* and *Capimali*.

(**Dee—Cap-mi-áli*) See the *48 Claves*. Dee places an accent on the third syllable. Both *i*'s likely take their long sound.

Also:

Capimali (kay-pii-MAY-lii)	Successively
"Capimao" (kay-pii-MAY-oh)	While
Capimaon (kap-ii-MAY-on)	Number of Time

Possible shared root:

Acocasb (ay-KOH-kasb)	Time
Cacacom (kay-SAY-som)	Flourish
"Cacocasb" (kay-KOH-kasb)	Another While
Cacrg (KAY-kurg)	Until
Casasam (kay-SAY-sam)	Abiding
Cocasb (KOH-kasb)	Time
Cocasg (KOH-kazh)	Times
Qcocasb (kwah-KOH-kasb)	Contents of Time

Compare from *Loagaeth*:

Cap

Note:

Also see *Pild* (continually).

Carbaf (kar-baf)* *v.* To Sink (i.e., To Stoop, To Dive)

8.33 . . . until this house fall and the dragon *sink*.

Pronunciation notes:

(**Dee—Car baf*) Two syllables.

Note:

This word is used to describe the dragon *stooping*—or diving to attack prey. The word *stoop* can also mean to descend from superior rank or moral standing—both of which make sense when applied to the dragon (or Satan).

Probable shared root:
"Abai" (a-bay) — Stooping

Carma (kar-ma) *v.* — To Come Out/To Arrive From/To Arise

Note:
See *TFR*, p. 32. Here, Dee is speaking with the Angel Madimi. Suddenly, Madimi halts the session and demands, "*Carma geta Barman.*" Dee asks her what this means, and she replies (in Latin, which roughly translates to:) "Come out of there, *Barma*." Madimi's command exorcises fifteen spirits from the body of Edward Kelley, the chief of whom is named Barma. After a short exchange (see *Gil*, etc.), Madimi banishes all fifteen spirits back to Hell "until the last cry." (That is, until the End Times.) Also see *Niis* (Come), *Nissa* (Come away!). *Carma Geta* is likely intended as an exorcism phrase, and not something one would use with the Angels. *Niis*, *Niisa*, etc. are appropriate for use with celestial beings.

Possible shared root:
Carmara (kar-mar-a) — n/a

Compare from *Loagaeth*:
Csrmax, Armax, Cardax

Carmara (or Marmara) (kar-mar-a) *prop. n.* — n/a

Possible shared root:
Carma (kar-ma) — To Come Out/To Arise

Note:
See the *Five Books*, pp. 184 and 187. *Carmara* is the title of the ruling King of the *Heptarchia*. In Dee's lifetime, the Heptarchic King of Venus—Baligon—held the title. Today, I presume it should be the King of Mercury—Bnaspol—though I do not know if he would hold the same title.

(Also see *Ga*, *Galvah*, *Hagonel*, *Mapsama*, *Murifri*, *Nalvage*, *Vaa*, and *Za*.)

Compare from *Loagaeth*:
Csrmax, Armax, Cardax

Casarm (kay-SARM)* *pron.* Whom

1.38 . . . *to whom* I made a law . . .
5.14 . . . *unto whom* I fastened pillars . . .

Pronunciation notes:
(**Dee—Casarm*) I assume just two syllables here. Also see *Casarmg*, *Casarman*, and *Casarmi*—which indicate the first *a* is long, and the accent is on the second syllable.

Also:

Casarma (kay-SAR-ma)	Whom
Casarman (kay-SAR-man)	Whom/(Under) Whose
Casarmg (kay-SAR-mij)	In Whom
Casarmi (kay-SAR-mij)	(Under) Whom

Also see:
Soba (whose)

Casarma (kay-SAR-ma)* *pron.* Whom

2.13 . . . *whom* I have prepared . . .

Pronunciation notes:
(**Dee—Casarma*)
(**Dee—Cas-arma*) See *48 Claves*. I assume three syllables here. Also see *Casarmg*, *Casarman*, and *Casarmi*, which indicate the first *a* is long. Other versions of this word indicate an accent on the second syllable.

Also:

Casarm (kay-SARM)	Whom
Casarman (kay-SAR-man)	Whom/(Under?) Whose
Casarmg (kay-SAR-mij)	In Whom
Casarmi (kay-SAR-mij)	(Under) Whom

Also see:
Soba (whose)

Casarman (kay-SAR-man)* *pron.* or *adj.* — Whom / (Under) Whose

11.22 . . . *of whom* it is measured . . .
**15.4 . . . *under whose* wings . . .

Pronunciation notes:
(*Dee 11.22—Ca sar man*) Three syllables. The first *a* is likely long.
(*Dee 11.22—Ca-sár-man*) See the *48 Claves*. Here, Dee places an accent upon the second syllable.

Note:
The *of* in the above translation (11.22) seems to be implied. The word *under* (in 15.4) is something more of a problem. At first it seems to be a mistake—however, there is also the instance of *Casarmi* (under whom) in Key Four.

**The transmission of Key Fifteen is missing from Dee's journals. We only have the English for this Key given later (see *TFR*, p. 193). Plus, the word appears in this location in Dee's *48 Claves*.

Also:

Casarm (kay-SARM)	Whom
Casarma (kay-SAR-ma)	Whom
Casarmg (kay-SAR-mij)	In Whom
Casarmi (kay-SAR-mij)	(Under) Whom

Also see:
Soba (whose).

Casarmg (kay-SAR-mij)* *pron.* — In Whom

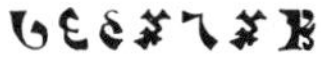

3.72 . . . *in whom* we say . . .
4.20 . . . *in whom* the second beginning of things . . .
7.14 . . . *in whom* the strength . . .

8.7 . . . made of hyacinth pillars, *in whom* the Elders . . .
18.12 . . . *in whom* the secrets . . .

Pronunciation note:

(**Dee 3.72; 8.7—Casarmg*)
(**Dee 4.20—Casarmg the g as in seurge*) Final *g* takes the soft "j" sound.
(**Dee 7.14—Ca sarmg. The g as dg armg*) Again, a soft "g" sound. Also, the first *a* appears long.
(**Dee 18.12—ca sar mg*) Three syllables. Again the *a* seems to take the long sound. Usually the *m* and the *g* would have to stand alone—as they do not combine naturally in English. However, in order to give the *g* its soft sound as Dee indicates, it is necessary to insert a vowel sound between the *m* and *g*. I suggest "mij."
(**Dee 3.72—Casármg*) See the *48 Claves*. Dee placed an accent on the second syllable.

Note:

The Angelical affix-word G (you) is not apparently intended in this spelling of *Casarmg*.

Also:

Casarm (kay-SARM)	Whom
Casarma (kay-SAR-ma)	Whom
Casarman (kay-SAR-man)	Whom/(Under) Whose
Casarmi (kay-SAR-mij)	(Under) Whom

Also see:

Soba (whose).

Casarmi (kay-SAR-mij)* *pron.* (Under) Whom

4.13 . . . *under whom* I have placed 9639 . . .

Pronunciation notes:

(**Dee—Ca sarmi*) Here, we are likely seeing one of Dee's typical substitutions of the letter *i* (that is—*j*) for the letter *g*. Both *Casarmg* and *Casarmi* are probably identical when spoken. However, note that Dee does not show the *i* as a separate syllable—so I have combined the *m* and *i* into the sound of "mij."

(**Dee—Casármi*) See the *48 Claves*. Dee places an accent on the second syllable.

Note:

What is confusing here is the addition of *under* to the word's definition. It repeats in Key Fifteen with the word *Casarman* (under whose).

Also:

Casarm (kay-SARM)	Whom
Casarma (kay-SAR-ma)	Whom
Casarman (kay-SAR-man)	Whom/(Under) Whose
Casarmg (kay-SAR-mij)	In Whom

Also see:

Soba (whose).

Casasam (kay-SAY-sam)* *n.* Abiding

18.16 . . . 6332 have *their abiding* . . .

Pronunciation note:

(**Dee—Ca fa fam*) Three syllables. I suspect that "Cafafam" is a mistake for *Casasam*. In Dee's English, *f* was often written in an elongated fashion that highly resembles an *s*. (I find this highly likely, because we also have the word *Cacacom* [flourish], which uses two *C*s instead of *S*s. Those *C*s could easily take the soft "s" sound.)

(**Dee—casâsam*) See the *48 Claves*. Here, Dee confirms that the *f*s shown in this word in *TFR* should be *s*'s instead. He also placed a circumflex over the second *a* to indicate its long sound.

I have adopted the accent from *Cacacom* (flourish).

Note:

Abiding seems to be used in this case as a noun, to mean "period of existence."

Also:

Cacacom (kay-SAY-som)	Flourish

Probable shared root:

Acocasb (ay-KOH-kasb)	Time

Cacrg (KAY-kurg)	Until
"Cacocasb" (kay-KOH-kasb)	Another While
Capimali (kay-pii-MAY-lii)	Successively
"Capimao" (kay-pii-MAY-oh)	While
Capimaon (kap-ii-MAY-on)	Number of Time
Capmiali (kap-mii-AY-lii)	Successively
Cocasb (KOH-kasb)	Time
Cocasg (KOH-kazh)	Times
Qcocasb (kwah-KOH-kasb)	Contents of Time

Note:
Also see *Pild* (continually).

Kelpadman (kel-pad-man) — n/a*

Note:
See the *Five Books*, p. 413. Kelley overhears many voices singing a song at some distance, and these are the words Dee recorded: *Pinzu-a lephe ganiurax kelpadman pacaph.* No translations are suggested.

Ceph (kef)* *prop. n.* — Letter Z

Note:
The name of the Angelical letter for Z. It is likely that these letter names have translations of their own. (For instance, note the Hebrew alphabet: the letter Z is named *Zain*, but *Zain* also translates as "sword.") However, such translations for the Angelical letters are never given. (See the *Five Books*, p. 270.)

Pronunciation notes:
(**Dee—Sounded like keph.*)

Compare from *Loagaeth*:
Cheph

Chiis (kiis)* *v.* — Are (They)

9.36 . . . cursed *are they* . . .

Pronunciation notes:

(**Dee—Chiis*) One syllable. In Early Modern English, a double *i* indicated the long vowel sound. This is further supported by Dee's phonetic notes for *Chis* (are). I suspect the second *i* in this word is a phonetic gloss.

Also:

Chis (kiis)	Are
"Chisda" (kiis-da)	Are There
Chiso (kiis-oh)	Shall Be
"Gchis" (jee-kiis)	Are
"Ichis" (jay-kiis)	Are
Zchis (zohd-kiis)	(They) Are

Note:

Note the usage of the letter *I* (Angelical for "is") through these words. Because both *I* and *Chis* are forms of "to be," it is possible that *I* forms the root of the *Chis* family of words.

Also see *Zchis* (they are).

Chirlan (kir-lan)* *v.* To Rejoice

7.16 . . .in whom the strength of men *rejoiceth* . . .

9.64 The God of Righteousness *rejoiceth* in them.

Pronunciation notes:

(**Dee 7.16; 9.64—Chir lan Kir*) Two syllables. The *Ch* in the first syllable is given the harder "K" (or "Kh") sound. Both vowels are likely short.

Chis (kiis)* *v.* Are

2.24 Stronger *are* your feet . . .

2.29 . . . mightier *are* your voices . . .

3.10 . . . six *are* the seats of . . .

3.14 . . . the rest *are* as sharp sickles . . .

3.20 . . . *are*, to are not, except by the hands . . .

4.22 . . . *are*, and wax strong . . .

4.26 . . . successively *are* the number of time . . .

4.29 . . . powers *are* as the first 456 . . .
6.3 . . . spirits of the fourth angle *are* nine . . .
8.9 . . . Elders *are* become strong . . .
9.15 . . . whose wings *are* of wormwood . . .
9.41 . . . in their eyes *are* millstones . . .
9.56 . . . upon their heads *are* marble . . .
10.2 . . . *are* numbered and harboured . . .
10.11 . . . *are* 22 nests of lamentation . . .
12.5 . . . and *are* 28 lanterns . . .
**15.6 . . . under whose wings *are* 6739 . . .
17.5 . . . whose wings *are* thorns . . .
30.19 . . . whose eyes *are* the brightness . . .

Pronunciation notes:

(**Dee 2.24—Chis [as Xis]*) The *X* is actually a Greek *Chi*—indicating the *Ch* has a "K" sound.

(**Dee 2.29—Chis [the I long]*) This note shows a long vowel sound for the *i*.

(**Dee 3.10—Chis as Kisse*) The *ss* represents a single "s" sound—as in *Kise*. The final *e* gives the *i* its long sound. We also see again that the *Ch* has a "K" sound.

(**Dee 3.14—Chis as Kis*)

(**Dee 3.20; 4.22, 26—Chis Kis*)

(**Dee 4.29; 6.3; 8.9; 9.15, 41, 56; 10.2, 11; 12.5; 17.5—Chis*)

(**Dee 30.19—Chis Kiss*)

(**Dee 2.29—chís*) See the *48 Claves*. I am unsure why Dee placed an accent on a single-syllable word—unless he had originally intended this particular instance to compound with the word before or after it.

Note:

**The transmission of Key Fifteen is missing from Dee's journals. We only have the English for this Key given later (see *TFR*, p. 193). Plus, the word appears in this location in Dee's *48 Claves*.

Compounds:

Chisholq (KIIS-hohl-kwa) [Chis + Holq]	Are Measured
Chismicaolz (kiis-mii-KAY-ohlz) [Chis + Micaolz]	Are Mighty
Chista (kiis-tay) [Chis + Ta]	Are as
Chistad (kiis-tad) [Chis + Ta + D]	Are as the Third
Dschis (dee-es-kiis) [Ds + Chis]	Which Are

Irgilchisda (ir-jil-KIIS-da) ["Irgil" + Chis + "Da"] — How Many Are There

Odchis (ohd-kiis) [Od + Chis] — And Are

Unalchis (yew-nal-kiis) [Unal + Chis] — These Are

Also:

Chiis (kiis) — Are (They)

"Chisda" (kiis-da) — Are There

Chiso (kiis-oh) — Shall Be

"Gchis" (jee-kiis) — Are

"Ichis" (jay-kiis) — Are

Zchis (zohd-kiis) — (They) Are

Note:

See note at *Chiis*.

Also see *Geh* (are/art)—which may be a more formal term.

"Chisda" (kiis-da) [Chis + "Da"] *comp.* — Are There

Compounds:

Irgilchisda (ir-jil-KIIS-da) ["Irgil" + Chis + "Da"] How many Are There

Chisholq (KIIS-hohl-kwa)* [Chis + Holq] *comp.* — Are Measured

9.24 . . . *are measured* with their ministers . . .

Pronunciation notes:

(**Dee—Chis hol q*) Three syllables. The final *q* stands alone. See *Chis* for further pronunciation notes.

(**Dee—chís hôlq*) See the *48 Claves*. Here, Dee placed an accent over the first syllable. He also placed a circumflex over the *o* to indicate its long sound.

Chismicaolz (kiis-mii-KAY-ohlz)* [Chis + Micaolz] *comp.* — Are Mighty

30.4 . . . *are mighty* in the parts of the earth . . .

Pronunciation notes:

(**Dee—Chis Micáolz Kis*) Four syllables, with an accent on the third syllable. (See *Micaolz*, where Dee places the accent on the same part of the word.) Dee also reminds us that the *Ch* has a "Kh" sound. See *Chis* for the long "i" sound in the first syllable. See *Micaolz* for the long "i" sound in the second syllable.

(**Dee—chis Micaólz*) See the *48 Claves*. Here, Dee indicates the accent on the fourth syllable instead. However, based on other versions of *Micaolz* (mighty), I have settled upon placing the accent over the third syllable.

Chiso (kiis-oh)* *v.* Shall Be

10.78 . . . her iniquity is, was, and *shall be* great . . .

Pronunciation notes:

(**Dee—Chi so K*) Two syllables. Dee indicates that the *Ch* should take the hard "K" (or "Kh") sound. Also, the *i* appears to take the long sound—which is supported by the long "i" sound in other versions of this word.

Note:

Also see *Trian* (shall be).

Also:

Chis (kiis)	Are
Chiis (kiis)	Are (They)
"Chisda" (kiis-da)	Are There
"Gchis" (jee-kiis)	Are
"Ichis" (jay-kiis)	Are
Zchis (zohd-kiis)	(They) Are

Note:

Often, an *o* affix indicates "of." However, it does not appear to hold true in this case.

Chista (kiis-tay)* [Chis + Ta] *comp.* Are as

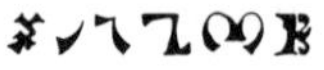

5.37 . . . whose numbers *are as* the first . . .

Pronunciation notes:

(**Dee—Chis ta . . .Kista*) Two syllables. The *Ch* takes a hard "Kh" sound. See *Chiis* for the long "i" sound.

Chistad (kiis-tad)* [Chis + Ta + D] *comp.* — Are as the Third

7.26 . . . *are as the third* and fourth . . .

Pronunciation notes:

(**Dee—Chis tad Kis*) Two syllables. Dee indicates that the *Ch* in the first syllable should take the harder "K" (or "Kh") sound. Also see the pronunciation notes for *Chis*.

Chr (kar)* *prop. n.* — "The Twentieth Aethyr" (To Be / Exist?)

30.3 . . . which dwell in *the twentieth aethyr* . . .

Note:

(**Dee—kar in palato very much.*) This means the *Ch* in this word is guttural (a hard sound made "in palato"—the back of the roof of the mouth, just at the throat)—a raspy "kh" sound. This (word 30.3) is the single space in the Key of the Aethyrs, which must be changed for each invocation—replacing word 30.3 with the name of the appropriate Aethyr. No established definitions were given for these names. However, if *Chr* means "to be / exist," do not confuse this with the verb *I* ("to be"—"is / are").

Chr contains the three Parts of the Earth *Zildron*, *Parziba*, and *Totocan*.

Possible shared root:

Chramsa (kraym-sa) — Be It Made with Power
Christeos (kris-TEE-os) — Let There Be

Chramsa (KRAYM-sa)* *v.* — Be It Made with Power**

Pronunciation note:

(**Dee—chrámsa —the first "a" very long.*) See the *Five Books*, p. 307. Dee adds an accent over the first *a*.

From *Loagaeth*:

(***Dee—A reverent word, [. . .] and is, be it made with power.*) See the *Five Books*, p. 307.

Possible shared root:

Chr (kar)	"The Twentieth Aethyr"
Christeos (kris-TEE-os)	Let There Be

Compare from *Loagaeth*:

Cramsa, Chramsa

Christeos (kris-TEE-os)* *v.* Let There Be . . .

30.47 . . . *let there be* division in her . . .

30.68 . . . and *let there be* no one creature equal . . .

30.79 . . . *let there be* no creature upon or within her . . .

Pronunciation notes:

(**Dee 30.47—Chris té os*)

(**Dee 30.68, 79—Chris te os*) Three syllables, with an accent on the second syllable. I assume a long "e" sound at the end of the second syllable. The *Ch* should take the "Kh" sound, as in the word *Christian*.

(**Dee 30.47, 68—christéos*) See the *48 Claves*. In these places, Dee again indicates an accent on the second syllable.

(**Dee 30.79—christêos*) See the *48 Claves*. Here, Dee used a circumflex over the *e* to indicate its long sound.

Note:

The similarity between this word and the word *Christ* in Greek (*Christos*)—meaning "the Anointed One." In ancient Gnosticism, the *Christos*—as distinct from Jesus—was the source of all life. The *Christos* was also known as the Word (*Logos*)—the agent of creation. (See John 1.) In Genesis 1, the first words spoken by the Creator are, "Let there be Light!"

Possible shared root:

Chr (kar)	"The Twentieth Aethyr"
Chramsa (kraym-sa)	Be It Made with Power

CIAL (sii-al)* 9996

9.26 . . . are measured with their ministers *9996*.

Pronunciation notes:

(**Dee—Ci al*) Two syllables. The *C* preceding an *I* should make a soft "s" sound—as in the English words *circle* and *circus*.

Note:

This word was not originally given with Key Nine. It was added later when Nalvage transmitted the English for the Key (see *TFR*, p. 191). This seems to have been the case with many of the numbers mentioned in the Keys.

Ciaofi (sii-ay-oh-fii)* *n.* Terror

8.48 . . . appear *to the terror* of the earth . . .

Pronunciation notes:

(**Dee—C I A O fi*) Dee's note is somewhat confusing. There is no *ao* letter combination in Early Modern English. Therefore, both letters should be sounded separately (as in the English word *chaos*). This leaves the initial *Ci*—which Dee writes as if they should each stand alone. However, these two letters do make a natural sound in English (as in *circle* and *circus*). Therefore, I suggest four syllables for this word, rather than the five Dee indicates in his phonetic note.

Cicle (sii-kayl)* *n.* Mysteries

1.78, (RFP), 30.152 Open *the mysteries of* your creation . . .

Pronunciation notes:

(**Dee 1.78—Call it Cicle*)

(**Dee 30.152—Cicle*) Dee gives us little to work with. I assume the initial *C* followed by an *i* should make an "s" sound (as in *circus* and *circle*). The *i* should take a long sound (based on Dee's phonetic note for *Cicles*).

Then, the final *le* following a consonant likely makes the "ayl" sound. (See the pronunciation notes for *Baltle* and *Bagle*.)

Also:

Cicles (sii-kayls) — Mysteries

Cicles (sii-kayls)* *n.* — Mysteries

5.52 Conclude us as receivers *of your mysteries* . . .

Pronunciation notes:

(*Dee—Ci cles*) Two syllables. I assume the initial *C* followed by an *i* should make an "s" sound (as in *circus* or *circle*). Also, the *cle* should make the sound of "kayl." (See the pronunciation notes for *Baltle* and *Bagle*.)

Also:

Cicle (sii-kayl) — Mysteries

Cinxir (sinks-ir)* *v.* — To Mingle

10.31 . . . live sulphur *myngled with* poison.

Pronunciation notes:

(*Dee—Cynx ir*) Two syllables. The initial *C* should take the "S" sound when preceding an *i*. Both vowels are short.

CLA (kla)* — 456

3.40 . . . over *456*, the true ages of time . . .

4.31 . . . are as the first *456*.

Pronunciation notes:

(**Dee 3.40; 4.31—Cla*) Dee appears to suggest one syllable.

Cnila (see-NII-la)* *n.* — Blood

9.49 . . . from their mouths run seas of *blood*.

Pronunciation notes:

(**Dee—Cni la*) This appears to be two syllables. However, it is unlikely that the *C* should blend with the *n*. (See *Cnoqod*, etc.) Therefore, it is more likely three syllables. The *i* should take its long sound.

(**Dee—Cníla*) See the *48 Claves*. Here, Dee placed an accent over the *i* in the second syllable.

Cnoqod (see-NOH-kwod)* *n.* (Unto) Servants

2.44 . . . move, therefore, *unto his servants* . . .

Pronunciation notes:

(**Dee—as C Nó Quod*) Three syllables, with an accent on the second syllable. Dee added a *u* in his note as a phonetic gloss—indicating the "kwah" sound.

(**Dee—c-nó-qod*) See *48 Claves*. This note agrees with the note in *TFR*.

Also:

Cnoquodi (see-noh-KWOH-dii) (With) Ministers
Cnoquol (see-NOH-kwol) Servants
Noco (NOH-kwoh) Servant

Note:

Also see *Lang* (Those Who Serve).

Cnoquodi (see-noh-KWOH-dii)* *n.* (With) Ministers

9.25 . . . are measured *with their ministers* 9996 . . .

Pronunciation notes:

(**Dee—Cno quo di*) Dee seems to indicate three syllables. However, other version of this word indicate the initial *C* should stand alone. Therefore, it is likely four syllables instead. The *u* in *Cnoquodi* and *Cnoquol* is likely a phonetic gloss. (It does not appear in *Cnoqod*, except in Dee's pronunciation note.)

(**Dee—Cnoquódi*) See the *48 Claves*. Dee placed an accent on the third syllable.

Also:

Cnoqod (see-NOH-kwod) — (Unto) Servants
Cnoquol (see-NOH-kwol) — Servants
Noco (NOH-kwoh) — Servant

Note:

Also see *Lang* (Those Who Serve).

Cnoquol (see-NOH-kwol)* *n.* — Servants

7.33 *O you servents of* mercy . . .

Pronunciation notes:

(**Dee—Cno quol kol*) Dee indicates that the *q* sounds like a "k" (as in the English words *kick* and *kite*). The *u* in *Cnoquol* and *Cnoquodi* is likely a phonetic gloss—making the *q* take more of a "kwah" sound. (The *u* does not appear in *Cnoqod*, except in Dee's pronunciation note.) See pronunciation note at *Cnoqod* for the accented syllable.

Also:

Cnoqod (see-NOH-kwod) — (Unto) Servants
Cnoquodi (see-noh-KWOH-dii) — (With) Ministers
Noco (NOH-kwoh) — Servant

Note:

Also see *Lang* (Those Who Serve).

"Coazior" (koh-ay-zhor) *v.* — To Increase

Compounds:

Arcoazior (ar-koh-ay-zhor) [Ar + "Coazior"] — That Increase

Note:

It is a long shot, but I suspect a connection between this word and the name of the Angel *Hecoa*, one of the Sons of Light. (Perhaps "Coa" is a root word.) This would give his name an etymology similar to his brother *Dmal*, whose name may contain *Mal* (increase).

Cocasb (KOH-kasb)* *n.* — Time

3.42 . . . the true ages of *time* . . .
10.55 . . . know any *time* there . . .

Pronunciation notes:

(**Dee 3.42—Cocasb*)

(**Dee 10.55—Co casb*) Two syllables. The *o* at the end of the first syllable should be long. The *a* appears to be short in this case.

I have adopted the accent from other versions of this word.

Also:

Acocasb (ay-KOH-kasb)	Time
"Cacocasb" (kay-KOH-kasb)	Another While
Cocasg (KOH-kazh)	Times
Qcocasb (kwah-KOH-kasb)	Contents of Time

Possible shared root:

Cacacom (kay-SAY-som)	Flourish
Cacrg (KAY-kurg)	Until
Casasam (kay-SAY-sam)	Abiding
Capimali (kay-pii-MAY-lii)	Successively
"Capimao" (kay-pii-MAY-oh)	While
Capimaon (kap-ii-MAY-on)	Number of Time
Capmiali (kap-mii-AY-lii)	Successively

Note:

Also see *Pild* (continually).

Cocasg (KOH-kazh)* *n.* — Times

10.37 . . . that 5678 *times* . . .
10.46 . . . thousand *times* as many . . .

Pronunciation notes:

(**Dee 10.37—Co casg g as dg*) Two syllables, with a soft final *g*. The *sg* likely blends into a soft *j* or "zhuh" sound. See *Vorsg* (over you) and *Caosg* (earth), where I also use the "zhuh" digraph in relation to the final letters *sg*. I indicate this rare digraph in my pronunciation as "zh."

(**Dee 10.46—Co Casg . . .gao dg*) Two syllables again. It is unclear what *gao* indicates.

I have adopted the accent from other versions of this word.

Also:

Acocasb (ay-KOH-kasb)	Time
"Cacocasb" (kay-KOH-kasb)	Another While
Cocasb (KOH-kasb)	Time
Qcocasb (kwah-KOH-kasb)	Contents of Time

Possible shared root:

Cacacom (kay-SAY-som)	Flourish
Cacrg (KAY-kurg)	Until
Casasam (kay-SAY-sam)	Abiding
Capimali (kay-pii-MAY-lii)	Successively
"Capimao" (kay-pii-MAY-oh)	While
Capimaon (kap-ii-MAY-on)	Number of Time
Capmiali (kap-mii-AY-lii)	Successively

Note:

Also see *Pild* (continually).

Collal (kol-lal)* *n.* — Sleeves/Sheaths

9.58 . . . upon their (hands) are marble *sleeves*.

Pronunciation notes:

(**Dee—Col lal*) Two syllables. Both vowels should take their short sounds.

Note:

This word indicates *sheaths*—so that these "sleeves" are in fact gloves of a sort.

Commah (KOM-mah)* *v.* — To Truss Together (Join)

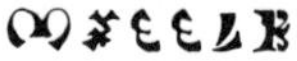

1.25 . . . and *trussed you together* like the palms of my hands . . .

Pronunciation notes:

(**Dee—COMMAH*) Dee gives us little clue here. In Early Modern English, a double consonant generally combined into one sound. This word likely has two syllables. I have adopted the accent from *Comselh* (circle).

Possible shared root:

Comselh (KOM-sel) Circle

Comselh (KOM-sel)* *n.* Circle

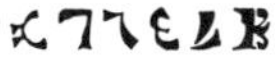

3.5 I am *a circle* on whose hands . . .

Pronunciation notes:

(**Dee—Com Selh*) Two syllables. I assume the final *h* is very faint if not entirely silent.

(**Dee—cómselh*) See *48 Claves*. Note the accent on the first syllable.

Possible shared root:

Commah (KOM-mah) Trussed Together

"Como" (koh-moh) *n.* Window

Compounds:

Comobliort (koh-moh-blii-ort) ["Como" + "Bliort"] Window of Comfort

Comobliort (koh-moh-blii-ort)* ["Como" + "Bliort"] *comp.* Window of Comfort

18.25 . . . be thou a *window of comfort* . . .

Pronunciation notes:

(**Dee—Co mo bli ort*) Four syllables. The *o*'s in the first and second syllables should both take their long sound. The *i* is also long.

Congamphlgh (KONG-am-filj)* *n.* Faith/Holy Ghost**

Pronunciation notes:

(**Dee—CÓNGAM-PHLGH —phlgh = filgh.*) See the *Five Books*, p. 316. Three syllables. Dee adds an accent over the *o*.

From *Loagaeth*:

(***Dee—Faith that revereth man's breast, the Holy Ghost.*) See the *Five Books*, p. 316.

Note:

Also see *Gono* (faith).

Conisbra (koh-NIS-bra)* *n.* The Work of Man

30.92 *The work of man* and his pomp . . .

Pronunciation notes:

(**Dee—Co nis bra*) Three syllables. I assume the *o* takes a long sound, because Dee placed the *n* at the head of the second syllable instead of at the end of the first.

(**Dee—Conísbra*) See the *48 Claves*. Here, Dee placed an accent over the *i* in the second syllable.

Note:

Neither of the usual Angelical words for "work" ("Aath" or *Vaun*) or mankind (*Cordziz*) appear within this word. Since Conisbra at least shares some common letters with *Cordziz*, I would assume *Conisbra* has "mankind" as its root.

Possible shared root:

Cordziz (KORD-ziz) Mankind

Const (konst)* *n.* Thunders

10.34 . . . These be *the Thunders* . . .

Pronunciation notes:

(**Dee—Const K*) One syllable. Dee indicates the *C* should take its harder "K" sound.

Note:

This is probably the generic Angelical word for "thunder"; however, the Key is referring to a group of Angels—referred to earlier in the Key as the *Coraxo* (Thunders)—rather than weather. Also see *Sapah* (Mighty Sounds), *Avavago* (Thunders), and *Coraxo* (Thunders).

Coraxo (koh-RAYKS-oh)* *prop. n.* Thunders of Judgment and Wrath

10.1 . . . *The Thunders of Judgment and Wrath* are numbered . . .

11.6 . . . They were five *Thunders* which flew into the East . . .

Pronunciation notes:

(**Dee 10.1—Co rax o*)

(**Dee 11.6—Co ráx o*) Three syllables, with an accent on the second syllable. Both *o*'s are long. Also, the Angel Illemese gives further information:

(**Illemese—Coraaxo*) See *TFR*, p. 200. The double *a* here shows that the *a* should also be long.

(**Dee 10.1; 11.6—Coráxo*) See the *48 Claves*. Dee again shows the accent over the second syllable.

Note:

The generic Angelical word for "thunder" is likely *Const*. The Thunders mentioned here and elsewhere in the Keys are groups of Angels. See *Avavago* (Thunders) and *Sapah* (Mighty Sounds). Note the Thunders, Lightnings, and Voices that proceeded from the Divine Throne in the vision of St. John (Book of Revelation). The Coraxo are mentioned only in Keys Ten and Eleven—both of which seem to relate to the Northern Quarter of the Universe.

Cordziz (KORD-ziz)* *n.* Mankind

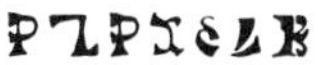

30.83 . . . *the reasonable creatures of earth (or men)*, let them vex . . .

Pronunciation notes:

(**Dee—Cord ziz*) Two syllables. I've kept the accent on the same syllable as in *Olcordziz* (made mankind).

Compounds:

Olcordziz (ohl-KORD-ziz) [Oln + Cordziz] — Made Mankind

Possible shared root:

Consibra (koh-NIS-bra) — Work of Man

Note:

Also see *Ollog* (men).

Cormf (kormf)* *n.* — Number

11.29 . . . whose *number* is 31 . . .

Pronunciation notes:

(**Dee—Cormf*) Note that this word sometimes ends with an *f* and sometimes with a *p*. I suspect this means that—in both cases—the *ph* digraph is intended. Dee seems to indicate one syllable here.

Also:

Cormfa (korm-FA) — Numbers
Cormp (kormf) — Numbered
Cormpo (korm-FOH) — Hath (Yet) Numbered
Cormpt (kormft) — Numbered

Shared root:

Sagacor (say-GAY-kor) — In One Number

Possible shared root:

Coronzom (kor-on-zom) — Satan, the Devil, the Enemy

Cormfa (korm-FA)* *n.* — Numbers

5.36 . . . whose *numbers* are as the first . . .

Pronunciation notes:

(**Dee—Cormfa*) Note that this word sometimes ends with an *f* and sometimes with a *p*. I suspect this means that—in both cases—the *ph* digraph is intended.

I have adopted the accent from *Cormpo* (hath numbered).

Also:

Cormf (kormf)	Number
Cormp (kormf)	Numbered
Cormpo (korm-FOH)	Hath (Yet) Numbered
Cormpt (kormft)	Numbered

Shared root:

Sagacor (say-GAY-kor)	In One Number

Possible shared root:

Coronzom (kor-on-zom)	Satan, the Devil, the Enemy

Cormp (kormf)* *v.* — To Number

4.9 . . . *numbered* 33 . . .
10.3 . . . are *numbered* and harboured . . .

Pronunciation notes:

(**Dee 4.9; 10.3—Cormp*) Note that this word sometimes ends with an *f* and sometimes with a *p*. I suspect this means that—in both cases—the *ph* digraph is intended.

Also:

Cormf (kormf)	Number
Cormfa (korm-FA)	Numbers
Cormpo (korm-FOH)	Hath Numbered, Yet Numbered
Cormpt (kormft)	Numbered

Shared root:

Sagacor (say-GAY-kor)	In One Number

Possible shared root:

Coronzom (kor-on-zom)	Satan, the Devil, the Enemy

Cormpo (korm-FOH)* *v.* Hath (Yet) Numbered

4.18 . . . none *hath yet numbered* but one . . .

Note:

The *-o* affix should indicate the word "of." Thus, the literal translation might be "of number"—meaning something that has been numbered. If so, then the proper English definition should be "hath numbered," and the "yet" is simply implied.

Pronunciation notes:

(**Dee—Corm po*) Two syllables. Note that this word sometimes ends with an *f* and sometimes with a *p*. I suspect this means that—in both cases—the *ph* digraph is intended.

(**Dee—cormpó*) See the *48 Claves*. Accent placed on the last syllable.

Also:

Cormf (kormf)	Number
Cormfa (korm-FA)	Numbers
Cormp (kormf)	Numbered
Cormpt (kormft)	Numbered

Shared root:

Sagacor (say-GAY-kor)	In One Number

Possible shared root:

Coronzom (kor-on-zom)	Satan, the Devil, the Enemy

Cormpt (kormft)* *v.* (Are) Numbered

30.140 . . . until the stars *be numbered.*

Pronunciation notes:

(**Dee—Cormpt*) Note that this word sometimes ends with an *f* and sometimes with a *p*. I suspect this means that—in both cases—the *ph* digraph is intended. Dee seems to indicate just one syllable for this word.

Also:

Cormf (kormf)	Number
Cormfa (korm-FA)	Numbers

Cormp (kormf) — Numbered
Cormpo (korm-FOH) — Hath (Yet) Numbered

Shared root:

Sagacor (say-GAY-kor) — In One Number

Possible shared root:

Coronzom (kor-on-zom) — Satan, the Devil, the Enemy

Coronzom (kor-on-zom) *prop. n.* — Satan, the Devil, the Enemy

Note:

See *TFR*, p. 92. Here Gabriel is discussing Adam's loss of the Angelical language when he fell from Paradise. In this telling, Gabriel refers to Satan as *Coronzom*: "So that in innocency the power of [Adam's] partaking with God, and with us [God's] good Angels, was exalted, and so became holy in the sight of God. Until that *Coronzom* (for so is the true name of that mighty Devil), envying his felicity, [. . .] began to assail him, and so prevailed."

The name *Coronzom* may predate Dee's journals in some form. Translator Rob Thomas (aka *Zadkiel*) has recorded his own search for a Barbarous Name found in the *Picatrix*: *Hacoronoz*—said in the text to be Greek. However, as Mr. Thomas notes, the name is likely a corruption of *ha Kronos* (the Chronos). *Chronos* is the Greek god of time, and the use of *ha* as "the" is drawn from Hebrew. (See the online discussion at http://groups.yahoo.com/group/solomonic/message/10778.)

I note that "succession of time" is an important subject in the Angelical Keys (see Cocasg and related words). Time, an aspect of the created realm, may be the principal domain of *Coronzom*.

Also note that this name appears incorrectly as *Coronzon* (with a final *n*) in *TFR*. The correct spelling can be found in Cotton Appendix 46, Part 1, folio 91.

Also see *Githgulcag* (likely a name for Lucifer) and *Telocvovim* (likely a name for the fallen Satan).

Possible shared root:

Cormfa (korm-FA) — Numbers
Cormp (kormf) — Numbered
Cormpo (korm-FOH) — Hath (Yet) Numbered

Cormpt (kormft) — Numbered
Sagacor (say-GAY-kor) — In One Number

Cors (kors)* *adj.* — Such

2.35 . . . a building *such* as is not but in the mind . . .

Pronunciation note:
(**Dee—Cors*) One syllable.

Also:
Corsi (kor-sii) — Such

Compounds:
Icorsca (ii-KORS-kay) [I + Cors + Ca] — Is Such as
Corsta (kors-tay) [Cors + Ta] — Such as

Corsi (kor-sii)* *adj.* — Such

8.53 . . . our comfort and *of such* as are prepared.

Pronunciation note:
(**Dee—Cor si*) Two syllables. The final *i* is likely a long vowel.

Also:
Cors (kors) — Such

Corsta (kors-tay)* [Cors + Ta] *comp.* — Such as

7.20 . . . *such as* work wonders . . .
30.125 . . . cast down *such as* fall . . .

Pronunciation notes:
(**Dee 7.20—Cors ta*)
(**Dee—Cor sta*) Two syllables.

Note:
Also see *Icorsca* (is such as).

Crip (krip)* *conj.* But

10.81 Come away, *but* not your noises.

Pronunciation notes:
(*Dee—Crip*) One syllable. Based on other versions of this word, I assume the *i* is a phonetic gloss.

Also:
"Crp" (krip) But

Note:
Crip (but) is usually a conjunction. Also see *Oq* (but), which is a preposition.

Croodzi (kroh-OD-zii)* *n.* Beginning (of Things)

4.21 . . . in whom *the second beginning of things* are . . .

Note:
There is no indication of the word *second* in *Croodzi*. Interestingly, the English for Key Four makes more sense without adding the word *second* here.

Pronunciation notes:
(*Dee—Cro od zi*) Three syllables.
(*Dee—croódzi*) See the *48 Claves*. An accent is placed on the second syllable.

Also:
Acroodzi (ak-roh-OD-zii) Beginning

Note:
Also see *Iaod* (beginning), *Iaodaf* (in the beginning), *Amgedpha* (I will begin anew), and *Nostoah* (it was in the beginning).

"Crp" (krip) *conj.* But

Compounds:
Crpl (krip-el) ["Crp" + L] But One

Also:

Crip (krip) — But

Note:

Crip (but) is a conjunction. However, for some reason, "Crp" is used in *Crpl* as a preposition. Also see *Oq* (but), a preposition.

Crpl (krip-el)* ["Crp" + L] *comp.* — But One

4.19 . . . none hath yet numbered *but one* . . .

Pronunciation notes:

(**Dee—CRPL*) Dee gives us little clue here. See the pronunciation note for Crip (but). Based on that, I suggest two syllables, with the *l* standing alone.

(**Dee—c-rp-l*) See the *48 Claves*. Dee seems to indicate three syllables here. However, I have settled on the two-syllable pronunciation.

Also:

Crip (kirp) — But

"Crus" (kroos)* *adj.* — More, Greater (?)**

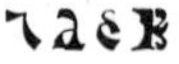

Note:

(***Dee—Canse signifieth mighty, and Cruscanse more mighty.*) See *Five Books*, p. 304. *Cruscanse* (more mighty) is found in *Loagaeth*, and *Canse* (mighty) was mentioned in a marginal note. *"Crus"* was not mentioned by itself, but it may indicate "more" or "greater."

Pronunciation note:

(**Dee—Pronounce as we do cruse a cup.*) See the *Five Books*, p. 306. Dee made this marginal note next to the entire word *Cruscanse*, but it obviously only indicates the first syllable *"Crus." Cruse a cup* is an archaic phrase, but the word cruse likely rhrymes with the English word *cruise*.

Also:

Cruscanse (kroos-kan-say) — More Mighty

Cruscanse (KROOS-kan-say) [*"Crus"* + *Canse*]* *comp.* More Mighty**

Pronunciation note:

(***Dee—crúscanse*) See the *Five Books*, p. 304. Dee adds an accent over the first *a*.

From *Loagaeth*:

(**Dee—Canse signifieth mighty, and Cruscanse more mighty.*) See *Five Books*, p. 304. *Cruscanse* (more mighty) is found in *Loagaeth*, but *Canse* (mighty) was mentioned only in a marginal note.

Note:

See also *Micaolz* (mighty), *Micalp* (mightier)

Kures (kyew-res) n/a (?)

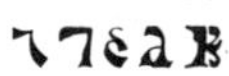

Note:

See *TFR*, p. 32. Here, the Angel Madimi has just interrupted the session to exorcise several demons from the body of Kelley. (See *Carma*.) These spirits came out of Kelley violently, scratching each other in the face and swarming about Madimi. To her, the spirits spoke in Angelical, *"Gil de pragma kures helech."* Dee asks Madimi what this means, and she replies in Latin, which roughly translates as: "We want to live here in our [friends]." (*Madimi* does not offer definitions for the individual words.)

When Dee asks who these "friends" are supposed to be, the spirits indicate Kelley as their place of habitation (probably meaning both Dee and Kelley). Madimi then banishes these spirits.

Pronunciation note:

I feel the *Ku* might make a "q" sound similar to "cu" in words like *cure* or *cute*.

Gal (D)

D (dee) * *n.* or *adj.* — Third

6.30 . . . the second and *the third* . . .

Pronunciation notes:

(**Dee—d*) A single letter standing alone sounds like the English name of the letter.

Note:

This is the word for "third," but not the number 3. It is a noun when something is referred to as "the third." However, it becomes an adjective when used with another noun, as in "the Third Flame."

Compounds:

Chistad (kiis-tad) [Chis + Ta + D] — Are as (the) Third
Dialprt (dii-AL-purt) [D + "Ialprt"] — Third Flame
Duiv (DOO-iv) [D + Div] — Third Angle

"Da" (dah) *pron.* — There

Compounds:

Irgilchisda (ir-jil-KIIS-da) ["Irgil" + Chis + "Da"] — How Many Are There
"Chisda" (kiis-da) [Chis + "Da"] — Are There

Note:

Also see *Geta* (There)

Damploz (DAM-ploz)* *n.* — Variety

30.30 . . . and her unspeakable *variety* . . .

Pronunciation notes:

(**Dee—Dám ploz*) Two syllables, accent on the first syllable.

(**Dee—dámploz*) See the 48 *Claves*. Dee again placed the accent on the first syllable.

DAOX (day-oks)* 5678

10.36 . . . thunders that *5678* times . . .

Pronunciation notes:

(**Dee—"Da" ox*) Two syllables. The *A* should be long.

(**Dee—dâox*) See the *48 Claves*. Here, Dee placed a circumflex over the *A* to confirm its long sound.

Note:

This word was not originally given with Key Ten. (It does appear there—see *TFR*, p. 131—but Dee may have added it at a later time.) It was added later when Nalvage transmitted the English for the Key (see *TFR*, p. 192). This seems to have been the case with many of the numbers mentioned in the Keys.

Darbs (darbs)* *v.* To Obey

5.45 . . . come you and *obey* your creation.

Pronunciation notes:

(**Dee—Darbs—one Syllable*) One syllable.

DARG (darj)* 6739

15.7 . . . whose wings are *6739* which weave . . .

Note:

The transmission of Key Fifteen is missing from Dee's journals. We have only the English given on *TFR*, p. 193. On that same page, Nalvage gives the phonetic note included in the following pronunciation notes.

Pronunciation notes:

(**Nalvage—Darg At large*) See *TFR*, p. 193. I assume this indicates that the final *g* should take a short sound, as in the English word *large*.

Darr (dar) *n.* — The Philosopher's Stone

From the *Alchemical Cipher*:

See *TFR*, pp. 387–89. The Angel Levanael says of this word, "*Audcal* is his Mercury. *Darr*, (in the Angelical tongue), is the true Name of the Stone." *Audcal* (gold) is here described as the alchemical Mercury (or essence) of the Philosopher's Stone.

Pronunciation note:

The *rr* is likely a hard "r" sound.

Darsar (dar-sar)* *adv.* — Wherefore / Therefore

6.31 *Wherefore*, hearken unto my voice.

Pronunciation notes:

(*Dee—Darsar*) Likely two syllables.

Note:

See also *Bagle* (for, wherefore, because) and *Lap* (for).

"Dax" (daks) *n.* — Loins

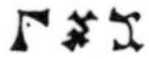

Compounds:

Daxil (daks-il) ["Dax" + "Yl"] — Thy Loins

Daxil (daks-il)* ["Dax" + "Yl"] *comp.* — Thy Loins

17.17 Gird up *thy loins* and harken.

Pronunciation notes:

(*Dee—Dax il*) Two syllables. I suspect the *i* takes the sound of a short *i* in this case, rather than the "y" sound of *Yls*, *Ylsi*, etc.

Dazis (daz-IS)* *n.* Heads

9.50 *Their heads* are covered with diamond . . .
10.27 . . . vomit out *the heads of* scorpions.

Pronunciation notes:
(**Dee 9.50—Daz is*)
(**Dee 10.27—Daz ís*) Two syllables. The accent is placed on the second syllable.
(**Dee—dazís*) See the *48 Claves*. Here, Dee again places the accent on the second syllable.

De (dee)* *prep.* Of

3.47 . . . the corners *of* your governments . . .

Pronunciation notes:
(**Dee—De, is my name*) In other words, the word *De* (of) should sound just like Dee's own name. The *e* takes the long sound.

Note:
There is only this one instance of the word *of* in the literal Angelical Keys. In a few other cases, the word of seems to be indicated by an -*o* affix (i.e., see Caosgo). Meanwhile, in the vast majority of cases the word *of* is absent from the Angelical, implied strictly by context.

Also see *TFR*, p. 32. Here, the Angel Madimi has just interrupted the session to exorcise several demons from the body of Kelley. (See *Carma*.) To Madimi, the spirits spoke in Angelical, "*Gil de pragma kures helech.*" (Note the word *De*.) Dee asks the Angel what this phrase means, and she replies in Latin, which roughly translates as, "We want to live here in our [friends]." (Madimi does not offer definitions for the individual words.)

Compare from *Loagaeth*:
De

Deo (dee-oh) *prop. n.* "The Seventh Aethyr"

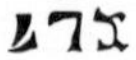

30.3 . . . which dwell in *the seventh aethyr* . . .

Note:
This (word 30.3) is the single space in the Key of the Aethyrs, which must be changed for each invocation—replacing word 30.3 with the name of the appropriate Aethyr. No established definitions were given for these names.

Deo contains the three Parts of the Earth *Opmacas*, *Genadol*, and *Aspiaon*.

Des (des) *prop. n.* "The Twenty-Sixth Aethyr"

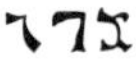

30.3 . . . which dwell in *the twenty-sixth aethyr* . . .

Note:
This (word 30.3) is the single space in the Key of the Aethyrs, which must be changed for each invocation—replacing word 30.3 with the name of the appropriate Aethyr. No established definitions were given for these names.

Des contains the three Parts of the Earth *Pophand*, *Nigrana*, and *Bazchim*.

Dialprt (dii-AL-purt)* [D + "Ialprt"] *comp.* Third Flame

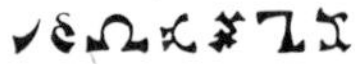

17.2 O thou *third flame* . . .

Pronunciation notes:
(**Dee—Di al pert*) Three syllables. The *i* seems to take a long sound. The *r* takes its extended "ur" (or "er") sound. I have adopted the accent from similar words.

Dilzmo (dilz-moh)* *v.* To Differ

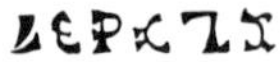

30.76 . . . *let them differ* in their qualities.

Pronunciation notes:

(**Dee—Dil zmo*) Dee indicates two syllables. However, I am unsure why he places the *z* in the second syllable—as that *should* indicate the *z* and likely the *m* both stand alone. However, that would make for three or four syllables. Dee likely intended *Dilz mo* instead.

Div (DII-vee) *n.* — Angle

Pronunciation note:

I have adopted the accent from *Sdiu* (fourth angle).

Compounds:

Sdiu (es-DII-vee) [S + Div]	Fourth Angle
Vivdiv (viv-DII-vee) [Viv + Div]	Second Angle
Duiv (DOO-iv) [D + Div]	Third Angle

Dlasod (dee-lay-sod) *n.* — Sulfur

From the *Alchemical Cipher*:

See *TFR*, pp. 387–89. The Angel Levanael says of this word, "*Dlasod* is Sulfur."

Note:

Also see *Salbrox* (Live Sulfur). Where Salbrox is the kind of sulfur one would find on a match, *Dlasod* refers to alchemical sulfur.

Dluga (dee-LOO-ga)* *v.* — To Give

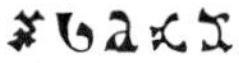

3.35 . . . *giving unto* every one of you . . .

Pronunciation notes:

(**Dee—Dluga*) See pronunciation note at *Idlugam* (is given). I assume the *D* in this word should stand alone, making three syllables.

Also:

"Dlugam" (dee-LOO-gam)	Given
Dlugar (dee-LOO-gar)	To Give

"Dlugam" (dee-LOO-gam) *v.* Given

Compounds:

Idlugam (id-LOO-gam) [I + "Dlugam"] Is given

Also:

Dluga (dee-LOO-ga) To Give

Dlugar (dee-LOO-gar) To Give

Dlugar (dee-LOO-gar)* *v.* To Give

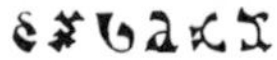

5.19 . . . and *gave them* vessels . . .

6.15 . . . *giving unto them* fiery darts . . .

Pronunciation notes:

(**Dee 5.19; 6.15—Dlugar*) See pronunciation note at Idlugam (is given). I assume the *D* in this word should stand alone, making three syllables.

Also:

Dluga (dee-LOO-ga) To Give

"Dlugam" (dee-LOO-gam) Given

Doalim (doh-ay-lim)* *n.* Sin

13.8 . . . to stir up wrath of *sin* . . .

Pronunciation notes:

(**Dee—Do a lim*) Three syllables. The *o* takes its long sound, and the *a* stands alone (instead of the two combining into one sound). The *i* appears to be short.

(**Dee—doâlim*) See the *48 Claves*. Here, Dee places a circumflex over the *a* to indicate its long sound.

Dobix (dob-iks)* *v.* To Fall

30.126 Cast down such as *fall*.

Pronunciation notes:

(**Dee—Dobix*) Likely two syllables. Both vowels appear to take their short sounds.

Note:

Also see *Loncho* (to fall).

Dodpal (dod-pal)* *v.* To Vex

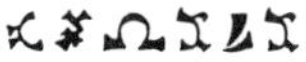

30.84 . . . *let them vex* and weed out one another.

Pronunciation notes:

(**Dee—Dod pal*) Two syllables.

Also:

Dodrmni (dod-rum-nii)	Vexed
Dods (dods)	To Vex
Dodsih (dod-sih)	Vexation

Dodrmni (dod-rum-nii)* *adj.* Vexed

30.55 . . . may be always drunken and *vexed* in itself . . .

Pronunciation notes:

(**Dee—Dod rm ni Dodrumni*) Three syllables. Plus, Dee has added an extra clue, showing us that *rm* should take a sound like *rum*.

Also:

Dodpal (dod-pal)	To Vex
Dods (dods)	To Vex
Dodsih (dod-sih)	Vexation

Dods (dods) *v.* To Vex

14.10 . . . *vexing* all creatures of the earth with age.

Note:

The transmission of Key Fourteen is missing from Dee's journals. We only have the English for this Key given later (see *TFR*, p. 193). Plus, the word appears in this location in Dee's *48 Claves*.

Also:

Dodpal (dod-pal)	(Let) Vex
Dodrmni (dod-rum-nii)	Vexed
Dodsih (dod-sih)	Vexation

Dodsih (dod-sih)* *n.* — Vexation

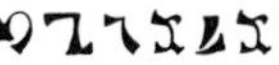

17.8 . . . to stir up *vexation* and . . .

Pronunciation notes:

(**Dee—Dod sih*) Two syllables. Both vowels seem to take their short sounds.

Also:

Dodpal (dod-pal)	To Vex
Dodrmni (dod-rum-nii)	Vexed
Dods (dods)	To Vex

Don (don) *prop. n.* — Letter *R*

Note:

The name of the Angelical letter for *R*. It is likely that these letter names have translations of their own. (For instance, note the Hebrew alphabet: the letter *R* is named *Resh*, but *Resh* also translates as "head" or "beginning.") However, such translations for the Angelical letters are never given. (See the *Five Books*, p. 270.)

"Donasdoga" (doh-NAS-dog-ay) — n/a

From *Loagaeth*:

See note at *Donasdogamatastos*.

Compounds:

Donadogamatastos (doh-NAS-dog-ay-MAT-az-tos)

[*"Donasdoga" + "Matastos"*] "Hellfire"

Donasdogamatastos (doh-NAS-dog-ay-MAT-az-tos)**

[*"Donasdoga"? + "Matastos"?*] *n.* "Hellfire"*

From *Loagaeth*:

(**Dee—The furious and perpetual fire enclosed for the punishment of them that are banished from the glory.*) See the *Five Books*, p. 321. This is likely a reference to the place of punishment prepared for the fallen Angels known as the Watchers in *1 Enoch*.

Pronunciation notes:

(***Dee—do násdoga mátastos—One word of 7 syllables: 4 in the first part and 3 in the last.*) See the *Five Books*, p. 321. Dee seems to indicate the first *o* and the second *a* should each be long. He places two accents in the word.

Note:

The fact that Dee places two accents in this word leads me to suspect this is a compound word. This may also explain why Dee points out that the first four syllables make up the "first part" and the final three the "last."

Compare from *Loagaeth*:

Donadocha, Doncha

Dooain (doh-OH-ay-in)* *n.* Name

3.68 . . . and (his) *Name* is become mighty . . .

12.20 . . . whose *name* amongst you is wrath.

Pronunciation notes:

(**Dee 3.68—Do o a in*)

(**Dee 12.20—Do ó a in*) Four syllables. The second *o* stands alone as the second syllable, and has the accent. The *a* also stands alone.

(**Dee 3.68—do-o-â-in*) See the *48 Claves*. Dee added a circumflex over the *a* to indicate the long vowel.
(**Dee 12.20—dooâin*) See the *48 Claves*. Dee shows the circumflex over the *a* again.

Also:

Dooaip (doh-OH-ay-ip)	In the Name
Dooiap (doh-OH-ii-ap)	In the Name

Possible shared root:

Omaoas (oh-may-OH-as)	Names

Dooaip (doh-OH-ay-ip)* *n.* (In the) Name

4.40 *In the name of* the Creator . . .

Pronunciation notes:

(**Dee—Do oa ip*) This appears to be three syllables. However, see the *48 Claves*:
(**Dee—Do-ó-â-io*) See the *48 Claves*. Here, Dee shows four syllables. There is an accent on the second syllable, and the *a* (standing alone) is given a circumflex to indicate its long sound. (Note that Dee also mistakenly wrote a final *o* on this word instead of the final *p*.)

Also:

Dooain (doh-OH-ay-in)	Name
Dooiap (doh-OH-ii-ap)	(In the) Name

Possible shared root:

Omaoas (oh-may-OH-as)	Names

Dooiap (doh-OH-ii-ap)* *n.* (In the) Name

3.59 *In the name of* the same your God . . .

Pronunciation notes:

(**Dee—Do o i ap*) Four syllables. The second *o* and the *i* each stand alone.
(**Dee—do-ó-î-ap*) See the *48 Claves*. Four syllables, with an accent on the third syllable. Dee also shows a circumflex over the *i* to indicate its long sound.

Also:

Dooaip (doh-OH-ay-ip) — (In the) Name
Dooain (doh-OH-ay-in) — Name

Possible shared root:

Omaoas (oh-may-OH-as) — Names

Dorpha (dor-fa)* *v.* — To Look About

4.5 . . . and *have looked about me* saying . . .

Pronunciation notes:

(**Dee—Dor pha*) Two syllables.

Also:

Dorphal (dor-fal) — To Look Upon (with Gladness)

Dorphal (dor-fal)* *v.* — To Look Upon (with Gladness)

5.8 . . . *looking with gladness upon* the earth . . .

Pronunciation notes:

(**Dee—Dorphal*) Likely two syllables.

Note:

I do not see *with gladness* indicated in the Angelical. If this were a compound, then the *L* (meaning "the first/one") would make this word mean "looking upon one." Instead, the word *Dorphal* is not a compound, and seems to have a tone of benevolence built into its definition—as to look over someone as a loved one.

Also:

Dorpha (dor-fa) — To Look About

Dosig (doh-sig)* *n.* Night

10.22 . . . which burn *night* and day . . .

Pronunciation notes:

(**Dee—Do sig*) Two syllables. I assume the *o* should take its long sound. I also assume the final *g* takes its hard sound.

Drilpa (dril-pa)* *adj.* Great

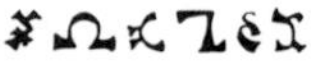

10.79 . . . is, was, and shall be *great.*
16.18 *Great* art thou in the God of . . .

Pronunciation notes:

(**Dee 10.79; 16.18—Dril pa*) Two syllables. The *i* takes a short sound.

Also:

Drilpi (dril-pii) Greater Than

Drilpi (dril-pii)* *adj.* Greater Than

9.43 . . . millstones *greater than* the earth . . .

Pronunciation notes:

(**Dee—Dril pi*) Two syllables. The first *i* appears to take its short sound, while the final *i* takes a long sound.

Also:

Drilpa (dril-pa) Great

Drix (driks)* *v.* To Bring Down

12.13 *Bring down* your train . . .

Pronunciation notes:

(**Dee—Drix*) One syllable.

Droln (drohln)* *adj.* or *adv.* Any

10.53 . . . neither know *any* (long) time here.

Pronunciation notes:

(**Dee—droln*) One syllable. I suggest a long sound for the *o*.

Drux (drooks)* *prop. n.* Letter *N*

Note:

The name of the Angelical letter for *N*. It is likely that these letter names have translations of their own. (For instance, note the Hebrew alphabet: the letter *N* is named *Nun*, but *Nun* also translates as "fish.") However, such translations for the Angelical letters are never given. (See the *Five Books*, p. 270.)

Pronunciation notes:

(**Dee—In sound, drovx.*) Dee uses a *v* here instead of a *u*. The word would look like *droux* in modern English. The *ou* letter combination could produce a long *o* or a long "u" sound. I have adopted the long *u*, because the word *Drux* is actually spelled with a *Van* (*U*).

Compare from *Loagaeth*:

*Adrux, Drux, Druz***

Note:

***Druz* was given in the margin of *Loagaeth*, Table One, side A, line 1—as an alternate form of *Drux*.

Ds (dee-es)* *pron.* Which/That

1.19 . . . *which* measureth your garments . . .
1.53 . . . him *that* liveth . . .
1.60 . . . *which* shineth as a flame . . .
5.32 . . . *which* are garnished with . . . lamps . . .
10.20 . . . *which* burn night and day . . .
10.35 . . . thunders *that* 5678 times . . .

10.49 . . . surges *which* rest not . . .
11.7 . . . thunders *which* flew into the east . . .
13.19 . . . power *which* is called amongst you . . .
**14.5 . . . *which* sit upon 24 seats . . .
**15.11 . . . *which* knowest the great name . . .
***16.5 . . . *which* hast thy beginning in glory . . .
18.6 . . . *which* openest they glory . . .
18.17 . . . *which* is called in thy kingdom joy . . .
30.22 . . . *which* provided you for the government . . .
30.147 . . . *which* hath sworn unto us . . .

Pronunciation notes:

(**Dee 1.19—DS*)

(**Dee 11.7; 18.6, 17; 30.22, 147—Ds*)

(**Dee 5.32; 10.20, 35, 49; 13.19—ds*) Likely a word of two syllables. Each letter pronounced on its own.

Note:

**The transmissions of Keys Fourteen and Fifteen are missing from Dee's journals. We only have the English for them given later (see *TFR*, p. 193). Plus, these words appear in these locations in Dee's *48 Claves*.

Note:

***The transmission of the first twelve words of Key Sixteen is missing from Dee's journals. We only have the English given for it on *TFR*, p. 194. However, they do appear in Dee's *48 Claves*.

Compounds:

Dsabramg (dee-say-bray-mig) [Ds + Abramg]	Which Prepared
Dsbrin (dee-es-brin) [Ds + "Brin"]	Which Have
Dschis (dee-es-kiis) [Ds + Chis]	Which Are
Dsi (dee-sii) [Ds + I]	Which Is
Dsinsi (dee-sin-sii) [Ds + "Insi"]	Which Walkest
Dsium (dee-sii-um) [Ds + "Ium"]	Which (Is) Called
Dsoado (dee-soh-ay-doh) [Ds + "Oado"]	Which Weave
Dsom (dee-som) [Ds + Om]	That Understand
Dsonf (dee-sonv) [Ds + Sonf]	Which Reign
Dspaaox (dee-SPAY-ay-oks) [Ds + Paaox]	Which Remain
Dspraf (dee-es-praf) [Ds + "Praf"]	Which Dwell

Also:

Dst (dee-es-tee) Which

Note:

The word *Ar* (that) is a conjunction, while the word *Ds* (which/that) is a pronoun.

Further:

Ds (dee-es) *conj.* And(?)

1.34 . . . *and* beautified your garments . . .
1.42 . . . *and* delivered you a rod . . .

Note:

It is difficult to accept that the word *and* is intended in these two instances. The word *which* does fit in both cases—even if it doesn't allow the English to sound quite as smooth. For the proper Angelical word for *and*, see *Od*.

Dsabramg (dee-say-bray-mig)* [Ds + Abramg] *comp.* Which Prepared

8.11 . . . *which I have prepared* for my own righteousness . . .

Pronunciation notes:

(**Dee—Dsabramg [g not as dg]*) Dee only tells us that the final *g* should take the hard sound rather than the soft "dg" (as in *hedge*) or "j" sound (as in *jump* and *just*). Otherwise, I assume the initial *D* should stand alone, while the *s* combines with the following vowel. (Further supporting this, see the pronunciation notes for *Dsi*.) Four syllables total.
(**Dee—dsa-bramg*) See the *48 Claves*. Here, Dee may be indicating a long sound for the first *a*. See notes for *Abramig* and *Abramg*, where we find that both *A*s should take the long sound.

Dsbrin (dee-es-brin)* [Ds + "Brin"] *comp.* Which Have

9.6 . . . *which have* vials 8 . . .
13.3 . . . *which have* 42 eyes . . .
**14.14 . . . *which have* under you 1636 . . .

Pronunciation notes:

(**Dee 9.6; 13.3—Ds brin*) This should be three syllables. (See the pronunciation of *Ds*.)

Note:

**The transmission of Key Fourteen is missing from Dee's journals. We only have the English for this Key given later (see *TFR*, p. 193). Plus, the word appears in this location in Dee's *48 Claves*.

Dschis (dee-es-kiis)* [Ds + Chis] *comp.* Which Are

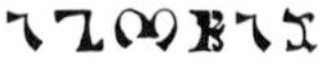

8.25 . . . *which are*, and shall not see death . . .

13.12 . . . making men drunken *which are* empty . . .

Pronunciation notes:

(**Dee8.25; 13.12—Ds chis*) I assume three syllables here. See the pronunciation notes for Ds (which) and *chis* (are).

Dsi (dee-sii)* [Ds + I] *comp.* Which Is

4.38 . . . God, *which is*, and liveth . . .

Pronunciation notes:

(**Dee—D SI*) I assume two syllables here—as Dee likely only intended for the *D* to stand alone. The *si* join to make a sound together.

Dsinsi (dee-sin-sii) [Ds + "Insi"] *comp.* Which Walkest

16.11 . . . *which walkest upon* the earth . . .

Note:

The transmission of the first twelve words of Key Sixteen is missing from Dee's journals. We only have the English given for it on *TFR*, p. 194. However, they do appear in Dee's *48 Claves*.

Dsium (dee-sii-um) [Ds + "Ium"] *comp.* Which (Is) Called

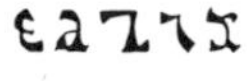

14.22 . . . *which is called* amongst you . . .

Note:

The transmission of Key Fourteen is missing from Dee's journals. We only have the English for this Key given later (see *TFR*, p. 193). Plus, the word appears in this location in Dee's *48 Claves*.

Dsoado (dee-soh-ay-doh)* [Ds + "Oado"] *comp.* Which Weave

15.8 . . . *which weave* the earth with dryness . . .

Note:

The transmission of Key Fifteen is missing from Dee's journals. We only have the English for this Key given later (see *TFR*, p. 193). Plus, the word appears in this location in Dee's *48 Claves*.

Pronunciation notes:

(**Dee—dsoâdo*) See the *48 Claves*. Likely four syllables. The initial *D* should stand alone, as it precedes a consonant (*s*) it does not naturally combine with in English. The *so* should form the second syllable, making the *o* take its long sound. The *a* takes a long sound, as Dee indicated with the circumflex.

Dsom (dee-som)* [Ds + Om] *comp.* That Understand

16.15 . . . *that understand* and separate creatures . . .

Pronunciation notes:

(**Dee—dsom*) Dee does not give us much of a clue. However, other compounds involving *Ds* (which) suggest that the initial *D* should stand alone, and the *som* should combine to form a second syllable.

Dsonf (dee-sonv)* [Ds + Sonf] *comp.* Which Reign

4.11 . . . *which reign in* the second angle . . .

12.2 . . . *that reign in* the south . . .

Pronunciation notes:

(**Dee—Dsonf*) The *D* should stand alone. However, the *s* blends into the rest of the word in a single syllable. See the pronunciation notes for *Sonf* (reign).

Dspaaox (dee-SPAY-ay-oks)* [Ds + Paaox] *comp.* Which Remain

8.22 . . . *which remain* in the glory . . .

Pronunciation notes:

(**Dee—Dspá a ox*) This is likely four syllables, as the *D* should most likely stand alone. The *sp* combine their sounds, as in the English words *spot* or *special*. The accent is on the second syllable. The first *a* takes a long sound, likely due to the letter combination *aa*. (Double vowels often indicated long vowel sounds in Early Modern English.)

(**Dee—ds pá-â-ox*) See the *48 Claves*. Dee again shows the accent on the first *a*. He also added a circumflex over the second *a* to indicate its long sound. This note seems to indicate that the *s* and the *p* do not combine together—although I have decided to stick with Dee's note from *TFR*.

Dspraf (dee-es-praf)* [Ds + "Praf"] *comp.* Which Dwell

30.2 . . . *which dwell* in the "1st Aethyr" . . .

Pronunciation notes:

(**Dee—Ds praf*) *Ds* should be two syllables, then "Praf" seems to have just one.

Dst (dee-es-tee)* *pron.* Which (Also)

3.24 . . . *which* sleep and shall rise . . .

4.24 . . . *which also* successively are . . .

Pronunciation notes:

(**Dee 3.24; 4.24—DST*) Most likely three syllables, each letter standing alone. Elsewhere, Dee indicates that *Ds* (that/which) has two syllables.

Also:

Ds (dee-es) Which/That

Note:

Also see *Ar* (that).

Duiv (DOO-iv)* [D + Div] *comp.* Third Angle

5.3 . . . have entered into *the third angle* . . .

Pronunciation notes:

(*Dee—Du iv*) Two syllables. Likely a long *u* followed by a short *i*.
(*Dee—du-i-v*) See the *48 Claves*. Here Dee seems to indicate three syllables. However, I have settled upon the two-syllable version in my pronunciation.
I have adopted the accent from *Sdiu* (fourth angle).

Note:

Duiv is not D + Viv—which would mean "third second." However, combining *D* (third) and *Div* (angle) only results in *Div*. (The repeated letter *D* would vanish.) The *u* is included to differentiate the word, although I am not sure why *u* is chosen.

Graph (E)

Eai* (ee-AY-ii) *prep.* — Amongst

Alternate spelling:

(**Dee 1.67—AAI The first a may be an A an O or an e*) Thus, there are two alternate spellings for *Aai* (amongst).

Pronunciation notes:

See *Aai* (amongst), which Dee indicates has three syllables.

Also:

Aai (ay-AY-ii)	Amongst (You)
Aaf (ay-AF)	Amongst
Aaiom (ay-AY-om)	Amongst (Us?)
Aao (ay-ay-OH)	Amongst
Oai (oh-AY-ii)	Amongst

"Ecrin" (EE-krin) *n.* — Praise

Compounds:

Odecrin (oh-dee-KRIN) [Od + "Ecrin"]	And the Praise (of)

Also:

Oecrimi (oh-EE-krim-ii)	To Sing Praises

Ednas (ed-nas)* *n.* — Receivers

5.51 Conclude us as *receivers of* your mysteries.

Pronunciation notes:

(**Dee—Ed nas*) Two syllables. Both vowels appear to take their short sounds.

(**Dee—ed-nas*) See the *48 Claves*. This note matches that from *TFR*.

Note:

This may also be the verb *to receive*. However, it is used in Key Five as a noun.

Ef (ef)* *v.* To Visit

12.12 . . . bind up your girdles and *visit us* . . .

Pronunciation notes:

(**Dee—Ef*) One syllable. The *E* is likely a phonetic gloss. (See *F*).

Also:

F (ef) Visit

Efafafe (ee-FAY-fay-fee)* *n.* Vials

9.7 . . . which have *vials* 8 of wrath . . .

Pronunciation notes:

(**Dee—E fa fa fe*) Four syllables. The initial *E* stands alone. The two *a*'s are each long vowels. The final *e* is uncertain—as it could be silent, or it could make a long "e" sound. I have chosen the long *e*.

(**Dee—efáfâfe*) See the *48 Claves*. Dee placed an accent on the second syllable. He also placed a circumflex over the second *a* to indicate its long sound.

Note:

This word is a palindrome. It is spelled the same forward as it is spelled backward.

Also:

Ofafafe (oh-FAY-fay-fee) Vials

El (el)* *prop. n.* The First

6.8 . . . whom *the First* hath planted . . .

Pronunciation notes:

(**Dee—el*) One syllable. The *E* is likely a phonetic gloss.

Compounds:

Gohel (GOH-hel) [Goho + El] Sayeth the First

Lel (el-el) [L + El] Same

Note:

This reminds me of the Hebrew Name of God: *El.*

Also compare to the name of the Angel *El* (or *L*), one of the Sons of the Sons of Light. His name literally translates as "The First."

Also:

"Lo" (loh)	The First
L (el)	The First
La (lah or el-ah)	The First
Lu (loo)	From One

"Elzap" (el-ZAP) *n.* — Course

Compounds:

Elzaptilb (el-ZAP-tilb) ["Elzap" + Tilb] — Her Course

Also:

"Lzar" (el-ZAR) — Courses

Elzaptilb (el-ZAP-tilb)* ["Elzap" + Tilb] *comp.* — Her Course

30.57 *Her course*, let it run with the heavens . . .

Pronunciation notes:

(**Dee—El zap tilb*) Three syllables. As we can see in the word "Lzar," (course) the *E* in *Elzaptilb* is a phonetic gloss only.

(**Dee—Elzáptilb*) See the *48 Claves*. Here, Dee placed an accent over the second syllable.

Em (em)* *n.* — Nine

6.4 The spirits of the fourth angle are *nine* . . .

Pronunciation notes:

(**Dee—Em*) One syllable. The *E* is not likely a phonetic gloss—see *M* (except).

Note:
I assume this is the word for "nine" rather than the actual number 9.

Emetgis (em-et-jis) *n.* Seal

15.16 . . . righteousness and *the seal of* honour.

Note:
The transmission of Key Fifteen is missing from Dee's journals. We only have the English for this Key given later (see *TFR*, p. 193). Plus, the word appears in this location in Dee's *48 Claves*.

Also note that the first four letters of this word are *Emet* (Hebrew for "truth"). This matches the name of Dee's Seal of Truth—or *Sigillum Dei Emet*. Perhaps this Seal of Truth and the Seal of Honor are one and the same.

Pronunciation note:
I assume the *g* takes the soft sound, as it precedes an *i* (as in the English words *giant* or *gibberish*).

Emna (em-na)* *n.* Here

10.56 . . . neither know any (long) time *here*.

Pronunciation notes:
(**Dee—Em na*) Two syllables.

Note:
Also see *Sem* (in this place).

EMOD (ee-mod)* 8763

16.14 . . . with feet *8763* that understand . . .

Pronunciation notes:
(**Dee—E mod*) Two syllables. The initial *E* stands alone.

Note:

This word was not originally given with Key Sixteen. It was added later when Nalvage transmitted the English for the Key (see *TFR*, p. 194). This seems to have been the case with many of the numbers mentioned in the Keys.

Enay (en-ay)* *n.* — Lord

7.8 . . . wherein *the Lord* hath opened His mouth . . .
12.17 . . . 3663 that *the Lord* may be magnified . . .

Pronunciation notes:

(**Dee 7.8—Enay*)
(**Dee12.17—E nay*) Two syllables. Dee indicates here (word 12.17) that the *E* can stand alone (ee-nay). However, consider that the spelling of *Enay* is actually a phonetic gloss. The word is one and the same with *NA* (en-ay). Dee's phonetic notes seem to indicate that either pronunciation is acceptable—although I have settled upon the "en-ay" version.

Compounds:

Zirenaiad (zii-er-NAY-ad) [Zir + Enay + Iad] I am the Lord (Your) God

Also:

NA (en-ay) — Lord

Eol (ee-OHL)* *v.* — Made

3.29 In the first, *I made you* stewards . . .

Pronunciation note:

(**Dee—EOL)* Dee gives us little clue here.
(**Dee—E-ól)* See the *48 Claves*. Two syllables, with an accent on the second syllable. The initial *E* stands alone.

Also:

Eolis (ee-OH-lis) — Making
Oln (ohln) — Made (of)

Note:
Also see *Ozazm* (to make) and *Ozazma* (to make).

Eolis (ee-OH-lis)* *v.* To Make

13.9 . . . *making* men drunken . . .

Pronunciation note:
(*Dee—E o lis*) Three syllables. The *E* and *o* each stand alone.
(*Dee—eôlis*) See the *48 Claves*. Here, Dee placed a circumflex over the *o* to indicate its long sound.
I have adopted the accent from *Eol* (made).

Also:

Eol (ee-OHL)	Made
Oln (ohln)	Made (of)

Note:
Also see *Ozazm* (to make) and *Ozazma* (to make).

Eophan (ee-oh-fan)* *n.* Lamentation

10.14 . . . 22 nests of *lamination* and weeping . . .

Pronunciation notes:
(*Dee—E o phan*) Three syllables. The intial *E* and the *o* each stand alone.
(*Dee—eôphan*) See the *48 Claves*. Here, Dee places a circumflex over the *o* to indicate its long sound.

"Eors" (ee-ORS)* n/a

Note:
This word appears nowhere in the Angelic system as of yet. It was originally dictated in the tenth Key as the word "thousand." However, this was corrected on page 192 of *TFR* with the word *Math* (10.45). "Eors" may have been merely a mistake on Kelley's part, and not an Angelical word at all (there were many difficulties in the reception of Key Ten).

Other such interferences with the transmission of the Keys were attributed to demonic spirits—see *Piamol.*

Pronunciation notes:

(**Dee—E órs*) Two syllables, with an accent on the second syllable. The initial *E* stands alone.

ERAN (ee-RAN)* 6332

18.14 . . . the secrets of truth *6332* have their abiding . . .

Pronunciation notes:

(**Dee—E ran*) Two syllables. The initial *E* stands alone.
(**Dee—erán*) See the *48 Claves*. Here, Dee placed an accent over the second syllable.

Note:

This word was not originally given with Key Eighteen. It was added later when Nalvage transmitted the English for the Key (see *TFR*, p. 194). This seems to have been the case with many of the numbers mentioned in the Keys.

Erm (erm) *n.* Ark/Refuge/Haven

1.45 . . . delivered you a rod with *the ark of* knowledge.

"Es" (es) *n.* Fourth

Compounds:

Odes (ohd-es) [Od + "Es"] And Fourth

Also:

S (es) Fourth

Note:

The *E* in "Es" is a phonetic gloss.
Also note this is the word for "fourth," but not the number 4. The word *fourth* could be a noun or adjective, but is used here as a noun.

Compare from *Loagaeth*:

Es

Esiasch (ee-sii-ash)* *n.* Brothers

5.26 . . . they are *the brothers of* the first and second . . .

Pronunciation notes:

(**Dee—E siach*) I suggest three syllables here. The initial *E* stands alone. Note that Dee indicates the sound of "ach" for *asch*. I assume this means the *ch* makes the "tch" sound (as in the English word *church*) instead of the harder "kh" sound. However, the preceding *s* would give the *ch* an extra soft sound, almost like a hard "sh."

(**Dee—esîach*) See the *48 Claves*. Note the circumflex over the I—indicating the long sound.

Ethamz (ee-THAM-zohd)* *v.* To Cover

9.51 Their heads *are covered with* diamond . . .

Pronunciation notes:

(**Dee—E tham Zod*) Three syllables. The initial *E* and the final *z* each stand alone. The *a* should take a short sound.

(**Dee—ethámz*) See the *48 Claves*. Here, Dee placed an accent over the second syllable.

"Etharzi" (eth-AR-zii) *n.* Peace

Compounds:

Fetharzi (feth-AR-zii) [F + "Etharzi"] Visit (Us) in Peace

Or (F)

F (ef) *v.* To Visit

Compounds:

Fbliard (ef-blii-ard) [F + "Bliard"] Visit (with) Comfort

Fcaosga (ef-kay-OS-ga) [F + Caosga] Visit the Earth

Fetharzi (feth-AR-zii) [F + "Etharzi"] Visit in Peace

Also:

Ef (ef) To Visit

Faaip (fay-AY-ip)* *n.* Voices (Voicings/Psalms?)

2.5 . . . understand your *voices* of wonder . . .

Pronunciation notes:

(**Dee—Fa á ip*) Dee indicates three syllables, the second *a* standing alone and accented.

(**Dee—Fa-á-ip*) See *48 Claves*. This note matches the one from *TFR*.

Possible shared root:

Farzem (farz-em) Uplifted Voices

Bia (bii-a) Voice

Note:

The word *Bia* appears to be Angelical for "voice"—as in one's speaking voice. *Faaip*, however, has the connotation of something that is said (as in to voice an opinion), or perhaps sung. Key Two gives me the impression that the Faaip ("voices" of wonder) are actually "songs" (or "voicings") of wonder—something akin to Psalms.

Also see *Luiahe* (song of honor).

Faboan (fay-boh-an)* *n.* Poison

10.32 . . . live sulphur myngled with *poison*.

Pronunciation notes:

(**Dee—Fa bo an*) Three syllables. The first *a* and the *o* take their long sounds.

(**Dee—fabôan*) See the *48 Claves*. Here, Dee placed a circumflex over the *o* to indicate its long sound.

Note:

See also *Tatan* (Wormwood).

Fafen (fay-fen)* *n.* Intent

3.43 . . . true ages of time, *to the intent that* from your highest . . .

Pronunciation notes:

(**Dee—Fafen*) The *e* likely gives the *a* a long sound.

Also:

Fafen (fay-fen)** Train

12.14 Bring down *your train* . . .

Pronunciation notes:

(***Dee—Fa fen*) Two syllables.

Note:

This is one of the few instances were a single Angelical word *appears* to have two completely separate definitions. The "train" in Key Twelve appears to have a triple meaning: (1) The poetry suggests the train of a royal robe or wedding gown. (2) It also suggests the meaning of "retinue"—so the Key is asking the Angels to descend with their servants and ministers. Finally, (3) a "train" can be defined as a "succession of events" or "consequences"—which best suits the word *Fafen* as a synonym of "intention." (As in a "train of thought.")

Fam (fam) *prop. n.* Letter *S / Sh*

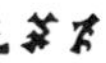

Note:

The name of the Angelical letter for *S / Sh*. It is likely that these letter names have translations of their own. (For instance, note the Hebrew alphabet:

the letter *S/Sh* is named *Shin*, but *Shin* also translates as "tooth.") However, such translations for the Angelical letters are never given. (See the *Five Books*, p. 270.)

Compare from *Loagaeth*:

Fam

Faonts (fay-onts)* *v.* — To Dwell (within)

5.11 . . . and *dwelling within* the brightness of the heavens . . .

Pronunciation notes:

(**Dee—Fa onts*) Two syllables. There is no *ao* letter combination in Early Modern English—each letter makes a separate sound—as in the English word *chaos*. The *a* is likely long.

Shared root:

Fargt (farj-et) — Dwelling Places

"Faorgt" (fay-or-jet) — Dwelling Place

"Faorgt" (fay-or-jet) *n.* — Dwelling Place

Compounds:

Odfaorgt (ohd-fay-or-jet) [Od + "Faorgt"] — And the Dwelling Place

Also:

Fargt (farj-et) — Dwelling Places

Faonts (fay-onts) — To Dwell (within)

Fargt (farj-et)* *n.* — Dwelling Places

30.89 And *the dwelling places*, let them forget . . .

Pronunciation notes:

(**Dee—Farg t Gad*) Two syllables. Dee's notation appears to indicate a hard *g* at the end of the first syllable, and the *t* stands alone. However, see the pronunciation for *Odfaorgt*, where we find the *g* can be soft, and combines with the *t* to indicate the sound of "dgt"—or "jet."

Also:

"Faorgt" (fay-or-jet) — Dwelling Place

Faonts (fay-onts) — To Dwell (within)

Farzm (farz-em) *v.* — Uplifted Voices (To Speak up)

1.48 . . . *you lifted up your voices* and swore . . .

Possible shared root:

Faaip (fay-AY-ip) — Voices (Psalms?)

Bia (bii-a) — Voices

Fbliard (ef-blii-ard)* [F + "Bliard"] *comp.* — Visit (with) Comfort

6.22 . . . *visit with comfort* the earth . . .

Pronunciation notes:

(**Dee—F bli ard*) Three syllables. The initial *F* stands alone. The *i* is likely long (as in the English words *dial* and *trial*).

(**Dee—f-bliard*) See the *48 Claves*. This note shows the *F* standing alone.

Fcaosga (ef-kay-OS-ga)* [F + Caosga] *comp.* — Visit the Earth

4.35 . . . arise you sons of pleasure and *visit the earth* . . .

Pronunciation notes:

(**Dee—F gaos ga*) Four syllables. Dee originally wrote this word as "Fgaosga"—which is apparently a mistake for *Fcaosga* (see *Caosga*). Therefore, the *g* in the second syllable is likely a *c* instead.

(**Dee—F caósga*) See the *48 Claves*. Note the accent on the third syllable.

Fetharzi (feth-AR-zii)* [F + "Etharzi"] *comp.* — Visit in Peace

5.47 . . . *visit us in peace* . . .

Pronunciation notes:

(**Dee—Feth ár zi*) Three syllables, with an accent on the second.

Dee originally had "Sfetharzi" written for this word—although his phonetic note excludes the *S*. (The Angelical itself does not require the *S* at all, as the word *F* indicates "visit.") It is possible that the *S* was merely held over from the end of the previous word (*Qaas*).

(**Dee—Feth-ar-zi*) See the *48 Claves*. This note essentially matches that from *TFR*.

Fifalz (fii-falz)* *v.* Weed Out

30.86 . . . let them vex and *weed out* one another.

Pronunciation notes:

(**Dee—Fi falz*) Two syllables.

Fisis (FIS-iis)* *v.* To Execute (i.e., Carry Out)

30.8 . . . and *execute* the judgment of the Highest.

Pronunciation notes:

(**Dee—fisise*) This appears to indicate two syllables. The final *e* in Dee's phonetic note indicates a long *i* in the second syllable.

(**Dee—físis*) See the *48 Claves*. Here, Dee placed an accent over the *i* in the first syllable.

Ged (G/J)

Ga (gay) *prop. n.* n/a

Pronuncation Note:

I have chosen the long "a" sound based upon the likely pronunciation of *Za*. (See *Za*.)

Note:

See *TFR*, pp. 228–29. The names of most of the Angels encountered by Dee and Kelley can be found in other parts of the Angelic system—such as the *Heptarchia* or Great Table (Watchtower) systems. However, *Ga* is one of the few entirely unique Angels that appeared to the two men. It was very late in the Angelical journals, after all of the essential Angelic magick had been transmitted. One day, Kelley saw three little creatures running around the floor of the room. It turned out that they were Angels from the Great Table (Watchtowers)—but their names were *not* derived according to the instructions Ave had previously given to Dee.

Ga says of himself: "I am the midst of the third [Tablet],* and the last of the spirit of life.** Understand in this temporal controversy, and conflict of man's soul. But not according to his eternal and immeasurable proportion." Dee notes, in Latin: "*Ga*—The Last of the Spirit of Life."

The three Angels, apparently jointly, say, "For even as the father, son and holy spirit are one, but of themselves and being dilated, is full of power, and many. So are we one particularly in power,*** but separated. Notwithstanding, spiritually of, and amongst, others, and dilated in the will of God, and into the branches of his determinations. But, particularly living, and jointly praising God."

Note:

*Dee notes the Angels are numbering the Watchtowers in an odd fashion. So that in this case, he points out, the numbering should follow: First = Eastern, Second = Western, Third = Southern, and Fourth = the Northern Watchtower. In the above text, I have added the bracketed [Tablet] in order to clarify the speech.

**Ga's name is found as the last two letters on the Line of the Holy Spirit (the horizontal arm of the Great Cross) of the Southern Watchtower Tablet.
(***On the next page Dee notes: *The three names make one name of 7 letters —Gazavaa.*)

I further note that all three of these names begin with capital letters on the Great Table (Watchtowers). Also, each one of them terminates once it hits the Great Cross, Black Cross, or the end of the Watchtower. We may have discovered an entirely new Angelic system in the Watchtowers.
(See *Vaa*, and *Za*. Also see *Carmara, Galvah, Hagonel, Mapsama, Murifri*, and *Nalvage*.)

Compare from *Loagaeth*:
Ga

"GA" (gah) 31

Compounds:
Iga (ii-gah) [I + "GA"] Is 31

Note:
This word was not originally given with Key Eleven. It was added later when Nalvage transmitted the English for the Key (see *TFR*, p. 193). This seems to have been the case with many of the numbers mentioned in the Keys.

Jabes (jay-bes) n/a

Note:
See the *Five Books*, p. 298, where the Angels use the phrase *Ne Ne Ne na Jabes*. But no definitions of these words are offered.

Pronunciation note:
The final *e* should make the *a* long.

Gah (jah)* *n.* Spirits

6.1 *The spirits of* the fourth angle . . .

Pronunciation notes:

(**Dee—Gah*) One syllable.

(**Dee—Iah.*) See the *Five Books*, p. 302. In most cases, a *g* followed by an *a* makes the hard "guh" sound. However, when this word appears in *Loagaeth*, Dee notes in the margin that it should begin with the soft "juh" sound. (Remember that *i* and *j* are interchangeable in Dee's English.)

Possible root for:

Gahoachma (jah-hohk-ma) I Am That I Am

Gahire (jah-hii-er) (A Name of God?)

Note:

The way the term *spirits* is used in Key Six indicates that this word does not indicate lower spirits, demons, fairies, etc. This is further supported by the appearance of this word as a root in two Names of God. Therefore, Gah would represent "pure spirits" or Angels—used in the same sense as we might describe the Holy "Spirit."

See *Tohcoth* (nature spirits).

Compare from *Loagaeth*:

Gah

Gahire (jah-hii-er) *prop. n.?* (A Name of God?)

Possible shared root:

Gah (jah) Spirits

Gahoachma (jah-hohk-ma) I Am That I Am

Note:

See *TFR*, p. 3. The Angel Murifri here speaks a prayer in Angelical, and Kelley can only overhear a few of the words: *Oh Gahire Rudna gephna oh Gahire.* It is unclear whether this represents a single Angelical phrase, or if they are disconnected words recorded by Dee as Kelley overheard them here and there in the prayer. No translations are suggested.

It seems likely, at least, that *Oh Gahire* is intended as a repeated phrase. *Oh* may indicate "Come and Bear Witness" and *Gahire* is likely a Name of God associated by root with *Gahoachma* (I Am That I Am). Therefore, *Oh Gahire* is likely an invocation of some aspect of God.

Gahoachma (jah-hohk-ma) *prop. n.* — I Am That I Am*

Possible shared root:

Gah (jah) — Spirits

Gahire (jah-hii-er) — (A Name of God?)

Note:

(**Dee—Gahoachma = I Am That I Am, Edward Kelley expounded it.*) See the *Five Books*, p. 322. The first words spoken by the Angelic voice in this session were, "I AM. Gahoachma." This is likely a proper Name of God, based upon the Hebrew name given to Moses at the Burning Bush: *Eheieh asher Eheieh* (I Am That I Am). It represents the pure and essential Divine Consciousness, without personality or duality.

I note that *Gah* (Spirit) seems to be the root of *Gahoachma*. I also note a similarity between the -hoachma portion of the word and the Hebrew *Hochmah* (Wisdom).

Gal (gal) *prop. n.* — Letter *D*

Note:

The name of the Angelical letter for *D*. It is likely that these letter names have translations of their own. (For instance, note the Hebrew alphabet: the letter *D* is named *Daleth*, but *Daleth* also translates as "door.") However, such translations for the Angelical letters are never given. (See the *Five Books*, p. 270.)

Also see *TFR*, pp. 34–35. This session is recorded entirely in Latin. Here we find this Angelical phrase spoken by "a Voice": *Garil zed masch, ich na gel galaht gemp gal noch Cabanladan.* (Note the word *gal.*) No translation or context is offered.

Compare from *Loagaeth*:

Gal

Galaht (gal-aht) n/a

Note:

See *TFR*, pp. 34–35. This session is recorded entirely in Latin. Here we find this Angelical phrase spoken by "a Voice": *Garil zed masch, ich na gel galaht gemp gal noch Cabanladan*. No translation or context is offered.

Galgol (gal-gol) n/a

Note:

See *Five Books*, p. 366. The Angel Illemese appears to Dee and Kelley with a bundle of empty boxes that he calls virtuous. When Dee asks for an explanation, Illemese says, "Will you have my bill? [. . .] I will show it. Serve it, where you list. *Iudra galgol astel.*" Dee states that he and Kelley do not understand, and wish to know how it can be served. But Illemese never offers definitions for these Angelical words.

I note a similarity between this word and the Hebrew word for "whirling," *Galgal*. The *Galgalim* are an order of Angels also known as the Wheels (*Auphanim*).

Galsagen (GAL-saj-en)* *prop. n.* or *v.?* Divine Power
Creating the Angel of the Sun**

Pronunciation note:

(*Dee—gálsagen*) See the *Five Books*, p. 307. Dee places an accent over the first *a*.

From *Loagaeth*:

(***Dee—The Divine power creating the Angel of the Sonne.*) See *Five Books*, p. 307. The word *Sonne* almost certainly means "Sun." See the *Five Books*, pp. 81–82, where Dee and Kelley meet an Angel named Salamian, who claims to be "mighty in the Sonne." There is ample evidence that Salamian is an

Angel of the Sun. Dee notes that his name can be found in the *Heptameron*, with that grimoire's "Call of Sunday." Later in the same session, the Archangel Raphael tells Dee to contact the Olympic solar Angel *Och*. (See the *Arbatel of Magic* for *Och*.) Then, still during the same session, Michael (Archangel of the Sun) claims that Salamian is under his direction.

Galsuagath (gals-vay-gath) n/a

Note:

See *TFR*, p. 22. Here, the guardian Angel of Lord Lasky of Poland says a prayer on Lasky's behalf, which ends with, "Grant this *Camascheth galsuagath garnastel zurah logaah luseroth*." No translation is offered.

Pronunciation note:

I have opted to pronounce the *u* as a *v* in this case, as it immediately precedes another vowel.

Galvah (gal-VAH)* *prop. n.* The End (or *Omega*)**

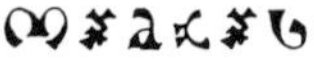

Pronunciation notes:

(**Dee, recording the words of Galvah—"My name is Galua'h"*) See *TFR*, p. 12. Galvah is likely two syllables, with the accent shown in the middle of the second syllable. The *u* takes the harder "v" sound.

Note:

(***Dee, recording the words of Galvah—"My name is Galua'h, in your language I am called Finis. [. . .] I am Finis, I am a beam of that Wisdom which is the end of man's excellency."*) See *TFR*, pp. 12–14. *Finis* is Latin for "the end." Galvah arrived after forty-eight Tables of *Loagaeth* had been delivered already, and it was her job to deliver the final Table. (Thus, seeing the Book through to its end.)

On p. 13, *Galvah* reveals that she is the Mother of the Daughters and the Daughters of the Daughters of Light. (This makes Her one and the same with "I AM," the mother of the Daughter of the Daughters named Madimi. See *TFR*, p. 27.)

On p. 14, we learn that *Galvah* is a proper name, and not the general word for "the end." (*Galvah: Understand my name particularly, and not generally.*)

Later on the same page, the Angel Ilemese refers to Galvah as "Wisdom." All of this information indicates that this entity is no less than *Sophia* of the Gnostics, the *Sheckinah* of Judaism, the Soul of the World of the Hermeticists, the Bride of God. "I AM" (a shortened form of the Name of God given to Moses: *I Am That I Am*) is likely her truest name. *Galvah*, therefore, is a specific title. It likely relates to the Greek *Omega* in the biblical phrase: "I Am the *Alpha* and the *Omega*." (See Revelation Ch 1:8.)

(Also see *Carmara, Ga, Hagonel, Mapsama, Murifri, Nalvage, Vaa*, and *Za* .)

Note:
See *Ul* for the general Angelical word for "the end."

Ganiurax (gan-ii-ur-ax) n/a

Note:
See the *Five Books*, p. 413. Kelley overhears many voices singing a song at some distance, and these are the words Dee recorded: *Pinzu-a lephe ganiurax kelpadman pacaph*. No translations are suggested.
Note that *Ganiurax* may have the *-ax* suffix, indicating action.

Garil (gar-il) n/a

Note:
See *TFR*, pp. 34–35. This session is recorded entirely in Latin. Here we find this Angelical phrase spoken by "a Voice": *Garil zed masch, ich na gel galaht gemp gal noch Cabanladan*. No translation or context is offered.

Garmal (gar-mal) n/a

Note:
See the *Five Books*, p. 415. This is part of a prayer recited jointly by the Archangels Michael, Raphael, and Uriel: "*Huseh Huseh Huseh garmal, Peleh Peleh Peleh pacaduasam.*" No translations are suggested.

Compare from *Loagaeth*:

Garmah, Garmes

Garnastel (gar-nas-tel) n/a

Note:

See *TFR*, p. 22. Here, the guardian Angel of Lord Lasky of Poland says a prayer on Lasky's behalf, which ends with, "Grant this *Camascheth galsuagath garnastel zurah logaah luseroth*." No translation is offered.

Also see:

Astel (ast-el) n/a

Gascampho (gas-KAM-foh)* *interr.* Why Didst Thou So?**

Pronunciation note:

(**Dee—gascámpho* or *gáscampho*) See the *Five Books*, p. 310. Dee places an accent over the second *a*, and then offers the alternative of placing the accent over the first *a* in a footnote. I have settled on the first option.

From *Loagaeth*:

(***Dee—"Why didst thou so?": as God said to Lucifer. The word hath 64 significations.*) See the *Five Books*, p. 310. This is likely a reference to Lucifer's rebellion in Heaven, or (more precisely) to the judgment of Lucifer afterward.

Gazavaa (gah-zah-vay) *prop. n.?* n/a*

Note:

(**Dee—The three names make one name of 7 letters—Gazavaa.*)

See *TFR*, pp. 228–29. A compound word made from the three Angels Ga, Za, and Vaa—who appear upon the Great Table (Watchtowers), but represent some hitherto unknown system of name-derivation. Dee created the compound *Gazavaa* when the three Angels told him, "For even as the father, son and holy spirit are one, but of themselves and being dilated,* is full of power, and many. So are we one particularly in power, but separated."

It is unclear if *Gazavaa* is a true Angelical word, or if Dee was merely taking the above words of the three Angels too literally. It appears to me that many further Angelical names might be derived from the Watchtowers, as we see with *Ga*, *Za*, and *Vaa*.

For a full account, see the notes with *Ga*, *Za*, and *Vaa*.

Note:

*"Dilated" would mean "spread out." In this case, it indicates the separation of the One God into the Trinity.

"Gchis" (jee-KIIS) *v.* — Are

Compounds:

Gchisge (jee-KIIS-jee) ["Gchis" + "Ge"] — Are Not

Also:

Chis (kiis) — Are
Chiis (kiis) — Are (They)
"Chisda" (kiis-da) — Are There
Chiso (kiis-oh) — Shall Be
"Ichis" (jay-kiis) — Are
Zchis (zohd-kiis) — (They) Are

Note:

"Gchis" and "Ichis" should be the same word—both are spelled the same in Angelical characters, with an initial Ged (*J*). See note at *Gchisge*.

Gchisge (jee-KIIS-jee)* ["Gchis" + "Ge"] *comp.* — Are Not

4.7 . . . *Are not* the Thunders of Increase numbered . . .?

Pronunciation notes:

(**Dee—G Chis ge*) Three syllables. The *i* and *j* are interchangeable in Dee's English. The *j* makes a soft "juh" sound, which is likely what Dee was hearing in both *Gchisge* and *Ichisge*. It is likely that both words begin with the Angelical Letter Ged (*J*).

Since Dee capitalized the second syllable, it *may* indicate the accent there. Also, see *Chis* and *Chiis* (are) for the long "i" sound.

(*Dee—G-chisge) See the 48 *Claves*. This looks like two syllables. However, three syllables are indicated elsewhere (including the word *Ichisge*).

Also:

Ichisge (jay-KIIS-jee) — Are Not

"Ge" (jee) *adv.* — Not

Compounds:

Gchisge (jee-KIIS-jee) ["Gchis" + "Ge"] — Are Not
Ichisge (jay-KIIS-jee) ["Ichis" + "Ge"] — Are Not
Tage (tayj) [Ta + "Ge"] — As (Is) Not

Compare from *Loagaeth*:

Ge, Ie

Note:

See also *Ip* (not), "Pam" (not), and *Ag* (none).

Gebofal (jeb-oh-fal) *n.* — "The Practice of the 49 Gates of Understanding"*

Note:

(**Dee recording the words of Levanael—"Now to the work intended, which is called in the Holy Art Gebofal. Which is not, (as the philosophers have written), the first step supernatural, but it is the first supernatural step naturally limited unto the 48 Gates of Wisdom; where your Holy Book beginneth."*) See *TFR*, p. 373. The Holy Book in question, of course, is the *Book of Loagaeth*. *Gebofal*, therefore, must be the Angelical name of the practice of opening the forty-eight Gates.

Ged (jed) *prop. n.* — Letter *G*/ *J**

Note:

The name of the Angelical letter for *G*/*J*. It is likely that these letter names have translations of their own. (For instance, note the Hebrew alphabet: the letter *G*/*J* is named *Gimel*, but *Gimel* also translates as "camel.") However, such translations for the Angelical letters are never given. (See the *Five Books*, p. 270.)

(**Dee—After that he said, One, One, One, Great, Great, Great!*) This does not appear to be a definition of Ged, but an invocation associated with the word in some way. See the letter *Med*, where another invocation is made along with the delivery of a letter.

Compare from *Loagaeth*:

Ged, Ied

Geh (jay)* *v.* Art (i.e., Are)

16.19 Great *art* thou in the God of . . .

Pronunciation notes:

(**Dee—Geh jeh*) One syllable. Dee indicates that the *G* should take a soft "j" sound. In Early Modern English, the *eh* would have combined to form a long "a" sound.

Note:

See also *Chis* (are). Perhaps *Geh* (art) is a term of formality or respect?

Compare from *Loagaeth*:

Geh, Ieh

Geiad (jej-AYD)* *prop. n.* Lord and Master

5.54 . . . *our Lord and Master* is all one . . .

Pronunciation notes:

(**Dee—Ge jad ie in as ien,** the iad as iade*) The word *Geiad* only appears in Dee's *48 Claves*. It is missing from *TFR* (perhaps from damage to the text?)—but Dee's slightly confusing phonetic note is still there. Based on this note, I believe Dee originally wrote *Geiad* in his journal (*TFR*) as "Ie iad"—divided into two syllables. The first syllable (*ie* or *ge*) sounds similar to "ien" ("jen")—that is, the *i* sounds like *j*, and the *e* takes its short sound. The second syllable (*iad*) must sound like the English word *jade*—with the *i* again taking the "j" sound.

I have adopted the accent from similar words.

Note:
**I believe that "ie in as ien" should be "ie *as in* ien."

Ge is translated elsewhere as "not"—though it is obviously not intended in this case.

Also:

Gohed (joh-ED)	One Everlasting . . .
Iad (yad)	God
"Iadoias" (jad-oh-JAS)	Eternal God
Iadpil (ii-AD-pil)	(To) Him
Iaida (jay-II-da)	The Highest
Iaidon (jay-II-don)	All Powerful
Ioiad (joh-JAD)	Him That Liveth Forever
Oiad (oh-ii-AD)	Of God
Piad (pii-AD)	Your God

Gel (jel) n/a

Note:
See *TFR*, p. 35. This session is recorded entirely in Latin. Here we find this Angelical phrase spoken by "a Voice": *Garil zed masch, ich na gel galaht gemp gal noch Cabanladan.* No translation or context is offered.

Compare from *Loagaeth*:
Gel, Geld

Gemeganza (jeem-gan-za) Your Will Be Done / As You Wish*

Note:
(**Dee—gemeganza = your will be done*) See the *Five Books*, p. 314. Dee here asks if he and Kelley can leave off for the night, as it is getting late. A voice responds, "*Gemeganza.*"

Gemp (jemp) n/a

Note:

See *TFR*, pp. 34–35. This session is recorded entirely in Latin. Here we find this Angelical phrase spoken by "a Voice": *Garil zed masch, ich na gel galaht gemp gal noch Cabanladan.* No translation or context is offered.

Gephna (jef-na) n/a

Note:

See *TFR*, p. 3. The Angel *Murifri* here speaks a prayer in Angelical, and Kelley can only overhear a few of the words: *Oh Gahire Rudna gephna oh Gahire.* It is unclear whether this represents a single Angelical phrase, or if they are disconnected words recorded by Dee as Kelley overheard them here and there in the prayer. No translations are suggested.

Ger (jer)* *prop. n.* Letter *Q/Qu*

Note:

The name of the Angelical letter for *Q/Qu*. It is likely that these letter names have translations of their own. (For instance, note the Hebrew alphabet: the letter *Q/Qu* is named *Qoph*, but *Qoph* also translates as "ear.") However, such translations for the Angelical letters are never given. (See the *Five Books*, p. 270.)

Pronunciation notes:

(**Dee—In sound, gierh.*) In Dee's notation *gierh*, the *gi* may be the same as *gj*—to indicate a soft "g" (or "j") sound. This is the pronunciation I have chosen for the word. However, it is also possible that the *ie* is intended to make an "ee" sound—so the word would sound like "jee-rr."

Compare from *Loagaeth*:

Ger

Geta (jet-a) *adv.* There

Note:

See *TFR*, p. 32. Here, Dee is speaking with the Angel Madimi. Suddenly, Madimi halts the session and demands, "*Carma geta Barman.*" Dee asks her what this means, and she replies (in Latin, which roughly translates to): "Come out of there, *Barma.*" Madimi's command exorcises fifteen spirits from the body of Edward Kelley, the chief of whom is named *Barma*. After a short exchange (see *Gil*, etc.), Madimi banishes all fifteen spirits back to Hell until the last cry. (That is, until the End Times.)

Carma Geta is likely intended as an exorcism phrase to command lesser spirits, and not something one would use with the Angels.

Note:

Also see "Da" (there).

Compare from *Loagaeth*:

Get

Gethog (jeth-og) *prop. n.* "A Divine Name From the *Sigillum Emeth*"

Note:

See the *Five Books*, p. 161 (*Hamuthz Gethog*). Kelley is having a vision of the Seven Biblical Days of Creation at this point—during which the Seven Ensigns of Creation are revealed. Oddly, the reception of one Ensign was interrupted by the reception of another. This interruption was marked by the sudden speaking of the words *Hamuthz Gethog*. (Dee does not attribute these words to any particular Angel. Much of the content of these sessions are merely attributed to "a Voice.") The "woman" who appears at these words creates the Sun, Moon, and Stars, and then presents her Ensign. (This happens to be the Ensign from which is drawn one of the Seals of the Watchtowers.) She then exits, and the interrupted vision continues.

No translation is given for *Hamuthz*, but *Gethog* is recognizable as one of the Divine Names encoded upon the Seal of Truth.

Compare from *Loagaeth*:

Gethgol

"Giar" (jii-ar) *n.* Harvest

Compounds:

Aziagiar (ay-zii-AY-jii-ar) ["Azia" + "Giar"] Like unto the Harvest

Pronunciation notes:

The vowel sound made by *ia* is unclear. However, we can find it in words like *dial*, *dialect*, or *William*. Based on this, I have assumed the sound should be a long *i* followed by a short *a*.

Gigipah (jij-ii-pah)* *n.* (Living) Breath

3.12 Six are the seats of *living breath* . . .

Pronunciation notes:

(**Dee—Gi gi pah*) Three syllables.

(**Dee—Gigîpah*) See *48 Claves*. Note that Dee places a circumflex over the second *i*—indicating its long sound. Thus, I assume the first *i* takes its short sound.

Gil (jil) n/a

Note:

See *TFR*, p. 32. Here, the Angel Madimi has just interrupted the session to exorcise several demons from the body of Kelley. (See *Carma*.) These spirits came out of Kelley violently, scratching each other in the face and swarming about Madimi. To her, the spirits spoke in Angelical, "*Gil de pragma kures helech*." Dee asks Madimi what this means, and she replies (in Latin, which roughly translates as:) "We want to live here in our [friends]." (Madimi does not offer definitions for the individual words.)

When Dee asks who these "friends" are supposed to be, the spirits indicate Kelley as their place of habitation (probably meaning both Dee and Kelley). Madimi then banishes these spirits.

Gisg (gizh) *prop. n.* Letter *T*

Note:

The name of the Angelical letter for *T*. It is likely that these letter names have translations of their own. (For instance, note the Hebrew alphabet: the letter *T* is named *Teth*, but *Teth* also translates as "serpent.") However, such translations for the Angelical letters are never given. (See the *Five Books*, p. 270.)

Githgulcag (jith-gul-kag) *prop. n.* Lucifer, Satan(?)

Note:

See *TFR*, p. 6. Here, an Angel (who is later identified as the Daughter of Light named *Aath*) tells Dee, "It is written that Pride was the first offense. *Githgulcag* knew not himself. Therefore he was ignorant. [. . .] You will grant me that pride is the greatest sin. Pride was the cause he knew not himself. Therefore Pride is the cause of Ignorance. Ignorance was the nakedness wherewithal you were first tormented,* and the first Plague that fell onto man was the want of Science." *Aath* appears to first explain the reason for Lucifer's Fall, and then ends her speech with a very Hermetic interpretation of the Fall from Eden.
Could *Githgulcag* have some indication of "ignorance"?

Note:

*See Genesis 3:7, "And the eyes of them both were opened, and they knew that they were naked."
Also see *Coronzom* (the Devil, Satan) and *Telocvovim* (likely a name for the fallen Lucifer).

Givi (jiv-ii)* *adj.* Stronger

2.23 . . . *stronger* are your feet than the barren stone.

Pronunciation notes:

(**Dee—Giui*) The letter *u* should probably sound like "v" when surrounded by vowels. The initial G should have a soft sound when preceding an *i*, and the final *i* likely has the long sound.

Note:

Also see *Umadea* (strong towers), *Umplif* (strength) and *Ugeg* (become strong).

Gizyax (jiz-wii-aks)* *n.* — Earthquakes

10.43 . . . a hundred mighty *earthquakes* . . .

Pronunciation notes:

(**Dee—Giz y ax*) Three syllables. The initial G should take the soft ("j") sound when preceding an *i*. The y stands alone.

Gmicalzo (jee-mii-KAYL-zoh)* *n.* — In Power (and Presence?)

6.37 . . . I move you *in power and presence* . . .

Pronunciation notes:

(**Dee—G-ni cál zo*) Likely four syllables, with an accent on the second syllable. Dee here indicates that the initial G stands alone. The *i* and *a* should take their long sounds (see *Micalzo*). Also note that Dee wrote an *n* in his phonetic note, but this is likely a mistake for *m*.

(**Dee—g-micálzo*) See the *48 Claves*. The initial G is again standing alone. The accent is again on the third syllable.

Compounds:

Gmicalzoma (jee-mii-KAYL-zoh-ma)
[Gmicalzo + "Oma"] — With a Power of Understanding

Also:

Micalp (mii-KALP) — Mightier
Micalzo (mii-KAYL-zoh) — Mighty
Micaoli (mii-KAY-oh-lii) — Mighty

Micaolz (mii-KAY-ohlz or mii-KAY-ohl-zohd) Mighty
Omicaolz (oh-mii-KAY-ohl-zohd) (Be) Mighty

Possible shared root:

Miketh (mii-KETH) "The True Measure of the Will of God in Judgment, Which Is by Wisdom"(?)

Note:

Also see *Umadea* (strong towers), *Umplif* (strength), *Ugeg* (become strong), *Vohim* (mighty), and *Nanaeel* (my power).

Gmicalzoma (jee-mii-KAYL-zoh-ma)* [Gmicalzo + "Oma"] *comp.*
Power of Understanding

30.33 . . . with *a power of understanding* to dispose all things . . .

Pronunciation notes:

(*Dee—Gmi cál zo ma*) Likely five syllables, with an accent on the third syllable. The G should stand alone, and the *i* and *o* should take their long sounds. Also, the first *a* is likely a long vowel—see *Micalzo* (mighty/power).

(*Dee—gmicálzôma*) See the *48 Claves*. Here, Dee again placed the accent upon the third syllable. He also placed a circumflex over the *o* to indicate its long sound.

Gnay (nay)* *v.* Doth (i.e., Does)

9.33 . . . as the rich man *doth* his treasure.
10.63 . . . as the heart of man *doth* his thoughts.

Pronunciation notes:

(*Dee 9.33; 10.63—Gnay*) One syllable. In Early Modern English, the digraph *Gn* began to take the sound of a hard *n*—such as in the English words *gnat* and *gnash*.

Gnetaab (nee-TAY-ab)* *n.* (Your) Governments

3.48 . . . the corners of *your governments* . . .

Pronunciation notes:

(**Dee—Gnetaab*) In Early Modern English, the letters *Gn* became a digraph that sounds like *n*. See *Netaab* (government) for further pronunciation notes.

(**Dee—gne-táab*) See the *48 Claves*. Likely three syllables, with an accent on the second syllable. The *e* likely takes a long sound.

Also:

Anetab (ay-NEE-tayb)	(In) Government
Netaab (nee-TAY-ab)	Your Governments
Netaaib (nee-TAY-ay-ib)	Government
Tabaam (tay-BAY-an)	Governor
Tabaord (tay-BAY-ord)	(Let) Be Governed
Tabaori (tay-BAY-oh-rii)	Govern
"Tabas" (tay-BAS)	Govern

Further:

Cab (kab)	Rod/Sceptor
Caba (ka-BA)	To Govern

Gnonp (non-pee) *v.* To Garnish

1.31 Whose seats *I garnished with* the fire . . .

Gohed (joh-ED)* *prop. n.?* "One Everlasting, All Things Descending Upon One"**

Pronuncation Note:

(**Dee—Gohed, pronounced as Iohed . . .*) See the *Five Books*, p. 304. Dee here shows the pronunciation of *Iohed*—showing the soft *G* (or *j*) sound. I have adopted the accent from similar words.

From *Loagaeth*:

(***Dee—Gohed, pronounced as Iohed, signifieth One Everlasting and all things Descending upon One, and Gohed Ascha is as much to say as One God.*) See the *Five Books*, p. 304.

Also:

Geiad (jej-AYD)	Lord and Master
Iaisg (hay-IZH)	Everlasting One . . . God
Ioiad (joh-JAD)	Him That Liveth Forever
"Iadoias" (jad-oh-JAS)	Eternal God

Gohel (GOH-hel)* [Goho + El] *comp.* Sayeth the First

2.41 . . . arise, *sayeth the First* . . .

Pronunciation notes:

(*Dee—Go hel*) Two syllables, and the *h* is audible. I assume the *e* is a phonetic gloss, as it is in the word *El* (The First).
(*Dee—góhel*) See *48 Claves*. The first syllable is given an accent.

Note:

I am uncertain why the final *o* of *Goho* was dropped here. Angelical usually only drops a letter in a compound if it is repeated twice. Note, for example, the compound *Zirenaiad*, formed of the words *Zir*, *Enay*, and *Iad*. We can see that the final *y* of *Enay* and the initial *I* of *Iad* combine into one letter in the compound.

Gohia (goh-HII-a)* *v.* (We) Say

3.73 . . . in whom *we say*, move . . .

Pronunciation notes:

(*Dee—Gohia*) I assume three syllables, with a long *i*. I have adopted the accent from other versions of this word.

Note:

Although this word is similar to the compound word *Gohoiad* (sayeth god), it is apparent that *Iad* does not serve as a root here at all.

Also:

Goho (goh-HOH)	To Say
Gohol (goh-HOHL)	To Say
Gohon (goh-HON)	Have Spoken

Gohulim (goh-HOO-lim) — It Is Said
Gohus (goh-US) — (I) say

Goho (goh-HOH)* *v.* — To Say

1.4 . . . *sayeth* the God of Justice . . .
3.2 Behold, *sayeth* your God . . .

Pronunciation notes:

(*Dee 1.4—GOHO*)

(*Dee 3.2—Goho*) Dee gives us little clue here. The initial *G* should take a hard sound when preceding an *o*. I suspect both *o*'s take a long sound.

(*Dee 1.4; 3.2—Gohó*) See *48 Claves*. The accent is shown on the second syllable.

Compounds:

Gohoiad (goh-HOH-ii-ad) [Goho + Iad] — Sayeth God
Gohel (GOH-hel) [Goho + El] — Sayeth the First

Also:

Gohia (goh-HII-a) — (We) Say
Gohol (goh-HOHL) — To Say
Gohon (goh-HON) — Have Spoken
Gohulim (goh-HOO-lim) — It Is Said
Gohus (goh-US) — (I) say

Compare from *Loagaeth*:

Goho, Gohor

Gohoiad (goh-HOH-ii-ad)* [Goho + Iad] *comp.* — Sayeth the Lord

8.13 . . . *sayeth the lord*, whose long continuance . . .

Pronunciation notes:

(*Dee—Go hó i ad*) This appears to be four syllables—though I find that it sounds more like three when spoken fluently. (Elsewhere, the word *Iad* is given the single-syllable pronunciation of "yad.") There is an accent on the second syllable.

(*Dee—gohó î-ad*) See the *48 Claves*. Dee again placed the accent on the second syllable. He also indicates that the *i* stands alone. (The circumflex over the *i* further indicates the long vowel sound.)

Gohol (goh-HOHL)* *v.* To Say

4.6 . . . *saying*, are not the thunders . . .
30.42 . . . rose up in the beginning, *saying* . . .

Pronunciation notes:
(**Dee 4.6—Go hol*)
(**Dee 30.42—Go hól*) Two syllables. The G before an *o* should take a hard sound (as in the English words *going* and *gone*). In the phonetic note for word 30.42, Dee places the accent on the second syllable.
(**Dee 4.6; 30.42—Gohól*) See the *48 Claves*. Accent again on the second syllable.

Also:

Gohia (goh-HII-a)	(We) Say
Goho (goh-HOH)	To Say
Gohon (goh-HON)	Have Spoken
Gohulim (goh-HOO-lim)	It Is Said
Gohus (goh-US)	(I) say

Compare from *Loagaeth*:
Goho

Goholor (goh-HOH-lor)* *v.* Lift Up

3.61 *Lift up*, I say, yourselves . . .

Pronunciation notes:
(**Dee—Goholor*) I suggest three syllables here. The *G* preceding an *o* is likely hard.
(**Dee—Gohólor*) See the *48 Claves*. Dee places the accent on the second syllable.

Note:

It is uncertain why this word "seems" to have *Goho* (to say) as a root. It may be a rare case of coincidentally similar spelling between unrelated Angelical words. Unfortunately, the English sense is not "uplifted voices" (see *Farzem*).

Compare from *Loagaeth*:

Gohor

Gohon (goh-HON)* *v.* Have Spoken

8.37 . . . the thunders *have spoken* . . .

Pronunciation notes:

(**Dee—Go hón*) Two syllables. The accent mark is placed on the second syllable. The first *o* should take its long sound.

(**Dee—gohón*) See the *48 Claves*. This note essentially matches that from *TFR*.

Also:

Gohia (goh-HII-a)	(We) Say
Goho (goh-HOH)	To Say
Gohol (goh-HOHL)	To Say
Gohulim (goh-HOO-lim)	(It Is) Said
Gohus (goh-US)	(I) say

Compare from *Loagaeth*:

Goho, Gohonp

Gohulim (goh-HOO-lim)* *v.* (It Is) Said

30.12 . . . to you *it is said*, behold . . .

Pronunciation notes:

(**Dee—Go hú lim*) Three syllables, with an accent on the second syllable.

(**Dee—gohúlim*) See the *48 Claves*. Here, Dee again placed an accent over the second syllable.

Also:

Gohia (goh-HII-a) — (We) Say
Goho (goh-HOH) — To Say
Gohol (goh-HOHL) — To Say
Gohon (goh-HON) — Have Spoken
Gohus (goh-US) — (I) say

Compare from *Loagaeth*:

Goho

Gohus (goh-US)* *v.* — (I) Say

3.62 Lift up, *I say*, yourselves!
12.24 Move, *I say*, and show yourselves.

Pronunciation notes:

(**Dee 3.62—Gohus*) Two syllables. I suggest a short "u" sound.

(**Dee—gohús*) See the *48 Claves*. Dee placed an accent on the second syllable.

Also:

Gohia (goh-HII-a) — (We) Say
Goho (goh-HOH) — To Say
Gohol (goh-HOHL) — To Say
Gohon (goh-HON) — Have Spoken
Gohulim (goh-HOO-lim) — (It Is) Said

Compare from *Loagaeth*:

Goho

Gon (gon) *prop. n.* — Letter *I*/Y

Note:

The name of the Angelical letter for *I/ Y*. It is likely that these letter names have translations of their own. (For instance, note the Hebrew alphabet: the letter *I* is named *Yod*, but *Yod* also translates as "hand.") However, such translations for the Angelical letters are never given. (See the *Five Books*, p. 270.)

Gono (gon-oh) *n.* Faith (Trust/Loyalty)

1.51 . . . and swore obedience *and faith* to him . . .

Note:

Also see *Congamphlgh* (Faith/Holy Ghost).

Gosaa (goh-say-ay)* *n.* Stranger

30.109 . . . let her be known, and another while *a stranger*.

Pronunciation notes:

(**Dee—Go sa a*) Three syllables. The final *a* stands alone. The other two vowels also appear to take their long sounds.

(**Dee—gosâa*) See the *48 Claves*. Here, Dee placed a circumflex over the first *a* to indicate its long sound.

Graa (gray)* *n.* Moon

1.16 . . . *the moon* is a through-thrusting fire . . .

Pronunciation notes:

(**Dee—GRAA*) Dee gives us little clue here. Likely, the double *a* indicates a long vowel, as we see in Early Modern English.

Compare from *Loagaeth*:

Gra

Graph (grakh-fa)* *prop. n.* Letter *E**

Note:

The name of the Angelical letter for *E*. It is likely that these letter names have translations of their own. (For instance, note the Hebrew alphabet: the letter *E* is named *Aleph*, but *Aleph* also translates as "ox/bull.") However, such translations for the Angelical letters are never given. (See the *Five Books*, p. 270.)

Pronunciation note:

(**Dee—The sound as Grakpha, in the throat.*) Dee adds the *k* in the center of this word, likely to indicate a throaty "kh" sound just before the "f" sound. I normally pronounce the word along the lines of "grah-fa."

Grosb (grozb)* *n.* or *v.* (Bitter) Sting

13.22 . . . is called amongst you *a bitter sting* . . .

Note:

Words 13.21 and 13.22 are both missing from Dee's journals. We only have the English given for this Key on *TFR*, p. 193. However, they do appear in Dee's *48 Claves*.

Note that the word *sting* should be a verb ("to sting"), but it is used in this case as a noun ("a sting").

Pronunciation notes:

(**Dee—GROSB*) Likely one syllable.

Shared root:

"Quasb" (kwazb) Destroy

Grsam (gur-sam)* *n.* Admiration

1.37 . . . beautified your garments with *admiration* . . .

Pronunciation notes:

(**Dee—as Gursam*) Usually, the *G* and *r* would combine to form a "Gr" sound. However, this should be followed by a vowel—such as in the words *great* and *grant*. In the case of *Grsam*, the first two letters are followed by a consonant. Therefore, the first two letters stand as a syllable of their own ("gur"), followed by the second syllable ("sam").

Gru (groo) *n.* or *v.?* To Cause, Bring About, Result

From *Corpus Omnium*:

Found in the post-Crucifixion portion of the Table, in the phrase *Gru Sor Iad* (Cause of the Actions of God).

Na (H)

Hagonel (hag-on-el) *prop. n.* n/a

Note:

See the *Five Books*, pp. 188–91. Hagonel is the title of the ruling Prince of the *Heptarchia*. (Not to be confused with the Son of the Sons of Light of the same name.) In Dee's lifetime, the Heptarchic Prince of Venus—Bagenol—held the title. Today, I presume it should be the Prince of Mercury—Blisdon—though I do not know if he would hold the same title.

(Also see *Carmara*, *Ga*, *Galvah*, *Mapsama*, *Murifri*, *Nalvage*, *Vaa*, and *Za* .)

Hamuthz (ham-oothz) n/a

Note:

See the *Five Books*, p. 161 (*Hamuthz Gethog*). Kelley is having a vision of the Seven Biblical Days of Creation at this point—during which the Seven Ensigns of Creation are revealed. Oddly, the reception of one Ensign was interrupted by the reception of another. This interruption was marked by the sudden speaking of the words *Hamuthz Gethog*. (Dee does not attribute these words to any particular Angel. Much of the content of these sessions are merely attributed to "a Voice.") The "woman" who appears at these words creates the Sun, Moon, and stars, and then presents her Ensign. (This happens to be the Ensign from which is drawn one of the Seals of the Watchtowers.) She then exits, and the interrupted vision continues.

No translation is given for *Hamuthz*, but *Gethog* is recognizable as one of the Divine Names encoded upon the Seal of Truth.

Hardeh (har-day) *v.?* To Read (?)

Pronunciation notes:

(*Dee—Amzes naghezes Hardeh—Note this to be pronounced roundly together.*) Perhaps this means the three words should be pronounced as if they were one.

Note:

See the *Five Books*, pp. 324–25. Here Kelley sees what the *Book of Loagaeth* looks like from the outside. It is covered in blue silk, and has the title *Amzes naghezes Hardeh* painted upon it in gold. Kelley says this signifies "the universal name of Him that created universally be praised and extolled forever."

However, also see *TFR*, p. 174, where the Angel Ave reveals that the title of Enoch's book was "Let Those That Fear God, and Are Worthy, Read." (Dee here notes: *The title of Enoch's books expounded into English.*) If this happens to be the real translation, then perhaps *Hardeh* indicates "to read."

Harg (harg)* *v.* To Plant

6.9 . . . the first *hath planted* a torment . . .

Pronunciation notes:

(**Dee—Harg argenton*) One syllable. Dee's phonetic note seems to be a form of the Latin *argentum* (silver). Both Patricia Shaffer (*DeesPronunciationNotes.rtf*) and my Latin dictionary suggest that *g* in Latin always takes the hard sound. Thus Harg has the sound of "arg" rather than "arj."

Helech (hel-ek) n/a (?)

Note:

See *TFR*, p. 32. Here, the Angel Madimi has just interrupted the session to exorcise several demons from the body of Kelley. (See *Carma*.) These spirits came out of Kelley violently, scratching each other in the face and swarming about Madimi. To her, the spirits spoke in Angelical, "*Gil de pragma kures helech*." Dee asks Madimi what this means, and she replies (in Latin), "We want to live here in our [friends]." (Madimi does not offer definitions for the individual words.)

When Dee asks who these "friends" are supposed to be, the spirits indicate Kelley as their place of habitation (probably meaning both Dee and Kelley.) Madimi then banishes these spirits.

Hoath (hohth)* *n.* True Worshiper

(RFP . . . *a true worshiper* of the highest.)

Pronunciation notes:

(**Dee—Call it Hoath.*) One syllable, rhyming with the English word *both*. The *oa* letter combination in Early Modern English makes a long "o" sound—as in the English words *boat* and *coat*.

Holdo (hol-doh)* *v.* To Groan

11.2 The mighty seat *groaned* . . .

Pronunciation notes:

(**Dee—Hol do*) Two syllables. The first *o* is short, while the second *o* takes its long sound.

Holq (HOL-kwah)* *v.* To Measure

1.20 . . . which *measureth* your garments . . .
11.23 . . . of whom *it is measured* . . .

Pronunciation notes:

(**Dee 1.20—HOLQ as Holquu*) The double *u* is literally a *w*. So, *quu* sounds like "kwah."

(**Dee 11.23—Hól q*) This note lets us know the word *Holq* has two syllables, with an accent on the first syllable.

(**Dee 1.20; 11.23—hol-q*) See *48 Claves*. Shows two syllables, with the *q* standing alone.

Compounds:

Chisholq (KIIS-hohl-kwa) [Chis + Holq] Are Measured

Hom (hom) *v.* To Live

1.54 . . . to him that *liveth* and triumpheth . . .

Shared root:

Homil (hom-il) — Ages

Homin (hom-in) — Age

Note:

Also see "Apila" (to live).

Homil (hom-il)* *n.* — (True) Ages

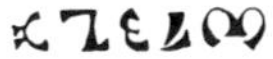

3.41 . . . over 456, the *true ages of* time . . .

Pronunciation notes:

(**Dee—Homil*) Likely two syllables.

Also:

Homin (hom-in) — Age

Shared root:

Hom (hom) — To Live

Homin (hom-in)* *n.* — Age

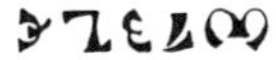

14.13 . . . vexing all creatures of the earth *with age* . . .

Pronunciation notes:

Likely two syllables.

Note:

The transmission of Key Fourteen is missing from Dee's journals. We only have the English for this Key given later (see *TFR*, p. 193). Plus, the word appears in this location in Dee's *48 Claves*.

Also:

Homil (hom-il) — Ages

Shared root:

Hom (hom) — To Live

Hoxmarch (hoks-mark) *v.* Fear (Stand in Awe of) God

Note:

See *TFR*, pp. 18–19. The Mother Galvah appears to Kelley in a rather dressed-up fashion. Dee asks her if she has put on her holiday clothes, but this is apparently not the case. She replies: "FEAR GOD. My Garment is called *HOXMARCH*, which in your speech is called . . ." Dee then replies, "It is Just Wisdom to fear the Lord. We acknowledge it to be an old and a true Lesson, and also the first step of the pathway to felicity." Galvah then goes on to reveal the final Table of *Loagaeth*.

Take special note that Dee's use of the word *fear* in this sense (as with the King James Bible, published at the same period of history), indicates "to stand in awe." The concept of "fear = terror" is not indicated by this.

Hubaio (hoo-BAY-ii-oh)* *n.* Lanterns

12.7 . . . 28 *the lanterns of* sorrow . . .

Pronunciation notes:

(**Dee—Hubá i o*) Four syllables, with an accent on the second. The *a* seems to take a long sound. The *i* and the final *o* each stand alone. The long *u* is indicated in the phonetic note for *Hubaro*.

(**Dee—hubíâo*) See the *48 Claves*. Dee seems to have switched the letters *a* and *i* in this notation. However, he does place an accent over the second syllable, and the circumflex over the *a* indicates its long sound. Based on the other versions of this word, I have settled upon the spelling found in *TFR*.

Also:

Hubar (hoo-BAR) Lamps

Hubaro (hoo-BAY-roh) (Living) Lamps

Compare from *Loagaeth*:

Hubra, Lubrah, Ubrah-ax, Vbrah, Subracah, Zubra, Zubrah

Hubar (hoo-BAR)* *n.* Lamps

5.33 . . . which are garnished with *continually burning lamps* . . .

Pronunciation notes:

(**Dee—Hubar*) Likely two syllables. The long *u* is indicated in the phonetic note for *Hubaro*. I have adopted the accent from other versions of this word.

Also:

Hubaio (hoo-BAY-ii-oh) — Lanterns
Hubaro (hoo-BAY-roh) — (Living) Lamps

Compare from *Loagaeth*:

Hubra, Lubrah, Ubrah-ax, Vbrah, Subracah, Zubra, Zubrah

Hubaro (hoo-BAY-roh)* *n.* — (Living/Burning) Lamps

17.11 . . . and hast 7336 living lamps going before . . .

Pronunciation notes:

(**Dee—Hu ba ro*) Three syllables. I suggest long *u*, *a*, and *o* sounds—as both of them fall as the very end of their syllables. I have adopted the accent from *Hubaio* (lanterns).

(**Dee—hubâro*) See the *48 Claves*. Here, Dee placed a circumflex over the *a* to indicate the long sound.

Also:

Hubaio (hoo-BAY-ii-oh) — Lanterns
Hubar (hoo-BAR) — Lamps

Compare from *Loagaeth*:

Hubra, Lubrah, Ubrah-ax, Vbrah, Subracah, Zubra, Zubrah

Hucacha (hoo-kay-cha) — n/a

Note:

See the *Five Books*, p. 310. Spoken during a longer prayer offered by "many voices": "It is good, O God, for you are goodness itself. And great because of the size of greatness itself. *Adgmach, adgmach, adgmach*! I am, and this pace is, holy. *Adgmach, adgmach, adgmach hucacha*."

Dee notes that "*Adgmach adgmach adgmach = Much Glory,*" but he offers no definition for *Hucacha*. Could *Hucacha* mean "This Place Is Holy"?

Huseh (hoo-say) n/a

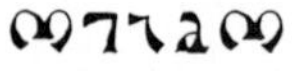

Note:

See the *Five Books*, p. 415. Part of a prayer recited jointly by the Archangels Michael, Raphael, and Uriel: *Huseh Huseh Huseh garmal, Peleh Peleh Peleh pacaduasam*. No translations are suggested.

Gon (*I*/*Y*)

Note that several words in this section begin with *Ged* (*G*, *J*) rather than *Gon* (*I*/*Y*). However, Dee spelled these particular words in English with an initial *I*, as that was an acceptable alternative to *J* in Early Modern English (John = Iohan, Justice = Iustice. In fact, the *J* as we know it is simply an elongated *I*.) Because of this, I have included those words in this section.

I (ii)* *v.* — Is/Are

1.13 . . . the sun *is* as a sword . . .
10.76 . . . *is*, was, and shall be . . .

Pronunciation notes:

(**Dee 1.13—a word by itself*)

(**Dee 10.76—I*) As we pronounce the word *I*.

Compounds:

Dsi (dee-sii) [Ds + I]	Which Is
Icorsca (ii-KORS-kay) [I + Cors + "Ca"]	Is Such as
Idlugam (id-LOO-gam) [I + "Dlugam"]	Is Given
Iga (ii-ga) [I + "GA"]	Is 31
Il (ii-el) [I + L]	Is One
Inoas (in-OH-as) [I + Noas]	Are Become
Isalman (ii-SAYL-man) [I + Salman]	Is a House
Ita (ii-tay) [I + Ta]	Is as
Ivonph (ii-VONV) [I + Vonph]	Is Wrath
Ivonpovnph (ii-VON-foh-unv) [I + "Vonpo" + "Vnph"]	Is Wrath in Anger
Pii (pii-ii) ["Pi" + I]	She Is
Ti (tii) ["T" + I]	It Is

Shared root:

Ip (ip)	Not
Ipam (ip-am)	Is Not
Ipamis (ip-am-is)	Can Not Be

Note:

The word *I* (is/are) appears to be a form of the verb "to be." Also see *Zir* (am, were, was).

Also see *Chis* (are) and *Geh* (art).

Also note the Angel *I*, one of the Sons of Light. His name literally translates as "is," "to be," or "to exist." (Perhaps "The Existent"?)

Ia (yah) n/a?

From *Loagaeth*:

This word is never given a definition. However, I have found it to be such a vital root word in the Angelical language, I decided to give it its own entry. It appears several times in *Loagaeth*. See *Iad* (God), *Iadnah* (Knowledge), *Ialprg* (Flame), etc. *Ia* appears to indicate many celestial or sacred concepts.

Note:

The similarity between this word and the Hebrew *Ia* (or *Yah*—God).

Compare from *Loagaeth*:

Iad, Iads, Ia-dron, Iaisg

Iad (yad)* *prop. n.* God

1.5 . . . sayeth *the God of* Justice . . .

Pronunciation notes:

(**Dee—Iad, as Yad*) The *I* has the sound of "y" rather than "j."

Compounds:

Bigliad (big-lii-ad) ["Bigl" + Iad?] (God) Our Comforter
Gohoiad (goh-HOH-ii-ad) [Goho + Iad] Sayeth the Lord
Iadbaloth (ii-ad-BAL-toh) [Iad + Balt + Toh] God (of) Righteousness
Iadoiasmomar (jad-oh-JAS-moh-mar)*
["Iadoias" + "Momar"] God Eternally Crowned
Sobaiad (soh-BAY-ad) [Soba + Iad] Whose God
Zirenaiad (zii-er-NAY-ad) [Zir + Enay + Iad] I Am the Lord (Your) God

Also:

Geiad (jej-AYD)	Lord and Master
"Iadoias" (jad-oh-JAS)	Eternal God
Iadpil (ii-AD-pil)	(To) Him
Iaida (jay-II-da)	The Highest
Iaidon (jay-II-don)	All Powerful
Iaisg (jay-IZH)	Everlasting One and Indivisible God
Ioiad (joh-JAD)	Him That Liveth Forever
Oiad (oh-ii-AD)	Of God
Piad (pii-AD)	Your God

Note:

See notes for *Iadbaltoh* (God of Righteousness).
Also see *Mad* (god, in the non-specific sense).

Probable root:

Ia (yah)	n/a

Iad as root? (Not referring to God):

Iadnah (yad-nah)	Knowledge
Iaiadix (yay-II-ad-iks)	Honor
Laiad (lay-II-ad)	Secrets of Truth

Note:

While this final group of words does not refer to God, the use of *Iad* as a root may indicate the lofty nature of these ideas.

Compare from *Loagaeth*:

Ia, *Iad*, *Iads*, *Ia-dron*

Compare from *Corpus Omnium*:

Iad appears in all four portions of the Table—taking up the cells in the outer corners. This is likely symbolic of the Horned Altars in the Tabernacle of Moses and the Temple of Solomon. (The same symbolism can be found upon Dee's Holy Table—which has the Angelical letter *Veh* [B] at the four corners.)

Iadbaltoh (ii-ad-BAL-toh)* [Iad + Balt + Toh] *comp.*

(Triumphant) God of Righteousness

9.63 . . . The God of Righteousness rejoiceth in them.

Pronunciation notes:

(**Dee—I ad bal toh*) Four syllables. The initial *I* stands alone—although it tends to blend with the second syllable when this word is spoken fluently. The *oh* in the last syllable makes a long "o" sound. The other syllables are all short.

(*Dee—Iadbáltoh) See the 48 Claves. Here, Dee placed an accent over the third syllable.

Also:

Baltle (bal-tayl) Righteousness

Note:

The similarity between *Iadbaltoh* and the ancient Gnostic name and title for the Creator: *Ialdabaoth*, the God of Righteousness.

Iadnah (yad-nah)* *n.* Knowledge

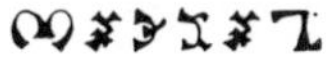

1.46 . . . ark of knowledge . . .

Pronunciation notes:

(**Dee—yadnah*) The *I* in this case takes the "y" sound. (Also see the pronunciation given for *Iad*).

(**Dee—Jadnah*) See *48 Claves*. Here Dee indicates the "j" sound. I have settled upon the "y" sound instead, as it is closer to the sound of related words (as we can see in each of the following compounds and related words).

Compounds:

Iadnamad (yad-nay-mad) [Iadnah + Mad?] Pure Knowledge

Probable root:

Ia (yah) n/a

Iad (yad) God

Probable shared root:

Iaiadix (yay-II-ad-iks)	Honor
Laiad (lay-II-ad)	Secrets of Truth

Compare from *Loagaeth*:

Ia, Iad

Iadnamad (yad-nay-mad)* [Iadnah + Mad?] *comp.?* — Pure Knowledge

30.157 . . . make us partakers of undefiled knowledge.

Pronunciation notes:

(**Dee—Iad na mad*) Three syllables. The *a* in the second syllable is likely long.

(**Dee—Iadnâmad*) See the *48 Claves*. Here, Dee places a circumflex over the second a to indicate its long sound.

Note:

This compound literally translates as "knowledge," "God," or "Godly Knowledge" (see *Mad*).

"Iadoias" (jad-oh-JAS) *prop. n.* — Eternal God

Compounds:

Iadoiasmomar (jad-oh-JAS-moh-mar) ["Iadoias" + "Momar"]	God Eternally Crowned

Also:

Ioiad (joh-JAD)	Him That Liveth Forever

Shared root:

Geiad (jej-AYD)	Lord and Master
Gohed (joh-ED)	One Everlasting . . .
Ia (yah)	n/a
Iad (yad)	God
Iadpil (ii-AD-pil)	(To) Him
Iaida (jay-II-da)	The Highest
Iaidon (jay-II-don)	All Powerful

Oiad (oh-ii-AD) (Of) God
Piad (pii-AD)
Your God

Iadoiasmomar (jad-oh-JAS-moh-mar)* ["Iadoias" + "Momar"] *comp.*
God Eternally Crowned

8.44 . . . *God is, was, and shall be crowned.*

Pronunciation notes:

(**Dee—Iad o i as mo mar*) This word appears to be six syllables—though I suspect it is only five. The first *o* stands alone. The *I* likely takes the hard "j" sound—as we see in *Ioiad* (Him That Liveth Forever)—thus I have used a Ged (J) in the Angelical spelling. Finally, the second *o* takes its long sound.

(**Dee—Jad-oiás-mômar*) See the *48 Claves*. Dee here indicates a "j" sound for the initial *I*—thus I have used a Ged (J) for this letter well. He places the accent over the second *a*, and a circumflex over the second *o* to indicate its long sound.

Iadpil (ii-AD-pil)* *prop. n.* (Unto) Him

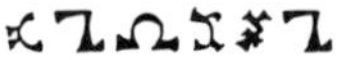

1.52 . . . faith *to Him* that liveth . . .

Pronunciation notes:

(**Dee—Call it IADPIL accent ad*) This note is haphazard. However, Dee seems to indicate that the letters *ad* stand as their own (accented) syllable. This means the *I* stands alone, and this word has three syllables.

(**Dee—Iädpil*) See *48 Claves*. There is a dieresis over the *a*, to indicate that it does not combine its sound with the initial *I*.

Also:

Geiad (jej-AYD)	Lord and Master
Iad (yad)	God
"Iadoias" (jad-oh-JAS)	Eternal God
Iaida (jay-II-da)	The Highest
Iaidon (jay-II-don)	All Powerful
Ioiad (joh-JAD)	Him That Liveth Forever

Oiad (oh-ii-AD) — (Of) God
Piad (pii-AD) — Your God

Probable root:

Ia (yah) — n/a

Iaiadix (yay-II-ad-iks)* *n.* — Honor

15.17 . . . seal of *honour* . . .

Note:

The transmission of Key Fifteen is missing from Dee's journals. We only have the English for this Key given later (see *TFR*, p. 193). Plus, the word appears in this location in Dee's *48 Claves*.

Pronunciation notes:

(**Dee—iaiâdix*) See the *48 Claves*. Dee placed an accent over the second *i*—which I assume is the second syllable. He also placed a circumflex over the second *a* to indicate its long sound. Compare to the pronunciation of *Laiad* (secrets of truth).

Probable shared root:

Ia (yah) — n/a
Iad (yad) — God
Iadnah (yad-nah) — Knowledge
Laiad (lay-II-ad) — Secrets of Truth

Iaial (jay-yal)* *v.* — To Conclude (To Judge)

5.50 . . . *conclude us as* receivers of your mysteries . . .

Note:

"Conclude" or "judge"—especially in the sense of Divine Judgment. In this place in the Keys, the speaker is asking the Angels to judge him worthy of the higher mysteries.

Pronunciation notes:

(**Dee—Ia ial*) Two syllables. Other words similar to *Iaial* seem to indicate a "j" sound for the first syllable—thus I have spelled this word with an initial Ged (J). (See Iaida, Iaidon, etc.)

(**Dee—ia-ial*) See the *48 Claves*. This note matches that from *TFR*.

Possible compound:

Oxiayal (ox-jay-al) [Tox? + Iaial] "The Mighty Seat" (i.e., Divine Throne)

Compare from *Loagaeth*:

Iaialgh

Iaida (jay-II-da)* *prop. n.* The Highest

(RFP) . . . the true worshiper of *the Highest* . . .

30.10 . . . the judgment of *the Highest* . . .

Pronunciation notes:

(**Dee 1.86—A word, Jaida*)

(**Dee 30.10—Ia—í da Ya*) There seem to be two pronunciations here—one taking the hard "j" sound and the other taking the soft "y" sound. I have settled on the "j" version in my pronunciation—along with an initial Ged (J) in the Angelical lettering—as that sound is found in many similar words. The note at 30.10 indicates three syllables, with the accent on the second syllable. Dee added the *Ya* to his notation to indicate the "y" sound for the initial *I* in that case.

(**Dee 1.RFP—Jaida*) See *48 Claves*. Dee indicates the "j" sound again.

(**Dee 13.RFP; 14.RFP; 15.RFP; 17.RFP; 18.RFP—Iaïda*) See the *48 Claves*. In these places, Dee added a dieresis over the second *i*, indicating that it should not join its sound with the previous vowel.

(**Dee 16.RFP; 30.10—Iaída*) See the *48 Claves*. Here, Dee again placed an accent on the *i* in the second syllable.

Also:

Geiad (jej-AYD) Lord and Master

Iad (yad) God

"Iadoias" (jad-oh-JAS) Eternal God

Iadpil (ii-AD-pil) (To) Him

Iaidon (jay-II-don)	All Powerful
Ioiad (joh-JAD)	Him That Liveth Forever
Oiad (oh-ii-AD)	Of God
Piad (pii-AD)	Your God

Possible compound:

Qadah (kwah-AY-dah) [Qaa + Iaida?]	Creator

Probable root:

Ia (yah)	n/a

Compare from *Loagaeth*:

Ia-dron

Iaidon (jay-II-don)* *prop. n.* — The All Powerful

2.39 . . . mind of *the All Powerful* . . .

Pronunciation note:

(**Dee—Ia í don*) Three syllables, with an accent on the second syllable. (**Dee—Ja-í-don*) See *48 Claves*. Same as in *TFR*. Note the "j" sound for the first syllable, and the initial Ged (J) in the Angelical lettering.

Also:

Geiad (jej-AYD)	Lord and Master
Iad (yad)	God
"Iadoias" (jad-oh-JAS)	Eternal God
Iadpil (ii-AD-pil)	(To) Him
Iaida (jay-II-da)	The Highest
Ioiad (joh-JAD)	Him That Liveth Forever
Oiad (oh-ii-AD)	Of God
Piad (pii-AD)	Your God

Probable root:

Ia (yah)	n/a

Compare from *Loagaeth*:

Ia-dron

Iaisg (jay-IZH)* *prop. n.* Everlasting One and Indivisible God**

Pronunciation note:

*(*Dee—ia-ísg)* See the *Five Books*, p. 307. Two syllables, with an accent on the second. This word likely begins with the "j" sound (see *Ioiad*), thus I have spelled it in Angelical with an initial Ged (J).

From *Loagaeth*:

(***Dee—Everlasting One and Indivisible God.*) See the *Five Books*, p. 307.

Also:

Geiad (jej-AYD)	Lord and Master
Gohed (joh-ED)	One Everlasting, All Things Descending Upon One
Ioiad (joh-JAD)	Him That Liveth Forever
"Iadoias" (jad-oh-JAS)	Eternal God

Probable root:

Ia (yah)	n/a

Compare from *Loagaeth*:

Ia, Ia-dron

Ialpirgah (YAL-pur-jah)* ["Ialprt" + "Pirgah"] *comp.* "Flames of the First Glory"

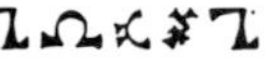

7.6 . . . amongst *the Flames of the First Glory* . . .

Pronunciation notes:

(**Dee—IAL pir gah Yal*) Three syllables. The first syllable likely takes an accent. Dee indicates that *Ial* should sound like "Yal." The *g* should take a soft "j" sound, as seen in other versions of the word *Prge*.

(**Dee—ial-pîrgah*) See the *48 Claves*. Dee places a circumflex over the second *i* to indicate a long sound. However, the long *i* does not appear in any other phonetic notes, for this or related words.

Note:

"Pirgah" is obviously a form of the word *Prge* (fire), and must mean "the First Glory" (i.e., the Light of Divinity, and possibly a reference to the rising Sun).

Also see *Ialpirt* (light), which seems to indicate Light from celestial beings.
Also see *Busd* (glory), which seems to indicate glory as in "wondrous."
Also see *Adgmach* (glory), which seems to indicate "adoration, praise."

Ialpirt (YAL-pert)* *n.* Light

18.3 . . . thou mighty *light* and burning flame . . .

Pronunciation notes:
(**Dee—Ol pirt*) The actual Angelical spelling of this word is not shown in Dee's journals. We only have his phonetic note, which shows the first syllable as *Ol*. However, this is corrected by Illemese later in the journals:
(*Illemese—al part*) See *TFR*, p. 200. Two syllables. This word is obviously the same as "Ialprt" (flame). Illemese drops the initial *I* (though I have retained it in my pronunciation, with the sound of "y"). The second *i* should be a phonetic gloss—which Illemese indicates with an *a* in his note.
I have adopted the accent from similar words.

Also:

Ialpon (YAL-pon)	Burn
Ialpor (YAL-por)	Flaming
"Ialprt" (YAL-pert)	Flame

Note:
These words (including compounds with "Ialprt") are used in the Keys to indicate Light as from a celestial being. The common-use nouns for a fire are *Vep* (flame) and *Prge* (fire). For verb forms, see *Ialpor* (flaming) and *Ialpon* (burn).

Ialpon (YAL-pon)* *v.* To Burn

10.21 . . . which *burn* night and day . . .

Pronunciation notes:

(**Dee—Jal pon Yal*) Two syllables. Dee appears to indicate that the initial *I* can take the "j" or "y" sound. I have settled upon the "y" sound, as it better matches other versions of this word. I have adopted the accent from similar words.

Also:

Ialpor (YAL-por)	Flaming
"Ialprt" (YAL-pert)	Flame
Ialpirt (YAL-pert)	Light

Note:

Ialpon (to burn) is a verb. *Ialpor* (flaming) is an adjective. The "Ialprt"/ *Ialpirt* family of words (flame, light) are nouns—specifically referring to the Light of celestial beings. The common-use nouns for a fire are *Vep* (flame) and *Prge* (fire).

Compare from *Loagaeth*:

Ia, Alpon

Ialpor (YAL-por)* *adj.* Flaming

9.5 . . . two edged swords *flaming* . . .

Pronunciation notes:

(**Dee—I AL por yal*) Dee indicates three syllables. However, the *I* must take the "y" sound. Because of this, it tends to blend with the second syllable (*al*) to make "yal." Therefore, I have given the word only two syllables in my pronunciation. (Further supporting this, see the pronunciation notes for *Ialpon*.)

I have adopted the accent from similar words.

Also:

Ialpon (YAL-pon)	Burn
"Ialprt" (YAL-pert)	Flame
Ialpirt (YAL-pert)	Light

Note:

See note at *Ialpon*.

Also compare the name of the Part of the Earth (and its Governor), *Yalpamb*. This could even be a compound (Ialpor + Pambt), or "Unto the Flame."

Compare from *Loagaeth*:

Ia

Ialprg (YAL-purj)* ["Ialprt" + "Prg"] *comp., prop. n.* — Burning Flame

18.4 . . . *burning flame* of comfort . . .

Pronunciation notes:

(*Dee—Ial purg*) Two syllables. The *r* takes its elongated "ur" sound. See "Prg", *Prge*, etc. for evidence that the final *g* should be soft. See *Ialpurg* for the accented first syllable.

Also:

Ialpurg (YAL-purj) ["Ialprt" + "Purg"] — Burning Flame(s)

Note:

The *u* in Ialpurg is a phonetic gloss.

"Ialprt" (YAL-pert) *n.* — Flame

Compounds:

Dialprt (dii-AL-purt) [D + "Ialprt"] — Third Flame
Lialprt (el-YAL-purt) [L + "Ialprt"] — First Flame
Vivialprt (viv-ii-AL-purt) [Viv + "Ialprt"] — Second Flame

Further compounds:

Ialprg (YAL-purj) ["Ialprt" + "Prg"] — Burning Flame(s)
Ialpirgah (YAL-pur-jah) ["Ialprt" + "Pirgah"] — Flames of the First Glory
Ialpurg (YAL-purj) ["Ialprt" + "Purg"] — Burning Flame(s)

Also:

Ialpirt (YAL-pert) — Light
Ialpon (YAL-pon) — Burn
Ialpor (YAL-por) — Flaming

Note:

All of these words are nouns, and they are all used to indicate Light as if from a celestial being. The common-use nouns for a fire are Vep (flame) and Prge (fire). For a verb form, see Ialpon (to burn). See Ialpor (flaming) for an adjective.

Ialpurg (YAL-purj)* ["Ialprt" + "Purg"] *comp., prop. n.* Burning Flame(s)

2.10 . . . *burning flames* have formed . . .

Pronunciation notes:

(**Dee—Ial purg*) Two syllables. The final *g* is likely soft—see the pronunciation notes for Prge (fire).

(**Dee—Iál-prg*) See *48 Claves*. Two syllables, with an accent on the first syllable. As we can see, the *u* is a phonetic gloss.

Also:

Ialprg (YAL-purj) ["Ialprt" + "Prg"] Burning Flame(s)

Compare from *Loagaeth*:

Ia

Iaod (YAY-ohd)* *n.* Beginning

5.30 . . . *the beginning of* their own seats . . .

30.16 . . . *the beginning of* comfort . . .

Pronunciation notes:

(**Dee 5.30; 30.16—I á od*) This would appear to have three syllables. However, also see *Iaodaf* (in the beginning), which indicates the initial *Ia* stand together. The accent is placed on the first syllable.

(**Dee 5.30—iáod*) See the *48 Claves*. Accent on the first syllable.

(**Dee 30.16—Jáod*) See the *48 Claves*. Dee seems to indicate the "j" sound for the initial *I*. However, see *Iaodaf* (in the beginning), which clearly indicates a "y" sound instead.

Also:

Iaodaf (YAY-oh-daf) (In the) Beginning

Note:

Also see *Acroodzi* (beginning), *Croodzi* (beginning of things), *Nostoah* (it was in the beginning).

Compare from *Loagaeth*:

Ia

Iaodaf (YAY-oh-daf)* *n.* (In the) Beginning

30.41 . . . rose up *in the beginning* . . .

Pronunciation notes:

(**Dee—Ia o daf Y*) Dee here indicates three syllables, and shows that the initial *I* takes the "y" sound. The first *a* seems to take its long sound. (Note also that it is followed by an *o*—as in the English word *chaos*.) Plus, see the pronunciation notes for *Iaod* (beginning).

(**Dee—iáodaf*) See the *48 Claves*. Here, Dee placed an accent upon the first syllable.

Also:

Iaod (YAY-ohd) Beginning

Note:

Also see *Acroodzi* (beginning), *Croodzi* (beginning of things), *Nostoah* (it was in the beginning).

Yarry (YAR-ee)* *n.* Providence

30.37 . . . *the providence of* Him who sits upon the Holy Throne.

Pronunciation notes:

(**Dee—Yar ry*) Two syllables. The initial *Y* should take the "yuh" sound, and the final *y* should take the "ee" sound. In Early Modern English, a double *r* is a regular "r" sound.

(**Dee—yárry*) See the *48 Claves*. Here, Dee indicates an accent on the first syllable.

Ich (ik)* *prop. n.* "The Eleventh Aethyr"

30.3 . . . which dwell in *the eleventh aethyr* . . .

Note:

This (word 30.3) is the single space in the Key of the Aethyrs, which must be changed for each invocation—replacing word 30.3 with the name of the appropriate Aethyr. No established definitions were given for these names.

Ich contains the three Parts of the Earth *Molpand*, *Usnarda*, and *Ponodol*.

Also see *TFR*, pp. 34–35. This session is recorded entirely in Latin. Here we find this Angelical phrase spoken by "a Voice": *"Garil zed masch, ich na gel galaht gemp gal noch Cabanladan."* No translation or context is offered. (Note the word *Ich*.)

Pronunciation notes:

(**Dee—ik*.) This means the *ch* in this word is hard, making a "kh" sound (as in the English word *ache*).

"Ichis" (jay-kiis) *v.* Are

Compounds:

Ichisge (jay-KIIS-jee) ["Ichis" + "Ge"] Are Not

Also:

Chis (kiis)	Are
Chiis (kiis)	Are (They)
"Chisda" (kiis-da)	Are There
Chiso (kiis-oh)	Shall Be
"Gchis" (jee-kiis)	Are
Zchis (zohd-kiis)	(They) Are

Note:

"Ichis" and "Gchis" are likely the same word—thus I have spelled this word with an initial Ged (J). See note at *Ichisge*.

Also see *Chis* (are).

Ichisge (jay-KIIS-jee)* ["Ichis" + "Ge"] *comp.* Are Not

3.21 . . . who are, *to are not*, except mine own hand . . .

Pronunciation notes:

(**Dee—I Chisge Kis*) Likely three syllables. Dee is not clear on the proper sound of the initial *I*—which could take the sound of "y" or "j." However, see *Gchisge* (are not), which indicates that both *Ichisge* and *Gchisge* should start with a soft "g" or "j" sound. (Note I have spelled the word with an initial Ged [J].) Finally, Dee indicates the *ch* should take the harder "k" sound.

(**Dee—i-chis-ge*) See the *48 Claves*. This note confirms three syllables for this word.

See *Gchisge* (are not) for the accented syllable.

Also:

Gchisge (jee-KIIS-jee) ["Gchis" + "Ge"] Are Not

Note:

The ungrammatical English phrase here—*to are not*—is probably a mistake on the part of Dee or Kelley. Apparently, the word *to* should read *and*, or perhaps *or*. However, the missing conjunction (*and/or*) is merely implied in the Angelical.

Also see *Chis* (are).

Icorsca (ii-KORS-kay)* [I + Cors + "Ca"] *comp.* Is Such as

9.72 . . . for the time *is such as* requireth comfort.

Pronunciation notes:

(**Dee—I cors ca Ka*) Three syllables. Dee indicates that the *c* in the last syllable should take the hard "k" sound. The initial *I* stands alone.

(**Dee—icórsca*) See the *48 Claves*. Here, Dee placed an accent over the second syllable.

Note:

See the similar *Corsta* (such as). Note that *ta* becomes *ca* here. For more info, see *Tabaam* (Governor), which becomes *Caba* in Key One. Also see *Ta* (as).

Idlugam (id-LOO-gam)* [I + "Dlugam"] *comp.* Is Given

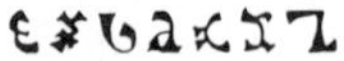

7.44 . . . this remembrance *is given* power . . .

Pronunciation notes:

(*Dee—Id lú gam*) Three syllables, with an accent on the second syllable. The *I* does not stand alone in Dee's note, and we know it takes the vowel sound ("i" rather than "j"), because it precedes a consonant.

(*Dee—idlúgam*) See the *48 Claves*. The accent is again shown on the second syllable.

Idoigo (ii-dee-oy-go)* *prop. n.* "Him Who Sits Upon the Holy Throne"

30.38 . . . the providence of *Him who sits upon the Holy Throne*.

Pronunciation notes:

(*Dee—I d oi go*) Dee seems to indicate four syllables here—with the initial *I* and *d* each standing alone. The *oi* should make an "oy" sound—as in the English words *oil* and *boil*.

Note:

This word appears as a Name of God upon the Eastern Watchtower of the Great Table of the Earth, ruling the Angels of medicine. Also, the title "Him Who Sits Upon the Throne" is common in biblical and *Merkavah* literature—such as *1 Enoch* and related texts like the Book of Revelation 4:9, 7:10, etc.

Iehusoz (jay-US-os)* *n.* (God's) Mercies

3.65 . . . *his mercies* flourish . . .

Pronunciation notes:

(*Dee—Jehusoz*) Three syllables. The initial *I* takes the consonant "J" sound—and I have thus spelled it with an initial Ged (J). The *eh* likely makes a long "a" sound, as in Early Modern English. No further long vowel sounds are indicated.

(*Dee—Iehúsoz*) See the *48 Claves*. Dee placed an accent on the second syllable.

Note:

The similarity between this word and Jesus in Greek (*Iesous*) and Hebrew (*Ieshuah*).

See also *Rit*, which probably stands for the more generalized concept of mercy.

Compare from *Loagaeth*:

Ihehudetha, Ihehudz, Ihehusch, Iehuscoth, Iehusa, Iehuded, Gehudan

Iga (ii-ga)* [I + "GA"] *comp.* Is 31

11.30 . . . whose number *is 31*.

Pronunciation notes:

(*Dee—I ga*) Two syllables. The *I* stands alone, and the *g* likely takes its hard sound.

Il (ii-el)* [I + L] *comp.* Is One

5.55 . . . our Lord and Master *is all one*.

Note:

Do not confuse this compound with the singular word "Yl" (thy).

Pronunciation notes:

(*Dee—i l*) Two syllables—both letters stand alone.

(*Dee—i-L*) See the *48 Claves*. This note matches that from *TFR*.

"Yl" (yil) *pron., sing.* Thy

Compounds:

Daxil (daks-il) ["Dax" + "Yl"] Thy Loins

Pronunciation note:

The "I" in this word element should sound like "y." Both letters form one syllable together. See *Yls*, *Ylsi*, etc.

Also:

Yls (yils) Thou

Note:

Do not confuse this word with the compound *Il* (is one).

Ili (Il-lii)* *n.* (The) First/(At) First

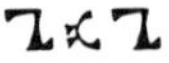

3.28 *In the first* I made you . . .

Pronunciation note:

(**Dee—ILI)* Dee give us little clue here.
(**Dee—í-lí)* See the *48 Claves*. Dee indicates two syllables. For some reason, he has accent marks on both *I*s. (I have left the accent on the first syllable in my pronunciation.) Both *I*s are likely long vowels.

Note:

This word is a palindrome, spelled the same forward and backward. Also see *La* (the First).

Probable root:

L (el) First, One

Yls (yils)* *pron., sing.* Thou

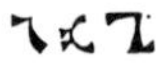

15.1 O *thou* the governor . . .
**16.1 O *thou* second flame . . .
16.20 . . . great art *thou* . . .
17.1 O *thou* third flame . . .
18.1 O *thou* mighty light . . .

Pronunciation notes:

(**Dee 17.1—ILS*)

(**Dee 16.20—Yls as Yils*)

(**Dee 18.1—Ils*) One syllable. Dee sometimes wrote this word with an initial *I*. However, he shows us in word 16.20 that the "Y" sound is intended. (I have used the *Y* in all versions of the word in this Lexicon.)

Note:

**The transmission of the first twelve words of Key Sixteen is missing from Dee's journals. We have only the English given on *TFR*, p. 194. Illemese also gives word 16.1 later, on *TFR*, p. 200. Plus, the word appears in Dee's *48 Claves*.

Also:

"Yl" (yil)	Thy
Ylsi (yil-sii)	Thee

Note:

These words indicate "you" in a singular sense—such as, "I am speaking to you." Also see *Nonci*, which indicates "you" in the plural sense—such as, "I am speaking to all of you."

Probable root:

L (el)	First

Possible shared root:

Aqlo (AY-kwah-loh)	Thy
Bolp (bohlp)	Be Thou

Ylsi (yil-sii)* *pron.* Thee

17.13 . . . living lamps going before *thee* . . .

Pronunciation notes:

(**Dee—Yl si*) Two syllables. The first syllable sounds like "yil," as shown with the phonetic notes for the word *Yls* (thou). The final *i* should take a long sound.

Also:

"Yl" (yil)	Thy
Yls (yils)	Thou

Note:

These words indicate "you" in a singular sense.
Also see *Nonci*, which indicates "you" in the plural sense.

Probable root:

L (el) — First, One

Possible shared root:

Aqlo (AY-kwah-loh) — Thy
Bolp (bohlp) — Be Thou

Imvamar (im-vay-mar)* *v.* — To Apply unto

3.77 . . . and *apply yourselves unto us* as unto partakers . . .

Pronunciation notes:

(**Dee—It is Im ua mar*) Likely three syllables. The *u* preceding an *a* likely takes the hard "v" sound.
(**Dee—Im-uâ-mar*) See the *48 Claves*. Dee places a circumflex over the first *a* to indicate the long vowel sound.

Note:

To "apply" something is to "bring it into action" or "put it into operation." Perhaps even more important here, it also means "to employ diligently or with close attention." (As in "to apply yourself to your studies.") Both of these senses of the word fit perfectly in Angelic invocations such as the Keys.

Inoas (in-OH-as)* [I + Noas] *comp.* — Are / Have Become

7.11 . . . and *they are become* 28 living dwellings . . .

Pronunciation notes:

(**Dee—In ó as*) Three syllables, with an accent upon the second syllable. In Early Modern English, the *oa* letter combination makes a long "o" sound (as in the English words *boat* and *coat*). Dee represents this by having the *o* stand alone in his phonetic note.
(**Dee—inóas*) See the *48 Claves*. The accent is again shown on the second syllable.

"Insi" (in-sii) *v.* To Walk

Compounds:

Dsinsi (dee-sin-sii) [Ds + "Insi"] Which Walkest

Ioiad (joh-JAD)* *prop. n.* Him That Liveth Forever

2.52 . . . I am of *Him that liveth forever* . . .

Pronunciation notes:

(**Dee—Ioiad*) Dee does not indicate a "y" sound here, nor does the *I* stand alone. Also note the existence of *Geiad* and *Gohed*—both starting with a soft "g" or "j" sound. Therefore I assume a "j" sound is intended for *Ioiad*, and I have spelled the word in Angelical with an initial Ged (J). I have adopted the accent from similar words.

Also:

"Iadoias" (jad-oh-JAS) Eternal God

Note:

I have found the title "He Who Lives Forever" attributed to God in *1 Enoch*, 6:1.

Probable root:

Ia (yah) n/a

Iad (yad) God

Shared root:

Geiad (jej-AYD) Lord and Master

Gohed (joh-ED) One Everlasting . . .

Iadpil (ii-AD-pil) (To) Him

Oiad (oh-ii-AD) (Of) God

Piad (pii-AD) Your God

Yolcam (yol-kam)* *v.* Bring Forth (i.e., To Bear)

30.127 *Bring forth* with those that increase.

Pronunciation notes:

(**Dee—Yol cam*) Two syllables.

Also:

Yolci (yol-sii) To Bring Forth

Yolci (yol-sii)* *v.* To Bring Forth

10.58 One rock *bringeth forth* 1000 . . .

Pronunciation notes:

(**Dee—Yol Ci*) Two syllables. The *c* likely takes the softer "s" sound, as it precedes an *i* (as in the English words *circle* and *circus*).

Also:

Yolcam (yol-kam) Bring Forth

Yor (yor)* *v.* To Roar

10.40 . . . *roar* with a hundred mighty earthquakes . . .

Pronunciation notes:

(**Dee—Yor*) One syllable, with an initial "Y" sound.

Ip (ip)* *adv.* Not

9.68 Come away, and *not* your vials.
10.82 Come away, but *not* your noises.

Pronunciation notes:

(**Dee 9.68; 10.82—Ip*) One syllable. The *I* should be short.

Compounds:

Odipuran (ohd-II-pew-ran) [Od + Ip + "Puran"] And Shall Not See
Pageip (pay-jee-ip) ["Page" + Ip] Rest Not

Probable root:

I (ii) Is

Note:

The word *Ip* appears to be a conjugation of *I*. The addition of the *p* accomplishes the transmutation of "to be"—or "is"—into "not be." See also *Ul* (end)—an antonymic transmutation of *L* (the first).

Probable root for:

Ipam (ip-am) [I + "Pam"] — Is Not
Ipamis (ip-am-is) [I + "Pamis"] — Can Not Be
Ripir (rii-PIR) — No Place

Note:

Also see "Ge" (not), Ag (none), "Pam" (not) and "Pamis" (cannot).

"Ip" (ip) *pron.* — Her

Compounds:

Ixomaxip (iks-oh-MAKS-ip) ["Ix" + Omax + "Ip"] — Let Her Be Known

In this example, the "Ip" obviously doesn't indicate *not*. It is uncertain, but it may indicate *her*. There is only one relative example (see below), which is itself just as uncertain.

Also:

"Pi" (pii) — She
Pii (pii-ii) ["Pi" + I] — She Is

Note:

Also see *Tilb* (her).

Ipam (ip-am) [I + "Pam"] *comp.* — Is Not

1.57 . . . whose *beginning is not* . . .

The Angelical for "beginning" (*Croodzi*) does not appear here.

Also:

Ipamis (ip-am-is) [I + "Pamis"] — Cannot Be

Note:

The word *I* (is/are) very likely stands for "is" in Ipam, and "be" in *Ipamis*. The change from "Pam" to "Pamis" seems to change the tense, and therefore the usage of *I*.

Probable shared root:

Ip (ip) Not

Ipamis (ip-am-is)* [I + "Pamis"] *comp.* Cannot Be

1.59 . . . nor end *cannot be* . . .

Pronunciation notes:

(**Dee—the A pronounced short*)

(**Dee—Ipâmis*) See *48 Claves*. Note the circumflex over the *a*—which should indicate a long sound. However, this conflicts with the short *a* Dee noted in *TFR*.

Also:

Ipam (ip-am) [I + "Pam"] Is Not

Note:

The word *I* (is/are) very likely stands for "is" in *Ipam*, and "be" in *Ipamis*. The change from "Pam" to "Pamis" seems to change the tense.

Probable shared root:

Ip (ip) Not

"Ipuran" (Il-pew-ran) [Ip + "Puran"] *comp.* Shall Not See

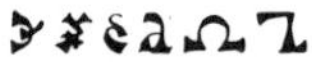

Compounds:

Odipuran (ohd-Il-pew-ran) [Od + Ip + "Puran"] And Shall Not See

"Irgil" (ir-jil) *comp.* How Many

Compounds:

Irgilchisda (ir-jil-KIIS-da) ["Irgil" + Chis + "Da"]

How Many Are There

Note:

Also see *Plosi* (as many).

Irgilchisda (ir-jil-KIIS-da)* ["Irgil" + Chis + "Da"] *comp.* How Many Are There

8.21 . . . *how many are there* which remain . . .

Pronunciation notes:

(*Dee—Ir gil chís da*) Four syllables, with an accent on the third syllable. Also see *Chis* (are) for more pronunciation notes.

(*Dee—Irgil chís da*) See the *48 Claves*. Dee again indicates the accent on the third syllable.

Yrpoil (yur-POY-il)* *n.* Division

30.48 . . . and let there be *division* in her . . .

Pronunciation notes:

(*Dee—Yr pó il*) Three syllables, with an accent on the second syllable. The *r* should likely take the "ur" sound. In Early Modern English, the *oi* letter combination should make an "oy" sound (as in the words *oil* and *boil*). See pronunciation notes for *Poilp* (divided).

(*Dee—yrpóil*) See the *48 Claves*. Here, Dee again placed the accent on the second syllable.

Also:

Poilp (poylp) Divided

Isalman (ii-SAYL-man)* [I + Salman] *comp.* Is a House

7.2 . . . *is a house* of virgins . . .

Pronunciation notes:

(*Dee—I Sal man*) Three syllables. The *I* stands alone. The capital *S may* indicate the accent.

(**Dee—isâlman*) See the *48 Claves*. Dee placed a circumflex over the first *a* to indicate its long sound.

Isro (iz-roh)* *comp.* Promise of

13.15 . . . Behold *the promise of* God . . .

Pronunciation notes:
(**Dee—Is ro*) Two syllables. I have represented the *s* as a *z* in my pronunciation, for a sound similar to the English word *is*. The final *o* is likely a long vowel.

Also:
Aisro (ay-ii-sroh) Promise of

Note:
It is possible that the *-o* affix (of) is in use here.
Also see *Sibsi* (covenant), *Surzas* (sworn), and *Znrza* (swore).

Ita (ii-tay)* [I + Ta] *comp.* Is as

8.2 . . . *is as* the 3rd heaven . . .

Pronunciation notes:
(**Dee—I ta*) Two syllables. The initial *I* stands alone.

Iudra (jood-ra) n/a

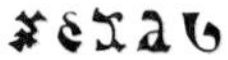

Note:
See *Five Books*, p. 366. The Angel Illemese appears to Dee and Kelley with a bundle of empty boxes that he calls virtuous. When Dee asks for an explanation, Illemese says, "Will you have my bill? [. . .] I will show it. Serve it, where you list. *Iudra galgol astel.*" Dee states that he and Kelley do not understand, and wish to know how it can be served. But Illemese never offers definitions for these Angelical words.

Pronunciation notes:

Because the initial *I* precedes a *u*, I suspect this word should begin with the "j" consonant sound. I have spelled the word in Angelical with an initial Ged (J).

"Ium" (jay-um) *v.* (Is) Called

Compounds:

Dsium (dee-sii-um) [Ds + "Ium"] Which Is Called

Also:

Iumd (jay-umd) (Is) Called

Note:

"Ium" / *Iumd* is translated as "is called." However, it is unlikely that this is a compound word, and thus the *I* should not stand for "is." (The pronunciation of the *i* as "j" may support this.) I have spelled this word in Angelical with an initial Ged (J).

Iumd (jay-umd)* *v.* (Is) Called

13.20 . . . which *is called* amongst you . . .
18.18 . . . which *is called* in thy kingdom . . .

Pronunciation notes:

(**Dee 13.20—J umbd*)

(**Dee 18.18—I umd*) Two syllables. The note Dee gave us with word 13.20 is the most useful. It lets us know that the initial *I* actually takes a "J" sound. For that reason, I have spelled this word in Angelical with an initial Ged (J). Then, Dee shows us that the first part of the second syllable sounds like "umb"—as in the English words *dumb* and *numb*. Therefore, the *u* takes its short sound.

Also:

"Ium" (jay-um) (Is) Called

Note:

See the note at "Ium."

Ivonph (ii-VONV)* [I + Vonph] *comp.* Is Wrath

12.22 . . . whose name amongst you *is wrath* . . .

Pronunciation notes:

(**Dee—I vonph*) Two syllables. The initial *I* stands alone. The *nph* should be similar to the *nf* in *Sonf* (reign). I have represented the sound in my pronunciation with an *nv*—where the *v* indicates a sound somewhere between a hard *f* and a very soft *v*.

I have adopted the accent from *Ivonpovnph* (is wrath in anger).

Ivonpovnph (ii-VON-foh-unv)* [I + "Vonpo" + "Vnph"] *comp.*

Is Wrath in Anger

17.15 . . . whose God *is wrath in anger* . . .

Pronunciation notes:

(**Dee—I von po vnph*) Four syllables. The initial *I* stands alone. The *p* in the third syllable is likely a *ph* digraph (see *Vonph*, *Vonpho*). The *o* in the third syllable is likely long. In the fourth syllable, Dee originally wrote a *v*—although it should take the "u" sound before a consonant. (Therefore, the *vn* should create the sound of "un"—with a short *u*.) Finally, the last three letters, *nph*, should be similar to the *nf* in words like *Sonf* (reign). I have written this sound as *nv* in my pronunciation—indicating a sound somewhere between a hard *f* and a very soft *v*.

(**Dee—i vónpôvnph*) See the *48 Claves*. Here, Dee placed an accent over the initial *o* in the second syllable. He also placed a circumflex over the second *o* to confirm its long sound.

Note:

This word is translated literally as "is wrath of wrath." The word *anger* is not actually indicated by the Angelical; it is simply a gloss to make the English make more sense. The basic idea is "intense wrath."

Further compounds:

Ivonph (ii-VONV) [I + Vonph] Is Wrath

Iurehoh (jur-AY-hoh)* *n.?* "What Christ Did in Hell"**

Pronunciation notes:

(**Dee—iuréhoh*) Because the initial *I* precedes a *u*, I suspect this word should begin with the "J" consonant sound. Thus, I have spelled this word in Angelical with an initial Ged (J). Then, the *eh* should make a long "a" vowel sound. Finally, the *oh* should combine to form a long "o" sound. Dee placed and accent over the *e*.

From *Loagaeth*:

(***Dee—This last word was hid a pretty while with a rim like a thin bladder before it. And when it was perfectly seen then there appeared a bloody cross over it. It is a word signifying what Christ did in hell.*) See the *Five Books*, p. 323. This is a reference to an obscure Christian legend (called *Descensus Ad Inferos*) in which Christ—during his three days in the Tomb—actually descended into Hell. While there, he literally stormed the place—smashing open gates, knocking down bridges, and liberating a number of souls who had been wrongly entrapped there. This is a controversial legend, mentioned in passing in the Apostles' Creed.

Iusmach (jus-mak) *adj.?* Begotten*

From *Loagaeth*:

(**Dee—Begotten.*) See the *Five Books*, p. 319.

Pronunciation notes:

Because the initial *I* precedes a *u*, I suspect this word should begin with the "J" consonant sound. Thus, I have spelled it in Angelical with an initial Ged (J).

"Ix" (iks) *v.* Let

Compounds:

Ixomaxip (iks-oh-MAKS-ip) ["Ix" + Omax + "Ip"] Let Her Be Known

Ixomaxip (iks-oh-MAKS-ip)* ["Ix" + Omax + "Ip"] *comp.*

Let Her Be Known

30.107 . . . one while *let her be known* . . .

Pronunciation notes:

(**Dee—Ix o máx ip*) This is likely four syllables, with an accent on the third syllable. The *o* stands alone.

Note:

While the word for "her" (*Tilb*) does not appear here, and the *-ip* obviously can't stand for "not," I should point out that the word for "she" appears as *Pi* in another isolated case.

Also note that the *omax* (knowest) element of this word has the *-ax* suffix to indicate action.

Izazaz (ii-zay-zaz)* *v.* To Frame (i.e., To Form)

2.11 . . . burning flames *have framed* within the depths of my jaws . . .

Pronunciation notes:

(**Dee—Izazaz*) Dee gives us little clue here.

(**Dee—I-zâ-zaz*) See *48 Claves*. Three syllables. The initial *I* stands alone. The first *a* has a circumflex, indicating that it takes its long sound.

Izizop (iz-is-op)* *n.* (Your?) Vessels

3.44 . . . that *from your highest vessels* and the corners . . .

Pronunciation notes:

(**Dee—Izizop*) Apparently three syllables. As we see in the pronunciation notes for *Zizop* (vessels), the second *z* takes on an "s" sound.

Note:

This is not a compound word, so the *I* does not indicate "is." I have noted that the word *I* can sometimes conjugate Angelical words in various ways. Therefore, perhaps the addition of *I* in this case indicates "your"?

Also:

Zizop (zis-op) Vessels

Ur (L)

L (el)* *prop. n.* — The First, One

2.8 . . . o you the second of *the first* . . .
5.27 . . . brothers of *the first* and second . . .

Pronunciation notes:

(**Dee 2.8—A word*)

(**Dee5.27—L*) Pronounced as we would the name of the letter *L*.

Compounds:

Agltoltorn (ag-el-tol-torn) [Ag + L + "Toltorn"]	No One Creature
Crpl (krip-el) ["Crp" + L]	But One
Il (ii-el) [I + L]	Is One
Lcapimao (el-ka-PII-may-oh) [L + "Capimao"]	One While
Lel (el-el) [L + El]	Same
Lialprt (el-YAL-purt) [L + "Ialprt"]	First Flame
Lnibm (el-nib-em) [L + "Nibm"]	One season
Lpatralx (el-PAY-tralks) [L + "Patralx"]	One Rock
Lsmnad (els-mad) [L + "Smnad"]	One Another

Also:

El (el)	The First
La (lah or el-ah)	The First
"Lo" (loh)	The First
Lu (loo)	From One

Note:

Compare to the name of the Angel *L* (or *El*), one of the Sons of the Sons of Light. His name literally translates as "The First."

Possible root for:

Aqlo (AY-kwah-loh)	Thy
Bolp (bohlp)	Be Thou
Daxil (daks-il)	Thy Loins
Ili (ii-EL-ii)	At First
Yls (yils)	Thou
Lil (el-il)	"The First Aethyr"

Ol (ohl)	I
Qaal (kwah-AY-el)	Creator
Ul (yewl)	End
Uls (yewls)	Ends

La (lah *or* el-ah)* *n.* The First

5.38 . . . *the first*, ends, and contents of time . . .

Pronunciation notes:

(*Dee—La*) Dee seems to indicate one syllable here. However, other words that have *L* (the first) as their root tend to pronounce the *L* as if it stands alone. I have offered both options in my pronunciation.

Also:

L (el)	The First
El (el)	The First
"Lo" (loh)	The First
Lu (loo)	From One

Note:

Also see *Ili* (at first).

Laiad (lay-II-ad)* *n.* Secrets of Truth

18.13 . . . in whom *the secrets of truth* . . .

Pronunciation notes:

(*Dee—La i ad*) Three syllables. The first *a* is likely long. The *i* stands alone.

(*Dee—Laíad*) See the *48 Claves*. Here, Dee placed an accent over the *i* in the second syllable.

Note:

Compare to the name of the Angel *Laidrom*, an Elder of the Southern Watchtower. It is possible that *Laidrom* is a compound of *Laiad* (secrets of truth) and *Om* (understand)—"He Who Understands the Secrets of Truth." (Unless, of course, *Rom* is a word unto itself.)

Probable root:

Ia (yah) — n/a

Iad (yad) — God

Probable shared root:

Iadnah (yad-nah) — Knowledge

Iaiadix (yay-II-ad-iks) — Honor

Lang (lang) *prop. n.* — Those Who Serve

From *Corpus Omnium*:

Associated with the post-Deluge quadrant of the Table. Translated in Latin as *Ministrantes* (Those Who Serve).

Compare from *Loagaeth*:

Lang, Langed

Note:

Also see *Cnoqod* (servants).

Lansh (lonsh)* *n.* — Exalted Power

1.7 . . . *in power exalted above* the firmaments . . .

Pronunciation notes:

(**Dee—LANSH as Lonsh*)

Also:

Lonsa (lon-sha) — Power

Lonshi (lon-shii) — Power

"Lonshin" (lon-shin) — Powers

Note:

Also see *Micalzo* (power/mighty), *Naneel* (my power).

Lap (lap)* *conj.* — For (Because)

(RFP) *For*, I am the servant . . .

2.32 *For*, you are become a building . . .

2.50 *For*, I am of him . . .

Pronunciation notes:

(**Dee 1.81—Call it Lap*)

(**Dee 2.32, 50—Lap*)

Note:

Also see *Bagle* (for), *Darsar* (wherefore)

Compare from *Loagaeth*:

Lap

Larag (lay-rag)* *conj.* Neither/Nor

10.51 . . . rest not *neither* know any (long) time here.

Pronunciation notes:

(**Dee—La rag*) Two syllables. The *a* is likely long. The final *g* is likely hard, as in the English words *rag* and *bag*.

Note:

The word *neither* can be a conjunction, adjective, or pronoun depending on use. Here in Key Ten, it is used as a conjunction.

"Las" (las) *adj.* Rich

Compounds:

Lasollor (las-OHL-or) ["Las" + "Ollor"] Rich Man

Compare from *Loagaeth*:

Las, Laz

Lasdi (las-dii)* *n.* (My) Feet

4.2 . . . I have set *my feet* in the south . . .

Pronunciation notes:

(**Dee—Las di*) Two syllables. The final *i* is likely a long vowel.

Also:

Lusd (lus-dee) Feet
Lusda (lus-da) Feet
Lusdan (lus-dan) Feet

Lasollor (las-OHL-or)* ["Las" + "Ollor"] *comp.* Rich Man

9.32 . . . as the *rich man* doth his treasure . . .

Pronunciation notes:

(**Dee—Las ol lor*) Three syllables. The *o* is likely long, while the other two vowels remain short. The two *ls* combine into a single sound, as in the English word *lesson*.

(**Dee—las óllor*) See the *48 Claves*. Here, Dee placed an accent over the second syllable.

Lava (lav-ah) *n.* Fervency/Humility?*

Note:

(**Dee—Laua Zuraah = Use humility in prayers to God, that is fervently pray. It signifieth, Pray Unto God*.) See the *Five Books*, p. 324. Between lines 46 and 47 of Table One of *Loagaeth*, some kind of stormy interference erupted in the shewstone. A voice then said the phrase "*Laua Zuraah*." The two men then prayed as instructed, and the interference cleared. It would appear that *Laua* indicates a specific attitude in prayer, which might mean fervency or humility. I don't believe *Laua* would be the standard Angelical word for either "fervent" or "humility."

Also compare this word to the name of the Part of the Earth (and its Angelic Governor), *Lauacon*.

Compare from *Loagaeth*:

Lauax

Lcapimao (el-kay-PII-may-oh)* [L + "Capimao"] *comp.* One While

30.106 . . . *one while* let her be known . . .

Pronunciation notes:

(**Dee—L ca pí ma o*) Five syllables, with an accent on the third syllable. The initial *L* and the final *o* each stand alone. Finally, I assume the *a* in the fourth syllable is long, because it is followed by an *o*.

(**Dee—L capîmao*) See the *48 Claves*. Here, Dee placed a circumflex over the *i* to indicate its long sound.

Lea (lee-ay) *prop. n.* "The Sixteenth Aethyr"

30.3 . . . which dwell in *the sixteenth aethyr* . . .

Note:

This (word 30.3) is the single space in the Key of the Aethyrs, which must be changed for each invocation—replacing word 30.3 with the name of the appropriate Aethyr. No established definitions were given for these names.

Lea contains the three Parts of the Earth *Cucarpt*, *Lauacon*, and *Sochial*.

Lel (el-el)* [L + El] *adv.* Same

30.73 . . . no creature upon or within her *the same* . . .

Pronunciation notes:

(**Dee—Lel*) Dee gives us little clue here. This could be a word of one or two syllables, depending on whether or not the initial *L* should stand alone. Since I have assumed this is a compound involving the word *L* (first), I have decided to allow the initial *L* to stand alone. (Note I have also assumed the *e* is a phonetic gloss.)

Note:

The basic concepts behind *L*/*El* are both "beginning" and "singularity." Thus, I feel it is important that it appears twice in this word—to indicate that two (or more) things are actually "one" (the same).

The word *same* can be an adjective, pronoun, or adverb, depending on use. Here in Key Thirty, it is used as an adverb.

Note:

Also see *Parach* (equal).

Lephe (leef-ay) n/a*

Note:

(**Dee—Life Lephe Lurfando is a strong charge to the wicked to tell the truth. This [the Angel] said to my demand of this phrase whereof I had mention many years since.*) See the *Five Books*, p. 308. *Life Lephe Lurfando* is a perfect phrase for use in goetic evocations, but we are never given specific definitions for each word.

(**Dee—Pinzu-a lephe ganiurax kelpadman pacaph.*) See the *Five Books*, p. 413. Kelley overhears many voices singing a song at some distance, and these are the words Dee recorded. No translations are suggested.

Compare from *Loagaeth*:

Lefa, Lefe, Leph, Life

Levithmong (lev-ith-mong)* *n.* Beasts of the Field

30.99 Let them become caves for *the beasts of the field*.

Pronunciation notes:

(**Dee—Levith mong*) Three syllables. I assume *mong* rhymes with the English word *song*.

Note:

The similarity between this word and *Leviathan*. Leviathan is a mythical sea creature mentioned in biblical literature (especially *1 Enoch*), who is destined to battle a mighty land creature named *Behemoth* during the End Times (apparently representing a clash of land and sea). It would appear that *Levithmong* (beasts of the field) is a combination of the *Leviathan* and *Behemoth* concepts.

Lialprt (el-YAL-purt)* [L + "Ialprt"] *comp.* First Flame

15.3 . . . the governer of *the First Flame* . . .

Note:

The transmission of Key Fifteen is missing from Dee's journals. We only have the English given for the Key on *TFR*, p. 193. However, Illemese gives the pronunciation later on *TFR*, p. 200. Plus, the word appears in Dee's *48 Claves*.

Pronunciation notes:

(**Illemese—L al purt*) See *TFR*, p. 200. Three syllables. Though Illemese seems to have dropped the sound of the *i*, I think this is merely because it barely makes a sound when this word is spoken fluently. I have retained it (sounding as "y") in my pronunciation.

(**Dee—Liálprt*) See the *48 Claves*. Here, Dee placed an accent over the *a* in the second syllable.

Life (liif) n/a*

Note:

(**Dee—Life Lephe Lurfando is a strong charge to the wicked to tell the truth. This [the Angel] said to my demand of this phrase whereof I had mention many years since.*) See the *Five Books*, p. 308. *Life Lephe Lurfando* is a perfect phrase for use in goetic evocations, but we are never given specific definitions for each word.

Compare from *Loagaeth*:

Lefa, Lefe, Leph, Life

Lil (el-il)* *prop. n.* "The First Aethyr"

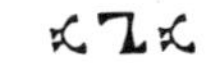

30.3 . . . which dwell in *the first aethyr* . . .

Pronunciation notes:

(**Dee—Lil*) Dee gives us little clue here. This could be a word of one or two syllables—depending on if the initial *L* should stand alone. Because this word indicates the First Aethyr and likely has *L* (the first) as its root, I will assume the *L* should stand alone.

Note:

Lil is the name—probably of a descriptive nature—of the first of the thirty Aethyrs. It holds the single space in the Key of the Aethyrs, which must be changed for each invocation, replacing Lil with the name of the next Aethyr, and then the next, and so on.

Lil contains the three Parts of the Earth *Occodon*, *Pascomb*, and *Valgars*.

Probable root:

L (el) — First

Lilonon (lii-loh-non)* *n.* — Branches

10.10 . . . whose *branches* are 22 nests . . .

Pronunciation notes:

(**Dee—Li lo non*) Three syllables. The *i* and the first *o* both appear to take their long sounds.

(**Dee—Lilônon*) See the *48 Claves*. Here, Dee uses a circumflex over the first *o* to indicate its long sound.

Limlal (lim-lal)* *n.* — Treasure

9.34 . . . as the rich man doth *his treasure*.

Pronunciation notes:

(**Dee—Lim lal*) Two syllables. Both vowels appear to take their short sounds.

Lin (lin) *prop. n.* — "The Twenty-Second Aethyr"

30.3 . . . which dwell in *the twenty-second aethyr* . . .

Note:

This (word 30.3) is the single space in the Key of the Aethyrs, which must be changed for each invocation—replacing word 30.3 with the name of the appropriate Aethyr. No established definitions were given for these names.

Lin contains the three Parts of the Earth *Ozidaia*, *Paraoan*, *Calzirg*.

Lit (lit) *prop. n.* — "The Fifth Aethyr"

30.3 . . . which dwell in *the fifth aethyr* . . .

Note:

This (word 30.3) is the single space in the Key of the Aethyrs, which must be changed for each invocation—replacing word 30.3 with the name of the appropriate Aethyr. No established definitions were given for these names.

Lit contains the three Parts of the Earth *Lazdixi*, *Nocamal*, and *Tiarpax*.

Lnibm (el-nib-em)* [L + "Nibm"] *comp.* — One Season

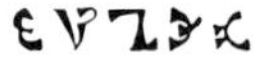

30.64 . . . *one season*, let it confound another . . .

Pronunciation notes:

(**Dee—L nib m*) Three syllables. The *L* and *m* each stand alone.

"Lo" (loh) *n.* — The First

Compounds:

Bazemlo (bas-em-loh) [Bazem + "Lo"] — The Midday the First

Talo (tay-el-oh) [Ta + "Lo"] — As the First

Also:

L (el) — First

El (el) — The First

La (lah or el-ah) — First

Lu (loo) — From One

Possible root for:

Aqlo (AY-kwah-loh) — Thy

Bolp (bohlp) — Be Thou

Ol (ohl) — I

Loagaeth (loh-gah)* *n.* Speech from God**

Pronunciation note:

(**Dee, recording the words of Galvah—"Touching the Book, it shall be called Logah: which in your language signifieth Speech from God. Write [it] after this sort: L O A G A E T H: it is to be sounded Logah. This word is of great signification, I mean in respect of the profoundness thereof."*) See *TFR*, p. 19. In Early Modern English, the *oa* letter combination makes a long "o" sound (as in the English words *boat* and *coat*). Dee recorded Galvah's phonetic explanation by dropping the *a* (*it shall be called Logah*). At the same time, we see that the final *eth* are entirely silent.

Note:

**This is the name of the Holy Book of forty-nine Tables transmitted to Dee and Kelley by the Archangel Raphael. It also appears as the first word of the forty-ninth Table in the Holy Book (see "Compare from *Loagaeth*" below).

Note the similarity between the Angelical *Loagaeth*, the Greek *Logos* (Word), and the Hebrew *Eth* (Spirit). It is interesting that both *Loagaeth* and *Logos* indicate "word/speech" and both are used in the biblical sense (as a reference to the God-Christ—see John 1, "In the Beginning was the Word . . . and the Word was God.").

Possible shared root:

Logaah (loh-gay-ah) n/a

Compare from *Loagaeth*:

Loagaeth, Loangah, Loggahah

Loe (loh-ee) *prop. n.* "The Twelfth Aethyr"

30.3 . . . which dwell in *the twelfth aethyr* . . .

Note:

This (word 30.3) is the single space in the Key of the Aethyrs, which must be changed for each invocation—replacing word 30.3 with the name of the appropriate Aethyr. No established definitions were given for these names.

Loe contains the three Parts of the Earth *Tapamal, Gedoons*, and *Ambriol*.

Logaah (loh-gay-ah) n/a

Possibly also:

Loagaeth (loh-gah) Speech from God

Note:

See *TFR*, p. 22. Here, the guardian Angel of Lord Lasky of Poland says a prayer on Lasky's behalf, which ends with, "*Grant this Camascheth galsuagath garnastel zurah logaah luseroth.*" No translation is offered.

Loholo (LOH-hoh-loh)* *v.* To Shine

1.61 . . . which *shineth as* a flame . . .

Pronunciation notes:

(**Dee—Call it Loholo. Long, the first syllable accented*) I assume that Dee intended all the *o*'s in this word to be long.

(**Dee—lóhôlo*) See *48 Claves*. The accent and circumflex match Dee's note from *TFR*.

"Lolcis" (LOL-sis) *n.* Bucklers

Compounds:

Talolcis (tay-LOL-sis) [Ta + "Lolcis"] As Bucklers

Loncho (lon-koh)* *v.* To Fall

8.30 . . . until this house *fall* and the dragon sink.

Pronunciation notes:

(**Dee—Lon cho or ko*) Two syllables. Dee indicates that the *ch* takes the harder "k" (or "kh") sound.

Note:

Also see *Dobix* (to fall).

Compare from *Loagaeth*:
Onchen

Londoh (lon-DOH)* *n.* Kingdoms

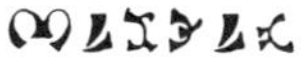

7.24 Whose *kingdoms* and continuance are as . . .

Pronunciation notes:
(**Dee—Lon dóh*) This appears to be two syllables, with an accent upon the second syllable.
(**Dee—londóh*) See *48 Claves*. Accent still on the second syllable.

Compounds:
Oslondoh (os-LON-doh) [Os + Londoh] 12 Kingdoms

Note:
The similarity between this word and the word *London*. Dee was very dedicated to the cause of the English empire—and many scholars suspect this word of bias on Dee's part rather than the Angels. For a parallel case, see *Madrid* (iniquity).

Also:
Adohi (ay-DOH-hii) Kingdom

Compare from *Loagaeth*:
Doh, Dohoh

Lonsa (lon-sha)* *n.* Power

3.37 . . . *power* successively over 456 . . .

Pronunciation notes:
(**Dee—Lonsa*) Likely two syllables. Based on the other versions of this word, I assume the *s* should make the *sh* digraph.

Also:
Lansh (lonsh) Exalted Power
Lonshi (lon-shii) Power
"Lonshin" (lon-shin) Powers

Lonshi (lon-shii)* *n.* Power

7.45 . . . this remembrance is given *power* . . .

Pronunciation notes:

(**Dee—Lon shi*) Two syllables. The *o* should be a short vowel, while the final *i* likely takes a long sound.

Compounds:

Lonshitox (lon-shii-toks) [Lonshi + Tox] His Power

Also:

Lansh (lonsh) Exalted Power

Lonsa (lon-sha) Power

"Lonshin" (lon-shin) Powers

"Lonshin" (lon-shin) *n.* Powers

Compounds:

Odlonshin (ohd-lon-shin) [Od + "Lonshin"] And Powers

Also:

Lansh (lonsh) Exalted Power

Lonsa (lon-sha) Power

Lonshi (lon-shii) Power

Lonshitox (lon-shii-toks)* [Lonshi + Tox] *comp.* His Power

13.18 . . . God and *his power* . . .

Pronunciation notes:

(**Dee—Lon shi tox*) Three syllables. The *i* is the only apparent long vowel.

(**Dee—Lon-shi-tox*) See the *48 Claves*. This note essentially matches that of *TFR*.

Lorslq (lors-el-kwah)* *n.* Flowers

2.1 . . . as *the flowers* in their beauty . . .

Pronunciation notes:

(**Dee—Lors l qua*) Three syllables, with the *l* and the *q* standing alone. (The *q* takes the sound of "kwah.")

(**Dee—lors-l-q*) See *48 Claves*. This note matches Dee's note from *TFR*.

Lpatralx (el-PAY-tralks)* [L + "Patralx"] *comp.* One Rock

10.57 . . . *one rock* bringeth forth 1000 . . .

Pronunciation notes:

(**Dee—L Pá tralx El*) Three syllables. The initial L stands alone, and Dee indicates that it sounds like "El." The first *a* is likely a long vowel. The accent is place on the second syllable.

Lrasd (el-RAZD)* *v.* To Dispose (To Place)

30.34 . . . *to dispose* all things according to . . .

Pronunciation notes:

(**Dee—L rásd*) Two syllables, with an accent on the second syllable. The intial *L* stands alone.

(**Dee—Lrásd*) See the *48 Claves*. Here, Dee again placed an accent on the second syllable.

Lring (el-ring)* *v.* To Stir Up

13.6 . . . 42 eyes *to stir up* wrath of sin . . .

Pronunciation notes:

(**Dee—LRING*) Dee does not indicate that the *r* should take its extended "ur" sound. Therefore, I suspect the *L* should stand alone in this word, making two syllables.

Note:

See also *Zixlay* (to stir up). I am not sure why these two words have the same definition.

Lsmnad (els-mad)* [L + "Smnad"] *comp.* One Another

30.87 . . . vex and weed out *one another* . . .

Pronunciation notes:

(**Dee—Ls mnad*) This note seems confusing at first. Dee indicates two syllables, yet there are still clusters of consonants in each one. In the first syllable, I assume the *l* is pronounced "el"—which allows it to combine naturally with the *s*. In the second syllable, I suspect the *mn* combines to form the same sound as in the English words *column*, *autumn*, and *solemn* (i.e., the *n* is effectively silent).

Note:

Also see *Symp* (another).

Lu (loo) *prep.?* From One*

From *Loagaeth*:

(**Dee—Lu = From one.*) See the *Five Books*, p. 322.

Also:

L (el) The First, One
El (el) The First
La (lah or el-ah) The First
"Lo" (loh) The First

Compare from *Loagaeth*:

Uloh

Luas (loo-akh)* *prop. n.* Those Who Praise (or, the Triumphant)

From *Corpus Omnium*:

Associated with the pre-Deluge quadrant of the Table, translated in Latin as *Laudantes* (Those Who Praise). They can alternately be called *Trimphantes* (Those Who Triumph).

Pronunciation notes:

(**Dee—Luach.*) Dee seems to note here that *Luas*, when spoken, should be ended with a throaty "kh" sound (like the *ch* in ache), instead of an "s" sound.

Compare from *Loagaeth*:

Luah

Lucal (loo-kal)* *n.* North

10.6 . . . harboured *in the north* in the likeness . . .

Pronunciation notes:

(**Dee—Lu cal*) Two syllables. The *u* takes its long sound. I assume the *c* takes its hard ("k") sound.

Luciftian (loo-sif-TII-an)* *n.* (Ornaments of) Brightness

7.19 . . . they are appareled with *ornaments of brightness* . . .

Pronunciation notes:

(**Dee—Lu cif tí an*) Four syllables, with an accent on the third syllable. I assume the *c* takes the soft sound, as in the Latin word *Lucifer*.

Also:

Luciftias (loo-SIF-tii-as) Brightness

Note:

The similarity between this word and the Latin *Lucifer* (light-bearer). See *Luciftias* (brightness) for more info.

Luciftias (loo-SIF-tii-as)* *n.* Brightness

30.20 . . . whose eyes are *the brightness of* the heavens . . .

Pronunciation notes:

(**Dee—Lu cíf ti as*) Four syllables, with an accent on the second syllable. The *c* should take the soft ("s") sound, as in the Latin word *Lucifer*.

(**Dee—Lucíftîas*) See the *48 Claves*. Here, Dee again placed the accent on the second syllable. He also placed a circumflex over the second *i* to indicate its long sound.

Also:

Luciftian (loo-sif-TII-an) (Ornaments of) Brightness

Note:

The similarity between this word and the Latin *Lucifer* (light-bearer). In Roman mythology, Lucifer was the name of the Venus star—which rose in the east just before dawn, thus heralding the approaching Sun. In Christian lore, Lucifer was the first and most beautiful among the Angels, but was cast down for his pride. The Angelical word *Luciftias* still represents brightness in the Heavens, and has no demonic connotations.

Luiahe (loo-JAY-hee)* *n.* Song of Honor

6.40 . . . whose works shall be *a song of honour* . . .

Pronunciation notes:

(**Dee—Lu ía he*) Three syllables, with an accent on the second syllable. Dee does not tell us if the *i* should take the sound of "y" or "j." (I have settled upon the "j" sound., and spelled the word in Angelical with a Ged [J] in this place.) The final *e* is also uncertain. It should remain silent while making the *a* a long vowel. However, Dee's phonetic note indicates three syllables—for which the *e* must make a sound along with the *h*. Whether the *e* should be long or short is unclear, although I have settled upon the long sound.

(**Dee—Lu-iá-he*) See the *48 Claves*. This note matches that from *TFR*.

Note:

Also see *Faaip* (voicing/psalm).

Lulo (loo-loh) *n.* Tartar (Mother of Vinegar)

From the *Alchemical Cipher*:

See *TFR*, pp. 387–89. The Angel *Levanael* says of this word, "*Roxtan* is pure and simple wine in herself. *Lulo* is her mother." Dee replies,

"There may be in these words some ambiguity." So *Levanael* explains more simply, "*Lulo* is Tartar, simply of red wine." (Tartar is Mother of Vinegar.)

It is not likely that *Lulo* is strictly tartar of *red* wine—but *Levanael* had established earlier in this session that red *Roxtan* (wine) was to be used for this alchemical experiment.

Lurfando (lur-fan-doh) n/a*

Note:

(**Dee—Life Lephe Lurfando is a strong charge to the wicked to tell the truth. This [the Angel] said to my demand of this phrase whereof I had mention many years since.*) See the *Five Books*, p. 308. *Life Lephe Lurfando* is a perfect phrase for use in goetic evocations, but we are never given specific definitions for each word.

In at least one case, Dee wrote that a *u* could make the sound of "f"—which was likely an indication of the "v" sound. Therefore, it is possible that *Lurfando* and *Lurvandah* are related.

Compare from *Loagaeth*:

Lurvandah

Lusd (lus-dee)* *n.* (Your) Feet

2.25 . . . stronger are *your feet* than the barren stone.

Pronunciation notes:

(**Dee—Lusd*) It would appear the one syllable is intended here. However, other versions of this word all have two syllables.

Also:

Lasdi (las-dii) (My) Feet

Lusda (lus-da) (Their) Feet

Lusdan (lus-dan) (With) Feet

Lusda (lus-da)* *n.* (Their) Feet

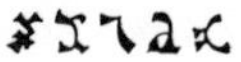

9.21 . . . have settled *their feet* in the west . . .

Pronunciation notes:

(**Dee—Lus da*) Two syllables.

Also:

Lasdi (las-dii) (My) Feet

Lusd (lus-dee) (Your) Feet

Lusdan (lus-dan) (With) Feet

Lusdan (lus-dan)* *n.* (With) Feet

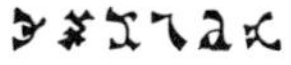

16.13 . . . which walkest upon the earth *with feet* 876 . . .

Pronunciation notes:

(**Dee—Lus dan*) Two syllables.

Also:

Lasdi (las-dii) (My) Feet

Lusd (lus-dee) (Your) Feet

Lusda (lus-da) (Their) Feet

Luseroth (lus-er-oth) n/a

Note:

See *TFR*, p. 22. Here, the guardian Angel of Lord Lasky of Poland says a prayer on Lasky's behalf, which ends with, "Grant this *Camascheth galsuagath garnastel zurah logaah luseroth*." No translation is offered.

Compare from *Loagaeth*:

Luseth, Luza, Luzan, Luzath, Luzed, Lusaz, Luzez, Uzed

"Lzar" (el-ZAR) *n.* — Courses

Compounds:

Sobolzar (soh-BOL-zar) ["Sobo" + "Lzar"] — Whose Courses

Also:

"Elzap" (el-ZAP) — Course

"Lzirn" (el-zirn) *n.* — Wonders

Compounds:

Vaulzirn (VOL-zern) ["Vau" + "Lzirn"] — Work Wonders

Note:

See also *Sald* (wonder), *Busd* (glory), and *Peleh* (Worker of Wonders?).

Also compare to the name of the Angel *Lzinopo*, an Elder of the Southern Watchtower. Perhaps his name means something akin to "He Who Works Wonders." Also compare to the name of the Angel *Iznr* or *Izinr*, an Angel of medicine also of the Southern Watchtower.

Tal (M)

M (em)* *conj.* or *prep.* — Except

3.22 . . . *except (by)* mine own hand . . .

Pronunciation notes:
(**Dee—EM it is a word*) Likely just one syllable.

Note:
See Oq (but), "Crp" (but).

Maasi (may-ay-sii)* *v.* — Laid Up (i.e., Stored Up)

10.17 . . . and weeping *laid up* for the earth . . .

Pronunciation notes:
(**Dee—Ma a si*) Three syllables. The double *a* should represent a long "a" sound in Early Modern English. Dee's note indicates two long *a*'s, but they nearly blend into one when this word is spoken fluently. The final *i* is likely long.
(**Dee—maâsi*) See the *48 Claves*. Here, Dee places a circumflex over the second *a* to indicate its long sound.

Mabberan (MAB-er-an) *adv.* — How Now(?)*

Pronunciation notes:
The first *a* of *Mabberan* is accented in Dee's journal. Also, I assume the first *a* takes its short sound, because it is followed by a double *b* (similar to the *a* in the English words *rabble* or *babble*).

Note:
(* *Vors Mabberan = how now: what hast thou to do with us?*) See the *Five Books*, p. 311. Here, several spirits appear and demand of Dee and Kelley, "*Vors Mabberan*?"—to which Dee makes his marginal notation above. Given the known definition of *Vors* (over, especially in a hierarchy), I assume this phrase is a challenge, as if to say, "What authority

do you have over us?" On its own, it is possible that *Mabberan* has some meaning akin to "What do you want?" or "Why have you bothered us?"

Mabza (MAB-za)* *n.* Coat

8.43 . . . and *the coat of* him that is . . .

Pronunciation notes:

(**Dee—Mab za*) Two syllables.

(**Dee—mábza*) See the *48 Claves*. Here, Dee adds an accent to the first syllable.

Mad (mad)* *n.* (Your) God, Pure/Undefiled

(RFP) . . . servant of *the same your God* . . .
3.60 . . . in the name of *the same your God* . . .
6.42 . . . the praise of *your God* . . .
13.16 . . . behold the promise of *God* . . .
30.15 . . . behold the face of *your God* . . .

Pronunciation notes:

(**Dee 1.84—Call it Mad.*)

(**Dee 3.60; 6.42; 13.16, 30.15—Mad.*)

Compounds:

Madzilodarp (mad-ZII-loh-darp) [Mad + "Zilodarp"] God of Conquest

Iadnamad (yad-nay-mad) [Iadnah + Mad?] Pure Knowledge

Probable root for:

"Madriax" (MAY-drii-yaks) Heavens

Madriiax (MAY-drii-yaks) Heavens

Madrid (MAY-drid) Iniquity

Note:

The proper Name of God in Angelical is *Iad. Mad*, on the other hand, indicates *god* in the generic sense. The word *your* is not directly indicated by the Angelical—though the change in spelling adequately suggests *some other god* as opposed to Iad Himself.

At the same time, note that Mad is used as a root in several cases to indicate things celestial or divine (*Iadnamad*, *"Madriax,"* and the antonymic *Madrid*).

Also see *Piad* (your God).

"Madriax"* (MAY-drii-yaks) *n.* Heavens

Note:

(**Dee—I think this word wanted as may appear by Madriax, about 44 words from the end.*) "Madriax" does not appear with this spelling in the Keys in *TFR*. Apparently, Dee did not receive the first word of the Key of the Aethyrs (word 30.1) until sometime after its transmission. (Illemese, who revealed this Key, gave only the English "O you heavens," but gave no Angelical for the phrase.) Dee found the proper word later in the Key—*Madriiax* (word 30.116). After adding *Madriiax* (with the *double i*) into space 30.1, Dee made the above note in the margin, spelling the word as *Madriax* (with a *single i*). However, also note the word *Oadriax* (lower Heavens) which also uses a single *i*—so this spelling, *Madriax*, is likely acceptable.

Pronunciation notes:

(**Dee 30.1—Madrîax*) See the *48 Claves*. Here, Dee spelled the word with only one *i*. He also placed a circumflex over the *i* to indicate its long sound.

See pronunciation notes for *Madriiax* (Heavens).

Also:

Madriiax (MAY-drii-yaks)	Heavens
Oadriax (oh-AY-drii-aks)	Lower Heavens

Probable root:

Mad (mad)	(Your) God, "Pure/Undefiled"

Madriiax (MAY-drii-yaks)* *n.* Heavens

30.1 *O you heavens* that dwell in the first Aethyr . . .

30.116 *O you heavens*, arise!

Pronunciation notes:

(**Dee 30.116—Má dri iax yax*) Three syllables, accent on the first syllable. The double *i* probably results in a long "i" sound in the second syllable. Dee places a "y" sound at the beginning of the third syllable, but it is barely audible when the word is spoken fluently.

(**Dee 30.1—Madrîax*) See the *48 Claves*. Here, Dee spelled the word with only one *i*. (See note at "Madriax.") He also placed a circumflex over the *i* to indicate its long sound.

(**Dee 30.116—Mádrîiax*) See the *48 Claves*. Here, Dee again placed an accent over the first syllable. He also placed a circumflex over the first *i* to indicate its long sound.

Note:

Note that the Heavens, in this case, are being addressed as living creatures. This is common in mystical systems such as Gnosticism or the Qabalah—where the Heavens (*Aeons*, *Sephiroth*) are treated as *both* celestial spheres and intelligent beings.

The Key of the Aethyrs is the only place where the Heavens are addressed as intelligent. Elsewhere, the standard word for "the Heavens" is *Piripsol / Piripson*.

Also see *Calz* (firmaments).

Also:

"Madriax" (MAY-drii-yaks)	Heavens
Oadriax (oh-AY-drii-aks)	Lower Heavens

Probable root:

Mad (mad)	(Your) God, Pure / Undefiled

Note:

Also see *Piripsol / Piripson* (The Heavens).

Madrid (MAY-drid)* *n.* Iniquity

9.38 Cursed are they whose *iniquities* they are.

10.75 . . . for *her iniquity* is, was, and shall be great.

Pronunciation notes:

(**Dee 9.38; 10.75—Ma drid*) Two syllables. The *a* should take a long sound. The *dr* combine into a single sound, as in the English words *drive* and *drop*.

I have adopted the accent from similar words.

Probable root:

Mad (mad) (Your) God, "Pure/Undefiled"

Note:

The similarities between this word and the city of Madrid, the capital of Spain. Dee was very dedicated to the cause of the English empire, and Spain was in contention with England, as Dee recorded his journals. Therefore, many scholars suspect this word of bias on Dee's part rather than the Angels. For a parallel case, see *Londoh* (kingdom).

Madzilodarp (mad-ZII-loh-darp)* [Mad + "Zilodarp"] *comp.*

God of Conquest

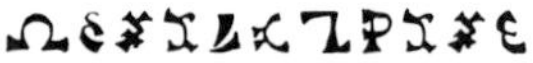

16.21 . . . great art thou in *the God of stretch forth and conquer* . . .

Pronunciation notes:

(**Dee—Mad zí lo darp*) Four syllables, with an accent on the second syllable. The *i* and the *o* each take their long sounds.

Note:

I have simplified "stretch forth and conquer" into the obvious definition of "conquest."

"Mal" (mal) *n.* Thrust, Arrow, Increase

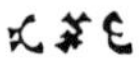

Compounds:

Malprg (mal-purj) ["Mal" + "Prg"] Through-thrusting Fire (i.e., Fiery Arrow)

Malpurg (mal-purj) ["Mal" + "Purg"] Fiery Arrows

Malpirgi (mal-per-jii) ["Mal" + "Pirgi"] Fires of Life and Increase

Note:

These words appear to show that "Mal" indicates the idea of arrows, rising, shooting, increase, etc.
Also see *Coazior* (increase).

Also note the Angel *Dmal*, one of the Sons of Light. "Mal" (arrow, increase) appears to be the root of his name.

Compare from *Loagaeth*:

Mal

Malpirgi (mal-per-jii)* ["Mal" + "Pirgi"] *comp.* — Fires of Life and Increase

3.52 . . . pouring down *the Fires of Life and Increase* . . .

Pronunciation notes:

(**Dee—Malpirgi*) Likely three syllables, with a long *i* at the end. Also, the first *i* in *Malpirgi* is likely a phonetic gloss. See *Malprg* and *Malpurg*.

Also:

Malprg (mal-purj) ["Mal" + "Prg"] — Through-thrusting Fire (i.e., Fiery Arrow)
Malpurg (mal-purj) ["Mal" + "Purg"] — Fiery Arrows

Malprg (mal-purj)* ["Mal" + "Prg"] *comp.* — Through-thrusting Fire (i.e., Fiery Arrow)

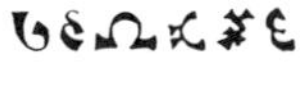

1.18 . . . the moon is *a through-thrusting fire* . . .

Pronunciation notes:

(**Dee—Malprg, as Malpurg*) Dee here shows us where to place the vowel sound. *Malprg* is likely the radical spelling of this word. See *Malpurg*, *Prge*, and *Malpirgi* for phonetic glosses. (The case of *Prge*—which follows the *g* with an *e* phonetic gloss—gives the final *g* its soft sound.)

Also:

Malpirgi (mal-per-jii) ["Mal" + "Pirgi"] — Fires of Life and Increase
Malpurg (mal-purj) ["Mal" + "Purg"] — Fiery Darts (Arrows)

Malpurg (mal-purj)* ["Mal" + "Purg"] *comp.* Fiery Darts/Arrows

6.16 . . . *fiery darts* to van the earth . . .

Pronunciation notes:

(**Dee—Mal purg*) Two syllables. The *u* is likely a phonetic gloss, and the final g should be soft. See pronunciation notes for *Malprg* and *Malpirgi*.

Also:

Malpirgi (mal-per-jii) ["Mal" + "Pirgi"] Fires of Life and Increase
Malprg (mal-purj) ["Mal" + "Prg"] Through-thrusting Fire (i.e., Fiery Arrow)

Mals (Makhls)* *prop. n.* Letter *P/Ph*

Note:

The name of the Angelical letter for *P/Ph*. It is likely that these letter names have translations of their own. (For instance, note the Hebrew alphabet: the letter *P/Ph* is named *Peh*, but *Peh* also translates as "mouth.") However, such translations for the Angelical letters are never given. (See the *Five Books*, p. 270.)

Pronunciation notes:

(**Dee—In sound machls.*) This is likely a soft "kh" sound (like the *ch* in *ache*, only softer) made just before the "*l*" sound. However, *Mals* is only one syllable. I tend to pronounce this word along the lines of "mahls."

Compare from *Loagaeth*:

Mals

Manin (man-in)* *n.* (In the) Mind

2.38 . . . but *in the mind of* the All Powerful.

Pronunciation note:

(**Dee—Manin*) Likely two syllables.

Maoffas (may-AHF-fas)* *adj.* Measureless

18.23 . . . in thy kingdom Joy, and *not to be measured.*

Pronunciation notes:

(**Dee—ma óf fas*) Three syllables, with an accent on the second syllable. The first *a* should be long and the *o* should be short, as in the English word *chaos*. The two *f*'s should combine into one sound, as we see in Early Modern English.

(**Dee—maóffas*) See the *48 Claves*. Here, Dee again indicated the accent on the second syllable.

MAPM (map-em)* 9639

4.15 I have placed *9639* whom none hath yet . . .

Pronunciation notes:

(**Dee—Map m*) Two syllables, the final *m* stands alone.

Mapsama (map-sam-a) *prop. n.* He That Speaks*

Note:

(**Dee records the words of Mapsama: "My name is called He That Speaks. I am one under Gabriel, and the name of Jesus I know and honour. My name is Mapsama."*) See *TFR*, pp. 138–39, 145ff. The names of most of the Angels encountered by Dee and Kelley can be found in other parts of the Angelic system—such as the Heptarchia or Great Table (Watchtower) systems. However, Mapsama is one of the few entirely unique Angels to appear to the two men. Mapsama appears to be connected to the political ambitions of Lord Lasky of Poland. He is also the Angel who delivered the instructions for the Book of Silver, which Dee never accomplished. (See also *Ga, Galvah, Murifri, Nalvage, Vaa,* and *Za.*)

Marb (marb)* *adj.* According to

30.36 . . . all things *according to* the providence . . .

Pronunciation notes:
(**Dee—Marb*) One syllable.

Marmara (mar-mar-a) *prop. n.* n/a

Note:
This is a variation of Carmara, the title of the ruling King of the *Heptarchia*. See the entry for *Carmara*.

Possible shared root:
Carma (kar-ma) To Come Out/To Arise

Masch (mask) n/a

Note:
See *TFR*, pp. 34–35. This session is recorded entirely in Latin. Here we find this Angelical phrase spoken by "a Voice": *"Garil zed masch, ich na gel galaht gemp gal noch Cabanladan."* No translation or context is offered.

Pronunciation note:
The *sch* letter combination should sound like "sk" (as in *school*). Note, also, that in the *Book of Loagaeth*, Dee gives the pronunciation for the word *Zuresch* as "zuresk"—further indicating the "sk" sound for *sch*.

Compare from *Loagaeth*:
Iemasch, Asch, Ascha, Aschah, Aschal, Ascham, Asche, Aschedh, Aschem, Ascheph, Aschi, Aschin, Aschma, Aschol, and probably *Dasch, Gascheth, Hasche, Pasch, Pascha, Pascheph, and maybe Iemasch, Surascha, Vascheth*

"Matastos" (MAT-az-tos) n/a

From *Loagaeth*:
See note at *Donasdogamatastos*.

Compounds:
Donadogamatastos (doh-NAS-dog-ay-MAT-az-tos)
[*"Donasdoga"* + *"Matastos"*] "Hellfire"

Matb (may-teb) *n.* One Thousand (1000)

10.45 . . . and *a thousand* times as many surges . . .

10.59 One rock bringeth forth *1000* . . .

Pronunciation notes:

Dee provided no phonetic notes for this word. See the pronunciation notes for *Matorb* (long, as in "period of time").

Note:

I suspect this is the word for "one thousand" rather than the numeral *1000*. Compare to *Torb* (one hundred) and *Matorb* (long period of time). This word was not originally given with Key Ten. It was added later when Nalvage transmitted the English for the Key (see *TFR*, p. 192). This seems to have been the case with many of the numbers mentioned in the Keys.

Compounds:

Matorb (may-torb) [Matb + Torb] Long (Period of Time)

Matorb (may-torb)* [Matb + Torb] *comp.* Long (Period of Time)

10.54 . . . neither know any *(long)* time here.

Pronunciation notes:

(**Dee—Ma torb*) Two syllables. The *a* should take its long sound.

Note:

There was no English given for *Matorb* in Dee's journals. However, it appears that the word is a compound of *Matb* (one thousand) and *Torb* (one hundred)—thus suggesting that the word is intended to indicate "a very long time." Similar, perhaps, to the Egyptian phrase "millions of years," which can indicate an eternity.

Maz (maz) *prop. n.* "The Sixth Aethyr"

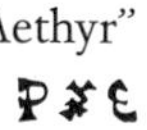

30.3 . . . which dwell in *the sixth aethyr* . . .

Note:

This (word 30.3) is the single space in the Key of the Aethyrs, which must be changed for each invocation—replacing word 30.3 with the name of the appropriate Aethyr. No established definitions were given for these names.

Maz contains the three Parts of the Earth *Saxtomp*, *Vavaamp*, and *Zirzird*.

Compare from *Loagaeth*:

Maz, Mazad

Med (med) *prop. n.* Letter *O*

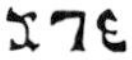

Note:

The name of the Angelical letter for *O*. It is likely that these letter names have translations of their own. (For instance, note the Hebrew alphabet: the letter *O* is named *Vav*, but *Vav* also translates as "stake" or "nail.") However, such translations for the Angelical letters are never given. (See the *Five Books*, p. 270.)

(*Dee—He said, Great is His Glory.*) This is not likely a translation of the word *Med*. See the letter *Ged*, where another invocation is made along with the delivery of a letter.

Miam (mii-AM)* *n.* Continuance

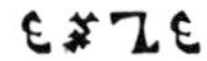

6.27 . . . in government and *continuance*.

Pronunciation notes:

(**Dee—Miam*) This is likely two syllables. Dee gives us little clue, but I assume the *i* should take a long sound.

(**Dee—miám*) See the *48 Claves*. Here, Dee places an accent over the *a* in the second syllable.

Compounds:

Odmiam (ohd-mii-AM) [Od + Miam] And Continuance

Also:

"Mian" Continuance

Note:

Seems to indicate "lifespan" or "continued existence."

"Mian" (mii-AN) *n.* Continuance

Pronunciation note:

I have adopted the accent from *Miam* (continuance).

Compounds:

Solamian (soh-LAY-mii-an) ["Sola" + "Mian"] Whose Continuance

Also:

Miam (mii-AM) Continuance

MIAN (mii-AN)* *3663*

12.15 . . . bring down your train *3663* that the Lord . . .

Pronunciation notes:

(**Dee—Mi an*) Two syllables. The *I* likely takes its long sound.

Note:

This word was not originally given with Key Twelve. It was added later when Nalvage transmitted the English for the Key (see *TFR*, p. 193). This seems to have been the case with many of the numbers mentioned in the Keys.

Do not confuse this word with "Mian" from *Solamian* (whose continuance).

Micalp (mii-KALP)* *adj.* Mightier

2.28 . . . *mightier* are your voices . . .

Pronunciation notes:

(**Dee—Mi calp*) Two syllables. The *i* is likely a long vowel. Also see *Micalzo*, where the accent is placed on the second syllable.

Also:

Gmicalzo (jee-mii-KAYL-zoh)	Power
Micalzo (mii-KAYL-zoh)	Mighty
Micaoli (mii-KAY-oh-lii)	Mighty
Micaolz (mii-KAY-ohlz or mii-KAY-ohl-zohd)	Mighty
Omicaolz (oh-mii-KAY-ohl-zohd)	(Be) Mighty

Possible shared root:

Miketh (mii-KETH)	"The True Measure of the Will of God in Judgment, Which Is by Wisdom"(?)

Note:

Also see *Umadea* (strong towers), *Umplif* (strength), *Ugeg* (become strong), *Vohim* (mighty).

Micalzo (mii-KAYL-zoh)* *n. or adj.* Mighty / Power

2.46 . . . show yourselves *in power* . . .
6.5 . . . *mighty in* the firmaments of waters . . .
**18.2 . . . thou *mighty* light and burning flame . . .

Pronunciation notes:

(**Dee 2.46—Micalzo*)

(**Dee 6.5—Micálzo*) Likely three syllables, with an accent on the second syllable. Also see *Micaolz*, where the *i* of the first syllable and the *a* of the second syllable are long.

(**Dee 6.5—micálzo*) See the *48 Claves*. Again the accent is on the second syllable.

Note:

**Word 18.2 was originally given as *Micaolz* (mighty). However, see *TFR*, p. 200, where Illemese gives the alternate pronunciation of "micalZo" (or *Micalzo*).

Also:

Gmicalzo (jee-mii-KAYL-zoh)	Power

Micalp (mii-KALP)	Mightier
Micaoli (mii-KAY-oh-lii)	Mighty
Micaolz (mii-KAY-ohlz or mii-KAY-ohl-zohd)	Mighty
Omicaolz (oh-mii-KAY-ohl-zohd)	(Be) Mighty

Possible shared root:

Miketh (mii-KETH)	"The True Measure of the Will of God in Judgment, Which Is by Wisdom"(?)

Note:

Also see *Umadea* (strong towers), *Umplif* (strength), *Ugeg* (become strong), *Vohim* (mighty).

Micaoli (mii-KAY-oh-lii)* *adj.* Mighty

9.1 A *mighty* sound . . .

Pronunciation notes:

(**Dee—Mi ca o li*) Four syllables. All of the vowels in this word are indicated as long. They all fall at the ends of their syllables, and the *o* itself stands alone.
(**Dee—Mi-cá-ôli*) See the *48 Claves*. Here, Dee placed an accent on the second syllable. He also placed a circumflex over the *o* to indicate its long sound.

Also:

Gmicalzo (jee-mii-KAYL-zoh)	Power
Micalp (mii-KALP)	Mightier
Micalzo (mii-KAYL-zoh)	Mighty
Micaolz (mii-KAY-ohlz or mii-KAY-ohl-zohd)	Mighty
Omicaolz (oh-mii-KAY-ohl-zohd)	(Be) Mighty

Possible shared root:

Miketh (mii-KETH)	"The True Measure of the Will of God in Judgment, Which Is by Wisdom" (?)

Note:

Also see *Umadea* (strong towers), *Umplif* (strength), *Ugeg* (become strong), *Vohim* (mighty).

Micaolz (mii-KAY-ohlz or mii-KAY-ohl-zohd)* *adj.* Mighty

3.70 . . . become *mighty* amongst us . . .
**18.2 . . . thou *mighty* light and burning flame . . .

Pronunciation notes:

(**Dee 3.70—Mi ca olz*)

(**Dee 18.2—Mi ca ol zod*) This word can be three or four syllables—depending on whether or not one extends the *z* to "zohd." (This word is further indication that the extended *z* is not a grammatical rule, but a phonetic flourish.) The *i* in the first syllable is likely long.

(**Dee 3.70—mi-cá-olz*) See the *48 Claves*. Dee places the accent on the second syllable.

(**Dee 18.2—Micaólz*) See the *48 Claves*. Here, Dee indicates the accent on the third syllable instead. Also note that he has dropped the extended "z" sound.

Note:

**For word 18.2, the Angel Illemese later gives an alternate pronunciation of "micalZo" (see *Micalzo*).

Compounds:

Chismicaolz (kiis-mii-KAY-ohlz) [Chis + Micaolz] Are Mighty

Also:

Gmicalzo (jee-mii-KAYL-zoh) Power
Micalp (mii-KALP) Mightier
Micalzo (mii-KAYL-zoh) Mighty*
Micaoli (mii-KAY-oh-lii) Mighty
Omicaolz (oh-mii-KAY-ohl-zohd) (Be) Mighty

Possible shared root:

Miketh (mii-KETH) "The True Measure of the Will of God in Judgment, Which Is by Wisdom" (?)

Note:

Also see *Umadea* (strong towers), *Umplif* (strength), *Ugeg* (become strong), *Vohim* (mighty).

Micma (mik-ma)* *v.* Behold

3.1 . . . *Behold*, sayeth your God . . .

3.64 . . . *Behold*, his mysteries flourish . . .

13.14 . . . *Behold* the promise of God . . .

**14.17 . . . *Behold* the voice of God . . .

30.13 . . . *Behold* the face of your God . . .

Pronunciation notes:

(**Dee 3.1, 64—Micma*)

(**Dee 13.14—Mic ma*) Two syllables.

(**Dee 30.13—Micma Mikma*) The *c* has a hard ("k") sound.

Note:

**The transmission of Key Fourteen is missing from Dee's journals. We only have the English for this Key given later (see *TFR*, p. 193). Plus, the word appears in this location in Dee's *48 Claves*.

Miinoag (mii-ii-noh-ayg)* *n.* Corners (Boundaries)

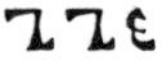

3.46 . . . and *the corners* of your governments . . .

Pronunciation notes:

(**Dee—Mi i no ag*) This appears to be four syllables. Note that each *i* is pronounced, as we might see in Middle English.

(**Dee—miinoâg*) See the *48 Claves*. Dee placed a circumflex over the *a*, indicating its long sound.

Note:

Also see *Unalah* (skirts).

Miketh (mii-KETH) *n.* "The True Measure of the Will of God in Judgment, Which Is by Wisdom"(?)

Pronunciation note:

I have adopted the accent from similar words, such as *Micaolz* (mighty).

Note:

See the *Five Books*, p. 354. Here, the Angel Illemese says of the *Book of Soyga*, "*Soyga* signifieth not *Agyos*. *Soyga alca miketh.*" (*Agyos* is Greek for "holiness," and is *Soyga* when spelled backward.) When Dee asked what these words meant, he was told, "The True Measure of the Will of God in Judgment, Which Is by Wisdom." Based on context, I feel that the word *Alca* probably means "to signify"—while *Miketh* (related, perhaps by root, to *Micaolz*) is translated as "the True Measure of the Will of God, etc."

Perhaps this long definition could be shortened to "God's Will in Judgment."

Possible shared root:

Micaolz (mii-KAY-olz *or* mii-KAY-ol-zohd) Mighty

Mir (mir)* *n.* Torment

6.10 . . . hath planted *a torment to* the wicked . . .

Pronunciation notes:

(**Dee—Mir*) One syllable.

Note:

This word appears to be in noun form ("a torment"), rather than in verb form ("to torment").

Mirc (mirk)* *prep.* Upon

9.54 . . . and *upon* their heads are marble . . .

**14.7 . . . which sit *upon* 24 seats . . .

30.70 . . . no creature *upon* or within her . . .

Pronunciation notes:

(**Dee 9.54; 30.70—Mirc Mirk*) One syllable, with a hard *c* at the end.

Note:

**The transmission of Key Fourteen is missing from Dee's journals. We only have the English for this Key given later (see *TFR*, p. 193). Plus, the word appears in Dee's *48 Claves*.

Molvi (mol-vii)* *n.* Surges

10.48 . . . a thousand times as many *surges* . . .

Pronunciation notes:

(**Dee—Mol ui*) Two syllables. The *o* takes its short sound. Dee originally wrote this word with a *u*—but the letter should make a "v" sound when preceding a vowel.

Mom (mom)* *n.* Moss (i.e., Dross?)

9.29 . . . gather up *the moss* of the earth . . .

Pronunciation notes:

(**Dee—Mom*) One syllable. I suggest a short *o*.

Note:

I have seen it suggested that "moss of the earth" is a reference to the dead—but I have not verified that yet. I have found the word *moss* used poetically in many cases, as a synonym for *dross*. (As in, "A rolling stone gathers no moss" or "Clearing the moss from your mind.") In just one case, I have found the phrase "I wish he would gather moss"—which appears to be a reference to death.

Also note this word is a palindrome, reading the same forward and backward.

Momao (MOH-may-oh)* *n.* Crowns

8.40 . . . for *the crowns of* the Temple . . .

Pronunciation notes:

(**Dee—Mo ma o*) Three syllables. Both *o*'s and the *a* should likely take their long sounds.

(**Dee—mómâo*) See the *48 Claves*. Here, Dee added an accent on the first syllable. He also placed a circumflex over the *a* to indicate its long sound.

Also:

"Momar" (MOH-mar) — To Crown

"Momar" (MOH-mar) *v.* — To Crown

Pronunciation note:

I have adopted the accent from *Momao* (crowns).

Compounds:

Iadoiasmomar (jad-oh-JAS-moh-mar) ["Iadoias" + "Momar"] — God Eternally Crowned

Also:

Momao (MOH-may-oh) — Crowns

Monasci (mon-ay-sii) *n.* — Great Name

15.13 . . . which knowest *the great name* Righteousness . . .

Pronunciation note:

I assume the *sci* letter combination is the same as in the words *science* or *scion*.

Note:

The transmission of Key Fifteen is missing from Dee's journals. We only have the English for this Key given later (see *TFR*, p. 193). Plus, the word appears in this location in Dee's *48 Claves*.

This likely indicates a Name of God.

Also see Dooain, which means *name* in the general sense.

Monons (moh-nons)* *n.* — Heart

10.61 . . . *the heart of* man . . .

Pronunciation notes:

(**Dee—Mo nons*) Two syllables. The first *o* takes its long sound.

Moooah (moh-oh-WAH)* *v.* — To Repent

30.104 For why? *It repenteth me* I made man.

Pronunciation notes:

(**Dee—Mo o Oah*) Three syllables. The second *o* stands alone. The third syllable is a bit obscure. The *oa* letter combination should make a long "o" sound (as in the English words *boat* and *coat*). However, Dee's phonetic note seems to indicate that the *a* should join with the *h*, leaving the preceding *o* to sound alone. Under that circumstance, the only way *Oah* could form one syllable is to sound like "wah." (Patricia Shaffer makes this suggestion in her *DeesPronunciationNotes.rtf.*)
(**Dee—Mooóâh*) See the *48 Claves*. Here, Dee placed an accent over the third *o* (which should be the third syllable). The *âh* should indicate a short "o" sound (as in the English words *father* and *fall*).

"Mospleh" (mos-play) *n.* — Horns

Compounds:

Qmospleh (kwah-mos-play) [Q + "Mospleh"] — Or the Horns

Moz (moz *or* moz-ohd)* *n.* — Joy, Joy of God

18.21 . . . called in thy kingdom *Joy*.

Pronunciation notes:

(**Dee—Moz*) Dee originally wrote this word as "Qzmoz." However, his phonetic note excludes the letters *qz*. Likewise, Dee recorded the word as "MOZ" in his *48 Claves*.

This exclusion is further supported by the appearance of *Moz* (to rejoice) on the *Corpus Omnium* Table. There, Nalvage reveals that *Moz* can also be pronounced with an extended *z* (see below)—so perhaps "Qz-moz" was a botched attempt to record the extended version of *Moz*.

Also From *Corpus Omnium*:

(**Dee—I pray you, is Mozod, a word of three letters or of five?*

Nalvage: In wrote three, it is larger extended.

Dee: Z extended is Zod.

Nalvage: Moz in itself signifieth Joy, but Mozod extended, signifieth the Joy of God.)

Found in the Pre-Deluge portion of the Table, in the phrase *Zir Moz Iad* (I Am the Joy of God). Apparently, Nalvage pronounced the word *Moz* as "mozod"—prompting Dee to ask how many letters *Moz* should have. Nalvage confirms that it should be written with three letters, but that "Mozod" is an extended pronunciation, expanding the definition of the word from "joy" to "joy of God." This is the first time we see such an extended *z* in Dee's records, although it will recur throughout the *48 Claves*.

Murifri (mur-if-rii) *prop. n.* n/a

Note:

See *TFR*, p. 3. The names of most of the Angels encountered by Dee and Kelley can be found in other parts of the Angelic system, such as the *Heptarchia* or Great Table (Watchtower) systems. However, *Murifri* is one of the few entirely unique Angels that appeared to the two men. He appeared to give further Heptarchic mysteries to Dee and Kelley—nearly the only Heptarchic information in *TFR*, concerning a talisman Dee wished to make for a sick woman. Murifri's name is found among the Tablets of the *Heptarchia*, but he is *not* one of the forty-nine good Angels, nor is the name derived by any instructions that the Angels gave to Dee. (His name appears in Table Three, which is associated with council and nobility.) No etymology is offered for Murifri's name.

(See also *Ga*, *Galvah*, *Mapsama*, *Nalvage*, *Vaa*, and *Za*.)

Drux (N)

NA (en-ay) *prop. n.* — The Name of the Trinity,* Lord

From *Loagaeth*:

(**Dee—The Name of the Trinity, One separable for a while.*) This means One God, but temporarily separable into Three. It appears many times throughout *Loagaeth*.

Note:

Also see the *Five Books*, p. 77. The Archangel Michael gives a small wafer marked *NA* as a Eucharist to Dee's Angel of profession.

See Agrippa's *Three Books*, Book III, chapter 11 (Of the Divine Names . . .): ". . . and the Name of God NA (Hebrew: *Nun, Aleph*) is to be invocated in perturbations and troubles."

Also:

Enay (en-ay) — Lord

Na (nakh)* *prop. n.* — Letter *H*

Note:

See the *Five Books*, p. 270. The name of the Angelical letter for *H*. It is likely that these letter names have translations of their own. (For instance, note the Hebrew alphabet: the letter *H* is named *Heh*, but *Heh* also translates as "window.") However, such translations for the Angelical letters are never given.

Pronunciation notes:

(**Dee—Hath./But in sound Nach as it were in the nose.*) Could *Hath* be what Dee calls the letter *H* in this case? Most of the time, when a word uses the *ch* digraph, it results in a sound like the "ch" in the word *ache* (a "kh" sound made in the throat). However, in this case, Dee tells us to make the sound in the nose, which is a much softer sound. I tend to pronounce the word along the lines of a nasal "nah."

(Note, also, that this pronunciation gives us a good clue that words like *Pa, Ga, Va*, etc., should have an "ah" vowel sound.)

Note:

Also see the *Five Books*, p. 298. This was at the very end of a session, after the curtain had been pulled to Kelley's vision in the stone. A voice was heard to say, "*Ne ne ne na Jabes.*" (Note the word *na*.) This is likely a praise of some sort, but no translation is offered.

Also see *TFR*, pp. 34–35. This session is recorded entirely in Latin. Here we find this Angelical phrase spoken by "a Voice": "*Garil zed masch, ich na gel galaht gemp gal noch Cabanladan.*" (Note the word *na*.) No translation or context is offered.

Compare from *Loagaeth*:

Na, Nah

Naghezes (naj-eez-es) *n.?* Worthiness(?)

Pronunciation notes:

(*Dee—Amzes naghezes Hardeh—Note this to be pronounced roundly together.*) Perhaps this means the three words should be pronounced as if they were one.

In the Angelical spelling above, I have assumed the *h* is a phonetic gloss and excluded it.

Note:

See the *Five Books*, pp. 324–25. Here Kelley sees what the *Book of Loagaeth* looks like from the outside. It is covered in blue silk, and has the title *Amzes naghezes Hardeh* painted upon it in gold. Kelley says this signifies "the universal name of Him that created universally be praised and extolled forever."

However, also see *TFR*, p. 174, where the Angel Ave reveals that the title of Enoch's book was "Let Those That Fear God, and Are Worthy, Read." (Dee, at that point, notes: "The title of Enoch's books expounded into English.") If this happens to be the real translation, then perhaps *Naghezes* indicates "to be worthy."

Nalvage (nal-vayj) *prop. n.* Earth-Fleer

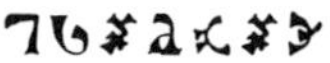

Note:

See *TFR*, p. 62ff. The names of most of the Angels encountered by Dee and Kelley can be found in other parts of the Angelic system, such as the *Heptarchia* or Great Table (Watchtower) systems. However, *Nalvage* is one of the few entirely unique Angels that appeared to the two men. He is the Angel who delivered the *Corpus Omnium*, the forty-eight Keys, and the ninety-one Parts of the Earth to Dee and Kelley. He appeared to be an Angel directly under the direction of Gabriel. Later (see *TFR*, p. 68), the Angel Madimi explains that Nalvage is a "close kinsman" of her mother (Galvah) and his name means *Fuga Terrestrium*—"Earth-Fleer" or "Avoidance of Earthly Things."

(See also *Ga, Galvah, Mapsama, Murifri, Vaa,* and *Za.*)

Nanaeel (nay-NAY-ee-el)* *n.* (My) Power

3.50 . . . you might work *my power.*

Pronunciation notes:

(*Dee—Na na e el*) Four syllables. The double *ee* actually makes the long "e" sound, followed by the final *l* which sounds like "el."

(*Dee—na-ná-ê-el*) See the *48 Claves*. Dee shows an accent on the second syllable. He also placed a circumflex over the first *e*, indicating the long sound.

Note:

This line in Key Three is spoken by God. Nanaeel does *not* represent "power" in the conventional sense of "strength" and "might." (See *Micaolz.*) Instead, Nanaeel is likely related to Ananael (secret wisdom)—meaning that Nanaeel is descriptive of a *kind* of divine power.

Possible shared root:

Ananael (an-AN-ee-el) Secret Wisdom

Nanba (nan-ba)* *n.* Thorns

17.6 . . . whose wings are *thorns* to stir up vexation . . .

Pronunciation notes:

(**Dee—Nan ba*) Two syllables.

Napeai (nay-pee-ay)* *n.* Swords

13.1 . . . O you *swords of* the south . . .

Pronunciation notes:

(**Dee—Na pe ai*) Three syllables. The first *a* and the *e* should take their long sounds. The *ai* (or *ay*) should make a long "a" sound, as in the English words *day* and *play*.

(**Dee—Napêai*) See the *48 Claves*. Here, Dee placed a circumflex over the *e* to indicate its long sound.

Also:

Napta (nap-ta) Two-edged Swords

Nazpsad (nayz-pee-sad) Sword

Closely related root:

Nazarth (nay-zarth) Pillars (of Gladness)

Nazavabh (nay-zay-VAB) (Hyacinth) Pillars

Note:

Apparently the "Naz" root holds some indication of "straightness," while "Nap" indicates "sharpness." The two come together in *Nazpsad* (sword).

Also compare to the name of the Angel *Bnapsen*, the Heptarchic King of Saturday. Perhaps his name contains some etymology of *sword*.

Compare from *Loagaeth*:

Nap, Napo, Napod

Napta (nap-ta)* *n.* (Two-edged) Swords

9.4 . . . with *two-edged swords* flaming . . .

Pronunciation notes:

(**Dee—Nap ta*) Two syllables.

Also:

Napeai (nay-pee-ay) — Swords
Nazpsad (nayz-pee-sad) — Sword

Closely related root:

Nazarth (nay-zarth) — Pillars (of Gladness)
Nazavabh (nay-zay-VAB) — (Hyacinth) Pillars

Note:

See note at *Napeai.*

Compare from *Loagaeth*:

Nap, Napo, Napod

Nazarth (nay-zarth)* *n.* — Pillars (of Gladness)

5.16 . . . I fastened *Pillars of Gladness* . . .

Pronunciation notes:

(**Dee—Na zarth*) Two syllables. The *a* at the end of the first syllable is likely long.

Note:

The similarity between this word and the word *Nazareth*—the town where Jesus supposedly grew up.

Also:

Nazavabh (nay-zay-VAB) — (Hyacinth) Pillars

Closely related root:

Napeai (nay-pee-ay) — Swords
Napta (nap-ta) — Two-edged Swords
Nazpsad (nayz-pee-sad) — Sword

Note:

See note at *Napeai.*

Nazavabh (nay-zay-VAB)* *n.* — (Hyacinth) Pillars

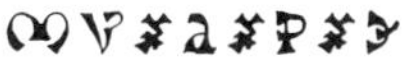

8.5 . . . third heaven made of *hyacinth pillars* . . .

Pronunciation notes:

(**Dee—Na za vábh*) Three syllables, with the accent on the third syllable. The first two *a*'s should be long, while the third *a* takes the short sound. The *bh* makes a soft "b" sound.

(**Dee—nazâvábh*) See the *48 Claves*. Dee placed a circumflex over the *a* in the second syllable to indicate its long sound. He again placed an accent on the last syllable.

Also:

Nazarth (nay-zarth) — Pillars (of Gladness)

Note:

Patricia Shaffer has suggested that "hyacinth" may be an indication of the stone lapis lazuli, rather than the plant.

Closely related root:

Napeai (nay-pee-ay) — Swords
Napta (nap-ta) — Two-edged Swords
Nazpsad (nayz-pee-sad) — Sword

Note:

See note at *Napeai*.

Nazpsad (nayz-pee-sad)* *n.* — Sword

1.15 . . . the sun is as a *sword* . . .

Pronunciation notes:

(**Dee—NAZPSAD*) Dee gives us little clue here. Most likely, the *p* must stand alone, since it does not make a natural sound when combined with the *z* or the *s* in English. Thus the word might be of three syllables. I have assumed the *a* takes a long sound based upon closely related words.

Also:

Napeai (nay-pee-ay) — Swords
Napta (nap-ta) — Two-edged swords

Closely related root:

Nazarth (nay-zarth) — Pillars (of Gladness)
Nazavabh (nay-zay-VAB) — (Hyacinth) Pillars

Note:

There appear to be two roots at work in *Nazpsad*—both "Naz" (straight/pillar) and "Nap" (sword/sharp).

Ne (nee) — n/a

Note:

See the *Five Books*, p. 298. This was at the very end of a session, after the curtain had been pulled to Kelley's vision in the stone. A voice was heard to say, "*Ne ne ne na Jabes.*" This is likely a praise of some sort, but no translation is offered.

Compare from *Loagaeth*:

Ne

Netaab (nee-TAY-ab)* *n.* — Government

3.34 . . . placed you in 12 seats of *government* . . .

Pronunciation notes:

(**Dee—Netaab*) Dee gives us little clue here. Instead, see his *48 Claves*:
(**Dee—ne-tâ-ab*) See the *48 Claves*. Dee indicates three syllables here. The *e* should take its long sound. The first *a* has a circumflex over it, indicating the long sound. See *Gnetaab* (your governments) for the accent on the second syllable.

Also:

Anetab (ay-NEE-tayb)	(In) Government
Gnetaab (nee-TAY-ab)	(Your) Governments
Netaaib (nee-TAY-ay-ib)	Government
Tabaam (tay-BAY-an)	Governor
Tabaord (tay-BAY-ord)	(Let) Be Governed
Tabaori (tay-BAY-oh-rii)	Govern
"Tabas" (tay-BAS)	Govern

Further:

Cab (kab)	Rod/Scepter
Caba (ka-BA)	To Govern

Netaaib (nee-TAY-ay-ib)* *n.* — Government

30.25 . . . provided you *for the government* of the earth . . .

Pronunciation notes:

(**Dee—Ne tá a ib*) Four syllables, with an accent on the second syllable. (**Dee—netáâib*) See the *48 Claves*. Here, Dee again placed the accent on the second syllable. He also placed a circumflex over the second *a* to indicate its long sound.

Also:

Anetab (ay-NEE-tayb)	(In) Government
Gnetaab (nee-TAY-ab)	(Your) Governments
Netaab (nee-TAY-ab)	Governments
Tabaam (tay-BAY-an)	Governor
Tabaord (tay-BAY-ord)	(Let) Be Governed
Tabaori (tay-BAY-oh-rii)	Govern
"Tabas" (tay-BAS)	Govern

Further:

Cab (kab)	Rod/Scepter
Caba (ka-BA)	To Govern

NI (nii)* — 28

7.12 . . . they are become *28* living dwellings . . .

Pronunciation notes:

(**Dee—Ni*) Dee seems to indicate a single syllable. I suggest a long "i" sound.

Note:

This word was not originally given with Key Seven. It was added later when Nalvage transmitted the English for the Key (see *TFR*, p. 199). This seems to have been the case with many of the numbers mentioned in the Keys.

Note:

See also *OB* (28).

Nia (nii-a) *prop. n.* "The Twenty-Fourth Aethyr"

30.3 . . . which dwell in *the twenty-fourth aethyr* . . .

Note:

This (word 30.3) is the single space in the Key of the Aethyrs, which must be changed for each invocation—replacing word 30.3 with the name of the appropriate Aethyr. No established definitions were given for these names.

Nia contains the three Parts of the Earth *Orcanir*, *Chialps*, and *Soageel*.

"Nibm" (nib-em) *n.* Season

Compounds:

Lnibm (el-nib-em) [L + "Nibm"] One Season

Nidali (nii-day-lii)* *n.* Noises

10.83 Come away, but not *your noises*.

Pronunciation note:

(**Dee—Ni da li*) Three syllables. All vowels appear to take their long sounds.

(**Dee—nidâli*) See the *48 Claves*. Here, Dee places a circumflex over the *a* to indicate its long sound.

Niis (nii-IS)* *v.* Come (Here)

5.43 . . . .*come you*, and obey . . .

8.46 . . . *come*, appear to the terror of the earth . . .

Pronunciation notes:

(**Dee 5.43—Ni is*)

(**Dee 8.46—Ni is, small sound of i*) Two syllables. The first *i* appears to take the long sound. Dee's note about the *"small sound of I"* likely indicates a short sound for the *i* in the second syllable.

I have adopted the accent from the other versions of this word.

Also:

Niisa (nii-II-sa) — Come Away
Niiso (nii-II-soh) — Come Away

Niisa (nii-II-sa)* *v.* — Come Away

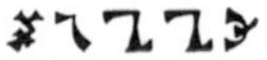

11.31 . . . *come away*! for I have prepared . . .

Pronunciation notes:

(**Dee—Ni í sa*) Three syllables, with an accent on the second syllable. Both *i*'s take their long sound. The word tends to sound more like two syllables when spoken fluently. (The double *i* would have combined to make a long "i" sound in Early Modern English.)

Also:

Niis (nii-IS) — Come (Here)
Niiso (nii-II-soh) — Come Away

Niiso (nii-II-soh)* *v.* — Come Away

8.34 . . . *come away*! for the Thunders have spoken . . .
8.38 . . . *come away*! for the crowns of the Temple . . .
9.66 . . . *come away*! and not your vials . . .
10.80 . . . *come away*! but not your noises . . .
11.15 . . . *come away*! and they gathered them together . . .

Pronunciation notes:

(**Dee 8.34, 38, 11.15—Ni í so*)

(**Dee 9.66; 10.80—Ni i so*) Three syllables, with an accent on the second syllable. Both *i*'s should take a long sound. The word tends to sound more like two syllables when spoken fluently. (The double *i* would have combined to make a long "i" sound in Early Modern English.)

(**Dee 8.34, 38; 9.66; 11.15—Niíso*) See the *48 Claves*. Dee again shows the accent over the second *i*.

Also:

Niis (nii-IS) — Come (Here)

Niisa (nii-II-sa) — Come Away

Noaln (noh-aln)* *v.* — May Be

30.51 . . . that the glory of her *may be* always drunken

Pronunciation note:

(**Dee—No aln*) Two syllables.

Also:

Noan (noh-an) — To Become

Noar (noh-ar) — Has Become

Noas (noh-as) — Have Become

Noasmi (noh-ays-mii) — (Let) Become

Note:

Compare this word to *Noalmr*, a Name of God in the Northern Watchtower, ruling the Angels of medicine. Thus, the name may contain an etymology of "to become."

Noan (noh-AN)* *v.* — To Become

2.33 For *you are become* a building . . .

3.5 . . . *you are become* the skirts of justice . . .

Pronunciation note:

(**Dee 2.33—No an*) Two syllables.

(**Dee 3.55—Noan*)

(**Dee 2.33—noán*) See *48 Claves*. The accent is placed on the second syllable.

Also:

Noaln (noh-aln) — May Be

Noar (noh-ar) — Has Become

Noas (noh-as) — Have Become

Noasmi (noh-ays-mii) — (Let) Become

Noar (noh-ar)* *v.* (Is) Become

3.69 His name *is become* mighty amongst us.

Pronunciation note:

(**Dee—Noar*) This would appear to rhyme with the English words "roar" and "boar." However, see *Noan* and *Noaln*—both of which are given two syllables.

Also:

Noaln (noh-aln) May Be
Noan (noh-an) To Become
Noas (noh-as) Have Become
Noasmi (noh-ays-mii) (Let) Become

Noas (noh-as)* *v.* To Become

5.5 The mighty sounds . . . *are become* as olives . . .
**11.19 and *became* the house of death.

Pronunciation note:

(**Dee 5.5—Noas*) This would appear to have a sound similar to the English words "toast" or "roast." However, see *Noan* and *Noaln*—both of which are given two syllables.

Note:

**This word was not given during the transmission of Key Eleven. Nor does it appear in Dee's *48 Claves*. We have only the English for the Key given on *TFR*, p. 193. Patricia Shaffer suggests this word here, and I have to agree.

Compounds:

Inoas (in-OH-as) [I + Noas] Are Become

Also:

Noaln (noh-aln) May Be
Noan (noh-an) To Become
Noar (noh-ar) Has Become
Noasmi (noh-ays-mii) (Let) Become

Noasmi (noh-ays-mii)* *v.* (Let) Become

30.97 His buildings, *let them become* caves . . .

Pronunciation note:

(*Dee—No as mi*) Three syllables. The final *i* is given its long sound—like the English word "my."

(*Dee—noâsmi*) See the *48 Claves*. Here, Dee placed a circumflex over the *a* to indicate its long sound.

Also:

Noaln (noh-aln)	May Be
Noan (noh-an)	To Become
Noar (noh-ar)	Has Become
Noas (noh-as)	Have Become

Nobloh (noh-bloh)* *n.* Palms (or, Palms of)

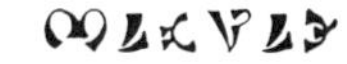

1.27 . . . trussed you together as *the palms of* my hands . . .

Pronunciation notes:

(*Dee—Nobloh*)

Note:

There is some possibility that the *-o* affix is in use here. If so, then the final *h* could be a phonetic gloss. Due to lack of evidence, I've stuck with Dee's spelling.

Noch (nok) n/a

Note:

See *TFR*, pp. 34–35. This session is recorded entirely in Latin. Here we find this Angelical phrase spoken by "a Voice": "*Garil zed masch, ich na gel galaht gemp gal noch Cabanladan.*" No translation or context is offered.

Compare from *Loagaeth*:

Nocas, Nochas

Noco (NOH-kwoh)* *n.* Servant

(RFP) . . . I am *a servant of* the same . . .

Pronunciation notes:

(*Dee—Call it Noco*) Two syllables. Note that other versions of this word are spelled with a *q* or *qu*. It is even likely that the word *Noco* should properly be spelled *Noqo*—with a *Ger* (Q) instead of *Veh* (C).
I have adopted the accent from other versions of this word.

Also:

Cnoqod (see-NOH-kwod)	(Unto) Servants
Cnoquodi (see-noh-KWOH-dii)	(With) Ministers
Cnoquol (see-NOH-kwol)	Servants

Note:

"Noquo" or "Noqo" may be the root for all words meaning "servant."

Also see *Lang* (Those Who Serve).

Noib (noh-ib)* *adv.* Yea (Yes)

10.7 . . . woe, woe, *yea* woe be to the earth . . .

Pronunciation notes:

(*Dee—No ib*) Two syllables. The *o* and *i* do not combine into one sound in this case. The *o* should take a long sound, and the *i* is likely short.

Nomig (noh-mig)* *adv.* or *adj.* Even (as)

10.60 . . . bringeth forth 1000 *even as* the heart of man . . .

Pronunciation notes:

(*Dee—No mig big*) Two syllables. The *o* is likely a long vowel. The final *g* seems to take a hard sound, as in the English word *big*.

Nonca (non-sa)* *pron., pl.* (To) You

30.11 . . . *to you* it is said, behold . . .

Pronunciation notes:

(**Dee—Nonca sa*) Two syllables. The *c* takes a soft sound.

Also:

Noncf (non-sef) — You
Nonci (non-sii) — You
Noncp (non-sef) — You

Note:

For *you* singular, see *Yls* (thou).

Noncf (non-sef)* *pron., pl.* — You

30.24 . . . provided *you* for the government . . .
30.32 . . . furnishing *you* with a power . . .

Pronunciation notes:

(**Dee 30.24—Noncf Nonsf*)
(**Dee 30.32—Non cf Nonsf*) Two syllables. Dee shows us here that the *c* takes it soft "s" sound. The *f* likely sounds like "ef," and (based on *Noncp*) I assume the word should end with *Mals* (Ph) rather than *Or* (F).

Also:

Nonca (non-sa) — (To) You
Nonci (non-sii) — You
Noncp (non-sef) — You

Note:

For *you* singular, see Yls (*thou*).

Nonci (non-sii)* *pron., pl.* — You

12.1 . . . *O you* that reign . . .

Pronunciation notes:

(**Dee—Non ci, si*) Two syllables. Dee indicates a soft "s" sound for the *c*. The final *i* is likely a long vowel.

Also:

Nonca (non-sa) — (To) You
Noncf (non-sef) — You
Noncp (non-sef) — You

Note:

For *you* singular, see Yls (*thou*).

Noncp (non-sef)* *pron., pl.* — You

11.34 . . . I have prepared for *you* . . .

Pronunciation notes:

(*Dee—Noncp Nonsp*) Two syllables. Dee shows us here that the *c* takes it soft "s" sound. I suspect the *p* is actually the digraph "ph"—as evidenced by the word *Noncf.*

Also:

Nonca (non-sa) — (To) You
Noncf (non-sef) — You
Nonci (non-sii) — You

Note:

For *you* singular, see Yls (*thou*).

"Nor" (nor) *n.* — Son

Compounds:

Norqrasahi (nor-kra-sa-hii) ["Nor" + "Qrasahi"] — Sons of Pleasure

Also:

"Norm" (norm) — Son/Sons
Noromi (noh-ROM-ii) — Sons

Note:

"Nor" appears to be the root here.

Compare from *Loagaeth*:

Nor

"Norm" (norm) *n.* Son/Sons

Compounds:

Normolap (nor-moh-lap) ["Norm" + "Olap"] Sons of Men

Also:

"Nor" (nor) Son

Noromi (noh-ROM-ii) Sons

Note:

"Nor" appears to be the root here.

Compare from *Loagaeth*:

Nor

Normolap (nor-moh-lap)* ["Norm" + "Olap"] *comp.* Sons of Men

4.47 . . . amongst *the sons of men*.

Pronunciation note:

(**Dee—Nor mo lap*) Three syllables. The second *o* should take the long sound.

(**Dee—Nor-mô-lap*) See the *48 Claves*. Also three syllables. Dee added a circumflex over the second *o* to indicate its long sound.

Note:

"Nor" appears to be the root here.

Compare from *Loagaeth*:

Nor

Noromi (noh-ROM-ii)* *n.* Sons

14.1 *O you sons* of fury . . .

Note:

The transmission of Key Fourteen is missing from Dee's journals. We only have the English for this Key given later (see *TFR*, p. 193). However, Illemese gives the pronunciation later in the journals on *TFR*, p. 200. Plus, the word appears in Dee's *48 Claves*.

Pronunciation notes:

(**Illemese—No Romi.*) See *TFR*, p. 200. I suggest three syllables. The first *o* and the final *i* should take their long sounds.

(**Dee—Norómi*) See the *48 Claves*. Here, Dee placed an accent over the second syllable.

Also:

"Nor" (nor) Son

"Norm" (norm) Son/Sons

Note:

"Nor" appears to be the root here.

Compare from *Loagaeth*:

Nor

Norquasahi (nor-kway-SAY-hii)* ["Nor" + "Qrasahi"] *comp.*

Sons of Pleasure

4.33 Arise *you sons of pleasure* and visit the earth . . .

Pronunciation notes:

(**Dee—Nor qua sa hi*) Four syllables. Dee originally wrote this word with an *r* after the *q*. However, he replaced the *r* with a *u* in his phonetic note (indicating that the *q* takes the sound of "kwah"—the *u* is obviously a phonetic gloss). He did the same in the *48 Claves*:

(**Dee—Nor quasáhi*) See the *48 Claves*. Note the accent on the third syllable.

Norz (norz)* *n.* Six

3.9 *Six* are the seats of living breath . . .

Pronunciation notes:

(**Dee—Norz*) One syllable.

Note:

This appears to be the word for "six" rather than the numeral 6.

Nostoah (nah-stah) *comp.* It Was in the Beginning*

From *Loagaeth*:

(**Dee—Nostah = It was in the beginning.*) See the *Five Books*, p. 323. "Nostah" is likely the pronunciation of *Nostoah*.

Note:

This seems similar to the Hebrew *Berashith* (It Was in the Beginning), the first word of Genesis. Much importance was placed upon this word in Jewish mysticism. (However, note that the very first word of the Holy *Book of Loagaeth* is *Zuresch*.)

Also see *Acroodzi* (beginning), *Croodzi* (beginning of things), *Iaod* (beginning), *Iaodaf* (in the beginning)

Nothoa (noth-OH-a)* *prep.* Amidst

1.22 . . . *in the midst of* my vestures . . .

Pronunciation notes:

(**Dee—Nothoa*) Likely three syllables.

(**Dee—nothóa*) See *48 Claves*. The accent is shown on the second syllable.

Note:

Also see *Zomdux* (amidst).

Med (O)

O (oh) — 5

11.5 . . . and they were *5* thunders which flew . . .

O (oh) *v.* — "Come, and Bear Witness"*

Note:

(**Dee—Befafes O, is to call upon him as on God. Befafes O, is as much to say, Come Befafes and bear witness.*) See the *Five Books*, p. 310. Dee is here using the Angel Befafes as an example. Note that O, by itself, seems to indicate "Come and Bear Witness."

Also see the *Five Books*, p. 258. Here, Raphael offers a long prayer, the very end of which is, "How great and innumerable are your [God's] gifts? *O remiges varpax. Kyrie eleyson.*"

Also:

Oh (oh) — "Come, and Bear Witness"(?)

Compare from *Loagaeth*:

O, Oh

"Oado" (oh-ay-doh) *v.* — To Weave

Compounds:

Dsoado (dee-soh-ay-doh) [Ds + "Oado"] — Which Weave

Oadriax (oh-AY-drii-aks)* *n.* — Lower Heavens

30.118 . . . *the lower heavens* beneath you . . .

Pronunciation notes:

(**Dee—O ádriax*) Likely four syllables, with an accent on the second syllable. The initial *O* stands alone. The first *a* likely takes its long sound—

based on the sound of similar words. The *i* likely takes a long sound, because it precedes an *a* (as in the English word *dial*).
(**Dee—oádriax*) See the *48 Claves*. Here, Dee again placed an accent over the *a* in the second syllable.

Also:

"Madriax" (MAY-drii-yaks) Heavens
Madriiax (MAY-drii-yaks) Heavens

Probable root:

Mad (mad) (Your) God, "Pure / Undefiled"

Note:

I have suggested that *Mad* is simply a modified form of *Iad*. The *I* of *Iad* (God) became the *M* of *Mad* (your God) to indicate something celestial and divine—yet not quite God Himself. Therefore, *Mad* is the root of "Madriax" (the Heavens). Now, with *Oadriax*, we seem to have a further progression of this same concept. The *M* of *Mad* gives way yet again in favor of the *O*, causing the word to indicate "the lower Heavens."

Oai* (oh-AY-ii) *prep.* Amongst

Alternate spelling:

(**Dee 1.67—AAI The first a may be an A an O or an e*) Thus, there are two alternate spellings for *Aai* (amongst).

Pronunciation notes:

See *Aai* (amongst), which Dee indicates has three syllables.

Also:

Aai (ay-AY-ii) Amongst (You)
Aaf (ay-AF) Amongst
Aaiom (ay-AY-om) Amongst (Us?)
Aao (ay-ay-OH) Amongst
Eai (ee-AY-ii) Amongst

Oali (OH-ay-lii)* *v.* To Place

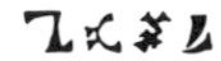

4.14 . . . under whom *I have placed* 9639 . . .

Pronunciation notes:

(**Dee—O a li*) Three syllables, the *O* and *a* each standing alone. I have adopted the accent from *Aala* (to place).

Also:

Aala (AY-ay-la) To Place

Probable shared root:

Alar (AY-lar) To Settle/Place
Aldi (AL-dii) Gathering
Aldon (AL-don) Gird Up
Allar (AL-lar) To Bind Up

Oanio (oh-AY-nii-oh)* *n.* Moment

10.39 . . . in the 24th part of *a moment* . . .

Pronunciation notes:

(**Dee—O a' ni o*) Four syllables. All of these vowels are given their long sounds. Accent placed on the second syllable.
(**Dee—oánîo*) See the *48 Claves*. Again, Dee indicates an accent on the second syllable, and a long "i" sound.

Probable shared root:

"Qanis" (kway-nis) Olives
Ooaona (oh-oh-AY-oh-na) Eyes
Ooanoan (oh-oh-AY-noh-an) (In Their?) Eyes

Note:

The similar spelling suggests these three words are connected. This might make sense for *Ooaona* (eyes): the word *Taqanis* (as olives) in Key Five appears to refer to the stars. In biblical literature, the word "eyes" is often used to indicate "stars." (Such as in the visions of St. John and Ezekiel, both of whom saw celestial Angels with wings "full of eyes.") If this is the case, then the shared root here may indicate "small units," which would explain its use to indicate a "moment" (Oanio).

OB (ob)* 28

12.6 . . . and are *28* the lanterns of sorrow . . .

Pronunciation notes:
(**Dee—Ob*) One syllable.

Note:
This word was not originally given with Key Twelve. It was added later when Nalvage transmitted the English for the Key (see *TFR*, p. 193). This seems to have been the case with many of the numbers mentioned in the Keys.
See also NI (28).

Obelison (oh-bel-is-on) *prop. n.* Pleasant Deliverer (a name of *Befafes*)*

Note:
(**Befafes: The Egyptians called me Obelison in respect of my nature.*
Dee: I pray you, what is the etymology of Obelison?
Befafes: A pleasant deliverer.) See the *Five Books*, pp. 234–45 (and the note added later by Dee on p. 201). Dee here encounters the Heptarchic Angel Befafes (Prince of Tuesday), who also claims the title *Obelison* (Pleasant Deliverer).

Also:
Obelisong (oh-bel-is-ong) Pleasant Deliverers

Obelisong (oh-bel-is-ong)* *n.* Pleasant Deliverers

4.44 . . . and show yourselves as *pleasant deliverers* . . .

Pronunciation notes:
(**Dee—Obelisong*) Likely four syllables. I am assuming a hard *g* at the end of the word, as it should combine naturally with the *n*, as in the English words *song* and *wrong*.

Also:
Obelison (oh-bel-is-on) Pleasant Deliverer (a name of *Befafes*)

Obloc (ob-lok)* *n.* Garland

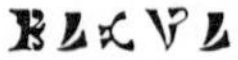

6.13 . . . and *a garland* to the righteous.

Pronunciation notes:

(**Dee—Ob loc*) Two syllables. The initial *O* seems to take the short sound (rather than standing alone).

Also:

Oboleh (OB-oh-lay) Garments

Note:

Both a *garland* and a *garment* are dressings. Also see *Qaa* (garments/creation).

Oboleh (OB-oh-lay)* *n.* Garments

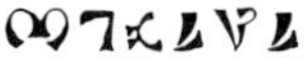

1.36 . . . beautified *your garments* with admiration . . .

Pronunciation notes:

(**Dee—óbôleh*) See *48 Claves*. Likely three syllables, showing the accent on the first syllable. The second *o* carries a circumflex, indicating the long sound.

Also:

Obloc (ob-lok) Garland

Note:

Take special note that the "garments" beautified in this part of Key One are likely the Heavenly Spheres (or celestial orbits). Generally depicted as a set of concentric circles, these could be easily represented poetically as "garlands."

Also see *Qaa* (garments/creation).

Obza (ob-za)* *n.* Half

9.12 . . . for two times and *a half*.

Pronunciation notes:

(**Dee—Ob za*) Two syllables.

Od (ohd *or* od)* *conj.* And

1.24 . . . *and* trussed you together . . .
1.65 . . . *and* reigneth among you . . .
1.71 . . . righteousness *and* truth . . .
RFP . . . *and* show yourselves . . . or . . . *and* appear . . .
2.27 . . . *and* mightier are your voices . . .
2.47 . . . *and* make me a strong seething . . .
3.26 . . . which sleep *and* shall rise . . .
3.31 . . . *and* placed you in 12 seats . . .
3.45 . . . *and* the corners of your government . . .
3.67 . . . *and* name is become mighty . . .
3.76 . . . descend *and* apply yourselves . . .
4.4 . . . *and* have looked around me . . .
4.34 . . . *and* visit the earth . . .
5.4 . . . *and* are become as olives . . .
5.10 . . . *and* dwelling in the brightness . . .
5.18 . . . *and* gave them vessels . . .
5.24 . . . *and* they are the brothers . . .
5.29 . . . *and* the beginning of their own seats . . .
5.40 . . . *and* the contents of time . . .
5.44 . . . come you *and* obey your creation . . .
5.48 . . . in peace *and* comfort . . .
6.12 . . . *and* a garland to the righteous . . .
6.18 . . . *and* 7699 continual workmen . . .
6.26 . . . *and* continuance as the second . . .
6.29 . . . second *and* third . . .
6.35 . . . *and* I moved you . . .
7.10 . . . *and* they are become 28 . . .
7.17 . . . *and* they are appareled . . .
7.29 . . . *and* places of comfort . . .
7.39 . . . *and* be mighty amongst us . . .
7.46 . . . *and* our strength waxeth . . .
8.18 . . . *and* like unto the harvest . . .

8.31 . . . house fall *and* the dragon sink . . .
8.42 . . . the Temple, *and* the coat . . .
8.50 . . . *and* to our comfort . . .
8.52 . . . *and* of such as are prepared . . .
9.11 . . . two times *and* a half . . .
9.17 . . . *and* of the marrow of salt . . .
9.23 . . . *and* are measured of their ministers . . .
9.45 . . . *and* from their mouths run seas . . .
9.53 . . . *and* upon their heads . . .
9.67 . . . Come away, *and* not your vials.
10.4 . . . *and* are harboured in the north . . .
10.15 . . . lamentation *and* weeping . . .
10.23 . . . burn night *and* day . . .
10.25 . . . *and* vomit out the heads of scorpions . . .
10.29 . . . scorpions *and* live sulphur . . .
10.44 . . . *and* a thousand times as many . . .
11.3 . . . *and* they were five thunders . . .
11.10 . . . *and* the Eagle spake . . .
11.13 . . . *and* cried with a loud voice . . .
**11.16 . . . *and* they gathered themselves together . . .
**11.18 . . . *and* became the house of death . . .
11.24 . . . *and* it is as they are . . .
12.4 . . . *and* are 28 lanterns . . .
12.11 . . . *and* visit us . . .
13.17 . . . God *and* His power . . .
***15.15 . . . *and* the seal of honour . . .
****16.8 . . . *and* shalt comfort the just . . .
16.16 . . . understand *and* separate . . .
17.18 . . . *and* hearken . . .
18.22 . . . *and* not to be measured . . .
30.7 . . . *and* execute the judgment . . .
30.27 . . . *and* her unspeakable variety . . .
30.39 . . . *and* rose up in the beginning . . .
30.46 . . . *and* let there be division . . .
30.54 . . . drunken *and* vexed . . .
30.60 . . . *and* as a handmaid . . .
30.67 . . . *and* let there be no creature . . .
30.78 . . . *and* let there be no one creature . . .

30.85 . . . vex *and* weed out . . .

30.88 . . . *and* the dwelling places . . .

30.93 . . . *and* his pomp . . .

30.136 . . . add *and* diminish . . .

30.154 . . . *and* make us partakers . . .

Pronunciation notes:

(**Dee 1.71—OD drawing the O long*)

(**Dee 1.24—As before OD*) Key One was transmitted backward, so 1.71 came before 1.24.

(**Dee 3.31; 8.18, 50, 52—OD*)

(**Dee 30.78—Od Long, or short*)

(**Dee 2.27, 47; 3.45, 67, 76; 4.4, 34; 5.4, 10, 18, 24, 29, 40, 44, 48; 6.12, 18, 35; 7.10, 17, 29, 39, 46; 8. 31, 42; 9.11, 17, 23, 45, 53, 67; 10,4, 15, 23, 25, 29, 44; 11.3, 10, 13, 24; 12.4, 11; 13.17; 16.16; 17.18; 18.22; 30.7, 27, 39, 46, 54, 60, 67, 85, 88, 93, 154—Od*)

(**Dee 6.26, 29—od*) Taking all of these notes together, I suggest a single syllable. The *O* may be long or short, though the long "oh" sound appears to dominate.

Note:

**Words 11.16 and 11.18 do not appear in Dee's journals, nor in the *48 Claves*. We have only the English given for the Key on *TFR*, p. 193. Patricia Shaffer suggests the words for 11.16–19, and I agree with her conclusion.

*** The transmission of Key Fifteen is missing from Dee's journals. We only have the English for this Key given later (see *TFR*, p. 193). Plus, the word appears in this location in Dee's *48 Claves*.

**** The transmission of the first twelve words of Key Sixteen is missing from Dee's journals. We only have the English given for it on *TFR*, p. 194. However, they do appear in Dee's *48 Claves*.

Compounds:

Odapila (ohd-ap-ii-la) [Od + "Apila"] And Liveth

Odbrint (ohd-brint) [Od + "Brint"] And Hast

Odcacocasb (ohd-kay-KOH-kazb) [Od + "Cacocasb"] And Another While

Odchis (ohd-kiis) [Od + Chis] And Are

Odecrin (oh-dee-KRIN) [Od + "Ecrin"]	And the Praise
Odes (ohd-es) [Od + "Es"]	And Fourth
Odfaorgt (ohd-fay-or-jet) [Od + "Faorgt"]	And the Dwelling Place
Odipuran (ohd-II-pew-ran) [Od + Ip + "Puran"]	And Shall Not See
Odmiam (ohd-MII-am) [Od + Miam]	And Continuance
Odlonshin (ohd-lon-shin) [Od + "Lonshin"]	And (Their) Powers
Odquasb (ohd-kwazb) [Od + "Quasb"]	And Destroy
Odugeg (ohd-yew-JEJ) [Od + Ugeg]	And Wax Strong
Odvooan (ohd-vay-ohn) [Od + Vooan]	And Truth
Odzamran (ohd-zam-ran) [Od + Zamran]	And Appear

Also:

Ot (oht) — And

Compare from *Loagaeth*:

Od

Odapila (ohd-ap-ii-la)* [Od + "Apila"] *comp.* — And Liveth

4.39 . . . God which is *and liveth.*

Pronunciation notes:

(**Dee—Od api la*) Likely four syllables. The final *i* in the second syllable is long.

(**Dee—od Apîla*) See the *48 Claves*. Dee added a circumflex over the *i* to indicate its long sound.

Odbrint (ohd-brint)* [Od + "Brint"] *comp.* — And Has

17.9 . . . *and hast* 7336 living lamps . . .

Pronunciation notes:

(**Dee—Od brint*) Two syllables. The initial *O* is likely long (see *Od*), while the *i* is likely short.

Odcacocasb (ohd-kay-KOH-kazb)* [Od + "Cacocasb"] *comp.*

And Another While

30.108 . . . *and another while* a stranger . . .

Pronunciation notes:

(*Dee—Od ca có casb) Four syllables, with an accent on the third syllable. The final letters *sb* can combine to make a sound—though it is an odd one to our modern language. I have rendered the sound in my pronunciation as "zb."

(*Dee—od cacócasb) See the *48 Claves*. Here, Dee again placed an accent over the third syllable.

Note:

See *Cocasb* (time).

Odchis (ohd-kiis)* [Od + Chis] *comp.*

And Are

6.24 . . . *and are* in government and continuance . . .

Pronunciation notes:

(**Dee—Od chif kif*) Two syllables. The *ch* takes the harder "k" (or "kh") sound. Dee originally wrote this word as "Odkif." However, we see elsewhere that the Angelical word for *are* is spelled as *Chis*. In Dee's time, the letter *s* was sometimes written in an elongated form that looks similar to a lowercase *f*. (See *Chis* or *Chiis* for further pronunciation notes.)

(**Dee—od chis*) See the *48 Claves*. Here, Dee confirms that the *f* in *TFR* should actually be an *s*.

Odecrin (oh-dee-KRIN)* [Od + "Ecrin"] *comp.*

And the Praise (of)

6.41 . . . a song of honour *and the praise of* your God . . .

Pronunciation notes:

(**Dee—O de crín*) Three syllables. The initial *O* stands alone. The *e* likely takes the long sound, as it rests at the end of its syllable. (Also see the pronunciation notes for *Oecrimi*.) The accent is placed upon the third syllable.

Odes (oh-DES)* [Od + "Es"] *comp.* And Fourth

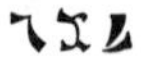

7.27 . . . as the third *and fourth* . . .

Pronunciation notes:

(*Dee—O des*) Two syllables. The *O* stands alone—that is, it makes a long sound. The *e* should be a phonetic gloss.

(*Dee—o dés*) See the *48 Claves*. Note the accent over the second syllable.

Odfaorgt (ohd-fay-ORJT)* [Od + "Faorgt"] *comp.* And the Dwelling Place

30.114 . . . the bed of an harlot, *and the dwelling place of* him . . .

Pronunciation notes:

(*Dee—Od fa orgt gt or dgt*) Three syllables. The *a* in the second syllable should be long, as it is followed by an *o* (as in the English word *chaos*). Dee indicates that the *g* in the final syllable should take a softer ("dg") sound.

(*Dee—od faórgt*) See the *48 Claves*. Here, Dee placed an accent upon the third syllable.

Odipuran (ohd-II-pew-ran)* [Od + Ip + "Puran"] *comp.* And Shall Not See

8.26 . . . which are *and shall not see* death . . .

Pronunciation notes:

(*Dee—Odí pu ran*) Four syllables, with an accent on the second syllable. The *i* and the *u* should each take their long sounds. I have given the *u* the sound of "yew"—as in the English words *pure* and *puce*.

(*Dee—odípûran*) See the *48 Claves*. Dee again shows the accent on the second syllable. He also added a circumflex over the *u*—confirming the long vowel sound.

Note:

It seems obvious that *Ip* should stand for "not" or perhaps "shall not" in this word. However, the word *Uran* appears earlier in Key Eight as the word "elders." Therefore, it is unlikely that this word is intended here as "see." It might be that the word is "Puran"—with the two *p*'s (between "Ip" and "Puran") combined as normal for Angelical compounds.

Odlonshin (ohd-lon-shin)* [Od + "Lonshin"] *comp.* And Powers

4.28 . . . *and their powers* are as the first 456 . . .

Pronunciation notes:

(**Dee—Od lonshin*) Three syllables.

Note:

There is no Angelical for *their* in the above.

Odmiam (ohd-MII-am)* [Od + Miam] *comp.* And Continuance

7.25 . . . whose kingdoms *and continuance* . . .

7.32 . . . .seats of mercy *and continuance* . . .

Pronunciation notes:

(**Dee 7.25—Od mi am, or Od Nuám*)

(**Dee 7.32—Od mí am*) I suspect that Dee had some confusion over the sound of word 7.25. However, by word 7.32, he seems to have settled upon his first assumption. Three syllables, with an accent on the second. The *i* should take the long sound.

Odo (od-oh)* *v.* To Open

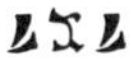

(RFP), 30.151 *Open* the mysteries of your creation . . .

18.7 . . . which *openest* the glory . . .

Pronunciation notes:

(**Dee 1.77—Call it ODO.*)

(**Dee 18.7; 30.151—Odo*) I suggest two syllables, the last *o* long.

Note:

This word is a palindrome, spelled the same forward and backward.

Odquasb (ohd-kwazb)* [Od + "Quasb"] *comp.* And Destroy

30.130 . . . *and destroy* the rotten . . .

Pronunciation notes:

(*Dee—Od Quasb*) This appears to be two syllables, so "Quasb" must be pronounced together as one syllable. (Also see *Grosb.*) I suspect the *u* is a phonetic gloss. (The Cotton MS of Dee's journals shows a final *z* on this word, but Dee did not include it in his phonetic note or in the *48 Claves.*)

Odugeg (ohd-yew-JEJ)* [Od + Ugeg] *comp.* And Wax Strong

4.23 . . . things are *and wax strong* . . .

Pronunciation notes:

(*Dee—Od Vgeg as Wedge*) There are three syllables here. Dee originally wrote this word with a *v*—however, it should take the "u" sound, as it precedes a consonant (see *Ugeg*). The first *g* should be soft, as it precedes an *e*. Dee notes that the final *g* is soft, as the *dg* in the English word *wedge*. Finally, see *Ugeg* for the accent.

Odvooan (ohd-voo-AN)* [Od + Vooan] *comp.* And Truth

3.58 . . . skirts of justice *and truth* . . .

Pronunciation notes:

(*Dee—Od vooen*) This should be three syllables. The double *o* should result in a long "u" sound—as in the English words *booth* and *shoot*. Dee gives the *a* the sound of "e" in his phonetic note—sounding like a schwa.

(*Dee—od vooán*) See the *48 Claves*. Here, Dee placed an accent upon the final syllable.

Note:

Dere here uses the fallen version of the word *Vooan* (truth). However, it should likely be the dignified version for the purpose of the Call. (See *Vooan* and *Vaoan*.)

Odzamran (ohd-zam-ran)* [Od + Zamran] *comp.* And Appear

4.43 . . . move *and show yourselves* . . .
30.143 . . . move *and appear* . . .

Pronunciation notes:

(**Dee 30.143—Od zamran*) Three syllables.

Oecrimi (oh-EE-kriim-ii)* *v.* To Sing Praises

7.4 . . . a house of virgins *singing praises* amongst . . .
7.37 . . . appear, *sing praises unto* the creator . . .

Pronunciation notes:

(**Dee 7.4—O écri mi*)

(**Dee 7.37—O é crimi*) This appears to be four syllables. The initial *O* and *e* each stand alone. The accent is placed on the second syllable. The first *i* seems to take the long sound.

(**Dee 7.4—oécrîmi*) See the *48 Claves*. Here, Dee again shows the accent on the *e*, and places a circumflex over the first *i* to indicate its long sound.

(**Dee 7.37—oëcrimi*) See the *48 Claves*. Dee placed a dieresis over the *e* to indicate that it does not combine its sound with the preceding *O*.

Also:

"Ecrin" (EE-krin) Praise

Ofafafe (oh-FAY-fay-fee)* *n.* Vials

9.69 Come away, and not *your vials*

Pronunciation notes:

(**Dee—O fa fa fe*) Four syllables. The initial *O* stands alone. The two *a*'s and the final *e* should take their long sounds.

(**Dee—ofáfâfe*) See the *48 Claves*. Here, Dee placed an accent over the *a* in the second syllable. He also placed a circumflex over the second *a* to indicate its long sound.

Also:

Efafafe (ee-FAY-fay-fee) Vials

Oh (oh) *v.* Come, and Bear Witness(?)*

Note:

See *TFR*, p. 3. The Angel *Murifri* here speaks a prayer in Angelical, and Kelley can only overhear a few of the words: *Oh Gahire Rudna gephna oh Gahire.* It is unclear whether this represents a single Angelical phrase, or if they are disconnected words recorded by Dee as Kelley overheard them here and there in the prayer. No translations are suggested. (It seems likely, at least, that *Oh Gahire* is intended as a repeated phrase.)

Also:

O (oh) Come, and Bear Witness*

Note:

(**Dee—Befafes O, is to call upon him as on God. Befafes O, is as much to say, Come Befafes and bear witness.*) See the *Five Books*, p. 310. Dee is here using the Angel Befafes as an example. Note that *O*, by itself, seems to indicate "Come and Bear Witness." The same is likely true of *Oh*, so that *Oh Gahire* is an invocation, likely of an aspect of God. (See *Gahire* for more.)

Compare from *Loagaeth*:

O, Oh

Ohio (oh-hii-oh)* *n.* Woe

10.65–70, 72 Woe, woe . . . yea woe be to the earth.

Note:
The Angel in Key Ten utters seven woes for the earth.

Pronunciation notes:
(**Dee—O hi o*) Three syllables. Both *O*s stand alone, and the *i* should take a long sound.
(**Dee—Ohîo*) See the *48 Claves*. Here, Dee places a circumflex over the *i*—confirming its long sound.

Ohorela (oh-hor-EL-a)* *v.* To Legislate

1.39 . . . to whom *I made a law* to govern the holy ones . . .

Pronunciation notes:
(**Dee—call it Ohorela*) I assume this should be four syllables.
(**Dee—ohoréla*) See *48 Claves*. The accent is places on the third syllable.

"Oi" (oh-ii) *adj.* or *pron.* This

Compounds:
Oisalman (oh-ii-SAYL-man) ["Oi" + Salman] This House

Note:
This can be a pronoun (as in "this is my cat"), but it is used in this case as an adjective (". . .until this house fall").

Oiad (oh-ii-AD)* *n.* (Of) God

**14.4 . . . the daughters of *the Just* . . .
14.19 . . . behold the voice *of God* . . .
18.9 . . . openest the glory *of God* . . .

Pronunciation notes:
(**Dee 18.9—O i ad*) Three syllables. The *O* and *i* each stand alone.
(**Dee 14.4, 19; 18.9—oîad*) See the *48 Claves*. Dee placed a circumflex over the *i* to indicate its long sound.
I have adopted the accent from similar words.

Note:

The transmission of Key Fourteen is missing from Dee's journals. We only have the English for this Key given later (see *TFR*, p. 193). Plus, the word appears in these locations in Dee's *48 Claves*.

**Others have suggested that word 14.4 should be *Balit* (the just). I would agree that Balit better fits the English in a literal sense. On the other hand, "the Just" in Key Fourteen might be a direct reference to God (as in the God of Justice), so that the English might better read ". . .the daughters of God." If so, then *Oiad* does fit better here.

Also:

Geiad (jej-AYD)	Lord and Master
Iad (yad)	God
"Iadoias" (jad-oh-JAS)	Eternal God
Iadpil (ii-AD-pil)	(To) Him
Ioiad (joh-JAD)	Him That Liveth Forever
Piad (pii-AD)	Your God

Probable root:

Ia (yah) n/a

Oisalman (oh-ii-SAYL-man)* ["Oi" + Salman] *comp.* This House

8.29 . . . until *this house* fall . . .

Pronunciation notes:

(**Dee—O i sal man*) Four syllables. Both the initial *O* and the *i* stand alone. (Rather than making the combined sound of "oy.")

(**Dee—O isâlman*) See the *48 Claves*. Here, Dee placed a circumflex over the first *a* to indicate its long sound.

I have adopted the accent from *Isalman* (is a house).

Ol (ohl)* *pron.* I

1.1 . . . *I* reign over you . . .

Pronunciation notes:

(**Dee—Ol*) One syllable.

Probable root:

L (el) — First, One

Probable shared root:

Aqlo (AY-kwah-loh) — Thy

Bolp (bohlp) — Be Thou

Note:

The pronoun *Ol* (I) is used only once in the Keys—as the very first word of Key One. I should point out, though it may or may not be important, that it is used by God to refer to Himself. It may also appear as a root in words like *Aqlo* (thy) and *Bolp* (be thou).

Compare from *Loagaeth*:

Ol

OL (oh-el)* — 24

10.38 . . . 5678 times *in the 24th part of* a moment . . .

14.8 . . . which sit on seats *24* . . .

Pronunciation notes:

(**Dee—O L*) Seems to be two syllables, each letter standing alone.

Note:

The transmission of Key Fourteen is missing from Dee's journals. We only have the English for this Key given later (see *TFR*, p. 193). Plus, the word appears in this location in Dee's *48 Claves*.

See *Ol* (I) above. These two words do not seem related. Note that *OL* (24) is given a different pronunciation than Ol (I).

Olani (oh-el-AY-nii)* *adv.* — Two Times (Twice)

9.10 . . . vials 8 of wrath *for two times* and a half.

Pronunciation notes:

(**Dee—O L a ni*) Four syllables. The *O*, *l*, and *a* each stand alone. It is unclear why the *l* is written as a capital.

(*Dee—oláni*) See the *48 Claves*. Here, Dee placed an accent over the *a* in the third syllable.

Also:

Pala (pay-la) — Two, separated
Pola (poh-la) — Two, together

Note:

Also see *Viv* (second).

"Olap" (oh-lap) *n.* — Men

Compounds:

Normolap (nor-moh-lap) ["Norm" + "Olap"] — Sons of Men

Also:

Ollog (ohl-log) — Men
"Ollor" (ohl-or) — Man
Olora (oh-loh-ra) — (Of) Man

Note:

Also see *Cordziz* (mankind).

Olcordziz (ohl-KORD-ziz)* [Oln + Cordziz] *comp.* — Made Mankind

30.105 . . . it rependeth me *I made man* . . .

Pronunciation notes:

(*Dee—Ol cord ziz*) Three syllables. All vowels appear to take their short sounds.
(*Dee—olcórdziz*) See the *48 Claves*. Here, Dee placed an accent on the second syllable.

Note:

It is not clear why *Oln* drops its *n* when compounded to *Cordziz*. However, since the English sense of this word is "I made mankind," it may be a play on words between *Oln* (made) and *Ol* (I).

Ollog (ohl-log)* *n.* Men

13.10 . . . making *men* drunken . . .

Pronunciation notes:

(**Dee—Ol log*) Two syllables. I suggest a long sound for the initial *O*.

Also:

"Olap" (oh-lap)	Men
"Ollor" (ohl-lor)	Man
Olora (oh-loh-ra)	(Of) Man

Note:

Also see *Cordziz* (mankind).

It is a long shot, but perhaps there is a relationship between this word and *Oloag*, a Name of God in the Northern Watchtower, ruling the Angels of medicine. Perhaps this is the God "of Man."

"Ollor" (ohl-lor) *n.* Man

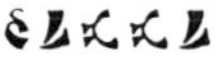

Compounds:

Lasollor (las-OHL-or) ["Las" + "Ollor"]	Rich Man

Also:

Ollog (ohl-log)	Men
"Olap" (oh-lap)	Men
Olora (oh-loh-ra)	(Of) Man

Note:

Also see *Cordziz* (mankind).

Oln (ohln)* *v.* Made (of)

8.4 . . . third heaven *made of* hyacinth pillars . . .

Pronunciation note:

(**Dee—Oln)* Dee seems to indicate a single syllable here.

Compounds:
Olcordziz (ohl-CORD-ziz) [Oln + Cordziz] Made Mankind

Note:
See note at *Olcordziz.*

Also:
Eol (ee-OHL) Made
Eolis (ee-OH-lis) Making

Compare from *Loagaeth*:
Olna, Olnah, Olneh, Olnoh

Olora (oh-loh-ra)* *n.* (Of) Man

10.62 . . . as the heart *of man* doth his thoughts.

Pronunciation notes:
(*Dee—O lo ra*) Three syllables. Both *O*s appear to take their long sounds. (*Dee—olôra*) See the *48 Claves*. Dee here placed a circumflex over the second *o* to indicate its long sound.

Also:
Ollog (ohl-log) Men
"Olap" (oh-lap) Men
"Ollor" (ohl-lor) Man

Note:
Also see *Cordziz* (mankind).

Also:
See note at *Ollog*.

Om (om)* *v.* To Understand / Know

2.4 . . . can the wings of the winds *understand* . . .
10.52 . . . neither *know* at any time . . .

Pronunciation notes:
(*Dee—Om*)

Compounds:

Dsom (dee-som) [Ds + Om] That Understand

Ixomaxip (iks-oh-MAKS-ip) ["Ix" + Omax + "Ip"] Let Her Be Known

Also:

Omax (oh-MAKS) Knowest

"Oma" (oh-ma) (Of) Understanding

"Omp" (omp) Understanding

Compare from *Loagaeth*:

Om

"Oma" (oh-ma) *n.* (Of) Understanding

Compounds:

Gmicalzoma (jee-mii-KAYL-zoh-ma) [Gmicalzo + "Oma"]
Power of Understanding

Also:

Om (om) Understand/Know

Omax (oh-MAKS) Knowest

"Omp" (omp) Understanding

Omaoas (oh-may-OH-as)* *n.* Names

30.91 . . . let them forget *their names* . . .

Pronunciation notes:

(**Dee—O ma o as*) Four syllables. Both *O*s stand alone. I suggest a long *a* at the end of the second syllable, because it is immediately followed by an *o*.

(**Dee—omaóas*) See the *48 Claves*. Here, Dee placed an accent on the *o* in the third syllable.

Apparent shared root:

Dooaip (doo-OH-ip) In the Name

Dooain (doo-OH-ay-in) Name

Dooiap (doo-OY-ap) In the Name

Note:

I assume that the combination of *oa* forms the root of these words.

Omax (oh-MAKS) *v.* To Know

15.12 . . . who *knowest* the great name . . .

Pronunciation notes:

(*Dee—ômax*) See the *48 Claves*. Likely two syllables. Dee placed a circumflex over the initial *O* to indicate its long sound. I have adopted the accent from *Ixomaxip* (let her be known).

Note:

The transmission of Key Fifteen is missing from Dee's journals. We only have the English for this Key given later (see *TFR*, p. 193). Plus, the word appears in this location in Dee's *48 Claves*.

This is likely an instance of the *-ax* suffix, indicating action.

Also:

Om (om) To Understand/Know
"Oma" (oh-ma) Understanding
"Omp" (omp) Understanding

Compound:

Ixomaxip (iks-oh-MAKS-ip) ["Ix" + Omax + "Ip"] Let Her Be known

Omicaolz (oh-mii-KAY-ohl-zohd)* *v.* (Be) Mighty

7.40 . . . *be mighty* amongst us . . .

Pronunciation notes:

(*Dee—O mi ca ol zod*) Five syllables. The initial *O* stands alone. The *i* should likely take its long sound. The *a* should also take its long sound—as it is followed by an *o* (as in the English word *chaos*). The final *z* stands alone.

I have adopted the accent from other versions of this word.

Also:

Gmicalzo (jee-mii-KAYL-zoh)	Power
Micalzo (mii-KAYL-zoh)	Power/Mighty
Micaoli (mii-KAY-oh-lii)	Mighty
Micaolz (mii-KAY-ohlz or mii-KAY-ohl-zohd)	Mighty
Micalp (mii-KALP)	Mightier

Possible shared root:

Miketh (mii-KETH) — "The True Measure of the Will of God in Judgment, Which Is by Wisdom" (?)

Note:

See also *Vohim* (mighty).

"Omp" (omp) *n.* — Understanding

Compounds:

Omptilb (omp-tilb) ["Omp" + Tilb] — Her Understanding

Also:

Om (om)	To Understand/Know
"Oma" (oh-ma)	(Of) Understanding
Omax (oh-MAKS)	Knowest

Note:

I am unsure if "Omp" is a proper element here, or if the compound should be Om + "Ptilb." (See "Ip" and "Pi"—both versions of "her.")

Omptilb (omp-tilb)* ["Omp" + Tilb] *comp.* — Her Understanding

30.101 . . . confound *her understanding* with darkness . . .

Pronunciation notes:

(*Dee—Omp tilb*) Two syllables. I find that this word, when spoken fluently, has a nearly silent *p*.

Note:

See note at "Omp."

Also:

See *Om* (know).

Ooanoan (oh-oh-AY-noh-an)* *n.* Eyes

9.40 *In their eyes* are millstones . . .

Pronunciation notes:

(*Dee—O o A no an*) Five syllables—though I find the word sounds more like four syllables when spoken fliently. The first two *O*s and the first *a* each stand alone. Dee might have capitalized the *A* to indicate the accent.

(*Dee—oöánôan*) See the *48 Claves*. Here, Dee placed a dieresis over the second *o* to indicate that it does not combine its sound with the previous vowel. He placed an accent over the *a* in the third syllable. Finally, he placed a circumflex over the third *o* to indicate its long sound.

Also:

Ooaona (oh-oh-AY-oh-na) Eyes

Probable shared root:

"Qanis" (kew-ay-nis) Olives

Oanio (oh-AY-nii-oh) Moment

Note:

The similar spelling suggests these four words are connected. This might make sense for *Ooanoan* (eyes): the word *Taqanis* (as olives) in Key Five appears to refer to the stars. In biblical literature, the word "eyes" is often used to indicate "stars." (Such as in the visions of St. John and Ezekiel, both of whom saw celestial Angels with wings "full of eyes.")

If this is the case, then the shared root here may indicate small units, which would explain its use to indicate a moment (*Oanio*).

Also compare the name of the Part of the Earth (and its Angelic Governor), *Ooanamb.*

Ooaona (oh-oh-AY-oh-na)* *n.* Eyes

13.5 . . . which have 42 *eyes* to stir up wrath . . .

Pronunciation notes:

(**Dee—O O Ao na.*) Dee indicates here that the two first *O*s should stand alone. Next, there is no *ao* letter combination In Early Modern English. Instead, the letters must make two sounds—as in the word *chaos*. That makes this a word of five syllables (although the double *O*s do tend to blend when this word is spoken fluently). I assume the last *a* is short, and the accent is on the third syllable, as indicated in the word *Ooanoan* (their eyes).

(**Dee—ooáôna*) See the *48 Claves*. Here, Dee placed the accent over the first *a* (which should be the third syllable). He also placed a circumflex over the third *o* to indicate its long sound.

Compounds:

Sabaooaona (say-bay-oh-oh-AY-oh-na) ["Saba" + Ooaona] Whose Eyes

Also:

Ooanoan (oh-oh-AY-noh-an) Eyes

Probable shared root:

"Qanis" (kew-ay-nis) Olives

Oanio (oh-AY-nii-oh) Moment

Ooge (oh-oj)* *n.* Chamber

2.21 . . . for *the chamber of* righteousness . . .

Pronunciation notes:

(**Dee—Ooge*) Dee gives us little clue here. Though, the final *e* likely makes the preceding *g* soft.

(**Dee—öoge*) See *48 Claves*. Note the dieresis over the first *O*, showing that its sound does not combine with the following *o*. (I suggest the first *O* takes the long sound, and the second takes the short sound.) Thus, this is likely a word of two syllables.

OP (oh-pee) 22

10.12 . . . are *22* nests of lamentation . . .

Note:
This word was not originally given with Key Ten. It was added later when Nalvage transmitted the English for the Key (see *TFR*, p. 192). This seems to have been the case with many of the numbers mentioned in the Keys.

Oq (oh-kwah)* *prep.* or *conj.* But/Except

2.37 . . . is not *but* in the mind of the all-powerful.

Pronunciation note:
(**Dee—O qua*) Two syllables, each letter stands alone. (The *q* makes the sound of "kwah.")
(**Dee—o-q*) See *48 Claves*. This note matches Dee's note from *TFR*.

Note:
Oq (but) is a preposition. See *Crip* (but), which is a conjunction.

Or (or)* *prop. n.* Letter *F*

Note:
The name of the Angelical letter for *F*. It is likely that these letter names have translations of their own. (For instance, note the Hebrew alphabet: the letter *F* is named *Peh*, but *Peh* also translates as "mouth.") However, such translations for the Angelical letters are never given. (See the *Five Books*, p. 270.)

Pronunciation note:
(**Dee—The voice seemed orh.*) Dee likely added this note to distinguish the sound of *Or* from the sound of *Ur*. (See the note at *Ur*.)

Compare from *Loagaeth*:
Or

Orh (or) *prop. n.* "A Spirit of Darkness"*

From *Loagaeth*:

(*Dee—The spirit Orh is the second in the scale of imperfections of darkness.*)
See the *Five Books*, p. 310.

Probable shared root:

Ors (ors) Darkness

Compare from *Loagaeth*:

Orh, Orho

Oroch (oh-ROK) *prep.* Under

14.15 . . . which have *under you* 1636.

Pronunciation notes:

I have adopted the accent from *Orocha* (beneath).

Note:

The transmission of Key Fourteen is missing from Dee's journals. We only have the English for this Key given later (see *TFR*, p. 193). Plus, the word appears in this location in Dee's *48 Claves*.

Also:

Orocha (oh-ROH-ka) Beneath

Possible shared root:

Orri (or-ii) Barren Stone
Ors (ors) Darkness
Orsba (ors-ba) Drunken
Orscor (ors-kor) Dryness
Orscatbl (ors-kat-bel) Buildings

Orocha (oh-ROH-ka)* *prep.* Beneath

30.119 . . . the lower heavens *beneath you*, let them serve . . .

Pronunciation notes:
(**Dee—O ro cha ka*) Three syllables. The *ch* takes a hard "k" (or "kh") sound, as in the English word *ache*.
(**Dee—orócha*) See the *48 Claves*. Here, Dee placed an accent upon the second syllable.

Also:

Oroch (oh-ROK)	Under

Possible shared root:

Orri (or-ii)	Barren Stone
Ors (ors)	Darkness
Orsba (ors-ba)	Drunken
Orscor (ors-kor)	Dryness
Orscatbl (ors-kat-bel)	Buildings

Orri (or-ii)* *n.* (Barren) Stone

2.26 . . . stronger are your feet than *the barren stone*.

Pronunciation notes:
(*Dee—Orri) Likely two syllables. A double *r* in Early Modern English represents a single "r" sound. The final *i* likely takes the long vowel sound.

Possible shared root:

Oroch (oh-ROK)	Beneath
Orocha (oh-ROH-ka)	Under
Ors (ors)	Darkness
Orsba (ors-ba)	Drunken
Orscor (ors-kor)	Dryness
Orscatbl (ors-kat-bel)	Buildings

Ors (ors)* *n.* Darkness

30.102 Confound her understanding with *darkness*.

Pronunciation notes:
(**Dee—Ors*) One syllable.

Also:

Orh (or)	A Spirit of Darkness

Possible shared root:

Oroch (oh-ROK)	Beneath
Orocha (oh-ROH-ka)	Under
Orri (or-ii)	Barren Stone
Orsba (ors-ba)	Drunken
Orscor (ors-kor)	Dryness
Orscatbl (ors-kat-bel)	Buildings

Compare from *Loagaeth*:

Oarz, Ors, Orse, Orze, Orsa, Orsat, Ors lah

Orsba (ors-ba)* *adj.* Drunken

13.11 . . . making men *drunken* which are empty.

30.53 . . . may always be *drunken* and vexed . . .

Pronunciation notes:

(**Dee 13.11; 30.53—Ors ba*) Two syllables.

Possible shared root:

Oroch (oh-ROK)	Beneath
Orocha (oh-ROH-ka)	Under
Orri (or-ii)	Barren Stone
Ors (ors)	Darkness
Orscor (ors-kor)	Dryness
Orscatbl (ors-kat-bel)	Buildings

Compare from *Loagaeth*:

Oarz, Ors, Orse, Orze, Orsa, Orsat, Ors lah

Orscatbl (ors-kat-bel)* *n.* Buildings

30.96 *His buildings*, let them become caves . . .

Pronunciation notes:

(**Dee—Ors cat bl*) Three syllables. In order for the final *bl* to form one syllable, the *l* must sound as "el."

Note:

It would seem that *Ors* (darkness) plays a role in this word—perhaps it is due to the comparison to caves. As far as I can tell, the root letters of *Tilb* (her) are not intended.

Also see *Trof* (a building).

Possible shared root:

Oroch (oh-ROK)	Beneath
Orocha (oh-ROH-ka)	Under
Orri (or-ii)	Barren Stone
Ors (ors)	Darkness
Orsba (ors-ba)	Drunken
Orscor (ors-kor)	Dryness

Compare from *Loagaeth*:

Oarz, Ors, Orse, Orze, Orsa, Orsat, Ors lah

Orscor (ors-kor) *n.* Dryness

15.10 . . . weave the earth with *dryness* . . .

Note:

The transmission of Key Fifteen is missing from Dee's journals. We only have the English for this Key given later (see *TFR*, p. 193). Plus, the word appears in this location in Dee's *48 Claves*.

Possible shared root:

Oroch (oh-ROK)	Beneath
Orocha (oh-ROH-ka)	Under
Orri (or-ii)	Barren Stone
Ors (ors)	Darkness
Orsba (ors-ba)	Drunken
Orscatbl (ors-kat-bel)	Buildings

Compare from *Loagaeth*:

Oarz, Ors, Orse, Orze, Orsa, Orsat, Ors lah

OS (os) 12

Compounds:

Thilnos (thil-nos) ["Thiln" + Os] 12 Seats

Oslondoh (os-LON-doh) [Os + Londoh] 12 Kingdoms

Compare from *Loagaeth*:

Os

Osf (os-ef) *n.* Discord

From *Corpus Omnium*:

Found in the Tribulation portion of the Table, in the phrase *Osf Ser Iad* (Discord and Sorrow of God).

Oslondoh (os-LON-doh)* [Os + Londoh] *comp.* 12 Kingdoms

3.8 . . . on whose hands stand *12 kingdoms*.

Pronunciation notes:

(**Dee—Os Lon doh [Os signifieth twelve.]*) Dee notes that this is a compound word. It has three syllables.

(**Dee—Os Lón-doh*) See the *48 Claves*. Other versions of *Londoh* show the accent on the "doh" syllable. However, when compounded with *Os*, the accent moves to the "Lon" syllable.

Ot* (ot) *conj.* And

Alternate spelling:

(**Dee 1.75—OD . . . or OT*)

Also:

Od (ohd) And

Othil (oh-THIL)* *n.* or *v.* Seats (of)/To Set

3.11 . . . six are *the seats of* living breath . . .
4.1 . . . *I have set* my feet in the south . . .

Note:
Perhaps Key Four should literally read "*the seats of* my feet are in the south," but this is stated better in English just as it is written in Key Four.

Pronunciation notes:
(**Dee 3.11—Othil*)
(**Dee 4.1—O thil*) Two syllables. The *O* stands alone.
(**Dee 3.11—óthil*) See *48 Claves*. Dee places the accent on the first syllable.
(**Dee 4.1—Othíl*) See *48 Claves*. Here, Dee places the accent on the second syllable. I have adopted this option in my pronunciation.

Compounds:
Othilrit (oh-THIL-rit) (Othil + Rit) Seats of Mercy

Also:
Thil (thil) Seats
Thild (thild) Seats
"Thiln" (thiln) Seats

Othilrit (oh-THIL-rit)* [Othil + Rit] *comp.* Seats of Mercy

7.3 . . . *the seats of mercy* and continuance . . .

Pronunciation notes:
(**Dee—O thil rit*) Three syllables. The *O* stands alone. The *i*'s should both take a short sound.
(**Dee—Othílrit*) See the *48 Claves*. Dee places an accent on the second syllable.

Oucho (oh-yew-choh)* *v.* To Confound

30.65 One season, *let it confound* another.

Pronunciation notes:

(**Dee—O v Cho Chose*) Dee shows us three syllables, with the *O* and the *u*/*v* standing alone. It is unlikely that Dee intended the *u* to sound like "vee," because the letter precedes a consonant. (Further supporting this is the "u" sound in other versions of this word.) Finally, Dee adds "chose"—to show us that the *ch* in the last syllable should make the "tch" sound (as in *church* and *chose*), and the *O* should be long.

Also:

Unchi (un-kii) To Confound
Urch (urk) The Confusers

Note:

It would appear that "uch" serves as a common root between these words.

Ovoars (oh-voh-ars)* *n.* Center

18.10 . . . the glory of God *to the center* of the earth.

Pronunciation notes:

(**Dee—O vo ors*) Three syllables. The initial *O* stands alone. Dee then shows a long "o" sound at the end of the second syllable. He may have mistakenly written an *o* in place of the *a* in the third syllable, or it is an error in *TFR*.

(**Dee—ouôars*) See the *48 Claves*. Dee places a circumflex over the second *o* to indicate its long sound. Note the *a* has returned to the third syllable.

Ovof (oh-vof)* *v.* To Magnify

12.18 . . . the Lord *may be magnified* whose name . . .

Pronunciation notes:

(**Dee—O vof*) Two syllables. The initial *O* stands alone.

OX (oks)* 26

8.6 . . . made of hyacinth pillars *26* in whom . . .

Pronunciation notes:

(**Dee—Ox*) One syllable.

Note:

This word was not originally given with Key Eight. It was added later when Nalvage transmitted the English for the Key (see *TFR*, p. 192). This seems to have been the case with many of the numbers mentioned in the Keys.

Oxex (oks-eks)* *v.* To Vomit (i.e., To Hurl Forth)

10.26 . . . and *vomit out* the heads of scorpions . . .

Pronunciation notes:

(**Dee—Ox ex*) Two syllables. The vowels both appear to take their short sounds.

Note:

This is not the Angelical word for *vomit* (a noun). Instead, this word is a verb, as in a volcano "vomiting" lava or a cannon "vomiting" flame. I notice this word falls just short of the *-ax* suffix, indicating action.

This word may share the masculine "Ox" root with the following:

Possible shared root:

Oxiayal (oks-AY-al) [Tox? + Iaial] Mighty Seat
Oxo (oks-oh) "The Fifteenth Aethyr"
Tox (toks) His

Oxiayal (oks-AY-al)* [Tox? + Iaial] *comp.* Mighty Seat (i.e., Divine Throne)

11.1 *The Mighty seat* groaned . . .

Pronunciation notes:

(**Dee—Ox í Ay al*) Dee heard four syllables, with an accent on the second syllable. However, Illemese corrected this later:

(*Illemese—Ox cai al. Sai*) See *TFR*, p. 200. Three syllables. The *c* used in the second syllable of *Illemese'* phonetic note takes an "s" sound—which I believe indicates the *second half* of the sound of "x." It appears to me that the accented *i* in Dee's phonetic note is not sounded at all in Illemese's version. It is unclear if the *i* should also be removed from the Angelical spelling of the word as well. (I have decided to leave it in.) Next, the letters *ai* or *ay* combine to form a long "a" sound—as in the English words *dais* and *day*. Finally, I have left the accent on the second syllable.

Possible shared root:

Oxex (oks-eks)	To Vomit
Tox (toks)	His

Note:

This reference to *Iaial* (conclude or judge), combined with the root of *Tox* (him/his), seems to make perfect sense when describing the Holy *Merkavah*—the Throne or "Judgment-Seat" of God.

Oxo (oks-oh) *prop. n.* "The Fifteenth Aethyr"

30.3 . . . which dwell in *the fifteenth aethyr* . . .

Note:

This (word 30.3) is the single space in the Key of the Aethyrs, which must be changed for each invocation—replacing word 30.3 with the name of the appropriate Aethyr. No established definitions were given for these names.

Note that this word is a palindrome, spelled the same forward and backward.

Oxo contains the three Parts of the Earth *Tahamdo, Nociabi,* and *Tastoxo*.

Possible shared root:

Oxex (oks-eks)	To Vomit
Tox (tox)	His

Ozazm (oz-az-em)* *v.* To Make (Me)

2.48 . . . and *make me* a strong seething . . .

Pronunciation notes:

(**Dee—Ozazm*) Likely three syllables.

Also:

Ozazma (oz-az-ma) To Make (Us)

Note:

Also see *Oln* (made) and *Eol* (made).

Ozazma (oz-az-ma)* *v.* To Make (Us)

30.155 . . . and *make us* partakers of undefiled knowledge.

Pronunciation notes:

(**Dee—Ozazma*) Likely three syllables.

Also:

Ozazm (oz-az-em) To Make (Me)

Note:

Also see *Oln* (made) and *Eol* (made).

Ozien (oh-ZEEN)* *n.* (Mine Own) Hand

3.23 . . . except by *mine own hand.*

Pronunciation notes:

(**Dee—Ozien*) I assume there should be two syllables here. The Early Modern English letter combination *ie* can make a long "e" sound. (It can also make a long "i" sound—but usually in combination with *ght*. So I have settled on the long "e" sound instead.)

(**Dee—ozíen*) See the *48 Claves*. Dee places the accent on the *i*—or the second syllable.

Also:

Azien (az-EEN) — (On Whose) Hands
Zien (zeen) — Hands

Probable shared root:

Ozol (oh-ZOHL) — Hands
Zol (zohd-OL) — Hands

Ozol (oh-ZOHL)* *n.* — Hands**

9.55 . . . and upon *their hands* are marble . . .

Pronunciation notes:

(**Dee—O zol*) Two syllables. The first *O* stands alone. Note how the *z* is not extended to "zohd" in this version of the word. (Compare to *Zol*.) This further supports the theory that the extended *z* is not a grammatical rule, but a lyrical flourish.
(**Dee—ózól*) See the *48 Claves*. Here, Dee placed accent marks over *both* syllables. It is unclear which syllable should take the accent. I have chosen the second syllable based on other versions of this word.

Note:

***Ozol* was translated as "heads" in Key Nine. However, this is apparently a mistake. *Zol* is elsewhere translated as "hands," and this makes much more sense in the English given for the Key.

Also:

Zol (zohd-OL) — Hands

Shared root:

Azien (az-EEN) — (On Whose) Hands
Ozien (oh-ZEEN) — (Mine Own) Hand
Zien (zeen) — Hands

Ozongon (OH-zohn-gon)* *n.* — Manifold Winds

2.31 . . . mightier are your voices than *the manifold winds*.

Pronunciation note:

(**Dee—Ozongon*)

(**Dee—ózôngon*) See *48 Claves*. Apparently three syllables. Dee places an accent on the first syllable. He also places a circumflex over the second *o*—indicating its long sound.

Also:

Zong (zong) Winds

Mals (P)

P (pee) 8

9.8 . . . which have *8* vials of wrath . . .

Pronunciation notes:

A letter standing alone sounds like the English name of that letter.

Note:

This word was not originally given with Key Nine. It was added later when Nalvage transmitted the English for the Key (see *TFR*, p. 191). This seems to have been the case with many of the numbers mentioned in the Keys.

Pa (pah) *prop. n.* Letter *B*

Note:

The name of the Angelical letter for *B*. It is likely that these letter names have translations of their own. (For instance, note the Hebrew alphabet: the letter *B* is named *Beth*, but *Beth* also translates as "house" or "dwelling.") However, such translations for the Angelical letters are never given. (See the *Five Books*, p. 270.)

Compare from *Loagaeth*:

Pa

"Paaox" (PAY-ay-oks) *v.* To Remain

Compounds:

Dspaaox (dee-SPAY-ay-oks) [Ds +" Paaox"] Which Remain

Also:

Paaoxt (PAY-ay-oxt) (Let) Remain

Note:

Compare this word to the name of the Angel *Paax* (an Angel of medicine of the Western Watchtower).

Paaoxt (PAY-ay-okst)* *v.* To Remain

30.133 No place, *let it remain* in one number.

Pronunciation notes:

(**Dee—Pa a oxt*) Three syllables. Both *a*'s appear to make the long vowel sound. The accent on the first syllable is taken from *Dspaaox*.

Also:

"Paaox" (PAY-ay-oks) To Remain

Note:

It is possible that the difference in spelling between "Paaox" and *Paaoxt* is merely a phonetic gloss.

Pacaduasam (pak-ad-yew-as-sam) n/a

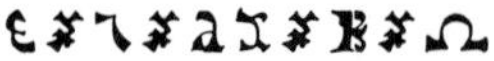

Note:

(*Dee—Huseh Huseh Huseh garmal, Peleh Peleh Peleh pacaduasam.*) See the *Five Books*, p. 415. This is part of a prayer recited jointly by the Archangels Michael, Raphael, and Uriel. No translations are suggested.

Possible shared root:

Pacaph (pak-af) n/a

Compare from *Loagaeth*:

Pacad, Pacadaah, Pacadabaah, Pacadura, Pachad, Pachadah, Pachadora, Pachadpha, and maybe *Paxchadma*

Pacaph (pak-af) n/a

Note:

See the *Five Books*, p. 413. Kelley overhears many voices singing a song at some distance, and these are the words Dee recorded: *Pinzu-a lephe ganiurax kelpadman pacaph*. No translations are suggested.

Note:

The similarity between this word and the Hebrew *Pachad* (fear).

Possible shared root:

Pacaduasam (pak-ad-yew-as-sam) n/a

Compare from *Loagaeth*:

Pacad, Pacadaah, Pacadabaah, Pacadura, Pachad, Pachadah, Pachadora, Pachadpha, and maybe *Paxchadma*

Padgze (paj)* *n.* "Justice From Divine Power Without Defect"**

Pronunciation notes:

(***Dee—Pagze/Pag.*) See the *Five Books*, p. 316. I suspect that Dee is indicating that *gze* should combine into a soft "g" (or "dg") sound. Thus, the word is one syllable, suggested by *Pag* in Dee's phonetic note.

From *Loagaeth*:

(**Dee—Justice from Divine Power without defect.*) See the *Five Books*, p. 316.

Paeb (pay-eb)* *n.* Oak

10.8 . . . *an oak* whose branches are 22 nests . . .

Pronunciation notes:

(**Dee—Pa eb*) Two syllables. The *a* appears to take its long sound. The *e* should be short.

(**Dee—p*æb) See the *48 Claves*. Here, Dee uses the "ash" (*æ*), which can make a short "a" sound or a long "e" sound. However, this conflicts with his two-syllable phonetic note in *TFR*. I have settled on the *TFR* version in this case.

"Page" (pay-jee) *v.* To Rest

Compounds:

Pageip (pay-jee-ip) ["Page" + Ip] Rest Not

Compare from *Loagaeth*:

Pagesgem, Pageh, Pagel, Arpagels, Arpaget, and maybe *Nagel.*

Pageip (pay-jee-ip)* ["Page" + Ip] *comp.* Rest Not

10.50 . . . which *rest not* neither know any long time . . .

Pronunciation notes:

(**Dee—Pa ge ip*) Three syllables. The *a* and *e* likely take long sounds. The *g*—preceding an *e*—should take the soft "j" sound.

(**Dee—pagêip*) See the *48 Claves*. Here, Dee placed a circumflex over the *e* to indicate its long sound.

Paid (pay-id)* *adv.* Always

30.52 . . . may be *always* drunken and vexed . . .

Pronunciation notes:

(**Dee—Pa id*) Dee here indicates two syllables.

Pal (pal)* *prop. n.* Letter *X*

Note:

The name of the Angelical letter for *X*. It is likely that these letter names have translations of their own. (For instance, note the Hebrew alphabet: the digraph *Tz* is named *Tzaddi*, but *Tzaddi* also translates as "fish hook.") However, such translations for the Angelical letters are never given. (See the *Five Books*, p. 270.)

Pronunciation notes:

(**Dee—The p being sounded remissly.*) The Latin word *remissus* means "to relax"—from which we get the English word *remiss* (to neglect or ignore). Therefore, the *P* in Pal must be very relaxed—nearly silent.

Compare from *Loagaeth*:

Pal

Pala (pay-la) *n.* Two, separated*

From *Loagaeth*:

(**Dee—Pola and Pala signify Two. Pola signifieth two together, and Pala signifieth two separated.*) See *Five Books*, p. 304. *Pola* (two together, or couple) appears in *Loagaeth*, while *Pala* is mentioned only in the marginal note. See also *Viv* (second).

Also:

Olani (oh-el-AY-nii) — Two Times, Twice
Pola (poh-la) — Two-together

"Pam" (pam) *adv.* Not

Compounds:

Ipam (ip-am) [I + "Pam"] — Is Not
Ipamis (ip-am-is) [I + "Pamis"] — Can Not Be

Note:

The words "Pam" and "Pamis" are very uncertain. In Angelical, the word *I* (is/are) becomes its own antonym in the form of *Ip* (not). However, both *Ipam* and *Ipamis* demand the essential form of the word *I* (for "is" and "be" respectively). That leaves "Pam" and "Pamis" as possible words. Of course, *Ip* could stand as a root here. See also *"Ge"* (not) and *Ag* (none).

Pambt (pamt)* *prep.* Unto (Me)

18.26 Be thou a window of comfort *unto me.*

Pronunciation notes:

(**Dee—Pambt*) One syllable. I suspect the *a* should take a short sound. The *b* in the letter combination *mb* is likely near-silent—as in the English words *comb* and *bomb*.

Note:

Also see *Tia* (unto) and *Pugo* (as unto).

"Pamis" (pam-is) *v.* Cannot

Compounds:

Ipam (ip-am) [I + "Pam"] Is Not

Ipamis (ip-am-is) [I + "Pamis"] Can Not Be

Note:

See note at "Pam."

Panpir (pan-per)* *v.* To Pour Down (Rain)

3.51 . . . *pouring down* the fires of life and increase . . .

Pronunciation notes:

(**Dee—Panpir*) Likely two syllables.

Paombd (pay-omd)* *n.* Members (Parts, Appendages)

30.75 All *her members*, let them differ . . .

Pronunciation notes:

(**Dee—Pa Ombd*) Dee indicates two syllables. I assume the *mb* represents the same sound as in the English words *comb*, *tomb*, and *bomb*. As for the vowel sounds, the note indicates a long *a* immediately followed by a short *o*—as in the English word *chaos*.

Papnor (pap-nor)* *n.* Remembrance (Memory)

7.43 For *to this remembrance* is given power . . .

Pronunciation notes:

(**Dee—Pap nor*) Two syllables. Both vowels are likely short.

Par (par)* *pron.* (In) Them

9.65 . . . the God of Righteousness rejoiceth *in them*.

Pronunciation notes:

(**Dee—Par*) One syllable.

Parach (pay-RAK)* *adj.* Equal

30.81 . . . no one creature *equal with* another . . .

Pronunciation notes:

(**Dee—Pa rach Ah Ach*) Two syllables. Dee seems to indicate that the final *ch* can take a softer "h" sound or a harder "kh" sound (as in the English word *ache*). I suggest a combination of the two, for a very soft "kh." (Also note the pronunciation of *Paracleda* (wedding), which uses a hard "c" sound.)

I have adopted the accent from *Paracelda*.

Probable shared root:

Paracleda (par-AK-lee-da) Wedding

Note:

Also see *Lel* (same).

Paracleda (par-AK-lee-da)* *n.* Wedding

2.17 . . . I have prepared as cups *for a wedding* . . .

Pronunciation notes:

(**Dee—Paracleda*) Should be four syllables. The *c* should take the hard sound when followed by an *l*—as in the English words *clean* and *climb*.

(**Dee—paráclêda*) See *48 Claves*. The accent is on the second syllable. The *e* has a circumflex, indicating its long sound.

Probable shared root:

Parach (pay-RAK) Equal

Note:

Also see *Pala* (two together, couple).

Paradial (pay-ray-DII-al)* *n.* Living Dwellings

7.13 . . . 28 *living dwellings* . . .

Pronunciation notes:

(**Dee—Pa ra dí al*) Four syllables, with an accent on the third syllable. (**Dee—paradíal*) See the *48 Claves*. The accent is again on the third syllable.

Note:

The word for "house" is given elsewhere as *Salman*. Here in Key Seven, however, this word is used after *Paradiz* (virgins) at 7.3. I assume these "living dwellings" are directly related to the Paradiz in some fashion.

Probable shared root:

Paradiz (pay-ray-DII-zohd) Virgins

Paradiz (pay-ray-DII-zohd)* *n.* Virgins

7.3 The east is a house of *virgins* . . .

Note:

There seems to be some relationship between Paradiz here, and the word *Paradial* (living dwellings) that appears later in the same Key. Paradial is obviously a special case, as the word for "house" is given elsewhere as *Salman*.

Pronunciation notes:

(**Dee—Pa ra di zod*) Four syllables. The *z* stands alone. Also, see *Paradial* (living dwellings) for the accent on the third syllable.

Probable shared root:

Paradial (pay-ray-DII-al) Living Dwellings

Parm (parm)* *v.* To Run

9.47 . . . from their mouths *run* seas of blood.

Pronunciation notes:

(**Dee—Parm*) One syllable.

Also:

Parmgi (parm-jii) (Let) Run

Parmgi (parm-jii)* *v.* (Let) Run

30.58 Her course, *let it run with* the heavens . . .

Pronunciation notes:

(**Dee—Parm gi*) Two syllables. The *g* preceding an *i* likely takes the soft sound.

Also:

Parm (parm) To Run

Pasbs (pas-bes) *n.* Daughters

14.3 . . . *the daughters* of the just . . .

Note:

The transmission of Key Fourteen is missing from Dee's journals. We only have the English for this Key given later (see *TFR*, p. 193). Plus, the word appears in this location in Dee's *48 Claves*.

"Patralx" (PAY-tralks) *n.* Rock

Compounds:

Lpatralx (el-PAY-tralks) [L + "Patralx"] One Rock

Paz (paz) *prop. n.* "The Fourth Aethyr"

30.3 . . . which dwell in *the fourth aethyr* . . .

Note:

This (word 30.3) is the single space in the Key of the Aethyrs, which must be changed for each invocation—replacing word 30.3 with the name of the appropriate Aethyr. No established definitions were given for these names.

Paz contains the three Parts of the Earth *Thotanp*, *Axziarg*, and *Pothnir*.

PD (pee-dee)* 33

4.10 . . . Thunders of Increase numbered *33* which reign . . .

Pronunciation notes:

(**Dee—PD Pe De*) Two syllables, each letter stands alone.

Peleh* (pee-lay) Worker of Wonders(?)

Note:

(**Dee—Huseh Huseh Huseh garmal, Peleh Peleh Peleh pacaduasam.*) See the *Five Books*, p. 415. This is part of a prayer recited jointly by the Archangels Michael, Raphael, and Uriel. No translations are suggested.

Note:

The Divine Name "PELE" appears on Dee's Ring of Solomon. This Name appears in Agrippa's *Three Books* . . . , Book III, chapter 11: (*Pele, signifieth with us, a worker or miracles, or causing wonders.*) In Hebrew, it is spelled *Peh, Lamed, Aleph*. (Also see "Lzirn"—To Work Wonders).

Compare from *Loagaeth*:

Peleh

PERAL (pee-AR-al)* 69636

5.34 . . . lamps *69636* whose numbers are . . .

Pronunciation notes:

(**Dee—Pe ó al*) Dee originally received this word as "Peoal," but it was later corrected to *Peral* (see *TFR*, p. 191). For my pronunciation, I have retained the structure of Dee's phonetic note, but applied it to the corrected word. It should therefore be three syllables, with an accent on the second. The *r* (instead of *o*) stands alone, and takes the accent.

(**Dee—Peóal*) See the *48 Claves*. This note essentially matches that from *TFR*. Dee did not correct the spelling of this word in the *48 Claves*.

Phama (fama) *v.* — I Will Give*

From *Loagaeth*:

(**Dee—Phamah/fama = I will give.*) See the *Five Books*, p. 320.

"Pi" (pii) *pron.* — She

Compounds:

Pii (pii-ii) ["Pi" + I] — She Is

Also:

"Ip" (ip) — Her

Note:

Also see *Tilb* (her).

Piad (pii-AD)* *n.* — (Your) God

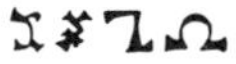

3.3 . . . behold, sayeth *your God* . . .

Pronunciation notes:

(**Dee—Pi ad*) Two syllables. Likely a long "i" sound. I have adopted the accent from similar words.

Also:

Geiad (jej-AYD)	Lord and Master
Iad (yad)	God
"Iadoias" (jad-oh-JAS)	Eternal God
Iadpil (ii-AD-pil)	(To) Him
Ioiad (joh-JAD)	Him That Liveth Forever
Mad (mad)	(Your) God
Oiad (oh-ii-AD)	Of God

Probable root:

Ia (yah) — n/a

Piadph (pii-AD-ef)* *n.* The Depths of (My) Jaws

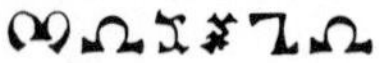

2.12 . . . burning flames have framed within *the depths of my jaws* . . .

Pronunciation notes:

(*Dee—Piadph*) Dee gives us little clue here.

(*Dee—pi-ádph*) See *48 Claves*. Likely three syllables. The *i* takes its long sound. The accent is on the second syllable.

Note:

This reference may be similar to "from the bottom of my heart" or even "deep in my gut." Otherwise, it may indicate "in my throat"—as the reference here in Key Two is to a song.

Piad (your God) does not appear to be intended in this case. It is perhaps a coincidental similarity in spelling.

"Piamol" n/a

Note:

Not an Angelical word. Dee and Kelley experienced problems during the reception of this word—intended for position 1.70 (righteousness). The Angels blamed the difficulty on interference from false spirits. This resulted in the erroneous transmission of "Piatol"—apparently a combination of the word preceding it in the Key (1.69—*Piap*) and the word actually intended here (1.70—*Baltle*). Dee's first attempt to correct the word—made while the false spirits continued to interfere—resulted in "Piamol." The next day, the Angels corrected it to *Baltle* (a form of *Balt*). See *Baltle*.

Piap (pii-ap) *n.* Balance

1.69 . . . *the balance of* righteousness . . .

"Piatol" n/a

Note:

Not an Angelical word. Dee and Kelley experienced problems during the reception of this word—intended for position 1.70 (righteousness).

The Angels blamed the difficulty on interference from false spirits. This resulted in the erroneous transmission of "Piatol"—apparently a combination of the word preceding it in the Key (1.69—*Piap*) and the word actually intended here (1.70—*Baltle*). Dee's first attempt to correct the word—made while the false spirits continued to interfere—resulted in "Piamol." The next day, the Angels corrected it to *Baltle* (a form of *Balt*). See *Baltle*.

Pibliar (pib-lii-AR)* *n.* Places of Comfort

7.30 . . . strong towers and *places of comfort.*

Pronunciation notes:

(**Dee—Pib li ar*) Three syllables. The first *i* should take a short sound, while the second *i* should take its long sound.

(**Dee—piblîar*) See the *48 Claves*. Dee places a circumflex over the second *i* to indicate the long sound.

I have adopted the accent from *Bliora* (comfort).

Also:

"Bigl" (big-el)	Comforter
"Bliard" (blii-ARD)	Comfort
Blior (blii-OR)	Comfort
Bliora (blii-OH-ra)	Comfort
Bliorax (blii-OH-raks)	To Comfort
Bliorb (blii-ORB)	Comfort
Bliors (blii-ORS)	Comfort
"Bliort" (blii-ORT)	Comfort

Pidiai (pii-dii-ay-ii)* *n.* Marble

9.57 . . . and upon their heads are *marble* sleeves.

Pronunciation notes:

(**Dee—Pi di a i*) Four syllables. The *a* and final *i* each stand alone.

Pii (pii-ii)* ["Pi" + I] *comp.* She Is

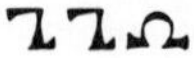

30.111 . . . *she is* the bed of an harlot . . .

Pronunciation notes:

(**Dee—Pi i*) Two syllables. I assume a long *i* in the first syllable. The *i* in the second syllable stands alone, also making a long "i" sound.

Pilah (pee-ii-lah)* *adv.* Moreover

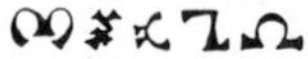

1.47 *Moreover*, you lifted up your voices . . .

Pronunciation notes:

(**Dee—Three syllables. P is distinctly sounded by itself.*)

(**Dee—Pïlah*) See *48 Claves*. There is a dieresis placed over the *i*, to indicate that the vowel stands alone.

Pild (pild)* *adv.* Continually

3.54 . . . upon the earth *continually*.

Pronunciation notes:

(**Dee—Pild*) Seems to be one syllable.

Note:

See also *Cocasb* (time), *Capimali* (successively), *Cacacom* (flourish).

Pilzin (pil-zin)* *n.* Firmaments of Waters

6.6 . . . mighty in the *firmaments of waters* . . .

Pronunciation notes:

(**Dee—Pilzin pilzen*) Likely two syllables.

Shared root:

Zlida (zohd-lida) To Water

Note:
Pilzin is a noun, while *Zlida* is a verb.

Pinzu (pin-zoo)* n/a

Note:
See the *Five Books*, p. 413. Kelley overhears many voices singing a song at some distance, and these are the words Dee recorded: *Pinzu-a lephe ganiurax kelpadman pacaph.* No translations are suggested.

Pronunciation notes:
(**Dee—This "a" was sounded to the end of pinzu as we use in english ballads, as with this word "down" is sounded as "downa, down a down a," etc.*) There is an extra "a" appended to Pinzu in Dee's journal (pin-zoo-ah). His marginal note explains this is merely a melodic flourish in the song, and not part of the word itself:

Pir (per) *n.* Holy (Ones)

1.41 . . . a law to govern the *holy ones* . . .

Note:
Apparently a reference to the celestial bodies / Angels.

Based on the words that seem to share *Pir* as their root, I suspect the *i* in *Pir* is a phonetic gloss.

Possible root for:

Piripsax (per-IP-saks)	The Heavens
Piripsol (per-IP-sol)	Heavens
Piripson (per-IP-son)	(Third?) Heaven
"Pirgah" (pur-jah)	The First Glory
"Pirgi" (pur-jii)	Fires
"Prg" (purj)	Flame
Prge (purj)	Fire
Prgel (pur-jel)	Fire
"Purg" (purj)	Flames

"Pirgah" (pur-jah) *n.* "The First Glory" (lit., Flames)

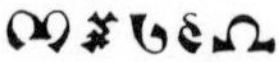

Compounds:

Ialpirgah (YAL-pur-jah) ["Ialprt" + "Pirgah"] Flames of the First Glory

Also:

"Pirgi" (pur-jii) Fires
"Prg" (purj) Flame
Prge (purj) Fire
Prgel (pur-jel) Fire
"Purg" (purj) Flames

Possible root:

Pir (per) Holy Ones

Note:

"Pirgah" is obviously a form of the word *Prge* (fire), and must mean "the First Glory"—that is, the Light of Divinity. (Possibly a reference to the rising Sun.)

Also see *Ialpirt* (light), which seems to indicate light from celestial beings.

Also see *Busd* (glory), which seems to indicate "wondrous."

Also see *Adgmach* (glory), which seems to indicate "adoration, praise."

"Pirgi" (per-jii) *n.* Fires

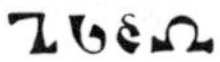

Compounds:

Malpirgi (mal-per-jii) ["Mal" + "Pirgi"] Fires of Life and Increase

Also:

"Pirgah" (pur-jah) The First Glory
"Prg" (purj) Flame
Prge (purj) Fire
Prgel (pur-jel) Fire
"Purg" (purj) Flames

Possible root:

Pir (per) Holy Ones

Note:

See *Prge* (fire).

Piripsax (per-IP-saks)* *n.* Heavens

30.59 . . . let it run with *the heavens* . . .

Pronunciation notes:

(**Dee—Pe rip sax*) Three syllables. Dee shows an *e* at the end of the first syllable, but it should take the short sound, as the letter is actually *i*.

(**Dee—perípsax*) See the *48 Claves*. Here, Dee places an accent over the *i* in the second syllable.

Also:

Piripsol (per-IP-sol) — Heavens

Piripson (per-IP-son) — (Third?) Heaven

Note:

Also see "Madriax" (Heavens) and *Oadriax* (Heavens).

Possible shared root:

Pir — Holy Ones

Piripsol (per-IP-sol)* *n.* Heavens

5.12 . . . the brightness of *the heavens* . . .

30.21 . . . the brightness of *the heavens* . . .

Pronunciation notes:

(**Dee 5.12—Pir ipsol*)

(**Dee 30.21—Pe ríp sol*) Three syllables, accent on the second syllable. Dee's note at 30.21 seems to indicate a long "e" sound in the first syllable—but his note at 5.12 does not show such. I have settled upon the short "e" sound.

(**Dee 5.12—péripsol*) See the *48 Claves*. Here, Dee moved the accent to the first syllable.

(**Dee 30.21—perípsol*) See the *48 Claves*. Here, Dee moved the accent back to the second syllable.

Also:

Piripson (per-IP-son) — (Third?) Heaven

Piripsax (per-IP-saks) — The Heavens

Note:

Also see "Madriax" (Heavens) and *Oadriax* (lower Heavens).

Possible shared root:

Pir — Holy Ones

Piripson (per-IP-son)* *n.* — (Third?) Heaven

8.3 . . . first, is as the *third heaven* . . .

Pronunciation notes:

(**Dee—Pi ríp son*) Three syllables, with an accent on the second syllable. The first *i* seems to take a long sound in Dee's phonetic note. However, other versions of this word clearly indicate a short "i" sound instead (which I have shown in my pronunciation as a short "e" sound).

(**Dee—pirípson*) See the *48 Claves*. The accent is again shown on the second syllable.

Note:

The word *D* (third) does not appear here. This could be a proper name for the third Heaven.

Also:

Piripsol (per-IP-sol) — Heavens

Piripsax (per-IP-saks) — The Heavens

Note:

Also see "Madriax" (Heavens) and *Oadriax* (lower Heavens).

Possible shared root:

Pir (per) — Holy Ones

Plapli (play-plii)* *n.* — Partakers (of)

3.79 . . . *partakers of* the secret wisdom . . .

30.156 . . . make us *partakers of* undefiled knowledge.

Pronunciation notes:

(**Dee 3.79—It is Plapli*)

(**Dee 30.156—Pla pli*) Two syllables, and none of these letters stand alone.

Plosi (ploh-sii)* *idiom* — As Many

10.47 . . . 1000 times *as many* . . .

Pronunciation notes:

(**Dee—Plo si*) Two syllables. The *o* and *i* should take their long sounds.

Note:

Also see "Irgil" (how many)

Poamal (poh-mal)* *n.* — Palace

1.64 . . . in the midst of *your palace* . . .

Pronunciation notes:

(**Dee—Poamal*) The Early Modern English letter combination *oa* makes a long "o" sound (as in the English words *boat* and *coat*). Therefore, I suspect this word should have two syllables.

Poilp (poylp)* *v.* — To Divide

8.45 . . . the crowns of the Temple and the coat of Him . . . are divided.

Pronunciation notes:

(**Dee—Poilp; one syllable*) Dee indicates one syllable for this word. Therefore, the *oi* letter combination should make an "oy" sound—as in the English words *boil* and *boy*.

Also:

Yrpoil (yur-POY-il) — Division

Pola (poh-la) *n.* — Two together, Couple*

From *Loagaeth*:

(**Dee—Pola and Pala signify Two. Pola signifieth two together, and Pala signifieth to separated.*) See *Five Books*, p. 304. *Pola* (two together, or couple) appears in *Loagaeth*, while *Pala* (two-separated) appears only in the marginal note.

See also *Viv* (second)

Also:

Olani (oh-el-AY-nii) — Two Times, Twice
Pala (pay-la) — Two, separated

Pop (pop) *prop. n.* — "The Nineteenth Aethyr"

30.3 . . . which dwell in the nineteenth aethyr . . .

Note:

This (word 30.3) is the single space in the Key of the Aethyrs, which must be changed for each invocation—replacing word 30.3 with the name of the appropriate Aethyr. No established definitions were given for these names.

Also note this word is a palindrome, spelled the same forward and backward.

Pop contains the three Parts of the Earth *Torzoxi*, *Abriond*, and *Omagrap*.

"Praf" (praf) *v.* — To Dwell

Compounds:

Dspraf (dee-es-praf) [Ds + "Praf"] — Which Dwell

Pragma (prag-ma) — n/a (?)

Note:

See *TFR*, p. 32. Here, the Angel Madimi has just interrupted the session to exorcise several demons from the body of Kelley. (See *Carma*.) These spirits came out of Kelley violently, scratching each other in the face and swarming about Madimi. To her, the spirits spoke in Angelical, "*Gil de pragma kures helech*." Dee asks Madimi what this means, and she replies (in Latin), "We want to live here in our [friends]." (Madimi does not offer definitions for the individual words.)

When Dee asks who these "friends" are supposed to be, the spirits indicate Kelley as their place of habitation. (Probably meaning both Dee and Kelley.) Madimi then banishes these spirits.

Prdzar (purd-zar)* *v.* To Diminish

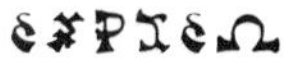

30.137 Add and *diminish* until the stars be numbered.

Pronunciation notes:

(**Dee—Prd zar Pur*) Two syllables. The *r* takes the "ur" sound.

(**Dee—prd-zar*) See the *48 Claves*. Dee again indicates two syllables.

Note:

Perhaps there is a relationship between this word and the Name of God *Ardza*, found on the Eastern Watchtower, ruling the Angels of medicine. If so, its attribute may be "to diminish" disease.

"Prg" (purj) *n.* Flame

Pronunciation notes:

See note at *Prge* (Fire).

Compounds:

Ialprg (YAL-purj) ["Ialprt" + "Prg"] Burning Flame

Malprg (mal-purj) ["Mal" + "Prg"] Through-thrusting Fire

Also:

"Pirgah" (pur-jah) The First Glory

"Pirgi" (pur-jii) Fires

Prge (purj) Fire

Prgel (pur-jel)	Fire
"Purg" (purj)	Flames

Possible root:

Pir (per)	Holy Ones

Note:

Both this word and *Vep* (flame) are nouns. For a verb form, see *Ialpon* (to burn). For an adjective form, see *Ialpor* (flaming). See also *Ialpirt* (light), which seems to indicate light from celestial beings.

Prge (purj)* *n.* Fire

1.32 . . . with *the fire of* gathering . . .

Pronunciation notes:

(**Dee—as purge*) The *e* in Prge is likely a phonetic gloss, giving the *g* its soft sound. See the following words for more of Dee's phonetic glosses upon "Prg."

Also:

"Pirgah" (pur-jah)	The First Glory
"Pirgi" (pur-jii)	Fires
"Prg" (purj)	Flame
Prgel (pur-jel)	Fire
"Purg" (purj)	Flames

Possible root:

Pir (per)	Holy Ones

Note:

See note at "Prg."

Prgel (pur-jel) *n.* Fire

9.3 A mighty guard of *fire* . . .

Pronunciation notes:

(**Dee—Pur gel*) Two syllables. The *r* takes the extended "ur" sound. The *g* should be soft before the letter *e*. The *e* in this word is likely a phonetic gloss. See note at *Prge* (fire).

Also:

"Pirgah" (pur-jah)	The First Glory
"Pirgi" (pur-jii)	Fires
"Prg" (purj)	Flame
Prge (purj)	Fire
"Purg" (purj)	Flames

Possible root:

Pir (per)	Holy Ones

Note:

See note at "Prg."

Priaz (prii-AYZ)* *pron.* or *adj.* Those

30.122 . . . govern *those* that govern . . .

Pronunciation notes:

(**Dee—Priáz*) Likely two syllables, with the accent on the second syllable. I assume the *i* takes a long sound, because it is followed by an *a* (as in the English *dial*). I have given the *a* its long sound based on the pronunciation of *Priazi* (those).

(**Dee—priáz*) See the *48 Claves*. Here, Dee again places the accent upon the second syllable.

Also:

Priazi (prii-AY-zii)	Those

Priazi (prii-AY-zii)* *pron.* or *adj.* Those

30.128 Bring forth with *those* that increase . . .

Pronunciation notes:

(**Dee—Pri á zi*) Three syllables. The *a* stands alone in the second syllable and takes the accent.

Also:

Priaz (prii-AYZ) Those

Pugo (pug-oh)* *prep.* As unto

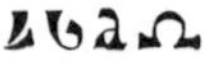

3.78 . . . unto us *as unto* partakers of the secret wisdom . . .

Pronunciation notes:

(**Dee—It is Pugo*) Likely two syllables, and I suggest a short *u* and a long final *o*.

Note:

Also see *Tia* (unto) and *Pambt* (unto).

"Puin" (pew-in) *n.* (Sharp) Sickles

Compounds:

Tapuin (TAY-pew-in) [Ta + "Puin"] As (Sharp) Sickles

"Puran" (pew-ran) *v.* To See

Compounds:

Odipuran (ohd-II-pew-ran) [Od + Ip + "Puran"] And Shall Not See

"Purg" (purj) *n.* Flames

Compounds:

Ialpurg (YAL-purj) ["Ialprt" + "Purg"] Burning Flames

Malpurg (mal-purj) ["Mal" + "Purg"] Fiery Darts (Arrows)

Also:

"Pirgah" (pur-jah) The First Glory

"Pirgi" (pur-jii)	Fires
"Prg" (purj)	Flame
Prge (purj)	Fire
Prgel (pur-jel)	Fire

Possible root:

Pir (per)	Holy Ones

Note:

See note at "Prg."

Ger (Q)

Q (kwah)* *conj.* Or

30.71 . . . no creature upon *or* within her . . .

Pronunciation notes:

(*Dee—Q*) One syllable. Likely takes the "kwah" sound.

Compounds:

Qmospleh [Q + "Mospleh"] Or the Horns

Qta [Q + Ta] Or as

Qaa (kwah-AY-ay)* *n.* Creation (or "Garments")

1.21 . . . measureth *your garments* . . .

(RFP) . . . open the mysteries of *your creation* . . .

30.153 Open the mysteries of *your creation.*

Pronunciation notes:

(**Dee 1.21—QAA three syllables*)

(**Dee 1.RFP—Call it QAA. Three syllables with accent on the last A*)

(**Dee 30.153—Q á a*) These notes tell us that each letter should stand by itself, making a word of three syllables. In one case (1.RFP), the accent is placed on the third syllable. Yet, elsewhere, it is placed on the second. I have opted for the second syllable accent, as we can also see in *Qaan* (creation).

(**Dee 1.21—Qa-a*) See *48 Claves*. Here, Dee indicates a word of two syllables instead.

(**Dee 11.RFP—Qaá*) See *48 Claves*. Dee indicates the accent on the third syllable.

(**Dee 12, 30.RFP—Qáa*) See *48 Claves*. Here, Dee indicates the accent on the second syllable.

(**Dee 13, 14, 15, 16, 17, 18.RFP—Qäa*) See *48 Claves*. Dee places a dieresis over the first *a*, giving it a long sound.

Note:

The first Key is the only place where *Qaa* is translated as "garments." I get the impression that this rogue definition of *Qaa* is meant to indicate "created forms" instead of clothing. It has been common to Western mysticism (Platonism, Neoplatonism, Gnosticism) to refer to the physical body (the created form) as a "garment" worn by the soul. (See Layton's *The Gnostic Scriptures*, p. 38, "Repentance and Elevation of Wisdom," where the word *garment* is used to refer to the body.)

Note that the common word for "garment" (or clothing) in Angelical is given as *Oboleh*, and related to the word *Obloch* (garland)—indicating a dressing.

Note also that *Zimz* (vestures) is *not* a reference to clothing.

Compounds?:

Qaal (kwah-AY-el) (Qaa + L)	Creator
Qadah (kwah-AY-dah) [Qaa + Iaida?]	Creator

Also:

Qaan (kwah-AY-an)	Creation
Qaaon (kwah-AY-ay-on)	Creation
Qaas (kwah-AY-as)	Creation

Qaal (kwah-AY-el)* [Qaa + L] *comp.* Creator

4.41 . . . in the name of *the Creator* . . .

Pronunciation notes:

(*Dee—Qa al*) Appears to be two syllables. However, also see the *48 Claves*:

(*Dee—Q-á-al*) See the *48 Claves*. Here Dee shows the proper three syllables, with an accent on the second syllable. The *Q* and the first *a* each stand alone.

Note:

The word *Qaa* is translated as "Creation." Combining this with *L* implies "the First Creator."

Also:

Qadah (kwah-AY-dah) [Qaa + Iaida?]	Creator

Qaan (kwah-AY-an)* *n.* Creation

3.81 . . . secret wisdom of *your creation* . . .

Pronunciation notes:

(*Dee—It is q á an*) Three syllables, with the accent on the second syllable.

(*Dee—Qáan*) See the 48 *Claves*. The accent is again on the second syllable.

Also:

Qaa (kwah-AY-ay) Creation (or Garments)
Qaaon (kwah-AY-ay-on) Creation
Qaas (kwah-AY-as) Creation

Qaaon (kwah-AY-ay-on)* *n.* Creation

6.43 . . . your God *in your creation* . . .

Pronunciation notes:

(*Dee—Q a a on*) Four syllables. The *Q* and both *a*'s stand alone.

(*Dee—Q-a-a-on*) See the 48 *Claves*. This note matches that from *TFR*. I have adopted the accent from other versions of this word.

Also:

Qaa (kwah-AY-ay) Creation (or Garments)
Qaan (kwah-AY-an) Creation
Qaas (kwah-AY-as) Creation

Qaas (kwah-AY-as)* *n.* Creation

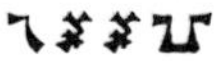

5.46 . . . obey *your creation* . . .

Pronunciation notes:

(*Dee—Q á as*) Three syllables, with an accent on the second syllable. The first *a* stands alone.

(*Dee—Q-á-as*) See the 48 *Claves*. This note matches that from *TFR*.

Also:

Qaa (kwah-AY-ay) — Creation (or Garments)
Qaan (kwah-AY-an) — Creation
Qaaon (kwah-AY-ay-on) — Creation

Qadah (kwah-AY-dah)* [Qaa + Iaida?] *comp.* — Creator

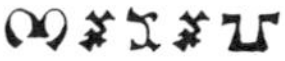

7.38 . . . sing praises unto *the creator*.

Note:

The word *Qaa* is translated as "Creation." Combining this with *Iaida* may imply the *Highest Creator*.

Pronunciation notes:

(*Dee—Q á dah*) Three syllables, with an accent on the second syllable. Both the *Q* and the *a* stand alone.
(*Dee—q-a-dah*) See the *48 Claves*. This note is essentially the same as that in *TFR*—without the accent mark.

Also:

Qaal (kwah-AY-el) — Creator

"Qanis" (kway-nis) *n.* — Olives

Compounds:

Taqanis (tay-kway-nis) [Ta + "Qanis"] — As Olives

Probable shared root:

Ooanoan (oh-oh-AY-noh-an) — (In Their?) Eyes
Ooaona (oh-ona) — Eyes
Oanio (oh-nii-oh) — Moment

Note:

The similar spelling suggests these three words are connected. This might make sense for *Ooaona* (eyes): the word *Taqanis* (as olives) in Key Five appears to refer to the stars. In biblical literature, the word "eyes" is often used to indicate "stars." (Such as in the visions of St. John and Ezekiel—who both saw celestial Angels with wings "full of eyes.")

If this is the case, then the shared root here may indicate "small units," which would explain its use to indicate a "moment" (*Oanio*).
Also see *Adroch* (olive mount).

Qcocasb (kwah-KOH-kasb)* *n.* Contents of Time

5.41 . . . the first, ends, and *contents of time* . . .

Pronunciation notes:
(**Dee—Q có casb*) Three syllables, with an accent on the second syllable. The *o* is likely long, as Dee shows it at the end of the second syllable.
(**Dee—Q-có-casb*) See the *48 Claves*. This note matches that from *TFR*.

Also:

Acocasb (ay-KOH-kasb)	Time
"Cacocasb" (kay-KOH-kasb)	Another While
Cocasb (KOH-kasb)	Time
Cocasg (KOH-kazh)	Times

Note:
Q translates in Angelical as "or," which would not fit the phrase here. Therefore, *Qcocasb* is not likely a compound of *Q* + *Cocasb*.

Possible shared root:

Cacacom (kay-SAY-som)	Flourish
Cacrg (KAY-kurg)	Until
Casasam (kay-SAY-sam)	Abiding
Capimali (kay-pii-MAY-lii)	Successively
"Capimao" (kay-pii-MAY-oh)	While
Capimaon (kap-ii-MAY-on)	Number of Time
Capmiali (kap-mii-AY-lii)	Successively

Note:
Also see *Pild* (continually)

Qmospleh (kwah-mos-play)* [Q + "Mospleh"] *comp.* Or the Horns

3.16 . . . as sharp sickles: *or the horns of* death . . .

Pronunciation notes:

(**Dee—Q Mos Pleh as two words*) Dee's statement indicates that *Qmospleh* is "as two words"—that is, a compound word. The *Q* stands alone.

(**Dee—Q mos-pleh*) See the *48 Claves*. This note matches the note in *TFR*.

"Qrasahi" (kra-sa-hii) *n.* — Pleasure

Compounds:

Norqrasahi (nor-kra-sa-hii) ["Nor" + "Qrasahi"] — Sons of Pleasure

Qta (kwah-tay)* [Q + Ta] *comp.* — Or as

2.18 . . . *or as* the flowers . . .

Pronunciation notes:

(**Dee—Quu Ta*) Two syllables. The *uu* in Early Modern English is a "w" sound—indicating that the Q should sound like "kwah."

(**Dee—Q-ta*) See *48 Claves*. Indicates two syllables.

Qting (kwah-tinj)* *n.* or *adj.?* — Rotten

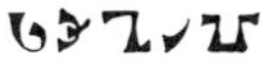

30.131 . . . and destroy *the rotten.*

Pronunciation notes:

(**Dee—Q ting dg*) Two syllables. The final *g* takes a soft "dg" (or "j") sound.

Note:

The word *rotten* is usually an adjective. However, it is used in Key Thirty as a noun ("the rotten").

QUAR (kwar) — 1636

14.16 . . . which have under you *1636.*

Note:

The transmission of Key Fourteen is missing from Dee's journals. We only have the English for this Key given later (see *TFR*, p. 193). Plus, the word appears in this location in Dee's *48 Claves*.

"Quasb" (kwazb) *v.* — To Destroy

Compounds:

Odquasb (ohd-kwazb) [Od + "Quasb"] — And Destroy

Note:

I suspect the *u* is a phonetic gloss.

Shared root:

Grosb (grozb) — Bitter Sting

Quiin (kwii-in)* *conj.* — Wherein

3.18 . . . *wherein* the creatures of the earth are . . .
7.7 . . . *wherein* the Lord hath opened his mouth . . .

Pronunciation notes:

(**Dee 3.18; 7.7—Qui in*) Two syllables. In Early Modern English, the double *i* makes a long "i" sound. The *n* essentially stands alone.

(**Dee 3.18—Qui-i-n*) See the *48 Claves*. Here, Dee shows three syllables. The second *i* and the *n* each stand alone.

(**Dee 7.7—qui-in*) See the *48 Claves*. This note essentially matches Dee's note in *TFR*. I have settled upon this two-syllable version of the word.

Note:

I assume the *u* in this word is a phonetic gloss.

Qurlst (kurlst)* *n.* — Handmaid

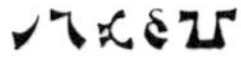

30.62 . . . as *a handmaid* let her serve them.

Pronunciation notes:

(**Dee—Qurlst Kurlst*) Likely just one syllable. The *Q* appears to make a hard "k" sound, while the *u* combines with the *r* to make an "ur" sound. I suspect the *u* is a phonetic gloss.

"Qzmoz" n/a

Note:

This is not likely an Angelical word at all. Dee originally wrote this word as "Qzmoz," but his phonetic note only indicated *Moz*. He also recorded the word as "MOZ" in his *48 Claves*. This same word (*Moz*) appears on the *Corpus Omnium* Table. There, Nalvage says that it can sound like "moz" or use the extended *z* for "mozod." Perhaps "Qzmoz" was a botched attempt to record the sound of the extended "mozod."

See *Moz* (joy, rejoice).

Don (R)

Raas (ray-as)* *n.* East

7.1 *The east* is a house of virgins . . .

Pronunciation notes:

(*Dee—Ra as*) Two syllables. In Early Modern English, a double vowel indicated a long sound—which Dee seems to indicate in the first syllable.

Also:

Raasy (ray-ay-see) East

Raasy (ray-ay-see)* *n.* East

11.9 . . . 5 thunders which flew into *the east* . . .

Pronunciation notes:

(*Dee—Ra a sy*) Three syllables. Both *a*'s take their long sound—and tend to blend into one sound when the word is spoken fluently. (In Early Modern English, a double *a* would simply indicate a long "a" sound.) The final *y* should make the sound of a long *e*—as in the English words *lazy* and *messy*.
(*Dee—raâsy*) See the *48 Claves*. Here, Dee placed a circumflex over the second *a* to indicate its long sound.

Also:

Raas (ray-as) East

Raclir (ray-kler)* *n.* or *v.* Weeping

10.16 . . . lamentation and *weeping* laid up for the earth . . .

Pronunciation notes:

(*Dee—Ra clir*) Two syllables. The *a* likely takes its long sound. The *c* appears to take its hard ("k") sound, as it combines with the *l*—as in the English words *clean* and *climb*.

Note:

Also compare with the name of the Angel *Rocle*, one of the Sons of the Sons of Light. If there is a connection, then *Rocle*'s name has the etymology of "to weep."

Remiges (rem-ii-jes) n/a

Note:

See the *Five Books*, p. 258. Here, Raphael offers a long prayer, the very end of which is, "How great and innumerable are your [God's] gifts? *O remiges varpax. Kyrie eleyson.*"

No translation is offered for this phrase, although I wonder if it is perhaps the Angelical for the Greek *Kyrie eleyson* (Lord have mercy), often used in Catholic prayer.

Restil (rest-el)* *v.* To Praise (Him?)

4.45 . . . *that you may praise him* amongst the sons of men.

Pronunciation notes:

(**Dee—Rest el*) Two syllables.

(**Dee—rest-el*) See the *48 Claves*. This note matches the note in in *TFR*.

Note:

See also *Oecrimi* (sing praises) and *Faaip* (voices).

Rii (rii-ii) *prop. n.* "The Twenty-Ninth Aethyr"

30.3 . . . which dwell in *the twenty-ninth aethyr* . . .

Note:

This (word 30.3) is the single space in the Key of the Aethyrs, which must be changed for each invocation—replacing word 30.3 with the name of the appropriate Aethyr. No established definitions were given for these names.

Rii contains the three Parts of the Earth *Vastrim*, *Odraxti*, and *Gomziam*.

Rior (rii-or)* *n.* Widow

8.20 . . . like unto the harvest of *a widow.*

Pronunciation notes:

(**Dee—Rior*) Dee gives us little clue here. I assume two syllables, with a long "i" sound.

Ripir (rii-PER)* *n.* No Place

30.132 . . . *No place,* let it remain in one number.

Pronunciation notes:

(**Dee—Ri pír*) Two syllables, with the accent on the second syllable. I suggest a long *i* at the end of the first syllable.

(**Dee—Ripír*) See the *48 Claves*. Dee again placed an accent over the *i* in the second syllable.

Note:

This word is a palindrome, spelled the same forward and backward.

Possible root:

Ip Not

Rit (rit)* *n.* Mercy

7.34 O you servants of *mercy* . . .

Pronunciation notes:

(**Dee—Rit*) One syllable, with a short vowel.

Compounds:

Othilrit (oh-THIL-rit) (Othil + Rit) Seats of Mercy

Rlodnr (rel-oh-din-ur) *n.* Alchemical Furnace / Athanor(?)

From the *Alchemical Cipher*:

See *TFR*, pp. 387–89. The Angel Levanael gives translations for all the *Alchemical Cipher* words except this one. However, from the deciphered message itself on p. 387, it would appear that *Rlodnr* is either an Alchemical Furnace (called an *Athanor*) or some process associated with the alchemical application of heat.

Ror (ror)* *n.* Sun

1.12 . . . *the sun* is as a sword . . .

Pronunciation notes:

(**Dee—Ror*) One syllable

Note:

This word is a palindrome, spelled the same forward and backward.

Roxtan (roks-tan) *n.* (Rectified?) Wine

From the *Alchemical Cipher*:

See TFR, pp. 387–89. The Angel Levanael says of this word, "*Roxtan*, is pure and simple wine in herself. *Lulo* is her mother." This could mean wine straight from the bottle. However, as this is an alchemical process, I suspect that "pure and simple wine in herself" could indicate rectified wine. (Rectification removes excess water and other impurities from the wine.)

Compare from *Loagaeth*:

Rox

Rudna (rud-na) n/a

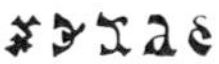

Note:

See *TFR*, p. 3. The Angel *Murifri* here speaks a prayer in Angelical, and Kelley can only overhear a few of the words: *Oh Gahire Rudna gephna oh Gahire*. It is unclear whether this represents a single Angelical phrase, or if they are disconnected words recorded by Dee as Kelley overheard them here and there in the prayer. No translations are suggested.

Fam (S)

S (es) *n.* or *adj.* Fourth

Compounds:

Sdiu (es-DII-vee) [S + Div] Fourth Angle

Also:

"Es" (es) Fourth

Note:

This is the word for "fourth," but not the numeral 4. The word is used here (the fourth angle) as an adjective.

Saanir (say-AY-ner)* *n.* Parts

30.5 . . . mighty in *the parts* of the earth . . .
30.45 . . . let her be governed by *her parts* . . .

Pronunciation notes:

(**Dee 30.5, 45—Sa á nir*) Three syllables, accent on the second. The *a* stands alone in the second syllable.

(**Dee 30.5, 45—saánir*) See the *48 Claves*. Dee again placed an accent over the second syllable.

"Saba" (SAY-bay) *adj.* Whose

Pronunciation note:

I have adopted the accent from *Asobam* (whom).

Compounds:

Sabaooaona (say-bay-oh-oh-AY-oh-na) ["Saba" + Ooaona] Whose Eyes

Also:

Asobam (ay-SOH-bam) (On) Whom
Sobam (SOH-bam) Whom
Sobca (SOB-kay) Whose

"Sobha" (sob-ha)	Whose
Soba (soh-ba)	Whose
"Sobo" (SOH-boh)	Whose
Sobra (SOB-ray)	Whose
"Sola" (SOH-lay)	Whose

Sabaooaona (say-bay-oh-oh-AY-oh-na) ["Saba" + Ooaona] *comp.*
Whose Eyes

30.18 . . . *whose eyes* are the brightness . . .

Pronunciation notes:
(**Dee—Sa ba o o áo na*) This may be a word of seven syllables—though it can sound more like six syllables when spoken fluently. (The two long "o" sounds run together.) The *ao* should make two sounds, as in the English word *chaos*. The accent is on the fifth syllable. The *a*'s in the first two syllables are long.
(**Dee—sabaooáôna*) See the *48 Claves*. Here, Dee again placed the accent over the *a* in the fifth syllable. He also placed a circumflex over the following *o* to indicate its long sound (thereby confirming that it should stand alone).

Sach (sak) *prop. n.* The Establishers/Supporters

From *Corpus Omnium*:
Associated with the post-Crucifixion portion of the Table, translated in Latin as *Confirmantes* (Those Who Establish).

Sagacor (say-GAY-kor)* *n.* "In One Number"

30.134 . . . no place, let it remain *in one number.*

Pronunciation notes:
(**Dee—Sa gá cor Kor*) Three syllables, with the accent on the second. It appears that Dee intended long *a*'s in the first two syllables. The *g*

should take its hard sound when preceding an *a*. Finally, Dee indicates that the *c* takes the hard "k" sound.

(**Dee—sagácor*) See the *48 Claves*. Here, Dee again placed an accent upon the second syllable.

Note:

The phrase "in one number" seems to indicate something like "constant" or "consistent."

Shared root:

Cormf (kormf)	Number
Cormfa (korm-FA)	Numbers
Cormp (kormf)	Numbered
Cormpo (korm-FOH)	Hath (Yet) Numbered
Cormpt (kormft)	Numbered

Salbrox (sal-broks)* *n.* Live (i.e., Burning) Sulfur

10.30 . . . scorpions and *live sulphur* mingled with poison.

Pronunciation notes:

(**Dee—Sal brox*) Two syllables. Both vowels are short.

Note:

Also see *Dlasod* (sulfur). Where *Salbrox* is the kind of sulfur one would find on a match, *Dlasod* refers to alchemical sulfur.

Sald (sald)* *n.* Wonder

2.6 . . . your voicings of *wonder* . . .

Pronunciation notes:

(**Dee—Sald*) One syllable.

Note:

Also see "Lzirn" (wonders) and *Busd* (Glory).

Salman (SAYL-man)* *n.* House

11.20 . . . *the house* of death . . .
**16.3 . . . *the house* of justice . . .

Pronunciation notes:
(**Dee—Sal man*) Two syllables. Both *a*'s appear to take their short sounds. However, see *Isalman* (is a house) and *Oisalman* (this house), which indicate a long sound for the first *a*. Finally, I have adopted the accent from *Isalman*.

Note:
**The transmission of the first twelve words of Key Sixteen is missing from Dee's journals. We only have the English given for it on *TFR*, p. 194. However, they do appear in Dee's *48 Claves*.

Compounds:

Isalman (ii-SAYL-man) [I + Salman]	Is a House
Oisalman (oh-ii-SAYL-man) ["Oi" + Salman]	This House

Samhampors (sam-HAM-pors)* n/a

Pronunciation note:
(**Dee—samhámpors*) See the *Five Books*, p. 302. Dee placed an accent over the second *a*.

From *Loagaeth*:
See the *Five Books*, p. 302. Note the similarity between this word and the Hebrew Name of God *Shem haMephoresh* (Name of Extension). See the note at *Semhaham*.

Possible shared root:

Sem (sem)	n/a
Semhaham (SEM-hah-ham)	n/a

Samvelg (sam-velj)* *n.* The Righteous

6.14 . . . and a garland to *the righteous*.

Pronunciation notes:

(**Dee—Samvelg*) I assume this should be two syllables. Dee does not indicate a hard or soft sound for the final *g*. I have settled upon a soft sound.

Note:

See also *Baltoh*, *Baltle*, and *Baeouib* (all translated as "righteousness").

Sapah (SAY-fah)* *prop. n.* Mighty Sounds (i.e., Thunders)

5.1 *The Mighty Sounds* have entered . . .

Pronunciation notes:

(**Dee—Sá pah*) Two syllables, with an accent on the first. Dee's phonetic note seems to indicate a hard "p" sound for the second syllable. However, see *TFR*, p. 200, where the Angel Illemese suggests "Saphah" as a pronunciation.

(**Dee—Sapáh*) See the *48 Claves*. In this case, Dee placed the accent on the second syllable.

Note:

The Mighty Sounds mentioned here, and the Thunders mentioned elsewhere in the Keys, are groups of Angels. See *Const* (thunders), *Avavago* (Thunders), and *Coraxo* (Thunders). The so-called *Sapah* (Mighty Sounds) are mentioned only in the fifth Key, which appears to relate to the Southern Quarter of the Universe.

Compare from *Loagaeth*:

Sapoh, Sappoh, Sepah, Sephah

Sdiv (es-DII-vee)* [S + Div] *comp.* Fourth Angle

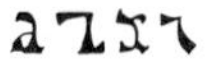

6.2 The spirits of *the fourth angle* . . .

Pronunciation notes:

(**Dee—S dí u es dí u*) Three syllables, with an accent on the second syllable. The the initial *S* and the final *u/v* stand alone.

(**Dee—s díu*) See the *48 Claves*. The accent is again shown on the second syllable.

Sem (sem) *n.?* In This Place*

From *Loagaeth*:
(**Dee—In this place.*) See the *Five Books*, p. 308.

Note:
Perhaps this word is similar to the English word *here*—although *Sem* seems to have a much more formal tone. See also *Emna* (here).

Possible shared root:
Samhampors (sam-HAM-pors) n/a
Semhaham (SEM-hah-ham) n/a

Compare from *Loagaeth*:
Zem

Semhaham (SEM-hah-ham) n/a*

Pronunciation note:
(**Dee—sémhaham*) See the *Five Books*, p. 310. Dee indicates an accent over the *e*.

From *Loagaeth*:
(**Dee—This word hath 72 significations.*) See the *Five Books*, p. 310. Note the similiarity between this word and the Hebrew *Shem haMephoresh* (Name of Extension). This is a Qabalistic Name of God composed of seventy-two individual names. Interestingly, the *Shem haMephoresh* seems to have an association with the twenty-four Elders (or Seniors) that appear in the Great Table of the Earth (Watchtowers). See my article "Shem haMephoresh: the Divine Name of Extension."

Possible shared root:
Sem (sem) n/a
Samhampors (sam-HAM-pors) n/a

Ser (ser) *n.* Sorrow

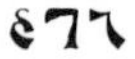

From *Corpus Omnium*:

Found in the Tribulation portion of the Table, in the phrase *Osf Ser Iad* (Discord and Sorrow of God).

Note:

Also see Tibibp (sorrow).

Siaion (sii-AY-ii-on)* *n.* Temple

8.41 . . . the crowns of *the temple* and the coat . . .

Pronunciation notes:

(*Dee—Si a i on*) Four syllables. Both *i*'s and the *a* should take their long sounds.

(*Dee—siáîon*) See the *48 Claves*. Dee added an accent over the *a* (second syllable). He also added a circumflex over the second *i* to indicate its long sound.

Note:

Perhaps there is some relationship between this word, and the name "Sion" (or Zion)—where the Holy Temple stood in Israel.

Siatris (sii-ay-TRIS)* *n.* Scorpions

10.28 . . . the heads of *scorpions* and live sulphur . . .

Pronunciation notes:

(*Dee—Si a trís*) Three syllables, with the accent mark placed in the middle of the third syllable. The first *i* and the *a* should take their long sounds.

(*Dee—siâtris*) See the *48 Claves*. Here, Dee placed a circumflex over the A to indicate its long sound.

Sibsi (sib-sii)* *n.* Covenant

30.145 . . . appear before *the covenant of* his mouth . . .

Pronunciation notes:

(**Dee—Sib si*) Two syllables.

Note:

Also see *Aisro / Isro* (promise of), *Surzas* (sworn), and *Znrza* (swore).

"Smnad" (sem-en-ad) *pron.* or *adj.* Another

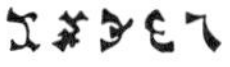

Compounds:

Lsmnad (el-sem-en-ad) [L + "Smnad"] One Another

Probable shared root:

Asymp (ay-simp) Another

Symp (simp) Another

Note:

The root here may be "sm" or "sym."

Soba (SOH-bay) *adj.* Whose

1.29 . . . *whose* seats I garnished . . .
1.56 . . . *whose* beginning is not . . .
5.35 . . . *whose* numbers are as the first . . .
7.23 . . . *whose* kingdoms and continuance . . .
10.9 . . . *whose* branches are 22 nests . . .
11.28 . . . *whose* number is 31 . . .
12.19 . . . *whose* name amongst you is wrath . . .
17.3 . . . *whose* wings are thorns . . .

Pronunciation notes:

(**Dee 5.35; 10.9; 11.28; 12.19—So ba*)

(**Dee 7.23;m 17.3—Soba*) Two syllables. The *o* should take its long sound. I have adopted the accent from *Asobam* (whom).

Compounds:

Sobaiad (soh-BAY-ad) [Soba + Iad] Whose God

Sabaooaona (say-bay-oh-oh-AY-oh-na) ["Saba" + Ooaona] Whose Eyes

Also:

Asobam (ay-SOH-bam)	(On) Whom
"Saba" (SAY-bay)	Whose
Sobam (SOH-bam)	Whom
Sobca (SOB-kay)	Whose
"Sobha" (SOB-hay)	Whose
"Sobo" (SOH-boh)	Whose
Sobra (SOB-ray)	Whose
"Sola" (SOH-lay)	Whose

Note:

Overall, the root of these words seems to be "Sob." However, *Soba* itself seems rather important in most cases.

See also *Casarm* (whom).

Compare from *Loagaeth*:

Sebas, Sebo, Sebra, Zeba

Sobaiad (soh-BAY-ad)* [Soba + Iad] *comp.* Whose God

17.14 . . . *whose God* is wrath in anger . . .

Pronunciation notes:

(**Dee—So bai ad*) Three syllables. The *o* takes its long sound. Dee also indicates that the *ai* (or "ay") combine to form a long "a" sound—as in the English words *day* and *play*.

(**Dee—sobaíad*) See the *48 Claves*. Here, Dee placed an accent over the *i* in the second syllable.

Sobam (SOH-bam)* *pron.* Whom

2.9 . . . *whom* the burning flames . . .

4.16 . . . *whom* none hath yet numbered . . .

6.7 . . . *whom* the First hath planted . . .

Pronunciation notes:

(**Dee 2.9—S o bam*)

(**Dee 4.16—So bam*)

(**Dee6.7—Sobam*) It would appear that Dee heard three syllables in Key Two—so that the *S* took the sound of "es." However, in later instances, the word had only two syllables. The three-syllable version of the word is likely a poetic or lyrical gloss, rather than a rule of pronunciation. I have adopted the accent from *Asobam* (whom).

Also:

Asobam (ay-SOH-bam)	(On) Whom
"Saba" (SAY-bay)	Whose
Soba (SOH-bay)	Whose
Sobca (SOB-kay)	Whose
"Sobha" (SOB-hay)	Whose
"Sobo" (SOH-boh)	Whose
Sobra (SOB-ray)	Whose
"Sola" (SOH-lay)	Whose

Also see:

Casarm (whom).

Sobca (SOB-kay)* *adj.* Whose

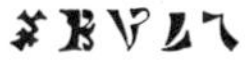

9.13 . . . *whose* wings are of wormwood . . .

9.37 . . . cursed are they *whose* iniquities . . .

Pronunciation notes:

(**Dee 9.13, 37—Sob ca ka*) Two syllables. The *c* takes a hard "k" sound. I have adopted the accent from *Asobam* (whom).

Also:

Asobam (ay-SOH-bam)	(On) Whom
"Saba" (SAY-bay)	Whose
Soba (SOH-bay)	Whose
Sobam (SOH-bam)	Whom
"Sobha" (SOB-hay)	Whose

"Sobo" (SOH-boh) Whose
Sobra (SOB-ray) Whose
"Sola" (SOH-lay) Whose

Also see:
Casarm (whom).

"Sobha" (SOB-hay) *adj.* Whose

Pronunciation note:
I have adopted the accent from *Asobam* (whom).

Compounds:
Sobhaath (sob-HAY-ath) ["Sobha" + "Aath"] Whose Works

Also:
Asobam (ay-SOH-bam) (On) Whom
"Saba" (SAY-bay) Whose
Soba (SOH-bay) Whose
Sobam (SOH-bam) Whom
Sobca (SOB-kay) Whose
"Sobo" (SOH-boh) Whose
Sobra (SOB-ray) Whose
"Sola" (SOH-lay) Whose

Also see:
Casarm (whom)

Sobhaath (sob-HAY-ath)* ["Sobha" + "Aath"] *comp.* Whose Works

6.38 . . . *whose works* shall be a song of honour . . .

Pronunciation notes:
(**Dee—Sob há ath*) Three syllables, with an accent on the second syllable. In Early Modern English, a double vowel indicated a long vowel—which Dee likely intends for the second syllable. Then a quick short *a* is sounded at the beginning of the third syllable.
(**Dee—sob-há-ath*) See the *48 Claves*. This note matches that from *TFR*.

Note:

See *Soba* (whose).

"Sobo" (SOH-boh) *adj.* — Whose

Pronunciation note:

I have adopted the accent from *Asobam* (whom).

Compounds:

Sobolzar (soh-BOL-zar) ["Sobo" + "Lzar"] — Whose Courses

Also:

Asobam (ay-SOH-bam)	(On) Whom
"Saba" (SAY-bay)	Whose
Soba (SOH-bay)	Whose
Sobam (SOH-bam)	Whom
Sobca (SOB-kay)	Whose
"Sobha" (SOB-hay)	Whose
Sobra (SOB-ray)	Whose
"Sola" (SOH-lay)	Whose

Also see:

Casarm (whom).

Soboln (soh-bohln)* *n.* — West

9.22 . . . settled their feet *in the west* . . .

Pronunciation notes:

(**Dee—So boln*) Two syllables, with a long *o* in the first syllable.

(**Dee—sobôln*) See the *48 Claves*. Here, Dee placed a circumflex over the second *o* to indicate that it, also, takes its long sound.

Note:

The similar spelling of *Soboln* (west) and *Sobolzar* (whose courses) appears to be coincidental. Unless the "courses" (Sobolzar) mentioned in Key Six are westward moving.

Sobolzar (soh-BOL-zar)* ["Sobo" + "Lzar"] *comp.* Whose Courses

6.21 . . . *whose courses* visit with comfort . . .

Pronunciation notes:

(*Dee—Sobol zar*) Should be three syllables.

(*Dee—sobólzar*) See the *48 Claves*. The accent is placed on the second syllable.

Note:

See note at *Soboln* (west).

Sobra (SOB-ray)* *adj.* Whose

1.10 . . . *in whose* hands the sun is as a sword . . .

Pronunciation notes:

(*Dee—Sobra*) Two syllables. The *o* appears short in this case. I have adopted the accent from *Asobam* (whom).

Also:

Asobam (ay-SOH-bam)	(On) Whom
"Saba" (SAY-bay)	Whose
Soba (SOH-bay)	Whose
Sobam (SOH-bam)	Whom
Sobca (SOB-kay)	Whose
"Sobha" (SOB-hay)	Whose
"Sobo" (SOH-boh)	Whose
"Sola" (SOH-lay)	Whose

Note:

Overall, the root of these words seems to be "sob." However, *Soba* itself seems rather important in most cases.

See also *Casarm* (whom).

Compare from *Loagaeth*:

Sebas, Sebo, Sebra, Zeba

"Sola" (SOH-lay) *adj.* Whose

Pronunciation note:

I have adopted the accent from *Asobam* (whom).

Compounds:

Solamian (soh-LAY-mii-an) ["Sola" + "Mian"] Whose Continuance

Also:

Asobam (ay-SOH-bam)	(On) Whom
"Saba" (SAY-bay)	Whose
Soba (SOH-bay)	Whose
Sobam (SOH-bam)	Whom
Sobca (SOB-kay)	Whose
"Sobha" (SOB-hay)	Whose
"Sobo" (SOH-boh)	Whose
Sobra (SOB-ray)	Whose

Also see:

Casarm (whom).

Solamian (soh-LAY-mii-an)* ["Sola" + "Mian"] *comp.* Whose Continuance

8.14 . . . *whose long continuance* shall be . . .

Note:

The word *long* is not indicated by the Angelical.

Pronunciation notes:

(**Dee—So lá mi an*) Four syllables. The accent is placed on the second syllable. I assume the *o*, the first *a*, and the *i* are all given their long sounds—as they fall at the ends of their syllables.

Note:

The similarity between this word and the name of the solar Angel *Salamian*. He is found in the *Heptameron*—associated with that grimoire's "Call of Sunday." This Angel also appeared to Dee and Kelley in the *Five Books*, pp. 81–82. There, Salamian claims to "rule in the heavens, and bear sway upon Earth . . . My name is Salamian, Mighty in the Sonne, worker of worldly actions . . . " Salamian also tells Dee that he is under the direction of Michael—who is the Archangel of the Sun.

Solpeth (sol-peth)* *v.* Harken (unto)/Listen to

6.32 Wherefore, *harken unto* my voice.

Pronunciation notes:

(**Dee—Sol peth*)

(**Dee—sol-peth*) See the *48 Claves*. These notes indicate two syllables. Both vowels appear to take their short sounds.

Note:

See also *Toatar* (harken).

Sonf (sonv)* *v.* To Reign

1.2 I *reign* over you, saith the God of Justice . . .

Pronunciation notes:

(**Dee—sonf*) Dee indicates a single syllable here. The *nf* tends to sound like "nv" when this word is spoken fluently.

Compounds:

Dsonf (dee-sonv) [Ds + Sonf] That Reign

Note:

Also see Bogpa (to reign).

Sor (sor) *n.* Action (especially that taken by a king)

From *Corpus Omnium*:

Found in the post-Crucifixion portion of the Table, in the phrase *Gru Sor Iad* (Cause of the Actions of God).

Surzas (sur-zas)* *v.* To Swear (Promise)

30.148 . . . which *he hath sworn* unto us . . .

Pronunciation notes:

(**Dee—Sur zas*) Two syllables. Based on the two forms of *Surzas* / *Znrza*, I suspect the *u* in this case is a phonetic gloss.

Also:

Znrza (snur-za) Swore

Note:

Also see *Aisro* / *Isro* (promise of) and *Sibsi* (covenant).

Symp (simp)* *pron.* or *adj.* Another

30.66 One season, let it confound *another* . . .

Pronunciation notes:

(**Dee—Symp*) One syllable.

Also:

Asymp (ay-simp) Another

Shared root:

"Smnad" (sem-en-ad) Another

Note:

The root here may be "sm" or "sym."

Gisg (T)

"T" (tee) *pron.* — It

Compounds:

Ti (tii) ["T" + I] — It Is

Ta (tay)* *prep.* or *conj.* — As

1.14 . . . sun is *as* a sword . . .
1.17 . . . moon *as* a through-thrusting fire . . .
1.26 . . . *as* the palms of my hands . . .
1.68 . . . *as* the balance of righteousness . . .
2.15 . . . *as* cups for a wedding . . .
8.54 . . . of such *as* are prepared . . .
9.31 . . . *as* the rich man doth his treasure . . .
11.26 . . . *as* they are whose number is . . .
30.61 . . . *as* a handmaid let her serve them . . .

Pronunciation notes:

(**Dee 1.14, 17, 26, 68—TA*)

(**Dee 2.15; 8.54; 9.31; 11.26; 30.61—Ta*) *Ta* is likely just one syllable. It is uncertain if the *a* should take a long or short sound. However, various compounds that begin with *Ta* indicate the long "a" sound.

Note:

For the most part, *Ta* (as) seems to be used as a preposition—often synonymous with the word *like*: i.e., "the sun is as a sword" = "the sun is like a sword." A prepositional *as* can also mean "in the role of," as we see in the phrase . . . *who reigneth amongst you as the balance of righteousness and truth*. *Ta* can also be a pronoun, when used in phrases like "Appear to our comfort . . . and such as are prepared." (In this case, *such as* is the same as "those who.")

Compounds:

Chista (kiis-tay) [Chis + Ta] — Are as
Chistad (kiis-tad) [Chis + Ta + D] — Are as (the) Third
Corsta (kors-tay) [Cors + Ta] — Such as

Ita (ii-tay) [I + Ta]	Is as
Qta (kwah-tay) [Q + Ta]	Or as
Tablior (TAY-blii-or) [Ta + Blior]	As (Continual) Comforters
Tage (tayj) [Ta + "Ge"]	As (Is) Not
Talo (tay-el-oh) [Ta + "Lo"]	As the First
Talolcis (tay-LOL-sis) [Ta + "Lolcis"]	As Bucklers
Taqanis (tay-kway-nis) [Ta + "Qanis"]	As Olives
Tapuin (tay-pew-in) [Ta + "Puin"]	As Sharp Sickles
Taviv (tay-viv) [Ta + Viv]	As the Second

Also:

"Ca" (kay)	As

Further:

"Ta" (tay) *conj.*	And(?)

Compounds:

Taviv (tay-viv) ["Ta" + Viv]	And(?) the Second

Tabaan (or Tabaam) (tay-BAY-an)* *n.* Governor

15.2 O thou, *the governor of* . . .

Note:

The transmission of Key Fifteen is missing from Dee's journals. We have only the English for the Key given on *TFR*, p. 193. However, this word is given later by Illemese, on *TFR*, p. 200.

It also appears in Dee's *48 Claves*—where it is spelled with an *n* instead of an *m* (*Tabaan*).

I have adopted the accent from *Tabaori* (to govern).

Pronunciation notes:

(**Dee—tabâan*) See the *48 Claves*. Dee gives us little clue here. He only placed a circumflex over the second *a* to indicate its long sound. The first *a* is possibly long as well, based on other versions of this word. This likely makes a word of three syllables. (I have settled upon the *Tabaan* version of this word in my pronunciation, because the *n* appears in other versions of this word.)

Also:

Anetab (ay-NEE-tayb)	(In) Government
Gnetaab (nee-TAY-ab)	(Your) Governments
Netaab (nee-TAY-ab)	Governments
Netaaib (nee-TAY-ay-ib)	Government
Tabaord (tay-BAY-ord)	(Let) Be Governed
Tabaori (tay-BAY-oh-rii)	To Govern
"Tabas" (tay-BAS)	To Govern

Further:

Cab (kab)	Rod/Scepter
Caba (ka-BA)	To Govern

Tabaord (tay-BAY-ord)* *v.* (Be) Governed

30.44 . . . *let her be governed by* her parts . . .

Note:

The word *her* is implied in the Angelical here only by context.

Pronunciation notes:

(**Dee—Ta ba ord*) Three syllables. The *a* preceding an *o* should take the long sound (as in the English word *chaos*). I have adopted the accent from *Tabaori* (to govern).

Also:

Anetab (ay-NEE-tayb)	(In) Government
Gnetaab (nee-TAY-ab)	(Your) Governments
Netaab (nee-TAY-ab)	Governments
Netaaib (nee-TAY-ay-ib)	Government
Tabaam (tay-BAY-an)	Governor
Tabaori (tay-BAY-oh-rii)	To Govern
"Tabas" (tay-BAS)	To Govern

Further:

Cab (kab)	Rod/Scepter
Caba (ka-BA)	To Govern

Tabaori (tay-BAY-oh-rii)* *v.* To Govern

30.121 . . . *govern* those that govern . . .

Pronunciation notes:

(*Dee—Tabá o ri*) Four syllables, with an accent on the second syllable. The first *a* should take a long sound, as seen in other versions of this word. The second *a* takes the long sound when preceding an *o* (as in the English word *chaos*). Dee shows that the *o* stands alone—taking its long sound.

(*Dee—Tabáôri*) See the *48 Claves*. Here, Dee again placed the accent on the second syllable. He also placed a circumflex over the *o* to indicate its long sound.

Also:

Anetab (ay-NEE-tayb) (In) Government
Gnetaab (nee-TAY-ab) (Your) Governments
Netaab (nee-TAY-ab) Governments
Netaaib (nee-TAY-ay-ib) Government
Tabaam (tay-BAY-an) Governor
Tabaord (tay-BAY-ord) (Let) Be Governed
"Tabas" (tay-BAS) To Govern

Further:

Cab (kab) Rod/Scepter
Caba (ka-BA) To Govern

"Tabas" (tay-BAS) *v.* To Govern

Pronunciation note:

I have adopted the accent from *Tabaori* (to govern).

Compounds:

Artabas (ar-tay-bas) [Ar + "Tabas"] That Govern

Also:

Anetab (ay-NEE-tayb) (In) Government
Gnetaab (nee-TAY-ab) (Your) Governments
Netaab (nee-TAY-ab) Governments

Netaaib (nee-TAY-ay-ib)	Government
Tabaam (tay-BAY-an)	Governor
Tabaord (tay-BAY-ord)	(Let) Be Governed
Tabaori (tay-BAY-oh-rii)	To Govern

Further:

Cab (kab)	Rod/Scepter
Caba (ka-BA)	To Govern

Note:

Compare to the name of the Part of the Earth (and its Angelic Governor) *Tabitom*. Perhaps this shares the "tab" root, and is perhaps even a compound with the word *Om* as well. Thus the name would mean "Governor of knowledge" or "wise Governor."

Tabges (tab-jes)* *n.* — Caves

30.98 . . . let them become *caves* for the beasts . . .

Pronunciation notes:

(*Dee—Tab ges*) Two syllables. The *g* followed by an *e* is likely soft.

Tablior (TAY-blii-or)* [Ta + Blior] *comp.* — As Comforters

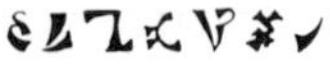

5.13 . . . as continual* comforters unto whom I have fastened . . .

Note:

(*The word *continual* is not represented in the Angelical.)

Pronunciation notes:

(*Dee—Tá blior*) Likely three syllables, with an accent on the first. See pronunciation notes for *Blior* (comfort) for the long "i" sound.

"Tad" (tad) [Ta + D] *comp.* — As the Third

Compounds:

Chistad (kiis-tad)* [Chis + Ta + D]	Are as the Third

Tage (tayj)* [Ta + "Ge"] *comp.* As (Is) Not

2.36 . . . such *as is not* but in the mind . . .

Pronunciation note:

(**Dee—Tage*) Appears to be one syllable. The final *e* would be silent, and it would make the *a* long. Rhymes with the English words *cage* and *rage*.

Tal (tzall)* *prop. n.* Letter *M**

Note:

The name of the Angelical letter for *M*. It is likely that these letter names have translations of their own. (For instance, note the Hebrew alphabet: the letter *M* is named *Mem*, but *Mem* also translates as "water.") However, such translations for the Angelical letters are never given. (See the *Five Books*, p. 270.)

Pronunciation notes:

(**Dee—In sound stall or xtall*) I suspect that Dee's "xt" is similar to the "tz" sound (as in Hebrew *Tzedek*)—which is somewhere between a "t" sound and a "z" sound ("tzuh").

Compare from *Loagaeth*:

Tal

Talho (tal-ho)* *n.* Cups

2.16 . . . I have prepared as *cups* for a wedding . . .

Pronunciation notes:

(**Dee—Talho*)

Talo (tay-el-oh)* [Ta + "Lo"] *comp.* As the First

4.30 . . . are *as the first* 456 . . .

Pronunciation notes:

(**Dee—Ta l o*) Three syllables. The *l* and *o* stand alone.

Talolcis (tay-LOL-sis)* [Ta + "Lolcis"] *comp.* As Bucklers

8.16 . . . shall be *as bucklers* to the stooping dragons . . .

Pronunciation notes:

(**Dee—Ta lol cis or sis*) Three syllables. Dee indicates that the *c* should take a soft ("s") sound.

(**Dee—ta lól-cis*) See the *48 Claves*. Here, Dee places an accent on the second syllable.

Tan (tan) *prop. n.* "The Seventeenth Aethyr"

30.3 . . . which dwell in *the seventeenth aethyr* . . .

Note:

This (word 30.3) is the single space in the Key of the Aethyrs, which must be changed for each invocation—replacing word 30.3 with the name of the appropriate Aethyr. No established definitions were given for these names.

Tan contains the three Parts of the Earth *Sigmorf*, *Avdropt*, and *Tocarzi*.

Tapuin (TAY-pew-in)* [Ta + "Puin"] *comp.* As (Sharp) Sickles

3.15 . . . the rest are *as sharp sickles* . . .

Pronunciation notes:

(**Dee—Ta pu in*) Three syllables. Dee originally spelled *Tapuin* with a *v* instead of a *u*. However, he indicates the "u" sound in his phonetic note.

(**Dee—tá pû-im*) See *48 Claves*. Note the accent on the first syllable. Dee added a circumflex over the *u* to indicate its long sound. Also note that Dee seems to have mistakenly spelled this word with a final *m* instead of an *n*.

Taqanis (tay-kway-nis)* [Ta + "Qanis"] *comp.* As Olives

5.6 . . . *as olives* in the olive mount . . .

Pronunciation notes:

(*Dee—Ta qu a nis*) This appears to be four syllables. I believe Dee's *qu* makes the same sound as *q* standing alone—"kwah." However, the *qu a* (or "kwah-ay") tends to blend into one sound when this word is spoken fluently.

(*Dee—ta qa-a-nis*) See the *48 Claves*. This note matches that from *TFR*.

Tastax (tas-taks)* *v.* Going Before (To Precede)

17.12 . . . lamps living *going before* thee.

Pronunciation notes:

(*Dee—Tas tax*) Two syllables. Both *a*'s take their short sounds.

Note:

This is likely an instance of the *-ax* suffix, indicating action.

Also compare this word with the name of the Part of the Earth (and its Angelic Governor) *Tastoxo*. This could even be a compound (Tastax + Tox) for "Going Before Him" or "He Who Precedes."

Tatan (tay-tan)* *n.* Wormwood

9.16 . . . whose wings are of wormwood . . .

Pronunciation notes:

(*Dee—Ta tan*) Two syllables. The first *a* is likely a long vowel.

Note:

Wormwood is a biblical reference to poison. In the Book of Revelation, a star named Wormwood falls to the Earth, and thereby poisons a third of the world's water supply.

See also *Faboan* (poison).

Compare from *Loagaeth*:
Tantas, Tantat

Taviv (tay-viv)* [Ta + Viv] *comp.* As the Second

6.28 . . . and continuance *as the second* and third . . .

Pronunciation notes:
(**Dee—Ta viv*) Dee indicates two syllables here.

Further:
Taviv (tay-viv)* ["Ta" + Viv] *comp.* And(?) Second

5.28 . . . brothers of the first *and second* . . .

Note:
Here is the only case where Ta (as) is strangely translated as "and." Could this be a mistake on the part of Dee or Kelley? Perhaps this word should be *Odviv*.
Also see *Taviv* (as the second).

Pronunciation notes:
(**Dee—Ta ui u*) Looks like three syllables, but it is most likely only two. Dee originally wrote this word with *u*'s instead of *v*'s—however, it is unlikely that he intended "u" sounds in this case. Instead, see word 6.28 (*Taviv*), which indicates the "v" sounds.

TAXS (taks-is)* *7336*

17.10 . . . and hast *7336* lamps living going before thee.

Pronunciation notes:
(**Dee—Taxs*) Probably two syllables, as in the English *taxes*. Also, see the following note:

Note:
(**Dee—Faxes or Faxis to be sounded. I find in the Call Taxs. I find also in some words T and F are indifferently used.*) See *TFR*, p. 194. This is an interesting

observation on Dee's part. Because the use of *T* or *F* is indifferent here, I have chosen to stick with the "T" sound in my pronunciation.

Teloah (TEE-loh-ah)* *n.* Death

8.27 . . . shall not see *death* until this house fall . . .

Pronunciation notes:

(**Dee—té lo ah*) Three syllables, with an accent on the first syllable. The *e* and the *o* should each take their long sounds.

(**Dee—téloâh*) See the *48 Claves*. Dee again shows the accent on the first syllable. The *âh* should indicate a short "o" sound (as in the words *father* and *fall*).

Also:

Teloch (tee-LOCH) Death

Teloch (tee-LOCH)* *n.* Death

3.17 . . . the horns of *death* . . .

11.21 . . . gathered them together in the house of *death* . . .

Pronunciation notes:

(**Dee 3.17—Teloch as och in hotch pot*)

(**Dee 11.21—Te loch hotch*) Two syllables, and the *ch* sounds as it does in the English words *church* and *chime*. However, also see *Telocvovim*, which suggests the *ch* may take the "ch" sound *or* the "kh" sound (as in the English word *ache*).

(**Dee—telóch*) See the *48 Claves*. Here, Dee placed an accent upon the second syllable.

Compounds:

Telocvovim (tee-LOCH-voh-vee-im) [Teloch + "Vovim"] Death Dragon

Also:

Teloah (TEE-loh-ah) Death

Telocvovim (tee-LOCH-voh-vee-im)* [Teloch + "Vovim"] *comp., prop. n.*

Death Dragon

30.115 . . . the dwelling place of *him that is fallen* . . .

Pronunciation notes:

(**Dee—Te lóc vo v im lotch, or loch*) Likely five syllables, with an accent on the second. The *c* at the end of the second syllable is actually a "ch" digraph (as in *church*). Finally, the *v* in the fourth syllable stands alone.

Note:

"Death Dragon" is the literal translation of *Telocvovim*, which itself is likely a proper noun for Satan—"Him That Is Fallen."

Also see *Githgulcag* (likely a name for Lucifer) and *Choronzon* (Satan, the Devil).

Tex (teks) *prop. n.*

"The Thirtieth Aethyr"

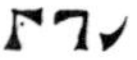

30.3 . . . which dwell in *the thirtieth aethyr* . . .

Note:

This (word 30.3) is the single space in the Key of the Aethyrs, which must be changed for each invocation—replacing word 30.3 with the name of the appropriate Aethyr. No established definitions were given for these names.

Tex contains the four Parts of the Earth *Taoagla*, *Gemnimb*, *Advorpt*, and *Doxinal*.

Thil (thil) *n.*

Seats

1.30 . . . whose *seats* I garnished . . .

*14.9 . . . upon 24 *seats* vexing all creatures . . .

Note:

*The transmission of Key Fourteen is missing from Dee's journals. We only have the English for this Key given later (see *TFR*, p. 193). Plus, the word appears in this location in Dee's 48 *Claves*.

Also:

Othil (oh-thil) Seats of

Thild (thild) Seats

"Thiln" (thiln) Seats

Thild (thild)* *n.* Seats

5.31 . . . *their own seats* which are garnished . . .

Note:

The word *own* does not seem to be indicated in the Angelical.

Pronunciation notes:

(**Dee—Thild, one Syllable*)

Also:

Othil (oh-thil) Seats of

Thil (thil) Seats

"Thiln" (thiln) Seats

"Thiln" (thiln) *n.* Seats

Compounds:

Thilnos (thil-nos) ["Thiln" + Os] 12 Seats of

Thilnos (thil-nos)* ["Thiln" + Os] *comp.* 12 Seats (of)

3.33 . . . placed you in *seats 12 of* government . . .

Pronunciation notes:

(**Dee—Thilnos*) Likely two syllables.

Ti (tii)* ["T" + I] *comp.* It Is

11.25 . . . *it is* as they are whose . . .

Pronunciation notes:
(**Dee—Ti*) One syllable. The *i* is likely a long vowel.

Tia (tii-a)* *prep.* Unto (Us)

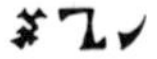

30.149 . . . he hath sworn *unto us* in his justice.

Pronunciation notes:
(**Dee—Tia*) Likely two syllables. I suggest a long *i*—because it is followed by an *a* (as in the English word *dial*).

Note:
Also see *Pambt* (unto) and *Pugo* (as unto).

Tianta (tii-AN-ta)* *n.* Bed

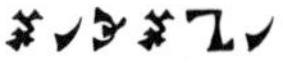

30.112 . . . she is *the bed of* an harlot . . .

Pronunciation notes:
(**Dee—Ti án ta*) Likely three syllables, with an accent in the middle of the second syllable. In the first syllable, I suggest a long *i*—because it is followed by an *a* (as in *dial*).

Tibibp (tib-ib-ip)* *n.* Sorrow

12.8 . . . the lanterns of *sorrow* . . .

Pronunciation notes:
(**Dee—Tibibp*) Dee gives us little clue for this word. I assume it should be three syllables. I would have assumed the final *p* stands alone, though Dee does not indicate such. Therefore, I have simply combined the *b* and *p* into the sound of "bip."

Note:
Also see *Ser* (sorrow).

Tilb (tilb)* *adj. or pron.* Her

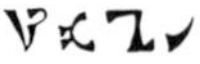

30.28 . . . *her* unspeakable variety . . .

Pronunciation notes:

(**Dee—Tilb*) One syllable.

Also:

Tiobl (tii-AHB-el) (Within) Her

Compounds:

Busdirtilb (buz-der-tilb) [Busdir + Tilb] Glory (of) Her

Elzaptilb (el-ZAP-tilb) ["Elzap" + Tilb] Her Course

Omptilb (omp-tilb) ["Omp" + Tilb] Her Understanding

Note:

Also see "Ip" (her) and "Pi" (she).

Tiobl (tii-AHB-el)* *pron.* (Within) Her

30.49 . . . let there be division *in her* . . .

30.72 . . . no creature upon or *within her* . . .

Pronunciation notes:

(**Dee 30.49—Ti óbil*)

(**Dee 30.72—Ti ob l*) Three syllables, with an accent on the second syllable. The *o* is not shown standing by itself, thus I assume it has a short sound. The second phonetic note (word 30.72) indicates the *l* stands alone.

(**Dee 30.49, 72—tióbl*) See the *48 Claves*. Here, Dee again placed an accent on the second syllable.

Also:

Tilb (tilb) Her

Note:

Also see "Pi" (she).

Tliob (tlii-ob)* *v.* To Separate (Classify?) Creatures

16.17 . . . that understand and *separate creatures*.

Pronunciation notes:

(*Dee—Tli ob*) Dee indicates two syllables—forcing the *Tl* to combine grudgingly into one sound. The *i* likely takes its long sound.

Note:

"To separate creatures" as into differing classifications. The entire phrase "that understand and separate creatures" appears to indicate intelligence or logical thought.

Toatar (toh-AY-tar)* *v.* Harken (To Listen)

17.19 Gird up thy loins and *harken*.

Pronunciation notes:

(*Dee—To a tar*) Three syllables. The *o* takes its long sound. The first *a* seems to stand alone.

(*Dee—toátar*) See the *48 Claves*. Here, Dee placed an accent over the *a* in the second syllable.

Note:

See also *Solpeth* (harken unto).

Also compare to the name of the Angel *Autotar*, an Elder of the Eastern Watchtower. Perhaps his name means "He Who Listens."

Tofglo (TOF-gloh)* *n.* All (Things)

30.35 . . . to dispose *all things* according to . . .

Pronunciation notes:

(*Dee—Tóf glo*) Two syllables, with the accent on the first syllable.

(*Dee—tófglo*) See the *48 Claves*. This note is essentially the same as that in *TFR*.

Note:

Also see *Ton* (all).

Toh (toh)* *v.* To Triumph

1.55 . . . him that liveth *and triumpheth* . . .

Pronunciation notes:

(*Dee—tóh*) See *48 Claves*. Note the accent mark over the *o*. (The previous word in the Key—*Hom*—is just one syllable without an accent. Thus, both words are likely to be taken together, with the accent on *Toh*.)

Possible compounds:

Baltoh (bal-toh) [Balt + Toh] Righteousness
Iadbaloth (ii-ad-BAL-toh) [Iad + Balt + Toh] God of Righteousness

Also:

"Toha" Triumph?

"Toha" (toh-ha) *n.* (My) Triumph?

Compounds:

Baltoha (bal-toh-ha) [Balt + "Toha"] (My?) Righteousness

Note:

The *-a* could be an affix added to the word *Toh* (triumph).

Also:

Toh (toh) Triumph

Tohcoth (toh-koth) *n.* "Nature Spirits"*

From *Loagaeth*:

(**Dee—This name comprehendeth the number of all the fairies—who are devils next to the state of man.*) See the *Five Books*, p. 315. In other words, *Tohcoth* indicates earthbound nature spirits. (Also see *Gah*, which likely means "pure spirits.")

Also see:

Tolham (tol-HAYM) All Creatures
Tolhami (tol-HAY-mii) (Upon) All Creatures
Toltorg (tol-TORJ) Creatures
Toltorgi (tol-TOR-jii) With (Her) Creatures
"Toltorn" (tol-TORN) Creature

Tolham (tol-HAYM) *n.* All Creatures

14.11 . . . vexing *all creatures* of the earth with age . . .

Pronunciation notes:

I have adopted the accent from *Tolhami.*

Note:

The transmission of Key Fourteen is missing from Dee's journals. We only have the English for this Key given later (see *TFR*, p. 193). Plus, the word appears in this location in Dee's *48 Claves*.

Here, the Angelical word *Caosgo* (of the earth) follows *Tolham*. See *Toltorg*.

Also:

Tolhami (tol-HAY-mii)	(Upon) All Creatures
Toltorg (tol-TORJ)	Creatures
Toltorgi (tol-TOR-jii)	With (Her) Creatures
"Toltorn" (tol-TORN)	Creature

Compare from *Loagaeth*:

Tohcoth

Tolhami (tol-HAY-mii)* *n.* (Upon) All Creatures

7.22 . . . such as work wonders *on all creatures*.

Pronunciation notes:

(**Dee—Tol há mi*) Three syllables, with an accent on the second syllable. The *a* and the final *i* likely take their long sounds.

(**Dee—tol-hâ-mi*) See the *48 Claves*. Note the circumflex over the *a*—indicating its long sound.

Also:

Tolham (tol-HAYM)	All Creatures
Toltorg (tol-TORJ)	Creatures
Toltorgi (tol-TOR-jii)	With (Her) Creatures
"Toltorn" (tol-TORN)	Creature

Compare from *Loagaeth*:
Tohcoth

Toltorg (tol-TORJ)* *n.* Creatures

3.19 . . . wherein *the creatures of the earth* are . . .

Pronunciation notes:
(**Dee—Toltorg org as in george*) Likely two syllables, with a soft *g* at the end. I have adopted the accent from other versions of this word.

Note:
The Angelical for "of the earth" (*Caosgo*) does not appear here. See *Tolham.*

Also:

Tolham (tol-HAYM)	All Creatures
Tolhami (tol-HAY-mii)	(Upon) All Creatures
Toltorgi (tol-TOR-jii)	With (Her) Creatures
"Toltorn" (tol-TORN)	Creature

Compare from *Loagaeth*: *Tohcoth*

Toltorgi (tol-TOR-jii)* *n.* (With) Creatures

5.23 . . . to water the earth *with her creatures* . . .

Pronunciation notes:
(**Dee—Toltórgi*) Likely three syllables, with an accent on the second syllable. The *g* preceding an *i* should take the soft ("j") sound.
(**Dee—toltórgi*) See the *48 Claves*. This note matches that from *TFR*.

Also:

Tolham (tol-HAYM)	All Creatures
Tolhami (tol-HAY-mii)	(Upon) All Creatures
Toltorg (tol-TORJ)	Creatures
"Toltorn" (tol-TORN)	Creature

Compare from *Loagaeth*:

Tohcoth

"Toltorn" (tol-TORN) *n.* Creature

Pronunciation note:

I have adopted the accent from other versions of this word.

Compounds:

Agtoltorn (ay-jee-tol-torn) [Ag + "Toltorn"] No Creature

Agltoltorn (ag-el-tol-torn) [Ag + L + "Toltorn"] No One Creature

Also:

Tolham (tol-HAYM) All Creatures

Tolhami (tol-HAY-mii) (Upon) All Creatures

Toltorg (tol-TORJ) Creatures

Toltorgi (tol-TOR-jii) With Creatures

Ton (ton)* *adj.* All

30.74 *All* her members, let them differ . . .

Pronunciation notes:

(**Dee—Ton*) One syllable.

Note:

Also see *Tofglo* (all things).

Also see Vomsarg, which is "All" (or Every One) used as a pronoun.

Tonug (too-nuj)* *v.* To Deface

30.95 . . . the work of man and his pomp, *let them be defaced*.

Pronunciation notes:

(**Dee—To nug g dg*) Two syllables. The final *g* takes the soft "j" sound.

Tooat (toh-OH-at)* *v.* To Furnish

30.31 . . . her unspeakable variety, *furnishing* you with . . .

Pronunciation notes:

(**Dee—To ó at*) Three syllables, with an accent on the second syllable. The *o* stands alone in the second syllable.

(**Dee—toóat*) See the *48 Claves*. Dee again placed the accent over the *o* in the second syllable.

Tor (tor) *prop. n.* "The Twenty-Third Aethyr" (To Rise?)

30.3 . . . which dwell in *the twenty-third aethyr* . . .

Note:

This (word 30.3) is the single space in the Key of the Aethyrs, which must be changed for each invocation—replacing word 30.3 with the name of the appropriate Aethyr. No established definitions were given for these names.

Tor contains the three Parts of the Earth *Ronoomb*, *Onizimp*, and *Zaxanin*.

Possible shared root:

Torgu (tor-GOO)	Arise
Torzu (tor-ZOOL)	Arise
Torzul (tor-ZOOL)	Shall Rise
Torzulp (tor-ZOOLP)	To Rise

Torb (torb) *n.* One Hundred

10.41 . . . roar *with a hundred* mighty earthquakes . . .

Note:

This word was not originally given with Key Ten. It was added later when Nalvage transmitted the English for the Key (see *TFR*, p. 192). This seems to have been the case with many of the numbers mentioned in the Keys.

This would appear to be the word for "one hundred" and not the numeral 100.

Compounds:

Matorb (may-torb) [Matb + Torb] — Long (period of time)

Torgu (tor-GOO)* *v.* — Arise

4.32 *Arise*, you sons of pleasure . . .

Pronunciation notes:

(*Dee—Torgu*) Likely two syllables. I assume the *g* should have a hard sound in front of a *u*, as in the English words *gulp* and *gun*. The final *u* itself likely has a long sound.

(*Dee—Torgú*) See the *48 Claves*. Note the accent on the last syllable.

Also:

Torzu (tor-ZOO) — Arise
Torzul (tor-ZOOL) — Shall Rise
Torzulp (tor-ZOOLP) — To Rise

Possible shared root:

Tor (tor) — "The Twenty-Third Aethyr"

Torzu (tor-ZOO)* *v.* — Arise

2.40 *Arise* sayeth the First.
30.117 O you heavens, *arise* . . .
30.141 *Arise*, move, and appear . . .

Pronunciation notes:

(*Dee 2.40—Torzú*) Dee places an accent on the final syllable.

(*Dee 30.117, 141—Tor zu*) Two syllables.

Also:

Torgu (tor-GOO) — Arise
Torzul (tor-ZOOL) — Shall Rise
Torzulp (tor-ZOOLP) — To Rise

Possible shared root:

Tor (tor) "The Twenty-Third Aethyr"

Note:

Compare to the name of the Part of the Earth (and its Angelic Governor) *Torzoxi*. It would appear that this name is a compound (Torzu + Tox), or "He Who Rises."

Torzul (tor-ZOOL)* *v.* (Shall) Arise

3.27 . . . which sleep and *shall rise.*

Pronunciation notes:

(**Dee—TORZUL*) Dee gives us little clue here. See pronunciation note for *Torzu* (arise). I have adopted the accent from other versions of this word.

Also:

Torgu (tor-GOO) Arise
Torzu (tor-ZOO) Arise
Torzulp (tor-ZOOLP) To Rise

Possible shared root:

Tor (tor) "The Twenty-Third Aethyr"

Torzulp (tor-ZOOLP)* *v.* To Rise

30.40 . . . and *rose up* in the beginning . . .

Pronunciation notes:

(**Dee—Tor zulp*) Two syllables. Based on the other versions of this word, I assume the *u* should have a long vowel sound.
I have adopted the accent from other versions of this word.

Also:

Torgu (tor-GOO) Arise
Torzu (tor-ZOO) Arise
Torzul (tor-ZOOL) Shall Rise

Possible shared root:

Tor (tor) — "The Twenty-Third Aethyr"

Tox (toks) *pron.* or *adj.* — His/Him

14.21 . . . the promise of *him* which is called . . .

Note:

The transmission of Key Fourteen is missing from Dee's journals. We only have the English for this Key given later (see *TFR*, p. 193). Plus, the word appears in this location in Dee's *48 Claves*.

Compounds:

Lonshitox (lon-shii-toks) [Lonshi + Tox] — His Power

Avavox (ay-vay-voks) ["Avav" + Tox] — His Pomp

Oxiayal (oks-AY-al) [Tox? + Iaial] — The Mighty Seat

Possible shared root:

Oxex (oks-eks) — To Vomit

Oxo (oks-oh) — "The Fifteenth Aethyr"

Note:

The root of these words may be "ox."

Tranan (tray-nan)* *n.* — Marrow

9.18 . . . and of *the marrow of* salt . . .

Pronunciation notes:

(**Dee—Tra nan*) Two syllables. The first *a* is likely a long vowel.

Trian (TRII-an)* *v.* — Shall Be

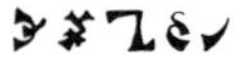

6.39 . . . whose works *shall be* a song of honour . . .

8.15 . . . whose long continuance *shall be* as bucklers . . .

Pronunciation notes:

(**Dee 6.39—Trian*)

(**Dee 8.15—Tri an*) Two syllables. The *i* is likely a long vowel, followed by a short *a*.

(**Dee 6.39—trian*) See the *48 Claves*. The accent is placed on the first syllable.

Note:
Also see *Chiso* (shall be).

Trint (trint) *v.* To Sit

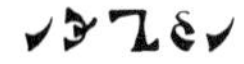

14.6 . . . which *sit* upon 24 seats . . .

Note:
The transmission of Key Fourteen is missing from Dee's journals. We only have the English for this Key given later (see *TFR*, p. 193). Plus, the word appears in this location in Dee's *48 Claves*.

Trof (trof)* *n.* or *v.?* A Building

2.34 . . . you are become *a building* such as . . .

Pronunciation note:
(**Dee—Trof*) Likely one syllable, as "Tr" makes a natural sound in English (as in *trial*, *try*, and *trouble*).

Note:
Also see *Orscatbl* (buildings). I suspect that *Trof* can also stand as the verb "to build."

Turbs (turbs)* *n.* (In) Beauty

2.20 . . . as the flowers *in their beauty* . . .

Pronunciation notes:
(**Dee—Turbs*) Likely one syllable.

Also:
Urbs (yurbs) Beautified

Van (U/V)

Vaa (vay) *prop. n.* n/a

Pronunciation note:
The double *a* In Early Modern English should indicate a long vowel sound.

Note:
See *TFR*, pp. 228–29. The names of most of the Angels encountered by Dee and Kelley can be found in other parts of the Angelic system—such as the *Heptarchia* or Great Table (Watchtower) systems. However, Vaa is one of the few entirely unique Angels that appeared to the two men. It was very late in the Angelic journals, after all of the essential Angelic magick had been transmitted. One day, Kelley saw three little creatures running around the floor of the room. It turned out that they were Angels from the Great Table (Watchtowers)—but their names were *not* derived according to the instructions Ave had previously given to Dee.

Note:
Vaa says of himself: "I am the last of the first, of the fourth.* And I have power to gather up the blessings of God, and to set them (if they be disdained) in a better soil." Dee notes, in Latin: "Transplanter of Gifts." And, a little further down the page: "*Vaa*—It is my duty to transplant the gifts of God."
The three Angels, apparently jointly, say, "For even as the father, son and holy spirit are one, but of themselves and being dilated, is full of power, and many. So are we one particularly in power,** but separated. Notwithstanding, spiritually of, and amongst, others, and dilated in the will of God, and into the branches of his determinations. But, particularly living, and jointly praising God."

Note:
*Dee notes the Angels are numbering the Watchtowers in an odd fashion. So that in this case, he points out, the numbering should follow: First = eastern, Second = western, Third = southern, and Fourth = the northern Watchtower. Vaa is found as the last three letters on the first line of the Northern Watchtower Tablet.

(***On the next page Dee notes: The three names make one name of 7 letters—Gazavaa.*) Further, I note that all three of these names begin with capital letters on the Great Table (Watchtowers). Also, each one of them terminates once it hits the Great Cross, Black Cross, or the end of the Watchtower. We may have discovered an entirely new Angelic system in the Watchtowers.

(See *Ga* and *Za*. Also see *Galvah*, *Mapsama*, *Murifri*, and *Nalvage*.)

Vabzir (vab-zer)* *n.* The Eagle

11.11 . . . and *the Eagle* spake and cried . . .

Pronunciation notes:

(**Dee—Vab zir*) Two syllables. Both vowels appear to take their short sounds.

Note:

This is a direct reference to one of the four Beasts of the Apocalypse. See Revelation, chapters 4ff.

Van (van) *prop. n.* Letter *U/V*

Note:

See the *Five Books*, p. 270. The name of the Angelical letter for *U/V*. It is likely that these letter names have translations of their own. (For instance, note the Hebrew alphabet: the letter *U/V* is named *Vav*, but *Vav* also translates as "nail" or "stake.") However, such translations for the Angelical letters are never given.

Compare from *Loagaeth*:

Van

"Vaoan" (vay-oh-AN)* *n.* Truth

1.72 . . . the balance of righteousness and *truth*.

Pronunciation notes:

(**Dee, recording the words of Nalvage—It is Vooan. It may be sounded Vaoan. Vooan is spoken with them that fall, but Vaoan with them that are, and are glorified. The devils have lost the dignity of their sounds.*) There are two acceptable spellings for this word (see *Vooan*). When working with earthbound or infernal spirits, the word should start with *Vo* (*Vooan*)—sounding akin to "voo-an." However, when working with Angels, the word should start with *Va* ("Vaoan")—sounding akin to "vay-oh-an."

(**Dee—vaoan*) See the *48 Claves*. Here, Dee uses the "Vaoan" spelling of the word, even though the *Vooan* spelling was given in *TFR*. (See *Odvooan* for the accented syllable.)

Note:

Also see *TFR*, p. 80. Here, the Angel Nalvage says of *Vooan*: "The word is, by interpretation, *Ignus vera mater*. The vain Philosophers do think it doth beget bodies. But, in truth, it conceiveth and bringeth forth." It seems that Nalvage accuses the "vain Philosophers" of regarding Vooan (Truth) as a male force (begetting bodies), but that Truth is in fact a feminine force (conceiving and bringing forth)—probably associating Truth with Gnostic images of the Goddess Wisdom (Sophia). The Latin that Nalvage uses to interpret the word—*Ignus vera mater*—seems to mean the "Fiery Truth of the Mother/Source."

Also:

Vooan (voo-AN) Truth

Varpax (var-paks) n/a

Note:

See the *Five Books*, p. 258. Here, Raphael offers a long prayer, the very end of which is, "How great and innumerable are your [God's] gifts? *O remiges varpax. Kyrie eleyson.*"

No translation is offered for this phrase, though I wonder if it is perhaps the Angelical for the Latin *Kyrie eleyson* (Lord have mercy), often used in Catholic prayer.

Note that *Varpax* may have the *-ax* suffix, indicating action.

Vasedg (vay-sej) *prop. n.* n/a

Note:

See the *Five Books*, p. 160. (*A voice: "Come, O Vasedg."*) Kelley is having a vision of the Seven Biblical Days of Creation at this point—where the Seven Ensigns of Creation are revealed. The call to Vasedg is answered by "a woman" who emerges from the darkness—except for her head—and presents a magickal tablet that produces "many things creeping out of it." She is then, temporarily, eclipsed by another woman who creates the Sun, Moon, and stars. When this other woman leaves, Vasedg steps fully into the light—revealing herself as an old crone. She retrieves clay from her tablet and creates birds with it. Finally, she says, "They are multiplied for your use" and exits the vision.

Note:

Compare this name to the name *Vasg*, an Angel of medicine of the Northern Watchtower.

"Vau" (vah) *v.* To Work

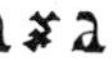

Compounds:

Vaulzirn (VOL-zern) ["Vau" + "Lzirn"] Work Wonders

Also:

Vaun (von) To Work

Vaulzirn (VOL-zern)* ["Vau" + "Lzirn"] *comp.* Work Wonders

7.21 . . . such as *work wonders* on all creatures.

Pronunciation notes:

(**Dee—Vául zirn*) Two syllables, with an accent on the first syllable. In Early Modern English, the *au* letter combination produces a short "o" sound (as in the English words *auburn* and *autumn*).

Vaun (von)* *v.* To Work

3.49 . . . *you might work* my power . . .

Pronunciation notes:

(**Dee—Vaun*) One syllable. In Early Modern English, the *au* letter combination produces a short "o" sound (as in the English words *auburn* and *autumn*).

Also:

"Vau" (vah) To Work

Ucim (yew-sim)* *v.* Frown Not (To Smile)

9.61 Happy is he upon whom they *frown not.*

Pronunciation notes:

(**Dee—U cim*) Two syllables. The *U* stands alone. The *c* should take its soft "s" sound when preceding an *i* (as in the English words *circus* and *circle.*)

Also:

Ulcinin (yewl-sii-nin) Happy (Is He)

Udl* (yew-del) *n.* The Rest

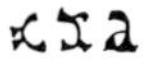

Alternate spelling:

(**Dee 3.13—Vndl It may be VdL or VndL"*) This is an alternate spelling for *Undl* (the rest).

Also:

Undl (und-el) The Rest

Veh (vay) *prop. n.* Letter *C/Ch/K*

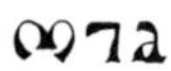

Note:

The name of the Angelical letter for *C/K*. It is likely that these letter names have translations of their own. (For instance, note the Hebrew alphabet: the letter *C/K* is named *Kaph*, but *Kaph* also translates as "fist" or "cupped hand.") However, such translations for the Angelical letters are never given. (See the *Five Books*, p. 270.)

Vep (vep)* *n.* Flame

1.62 . . . which shineth as *a flame* . . .

Pronunciation notes:

(**Dee—It is called Vep*) I assume the *e* in this word is a phonetic gloss. See the word *Vp* in *Loagaeth*.

Note:

Both *Vep* and *Prge* (fire) are nouns. For a verb form, see *Ialpon* (to burn). For an adjective, see *Ialpor* (flaming).

Compare from *Loagaeth*:

Vp

Ugear (yew-JEE-ar)* *n.* Strength (of Men)

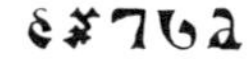

7.15 . . . in whom *the strength of men* rejoiceth . . .

Pronunciation notes:

(**Dee—V gé ar*) Three syllables. The accent is on the second syllable. Dee originally wrote this word with an initial *V*—however, it should take the "u" sound, as it precedes a consonant. The *g* is likely soft, as it precedes an *e* (as in the English words *gentle* and *gender*). Also, the *e* in the second syllable appears to take a long sound (likely due to the *ea* letter combination—as in the English words *eat* and *seat*).

(**Dee—vgéar*) See the *48 Claves*. The accent is again shown on the second syllable.

Also:

Ugeg (yew-JEJ)	Become Strong
Ugegi (yew-JEE-jii)	Waxeth Strong

Note:

Also see *Umadea* (strong towers), *Umplif* (strength), and *Vohim* (mighty). Note how all these words for "strength" begin with *U*/*V*. But, also see *Micaolz* (mighty).

Ugeg (yew-JEJ)* *v.* — Become Strong

8.10 . . . the Elders are *become strong* . . .

Pronunciation notes:

(**Dee—V geg*) Two syllables. Dee originally wrote this word with an initial *V*—however, it should take the "u" sound, as it precedes a consonant. The accent on the second syllable is found in the pronunciation notes at *Ugear* (strength of men). The first *g* should be soft, as it precedes an *e*. The final *g* is indicated as soft in Dee's phonetic notes for *Odugeg* (and wax strong).

Compounds:

Odugeg (ohd-yew-JEJ) [Od + Ugeg]	And Wax Strong

Also:

Ugear (yew-JEE-ar)	Strength (of Men)
Ugegi (yew-JEE-jii)	Waxeth Strong

Note:

See note at *Ugear*.

Ugegi (yew-JEE-jii)* *v.* — To Wax (Become) Strong

7.48 . . . our strength *waxeth strong* in our comforter.

Pronunciation notes:

(**Dee—V Ge gi*) Three syllables. Dee originally wrote this word with an initial *V*—however, it should take the "u" sound, as it precedes a consonant. The accent falls upon the second syllable, which Dee capitalized

(see pronunciation notes for *Ugear*). The *e* is likely long. The second *g* should take the soft "j" sound, as it precedes an *i* (as in the English words *giant* and *gyrate*).
(**Dee—vgêgi*) See the *48 Claves*. Note the circumflex over the *e* to indicate its long sound.

Also:
Ugear (yew-JEE-ar) — Strength (of Men)
Ugeg (yew-JEJ) — Become Strong

Note:
See note at *Ugear*.

Viiv (vii-iv)* *n.* — Second

2.7 . . . O you *the second of* the first . . .

Note:
The words *O you* are not indicated in the Angelical.
Also, this is the word for "second," but not the numeral 2.

Pronunciation notes:
(**Dee—Vi iv*) Two syllables—although, when spoken fluently, they tend to blend together. In Early Modern English, a double *i* indicated a long "i" sound. (I suspect the second *i* in *Viiv* is just a phonetic gloss.)
(**Dee—vi-iv*) See *48 Claves*. This note matches the one from *TFR*.

Also:
Viv (vii-iv) — Second

Virq (vir-kwah)* *n.* — Nests

10.13 . . . are 22 *nests of* lamentation . . .

Pronunciation notes:
(**Dee—Vir q quu*) Two syllables. The *q* stands alone, and Dee indicates that it should sound like "kwah." (The *uu* is the same in Early Modern English as our modern *w*—so Dee's note indicates "quu" or "qw" as the sound of the second syllable.)

Viv (viv) *n.* Second

Compounds:

Taviv (tay-viv) [Ta + Viv] As the Second
Taviv (tay-viv) ["Ta" + Viv] And(?) Second
Vivialprt (viv-ii-AL-purt) [Viv + "Ialprt"] Second Flame
Vivdiv (viv-DII-vee) [Viv + Div] Second Angle

Also:

Viiv (vii-iv) Second

Note:

This is the word for "second," but not the numeral 2.
Compare this word to the name of the Part of the Earth (and its Angelic Governor) *Vivipos.*

Vivdiv (viv-DII-vee)* [Viv + Div] *comp.* Second Angle

4.12 . . . which reign in *the second angle* . . .

Pronunciation notes:

(**Dee—Vi v di v*) Seems to be four syllables. The second and third *v*'s appear to stand alone.
(**Dee—viv-di-v*) See the *48 Claves*. Here, Dee indicates three syllables instead.
I have adopted the accent from *Sdiu* (fourth angle).

Vivialprt (viv-ii-AL-purt)* [Viv + "Ialprt"] *comp.* Second Flame

**16.2 O thou *Second Flame* . . .

Note:

**The transmission of the first twelve words of Key Sixteen is missing from Dee's journals. We only have the English given for it on *TFR*, p. 194. However, Illemese gives his phonetic note for this word later, on *TFR*, p. 200. It also appears in Dee's *48 Claves*.

Pronunciation notes:

(**Illemese—vivi a purt*) See *TFR*, p. 200. Four syllables. The *r* takes the "ur" sound. Although Illemese dropps the sound of the *l*, I have retained it in my pronunciation. Also see pronunciation notes for *Ialprg* (burning flames).

(**Dee—viuiâlprt*) See the *48 Claves*. Here, Dee placed an accent over the second *i*—which should be the second syllable. He also placed a circumflex over the *a* to indicate a long vowel. However, all other versions of "Ialprt," *Ialprg*, etc., indicate a short *a* in the same place. (I have settled upon the short *a* sound in my pronunciation.)

I have adopted the accent from similar words.

Ul (yewl)* *n.* — End

1.58 . . . nor *end* cannot be . . .

Pronunciation notes:

(**Dee—Call it UL, with such sound to U as we pronounce yew, whereof bows are made.*) It is hard to tell if Dee intended one or two syllables for this word. I have settled upon a single syllable.

Also:

Uls (yewls) — Ends

Probable root:

L (el) — First

Note:

The two instances of *end* are interesting. *L* by itself indicates *the first* or *beginning*, while its usage here is antonymic. See also *I* (is/are), which transmutes into its antonym by the addition of the letter *p*: *Ip* (not)

Ulcinin (yewl-SII-nin)* *adj.* — Happy

9.59 *Happy is he* upon whom they frown not.

Pronunciation notes:

(**Dee—Ul ci nin*) Three syllables. Dee originally wrote this word with an initial *V*—but he clearly shows the "u" sound in his phonetic note.

(The *U/V* precedes a consonant, so it should take the "u" sound.) The *c* should take its soft "s" sound when preceding an *i*. The first *i* should be long, while the second *i* is short.
(**Dee—vlcínin*) See the *48 Claves*. Here, Dee placed an accent over the *i* in the second syllable.

Also:
Ucim (yew-sim) Frown Not (Smile)

Uls (yewls)* *n.* Ends

5.39 . . . first, *ends*, and contents of time . . .

Pronunciation notes:
(**Dee—Uls*) One syllable. Dee originally wrote this word as "Vls"—but his note clearly shows the "u" sound. See the pronunciation note at *Ul* (end) for more info.

Also:
Ul (yewl) End

Probable root:
L (el) First

Note:
See note at *Ul*.

Umadea (yew-MAY-dee-a)* *n.* Strong Towers
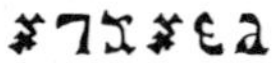

7.28 . . . *strong towers* and places of comfort . . .

Pronunciation notes:
(**Dee—V má de a*) Dee originally wrote this word as "Vmadea." However, in Early Modern English, a *v* followed by a consonant would have to take the "u" sound. (This is further supported by the related word *Umplif.*) *Umadea* appears to be four syllables, with an accent on the second syllable. The V/*U* stands alone. The *e* should likely take the long sound, as the *ea* letter combination does result in a long *e* (as in the

English words *reading* and *seat*). I suspect the final *a* (though it is written by itself) makes a short sound.

(*Dee—vmádêa) See the *48 Claves*. The accent is still on the second syllable. The *e* has a circumflex over it to indicate the long sound.

Probable shared root:

Umplif (um-plif) Strength

Note:

Also see *Ugeg* (become strong), *Vohim* (mighty). Note how all these words for "strength" begin with a *U/V*. But, also see *Micaolz* (mighty).

Uml (um-el)* *v.* To Add

30.135 *Add* and diminish until the stars . . .

Pronunciation notes:

(*Dee—Vm l*) Two syllables. The *l* stands alone. Dee originally spelled this word with a *V*—but the pronunciation note indicates that it should combine with the *m* in a single syllable. If so, then it could make the sound of "vem" or it could simply take the sound of "um" instead. Since Dee offers no clue, I have opted for the "u" sound instead of "v."

Umplif (um-plif)* *n.* Strength

7.47 . . . and our strength *waxeth strong* . . .

Pronunciation notes:

(*Dee—Umplif*) Dee originally wrote this word as *Vmplif*. However, his phonetic note clearly indicates the "u" sound. Likely two syllables, with short vowel sounds.

Probable shared root:

Umadea (yew-MAY-dee-a) Strong Towers

Note:

Also see *Givi* (stronger), *Umadea* (strong towers), *Ugeg* (become strong), and *Vohim* (mighty). Note how all these words for "strength" begin with *U/V*.

Un (und)* *prop. n.* Letter *A*

Note:

See the *Five Books*, p. 270. The name of the Angelical letter for *A*. It is likely that these letter names have translations of their own. (For instance, note the Hebrew alphabet: the letter *a* is named *Aleph*, but *Aleph* also translates as "ox/bull.") However, such translations for the Angelical letters are never given.

Pronunciation notes:

(**Dee—The sound seemed und.*) Likely just one syllable. The *u* in Dee's phonetic note could indicate a "yew" sound (as in *ubiquitous*) or an "uh" sound (as in *under*). I am unsure which is intended, but I have chosen to go with the "uh" sound.

Compare from *Loagaeth*:

Un

Unal (yew-NAL)* *pron.* These

9.27 *These* gather up the moss of the earth . . .

Pronunciation notes:

(**Dee—V nal*) Two syllables. Dee wrote this word with a "V"—though the letter should take a "u" sound because it precedes a consonant.

(**Dee—Unál*) See the *48 Claves*. Here, Dee placed an accent over the second syllable. He also confirms the "u" sound for the initial letter.

Note:

The word *these* can be an adjective (as in "these books"). However, it is used in the Keys as a pronoun, being used in place of the subject noun.

Compounds:

Unalchis (yew-nal-kiis) [Unal + Chis] These Are

Unalah (un-al-ah)* *n.* Skirts

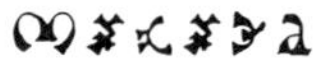

3.56 . . . you are become *the skirts of* justice and truth.

Pronunciation notes:

(**Dee—Unalah*) Likely three syllables. Dee did not write the *U* standing alone, which seems to indicate that it combines with the *n* (making a short "u" sound).

Note:

Also see *Miinoag* (corners/boundaries).

Unalchis (yew-nal-kiis)* [Unal + Chis] *comp.* These Are

10.33 . . . *these be* the Thunders . . .

Pronunciation notes:

(**Dee—U nal ckis*) Three syllables. The initial *U* stands alone. The *ch* in the final syllable takes a hard "ck" sound. (See *Chis* for further pronunciation notes.)

(**Dee—Vnâl-chis*) See the *48 Claves*. Here, Dee placed a circumflex over the *a* to indicate a long vowel sound. The initial *V* takes the "u" sound.

Note:

See note at *Unal*.

Unchi (un-kii)* *v.* To Confound

30.100 *Confound* her understanding . . .

Pronunciation notes:

(**Dee—Un chi Ki*) Two syllables. The *ch* in the second syllable takes the harder "kh" sound—as in the English word *ache*.

Also:

Oucho (oh-yew-choh) (Let) Confound

Urch (yurk) The Confusers

Note:

It would appear that "uch" serves as a common root between these words.

Undl (und-el)* *n.* The Rest

3.13 . . . *the rest* are as sharp sickles . . .

Pronunciation notes:

(*Dee—Vnd L*) Two syllables. Dee originally wrote this word with an initial *V*. The *V* likely takes the sound of "u"—because it precedes a consonant. The *l* stands alone.

(*Dee—und-l*) See *48 Claves*. Here, Dee confirms the initial "u" sound as well as the stand-alone *l*.

Also:

Udl (yew-del) The Rest

Unig (yew-nig)* *v.* To Require

9.73 . . . the time is such as *requireth* comfort.

Pronunciation notes:

(*Dee—V nig*) Two syllables. Dee wrote this word with an initial *V*. However, because it precedes a consonant, it more likely takes the "u" sound.

Uniglag (yew-nii-glag)* *v.* To Descend

3.75 . . . move, *descend*, and apply yourselves . . .

Pronunciation notes:

(*Dee—Uniglag*) I assume three syllables here, with a hard *g* in the second and third syllables.

(*Dee—vnîglag*) See the *48 Claves*. Dee placed a circumflex over the *i* to indicate the long sound.

I have adopted the long "u" sound from the similarly spelled *Unig* (to require).

"Vnph" (unv) *n.* Anger

Pronunciation note:

Following the *n*, the *ph* likely has a soft "v" sound. (See the pronunciation notes for *Sonf*.)

Compounds:

Ivonpovnph (ii-VON-foh-unv) [I + "Vonpo" + "Vnph"] Is Wrath in Anger

"Vonpovnph" (VON-foh-unv) ["Vonpo" + "Vnph"] Wrath in Anger

Also:

Vonph (vonv) Wrath

Vonpho (von-foh) (Of) Wrath

"Vonpo" (von-foh) Wrath

Possible shared root:

Vohim (VOH-im) Mighty

"Vonin" (voh-NIN) Dragon

Vonph (vonv)

Wrath

"Vovim" (voh-VIM) Dragon

Vovina (voh-VII-na) Dragon

Vohim (VOH-im)* *adj.* Mighty

10.42 . . . with a hundred *mighty* earthquakes . . .

Pronunciation notes:

(**Dee—Vóh-im*) Two syllables, with an accent on the first syllable.

(**Dee—vóhim*) See the *48 Claves*. Here, Dee again indicates the accent on the first syllable.

Possible shared root:

"Vnph" (unv) Anger

"Vonin" (voh-NIN) Dragon

Vonph (vonv)	Wrath
Vonpho (von-foh)	(Of) Wrath
"Vonpo" (von-foh)	Wrath
"Vovim" (voh-VIM)	Dragon
Vovina (voh-VII-na)	Dragon

Note:

Also see *Umadea* (strong towers), *Umplif* (strength), *Ugeg* (become strong). Note how all these words for "strength" begin with *U*/V. But, also see *Micaolz* (mighty).

Compare from *Loagaeth*:

Voh, Voha

Vomzarg (vom-sarj)* *pron.* Every One/All

3.36 . . . giving unto *every one of you* power . . .

Pronunciation notes:

(**Dee—Vomsarg, arg as in barge*) Likely two syllables, with a soft *g* at the end.

Note:

The word *all* can be an adjective ("all books") or a pronoun ("justice for all"). The word *every* is simply an adjective—but the word *Vomzarg* translates as "every one," which is synonymous with *all* used as a pronoun.

See also *Ton*, which is "all" used as an adjective.

"Vonin" (voh-NIN) *n.* Dragons

Pronunciation note:

I have adopted the accent from *Vovina* (dragon).

Compounds:

Abaivonin (ay-bay-II-voh-nin) ["Abai" + "Vonin"]	Stooping Dragons

Note:

Stooping here means "diving," as an eagle stooping for its prey.

Also:

"Vovim" (voh-VIM)	Dragon
Vovina (voh-VII-na)	Dragon

Possible shared root:

Vohim (VOH-im)	Mighty
"Vnph" (unv)	Anger
Vonph (vonv)	Wrath
Vonpho (von-foh)	(Of) Wrath
"Vonpo" (von-foh)	Wrath

Vonph (vonv)* *n.* Wrath

13.7 . . . to stir up *wrath of* sin . . .

Pronunciation notes:

(**Dee—Vonph*) One syllable. I assume the *nph* is similar to the *nf* we see in words like *Sonf* (reign). I have indicated this in my pronunciation with "nv." The *v* indicates a sound somewhere between a hard *f* and a very soft *v*.

Compounds:

Ivonph (ii-VONV) [I + Vonph]	Is Wrath

Also:

"Vnph" (unv)	Anger
Vonpho (von-foh)	(Of) Wrath
"Vonpo" (von-foh)	Wrath

Possible shared root:

Vohim (VOH-im)	Mighty
"Vonin" (voh-NIN)	Dragon
"Vovim" (voh-VIM)	Dragon
Vovina (voh-VII-na)	Dragon

Vonpho (von-foh)* *n.* (Of) Wrath

1.9 . . . the firmaments *of wrath* . . .

9.9 . . . vials eight *of wrath* . . .

Pronunciation notes:

(**Dee 1.9—Vonpho*)

(**Dee 9.9—Von pho*) Two syllables.

Also:

Vonph (vonv)	Wrath
"Vnph" (unv)	Anger
"Vonpo" (von-foh)	Wrath

Possible shared root:

Vohim (VOH-im)	Mighty
"Vonin" (voh-NIN)	Dragon
"Vovim" (voh-VIM)	Dragon
Vovina (voh-VII-na)	Dragon

"Vonpo" (von-foh) *n.* Wrath

Compounds:

Ivonpovnph (ii-VON-foh-unv) [I + "Vonpo" + "Vnph"]	Is Wrath in Anger
"Vonpovnph" (VON-foh-unv) ["Vonpo" + "Vnph"]	Wrath in Anger

Also:

"Vnph" (unv)	Anger
Vonph (vonv)	Wrath
Vonpho (von-foh)	(Of) Wrath

Possible shared root:

Vohim (VOH-im)	Mighty
"Vonin" (voh-NIN)	Dragon
"Vovim" (voh-VIM)	Dragon
Vovina (voh-VII-na)	Dragon

"Vonpovnph" (VON-foh-unv) ["Vonpo" + "Vnph"] *comp.* Wrath in Anger

Compounds:

Ivonpovnph (ii-VON-foh-unv) [I + "Vonpo" + "Vnph"] Is Wrath In Anger

Vooan (voo-AN)* *n.* Truth**

1.72 . . . the balance of righteousness and *truth.*

Pronunciation notes:

(**Dee, recording the words of Nalvage—It is Vooan. It may be sounded Vaoan. Vooan is spoken with them that fall, but Vaoan with them that are, and are glorified. The devils have lost the dignity of their sounds.*) Thus, there are two acceptable spellings for *Vooan*. When working with earthbound or infernal spirits, the word should start with *Vo* (*Vooan*)—sounding akin to "voo-an." However, when working with Angels, the word should start with *Va* ("Vaoan")—sounding akin to "vay-oh-an."

(**Dee—vaoan*) See the *48 Claves*. Here, Dee uses the "Vaoan" spelling of the word, even though *Vooan* was given in *TFR*. (See *Odvooan* for the accented syllable.)

Note:

(***Dee recording the words of Nalvage—The word is, by interpretation, Ignus vera mater. The vain Philosophers do think it doth beget bodies. But, in truth, it concieveth and bringeth forth."*) See *TFR*, p. 80. It seems that Nalvage accuses the "vain Philosophers" of regarding Vooan (Truth) as a male force (begetting bodies), but that Truth is in fact a feminine force (conceiving and bringing forth)—probably associating Truth with Gnostic images of Wisdom (Sophia). The Latin that Nalvage uses to interpret the word—*Ignus vera mater*—seems to mean the "Fiery Truth of the Mother/Source."

Compounds:

Odvooan (ohd-voo-AN) [Od + Vooan] And Truth

Also:

"Vaoan" (vay-oh-AN) Truth

Vors (vorz)* *prep.* Over

3.39 . . . power successively *over* 456 . . .

Pronunciation notes:

(*Dee—VORS*) One syllable. See the pronunciation note for *Vorsg*.

Also:

Vorsg (vorzh) Over (You)

Note:

Also see the *Five Books*, p. 311. Here, several spirits appear and demand of Dee and Kelley, "Vors Mabberan?" Dee records (*Vors Mabberan = how now: what hast thou to do with us?*) Given the known definition of *Vors* (over—especially in a hierarchy), I assume this phrase is a challenge as if to say, "What authority do you have over us?" Dee responds by reciting a prayer that sends these spirits fleeing.

Compare from *Loagaeth*:

Vor, Vors, Vorza, Vorzad, Vorzed

Vorsg (vorzh)* *prep.* Over (You)

1.3 . . . I reign *over you*, sayeth the God of Justice . . .

Pronunciation notes:

(*Dee—Vorsg*) It is unclear if Dee intends this word to be one syllable or not. The *g* may stand alone, or it could combine with the *s* to make a kind of "zhuh" digraph. I have chosen the latter, and have presented it as "zh" in my pronunciation.

Also:

Vors (vorz) Over

Compare from *Loagaeth*:

Vor, Vors, Vorza, Vorzad, Vorzed

"Vovim" (voh-VIM) *n.* Dragon

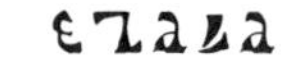

Pronunciation note:

I have adopted the accent from *Vovina* (dragon).

Compounds:

Telocvovim (tee-LOCH-voh-vee-im) [Teloch + "Vovim"] Death Dragon

Also:

"Vonin" (voh-NIN)	Dragons
Vovina (voh-VII-na)	Dragon

Possible shared root:

Vohim (VOH-im)	Mighty
"Vnph" (unv)	Anger
Vonph (vonv)	Wrath
Vonpho (von-foh)	(Of) Wrath
"Vonpo" (von-foh)	Wrath

Vovina (voh-VII-na)* *n.* Dragon

8.32 . . . until this house fall and *the dragon* sink . . .

Pronunciation notes:

(**Dee—Vo uí na*) Three syllables, with an accent on the second syllable. The *o* and the *i* should take their long sounds. Dee originally wrote this word with a *U* in the second syllable. However, the *U*/V should take the "v" sound when preceding a vowel. (Further supporting this, see the pronunciation notes for *Taviv*, as well as other versions of *Vovina*.)

(**Dee—Vouína*) See the *48 Claves*. Dee again indicates the accent on the second syllable.

Also:

"Vonin" (voh-NIN)	Dragon
"Vovim" (voh-VIM)	Dragon

Possible shared root:

Vohim (VOH-im)	Mighty
"Vnph" (unv)	Anger

Vonph (vonv)	Wrath
Vonpho (von-foh)	(Of) Wrath
"Vonpo" (von-foh)	Wrath

Upaah (yew-pay-ah)* *n.* Wings

2.2 Can *the wings* of the winds understand . . .
9.14 . . . whose *wings* are of wormwood . . .
17.4 . . . whose *wings* are thorns to stir up vexation . . .

Pronunciation notes:

(**Dee 2.2; 9.14; 17.4—V pa ah*) Three syllables. Dee originally wrote this word with an initial *V*. However, it should take the "u" sound because it precedes a consonant. The second syllable probably has a long *a*.
(**Dee 2.2—v-pa-âh*) See *48 Claves*. Three syllables. Note the circumflex over the second *a*. This is not the only case where "âh" seems to indicate the short "o" sound (as in the English words *father* and *fall*).
(**Dee 9.14; 17.4—vpâah*) See *48 Claves*. Here, Dee places the circumflex on the first *a* instead.

Also:

Upaahi (yew-pay-hii)	Wings

Upaahi (yew-pay-hii)* *n.* Wings

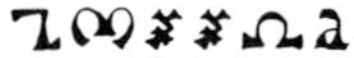

15.5 . . . under whose *wings* are 6739 . . .

Note:

The transmission of Key Fifteen is missing from Dee's journals. We only have the English for this Key given later (see *TFR*, p. 193). Plus, the word appears in this location in Dee's *48 Claves*.

Pronunciation notes:

(**Dee—vpaáhi*) See the *48 Claves*. Likely three syllables. Dee originally wrote this word with an initial *V*. However, it should take the "u" sound because it precedes a consonant. He placed an accent over the second *a*, which is possibly the second syllable. In Early Modern English, a double *a* should indicate the long "a" sound.

Also:

Upaah (yew-pay-ah) Wings

Ur (owr)* *prop. n.* Letter *L*

Note:

The name of the Angelical letter for *L*. It is likely that these letter names have translations of their own. (For instance, note the Hebrew alphabet: the letter *L* is named *Lamed*, but *Lamed* also translates as "ox-goad.") However, such translations for the Angelical letters are never given. (See the *Five Books*, p. 270.)

Pronunciation notes:

(**Dee—In sound our or ourh.*) I would assume this word rhymes with the English word *hour*.

Compare from *Loagaeth*:

Vr

Uran (yew-RAN)* *n.* Elders

8.8 . . . in whom *the Elders* are become strong . . .

Note:

This is apparently a direct reference to the twenty-four Elders of the Apocalypse (see Revelation, chapter 4).

Pronunciation notes:

(**Dee—V rán*) Two syllables, with the accent on the second syllable. Dee shows a *V* at the beginning of this word—however, in Early Modern English, a *U*/*V* before a consonant should take the vowel ("u") sound.

(**Dee—Vrán*) See the *48 Claves*. Again the accent is placed on the second syllable.

Compare from *Loagaeth*:

Uran

Urbs (yurbs) *v.* To Beautify

1.35 . . . which *beautified* your garments . . .

Also:

Turbs (turbs) In Beauty

Urch (yurk) *prop. n.* The Confusers

From *Corpus Omnium*:

Associated with the Tribulation portion of the Table, translated in Latin as *Confundantes* (The Confusers)—which has a connotation of "to dissolve back to chaos."

Also:

Oucho (oh-yew-choh) (Let) Confound

Unchi (un-kii) Confound

Note:

It would appear that "uch" is the shared root between these words.

Compare from *Loagaeth*:

Urchan

Urelp (yer-elp)* *n.* (A Strong) Seething

2.49 . . . and make me *a strong seething* . . .

Pronunciation note:

(**Dee—Vrelp*) This seems to be two syllables, which means the initial *V* likely takes its soft "u" sound.

Note:

There have been suggestions that this word should be translated as "see-thing," indicating that the speaker of the Key is asking to be granted visions. I find this unlikely. The speaker of the Key is attempting to "stir up" the Angels, and the English might thus better read " . . . and make (for) me a strong seething."

Also note that *seething* would normally be an adjective (as in "he displayed a seething anger"). However, in Key Two, it is used as a noun.

Uta (yew-tay) *prop. n.* "The Fourteenth Aethyr"

30.3 . . . which dwell in *the fourteenth aethyr* . . .

Note:
This (word 30.3) is the single space in the Key of the Aethyrs, which must be changed for each invocation—replacing word 30.3 with the name of the appropriate Aethyr. No established definitions were given for these names.

Uta contains the three Parts of the Earth *Tedoond*, *Vivipos*, and *Ooanamb*.

Uti (yew-tii) *prop. n.* "The Twenty-Fifth Aethyr"

30.3 . . . which dwell in *the twenty-fifth aethyr* . . .

Note:
This (word 30.3) is the single space in the Key of the Aethyrs, which must be changed for each invocation—replacing word 30.3 with the name of the appropriate Aethyr. No established definitions were given for these names.

Uti contains the three Parts of the Earth *Mirzind*, *Obvaors*, and *Ranglam*.

UX (yewks)* 42

13.4 . . . which have *42* eyes to stir up . . .

Pronunciation notes:
(**Dee—Ux*) Likely just one syllable. It is unclear if the *U* should be long or short. I have settled upon the long sound.

Note:

This word was not originally given with Key Thirteen. It was added later when Nalvage transmitted the English for the Key (see *TFR*, p. 193). This seems to have been the case with many of the numbers mentioned in the Keys.

Pal (X)

There are no Angelical words (to date) that begin with the letter *Pal* (X). Usually, a word beginning with an *X* will take a "z" sound (as in the English words *xylophone* and *xenophobe*). Therefore, I assume that any such word in Angelical would begin with a *Ceph* (Z) instead.

Ceph (Z)

Za (zay)* *prop. n.* n/a

Pronunciation note:

(**Dee: Zaa*) Dee spells the Angel *Za*'s name with two *a*'s in a marginal notation (see the note below), which may indicate the long "a" sound.

Note:

See *TFR*, pp. 228–29. The names of most of the Angels encountered by Dee and Kelley can be found in other parts of the Angelic system, such as the *Heptarchia* or Great Table (Watchtower) systems. However, Za is one of the few entirely unique Angels that appeared to the two men. It was very late in the Angelic journals, after all of the essential Angelic magick had been transmitted. One day, Kelley saw three little creatures running around the floor of the room. It turned out that they were Angels from the Great Table (Watchtowers), but their names were *not* derived according to the instructions Ave had previously given to Dee.

Za says of himself: "I am the second of the third,* which dwell in the spirit, and power of God in earth.** I have power to scourge them that resist the power, will and commandment of God. And I am one of those that stand, and is perpetual." Dee notes, in Latin: "*Zaa*—Scourger of resistance to the power, will and commandment of God."

The three Angels, apparently jointly, say, "For even as the father, son, and holy spirit are one, but of themselves and being dilated, is full of power, and many. So are we one particularly in power,*** but separated. Notwithstanding, spiritually of, and amongst, others, and dilated in the will of God, and into the branches of his determinations. But, particularly living, and jointly praising God."

Note:

*Dee notes the Angels are numbering the Watchtowers in an odd fashion. So that in this case, he points out, the numbering should follow: First = eastern, Second = western, Third = southern, and Fourth = the northern Watchtower. Za is found as the last two letters in the upper-left subquadrant of the Southern Watchtower Tablet.

**In Dee's diagram of the Holy City (see Geoffrey James' *Enochian Magick of Dr. John Dee*, p. 103), the Southern Gates are associated with the zodiacal triplicity of Earth.

(*** *On the next page Dee notes: The three names make one name of 7 letters-Gazavaa.*) I note that all three of these names begin with capital letters on the Great Table (Watchtowers). Also, each one of them terminates once it hits the Great Cross, Black Cross, or the end of the Watchtower. We may have discovered an entirely new Angelic system in the Watchtowers.

(See *Ga* and *Vaa*. Also *Galvah*, *Mapsama*, *Murifri*, and *Nalvage*.)

Zaa (zay) *prop. n.* "The Twenty-Seventh Aethyr"

30.3 . . . which dwell in *the twenty-seventh aethyr* . . .

Note:

This (word 30.3) is the single space in the Key of the Aethyrs, which must be changed for each invocation—replacing word 30.3 with the name of the appropriate Aethyr. No established definitions were given for these names.

Zaa contains the three Parts of the Earth *Saziami*, *Mathula*, and *Orpanib*.

Zacam (ZAY-kam) *v.* To Move

6.36 . . . I have talked of you and *I move you* . . .

Pronunciation notes:

(**Dee—Za cam*) Two syllables. I would suggest the *a* takes a long sound, as it falls as the end of its syllable.

(**Dee—zácam*) See the 48 *Claves*. The accent is placed on the first syllable.

Note:

Remember that both *I* and *you* are generally implied in Angelical. Neither of these pronouns is indicated in the word itself.

Also:

Zacar (ZAY-kayr *or* ZOHD-ay-kayr) Move

Zacar (ZAY-kayr *or* ZOHD-ay-kayr)* *v.* Move

1.73 . . . *move*, therefore . . .
2.42 . . . *move*, therefore . . .
3.74 . . . *move*, descend . . .
4.42 . . . *move*, and show yourselves . . .
7.35 . . . *move*, appear . . .
12.23 . . . *move*, I say . . .
(RFP) . . . *move*, and show yourselves . . .
30.142 . . . *move* and appear . . .

Pronunciation notes:

(**Dee 1.73—Call it Zacar. E must come after R: but without number, and so it is Zacare*) Nalvage was still giving numbers with each letter of the words at this point. However, the letter *e* was not drawn from the Tables of *Loagaeth*, so it is "without number." Instead, it was only appended to the word in Dee's phonetic note to indicate that the preceding *a* should be long. It is purely a phonetic gloss.

(**Dee 2.42; 4.42; 30.142—Zacar*)

(**Dee 7.35—Za car*) This note suggests two syllables.

(**Dee 3.74—Zod a car*) Here, Dee indicates that the Z should stand alone, making the "zohd" sound (producing three syllables instead of two). Since this is not indicated in other instances of the word, I suspect the extended Z is a poetic or lyrical gloss, rather than a rule of pronunciation. Finally, note that words 7.35 abd 3.74 each indicate a long *a* in the first syllable.

(**Dee 1.73; 11.RFP—ZACARe*) See the *48 Claves*. In these places, Dee placed a lowercase *e* at the end of the word—supporting the note in *TFR*, word 1.73.

Finally, I have adopted the accent from the word *Zacam* (to move).

Note:

Could there be a relationship between this word and the name of *Acar*, an Angel of fire in the Northern Watchtower?

Also:

Zacam (ZAY-kam) To Move

Zamran (zam-ran)* *v.* To Appear

1.76 ...move, therefore, and *show yourselves*...

2.45 ...move, therefore, and *show yourselves*...

(RFP) ...move, therefore, and *show yourselves*...**

7.36 ...move, *appear*, sing praises...

8.47 ...*appear* to the terror of the earth...

11.35 ...move, therefore, and *show yourselves*...

12.26 ...move, I say, and *show yourselves*...

Pronunciation notes:

(**Dee 1.76—Call it Zamran*)

(**Dee 2.45—Zamran*)

(**Dee 7.36; 8.47—Zam ran*) Two syllables

Note:

**The wording of the RFP does change slightly in some of the Keys. See either the Angelical Keys cross-reference (chapter 2) or the Angelical Psalter (in volume I).

Compounds:

Odzamran (ohd-zam-ran) [Od + Zamran] And Appear

Zax (zaks) *prop. n.* "The Tenth Aethyr"

30.3 . . . which dwell in *the tenth aethyr* . . .

Note:

This (word 30.3) is the single space in the Key of the Aethyrs, which must be changed for each invocation—replacing word 30.3 with the name of the appropriate Aethyr. No established definitions were given for these names.

Zax contains the three Parts of the Earth *Lexarph*, *Comanan*, and *Tabitom*.

Zchis (zohd-kiis)* *v.* (They) Are

5.25 . . . *they are* the brothers . . .
9.39 . . . whose iniquities *they are* . . .
11.27 . . . as *they are* whose number is 31 . . .

Pronunciation notes:

(**Dee 5.25; 11.27—Zod chis*)

(**Dee 9.39—Zod Chis kis*) Two syllables. The *ch* makes the harder "k" (or "kh") sound. See the pronunciation notes for *Chis* (are) for the long "i" sound.

(**Dee 5.25; 11.27—z-chis*) See the *48 Claves*. Notes two syllables, with the Z standing alone.

Also:

Chis (kiis)	Are
Chiis (kiis)	Are (They)
"Chisda" (KIIS-da)	Are There
Chiso (kiis-oh)	Shall Be
"Gchis" (jee-kiis)	Are
"Ichis" (jjay-kiis)	Are

Zed (zed) n/a

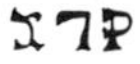

Note:

See *TFR*, pp. 34-35. This session is recorded entirely in Latin. Here we find this Angelical phrase spoken by "a Voice": "*Garil zed masch, ich na gel galaht gemp gal noch Cabanladan.*" No translation or context is offered.

Zen (zen) *prop. n.* "The Eighteenth Aethyr"

30.3 . . . which dwell in *the eighteenth aethyr* . . .

Note:

This (word 30.3) is the single space in the Key of the Aethyrs, which must be changed for each invocation—replacing word 30.3 with the name of the appropriate Aethyr. No established definitions were given for these names.

Zen contains the three Parts of the Earth *Nabaomi*, *Zafasai*, and *Yalpamb*.

Zid (zid) *prop. n.* "The Eighth Aethyr"

30.3 . . . which dwell in *the eighth aethyr* . . .

Note:

This (word 30.3) is the single space in the Key of the Aethyrs, which must be changed for each invocation—replacing word 30.3 with the name of the appropriate Aethyr. No established definitions were given for these names.

Zid contains the three Parts of the Earth *Zamfres*, *Todnaon*, and *Pristac*.

Zien (zeen)* *n.* Hands

1.28 . . . the palms of *my hands* . . .

Pronunciation notes:

(**Dee—Zien*) I assume there should be one syllable here. The Early Modern English letter combination *ie* makes a long "e" sound—as in the English words *grieve* and *believe*.

Also:

Azien (az-EEN) (On Whose) Hands

Ozien (oh-ZEEN) (Mine Own) Hand

Probable shared root:

Ozol (oh-ZOHL) Hands

Zol (zohd-OL) Hands

Zildar (zil-dar)* *v.* Fly into

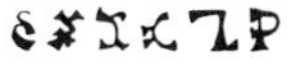

11.8 . . . Thunders which *flew into* the east . . .

Pronunciation notes:

(**Dee—Zil dar*) Two syllables. Both vowels appear to take their short sounds.

Possible shared root:

Zylna (zil-na) "Within"

"Zilodarp" (ZII-loh-darp) Stretch Forth / Conquest

Note:

Compare this word to the name of the Part of the Earth (and its Angelic Governor), *Zildron*. Thus, there is an etymology of "to fly" in his name.

"Zilodarp" (ZII-loh-darp) *n.* Stretch Forth / Conquest

Compounds:

Madzilodarp (mad-ZII-loh-darp) [Mad + "Zilodarp"] God of Conquest

Note:

I have simplified "stretch forth and conquer" into the obvious: "conquest." However, based upon the words that might share a root with this word, I suggest that "stretch forth" is the base of "Zilodarp."

Possible shared root:

Zildar (zil-dar) Fly into

Zylna (zil-na) "Within"

Zim (zim) *prop. n.* "The Thirteenth Aethyr" (Entrance or Territory?)

30.3 . . . which dwell in *the thirteenth aethyr* . . .

Note:

This (word 30.3) is the single space in the Key of the Aethyrs, which must be changed for each invocation—replacing word 30.3 with the name of the appropriate Aethyr. No established definitions were given for these names.

Zim contains the three Parts of the Earth *Gecaond*, *Laparin*, and *Docepax*.

Possible shared root:

Zimii (ZII-mii) To Enter

Zimz (zimz) Vestures (Territories)

Zimii (ZII-mii)* *v.* To Enter

5.2 The Mighty Sounds *have entered into* the third angle . . .

Pronunciation notes:

(**Dee—Zi mii*) Two syllables. The first *i* is likely a long sound. The double *i*'s in the second syllable would form a long "i" sound in Early Modern English.

(**Dee—zímii*) See the *48 Claves*. Note the accent on the first syllable.

Possible shared root:

Zim (zim) "The Thirteenth Aethyr"

Zimz (zimz) Vestures (Territories)

Zimz (zimz)* *n.* Vestures (Territories)

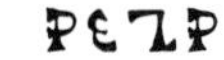

1.23 . . . in the midst of *my vestures* . . .

Pronunciation notes:

(**Dee—Zimz*) Probably one syllable.

Note:

The word *vestures* would not have indicated clothing to Dee and Kelley. Instead, it would have indicated property or territories— especially those given by a king. (It is the root of our modern words *investiture* and *investment.*)

Note that the word *garment* in Angelical is given as *Oboleh*, and related to the word *Obloch* (garland)— indicating a wrapping. Also see *Qaa* (creation).

Possible shared root:

Zim (zim) "The Thirteenth Aethyr"

Zimii (ZII-mii) To Enter

Zip (zip) *prop. n.* "The Ninth Aethyr"

30.3 . . . which dwell in *the ninth aethyr* . . .

Note:

This (word 30.3) is the single space in the Key of the Aethyrs, which must be changed for each invocation—replacing word 30.3 with the name of the appropriate Aethyr. No established definitions were given for these names.

Zip contains the three Parts of the Earth *Oddiorg, Cralpir,* and *Doanzin.*

Zir (zer)* *v.* Am, Were, Was

2.51 ...*I am* of him...

3.4 ...*I am* a circle...

Pronunciation note:

(**Dee 2.51; 3.4—Zir*) One syllable.

Note:

As is most often the case in Angelical, the pronoun (*I*) is simply implied.

Compounds:

Zirenaiad (zii-er-NAY-ad) [Zir + Enay + Iad]

I Am The Lord (Your) God

Also:

Zirdo (zer-DOH)	Am
Zirom (zer-OM)	Were
Zirop (zii-ROP)	Was

Compare from *Corpus Omnium*:
Found in the pre-Deluge portion of the Table, in the phrase *Zir Moz Iad* (I am the Joy of God).

Note:
Zir appears to be a form of the verb *to be*. Compare to *I* (is/are).

Also compare with the name of the Part of the Earth (and its Angelic Governor) *Zirzird*. It could be that this name is similar to the biblical Name of God "I Am That I Am." (Also, the Mother of Angels, *Galvah*, once introduced herself as "I Am.")

Zirdo (zer-DOH)* *v.* Am

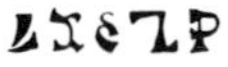

(RFP) . . . *I am* the servant . . .

Pronunciation notes:
(**Dee 1.83—Call it Zirdo*) I have adopted the accent from *Zirop* (was).

Also:

Zir (zer)	Am
Zirom (zer-OM)	Were
Zirop (zii-ROP)	Was

Zirenaiad (zii-er-NAY-ad)* [Zir + Enay + Iad] *comp.*
I Am the Lord (Your) God

4.37 . . . For, *I am the Lord your God* . . .

Pronunciation notes:
(**Dee—Zire nai ad*) Four syllables. In the first syllable, the final *e* gives the *i* its long sound. ("Zire" likely rhymes with the English words *fire* and *desire*.) In the second syllable, the Early Modern English letter com-

bination *ai* (or "ay") makes the long "a" sound—as in the English words *dais* and *day*.
(**Dee—Zirenáiad*) See the *48 Claves*. Note the accent on the third syllable.

Note:
The *e* and *a* in "enay" are phonetic glosses. See *Enay* (Lord).

Zirom (zer-OM)* *v.* Were

11.4 . . . *they were* five thunders . . .

Pronunciation notes:
(**Dee—Zir om*) Two syllables. Both vowels seem to take their short sounds. I have adopted the accent from *Zirop* (was).

Also:

Zir (zer)	Am
Zirdo (zer-DOH)	Am
Zirop (zii-ROP)	Was

Zirop (zii-ROP)* *v.* Was

10.77 . . . is, *was*, and shall be great . . .

Pronunciation notes:
(**Dee—Zi róp*) Two syllables. The accent mark is on the second syllable. The *i* should be long, while the *o* is likely short.
(**Dee—ziróp*) See the *48 Claves*. Again shows an accent over the second syllable.

Also:

Zir (zer)	Am
Zirdo (zer-DOH)	Am
Zirom (zer-OM)	Were

Zixlay (ziks-lay)* *v.* To Stir Up

17.7 . . . thorns *to stir up* vexation . . .

Pronunciation notes:

(**Dee—Zix lay*) Two syllables. The *i* is short, but the *ay* combine to form a long "a" sound.

Note:

Also see *Lring* (to stir up).

Zizop (zis-op)* *n.* Vessels

5.20 . . . gave them *vessles* to water the earth . . .

Pronunciation notes:

(**Dee—Zisop*) Appears to be three syllables. Note the second *z* takes on more of an "s" sound in pronunciation.

Also:

Izizop (iz-is-op) (Your?) Vessels

Note:

Compare this word to the name *Sisp* (or *Siosp*), an Angel of Water in the Northern Watchtower. I find it interesting that the name of an Angel of Water is similar to the *Zizop* (vessels) that are used in Key Five "to water the earth."

Also compare the names *Ziza*, *Izaz*, *Zazi*, and *Aziz,* the four Angels of Secrets from the Northern Watchtower.

Zlida (zohd-lid-a)* *v.* To Water

5.21 . . . vessels *to water* the earth . . .

Pronunciation notes:

(**Dee—Zod-lida. It is a Word and a letter. Zod lida. Z lida*) There was some confusion at this point in the session, so Dee ended up writing three distinct phonetic notes for this word. All of them indicate the same thing: the initial Z stands alone (. . . *and a letter*)—probably because it is followed by a consonant.

(**Dee—z-lida*) See the *48 Claves*. This note matches that in *TFR*.

Shared root:

Pilzin (pil-zin) Waters

Note:

Zlida is a verb, while *Pilzin* is a noun.

Zna (snay) *adj.* Motion (Action)

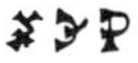

From *Corpus Omnium*:

Found in the post-Deluge portion of the Table, in the phrase *Zna Bab Iad* (Moving Dominion of God).

Pronunciation notes:

Dee may have intended *Zn* to make a unified sound akin to "sn" (as in *snake*, *snap*, etc.). See the pronunciation given for *Znurza* (swore).

Znrza (snur-za)* *v.* To Swear

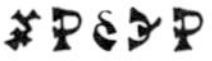

1.49 . . . you lifted up your voices *and swore* obedience.

Pronunciation notes:

(**Dee—as Znursa*) It is difficult to be certain, but it would appear Dee intended for the *Zn* to make a sound akin to "sn" (as in *snake*, *snap*, etc.). Then, the *r* takes the "ur" sound when surrounded by consonants with which it can't combine (in this case, *n* and Z).

Also:

Surzas (sur-zas) Sworn

Note:

Also see *Aisro*/*Isro* (promise of) and *Sibsi* (covenant).

Zol (zohd-OL)* *n.* Hands

1.11 . . . in whose *hands* the sun is as a sword . . .

Pronunciation notes:

(**Dee—Zol . . . zod, as ol*) Indicates that the Z should possess its extended "zohd" sound. This extension is likely a poetic or lyrical gloss, rather than a grammatical rule. (Note that other versions of the word do not have the extended "zohd" sound.)

(**Dee—z-ol*) See *48 Claves*. Two syllables, with the Z standing alone.

I have chosen to place the accent on the second syllable for two reasons. First, both *Asien* (hands) and *Ozien* (hand) are accented on the second syllable. Second, the extended "zohd" sound is likely a lyrical gloss, and not an inherent part of the word itself.

Also:

Ozol (oh-ZOHL) Hands

Probable shared root:

Azien (az-EEN) (On Whose) Hands

Ozien (oh-ZEEN) (Mine Own) Hand

Zien (zeen) Hands

Zom (zom) *prop. n.* "The Third Aethyr" (To Encompass?)

30.3 . . . which dwell in *the third aethyr* . . .

Note:

This (word 30.3) is the single space in the Key of the Aethyrs, which must be changed for each invocation—replacing word 30.3 with the name of the appropriate Aethyr. No established definitions were given for these names.

Zom contains the three Parts of the Earth *Samapha*, *Virooli*, and *Andispi*.

Possible shared root:

Zomdux (zom-dooks) Amidst (i.e., "encompassed by")

Zomdux (zom-dooks) *prep.* Amidst (i.e.,"encompassed by")

1.63 . . . shineth as a flame *in the midst of* your palace.

Possible shared root:

Zom (zom) "The Third Aethyr"

Note:

Also see *Nothoa* (Amidst).

Zonac (zoh-nak)* *v.* Appareled (with)

7.18 . . . and *they are appareled with* ornaments . . .

Pronunciation notes:

(**Dee—Zo nac*) Two syllables. The *o* is likely long, while the *A* should take a short sound. I assume the *c* at the end of a word would take its hard sound.

Zong (zong)* *n.* Winds

2.3 Can the wings of *the winds* understand . . .

Pronunciation notes:

(**Dee—Zong*)

Also:

Ozongon (oh-zong-on) Manifold Winds

Zonrensg (zon-renj) *v.* To Deliver

1.43 . . . *delivered you* a rod . . .

Zorge (zorj)* *v.* Be Friendly unto Me

(RFP) *Be friendly unto me.*

Pronunciation notes:

(**Dee 1.RFP—Call it Zorge [Of one syllable]*) The final *e* indicates a soft "g" sound. It probably rhymes with *George* and *gorge*.

Zumvi (zum-vii)* *n.* Seas

9.48 . . . from their mouths run *seas of* blood.

Pronunciation notes:

(**Dee—Zum vi*) Two syllables. The *u* should take its short sound. The final *i* should take a long sound.

Zuraah (zur-AY-ah) *n.?* Prayer?*

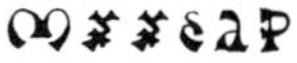

Note:

(**Dee—Laua Zuraah = Use humility in prayers to God, that is fervently pray. It signifieth, <u>Pray Unto God</u>.*) See the *Five Books*, p. 324. Between lines 46 and 47 of Table One of *Loagaeth*, some kind of stormy interference erupted in the shewstone. A voice then said the phrase "*Laua Zuráah.*" The two men then prayed as instructed, and the interference cleared. It would appear that *Zuraah* indicates prayer to the Highest God.

Pronunciation notes:

The first *a* of *Zuraah* is accented in Dee's journal. The double *a* should result in a long "a" sound.

Possibly also:

Zurah (zur-AH) n/a

Zure (zur-AY) n/a

Zuresch (zur-ESK) n/a

Compare from *Loagaeth*:

Zurad, *Zuram*, *Zurath*, *Zureheffa*, *Zurehoh*, *Zureoch*, *Zuresch*, and *Zureth*

Zurah (zur-AH) n/a

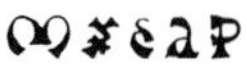

Pronunciation note:

I have adopted the accent from *Zuraah*.

Note:

See *TFR*, p. 22. Here, the guardian Angel of Lord Lasky of Poland says a prayer on Lasky's behalf, which ends with, "Grant this *Camascheth galsuagath garnastel zurah logaah luseroth*." (Note the word *Zurah*.) No translation is offered.

Possibly also:

Zuraah (zur-AY-ah) Prayer?

Zure (zur-AY) n/a

Zuresch (zur-ESK) n/a

Compare from *Loagaeth*:

Zurad, *Zuram*, *Zurath*, *Zureheffa*, *Zurehoh*, *Zureoch*, *Zuresch*, and *Zureth*

Zure (zur-AY) n/a

Pronunciation note:

I have adopted the accent from *Zuraah*.

Note:

See the *Five Books*, p. 276. Here, Kelley is once again convinced the Angels are evil devils sent to lead humans astray. The Archangel Raphael holds his hands to Heaven (in what appears to be exasperation) and exclaims, "*Camikas Zure*!" No translation is suggested.

Possibly also:

Zuraah (zur-AY-ah) Prayer?

Zurah (zur-AH) n/a

Zuresch (zur-ESK) n/a

Compare from *Loagaeth*:

Zurad, *Zuram*, *Zurath*, *Zureheffa*, *Zurehoh*, *Zureoch*, *Zuresch*, and *Zureth*

Zuresch (zur-ESK) n/a

Pronunciation note:

I have adopted the accent from *Zuraah*.

From *Loagaeth*:

See the *Five Books*, pp. 288 and 291. This is one of the thousands of untranslated words from the Tables of *Loagaeth*. I have included it here merely because I have discussed it more than once in the text of this study. It is the first word of *Loagaeth* itself (Table One, side A, Word 1), and Raphael made a point that it was to be of seven letters.

Possibly also:

Zuraah (zur-AY-ah)	Prayer?
Zurah (zur-AH)	n/a
Zure (zur-AY)	n/a

Compare from *Loagaeth*:

Zurad, *Zuram*, *Zurath*, *Zureheffa*, *Zurehoh*, *Zureoch*, *Zuresch*, and *Zureth*

Zylna (zil-na)* *prep.* Within (Itself)

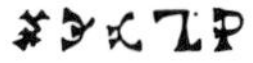

30.56 . . . may be always drunken and vexed *in itself.*

Pronunciation notes:

(**Dee—Zyl na*) Two syllables. Remember the *y* could also be written as an *i*—so the word could also appear as *Zilna*.

Possible shared root:

Zildar (zil-dar)	Fly into
"Zilodarp" (ZII-loh-darp)	Stretch Forth / Conquest

An English to Angelical Dictionary

If you are using this Lexicon to create new prayers and invocations (or to convert existing texts into Angelical), then you are likely to begin here. Simply look up the English word you wish to translate, and you will find the Angelical word, all of its alternate versions, and reference pointers to similar, related, or synonymous words. Decide which version best fits your intent, and then look up the word in the Lexicon itself to see how it is properly used—and much more.

This dictionary is expanded. Because of the fluid definitions associated with Angelical words, I was able to use a thesaurus to to generate a larger pool of interrelated words and concepts. This makes it more likely that you will find the word you are looking for, or at least something closely related.

Tips on Translating English into Angelical

Based on my overall study of the language, I would like to offer some basic tips on translating English texts into Angelical. First of all, write out the text as it exists in English. Then follow these steps:

- Mark out articles (*a*, *an*, and *the*). Articles do not exist at all in Angelical. The word *of* is also unnecessary most of the time, although there does exist an Angelical word for it (*De*), so it can be used if you feel it is unavoidable.
- Mark out most adjectives. You can check the English to Angelical to see if your adjective—or something similar—exists. If it does not, you can drop the adjective, and consider it implied in the Angelical. As an example, if you want to translate the words *a bitter sting*, you would only need to look up the word *sting*. There is no Angelical word for *bitter*, but that adjective is implicit in the Angelical word *Grosb* (bitter sting). The same word might translate as "horrible sting," "painful sting," "poisonous sting," and so forth.
- Also remember that Angelical compounds are often formed between nouns and the possessive adjectives (*his*, *her*, *their*), demonstrative and relative pronouns (*which/that*, *this*, *those*), conjunctions (*and*, *or*, *but*), and the forms of *to be* (*is*, *are*, *were*) that indicate them. Therefore, try

linking these words together in the English text, and see if they form natural compounds in Angelical.

- You can take most noun phrases and verb phrases and reduce them to their basic concepts. For instance, consider the sentence *He was running swiftly*. The verbal phrase *was running swiftly* might be represented sufficiently by the Angelical for "to run." Thus *He was running swiftly* could be represented with the single Angelical word *Parm*. Or, another example: *The great sea of the western region* would become just three words: *Drilpa zumvi soboln* ("great sea west"). (Especially look at column 4 of the Angelical cross-reference, to see how simple Angelical translates into elaborate English.)
- If you've written something for which there is no (current) Angelical translation, try re-wording your text. Endeavor to say the same thing in a different way, and see if the Angelical exists for such alternate wording. (A thesaurus can be a big help in this process.) At the same time, you can browse through this English-to-Angelical section for alternate words that might fit your intent.

These are just a few simple suggestions that will allow you to convert English text into a format easily translatable into Angelical. I also strongly suggest that you study the "Angelical Linguistics" chapter, in order to get a better feel for how Angelical grammar works. With these tools at your disposal, you should have little trouble writing and translating Angelical texts.

1
See First, One

2
See Second

3
See Third

4
See Fourth

5
O

6
See Six

8
P

9
See Nine

12
OS

12 Kingdoms
Oslondoh

12 Seats
Thilnos

19
AF

22
OP

24
OL

26
OX

28
OB, NI

31
"GA"

33
PD

42
UX

100
See Hundred

456
CLA

1000
See Thousand

1636
QUAR

3663
MIAN

5678
DAOX

6332
ERAN

6739
DARG

7336
TAXS

7699
ACAM

8763
EMOD

9639
MAPM

9996
CIAL

69636
PERAL

A (Un)

Abide
Casasam (Abiding)
See also Continue, Dwell, Remain

Able
See Can

Abound
See Flourish

Accomplish
See Execute

According
Marb (According to)

Achieve
See Execute

Action
Sor (Action, especially that taken by a king)
Zna (Motion, Action)
See also Move, Motion, Rest Not, Stir

Add
Uml (To Add)
See also Increase

Administer
See Apply

Admiration
Grsam (Admiration)
See also Adoration, Glory, Praise

Adoration
Adgmach (Glory, Adoration, Praise)
See also Glory, Praise, Admiration

Adornment
See Garnish

Advance
"Ar" (To Advance Upon)

Aeon
See Age

Affix
See Bind, Fasten, Truss Together

Afflict/Affliction
See Torment

Age
Homil (Ages)
Homin (Age)
See also While, Period, Season, Time

Agony
See Torment

Ahead
See Before

All
Tofglo (All Things)
Ton (All)
See also Every One

"All Powerful"
Iaidon (the All Powerful God)
See also God, Lord

Always
Paid (Always)

Am
Zir (I Am)
Zirdo (I Am)
See also Are, Is, Was, Were

Amidst
Nothoa (Amidst)
Zomdux (Amidst/Encompassed by)
See also Among, Center

Among
Aai (Amongst You)
Aaf (Amongst)
Aaiom (Amongst Us)
Aao (Amongst)
Eai (Amongst)
Oai (Amongst)
See also Amidst, Center

Amplify
See Magnify

And
Ds (And?)
Od (And)
Ot (And)

And Another While
Odcacocasb

And Appear
Odzamran

And Are
Odchis

And Continuance
Odmiam

And Destroy
Odquasb

And the Dwelling Place
Odfaorgt

And Fourth
Odes

And Has
Odbrint

And Liveth
Odapila

And Powers
Odlonshin

And the Praise
Odecrin

And the Second
Taviv(?)

And Shall Not See
Odipuran

And Truth
Odvooan

And Wax Strong
Odugeg

Angels/Angelic Orders
(It is unclear if these are Angelic Orders or simply different Angelical words for *Angel*.)
Avavago (Thunders of Increase)
Const (Thunders)
Coraxo (Thunders of Judgment and Wrath)
Ialpurg (Burning Flames)
Lang (Those Who Serve)
Luas (Those Who Praise, or The Triumphant)
Pir (Holy Ones)
Sach (The Establishers/Supporters)
Sapah (Mighty Sounds)
Urch (The Confusers)
See also Divine Names, Spirits. (Also see Star, a common biblical term for an Angel.)

Anger
"Vnph" (Anger)
See also Fury, Wrath

Angle
Div

Animal
See Beast, Creature

Another
Asymp (Another)
"Smnad" (Another)
Symp (Another)

Any
Droln (Any)

Apparel
Zonac (Appareled with, Cloathed)
See also Garment, Garland

Appear
Zamran (To Appear)
See also Arise

Appendage
See Member

Apply
Imuamar (To Apply unto)

Are
Chiis (Are)
Chis (Are)
"Gchis" (Are)
Geh (Are/Art)
I (Is, Are)
"Ichis" (Are)
Zchis (They Are)
See also Is, May Be, Shall Be, Was, Were

Are as
Chista

Are as the Third
Chistad

Are Become
Inoas

Are Measured
Chisholq

Are Mighty
Chismicaolz

Are Not
Gchisge (Are Not)
Ichisge (Are Not)

Are There
"Chisda"

Arise/Rise
Torgu (Arise)
Torzu (Arise)
Torzul (Shall Rise)
Torzulp (To Rise)
See also Lift Up, Appear

Ark
Erm (Ark)
See also Harbor

Arrogance
See Pomp

Arrow
"Mal" (Thrust, Arrow, Increase)

Art
See Are

As
"Ca" (As?)
Ta (As)

As Bucklers
Talolcis

As Comforters
Tablior

As the First
Talo

As Many
Plosi (As Many)
See also Many

As is Not
Tage

As Olives
Taqanis

As the Second
Taviv

As Sickles
Tapuin

As the Third
"Tad"

Assortment
See Variety

Asylum
See Ark, Harbor

***Athanor* (Alchemical Furnace)**
Rlodnr (Alchemical Furnace or Heat)

Attach
See Bind, Fasten, Truss Together

Attend
See Apply, Appear

Attire
See Apparel, Garment, Garland

Attractive
See Beauty

Authority
See Dominion

"Avoidance of Earthly Things"
See "Earth-Fleer"

B (Pa)

Balance
Piap (Balance)

Bane
See Torment

Barb
See Thorn

Barrier
See Buckler

Be
See Am, Are, Become, Is, Let There Be, Not, Shall Be, Was, Were

Bear
See Bring Forth

Bear Witness
O (Come and Bear Witness)
Oh (Come and Bear Witness?)

Beast
Levithmong (Beasts of the Field)
See also Creature

Beauty
Turbs (Beauty)
Urbs (Beautified)

Because
Bagle (For, Wherefore, Because)
Baglen (Because)
See also For, Therefore, Wherefore

Become
Inoas (Are/Have Become)
Noaln (May Be)
Noan (To Become)
Noar (Has Become)
Noas (Have Become)
Noasmi (Let Become)

Become Strong
Ugeg (Become Strong)
Ugegi (Become/Grow Strong)
See also Strong

Bed
Tianta (Bed)

Before
Aspt (Before, In Front)
See also Precede

Be Friendly unto Me
Zorge (Be Friendly unto Me)

Beginning
Acroodzi (Beginning)
Amgedpha (I Will Begin Anew)
Croodzi (Beginning of Things)
Iaod (Beginning)
Iaodaf (In the Beginning)
Nostoah (It Was in the Beginning)

Begotten
Iusmach (Begotten)

Behold
Micma (Behold)
See also Look, See

Be It Made with Power
Chramsa
See also Let There Be

Beneath
Oroch (Under)
Orocha (Beneath)
See also Under

Between
See Amidst, Among

Bind
Alar (To Settle, To Place)
Allar (To Bind Up)
See also Set, Settle, Place, Plant

Blood
Cnila (Blood)

Boil
See Seethe

Bolt
See Arrow

Born
See Begotten

Boundaries
See Corners

Branch
Lilonon (Branches)

Breath
Gigipah (Living Breath)

Brightness
Luciftian (Ornaments of Brightness)
Luciftias (Brightness)
See also Light, Shine

Bring Down
Drix (To Bring Down)
See also Cast Down

Bring Forth
Yolcam (To Bring Forth/Bear)
Yolci (To Bring Forth)

Brother
Esiasch (Brothers)

Buckler
"Lolcis" (Bucklers)

Building
Orscatbl (Buildings)
Trof (Building)
See also House, Dwelling

Bulwark
See Buckler

Burn
Ialpon (To Burn)
Ialpor (Flaming)
See also Fire, Flame, Shine

Burning Flame
Ialprg (Burning Flame)
Ialpurg (Burning Flames)

But
Crip (But)
"Crp" (But)
Oq (But/Except)
See also Except

But One
Crpl

C (Veh)

Call
"Ium" (Is Called)
Iumd (Is Called)

Can
Adgt (Can)

Cannot
"Pamis" (Cannot)
Ipamis (Cannot Be)
See also No/None, Not

Carry Out
See Execute

Cast Down
Adrpan (Cast Down)
See also Bring Down

Cause
Gru (To Cause, Bring about, Result)

Cave/Cavern
Tabges (Caves)

Celebrate
See Rejoice

Center
Ovoars (Center)
See also Amidst

Chamber
Ooge (Chamber)

Characteristic
See Quality

Christ in Hell
Iurehoh (What Christ Did in Hell)

Churn
See Mingle, Seethe

Circle
Comselh (Circle)

Classify
See Separate Creatures

Clothed
See Apparel, Garment, Garland

Coat
Mabza (Coat)

Come
Carma (Come Out)
Niis (Come Here)
Niisa (Come Away)
Niiso (Come Away)

Come and Bear Witness
O (Come and Bear Witness)
Oh (Come and Bear Witness?)

Comfort
"Bigl" (Comforter?)
Bigliad (In Our Comforter)
"Bliard" (Comfort)
Blior (Comfort)
Bliora (Comfort)
Bliorax (To Comfort)
Bliorb (Comfort)
Bliors (Comfort)
"Bliort" (Comfort)
Pibliar (Places of Comfort)

Command
See Dominion, Government

Conceit
See Pomp

Conclude
Iaial (To Conclude, Judge)
See also Judgment

Conflict
See Differ, Discord

Confound
Oucho (Confound)
Unchi (To Confound)
Urch (The Confusers)
See also Confuse

Confuse
Urch (The Confusers)
See also Confound

Connect
See Fasten, Truss Together

Conquer
See Stretch Forth / Conquest

Conquest
See Stretch Forth / Conquest

Consistent/Constant?
See "In One Number," Always

Container
See Cup, Vessel, Vial

Continue
Miam (Continuance)
"Mian" (Continuance)
Pild (Continually)
See also Successive, Abide, Remain

Corner
Miinoag (Corners—Boundaries)
See also Skirt

Corrupt
See Rotten

Count
See Number (especially "Numbered")

Countenance
See Face

Couple
Pola (Two, together / Couple)
See also Together, Two, Wedding

Course
"Elzap" (Course)
"Lzar" (Courses)

Covenant
Sibsi (Covenant)
See also Promise, Swear

Cover
Ethamz (To Cover)

Creation
Qaa (Creation / Garments)
Qaan (Creation)
Qaaon (Creation)
Qaas (Creation)
See also Creator

Creator
Qaal (Creator)
Qadah (Creator)
See also Creation

Creature
Tolham (All Creatures)
Tolhami (Upon All Creatures)
Toltorg (Creatures)
Toltorgi (With Creatures)
"Toltorn" (Creature)
See also Beast

Crown
Momao (Crowns)
"Momar" (To Crown)

Cry
Bahal (Cry Loudly)
See also Weep

Cup
Talho (Cups)
See also Vessel, Vial

Curse
Amma (Cursed)
See also Wicked

D (Gal)

Damn/Damned
See Curse

Dark
Ors (Darkness)

Dart
See Arrow, Fiery Arrow/Dart

Daughter
Pasbs (Daughters)

Dawning
See Beginning

Day
Basgim (Day)
See also Midday

Death
Teloah (Death)
Teloch (Death)

Death Dragon
Telocvovim (Death Dragon, "Him That Is Fallen")
See also Devil, Lucifer, Satan

Decorate
See Garnish

Deep
See Sea

Deface
Tonug (To Deface)
See also Destroy

Defense
See Buckler

Deliver
Zonrensg (To Deliver)
Obelison (Pleasant Deliverer, the Angel Befafes)
Obelisong (Pleasant Deliverers)
See also Bring Forth

Demand
See Require

Depths of My Jaws
Piadph (Depths of My Jaws)

Descend
Uniglag (To Descend)
See also Fall, Sink, Stoop

Destroy
"Quasb" (To Destroy)
See also Deface

Devil, The
Coronzom
Githgulcag
Telocvovim (Death Dragon, "Him That Is Fallen")
See also Satan, Lucifer

Devoid
See Empty

Diamond
Achildao (Diamond)

Differ
Dilzmo (To Differ)

Diminish
Prdzar (To Diminish)

Discord
Osf (Discord)

Dispose
Lrasd (To Dispose, To Place)

Dive
See Sink, Stoop, Fall

Diversity
See Variety

Divide
Poilp (Divided)
Yrpoil (Division)
See also Separate

Divine Names
Baeovib (Righteousness)
El (The First)
Enay (Lord)
Gahoachma (I Am That I Am)
Galsagen (Divine Power Creating the Angel of the Sun)
Galvah (The End/*Omega*)
Geiad (Lord and Master)
Gohed (One Everlasting, All Things Descending Upon One)
Iad (God)
"Iadoias" (Eternal God)
Iadpil (Unto Him)
Iaida (The Highest)
Iaidon (The All Powerful)
Ia-isg (Everlasting One and Indivisible God)
Idoigo (Him Who Sits upon the Holy Throne)
Ioiad (Him That Liveth Forever)
L (The First, One)
NA (The Trinity, Lord)
See also Angelic Orders

"Divine Power Creating the Angel of the Sun"
Galsagen

Divine Throne, The
See Mighty Seat

Division
See Divide

Do/Does (Doth)
Gnay (Doth)

Dominance
See Dominion

Dominion
Bab (Dominion)
See also Government, Kingdom

Doth
See Do/Does

Dragon
"Vonin" (Dragons)
"Vovim" (Dragon)
Vovina (Dragon)

Dress
See Apparel, Garment, Garland

Dross
See Moss

Drunk
Orsba (Drunken)

Dry
Orscor (Dryness)

Dwell/Dwelling
Faonts (To Dwell within)
"Faorgt" (Dwelling Place)
Fargt (Dwelling Places)
"Praf" (To Dwell)
See also Living Dwellings, Building, House

E (Graph)

Eagle
Vabzir (Eagle)

Earth
Caosg (Earth)
Caosga (Earth)
Caosgi (Earth)
Caosgin (Earth)
Caosgo (Of the Earth)
Caosgon (Unto the Earth)

"Earth-Fleer"
Nalvage (Earth-Fleer, or Avoidance of Earthly Things)

Earthquakes
Gizyax (Earthquakes)

East
Raas (East)
Rassy (East)

Elder
Uran (Elders)

Empty
Affa (Empty)

End
Ul (End)
Uls (Ends)
See also Omega

Endure
See Abide

Enigma
See Mystery

Enjoyment
See Pleasure, Joy

Enlarge
See Magnify

Enter
Zimii (To Enter)

Eon
See Age

Equal
Parach (Equal)
See also Same

Era
See Age

Essence
See Marrow

Establish
Sach (The Establishers)

Eternal God
"Iadoias" (Eternal God)
See also Everlasting, Him That Liveth Forever, God, Lord

Even
Nomig (Even as)

Everlasting
Ia-isg (Everlasting One and Indivisible God)
Gohed (One Everlasting...)
See also God, Eternal God, Him That Liveth Forever, Lord

Every One
Vomzarg (Every One / All)
See also All

Everything

See All

Exalted

See Great

Except

Oq (But/Except)

M (Except)

See also But

Excite

See Stir

Execute

Fisis (To Execute, Carry Out)

Eye

Ooanoan (Eyes)

Ooaona (Eyes)

F (Or)

Face
Adoian (Face)

Faith
Congamphlgh (Faith / Holy Ghost)
Gono (Faith / Trust / Loyalty)

Fall
Dobix (To Fall)
Loncho (To Fall)
See also Descend, Sink, Stoop

Fashion
See Frame

Fasten
Amipzi (To Fasten)
See also Truss Together

Fate
See Providence

Fear God
Hoxmarch (To Fear God)
See also Those That Fear God

Feet
Lasdi (Feet)
Lusd (Feet)
Lusda (Feet)
Lusdan (Feet)

"Fervency"
Laua (Fervency / Humility—an attitude in prayer?)

Fiery Arrow / Dart
Malprg (Through-thrusting Fire, Fiery Arrow)
Malpurg (Fiery Arrows)
See also Fires of Life and Increase

Fire
"Pirgi" (Fires)
Prge (Fire, Flame, Flames)
Prgel (Fire)
See also Burn, Flame, Light

Fires of Life and Increase
Malpirgi
See also Fiery Arrow, Through-thrusting Fire

Firmament
Calz (Firmaments)
See also Heaven, Firmaments of Waters

Firmaments of Waters
Pilzin (Firmaments of Waters)
See also Firmament, Heaven, Water

First
El (The First, God)
"Elo" (The First)
Ili (The First)
L (One, The First, God)
La (The First)
Lu (From One)

First Flame
Lialprt

First Glory
"Pirgah" (The First Glory)
See also Flame, Fire

Flame
Ialpirt (Light, Flame)
Ialpor (Flaming)
"Ialprt" (Light, Flame)
"Prg" (Fire, Flame, Flames)
Prge (Fire, Flame, Flames)
"Purg" (Fire, Flame, Flames)

Vep (Flame)
See also Burn, Fire, Light

Flames of the First Glory
Ialpirgah

Flourish
Cacacom (To Flourish)

Flower
Lorslq (Flowers)

Fly Into
Zildar (Fly into)
See also Within

Foot
See Feet

For
Bagle (For, Wherefore, Because)
Lap (For)
See also Therefore, Wherefore, Because

Forget
Bams (To Forget)

Form
See Frame

Fourth
"Es" (Fourth)
S (Fourth)

Fourth Angle
Sdiv

Frame
Izazaz (To Frame, To Form)

Friendly
See Be Friendly unto Me

Front
Aspt (Before, In Front)
See also Face

Frown Not
Ucim (Frown Not)
See also Happy

"Furious and Perpetual Fire Enclosed for the Punishment of Them That Are Banished From the Glory"
See Hellfire

Furnace
See Athanor (Alchemical Furnace)

Furnish
Tooat (To Furnish)
See also Provide

Fury
Bagie (Fury)
Baltim (Fury, or Extreme Justice)
See also Anger, Wrath

G (Ged)

Garb
See Apparel, Garment, Garland

Garland
Obloc (Garland)
See also Garment

Garment
Oboleh (Garments)
Qaa (Garments / Creation)
See also Apparel, Garland

Garnish
Gnonp (To Garnish)

Gather
Aldi (To Gather)
Aldon (Gird Up, Gather Together)
See also Gird, Harvest

Gird
Aldi (To Gather)
Aldon (Gird Up, Gather Together)
See also Gather, Bind

Girdle
Atraah (Girdles)

Give
Dluga (To Give)
"Dlugam" (Given)
Dlugar (To Give)
Phama (I Will Give)

Glory, Glorious
Adgmach (Glory, Adoration, Praise)
Busd (Glory, Glorious)
Busdir (Glory, Glorious)
"Pirgah" (Glory)
See also Admiration, Adoration, Praise, Magnify, Wonder

Glory of Her
Busdirtilb

Go Before
See Precede

God
Geiad (Lord and Master)
Iad (God)
"Iadoias" (Eternal God)
Iadpil (To Him)
Iaida (The Highest)
Iaidon (All Powerful)
Ia-isg (Everlasting One and Indivisible God)
Idoigo (Him Who Sits upon the Holy Throne)
Ioiad (Him That Liveth Forever)
Mad (A God, Your God)
Oiad (Of God)
Piad (Your God)
See also First, God of Righteousness, Lord, Worker of Wonders

God Eternally Crowned
Iadoiasmomar (God Is, Was, and Shall Be Crowned)

God Is, Was, and Shall Be Crowned
See God Eternally Crowned

God of Righteousness
Iadbaltoh
See also God, Lord

God of Stretch Forth and Conquer
Madzilodarp (God of Conquest)

Gold

Audcal (Alchemical Gold, Alchemical Mercury)

Govern/Government/Governor

Anetab (In Government)
Caba (To Govern)
Gnataab (Your Governments)
Netaab (Governments)
Netaaib (Government)
Tabaam (Governor)
Tabaord (Be Governed)
Tabaori (To Govern)
"Tabas" (To Govern)
See also Steward, Dominion, Reign

Great

Drilpa (Great)
Drilpi (Greater Than)

Great Name

Monasci (Great Name)

Groan

Holdo (To Groan)

Grow

See Flourish

Grow Strong

Ugeg (Become Strong)
Ugegi (Become/Grow Strong)
See also Strong

Guard

Bransg (A Guard)

H (Na)

Half
Obza (Half)

Hand
Azien (Hands)
Ozien (My Own Hand)
Ozol (Hands)
Zien (Hands)
Zol (Hands)

Handmaid
Qurlst (Handmaid)
See also Minister, Servant

Happy
Ulcinin (Happy)
See also Frown Not

Harbor
Blans (To Harbor)
See also Ark

Harlot
Ababalond (Harlot)

Harmony
See Balance

Harvest
"Giar" (Harvest)
See also Gather

Has
See Have / Has

Have/Has
"Brin" (Have)
"Brint" (Has)
Brints (To Have)

Haven
See Ark, Harbor

He
See Him, His

"He That Speaks"
Mapsama

Head
Dazis (Heads)

Hear
See Listen

Hearken
See Listen

Heart
Monons (Heart)

Heaven
"Madriax" (Heavens)
Madriiax (Heavens)
Oadriax (Lower Heavens)
Piripsax (Heavens)
Piripsol (Heavens)
Piripson (Third? Heaven)
See also Firmament

Hellfire
Donasdogamatastos (The Furious and Perpetual Fire Enclosed for the Punishment of Them That Are Banished From the Glory)

Her
"Ip" (Her)
Tilb (Her)
Tiobl (Within Her)
See also She

Her Course
Elzaptilb (Her Course)

Her Understanding
Omptilb

Here
Emna (Here)
Sem (In This Place)

Highest
Iaida (The Highest)
See also God, Lord

Him
Iadpil (Unto Him—God)
Tox (His, Him)
See also His

"Him That Is Fallen"
Telocvovim (Death Dragon, "Him That Is Fallen")
See also Devil, Lucifer, Satan

"Him That Liveth Forever"
Ioiad (Him That Liveth Forever)
See also Eternal God, God, Lord

"Him Who Sits upon the Holy Throne"
Idoigo (Him Who Sits upon the Holy Throne)
See also God, Lord

His
Tox (His, Him)
See also Him

His Pomp
Avavox

His Power
Lonshitox

Hollow
See Empty

Holy
Pir (Holy Ones)
See also Angels

"Holy Ghost"
Congamphlgh (Faith/Holy Ghost)

Honor
Iaiadix (Honor)

Horn
"Mospleh" (Horns)

House
Salman (House)
See also Building, Dwelling

How Many
"Irgil" (How Many)
See also Many

How Many Are There
Irgilchisda

How Now
Mabberan (How Now?)

Humility
Laua (Fervency/Humility—an attitude in prayer?)

Hundred
Torb (One Hundred)

Hyacinth Pillars
See Pillar

I (Gon)

I
Ol (I)

"I Am That I Am"
Gahoachma

I Am the Lord (Your) God
Zirenaiad

"I Desire Thee, O God"
Arphe

In Front
See Before

"In One Number"
Sagacor (In One Number)

"In This Place"
Sem
See also Here

Increase
"Coazior" (To Increase)
"Mal" (Thrust, Arrow, Increase)
See also Add

Ineffable
See Unspeakable

Iniquity
Madrid (Iniquity)
See also Sin

Intent
Fafen (Intent, Train)

Is
I (Is, Are)
See also Am, Are, Is Not, May Be, Shall Be, Let There Be, Was, Were

Is 31
Iga

Is As
Ita

Is Given
Idlugam

Is a House
Isalman

Is Not
Ipam (Is Not)
Ipamis (Cannot Be)
See also No/None, Not

Is One
Il

Is Such As
Icorsca

Is Wrath
Ivonph
See also Is Wrath in Anger

Is Wrath in Anger
Ivonpovnph
See also Is Wrath

It
"T" (It)

It Is
Ti

J (Ged)

Join
See Fasten, Truss Together

Joy
Moz (Joy, Joy of God)
See also Pleasure

Judgment
Balzizras (Judgment)
See also Conclude

Just/Justice
Balit (The Just)
Balt (Justice)
Baltan (Justice)
Baltim (Extreme Justice, or Fury)
Padgze (Justice From Divine Power Without Defect)

K (Veh)

Kindness
See Mercy

Kingdom
Adohi (Kingdom)
Londoh (Kingdom)
See also Dominion

Know
See Knowledge, Understand

Knowledge
Iadnah (Knowledge)
Iadnamad (Pure Knowledge)
See also Understand

L (Ur)

Laborer
See Workmen

Laid Up
Maasi (Laid up, Stored)

Lamentation
Eophan (Lamentation)
See also Sorrow, Woe

Lamp, Lantern
Hubaio (Lanterns)
Hubar (Lamps)
Hubaro (Living Lamps)
See also Lantern

Law
See Legislate

Lead
See Before

Legislate
Ohorela (To Legislate)

Let
"Ix" (Let)

Let Her Be Known
Ixomaxip

Let There Be
Christeos (Let There Be)
See also Are, Shall Be

Lift Up
Goholor (Lift Up)
See also Arise

Light
Ialpirt (Light, Flame)
"Ialprt" (Light, Flame)
See also Brightness, Flame, Shine

Like
"Azia" (Like unto)
Aziazor (Likeness of)

Like unto the Harvest
Aziagiar

Limb
See Branch, Member

Limitless
Maoffas (Measureless)

Listen
Solpeth (Hearken, To Listen)
Toatar (Hearken, To Listen)

Live
"Apila" (To Live)
Hom (To Live)

Living Breath
Gigipah (Living Breath)

Living Dwellings
Paradial (Living Dwellings)
See also Dwell/Dwelling

Loathsome
See Rotten

Loins
"Dax" (Loins)

Long
See Age, Period, Time, While

Look
Dorpha (To Look about)
Dorphal (Looking with Gladness Upon)
See also Behold, See

Lord
Enay (Lord)
Geiad (Lord and Master)
NA (Lord, the Trinity)
See also God

Lower Heavens
Oadriax (Lower Heavens)
See also Heaven

Loyalty
See Faith

Lucifer
Coronzom
Githgulcag
Telocvovim (Death Dragon, "Him That Is Fallen")
See also Devil, Satan

M (Tal)

Made/Make
Eol (Made)
Eolis (Making)
Oln (Made of)
Ozazm (To Make)
Ozazma (To Make)

Made a Law
See Legislate

Made Mankind
Olcordziz

Magnify
Ovof (To Magnify)
See also Adoration, Glory, Praise

Make
See Made/Make

Man
"Olap" (Men)
Ollog (Men)
"Ollor" (Man)
Olora (Of Man)
See also Mankind, Work of Man

Mankind
Cordziz (Mankind)
See also Man

Mansion
See Palace

Many
"Irgil" (How Many)
Plosi (As Many)

Marble
Pidiai (Marble)

Marrow
Tranan (Marrow)

Master
Geiad (Lord and Master)
See also Lord

May Be
Noaln (May Be)
See also Are, Become, Let There Be, Shall Be

Measure
Holq (To Measure)
Maoffas (Measureless)

Member
Paombd (Members, Parts, Appendages)
See also Part

Memory
See Remember

Men
See Man, Mankind

Mercury
Audcal (Alchemical Gold, Alchemical Mercury)

Mercy
Iehusoz (God's? Mercies)
Rit (Mercy)

Midday
"Bazem" (Midday)
Bazemlo (Midday the First)
See also Day

Middle
See Amidst, Center

Midst
See Amidst

Mighty
Canse (Mighty)
Cruscanse (More Mighty)
Micalp (Mightier)
Micalzo (Mighty, Power)
Micaoli (Mighty)
Micaolz (Mighty)
Omicaolz (Be Mighty)
Vohim (Mighty)
See also Strong, Power

Mighty Seat
Oziayal (Mighty Seat—Throne of God)
See also "Him Who Sits upon the Holy Throne"

Millstone
Aviny (Millstones)

Mind
Manin (In the Mind)

Mingle
Cinxir (To Mingle)

Minister
Cnoquodi (Ministers)
See also Handmaid, Servant

Misery
See Torment

Mix
See Mingle

Moment
Oanio (Moment)

Moon
Graa (Moon)

More
"Crus" (More, Greater?)

More Mighty
Cruscanse

Moreover
Pilah (Moreover)

Moss
Mom (Moss, Dross?)

"Mother of Vinegar"
See Tartar

Motion
Zna (Motion, Action)
See also Action, Move, Rest Not, Stir

Mount of Olives
See Olive Mount

Mourning
See Sorrow, Lamentation

Mouth
Butmon (Mouth)
Butmona (Mouth)
Butmoni (Mouths)

Move
Zacam (To Move)
Zacar (Move)
See Action, Motion, Rest Not, Stir

Mystery
Cicle (Mysteries)
Cicles (Mysteries)
See also Secret

N (Drux)

Name
Dooain (Name)
Dooaip (In the Name)
Dooiap (In the Name)
Monasci (Great Name)
Omaoas (Names)

Need
See Require

Neither
Larag (Neither/Nor)
See also No/None, Not

Nest
Virq (Nests)

Night
Dosig (Night)

Nine
Em (Nine)

No/None
Ag (No, None)
See also Not, Neither

No Creature
Agtoltorn

Noise
Nidali (Noises)

None
See No, Neither

Noon
See Midday

No One
"Agl"

No One Creature
Agltoltorn

No Place
Ripir (No Place)

"Nor"
See Neither

North
Lucal (North)

Not
"Ge" (Not)
Ip (Not)
Ipam (Is Not)
Ipamis (Can Not Be)
"Pam" (Not)
"Pamis" (Cannot)
See also Cannot, Neither, No/None

Number
Capimaon (Number of Time)
Cormf (Number)
Cormfa (Numbers)
Cormp (Numbered)
Cormpo (Hath Yet Numbered)
Cormpt (Numbered)
Sagacor ("In One Number"—Consistent/Constant?)
See also Successive

O (Med)

Oak
Paeb (Oak)

Obedience
Adna (Obedience)
See also Obey

Obey
Darbs (Obey)
See also Obedience

Ocean
See Sea

Of
De (Of)

Olive
"Qanis" (Olives)

Olive Mount
Adroch (Olive Mount)

***Omega* (The End)**
Galvah (The End—*prop. n.*)
See also End

One
L (One, The First—God)
Lu (From One)
See also First

One Another
Lsmnad

"One Everlasting, All Things Descending Upon One"
Gohed
See also One, Lord, God

One Rock
Lpatralx

One Season
Lnibm

One While
Lcapimao

Only
See But

Open
Odo (To Open)

Or
Q (Or)

Or as
Qta

Organize
See Dispose

Or the Horns
Qmospleh

Over
Vors (Over)
Vorsg (Over You)

P (Mals)

Pair
See Couple

Palace
Poamal

Palm
Nobloh (Palms of the Hands)

Part
Saanir (Parts)
See also Member

Partake
Plapli (Partakers)

Peace
"Etharzi" (Peace)

Perform
See Execute

Period
Matorb (Long, period of time)
See also Age, Time, While

Persecute
See Torment

Persist
See Abide

Philosopher's Stone
Darr (The Philosopher's Stone)

Pillar
Nazarth (Pillars of Gladness)
Nazavabh (Hyacinth Pillars)
See also Strong Towers

Place
Aala (To Place)
Oali (To Place)
See also Bind, Dispose, Set, Settle, Sit, Plant

Places of Comfort
Pibliar (Places of Comfort)

Plant
Harg (To Plant)
See also Bind, Place, Set, Settle, Sit

Pleasant Deliverer
Obelisong (Pleasant Deliverers)
Obelison (Pleasant Deliverer, the Angel *Befafes*)

Pleasure
"Qrasahi" (Pleasure)
See also Joy

Plummet
See Fall, Sink, Stoop

Poison
Faboan (Poison)
See also Wormwood

Pomp
"Avav" (Pomp)

Pour
Panpir (To Pour Down)

Power
Gmicalzo (In Power)
Iaidon (The All Powerful—God)
Lansh (Exalted Power)
Lonsa (Power)
Lonshi (Power)
"Lonshin" (Powers)

Micalzo (Power, Mighty)
Nanaeel (My Power)
See also Mighty, Strong

Power of Understanding
Gmicalzoma

Praise
Adgmach (Glory, Adoration, Praise)
"Ecrin" (Praise)
Luas (Those Who Praise or The Triumphant)
Oecrimi (To Sing Praises)
Restil (To Praise Him?)
See also Admiration, Adoration, Glory, Magnify

Pray/Prayer
Zuraah (Prayer?)

Precede
Tastax (Going Before, To Precede)
See also Before

Prepare
Abramig (To Prepare)
Abramg (To Prepare)
See also Provide

Pretty
See Beauty

Pride
See Pomp

Produce
See Bring Forth

Promise
Aisro (To Promise)
Isr (Promise?, A Son of the Sons of Light)
Isro (Promise of)
See also Covenant, Swear

Prosper
See Flourish

Prostitute
See Harlot

Provide
Abraassa (To Provide)
See also Prepare, Furnish

Providence
Yarry (Providence)

Psalm
See Song

Pure (Undefiled)
Mad (Your God, "Pure/Undefiled")

Pure Knowledge
Iadnamad

Put
See Place

Q (Ger)

Quality
Aspian (Qualities, Characteristics)

R (Don)

Rage
See Fury, Wrath

Rain
See Pour

Raise
See Lift Up, Arise

Read
Hardeh (To Read?)

"Reasonable Creature"
See Man, Mankind

Receive
Ednas (Receivers)

Recollection
See Remember

Refuge
See Ark, Harbor

Regret
See Repent

Reign
Bogpa (To Reign)
Sonf (To Reign)
See also Govern

Rejoice
Chirlan (To Rejoice)

Remain
"Paaox" (To Remain)
Paaoxt (Let Remain)
See also Abide, Continue

Remainder
See Rest

Remember
Papnor (Remembrance, Memory)

Repent
Moooah (To Repent)

Require
Unig (To Require)

Rest
"Page" (To Rest)
Udl (The Rest)
Undl (The Rest)
See also Sleep

Rest Not
Pageip
See also Action, Move

Rich
"Las" (Rich)

Rich Man
Lasollor

Righteous
Baeovib (Righteousness)
Baltle (Righteousness)
Baltoh (Righteousness)
Baltoha (My Righteousness)
Samvelg (The Righteous)

Rise
See Arise

Roar
Yor (To Roar)

Rock
"Patralx" (Rock)
See also Stone

Rod
Cab (Rod/Scepter)

Room
See Chamber

Rotten
Qting (Rotten)

Rule
See Govern, Reign

Run
Parm (To Run)
Parmgi (Let Run)

S (Fam)

Safeguard
See Buckler

Salt
Balye (Salt)

Same
Lel (Same)
See also Equal

Sanctuary
See Ark, Harbor

Satan
Coronzom
Githgulcag
Telocvovim (Death Dragon, "Him That Is Fallen")
See also Devil, Lucifer

Say
Gohia (We Say)
Goho (To Say)
Gohol (To Say)
Gohon (Have Spoken)
Gohulim (It Is Said)
Gohus (I Say)
See also Speak, Talk

Sayeth the First
Gohel

Sayeth the Lord
Gohoiad

Scepter
See Rod

Scorpion
Siatris (Scorpions)

Scourge
See Torment

Scythe
See Sickle

Sea
Zumvi (Seas)

Seal
Emetgis (Seal)

Season
"Nibm" (Season)
See also Period, Age

Seat
Othil (Seats)
Thil (Seats)
Thild (Seats)
"Thiln" (Seats)
See also Mighty Seat

Seats of Mercy
Othilrit
See also Mighty Seat

Second (2nd)
Viiv (Second)
Viv (Second)
See also Two

Second (unit of time)
See Moment

Second Angle
Vivdiv

Second Flame
Vivialprt

Secret
Ananael (Secret Wisdom)

Laiad (Secrets of Truth)
See also Mystery

Secrets of Truth
Laiad (Secrets of Truth)

Secret Wisdom
Ananael (Secret Wisdom)

See
"Puran" (To See)
See also Behold, Look

Seethe
Vrelp (Strong Seething)

Senior
See Elder

Separate
Pala (Two, separated)
See also Two, Divide, Separate Creatures

Separate Creatures
Tliob (To Separate Creatures, Classify?)
See also Separate

Servant
Cnoqod (Servants)
Cnoquol (Servants)
Lang (Those Who Serve)
Noco (Servant)
See also Handmaid, Minister, Serve

Serve
Aboapri (To Serve)
Booapis (To Serve)
See also Servant

Set
Othil (To Set/Seat)
See also Bind, Place, Plant, Settle, Sit

Settle
Alar (To Settle, To Place)
Allar (To Bind Up)
See also Set, Sit, Bind, Place, Plant

Shall Be
Chiso (Shall Be)
Trian (Shall Be)
See also Are, Let There Be, May Be

Shall Not See
"Ipuran"

She
"Pi" (She)
See also Her

Sheath
See Sleeve

She Is
Pii

Shelter
See Harbor, Ark

Shine
Loholo (To Shine)
See also Burn, Brightness

Show Yourself
See Appear

Sibling
See Brother

Sickle
"Puin" (Sickles)

Signify
Alca (To Signify?)

Sin
Doalim (Sin)
See also Iniquity

Sing Praises
Oecrimi (To Sing Praises)
See also Praise

Sink
Carbaf (Sink)
See also Fall, Descend, Stoop

Sit
Trint (To Sit)
See also Place, Set, Settle

Six
Norz (Six)

Skirt
Unalah (Skirts)
See also Corner

Sleep
Brgda (To Sleep)
See also Rest

Sleeve
Collal (Sleeves/Sheaths)

"Slimy Things Made of Dust"
Apachana (The Slimy Things Made of Dust)

Smile
See Frown Not
See also Happy

Sol
See Sun

Son
"Nor" (Son)
"Norm" (Son/Sons)
Noromi (Sons)

Song
Faaip (Voicings, as in Songs or Psalms)
Luiahe (Song of Honor)

Sons of Men
Normolap

Sons of Pleasure
Norquasahi

Sorrow
Ser (Sorrow)
Tibibp (Sorrow)
See also Lamentation, Woe

South
Babage (South)
Babagen (South)

Speak
Brita (To Speak of, Talk About)
Camliax (Spake, Spoke)
See also "He That Speaks," Talk, Say

Speech from God
Loagaeth (Speech from God—the Holy Book)

Spirit
Gah (Spirits—Angels?)
Tohcoth (Nature Spirits)

Staff
See Rod

Stand
Biab (To Stand)

Star
Aoiveae (Stars)

Start
See Beginning

Steward
Balzarg (Stewards)
See also Governor

Sting
Grosb (Bitter Sting)

Stir
Lring (To Stir Up)
Zixlay (To Stir Up)
See also Action, Mingle, Motion, Move, Rest Not, Seethe

Stone
Orri (Barren Stone)
See also Rock, Philosopher's Stone

Stoop
"Abai" (Stoop)
See also Fall, Descend, Sink

Stooping Dragons
Abaivonin

Store
See Laid up

Stranger
Gosaa (Stranger)

Strength
Umplif (Strength)
Ugear (Strength of Men)
See also Strong

Stretch Forth/Conquest
"Zilodarp" (Stretch Forth/Conquest)

Strong
Givi (Stronger)
Ugear (Strength of Men)
Ugeg (Become Strong)
Ugegi (Become/Grow Strong)
Umadea (Strong Towers)
Umplif (Strength)
See also Mighty, Power, Strength

Strong Towers
Umadea (Strong Towers)
See also Pillar

Subtract
See Diminish

Successive
Capimali (Successively)
Capmiali (Successively)
See also Number

Such
Cors (Such)
Corsi (Such)

Such As
Corsta

Sulfur
Dlasod (Alchemical Sulfur)
Salbrox (Live Sulfur)

Sun
Ror (Sun)

Surge
Molvi (Surges)

Surround
See Circle

Surrounded
See Amidst, Among

Swear

Surzas (To Swear)

Znrza (Swore)

See also Covenant, Promise

Sword

Napeai (Swords)

Napta (Two-edged Swords)

Nazpsad (Sword)

T (Gisg)

Talk
Brita (To Speak of, Talk about)
See also Speak, Say

Tartar
Lulo (Tartar, Mother of Vinegar)

Temple
Siaion (Temple)

Territories
See Vestures

Terror
Ciaofi (Terror)

That
Ar (That)
Ds (Which/That)
See also Which, These, Those

That Govern
Artabas

That Increase
Arcoazior

That Understand
Dsom

Thee
See You

Them
Par (Them)

There
"Da" (There)
Geta (There)

Therefore
"Ca" (Therefore)
Darsar (Wherefore, Therefore)
See also For, Because, Wherefore

These
Unal (These)
See also This, Those

These Are
Unalchis

They
See Them

Third
D (Third)

Third Angle
Duiv

Third Flame
Dialprt

This
"Oi" (This)
See also That, These, Those

This House
Oisalman

Thorn
Nanba (Thorns)

Those
Priaz (Those)
Priazi (Those)
See also That, This, These

Those That Fear God
Amzes ("Those That Fear God"?)
See also Fear God

Thou
See You, Yourself

Thought
Angelard (Thoughts)

Thousand
Matb (One Thousand)

Throne (of God)
See Mighty Seat

Through-thrusting Fire
See Fiery Arrow

Thrust
"Mal" (Thrust, Arrow, Increase)

Thunder
Avavago (Thunders of Increase)
Const (Thunders)
Coraxo (Thunders)
Sapah (Mighty Sounds)

Thy
Aqlo (Thy)
"Yl" (Thy)
See also You, Yourself

Time
Acocasb (Time)
Capimaon (Number of Time)
Cocasb (Time)
Cocasg (Times)
Qcocasb (Contents of Time)
See also Age, Period, Season, While

To
See Unto

Together
Pola (Two, together/Couple)
See also Couple, Two, Wedding

Torment
Mir (Torment)
See also Vex

Torture
See Torment

Tower
See Strong Towers, Pillar

Train
Fafen (Train, Intent)

Treasure
Limlal (Treasure)

Trinity
NA (Lord, Trinity)

Triumph
Luas (Those Who Praise or The Triumphant)
Toh (To Triumph)
"Toha" (Triumph)

Troop
See Guard

"True Measure of the Will of God in Judgment, Which is by Wisdom"
Miketh

True Worshiper
Hoath (True Worshiper)

Truss Together
Commah (To Truss Together/Join)
See also Fasten, Bind

Trust

See Faith

Truth

"Vaoan" (Truth—Higher)

Vooan (Truth—Lower)

Twice

See Two

Two

Pala (Two-separated)

Pola (Two-together, Couple)

Olani (Two Times, Twice)

See also Second

U (Van)

Undefiled
See Pure

Under
Oroch (Under)
Orocha (Beneath)
See also Beneath

Understand
Om (To Understand/Know)
"Oma" (Of Understanding)
Omax (To Know)
"Omp" (Understanding)
See also Knowledge

Unspeakable
Adphaht (Unspeakable)

Until
Cacrg (Until)

Unto
Pambt (Unto Me)
Pugo (As unto)
Tia (Unto Us)

Upon
Mirc (Upon)

V (Van)

Vacant
See Empty

Van
"Ar" (To Van, i.e., to Advance Upon)

Van the Earth
Arcaosgi (To Van the Earth)

Vanity
See Pomp

Variety
Damploz (Variety)

Vessel
Izizop (Your Vessels)
Zizop (Vessels)
See also Cup, Vial

Vestment
See Apparel, Garment, Garland

Vesture
Zimz (Vestures, Territories)
See also Garment

Vex
Dodpal (To Vex)
Dodrmni (Vexed)
Dods (To Vex)
Dodsih (Vexation)
See also Torment

Vial
Efafafe (Vials)
Ofafafe (Vials)
See also Cup, Vessel

Victory
See Triumph

Vinegar, Mother of
See Tartar

Virgin
Paradiz (Virgins)

Visage
See Face

Visit
Ef (Visit)
F (Visit)

Visit in Peace
Fetharzi

Visit the Earth
Fcaosga

Visit with Comfort
Fbliard

Voice
Bia (Voices)
Bial (Voice)
Bien (My Voice)
Bahal (Cry with a Loud Voice)
Faaip (Voicings—as in Songs or Psalms)
Farzem (Uplifted Voices)

Void
See Empty

Vomit
Oxex (To Vomit)

W

Walk
"Insi" (To Walk)

Want
See Require

Was
Zirop (Was)
See also Am, Are, Is, Were

Water
Pilzin (Waters)
Zlida (To Water)

Wax Strong
Ugeg (Become Strong)
Ugegi (Become / Grow Strong)
See also Strong

Wealthy
See Rich

Weave
"Oado" (To Weave)

Wedding
Paracleda (Wedding)
See also Couple, Together

Weed Out
Fifalz (Weed Out)

Weep
Raclir (Weeping)

Were
Zirom (They Were)
See also Am, Are, Is, Was

West
Soboln (West)

Wherefore
Bagle (For, Wherefore, Because)
Darsar (Wherefore, Therefore)
See also For, Because, Therefore

Wherein
Quiin (Wherein)

Which
Ds (Which / That)
Dst (Which Also)
See also That, This

Which Are
Dschis

Which Dwell
Dspraf

Which Have
Dsbrin

Which Is
Dsi

Which Is Called
Dsium

Which Prepared
Dsabramg

Which Reign
Dsonf

Which Remain
Dspaaox

Which Walkest
Dsinsi

Which Weave
Dsoado

While
"Cacocasb" (Another While)
"Capimao" (While)
See also Age, Period, Season, Time

Whom/Whose
Asobam (On Whom)
Casarm (Whom)
Casarma (Whom)
Casarman (Whom/Under Whose)
Casarmg (In Whom)
Casarmi (Under Whom)
"Saba" (Whose)
Soba (Whose)
Sobam (Whom)
Sobca (Whose)
"Sobha" (Whose)
"Sobo" (Whose)
Sobra (Whose)
"Sola" (Whose)

Whore
See Harlot

Whose Continuance
Solamian

Whose Courses
Sobolzar

Whose Eyes
Sabaooaona

Whose God
Sobaiad

Whose Works
Sobhaath

Why
See Wherefore

"Why Didst Thou So?"
Gascampho

Wicked
Babalon (Wicked)
See also Curse

Widow
Rior (Widow)

Will
See Your Will Be Done

Wind
Ozongon (Manifold Winds)
Zong (Winds)

Window
"Como" (Window)

Window of Comfort
Comobliort

Wine
Roxtan (Rectified Wine)

Wing
Upaah (Wings)
Upaahi (Wings)

Winnow
See Van

Wisdom
See Secret Wisdom, Knowledge, Understand

"With Humility We Call Thee, with Adoration of the Trinity"
Argedco

Within
Zylna (Within Itself)

Woe
Ohio (Woe)
See also Sorrow, Lamentation

Wonder
Sald (Wonder)
"Lzirn" (Wonders)
See also Glory

Work
"Aath" (Works)
"Vau" (To Work)
Vaun (To Work)

Work of Man
Conisbra (The Work of Man)
See also Man, Mankind

Workmen
Canal (Workmen)

Work Wonders
Vaulzirn

Worker of Wonders
PELE (Worker of Wonders)
Peleh (Worker of Wonders?)
See also God

World
See Earth

Wormwood
Tatan (Wormwood)
See also Poison

Worship
See True Worshiper

Worthy
Naghezes (To Be Worthy?)

Wrath
Vonph (Wrath)
Vonpho (Of Wrath)
"Vonpo" (Wrath)
See also Anger, Fury

Wrath in Anger
"Vonpovnph"

X (Pal)

There are no Angelical words in Dee's records that translate into English words beginning with the letter *X*.

Y (Gon)

Yea
See Yes

Yell
See Cry

Yes
Noib (Yea, Yes)

You (pl.)
Nonca (You)
Noncf (You)
Nonci (You)
Noncp (You)
See also You (sing.), Yourself

You (sing.)
Bolp (Be Thou)
Yls (Thou)
Ylsi (Thee)
See also You (pl.), Yourself, Thy

Your
See Thy

Your Loins
Daxil

Yourself
Amiran (Yourselves)
See also You (sing.)

Your Will Be Done
Gemeganza

Z (Ceph)

There are no Angelical words in Dee's records that translate into English words beginning with the letter Z.

Bibliography

Adler, Aufsteigender. *Soyga/Agyos: Tractatus Astrologico Magicus Aldaraia sive Soyga Vocor, Flight of the Condor—Contemporary Shamanism* (2001) (Online at http://www.kondor.de/enoch/soyga/Soyga_starte.htm.)

Agrippa, Henry C. (edited by Stephen Skinner and trans. by Robert Turner). *The Fourth Book of Occult Philosophy*. Berwick, ME: Ibis Press, 2004.

———. (edited by Donald Tyson and trans. by James Freake). *Three Books of Occult Philosophy*. St. Paul, MN: Llewellyn, 1992.

Allan, Jim, ed. *An Introduction to Elvish*. Hayes, UK: Bran's Head Books, 1978.

Ashe, Steven. *Qabalah of 50 Gates*. Glastonbury, UK: Glastonbury Books, 2006.

Bible, The. King James Version. (See *BibleGateway.com*, http://www.biblegateway.com.)

Bouwsma, William J. *Concordia Mundi: The Career and Thought of Guillaume Postel, 1510–1581*. Cambridge, MA: Harvard University Press, 1957.

Budge, E. A. Wallis, trans. *The Egyptian Book of the Dead: The Papyrus of Ani in the British Museum*. New York: Dover, 1967.

Charles, R. H., ed., and W. R. Morfill, trans. *The Book of the Secrets of Enoch*. Escondido, CA: Book Tree, 1999. First published in 1896. (This is *2 Enoch*, "The Slavonic Book of Enoch.")

Charlesworth, James H., ed. *The Old Testament Pseudepigrapha, vol. 1*. Garden City, NY: Doubleday, 1983. (Includes *1 Enoch*, "The Ethiopic Book of Enoch"; *2 Enoch*, "The Slavonic Book of Enoch"; and *3 Enoch*, "The Hebrew Book of Enoch.")

Clulee, Nicholas H. *John Dee's Natural Philosophy: Between Science and Religion*. London: Routledge, 1988.

Dalley, Stephanie. *Myths from Mesopotamia : Creation, the Flood, Gilgamesh, and Others*. Oxford: Oxford University Press, 1998.

Dan, Joseph. *The Ancient Jewish Mysticism*. Tel Aviv, Israel: MOD Books, 1993.

Davidson, Gustav. *A Dictionary of Angels, Including the Fallen Angels*. Reissue edition. New York: Free Press, 1994.

Dee, John. *A True and Faithful Relation of What Passed For Many Years Between Dr. John Dee [. . .] and Some Spirits*. New York: Magickal Childe, 1992. First published in 1659. Other editions also available. A PDF version is available at *The Magickal Review*, http://www.themagickalreview.org/enochian/tfr.php (accessed March 1, 2010).

Dee, John. (Peterson, Joseph H., ed.). *John Dee's Five Books of Mystery: Original Sourcebook of Enochian Magic*. Boston: Weiser, 2003.

———. *Mysteriorum Libri Quinti: or, Five Books of Mystical Exercises of Dr. John Dee*. Magnum Dyfed, UK: Opus Hermetic Sourceworks, 1985.

Eliade, Mircea. *Shamanism: Archaic Techniques of Ecstasy*. Princeton, NJ: Princeton University Press, 2004.

"Enochian-l" (e-mail list). http://www.gnostica.net/mailman/listinfo/enochian-l.

Ginzberg, Louis. *Legends of the Bible*. New York: Simon and Schuster, 1956.

Godwin, Malcolm. *Angels: An Endangered Species*. New York: Simon and Schuster, 1990.

Harkness, Deborah E. *John Dee's Conversations with Angels: Cabala, Alchemy, and the End of Nature*. Cambridge: Cambridge University Press, 1999.

———. *The Scientific Reformation: John Dee and the Restitution of Nature*. (Unpublished PhD thesis, University of California, Davis, 1994.)

Heidrick, Bill. "The Star Sponge and the Fifty Gates, Two Passages to Attainment." *Thelema Lodge Calendar*, 5/90 e.vol. "From the Out Basket" (copyright 1975 and 1990). Online at http://www.digital-brilliance.com/kab/50gates.txt (accessed March 1, 2010).

Heinlein, Robert. *Stranger in a Strange Land*. New York: Putnam, 1961.

James, Geoffrey. *The Angel Summoner*. St. Paul, MN: Llewellyn, 1998.

———. *The Enochian Magick of Dr. John Dee*. St. Paul, MN: Llewellyn, 1994.

Kaplan, Aryeh. *Sepher Yetzirah: The Book of Creation*. York Beach, ME: Weiser, 1997.

Kircher, Athanasius. *Oedipus Aegyptiacus*. Online at http://www.billheidrick.com/Orpd/AKir/AKOeAeII.htm (accessed March 1, 2010).

Krakovsky, Levi Isaac. *Kabbalah: The Light of Redemption*. Brooklyn, NY: Kabbalah Foundation, 1950.

Laurence, Richard, trans. *The Book of Enoch the Prophet*. Bensenville, IL: Lushena Books, 2001. First published in 1883. Also online at http://www.livius.org/ei-er/enoch/enoch.htm.

Laycock, Donald. *The Complete Enochian Dictionary: A Dictionary of the Angelic Language as Revealed to Dr. John Dee and Edward Kelley*. Revised edition. York Beach, ME: Red Wheel/Weiser, 2001.

Layton, Bentley, trans. *The Gnostic Scriptures*. New York: Doubelday, 1995.

Leitch, Aaron. "The Angelic Alphabet." Found online at http://kheph777.tripod.com/art_angelical_alphabet.pdf.

———. "Gnosticism: Sethian to Valentinian." *Diamond Fire* magazine, Winter 2003. (Also online at http://kheph777.tripod.com/)

———. "Introduction to the Hebrew Alphabet." *Diamond Fire* magazine, Summer 2004. Also online at http://kheph777.tripod.com/.

———. *John Dee's Journals Abridged: The Angelic Language, Loagaeth, the Parts of the Earth and the Great Table of the Earth.* (working title) Unpublished manuscript, 2004.

———. *Secrets of the Magickal Grimoires: The Classical Texts of Magick Deciphered.* St. Paul, MN: Llewellyn, 2005.

———. "Shem haMephoresh: Divine Name of Extension." *Diamond Fire* magazine, Fall 2003. Also online at http://kheph777.tripod .com/.

———, (moderator). *The Solomonic Yahoo Group.* http://groups.yahoo .com/group/solomonic.

Liber Loagaeth. Online at http://www.geocities.com/peripsol/Enoch /5LiberLoagaeth.htm.

Magickal Review, The. http://www.themagickalreview.org/

———., ed. *Enochian Manuscripts Online.* Digital scans of the British Library microfilms: MSS. Sloane 3188, 3189, 3191, and Cotton Appendix MS. XLVI Parts I and II. (Online at http://themagickalreview .org/enochian/)

Mastros, Sara Leanne. "The Fifty Gates of Understanding." Online at http://www.ugcs.caltech.edu/~abszero/mine.html.

Mathers, S. L. MacGregor, ed. and trans. *The Key of Solomon the King.* Mineola, NY: Dover, 2009.

McLean, Adam, ed. *A Treatise on Angel Magic.* San Francisco: Weiser, 2006.

Odeberg, Hugo, trans. and ed. *3 Enoch; or the Hebrew Book of Enoch.* New York: Ktav Publishing, 1973.

Orwell, George. *Nineteen Eighty-Four.* New York: Harcourt, Brace, 1949.

Peterson, Joseph H., ed. *John Dee's Five Books of Mystery.* York Beach, ME: Weiser, 2003.

———. *Liber Loagaeth or Liber Mysteriorum, Sextus et Sanctus,* 1997. Online at http://www.esotericarchives.com/dee/sl3189.htm (accessed

October 22, 2009). The full text of *Loagaeth* can be purchased on CD from this webpage.

———. *Twilit Grotto: Archives of Western Esoterica*. Online at http://www.esotericarchives.com (accessed October 22, 2009).

Radiant, Callisto, ed. *Enochian Linguistics*. Online at http://www.madimi.com/enochlng.htm (accessed October 22, 2009).

Reeds, Jim. "Breakthrough in Renaissance Cryptography: A Book Review." *Cryptologia* magazine, January 1999. Available online at http://findarticles.com/p/articles/mi_qa3926/is_199901/ai_n8848725/ (accessed October 22, 2009).

———. "John Dee and the Magic Tables in the Book of Soyga." In Clucas, Stephen, ed. *John Dee: Interdisciplinary Studies in English Renaissance Thought*. Dordrecht, The Netherlands: Springer, 2006. Also available online at http://www.dtc.umn.edu/~reedsj/soyga (accessed October 22, 2009).

———. "Solved: The Ciphers in Book III of Trithemius's Steganographia," *Cryptologia* magazine, October 1998. Available online at http://www.dtc.umn.edu/~reedsj/steg.html (accessed October 22, 2009).

Reuchlin, Johann. *On the Art of the Kabbalah: De Arte Cabalistica*. Trans. by Martin Goodman and Sarah Goodman. Lincoln, NE: University of Nebraska Press, 1993.

Rogers, William E., and Diana Ervin. *The History of English Phonemes*. Online at http://alpha.furman.edu/~wrogers/phonemes/ (Greenville, SC: Furman University, 2000). See particularly the section entitled "Early Modern English: 1500–1800 C.E.," online at http://alpha.furman.edu/~wrogers/phonemes/phone/eme (accessed October 22, 2009).

Rowe, Benjamin. "A Note on Fifteenth Century Syntax and Interpretation." Originally posted to the "Enochian-l" e-mail list. Also available online at http://www.madimi.com/syntint.htm (accessed March 1, 2010).

Sandars, N. K., trans. *The Epic of Gilgamesh: An English Version with an Introduction*. London: Penguin, 1972.

Scholem, Gershom (trans. by Ralph Manheim). *On the Kabbalah and Its Symbolism*. (Original German title: *Zur Kabbala und ihrer Symbolik*.) New York: Schocken, 1996.

Scrolls From the Dead Sea. Library of Congress exhibition (2002). Online at http://www.loc.gov/exhibits/scrolls/toc.html (accessed October 29, 2009).

Shaffer, Patricia. *DeesPronunciationNotes.RTF*. Online at http://kheph777.tripod.com/DeesPronNotes.doc (accessed March 1, 2010).

Sichos in English.org. *Chasidic Discourses*. Online at http://www.sichosinenglish.org/cgi-bin/calendar?holiday=pesach10441 (accessed March 1, 2010).

Simpson, D. P. *Cassell's Latin Dictionary: Latin-English, English-Latin*. London: Cassell, 1977.

Skinner, Stephen, and David Rankine. *The Practical Angel Magic of Dr. John Dee's Enochian Tables*. Singapore: Golden Hoard Press, 2005.

A Specimen of the Tables or Book of Enoch. Online at http://www.geocities.com/peripsol/Enoch/5SampleTable.html.

Szönyi, György E. *John Dee's Occultism: Magical Exaltation Through Powerful Signs*. Albany, NY: State University of New York Press, 2004.

Tolkien, J. R. R. *The Hobbit*. Boston: Houghton Mifflin, 1997. First published in 1937.

———. *The Lord of the Rings*. Boston: Houghton Mifflin, 1993. First published in 1955.

Typo.cz and DesignIQ.cz. *Diacritics: All You Need to Design a Font with Correct Accents*. Online at http://diacritics.typo.cz/index.php (accessed October 22, 2009).

Tyson, Donald. *Enochian Magic for Beginners: The Original System of Angel Magic*. St. Paul, MN: Llewellyn, 2002. First published in 1997.

———. *The Power of the Word: The Secret Code of Creation*. St. Paul, MN: Llewellyn, 2004.

———. *Tetragrammaton: The Secret to Evoking Angelic Powers and the Key to the Apocalypse*. St. Paul, MN: Llewellyn, 2002.

Vinci, Leo. *GMICALZOMA!: An Enochian Dictionary*. London: Regency Press, 1976.

Warnock, Christopher. *Renaissance Astrology*. Online at http://www.renaissanceastrology.com/ (accessed October 22, 2009).

Westcott, W. Wynn, trans. (Edited by Darcy Kuntz.) *Sepher Yetzirah: The Book of Formation and the Thirty-Two Paths of Wisdom with Hebrew Text*. Sequim, WA: Holmes, 1996.

Wheelock, Frederic M. *Wheelock's Latin, Sixth Edition Revised*. New York: HarperResource, 2005.

Whitaker, William. *Words, Latin to English* (a Latin-to-English dictionary). Online at http://lysy2.archives.nd.edu/cgi-bin/words.exe (accessed October 22, 2009).

Whitby, Christopher. *John Dee's Actions with Spirits: 22 December 1581 to 23 May 1583*. New York: Garland, 1988.

Wilson, Robert Anton. *Prometheus Rising* (reprint edition). Phoenix, AZ: New Falcon, 1992.

Yahsanet Studies. *The Fifty Gates of Understanding* (in *A Study of the Book of Revelation*). Online at http://www.yashanet.com/studies/revstudy/fifty-gates.htm (accessed March 1, 2010).

Yates, Frances A. *The Rosicrucian Enlightenment*. London: Routledge, 2001.

Zalewski, Pat. *Golden Dawn Enochian Magic*. St. Paul, MN: Llewellyn, 1990.

———. *The Kabbalah of the Golden Dawn*. St. Paul, MN: Llewellyn, 1993.

Original Manuscripts

The following manuscripts are included for reference. All of these manuscripts can be found, under the manuscript numbers given here, at the British Museum in London:

Cotton Appendix 46, parts 1–2 (Published as *A True and Faithful Relation . . .*, Casaubon.)

"Sloane MS 3188" (Published as *John Dee's Five Books of Mystery*, Peterson.)

"Sloane MS 3189" (Kelley's handwritten copy of the *Book of Loagaeth*. See Peterson and *The Magickal Review*.)

"Sloane MS 3190" (A copy of *A True and Faithful Relation . . .*, unpublished.)

"Sloane MS 3191" (Dee's grimoire. Published as *The Enochian Magick of Dr. John Dee*, James.)

Further Reading

These texts also come highly recommended in the study of general Enochiana and the occult world of Dr. John Dee and Sir Edward Kelley:

Chase, Steven, trans. *Angelic Spirituality: Medieval Perspectives on the Ways of Angels*. New York: Paulist Press, 2002.

Clucas, Stephen, ed. *John Dee: Interdisciplinary Studies in English Renaissance Thought*. Dordrecht, The Netherlands: Springer, 2006. (Includes Jim Reeds' "John Dee and the Magic Tables in the Book of Soyga.")

Eco, Umberto. *The Search for the Perfect Language*. Oxford, UK: Blackwell, 1997.

Farmer, S. A. *Syncretism in the West: Pico's 900 Theses (1486): The Evolution of Traditional Religious and Philosophical Systems*. Tempe, AZ: MRTS, 1998.

French, Peter J. *John Dee: The World of an Elizabethan Magus*. London: Routledge, 1987.

Karr, Don. *Notes on Editions of Sepher Yetzirah in English* (1991, 2007). Online at http://www.digital-brilliance.com/kab/karr/syie.pdf.

Pseudo-Dionysius, the Areopagite. (Translated by Colm Luibheid.) *Pseudo-Dionysius: The Complete Works*. New York: Paulist Press, 1987.

VanderKam, James C. *Enoch: A Man for All Generations*. Columbia, SC: University of South Carolina Press, 1995.

Woolley, Benjamin. *The Queen's Conjurer: The Science and Magic of Dr. John Dee, Adviser to Queen Elizabeth I*. New York: Henry Holt, 2001.

To Write to the Author

If you wish to contact the author or would like more information about this book, please write to the author in care of Llewellyn Worldwide and we will forward your request. Both the author and publisher appreciate hearing from you and learning of your enjoyment of this book and how it has helped you. Llewellyn Worldwide cannot guarantee that every letter written to the author can be answered, but all will be forwarded. Please write to:

Aaron Leitch
℅ Llewellyn Worldwide
2143 Wooddale Drive
Woodbury, MN 55125-2989, U.S.A.

Please enclose a self-addressed stamped envelope for reply, or $1.00 to cover costs. If outside the U.S.A., enclose an international postal reply coupon.

Many of Llewellyn's authors have websites with additional information and resources. For more information, please visit our website at http://www.llewellyn.com.

Praise for The Angelical Language, Volumes I and II

"*The Angelical Language* is the single most comprehensive text ever written on the subject of the Enochian magical system and language of Elizabethan luminary, Dr. John Dee. This two-volume magnum opus demonstrates Aaron Leitch's familiarity with practical magic as well as his skill as a meticulous researcher. A must-have book."
—**CHIC CICERO AND SANDRA TABATHA CICERO,** Chief Adepts of the Hermetic Order of the Golden Dawn

"This extensive tome, ten years in the making, is a profound step in the evolution of magickal understanding. Though debate continues to surround the 'legitimacy' of Dee and Kelley's Enochian system, its influence on modern magick is undeniable. Aaron Leitch has taken it upon himself to deeply explore the ins and outs of the Angelical Language, examining its linguistics and origins with accuracy and an eye for detail. For serious practitioners interested in an approach to Enochia that is both scholarly and mystical, I can't suggest this book highly enough."
—**RAVEN DIGITALIS,** author of *Shadow Magick Compendium* and *Planetary Spells and Rituals*

"The most in-depth analysis of the Enochian alphabet and the Enochian language that has appeared to date."
—**DONALD TYSON,** author of *Necronomicon*

"Aaron Leitch is to be congratulated on producing what is surely by far the most lucid, thorough, practical, and coherent study of the apparently diverse workings of Dr. John Dee and Edward Kelley to date."
—**DAVID RANKINE AND SORITA D'ESTE,** authors of *Practical Elementary Magick*

"A tremendous amount of original research and creative effort have gone into this work, and it represents a fascinating—if difficult—study of the Angelic language from a specific individual's understanding of it, and is worthy of its competition. It is a deep, learned, and intense work, an Enochian scholar's tour de force of his subject."
—**OSBORNE PHILLIPS,** coauthor of *Planetary Magick* and *Mysteria Magica*

The ANGELICAL LANGUAGE

About the Author

Aaron Leitch has been a scholar and spiritual seeker for over three decades. He is an ordained Gnostic Priest and a member of the Hermetic Order of the Golden Dawn, the Societas Rosicruciana in America, and the academic Societas Magica. His writings cover such varied fields as religion and mythology (from ancient Middle Eastern to Renaissance European), Solomonic mysticism, shamanism, Neoplatonism, Hermeticism and alchemy, traditional Wicca and Neopaganism, and more. He is the author of *Secrets of the Magickal Grimoires*, *The Angelical Language*, Volumes I and II, and the *Essential Enochian Grimoire*. He also has edited and/or contributed to various projects concerning the Western occult mysteries. Leitch and his wife cofounded Doc Solomon's Occult Curios, which caters to those exploring the old magick.

Visit his blog at AaronLeitch.wordpress.com, his Facebook @Kheph777, and Doc Solomon's at DocSolomons.com/wp/shop.

The ANGELICAL LANGUAGE

VOLUME I

The Complete History and Mythos of the Tongue of Angels

BASED ON THE JOURNALS OF
DR. JOHN DEE AND EDWARD KELLEY

AARON LEITCH

LLEWELLYN
WOODBURY, MINNESOTA

Second Edition
First Printing, 2025

Cover design by Kevin R. Brown
Editing by Brett Fechheimer
Interior illustrations are public domain, provided by the author

Library of Congress Cataloging-in-Publication Data (Pending)
ISBN: 978-0-7387-8135-8

Llewellyn Publications
A Division of Llewellyn Worldwide, Ltd.
2143 Wooddale Drive
Woodbury, Minnesota 55125-2989, U.S.A.
www.llewellyn.com

Printed in China

FSC www.fsc.org
MIX
Paper | Supporting responsible forestry
FSC™ C007683

Other books by Aaron Leitch

The Essential Enochian Grimoire:
An Introduction to Angel Magick from Dr. John Dee to the Golden Dawn
(Llewellyn)

Llewellyn's Complete Book of Ceremonial Magick:
A Comprehensive Guide to the Western Mystery Tradition (contributor)
(Llewellyn)

Secrets of the Magickal Grimoires:
The Classical Texts of Magick Deciphered
(Llewellyn)

Ritual Offerings (editor and contributor)
(self-published)

The Spirit-Magick of Abramelin
(self-published)

The Enochian Saga: Exploring the Angelic Journals of Dr. John Dee
(self-published)

A Course in the Tongue of Angels
(self-published)

Codex Septemgenius
(self-published)

Doc Solomon's Occult Calendar
(self-published)

Contents

Acknowledgments

I wish to acknowledge Mr. Geoffrey James, Joseph Peterson, Donald Tyson, the late Donald Laycock, and the awesome folks at TheMagickal Review.org. Without their work, Dee's original system of mysticism would have lain hidden in the *Five Books of the Mysteries* and *A True and Faithful Relation* . . . for God knows how long. Their books and resources were indispensable as reference material in my own studies. (Special thanks must also go to Joseph Peterson and to Ian Rons of *The Magickal Review*, for granting me permission to use their publications of Dee's journals, and the best Enochian font ever made—the "Kelley Angelic" font.)

In the same spirit, I wish to acknowledge Patricia Shaffer. Her work on gathering Dee's pronunciation notes for the Angelical Keys was an indescribable help to me! Finally, I also thank her for taking the time to work with me, and to answer all of my challenges to her work. I also wish to thank everyone on the Enochian-l e-mail list (at gnostica.net), who collectively make up the very elite of Enochian scholarship.

I would also like to mention Ben Rowe (aka "Josh Norton"), who was one of the brightest minds in Enochian scholarship of the late twentieth and early twenty-first centuries. Like James, Peterson, Laycock, and the others, he was instrumental in the resurrection of Dee's lost system of Angelic Magick. I know you're studying with the Pir now, Mr. Rowe!

A special kind of thanks goes to Robert Heinlein, and his work *Stranger in a Strange Land*. He told us all about the miracles one could accomplish if one would only take the time to learn a language that transcends human thought.

I wish also to thank those from my personal life who allowed me access to Dee's records (before *The Magickal Review* gave them to the world!). Thanks to Steve for swelling my head just enough to keep plugging away at this weirdness, as well as for helping me get the images and diagrams in order. Thanks to Austin, without whom I would never have had the computer equipment to get onto the Internet ten years ago, nor to write this material. Of course, thanks must go to Carrie, for enduring ten long years of this project! Thanks also to Jessica for reviewing and editing the chapters of volume I with a fresh eye.

I would also like to show my appreciation for Llewellyn's expert readers. They must have seen much potential in this project, because they sacrificed a *lot* of their own time to make page-by-page constructive criticisms and editing suggestions. The final project is much better thanks to their efforts.

I also find it most appropriate to give my thanks to the acquisitions, production, and art departments at Llewellyn Worldwide, especially Kevin R. Brown, Donna Burch, Brett Fechheimer, and Elysia Gallo. Each of you has gone above and beyond on every aspect of this project. You took a great book and made it exceptional. Thank you.

I further dedicate this work to the memory of Travis Meeks (aka "Doc Fox"). You helped me much more than you knew. And to A. J. Rose, my first and greatest fan. I love you both!

Introduction to Volume I

The work you are now holding is the end product of an intensive ten-year project. In fact, this undertaking was so massive, I had little choice but to split it between two volumes—the first of which you are currently reading. If you are at all familiar with Dr. John Dee, Sir Edward Kelley, and/or their system of Angelic magick, you may be shocked (and I hope delighted) to discover this is *not* a typical book about "Enochian" magick. Instead, it is an exhaustive analysis of the Angelical tongue recorded in Dee's magickal journals—including its history (regarding its reception by Dee), its mythology (as expounded to Dee by the Angels), and (in volume II) its grammar and linguistics. This work does not merely *present* Angelical, but will actually help the student *understand* the language.

By the year 1997, I was firmly dedicated to a study of classical Angelic magick—such as we find in the medieval Solomonic cycle, the *Sacred Magic of Abramelin the Mage*, and of course the "Enochian" magick of Dee and Kelley. Among these often diverse systems of mysticism, I must admit none puzzled and fascinated me more than that preserved in Dr. Dee's journals.

John Dee (1527–1608) was a world famous mathematician, scholar, and inventor. He was also a mystic and an astrologer, in which capacity he acted as an advisor to Queen Elizabeth I. (It was Dee who, in 1559, cast a horoscope to choose the most fortunate time for Elizabeth's coronation.) There is even a long-standing tradition that Dee was England's first official spy—traveling across Europe on the queen's business, but under the guise of an eccentric old wizard.

Dee was interested in Angelic magick throughout his life, but his real work did not begin until he met one Edward Kelley (introduced to him as Edward Talbot) in the year 1582 CE. Kelley (1555–97) has an uncertain and perhaps dark history, but we can be certain that he was an avid student of alchemy. This was likely what brought him to Dee.

During their very first meeting, Dee learned that Kelley had a knack for mediumship that he himself lacked. Dee performed an invocation to bring Angels into his mystical shewstone, and Kelley was able to see, hear, and speak to the Angels with ease. Thereafter, the two men formed a years-long partnership dedicated to a series of Angelic séances. They began by contacting one of the seven planetary Archangels—Annael, ruler of Venus—who claimed to be the current successive ruler of the cosmos.[1] Annael, then, introduced the men to the four Archangels known as Michael, Gabriel, Raphael, and Uriel. It was these four Angels, and lesser Angels directed by them, who delivered the entirety of Dee's magickal systems. The séances effectively ended by 1587, and the two men went their separate ways by 1589.

Dee recorded his Angelic sessions in several journals, and condensed the main points of the magick into a grimoire. Before he died, he hid a number of his journals and the grimoire in the false bottom of a wooden chest. After his death, the papers remained hidden there for over fifty years. The chest was sold to a confectioner as a gift for his wife, who owned the chest for twenty years before the papers were finally discovered. An illiterate maid used several pages to kindle fires, but the wife eventually discovered this and rescued what remained.

Finally, her second husband sold the papers to Elias Ashmole (1617–92), the famous English Mason, mystic, and scholar. Ashmole discovered that the papers included Dee's journals from December 1581 to May 1583 (comprising the *Five Books of the Mysteries,* in which we find the bulk of the *Heptarchic* system and parts of the *Loagaeth* system), a copy of the Angelical *Book of Loagaeth*, and Dee's personal grimoire.

These three are preserved today in the British Museum in London as Sloane MSS 3188, 3189, and 3191, respectively.

Apparently, Dee did not hide all of his journals. After his passing, several of them were sold with Dee's library—purchased, along with some of Dee's Angelic magick tools, by the antiquarian Sir Robert Bruce Cotton. These journals pick up where Ashmole's leave off, beginning at May 1583 and ending at April 1587. Cotton passed these journals on to his son Sir Thomas Cotton, and they are preserved today in the British Museum as Cotton appendix 46, parts 1 and 2.

It was in the Cotton library that Meric Casaubon discovered them. Somewhere, Casaubon also obtained journals covering March to September of 1607. He combined these (composed of thirteen individual books) into the compendium entitled *A True and Faithful Relation of What Passed for Many Years Between Dr. John Dee [. . .] and Some Spirits*. Published in 1659, this work contains the remainder of the Heptarchic system, the bulk of instruction concerning *Loagaeth* and the Angelical Keys, and Dee's advanced magick involving the Parts of the Earth and the Great Table of the Earth (or Watchtowers). A copy of this book is preserved as Sloane MS 3190.

Although most of Dee's journals were lost for a time, aspects of his Angelical language survived to have a profound influence upon Western esotericism. This was largely through Dee's grimoire (Sloane 3191), which contained a section entitled the *48 Claves Angelicae* (48 Angelical Keys),[2] as well as a section of invocations for the Angels of the four quarters of the Universe.[3] The latter section is called the *Book of Supplication* by modern scholars, because Dee was instructed by the Angels to write supplications to invoke the Angels whose names are contained in the Great Table of the Earth (or the "Watchtowers" of the four quarters).

Unfortunately, instructions for the correct use of these systems were not included in Dee's groimoire (likely because the grimoire was simply his working notes, intended for his personal use.) Therefore, mystics began to adopt Dee's material into the structure of their own systems, and even expanded the material on the same basis. The invocations contained in the *Book of Supplication* were expanded until the book was ten times its original size, and the *48 Claves Angelicae* were applied directly to the four Watchtowers.[4] This "neo-Enochian" system eventually made it into the hands of the esoteric Masons who, in 1888, founded the Hermetic Order known as the Golden Dawn.[5]

The study of Enochian magick through most of the twentieth century descended almost entirely from the Golden Dawn and those who followed (such as Aleister Crowley's Thelema, the Aurum Solis, and many others). Even when students returned to Dee's original manuscripts, they merely continued the tradition of adopting into their own systems bits and pieces of what they found. This is no surprise, because Dee's journals were obscure at best—the handwriting was hard to decipher, the material was scattered throughout the books, and Dee's English was archaic. In the end, most of Dee's original material was ignored.

It wasn't until the later years of the twentieth century that scholars began to take a fresh interest in the Dee journals, and what these journals had to say about the skeletal material found in his grimoire. The first such scholar was Donald Laycock, who published *The Complete Enochian Dictionary* in 1978. This book was transitional between standard "neo-Enochian" and the newer study of Dee's original material (which I call "Dee-purist"). While Laycock included all the Angelical words he could find from the systems of the Golden Dawn and Aleister Crowley, Dee's versions of the words formed the basis of Laycock's work.[6] Moreover, Laycock's preface to his *Dictionary* was the first to delve deeply into actual journal entries written by Dee and Kelley.

The next groundbreaking work on Dee's system, Geoffrey James' *The Enochian Evocation of Dr. John Dee*, was published just a few years later, in 1984. (In 1994 it was re-published under the title *The Enochian Magick of Dr. John Dee*.) This book was mostly a presentation of Dee's grimoire (Sloane 3191), along with a preface, several quotes from Dee's diary outlining the mythology behind the system, and several appendices that nicely complimented Laycock's preface. James also created a cross-reference system for the words of the Keys. For example, the seventh word of the first Key would have the cross-reference number "1.7." These numbers are extremely useful for study purposes, and make the Angelical words of the Keys easy to locate.

I must also mention the publication in 1997 of Donald Tyson's *Enochian Magic for Beginners: The Original System of Angel Magic.* Although many scholars take issue with Tyson's *interpretation* of Enochian magick, it cannot be denied that his book was the first to focus upon Dee's journals from start to finish. Therefore, this book stands with Laycock's *Dictionary* and James' *Enochian Evocation* as one of the few printed resources available for "Dee-purist" Enochiana.

Finally, by the turn of the twenty-first century, the Internet had revolutionized research and scholarship of all kinds. Enochian studies were no exception, and I eventually joined a mailing list called "Enochian-l"—where I found many of the top minds in this field of study: Ben Rowe, Clay Holden, Patricia Shaffer, Callisto Radiant, Christeos Pir, Dean Hildebrandt, Al Billings, Runar Karlsen . . . and the list could go on! These folks spent hours of their time discussing Dee's system, answering questions, uploading obscure Enochian material to websites, and mailing manuscripts to one another.[7] Thanks to these wonderful people, Dee-purist Enochian scholarship was no longer open only to those few who could gain reading time at the British Museum.

That is where I found myself in 1997, a member of this new generation of Enochian students. I was certainly interested in all aspects of Dee's system, but it was the Angelical language of the forty-eight Keys that fascinated me the most. I had been learning from the sources mentioned above, but the scholars with whom I communicated pointed out the texts' many shortcomings. (I will cover these in the introduction to volume II.)

In the end, I discovered I had little choice but to start from scratch—going back to Dee's journals and beginning a truly exhaustive page-by-page analysis. This meant sifting through hundreds of entries packed with material both relevant and irrelevant (not to mention judging which was which!). Dee's journals are not mere records of his séances, but include an entire saga of mysticism, political intrigue, personal drama, historical record, Angelic sermons, and so much more!

The Scope of This Work

I initially wrote the two parts of *The Angelical Language* as a single volume. I had, in fact, intended to provide a brief overview of the history and mythology of the language, then jump right into the linguistics. However, I quickly found my brief overview expanding into several long chapters—all containing information vital to an overall understanding of Angelical. Once it was all done, I realized I had either one *very* large textbook to publish, or two separate yet interdependent books of smaller size. I opted for the two-volume approach, so as not to frighten potential students with an overwhelming "doorstop" of a book!

This first volume—*The Complete History and Mythos of the Tongue of Angels*—explores the reception of the language by Dee and Kelley, and the biblical mythology behind the language as related to them by the Angels. This alone is a groundbreaking resource, as the full saga of Dee's reception of the magick has never before been told in such depth. You will find in these pages detailed and concise descriptions of aspects of Dee's work that are often ignored or marginalized in other books on "Enochian magick."

Chapter 1, for example, outlines several of the mystical traditions that influenced Dee's work. I briefly explain the Qabalistic concept of the "Fifty Gates of Understanding" and a related Jewish observance called "Counting the Omer." It involved a series of meditations by which the faithful could pass through the fifty Gates of the Tree of Life to gain an ever-increasing understanding of God and the Universe. If you understand this tradition while reading Dee's journals, there can be little doubt that this practice fascinated him, and played an important role in the mysticism he received from the Angels.

The same chapter then goes on to explain the true Enochian tradition. By this I do not mean Dee's magick—but rather a centuries-old tradition surrounding the biblical prophet Enoch. I briefly outline the existing Apocryphal Books of Enoch, as well as the mythos contained within them about Enoch's journeys into the Heavens to meet with God and His Angels, and to record the mysteries he found there. This, too, had a profound impact on Dee. As you shall see in this book, much of Dee's motivation in talking to the Angels was his hope of recovering the lost wisdom that Enoch himself had once revealed to mankind.

Finally, chapter 1 ends with a short overview of an obscure text called the *Book of Soyga*. Many have heard mention of this book, but few know very much about it. Yet it was a grimoire that so fascinated Dee that it became absolutely foundational to the magick he received from his Angels. If you want to know why Dee's system is overflowing with large indecipherable letter-Tables and magickal squares, you first have to understand the Tables found in the *Book of Soyga*. Once you have read the first chapter in this book, you will understand what that little grimoire was all about, and exactly how it influenced Dee.

Chapter 2, then, leads us directly into Dee's own book of indecipherable magickal Tables, called the *Book of Loagaeth* (the "Book of the Speech from God"). This book is another aspect of Dee's work that is often mentioned by Enochian scholars, but hardly ever explained in any depth. It is either marginalized to the point that students assume it is unimportant to their studies of Dee's magick, or it is presented in a fashion *entirely* removed from the context of his journals. Yet, in truth, it is the very heart and soul of the entire system of magick Dee received from the Angels—linking together what Enochian scholars often assume are three distinct branches of the system.

The *Book of Loagaeth* had an even larger scope, besides. It was not presented as a grimoire at all. Instead, it was called the Book of Enoch—not the Apocryphal biblical text, but the actual Celestial Tablets that Enoch was said to have copied during his journeys through the Heavens. It was said to be one and the same with the "Book of Life" or the "Book of the Lamb" described in the Revelation of St. John—sealed with seven seals and opened only by Christ himself during the final Tribulation of the earth.

Now, for the first time ever, I have presented the entire saga of the *Book of Loagaeth* in every detail—explaining what the book meant to Dee and Kelley, what the Angels had to say about its impact on the world, and (of course) the central role it plays in the entirety of Dee's "Enochian magick."

From there, beginning in chapter 3, I continue to outline and explain the saga of the Angelical language itself. Dee did not merely receive a few magickal orations to use in summoning Angels. In fact, the forty-eight Angelical Keys were presented as the means to "open" and access the mystical knowledge encoded into the Tables of *Loagaeth*. Besides this, the Angels communicated much information about their language to Dee and Kelley—some of which falls outside the realm of the Keys, and is sadly ignored by (or unknown to) most Enochian students. Therefore, I have explained in this book every scrap of information the Angels shared with Dee about the Keys and the language in which they are written. (I even include a bonus addendum that analyzes the English translations of the Keys given by the Angels—which also sheds much light on the meaning and purpose of both the Keys and the celestial tongue.)

To make this volume complete, I also decided to include a chapter on the instructions given to Dee on how to use the forty-eight Keys with the *Book of Loagaeth*. Yet even this is not standard "Enochian" magick material! Students have long been confused about the proper application of the forty-eight Keys, and have even argued that they have no relation at all to *Loagaeth*! In chapter 4, you will find the records set straight, and I am sure you will have little doubt how the Angels intended Dee to use the system!

Finally, in chapter 5, I focus entirely on the Angelical language itself. If you read the first four chapters diligently, then you will—at last!—be able to understand what the Angels had to say about their tongue in its proper context. You will understand the intentions of both Dee and the Angels in relation to such things as the Fifty Gates of Understanding, Counting the Omer, and the Book of Enoch.

I also fully explain how Dee was instructed to use the language beyond the *Book of Loagaeth*, and why I consider Angelical the true Sacred Language of the West. I have even ended this section with an addendum explaining exactly how to use the language within the scope of Solomonic-style Renaissance occultism: in the generation of Angelic Names, the creation of Sigils, and the making of Magickal Talismans.

Finally, I have decided to end this volume with an Angelical Psalter. This is something of a bridge between this volume and the second volume. It is a presentation of all forty-eight Keys—shown with proper Angelical/English translations and my own pronunciation key—all organized in such a way the practicing student can use the Psalter in practical work (meaning one can hold the Psalter open and read directly from it during ritual or prayer). I do not spend much time explaining the rationale behind my pronunciations or translations, as these will be covered in exhaustive depth in volume II. This first volume is perfect for anyone who wishes to learn *about* the Angelical tongue, without necessarily wishing to sit down and *learn* the language.

Whether you are interested in Renaissance Angel magick, or you are simply interested in the study of Angels themselves, I am sure you will find this volume to be an indispensable resource. Few mystics beyond Dee and Kelley have recorded such extensive journals concerning their encounters and interactions with Angelic beings! Yet, so few have truly studied or understood what is found in those journals. Therefore, I hope you will find this text a must-have for your study of Angelology.

Zorge,
Aaron Leitch
March 2009

Endnotes

1 See the *Arbatel of Magic* (a new translation by Joseph H. Peterson, *Arbatel—Concerning the Magic of the Ancients*, was published by Ibis Press of Lake Worth, FL in 2009), as well as Trithemius' *De Septum Secundeis* (for example, online at http://www.renaissanceastrology.com/heavenlyintelligences.html), for descriptions of this universal rulership by the Seven Archangels. Dee was familiar with both texts.

2. See James, Geoffrey. *The Enochian Magick of Dr. John Dee*. St. Paul, MN: Llewellyn, 2002, p. 65.

3. See James, *The Enochian Magick of Dr. John Dee*, p. 117. There were several other sections in the grimoire, but only the two mentioned thus far are relevant here. The others are the *Heptarchia Mystica*, and *Earthy Knowledge and Victory* (i.e., the 91 Parts of the Earth).

4. Though ultimately in error, there was good reason for modern mystics to assume the Keys should apply to the Watchtowers. The final Angelical Key contains an invocation for use with the "91 Parts of the Earth," and the names of those Parts are used to make up the Great Table of the Earth. (Shown in Sloane 3191, in a section entitled "Earthly Knowledge and Victory.") Thus, it seemed natural to assume the first eighteen Keys also applied to the Watchtowers—the first two standing alone as Grand Orations, and the remaining sixteen addressing the sixteen subdivisions of the four Watchtowers.

5. Reference the Golden Dawn's "Book H"—their foundational Enochian document. The entire story leading from Dee's original papers to "Book H" is contained in Stephen Skinner and David Rankine's book, *The Practical Angel Magic of Dr. John Dee's*

Enochian Tables (Singapore: Golden Hoard Press, 2005). That is the only book so far to tackle this important historical thread.

6. Dee's words formed the basic entires for Laycock's dictionary, and the Golden Dawn and Crowley recensions were included for comparison.
7. Today the amount of Enochian material available online is enormous—including scanned copies of Dee's handwritten journals. See, for example, http://www.themagickalreview.org/enochian/.

Chapter One

The Gates of Heaven and the Enochian Tradition

In order to understand where John Dee and his Angels were going with their magickal system, it is important to understand first where they were coming from. There are several important historical threads to trace from classical European mysticism to their convergence in the scrying sessions of Dee and Kelley. Without taking these foundational influences upon both men into account, their mystical system can often appear an incomprehensible jumble of magickal squares and arcane language.

There are many such threads to trace beneath the whole of Dee's system—such as ancient Gnosticism, the Qabalah, Hermeticism, alchemy, Agrippa's *Occult Philosophy*, and the Neoplatonic revival of the medieval and Renaissance eras. However, in this text, we are only concerned with the Angelical language and its intended magickal application as revealed by Dee's celestial contacts.

In this vein, it will be necessary to outline some aspects of the Qabalah—particularly the mystical models known as the Tree of Life and the fifty Gates of *Binah* (Understanding). We will also need to know something about the ancient Book of Enoch, and its effect upon the magickal system received by Dee and Kelley. This Apocryphal biblical text (the oldest known Apocrypha) was not in Dee's possession in the sixteenth century, but the legends based upon it—collectively called

"Enochian"—were current and popular in the occult circles of Dee's time.

Finally, this chapter will cover a subject that just may enjoy the status of "most obscure" when it comes to influences upon Dee's work: the mysterious *Book of Soyga*. This text was in Dee's possession—and the references he makes to *Soyga* in his journals were for hundreds of years the only hints we had of its existence. Relatively recently, in 1994, two copies of the book (one of which is likely the very copy that belonged to Dee) were finally discovered in England. The text has since been deciphered, and an analysis of the work will be included in this chapter. In this and the following chapter, we will see exactly what relationship this book has to the Qabalah and the Book of Enoch, and the influence it had on the magick Dee and Kelley received from the Angels.

Therefore, we will leave our two Renaissance mages behind for now—and explore these particulars of the occultism that form the foundation of Dee's Angelical language and the famed *Book of Loagaeth*.

The Fifty Gates of Binah

> The world was created with Fifty Gates of Understanding . . . [Talmud, Rosh haShanah 21b]

> In that Temple [of Binah] there are fifty gates, which are supposed to be closed, meaning that they block the flow of Lights. There are forty-nine gates engraved upon the 'four winds' of the world. One gate has no direction; it is not known whether it faces up or down. This is how this gate remains closed. Inside the gates is a lock with a tiny and narrow keyhole. This lock is marked and known only by the impression of the key. And no one is to know about this narrow keyhole without having the key [*Sepher Zohar*, Prologue, "The Locked and the Unlocked," verses 43–44].[1]

The Tree of Life is mentioned in Genesis (2:9) and the Revelation of St. John (2:7, 22:2), and is said to bear the fruits of God's graces.[2] As used by mystics (especially in the later Hermetic Qabalah), it has become a stylized diagram of the spheres of Heaven—including the planetary spheres, the fixed stars, and the Divine Source above all. These spheres—each

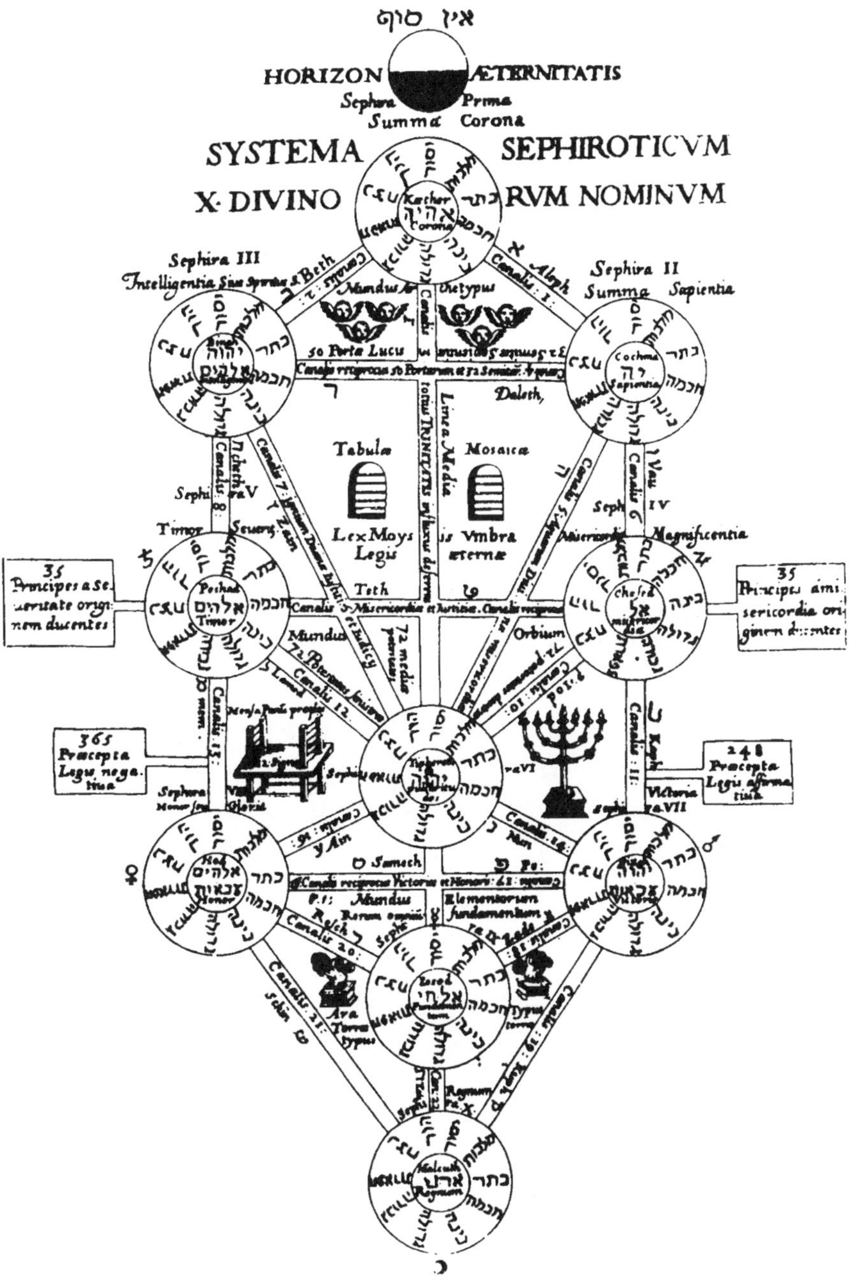

Kircher's Tree of Life

representing one of the divine "fruits"—are called *Sephiroth* (singular: *Sephirah*) in Hebrew. One interpretation of this word is "to say"—indicating that each of the Sephiroth upon the Tree is associated with one of the ten creative instances of "God said . . . " in Genesis 1.

In the teachings of the Hebrew Qabalah, there are seven primary Sephiroth (or aspects of God):[3] beginning with *Chesed* (Mercy), and then *Gevurah* (Severity), *Tiphareth* (Majesty), *Netzach* (Victory), *Hod* (Splendor), *Yesod* (Foundation), and *Malkuth* (Kingdom). These represent the seven principal characteristics of God as illustrated throughout the Torah.

Each Sephirah is further represented in sacred Scripture by one of the Seven Patriarchs (the *Ushpizin*): Abraham, Isaac, Jacob, Joseph, Moses, Aaron, and David.[4] Biblical legend depicts these heroes acting on behalf of Yahweh within the context of one or more of the Sephiroth. To note but a few examples: Abraham acts from Chesed (Divine Mercy), because he was allowed to spare his son from sacrifice. Isaac, meanwhile, acts from Gevurah (Divine Severity) because he was, in fact, almost sacrificed in blood. David, the first king of Israel, acts from Malkuth (the Kingdom) because he established God's Kingdom upon the Earth.

Further, the seven primary Sephiroth correspond to the Seven Days of Creation, the seven days of the week, the seven planets,[5] and all related mystical considerations of the number seven. The three Sephiroth above these seven—*Kether* (Crown), *Chockmah* (Wisdom), and *Binah* (Understanding)—are considered "hidden Sephiroth" that are in many ways a separate system unto themselves. The physical man has no part in these transcendent levels of Deity—yet it is toward this Supernal Triad that the devout must aspire. It is the work of a lifetime, and the higher Spheres are gained only upon death and re-union with God.

In this section, we are going to discuss just one Qabalistic mystery based upon the Sephiroth: the Fifty Gates of Understanding, contained within a Jewish custom known as the "Counting of the Omer." An *Omer* is simply a generic biblical term for a "unit of measurement," and in particular a unit (or sheaf) of wheat. Leviticus 23:15–16 instructs:

> And ye shall count unto you from the morrow after the Sabbath, from the day that ye brought the sheaf (Omer) of the wave offering; seven Sabbaths shall be complete: Even unto the morrow after the seventh

> Sabbath shall ye number 50 days; and ye shall offer a new meat offering unto the Lord.

This Torah commandment outlines a specific period of time falling between Passover[6] and, fifty days later, the observance of *Shavu'ot*. Primarily, each of these holidays is an agricultural observance: Passover marks the beginning of the harvest season in Israel, and Shavu'ot the end of the season and its first fruits. From the devotional perspective, Passover celebrates the sparing of the Hebrew slaves in Egypt from the Plague of Death, and the commencement of the Exodus. Seven weeks then follow until Shavu'ot, which celebrates the arrival of the Israelites at Mount Sinai and the reception of the Ten Commandments. This period of seven times seven days (seven weeks or forty-nine days) plus the day of the Reception totals the fifty days of the Counting of the Omer as prescribed in Leviticus.

From this point, a mystical interpretation of the Torah must be adopted, similar to that found throughout the *Sepher haZohar* and other foundational Qabalistic texts. By leaving the civilization of Egypt behind them in favor of the wilderness, the Israelites were both literally and philosophically removing themselves from the World of Man. At the same time, they were journeying *toward* the Divine Light as symbolized by Mount Sinai and their meeting with God. Therefore, it is necessary for the devout to make this same philosophical journey each year—repenting and leaving behind the worldly sins of humanity, and striving through the emotional wilderness to attain union with God and His Law (Torah).

This is the fifty-day practice of the "Counting of the Omer." Every night, a blessing is recited, and then the numbering of the day is stated. (For instance, twelve days into the process, one would state, "Today is twelve days, which is one week and five days of the Omer.") It revolves around the concept of *Teshuvah* (Repentance), and is marked by focus upon Torah study, prayer, and observance of the Commandments. Each day, a sin or other spiritual hindrance that has infected one's soul throughout the year (by association with the World of Man, or "Egypt") must be relinquished. This is known as removing oneself from the Fifty Gates of Impurity.

In order to accomplish this, a different "aspect (*midot*) of God" is singled out every day for devotional contemplation. It is these fifty (really, forty-nine) aspects of God, based upon the seven Sephiroth, that comprise the *Nun Sha'arei Binah* (Fifty Gates of Understanding). By successfully exiting a Gate of Impurity, one necessarily enters its corresponding Gate of Understanding.

Students of the Qabalah will recognize the Hebrew word for *understanding* (Binah) as the name of an eighth "hidden" Sephirah—which lies immediately above the abyss that separates the Highest Divinity from the lower seven Sephiroth. It is true that the fifty Gates are related directly to this eighth Sephirah. It is understanding of both God and the self that is sought by the devout during the Counting of the Omer—an attempt to bridge the span of the abyss (that is, to reconcile) between God and mankind. Therefore, Binah—in its entirety—is considered the Fiftieth Gate, thrown open only by opening all the previous forty-nine.

The opening of this final Gate falls on the day of Shavu'ot, and is thus not actually counted among the 7 x 7 preceding days. It corresponds instead to the completion of the work, the reception of Divine revelation, or the reception of the Commandments by the ancient Israelites on the fiftieth day of the Exodus. The previous forty-nine Gates are, in fact, Gates of entrance to the Sephirah Binah—and all forty-nine must be passed before the real Binah can be reached. (Seven is a mystical number of completion—as seen in the Days of Creation: six days of work followed by rest after completion on the seventh. The number 49 is seven successive sevens, and therefore represents the completion of the physical, and entrance into the spiritual realm.)

Reaching this height does *not*, however, represent passing through the Fiftieth Gate of Binah—which corresponds to the Creator. That final Gate cannot be entered by a living human being—as it technically lies across the abyss in the realm of pure (Supernal) Deity. This Gate is reserved, instead, for the Messiah—who will open the Fiftieth Gate in the "End Times" and bring about the destruction of the World of Man. According to the Talmud, only Moses has passed through this Gate, and then only upon his death. The Jewish mystic passing through the forty-nine Gates would be rewarded with a day of prophetic revelation,

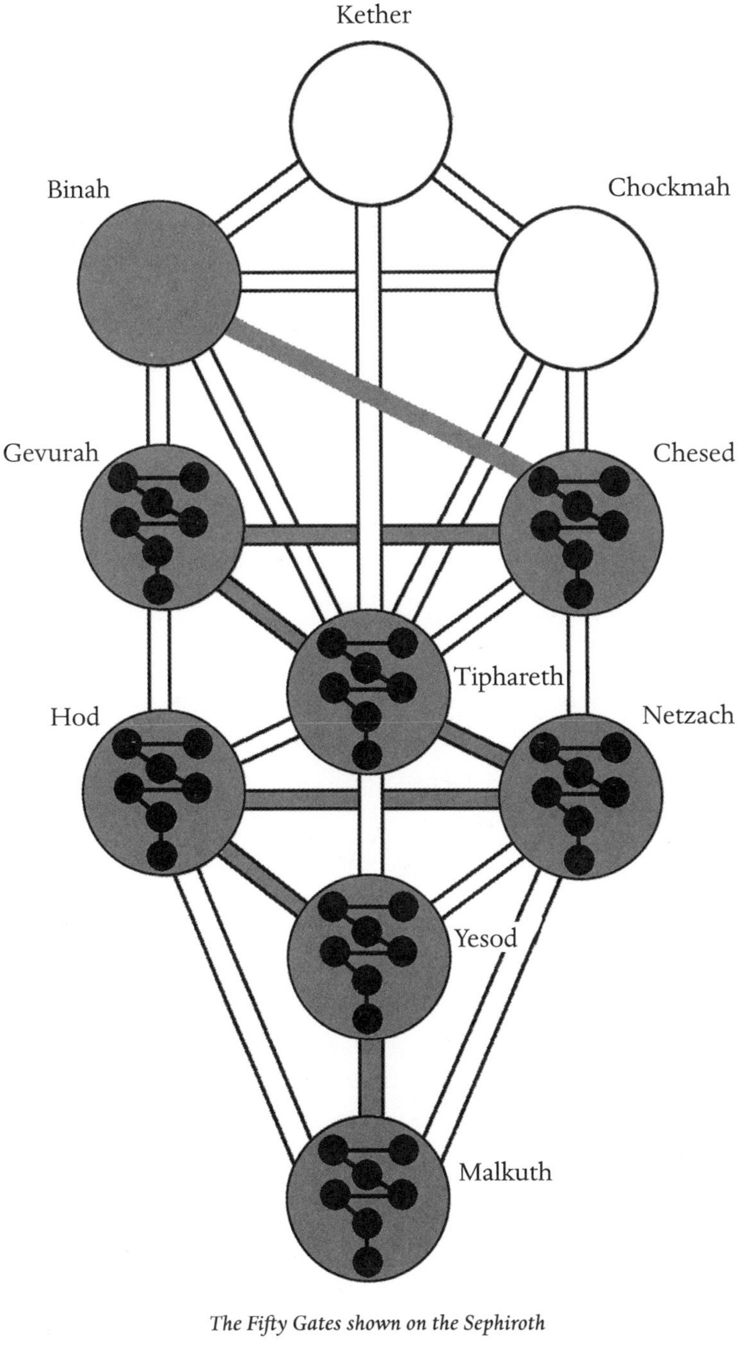

The Fifty Gates shown on the Sephiroth

and an experience of closeness with the Divine. However, come back to earth he must, until the time of his own passing.

As can be seen from the diagram on the previous page, each of the seven lower Sephiroth is divided into seven sub-Sephiroth. Thus, within the context of God's Mercy (Chesed), we find the Mercy of Mercy (or pure Chesed), the Severity of Mercy, the Majesty of Mercy, the Victory of Mercy, the Splendor of Mercy, the Foundation of Mercy, and the Kingdom (or application) of Mercy.

During the first week of the Counting of the Omer, Divine Mercy would be the overall focus, along with the lessons taught by the patriarch Abraham. On the first day, the aspirant would invoke the Mercy of God's Mercy, and would apply himself to the virtue of study. On the second day, the aspirant would invoke the Severity of God's Mercy, and practice the virtue of attentive listening. This process continues for seven days—all associated with Chesed—until the Kingdom of Mercy is reached:

Day 1: *Chesed of Chesed*—Study[7]
Day 2: *Gevurah of Chesed*—Attentive listening
Day 3: *Tiphareth of Chesed*—Orderly speech
Day 4: *Netzach of Chesed*—Understanding
Day 5: *Hod of Chesed*—Intuitive Insight
Day 6: *Yesod of Chesed*—Awe
Day 7: *Malkuth of Chesed*—Reverence

The second week would then focus upon Isaac and Gevurah—beginning with the Mercy of Severity, and continuing to the Kingdom of Severity on the seventh day (the fourteenth of Counting the Omer). The third week highlights the seven subsets of Tiphareth, the fourth week those of Netzach, the fifth those of Hod, the sixth those of Yesod, and the seventh focuses upon Malkuth. All forty-nine days have virtues associated with them for study, meditation, and practice. Finally, Shavu'ot falls on day fifty—when the dedicated aspirant will receive prophetic insight into his own soul, and into the Mind of God.

It might strike some as odd that this list appears to run backward. God exists above the highest Gate, while man resides at the opposite end in Malkuth of Malkuth—the lowest and darkest position in the scheme.

Thus, it might seem logical to assume that one should begin at this lowest point and move upward toward the Divine Source. However, this does not appear to be the traditional practice for the Fifty Gates—nor with many related mystical exercises. Instead, it was common to begin at the highest point, and work backward toward Earth. For instance, the *Merkavah* mystics—Hebrew shamans from whom much of the Qabalah was drawn after the thirteenth century—were known to achieve the Vision of God through fasting, prayer, and (some believe) sacramental drugs. Then, they would turn back toward Earth and "ride" downward through the Seven Heavenly Palaces.[8]

A similar idea seems to be at work with the Fifty Gates of Understanding. Because prophecy flows from the Divine to the heart of man, it is necessary to invoke the Gates from the highest available to us (Chesed of Chesed) downward toward the physical realm (Malkuth of Malkuth). The impenetrable Fiftieth Gate of Binah itself is actually the first in the list—but it is passed over in silence, and symbolized instead by the final day of Shavu'ot. The revelation that comes through the Fiftieth Gate—since it cannot be attained by human effort alone—is regarded as a gift handed down from God.

The Hermetic Gates of Intelligence

Later Christian mysticism (during and after the Renaissance era) obtained a somewhat different scheme for the Fifty Gates—as we shall see here in the "Hermetic Gates of Intelligence." Whereas the Jewish mystics were centered upon spiritual devotion, the Hermetic mages were scientists at heart. Their spiritual pursuits were grounded in practices such as alchemy, astronomy/astrology, and mathematics. Therefore, the Fifty Gates became those of "Intelligence" rather than "Understanding," and were based upon an almost Darwinian progression of evolution.

This scheme was first presented in 1652 CE by Athanasius Kircher, in his *Oedipus Aegyptiacus*[9]—the same text from which the Hermetic Order of the Golden Dawn would later draw their standard version of the Qabalistic Tree of Life. In the late 1800s, one of the founders of the Golden Dawn, W. Wynn Westcott, appended a slightly altered version of the

Gates of Intelligence to the *Sepher Yetzirah*. This is the most popular and readily available version:[10]

First Order: Elementary

1. Chaos, Hyle, the first matter
2. Formless, void, lifeless
3. The Abyss
4. Origin of the Elements
5. Earth (no seed germs)
6. Water
7. Air
8. Fire
9. Differentiation of qualities
10. Mixture and combination

Second Order: Decad of Evolution

11. Minerals differentiate
12. Vegetable principles appear
13. Seeds germinate in moisture
14. Herbs and trees
15. Fructification in vegetable life
16. Origin of low forms of animal life
17. Insects and reptiles appear
18. Fishes, vertebrate life in the waters
19. Birds, vertebrate life in the air
20. Quadrupeds, vertebrate earth animals

Third Order: Decad of Humanity

21. Appearance of Man
22. Material human body
23. Human soul conferred
24. Mystery of Adam and Eve
25. Complete Man as the Microcosm
26. Gift of five human faces acting exteriorly
27. Gift of five powers to the Soul

28. Adam Kadmon, the Heavenly Man
29. Angelic beings
30. Man in the image of God

Fourth Order: World of Spheres

31. The Moon
32. Mercury
33. Venus
34. Sol
35. Mars
36. Jupiter
37. Saturn
38. The Firmament
39. The Premium Mobile
40. The Empyrean Heaven

Fifth Order: The Angelic World (modified)[11]

41. Angels
42. Archangels
43. Principalities
44. Virtues (or Authorities)
45. Powers
46. Dominations
47. Thrones
48. Cherubim
49. Seraphim

Sixth Order: the Archetype

50. God. Ain Soph. He Whom no mortal eye hath seen, and Who has been known to Jesus the Messiah alone.

Westcott prefaces the above list with a note that illustrates the scientific (rather than devotional) nature of the Fifty Gates of Intelligence:

> Attached to some editions of the *Sepher Yetzirah* is found this scheme of Kabalistic classification of knowledge emanating from the Second

> *Sephira Binah*, Understanding, and descending by stages through the angels, Heavens, humanity, animal and vegetable and mineral kingdoms to Hyle and the chaos. The Kabalists said that one must enter and pass up through the Gates to attain to the Thirty-Two Paths of Wisdom; and that even Moses only passed through the forty-ninth Gate, and never entered the fiftieth.

We can see that the list has been changed from a devotional invocation for a gift from God into a Qabalistic "classification of knowledge."

Also, we can see that the practice of the Fifty Gates has been reversed in order to follow the more logical "from bottom upward" progression. (Remember, the Qabalists actually said one should enter and pass *downward*, not upward, through the Gates.) Therefore, the Hermetic system does not begin at the highest Gate, passing silently over the unattainable Gate of Binah. Instead, it begins at the lowest point (chaos, hyle) and progresses upward toward the hidden Fiftieth Gate and the Divine. This ascension is a hallmark of the Hermetic practices (as opposed to the traditional descending practices of Hebrew Qabalists and Merkavah mystics)—and can be seen in the modern Hermetic practice of initiation upon the Tree of Life from Malkuth upward toward Kether.

The Gates of Intelligence, as previously mentioned, incorporate a progression of natural evolution and (subsequent) human spiritual evolution. The Hermetic aspirant was intended to progressively study and experience (i.e., come to understand) each of the elements outlined in the list—meaning that one must engage in alchemy, astrology, ceremonial magick, and more in order to explore and bond with each of these concepts. (This reflects the attitude of the "renaissance man." We see the attitude at work in men such as John Dee, who felt that acquiring all human—and more than human—knowledge was key to enlightenment.) As the fifty progressive Gates reflect the natural evolutionary advancement of life in the Universe, the individual mage was to follow its pattern for personal evolution.

In Westcott's prefatory note to this list, Moses seems to have been demoted—gaining credit only for passing through Gate Forty-nine rather than the fiftieth. However, the statement may be a simple reference to the fact that the prophet (according to the Talmud) only obtained forty-nine Gates by his own efforts. The Christian author may or may not have known that Moses was supposed to have passed through the Fiftieth Gate upon his death.

Similarly, the "Sixth Order" includes a note assuring us that no mortal eye has seen the Fiftieth Gate (which matches tradition), and that Jesus alone has passed through it. The latter idea (apparently attributed to Kircher himself) is a Christianized recension of the traditional view that the Gate is reserved for the Messiah. To the Judaic mystic, this means that the Gate is sealed and will remain so until the advent of the final Tribulations and the coming of the Messiah (who is *not* equated with the prophet Jesus). To the Christian Hermeticist, however, the Messiah has already come and gone—meaning that the Fiftieth Gate was opened during Jesus' translation to Heaven. More than likely, this goes along with the view that the Gate will be opened by Jesus a second time during the Apocalypse.

Note, also, that Westcott's list that equates Gate Fifty with the *Ain Soph* (Limitless)—the realm of pure Divinity that properly resides above even the highest Sephirah of Kether. However, if these are the Gates of Binah (which resides beneath Kether), this should not be the case at all. It is my own assumption that the three hidden and Supernal Sephiroth are simply being lumped together and equated with the Limitless Divinity within which they reside. Christian Qabalists often associated these with the Trinity: Kether (the Crown) as God, Chockmah (Wisdom) as the Holy Spirit, and Binah (whose Hebrew name contains the root *Ben*—Son) as the Messiah.

Finally, we can see that this Hermetic list has lost its traditional 7 x 7 categorization. Instead, the Gates of Intelligence are divided into "Orders" of ten—reflecting the Christian Qabalists' obsession with the ten Sephiroth of the Tree of Life. (As we see in the Golden Dawn, nearly everything that can be divided into groupings of ten is presented as such. In this mindset, it is inconceivable to interpret a list of fifty Gates as anything other than a 5 x 10 equation.) Of course, the isolation of the Fiftieth Gate is preserved in the Hermetic system—leaving the "Fifth Order" of Gates with merely nine. This might at first appear to be problematic, but we find the solution by adopting the Pseudo-Dionysus list of Angelic Choirs—containing only nine Orders of Angels (3 x 3) rather than the ten found upon the Tree of Life. This frees up the Fiftieth Gate for its presentation (or occlusion) as hidden and unattainable.

The Book of Enoch

> [Uriel] said, "O Enoch, look on the Book which Heaven has gradually distilled; and, reading that which is written within it, understand every part of it." Then I looked on all which was written, and understood all, reading the Book and everything written in it, all the works of man." [*1 Enoch*, chapter 80, vol. 1–2, Charlesworth]

> And Pravuil told me: "All the things that I have told you, we have written. Sit and write all the souls of mankind . . . for all souls are prepared to eternity, before the formation of the world. . . . and I wrote out all things exactly, and wrote three hundred and sixty-six books." [*2 Enoch* 23:2–3, Charles]

> " . . . from my Heavenly vision and from the voice of the holy Angels have I acquired knowledge, and from the Tablet[s][12] of Heaven have I acquired Understanding." [*1 Enoch*, chapter 92, vol. 3, Charlesworth]

The patriarch Enoch (Hebrew: *Chanock*) appears in canonical Scripture in at least three places. The first reference is in Genesis 5:18–24, within a longer list of genealogies.[13] Enoch is said to have walked this earth for 365 years,[14] during which time he fathered Methuselah. (Methuselah is famous for the grossly extended span of his life—just short of one thousand years!) Methuselah, then, fathered Lamech, who in turn fathered the patriarch Noah. Meanwhile, the saga of Noah's great-grandfather Enoch is summed up cryptically in verses 23–24:

> And all the days of Enoch were three hundred and sixty five years: And Enoch walked with God: and he was not; for God took him.

Each and every generation outlined in this section of Genesis contains the birth, years of life, and death of the patriarchs. Enoch alone is given no time of death, and is (apparently) described as having been taken bodily into the Heavens by God. (This honor was shared by only one other human being in the canonical Bible: the prophet Elijah.[15]) This quirk in the wording of Genesis has fascinated Judeo-Christian devotees and mystics for thousands of years, and has served as the basis for the later traditions (such as Merkavah) based upon Enoch and his experiences in the Heavens.

The second biblical reference to Enoch is, in fact, a product of these Enochian traditions.[16] It is found in the New Testament, Hebrews 11:5, where we find a solid explanation of what happened to Enoch when "God took him":

> By faith Enoch was translated that he should not see death; and was not found, because God had translated him: for before his translation he had this testimony, that he pleased God.

The use of the word *translated* here indicates a person who has been taken bodily into Heaven, as opposed to someone who has ascended into the Heavens after death.

The third reference to Enoch in the Bible returns to the cryptic. We also find this one in the New Testament, the Epistle of Jude, verse 14:

> And Enoch also, the seventh from Adam, prophesied of these, saying, Behold, the Lord cometh with ten thousands of his saints.

This third reference was something of a problem for later (and many current) Christian authorities. It canonizes the words of Enoch—but there are no writings of the prophet found anywhere in the Bible!

Instead, we have to turn to that huge collection of "unofficial" biblical documents known as the Apocrypha. In most cases, these books have been excluded from the canon—by both Christian and Jewish authorities—because of their mystical (and often very Pagan) nature.

In the early days of Christianity, before the Bible was canonized, there were actually several books attributed to Enoch in use by various churches. Three of them are known to us today. The first Book of Enoch (*1 Enoch*) is the oldest known Apocrypha—having been composed (most likely) during or directly after the Hebrew captivity in Babylon. (We will return to this subject shortly.) It was known to ancient scholars—such as St. Irenaeus during the early Common Era—but was lost for nearly a thousand years during Roman Catholic world dominance. Then, in 1773, the famous explorer James Bruce discovered three copies of *1 Enoch* in Abyssinia. This was later called the "Ethiopic" Book of Enoch—because it was written in Ethiopian. However, the oldest copies were likely written in Aramaic or Hebrew. As it turns out, this is the very same text from which the Epistle of Jude draws its quote. Over the ensuing years, several portions of the same text—in Greek this time—have been found. Finally, in the late 1940s and early 1950s, the famous Dead Sea Scrolls were discovered near Qumran. Among the texts recovered from this library was *1 Enoch* (now in Aramaic)—officially making the book part of the Dead Sea collection.

The second Book of Enoch (*2 Enoch*, or the "Slavonic" Book of Enoch) is actually titled the *Book of the Secrets of Enoch*. This was discovered in 1886 in the Belgrade public library by a professor Sokolov, although it was not translated for ten more years. It is generally assumed the text was compiled—and perhaps altered—by Christian editors sometime after the dawn of the Common Era, although much of its content is likely much older. (It may be dependent on *1 Enoch* itself.)

In 1922, the scholar Hugo Odeberg translated the "Hebrew" Book of Enoch (*3 Enoch*). This is another principally Merkavah-class text, depicting the heavenly ascensions of the second-century Rabbi Ishmael. It contains legends concerning Enoch's shamanic translation from mortal man into the fiery Archangel Metatron (the Scribe, and Voice of God—both jobs suited to the role of a prophet-made-celestial). Most significantly, this work had an influence upon the *Sepher haZohar*—a principal text of the Qabalah written in the thirteenth century.

The legend of Enoch weaves its way back to the Captivity in Babylon (circa 600 BCE). At the time, *1 Enoch* was simply a biblical text similar to the Books of Daniel, Isaiah, Ezekiel, or (later) the Revelation of St. John. Like these latter four, the Book of Enoch was an apocalyptic writing—outlining various Divine communications between Enoch and God. It stands out in history as (perhaps) the first biblical text in which the Hebrew God promises retribution against the entire world for mistreatment of the Israelites. It is the source book for all of the above-mentioned biblical Scriptures, and many further besides.[17]

This book gave birth to the widespread Judeo-Christian mindset that assumes "God will someday punish and destroy all of our enemies." It was written by a people who had been defeated and carried into a foreign land against their will. It was written to help alleviate some of the anger and resentment that the Israelite people felt against their Babylonian captors. To this day, Babylon (along with Egypt) remains a biblical symbol of wrongdoing and social degeneration.[18]

Nevertheless, the captive Israelites seem to have adopted quite a bit of Babylonian cosmology, along with no small amount of Babylonian mythology. *1 Enoch* itself is overflowing with Babylonian astronomy, stories of Angels that mirror older Pagan Mesopotamian tales, and a description of an ascent through the Heavens—a very Chaldean concept.

It is this ascent through the Heavens by Enoch that concerns us the most. *1 Enoch* states that the patriarch was lifted into Heaven by Angelic guides. However, there are other legends asserting that Enoch flew into the sky in a chariot of fire.[19] These, of course, are the legends associated with the Merkavah (Chariot) tradition, by Hebrew shamans who desired to follow in Enoch's footsteps. The various books attributed to Enoch, along with such books as Revelation and Ezekiel, are Merkavah texts—in which prophets are taken to the very Throne of God and taught the mysteries of the Universe in Angelic colleges.

Needless to say, the rise of Merkavah mysticism brought along with it an occult fad for Enochian mythos. When the texts were hidden away or destroyed in the first centuries of the Common Era, the legends of Enoch lived on—and perhaps prospered. The fact that the Books of Enoch had become the *Lost* Books of Enoch merely strengthened their popularity among occultists, adding to the already passionate tales a deep air of mystery and the slight irritation of lost ancient wisdom. The interest in Enoch as a patron of Merkavah riders and Gnostic ascenders was still in vogue in sixteenth-century Europe—paralleled by the similar fad that existed for Solomon and his Keys of magick.

From a practical standpoint, the *Mah'aseh Merkavah* (Work of the Chariot) generally had three principal goals. The first was the gaining of the vision of the Merkavah itself—the Throne of God in the highest Heaven, uplifted by the mighty *Cherubim* and surrounded by its Choirs of ministering Angels.[20] Secondly, the Merkavah Rider wished to journey through the celestial spheres—passing through the seven Palaces (*Hekhaloth*) of

Heaven by way of various talismans and passwords—a practice not far removed from the entrance of the Fifty Gates of Understanding.

There also existed a third, almost hidden, objective to gaining entrance to the Heavenly Halls. The truly adept, through a lifetime of dedication, might be allowed a glimpse within the Celestial Book of Enoch. Do not confuse this with such human-created works as *1 Enoch*, *2 Enoch*, or *3 Enoch*! Those Apocryphal texts are, in fact, merely legends *about* the true Book (or Books) of Enoch—written many generations after the patriarch's supposed lifetime. In such literature, the Celestial Book of Enoch is addressed by the terms "Tablets of Heaven" or "Book of Life."

At the beginning of this section, I quoted several instances from Enochian literature wherein the patriarch beholds and then copies the content of the Tablets of Heaven. This is the very same Book that legends such as the Revelation of St. John describe—the seven seals of which only the coming Messiah is worthy to break.[21] Thus, granting Enoch the privilege to view and *copy* the Celestial Book of Life was a gift from God much akin to Moses' entrance of the Fiftieth Gate of Understanding. (Except in Enoch's case, God was granting the gift to the entire world, by delivering the contents of the Tablets into human hands.)

The Enochian legends hold (in some cases) that Enoch filled 366 hand-written books before he completed his transcription.[22] Then, upon his translation into Heaven, he was transfigured into the Archangel Metatron—appointed to the position of Scribe within God's Court (with full authority to speak for the Creator!), and thereby granted stewardship of the Tablets for eternity. As for the hand-written copies he penned while still in the flesh, they've had a rather turbulent history.

The concept of the Tablets of Heaven is not at all confined to the Merkavah tradition. Stories about it appear again and again throughout history and all over the world. It has various mythologies and various names, but they all boil down to the same basic ideas. Many cultures also have a parallel concept of a Divine Record Keeper, who records every single event that takes place in the world, along with all the secrets of Heaven.

In a similar Judaic legend, the Archangel *Raziel* (whose name means "Secrets of God") holds the heavenly scribal position. He is said to stand before the Divine Throne, just behind the Veil, writing down everything that occurs in the Royal Court of *Elohim* (which is the origin of everything that happens in existence). Legend holds that this book (*Sepher Raziel*)[23] was given to Adam, but it was stolen by jealous Angels and tossed into the sea.[24] The book was finally recopied by Enoch, passed through Methuselah and Lamech, and finally to his great-grandson Noah. (It contained the blueprints for the Ark.) At length, it was passed down to Solomon, and granted the king his world-famous wisdom and magickal power. Then, it disappeared yet again when Solomon fell from Yahweh's good graces.

In ancient Egypt, the precursor of the Raziel myth involved Thoth (*Djehuti*)—the Ibis-headed God who invented writing and words. In Pagan Egypt, Djehuti represented what the later Gnostics would call the *Logos* (Word).[25] The Logos is the creative principle of the Divine—the Word of Creation used by God (or, in Egypt, Ra) to fashion the world. Thoth was the God of all language and communication, and (like Raziel) was a keeper of the Divine Secrets of the Heavens. The *Book of Thoth* appears in Egyptian legend in the same manner as the *Sepher Raziel*—as a much-sought-after but ever-elusive tome of ultimate knowledge.[26]

There are other examples of this Book in world history—such as the Eastern concept of the "Akashic Records," or the ancient Babylonian "Tablet of Destinies"—stolen from the Father God and gifted to humanity by the goddess Ishtar. In all cases, we have references to an astral compendium of all knowledge and wisdom, which can be accessed only by adepts who learn how to gain entrance to the record itself.

There have been various attempts to actually write this great Book here in the physical. The medieval grimoire entitled *Sepher Raziel* is one example. The deck of Tarot cards is another. (This is likely why Aleister Crowley named his own Tarot deck the *Book of Thoth*.) Even the Torah is described by medieval Jewish mystics as a mere earthly reflection of the *real* Torah in Heaven.[27] Another, more obscure, example is found in the little-known *Book of Soyga*.

The *Book of Soyga (Aldaraia Sive Soyga Vocor)*

Dee: Is my *Book of Soyga* of any excellency?

Uriel: That book was revealed unto Adam in Paradise by God's good angels.

Dee: [. . .] Oh my great and long desire hath been to be able to read those Tables of *Soyga*. [*Five Books of Mystery*, March 10, 1582]

For centuries, all that was known about the mysterious medieval grimoire called the *Book of Soyga* (or *Aldaraia*) came from a few scattered references in Dr. John Dee's journals, and from reproductions of eight of *Soyga*'s Tables appended to the back of Dee's own *Book of Loagaeth*.[28]

Dee obviously held the *Book of Soyga* in high regard. His inclusion of some of its Tables with, and similarity to, his Tables of *Loagaeth* have always hinted at a connection between *Soyga* and Dee's Angelic magick. However, with such a small amount of information on the *Book of Soyga* available, there was no hope of tracing a historical thread.

This finally changed in 1994, when scholar Deborah Harkness discovered two copies of the text: one in the Bodleian Library (Bodley MS 908) and the other at the British Library (Sloane MS 8—which may have been Dee's copy). Each of them had been cataloged under the alternate title *Aldaraia*—thereby misleading generations of Dee scholars who had been seeking a book entitled *Soyga*. Unfortunately, since the rediscovery there has been little written about the *Book of Soyga*, and no copy of the book itself has yet been offered for publication.

The conversation quoted at the head of this section took place between Dee and the Archangel Uriel in March of 1582. In response to Dee's questions about *Soyga*, Uriel suggested that only the Archangel Michael could reveal the mysteries of the Tables. However, as far as we know, Dee never asked Michael to explain them.

At some point during the next year, Dee appears to have misplaced his copy of the *Book of Soyga*. In April of 1583, Dee asked the Angel Illemese[29] for information about his lost "Arabic book of Tables and numbers."[30] Unfortunately, Illemese did not regard the *Book of Soyga* with the same esteem as Uriel—instead calling it a work of false witchcrafts. After some discussion on the matter, Dee finally changed the subject to the (also lost) Book of Enoch, which Illemese promises to deliver.[31]

Meanwhile, let us explore this obscure *Book of Soyga*. The *Soyga* Tables are large magickal squares (36 x 36 cells) filled with letters generated by a keyword (one associated with each Table) via some unknown cipher algorithm. The cipher was so complicated that even the genius of Dee couldn't break it—hence his "great and long desire" to finally read the text!

The best study of the text to date is *John Dee and the Magic Tables in the Book of Soyga*, by Jim Reeds.[32] His interest in *Soyga* arises from the encrypted Tables, and he has actually succeeded in deciphering them where Dee failed. However, it is not necessary to go into detail on his cryptographic work here. Nothing mystical was revealed by finding the method used to generate the Tables (i.e., they did not produce a readable scripture; instead, the letters represent a mathematical algorithm). The magick is likely inherent in the keyword upon which each Table is based, but there has been no work yet toward exploring the linguistic origins of the keywords.[33]

Of more interest to us here, Reeds also offers a (relatively) detailed description of the entire *Book of Soyga*—which he took from microfilm copies of the manuscripts. He assigns it roughly to the late medieval period, and the texts he studied (the Sloane and Bodley manuscripts) are both of the sixteenth century. It is the Sloane version of the manuscript that also bears the title *Aldaraia sive Soyga vocor*, although both copies were cataloged under that title. The same copy also identifies the text as an astrological mystery—*Tractatus Astrologico Magicus*—which is hardly uncommon for a text of its period. (At the time, astrology was in the mainstream of medical practice.)

Soyga is principally divided into three parts, called respectively *Liber Aldaraia*, *Liber Radiorum*, and *Liber Decimus Septimus*. There also follow several unnamed additions to the text, ending with the thirty-six Magickal Tables that so fascinated and inspired the heart of John Dee.

The full Latin text actually begins as a rather typical medieval grimoire. If one has seen a copy of the *Key of Solomon the King*, one has seen an example of this kind of literature. There are lists of demonologies, and conjurations full of classic (probably Gnostic-descended) barbarous invocations:

> Adracty, Adaci, Adai, Teroccot, Terocot, Tercot, Herm, Hermzm, Hermzisco, Cotzi, Cotzizi, Cotzizizin, Zinzicon, Ginzecohon, Ginchecon, Saradon, Sardon, Sardeon, Belzebuc, Belzscup, Belcupe, Saraduc, Sarcud, Carc, Sathanas, Satnas, Sacsan, Contion, Conoi, Conoison, Satnei, Sapnn, Sappi, Danarcas, Dancas, Dancasnar [*Aldaraia*, Bodley MS 908, folio 51]

Both copies of the grimoire also refer to Adam (to whom, Uriel told Dee, this book was given in Paradise) by the mystical name of "Zadzaczadlin." As we progress in our study of Dee's Angelic magick, we shall see how similar his work is to this material.

Again, like the *Key of Solomon*, it is both astrology and alchemy that form the heart of *Soyga*'s magickal spells—classical aspects of medieval Christian proto-Hermetic mysticism. This gives us some major clues into the core philosophy behind the mysteries transmitted to Dee and Kelley—which are also overflowing with alchemical and astrological references.

Reeds points out that *Soyga* is somewhat unique in the fact that it does not claim any mythological authority. It is not written by any pseudo-Enoch or pseudo-Solomon, and even the claim of ownership by Adam in Paradise comes from Uriel speaking through Edward Kelley rather than from the text itself. This suggests to me that the book was a practicing mage's workbook, rather than something written exclusively for publication.

On the other hand, it does make reference to several medieval medical treatises—mysterious books called *Liber E* and *Liber Os*. This is perhaps less significant to Dee's Angelic magick than it is to the later Rosicrucian movement. There is some evidence to suggest Dee's involvement in (or influence upon) the founding of the movement in early Renaissance Germany.[34] The foundational document of that movement—the *Fama Fraternitatus*, published by physicians in the mid-1600s (after Dee's death)—contains many obscure references to texts such as *Liber M*, *Liber I*, and *Liber T*.

More relevant to Dee's Enochian system is the stress upon mystical writing in the *Book of Soyga*—especially the practice of writing backwards (mimicking the right-to-left nature of Hebrew). Words such as *Sipal* (Lapis), *Munob* (*Bonum*—Latin for Good), and *Retap Retson* (*Pater Noster*) are used throughout the text, and even the title of the book is a reversal of the Greek word *Agyos*, meaning "Holy."

Reeds describes an abundance of the same kind of gematria and wordplay as found in Book II of Agrippa's *Occult Philosophy*. Letters are assigned numerical values (again like Hebrew) as well as occult correspondences, and are then recombined and permutated in various fashions to create magickal Names of Power.

Finally, the book contains the famous thirty-six Tables of *Soyga* (which are discussed within the *Liber Radiorum* section of the grimoire). Space does not permit a full discussion of magickal squares here.[35] It is only needful to point out that such squares were very popular among Hermeticists and Qabalists during the Middle Ages and the Renaissance (roughly Dee's time). Their focus upon gematria and mathematics fascinated great scientific minds such as Dee, Trithemius, and others.

The Tables of *Soyga* are all thirty-six rows by thirty-six columns in size, and the keyword provided for each is exactly six letters long. This is necessary to the magickal square itself—so that the keyword will fit properly into the Table. The keyword is repeatedly written down the left-hand column of each page—in a once-forward and once-backward pattern[36]—a total of six times. Thus we have 6 words x 6 letters = 36 squares. (Because the number six is obviously the basis for this mystery, it is no wonder that Uriel directed Dee to question Michael—the Angel of the Sun and the sixth Sephirah, Tiphareth, in many classical Qabalistic texts.)

Each Table is also labeled with the name of the occult force it supposedly embodies. Tables 1–12 bear the names of the signs of the zodiac in order from Aries to Pisces, and Tables 13–24 repeat the same names again. I would assume these represent the positive aspects of the signs followed by the negative—a common twenty-four-fold view of the zodiac when associated with the twenty-four Elders of the Apocalypse. The following seven Tables, 25–31, are labeled with the names of the seven planets in their proper Qabalistic or Chaldean order (from highest to lowest). The next four, Tables 32–35, then bear the names of the four earthly elements. The collection finally ends with Table 36, which stands alone with the label of *Magistri*—opened with the keyword *MOYSES*.

From what we've seen so far, it is quite possible to draw a connection between the Tables of *Soyga* and the mythological *Sepher Raziel*/ Book of Enoch. Uriel told Dee that *Soyga* was revealed to Adam by good Angels before the Fall from Eden—which parallels the legend of *Sepher Raziel*. The fact that it contains Tables referring to all of the occult forces of the Universe suggests that it, too, is intended as the all-encompassing Book of Life. It even possesses thirty-six Tables exactly, which would have rested well upon legends of Enoch and his 366 books.

We can also find some relation between the Tables of *Soyga* and the Gates of Understanding. For instance, their progression from zodiac, to the planets, to the four earthly elements demonstrates the same kind of downward progression from highest to lowest found with the traditional (Judaic) fifty-Gates system. Moreover, the final Table of *Soyga*—like the final Gate of Understanding—is isolated from the rest of the group and reserved only for the adept. (The keyword for this Table—*MOYSES*—even hints at the only patriarch given credit for passing the Fiftieth Gate of Binah.)

Finally, the labeling of the last Table of *Soyga* as that of *Magistri* (adepthood) indicates the entire set may have an initiatory purpose. Although we do not know how the Tables were intended for magickal use, it is not a stretch in logic to assume they—like all magickal squares—acted as talismanic gateways of some sort. Likely, a mage would have successively invoked the forces embodied in each Table, thereby passing through each Gate in an effort to receive magickal power and Divine revelation from God. In the following chapters, we shall see that this is how Dee's Angelic contacts instructed him to use his own *Book of Loagaeth*.

Endnotes

1. The *Zohar* Online: http://www.kabbalah.com/k/index.php/p=zohar/zohar (accessed November 2, 2009).
2. "And out of the ground made the Lord God to grow [. . .] the Tree of Life also in the midst of the garden, and the Tree of Knowledge of good and evil." [Genesis 2:9]

"To him that overcometh will I give to eat of the Tree of Life, which is in the midst of the paradise of God." [Revelation 2:7]

"In the midst of the street [. . .], and on either side of the river, was there the Tree of Life, which bare twelve manner of fruits, and yielded her fruit every month: and the leaves of the tree were for the healing of the nations." [Revelation 22:2]

3. Although there are ten Sephiroth, three of the them are transcendent, leaving only seven accessible to man.
4. Along with the Seven Matriarchs: Sarah, Rebecca, Rachel, Leah, Miriam, Hannah, and Deborah.
5. Remember that the Hermetic or Rosicrucian Qabalah—such as used by the Hermetic Order of the Golden Dawn—is not always similar to older Judaic systems. The Jewish Qabalist does not necessarily place Saturn within Binah.
6. The fifteenth day of *Nisan*, the first month on the Hebrew calendar, falling in March / April.
7. See *The Fifty Gates of Understanding*, http: / / www.yashanet.com / studies / revstudy / fifty-gates.htm, for this list of virtues (accessed November 2, 2009).
8. Merkavah texts such as the Book of Enoch depict the patriarch gaining the Divine Vision, and then touring the Heavens with various Archangels as guides.
9. Athanasius Kircher, *Oedipus Aegyptiacus,* vol. II, p. 319. See http: / / www.billheidrick .com / Orpd / AKir / AKOeAeII.htm.
10. Please see *The Kabbalah of the Golden Dawn* by Pat Zalewski (St. Paul, MN: Llewellyn, 1993) for more information. Also see the bibliography of this book for more interpretations of the Fifty Gates of Understanding.
11. The Fifth Order usually contains a confused mixture of the nine Angelic Choirs of Pseudo-Dionysus with a truncated hierarchy of the Angels of the Tree of Life. It results in a misleading list of Hebrew names with utterly inaccurate "translations." Because nine Choirs are called for in this Order of Gates, and the Tree of Life hierarchy properly includes ten Choirs, I have opted to retain the classical nine-Choir scheme as found in Agrippa's *Three Books of Occult Philosophy*, Book II, "The Scale of the Number Nine."
12. This is singular in the text. However, chapter 105, vol. 16 of *1 Enoch* refers to Tablets in the plural, so I have duplicated the reference here.
13. The first time by the name *Enoch*. He appears as "Enosh" in a parallel list given previously in the same chapter of Genesis. (There is also an "Enoch" described as the son of Cain in Genesis, chapter 4, but this person does not appear to be related to the patriarch.)
14. Note the Egyptian / Gnostic-flavored reference to the number of days in a year.
15. Jesus of the New Testament notwithstanding. Very much like the translation of Jesus, however, both Enoch and Elijah are said to have become purely spiritual (Angelic) beings upon their ascension. Enoch became *Metatron*, and Elijah became *Sandalphon*.

16. *Enochian* indicates "of Enoch." In relation to Dee's magick, the term "Enochian" merely refers to the *type* of system—similar to saying other medieval systems are "Solomonic."
17. Lyman Abbott's introduction to *The Book of Enoch the Prophet* is highly recommended. See the bibliography of this book, under Laurence.
18. Note the "Whore of Babylon" in the Book of Revelation.
19. Elijah is said to have ascended in the same manner. The song "Chariots of Fire" by Vangelis (Evangelos Odysseas Papathanassiou) is named after this biblical convention.
20. See Revelation, chapter 4.
21. See Revelation, chapter 5.
22. I assume this breaks down to 365 + 1. The number of days in a year played an important role in ancient Gnostic mythos, as did the concept of a singular Divine Source.
23. *Sepher Raziel* = Book of the Secrets of God. This is the name of the Tablets of Heaven in this case. The medieval Jewish grimoire of the same title is merely based upon this legend, purporting to be the earthly copy.
24. See *Legends of the Bible*, by Louis Ginzberg (New York: Simon and Schuster, 1956).
25. See John, chapter 1. The Gnostics associated the Logos with Jesus, rather than the older Djehuti.
26. See David C. Scott, *The Gods of Ancient Egypt—The Book of Thoth* (2004). Online at http://touregypt.net/godsofegypt/thebookofthoth.htm (accessed November 2, 2009).
27. Intense study of the written Scripture, after invoking the Archangelic Prince of the Torah (none other than Metatron under various names) for guidance, was a means toward achieving divine revelation, and thus visions of the Celestial Torah. Joseph Dan's *The Ancient Jewish Mysticism* (Tel Aviv, Israel: MOD Books, 1993) has come highly recommended for this subject. See the bibliography of this book.
28. We will return to the subject of *Loagaeth* in the following chapter.
29. An Angel from Dee's Heptarchic system of magick.
30. *Soyga* is actually a Latin manuscript. However, there are many magickal names in it that appear to be of Arabic origin or influence.
31. This turns out to be in the form of the *Book of Loagaeth*. See the next chapter.
32. Mr. Reeds (his website is http://www.dtc.umn.edu/~reedsj/) is a professional cryptologist. See the bibliography of this book for his work on *Soyga*.
33. Presumably, each keyword has a mystical relationship with an astrological or elemental force, which would then be embodied in its corresponding Table. Reeds calls them arbitrary, but I tend to disagree with such an assumption. They are more likely corruptions of various Hebrew, Greek, and Latin words, as well as other words.
34. See *The Rosicrucian Enlightenment* by Frances Yates (London: Routledge, 2001).
35. A great dissertation on magickal squares can be found in an appendix, by Donald Tyson, in Llewellyn's 1992 publication of Agrippa's *Three Books of Occult Philosophy*.

36. Note the similarity here to the practice of the *Shem haMephoresh*. This seventy-two-fold Name of God is obtained by writing three verses from Exodus in a pattern called "as the ox plows": the first line written right to left, the next line (written underneath the first) from left to right, and the final line written right to left again.

Chapter Two

John Dee's Book of Enoch (The *Book of Loagaeth*)

> And I saw in the right hand of Him that sat on the Throne a Book with writing upon both sides, sealed with seven seals. And I saw a mighty angel proclaiming with a loud voice, "Who is worthy to open the Book, and to loose the seals thereof?" And no man in Heaven, nor in earth, neither under the earth, was able to open the Book, neither to look thereon. [Revelation 5:1–5]

> O Book, Book, Book, life to the good, but truly death itself for the wicked. Great are the wonders sealed up inside you, and great is the name of your Seal. The light of my medicine, for you. [Archangel Raphael, *Five Books of Mystery*, p. 274]

The traditions outlined in the previous chapter converged in Europe in 1583 CE, within the magickal journals of Dr. John Dee and Edward Kelley.[1] These journals record the Christian esotericism the men received from their Angelic contacts—with a heavy focus upon the biblical books of Genesis and the Revelation of St. John, and the foundational assumption that Dee and Kelley were already living within the "End Times"—when the Antichrist would plunge the world into Tribulation and chaos. At the heart of all of this stood the Christian version of Enoch's Celestial Tablets, known in this case as the "Book of Life" or the "Book of the

Lamb." (See Revelation 5—part of which is quoted at the head of this chapter.)[2]

The bulk of what Dee and Kelley received from their Angels was a system of mysticism, by which one might gain access to the mysteries contained within the Book of the Lamb. As we shall see in this chapter, Dee's mysticism combines elements of the fifty Gates of Binah, the practice of the Counting of the Omer, encoded magickal Tables similar to those of the *Book of Soyga*, and the legends of Enoch's Celestial Tablets.

Of course, neither Dee nor Kelley would have had access to the Apocryphal Books of Enoch in the late 1500s. As we saw in chapter 1, these were not rediscovered until the eighteenth century and later. An avid seeker of the fabled Book of Enoch, Dee may certainly have tracked down a few scraps of text here and there, but a full copy of any of the Enochian texts ultimately eluded him.[3]

However, the legends that began with these books were current and popular in Dee's time. (Merkavah mysticism had long fascinated Hermeticists and mystics of the West.) John Dee—a Hermeticist, alchemist, and mystic—had a particular interest in these legends, as he records in his own words:

> O God . . . I have read in thy books and records how Enoch enjoyed thy favor and conversation. With Moses thou wast familiar. And also that to Abraham, Isaac and Jacob, Joshua, Gideon, Esdras, Daniel, Tobias, and sundry others, thy good Angels were sent, by thy disposition, to instruct them, inform them, help them, yea in worldly and domestical affairs; yea and sometimes to satisfy their desires, doubts and questions of thy Secrets. And, furthermore, considering the Shewstone, which the high priests did use—by thy own ordering—wherein they had Lights and Judgments in their great doubts.[4] And considering also that thou (O God) didst not refuse to instruct thy prophets (then, called Seers) to give true answers to common people of things economical, as Samuel [did] for Saul . . .[5]
>
> And remembering the good counsel thy good Apostle James giveth, saying, "If any of you lack wisdom, let him ask of God, that giveth to all men liberally, and upbraideth not; and it shall be given him." And

> that Solomon the Wise, did so, even immediately by thy self, attain to his wonderful wisdom.
>
> Therefore, seeing I was sufficiently taught and confirmed, that this wisdom could not be attained by man's hand,[6] or by human power, but only from thee (O God) indirectly, or directly.[7] [*Five Books of Mystery*, Preface, pp. 58–59]

Thus it is no surprise that, when Dee finally made contact with Angelic beings, the legends of the ancient prophet Enoch were of some importance. For instance, Dee once asked the Angel Illemese about the Apocryphal Book of Enoch, as mentioned in the Epistle of Jude:

> **Dee:** Belike then, they were delivered from one to another by tradition or else Enoch his book, or prophesy, doth—or may seem to be—written in the same language. Because mention is made of it in the New Testament in Jude his Epistle where he hath said, "Enoch also, the seventh from Adam, prophesied of these . . .[8]
>
> **Illemese:** I must distinguish with you. Before the flood, the spirit of God was not utterly obscured in men. Their memories were greater, their understanding more clear, and their traditions, most unsearchable. Nothing remained of Enoch but (and if it please your mastership) might have been carried in a cart. I can not bring you the brass, but I can shew you the books. [*Five Books of Mystery*, pp. 354–55]

Illemese here speaks of the Enochian mythos as it has existed for centuries—including the central role of the biblical Deluge in the loss of the Wisdom of Enoch.

Another Angel to discuss the prophet Enoch with Dee and Kelley was named Ave, who offers a rather detailed version of the legend of Enoch. In fact, Ave's Enochian speeches[9] are the principal reasons why Dee's journals are classified as "Enochian" literature.[10] Ave says:

> The Lord appeared unto Enoch, and was merciful unto him, opened his eyes, that he might see and judge the earth, which was unknown unto his Parents, by reason of their fall.[11] For the Lord said, Let us shew unto Enoch, the use of the earth. And lo, Enoch was wise, and full of the spirit of wisdom. And he said unto the Lord, Let there be remembrance

of thy mercy, and let those that love thee taste of this after me. O let not thy mercy be forgotten. And the Lord was pleased.

And after fifty days Enoch had written, and this was the Title of his books, *Let Those That Fear God, and Are Worthy, Read.*

But behold, the people are waxed wicked, and became unrighteous, and the Spirit of the Lord was far off, and gone away from them. So that those that were unworthy began to read. And the Kings of the earth said thus against the Lord, What is it that we cannot do? Or who is he, that can resist us?

And the Lord was vexed, and he sent in amongst them an hundred and fifty Lions, and spirits of wickedness, error, and deceit. And they appeared unto them, for the Lord had put them between those that are wicked, and his good Angels. And they began to counterfeit the doings of God and his power, for they had power given them so to do, so that the memory of Enoch washed away. And the spirits of error began to teach them Doctrine, which from time to time unto this age, and unto this day, hath spread abroad into all parts of the world, and is the skill and cunning of the wicked. Hereby they speak with Devils. Not because they have power over the Devils, but because they are joined unto them in the league and Discipline of their own Doctrine.

For behold, in the knowledge of the mystical figures, and the use of their presence is the gift of God delivered unto Enoch, and by Enoch his request to the faithful, that thereby they might have the true use of Gods creatures, and of the earth whereon they dwell. [*A True and Faithful Relation*, p. 174]

This legend suggests that the wickedness of mankind (presumably before the Great Deluge) was the result of giving too much knowledge into the hands of those who were not ready. ("Those who were unworthy began to read.") After this, the wisdom contained in the Tablets of Enoch was obscured among humanity. Ave then continues:

Now hath it pleased God to deliver this Doctrine again out of darkness, and to fulfill His promise with thee (for the Books of Enoch), to whom he sayeth as he said unto Enoch, "Let those that are worthy understand this, by thee, that it may be one witness of my promise toward thee." Come therefore, O thou Cloud, and wretched darkness, come forth I say out of this Table: for the Lord again hath opened the earth: and she shall become known to the worthy. [*A True and Faithful Relation*, p. 174]

Therefore, the Angels' plan was to deliver the Celestial "Book of Enoch" to Dee and Kelley. (We shall explore their motives for this revelation.) In fact, by the time Dee recorded these words from Ave, he had already received the entire text of a "Holy Book" written in the Angelical language. However, it was not directly referred to as the "Book of Enoch" until Ave does so later in the journals:

My brother, I see thou dost not understand the mystery of this Book, or work, thou hast in hand. But I told thee, it was the knowledge that God delivered unto Enoch. [*A True and Faithful Relation*, p. 196]

And so, let us take an in-depth look at this Doctrine—delivered again out of darkness:

The Holy *Book of Loagaeth* (Speech from God)

Dee and Kelley had already been at work with the Angels for some time, receiving the particulars of the Angelic scrying tools and the Heptarchic[12] system. (This comprises the bulk of books One through Four of Dee's *Five Books of the Mysteries*—Sloane MS 3188.)[13] Book Five, then, is where we find the first descriptions of a new "Holy Book." The next manuscript in the Sloane collection—MS 3189—contains the Holy Book itself. This is technically classified as the *Sixth and Holy Book of the Mysteries*, and is also called the *Book of Enoch* and the *Book of Loagaeth* (Speech from God).[14]

The Holy Book was formally introduced to Dee and Kelley, by the Archangel Raphael, with these words:

Behold! Behold, yea, let Heaven and earth behold: For with this, they were created. And it is the voice and speech of Him, which proceeded from the First, and is the First, whose glorious Name be exalted in his own horn of honor. Lo, this it is. And it is truth; whose truth shall endure forever. [*Five Books of Mystery*, p. 268]

The concept of "He who proceeded from the First, and is the First" comes from ancient Gnosticism. In Gnostic mythology, the *Christos* (or

Logos—Word) was born directly and entirely from the Divine Source itself. Therefore, the Logos was both God *and* the Son of God—two facets of the same gem. See the Book of John, chapter 1: "In the beginning was the Word, and the Word was with God, and the Word was God."

Note, also, that Raphael claims this Book contains the "voice and speech" of the Christos, and that both Heaven and earth were created therewith. (Dee notes in the margin: "The Book, the first language of God-Christ.") This is another ancient Gnostic concept related directly to the Christos. To the Gnostics, the Highest God was far removed from the imperfect physical realm. However, the Christos was an active and creative aspect of Divinity. All things in the Universe were created after patterns established by the Christos. Once again, see the Book of John, chapter 1: "All things were made by him, and without him was nothing made . . . In him was life, and the life was the light of mankind."

Therefore, we have in this Holy Book the very words that the God-Christ used to create the Universe. (See Genesis chapter 1, where each phase of creation is initiated with the words "God said . . . " Consider that Dee's Holy Book will eventually be entitled *Loagaeth*, the Speech from God.)

Three Types of Knowledge

The biblical Creation is not the whole of what is contained within the Book. Later in the journals (in the appendix to the *Five Books*), Dee records a conversation with the Angel Illemese[15] that expands our understanding of the nature of the Holy Book:

> It only consisteth in the mercy of God, and the Characters of these books. For, behold, as there is nothing that cometh or springeth from God, but it is as God, and hath secret Majestical and inexplicable Operation in it: So every letter here bringeth forth the Names of God. But, indeed, they are but one Name; but according to the local and former being, do comprehend the universal generation corruptible and incorruptible of every thing. It followeth, then, it must needs comprehend the end of all things. Thus much, hitherto. [*Five Books of Mystery*, p. 382]

This is the first time we are told that the Book is associated not only with Creation, but also comprehends (encompasses) "the end of all things." Remember my statement at the beginning of this chapter, that both Genesis and the Revelation of St. John play prominent roles in this system.

Later in the appendix to the *Five Books*, Dee and Kelley make contact with the Archangel Uriel. This entity, too, has something to say concerning the contents of the Holy Book:

> This book, and holy key, which unlocketh the secrets of God His determination—as concerning the beginning, present being, and end of this world—is so reverent and holy, that I wonder (I speak in your sense) why it is delivered to those that shall decay. So excellent and great are the Mysteries therein contained, above the capacity of man. [*Five Books of Mystery*, p. 393]

So, the mystical text comprehends the beginning, present, *and* end of the Universe. In other words, all things in Creation and Time are represented in the Holy Book. (Just like the Celestial Tablets, *Sepher Raziel*, and *Book of Thoth*, described in chapter 1.) Uriel later returns to this subject, revealing the three types of knowledge contained in the text:

> For it is said before that the Book containeth three types of knowledge:
> 1. The knowledge of God, truly.
> 2. The number and doing of His Angels, perfectly.
> 3. The beginning and ending of Nature, substantially.
> And this hath answered a great doubt. [*Five Books of Mystery*, p. 399]

Later in the journals, after Dee and Kelley have received all but the last page of the Book, a female entity named Galvah—apparently the Mother of Angels, as we shall see later—takes over the sessions. She speaks further about the nature and contents of the Holy Book:

> For herein is the creation of Adam with his transgression. The Dignity and wisdom he had. The error and horror wherein he was drowned, yea herein is the power spread of the highest working in all creatures. [. . .]
>
> The life of all things is here known: The reward of death for those who are rewarded for life. [. . .]

> Whatsoever hath been from the beginning (since it was said in Divine Determination, Be it done) is here enclosed. [*A True and Faithful Relation,* p. 18]

Still later in Dee's journals, an Angel by the name of Nalvage offers his own description of the Book:

> These Tables are to be written, not by man, but by the finger of her which is mother of Virtue.[16] Wherein the whole World, (to flesh incredible) all Creatures, and in all kinds, are numbered, in being, and multitude. The measure and proportion of that substance, which is Transitory, and shall wax old. These things and mysteries are your parts, and portions sealed, as well by your own knowledge, as the fruit of your Intercession. The knowledge of Gods Creatures. [*A True and Faithful Relation*, p. 64]

I note that Nalvage above refers to a "substance" that is transitory (that is to say, mortal) and will grow old. This substance is likely the "material essence"—or physical matter of the Universe—described by Plato. (Plato actually described three essences, which were also adopted by the Gnostics: The first is the spiritual essence, which is pure and immortal. The second is the material essence, which is mortal and will eventually die. The third is the animate essence, which is a mixture of the previous two. Human beings are composed of the animate essence.)

The Last Prophecy of the World

The Angels also had a few things to say about the Holy Book and its relation to the Christian concept of the End Times. (Keep in mind that Dee was a devout Christian in sixteenth-century Europe. He would have taken the subject of the End Times very seriously, and would have firmly believed they were near.)

During one of their sessions with Uriel, the Archangel told the two men that the testimony of the Holy Book heralds the Second Coming (of Christ), and will not be reserved for a single nation or people:

> The second of the greatest prophesie, is this, O ye mortal men! For the first was of Himself, that He should come.[17] And this, is from Him, in respect that He will come.[18] Neither are you to speak the words of this

> Testimony in one place, or in one people, but that the Nations of the whole world may know that there is a GOD which forgetteth not the truth of His promise, nor the safeguard of His chosen, for the greatness of His glory. [*Five Books of Mystery*, p. 394]

In this same session, Uriel warns the two men (at length) to prepare, for the Antichrist is already born and the End Times are at hand. In fact, Uriel associates the reception of *Loagaeth* by Dee and Kelley with the initiation of the Tribulation.[19]

> For why? The Lord hath sent His angels already to visit the earth, and to gather the sins thereof together, that they may be weighed before him in the balance of Justice. And then is the time that the promise of God shall be fulfilled. Doubt not, for we are good Angels. [*Five Books of Mystery*, p. 394]

Later, the Archangel Gabriel elaborates upon the Tribulation, highlighting the advent of the Holy Book (the "Last Prophecy of the World") and the involvement of Dee and Kelley in the End Times:

> But in you two is figured the time to come. For many shall cleave unto the Lord, even at the first call.[20] [. . .]
>
> And these are the latter days. And this is the last Prophesie of the World.[21] Now! Now, shall one King rise up against another, and there shall be bloodshed throughout all the World. Fighting between the Devil his Kingdom, and the Kingdom of Light.
>
> As for you, thus sayeth the Lord: I . . . have delivered unto you the Testimony of my Spirit to Come. For, my Barn hath been long without Threshers. And I have kept my flails for a long time hid in unknown places. Which flail is the Doctrine that I deliver unto you. Which is the Instrument of thrashing, wherewith you shall beat the sheafs, that the Corn which is scattered, and the rest may be all one. [*A True and Faithful Relation*, p. 161]

The last lines of Gabriel's above speech invoke the image of threshing wheat in a barn as an analogy to the Tribulation and the threshing of the "wheat from the chaff" among human souls. Most important for us here, we see that the Doctrine of *Loagaeth* is described as the flail that shall be the "instrument of thrashing."

Returning to Uriel's sermon about the End Times, we find the Archangel reveals what may be the most profound words yet in relation to the Holy Book:

> Out of this shall be restored the holy books, which have perished even from the beginning, and from the first that lived.[22] And herein shall be deciphered perfect truth from imperfect falsehood, True religion from false and damnable errors with all Arts, which are proper to the use of man, the first and sanctified perfection. Which when it hath spread a while, THEN COMETH THE END. [*Five Books of Mystery*, p. 395]

Thus, according to Uriel, the Angels were seeding this "Testimony" into the world through Kelley and Dee. The influence of the Book was to spread among humanity for a time, and then would come the end of the World of Man and the establishment of God's kingdom. (See the final chapter of the Revelation of St. John.)

What is so profound here is Uriel's suggestion that this Book will "restore the holy books" and "decipher . . . true religion." Dee and Kelley encountered several Angels who referred to the Holy Book as a new "Testimony" or "Doctrine"—Uriel included:

> Behold, Behold, Mark O, and Behold. Each line hath stretched himself even to his end, and the Midst is glorious to the good, and dishonor to the wicked. Heaven and earth must decay. So, shall not the words of this Testimony. [*Five Books of Mystery*, p. 328]

The Angel Nalvage also refers to a Doctrine when giving his own explanation of the virtues of the Holy Book:

> In our Doctrine there is nothing taught but the state of the world, here, and to come. The prophecies of time, and the knitting up of God his mysteries, opened from time to time, to those that are his sanctified: as testimonies in the Creation and Operation of his Creatures; whereof this Doctrine is a part. The Prophets in their times were not ignorant by revelation of the good will of their Creator. The Apostles, in Christ his Kingdom, were made partakers of the mysteries to come . . . So that this Doctrine is the mysteries of the word of God, sealed from the beginning, now delivered unto man, for that Reformation which must be in One unity established unto the end. [. . .] The fruit of our Doctrine

> is that God should be praised. [. . .] The very key and entrance into the secret mysteries of God (in respect of His determination on earth), bringing with it reward in the end of eternal glory, which is the greatest Treasure. [*A True and Faithful Relation,* p. 64]

Considering the time and place in which Dee lived, Nalvage is treading on some dangerous religious ground in this speech. He points out that revelations were given to the Prophets of old—from whence we get the Old Testament of the Bible. Then, revelations were opened to the Apostles of Christ—whereby we derived the New Testament of the Bible. Therefore, Nalvage is here suggesting that new prophecies will be revealed through Dee's Holy Book—which would logically result in an entirely new Testament. Several weeks later, Nalvage returns to the subject of this new Doctrine:

> And lo, He called you, and you became drunken, and foolish with the spirit of God: And it was said Descend, for he calleth, and hath called. And Raphael that brought up the prayers descended: and he was full with the power, and spirit of God:[23] and it became a Doctrine, such was never from the beginning. [. . .]
>
> This selfsame Art is it, which is delivered unto you as an infallible Doctrine, containing in it the waters which run through many Gates: even above the Gate of Innocence, wherein you are taught to find out the Dignity and Corruption of nature. Also, [you will be][24] made partakers of the secret judgments of the Almighty to be made manifest, and to be put into execution. [*A True and Faithful Relation,* p. 77]

Later in the journals, Nalvage and the Archangel Gabriel (his superior) are speaking in unison about this same Doctrine:

> These things, that is to say, this Doctrine, delivered by us, is of God; and of his mercies granted unto you, which cannot be in vain. And therefore to be performed, for the secret determinations of God are unknown unto us. [*A True and Faithful Relation,* p. 92]

The idea of a brand-new Doctrine or Testament was quite alarming to Christians of Dee's time—especially as the Church was already segmenting into Catholic and Protestant sects. For instance, Meric Casaubon, who published many of Dee's journals in *A True and Faithful Relation* in 1659, had this to say of the Holy Book:

> This Book (had things succeeded) should have been instead of a Bible; as the *Al Koran*,[25] (and much of the same subject), is among the Islamic peoples.[26] [. . .] A very effectual way to draw people, under color of a New Law, new lights, and Doctrines . . . from Heaven. [*A True and Faithful Relation*, VI, p. 10]

This description from Casaubon may be a bit unfair. While the Holy Book is certainly described by the Angels as a Doctrine delivered from God to mankind, they never indicated to Dee and Kelley that it would *replace* any existing Scripture. Instead, it would "restore" all of the world's holy books (i.e., by removing errors from them that have crept in over generations). This would be much more in line with Dee's Hermetic thinking—as he would have recognized all religions and their scriptures as containing some amount of Truth and some amount of error. He would have been looking for a Universal Religion (akin to Gnosticism) that underlay all existing religions.

The last entity to appear for Dee and Kelley, during the reception of the Holy Book, was the Mother of Angels, Galvah. Before delivering the final page of the Book, Galvah provides the following important information:

> Touching the Book, it shall be called Logah: which in your language signifieth Speech from God. Write after this sort L O A G A E T H:[27] it is to be sounded Logah. This word is of great signification, I mean in respect of the profoundness thereof. [*A True and Faithful Relation*, p. 19]

Note that Galvah has just named the Holy Book *Loagaeth* (pronounced "loh-gah"), which signifies "speech from God." Even though all but the final page of the Book had been transmitted previously, it was never referred to as *Loagaeth* until Galvah did so. (As we shall see later in this chapter, the Holy Book bears Angelic words other than *Loagaeth* on its cover. However, these words are not necessarily the proper title of the Book itself.)

In the same session, Galvah also adds:

> Happy are they, which are covered with the Pearls of Righteousness, and on whose head there is a Garland of gladness: For unto those belongeth to taste of the Fountain of true wisdom. Is it not written of this book, that it teacheth nature in all degrees? The judgment hereof is Intellectual. [. . .]
>
> How thou art God knoweth: But comfort yourselves in this; that neither this Testimony can perish, neither unto you can remain any slavery. [*A True and Faithful Relation*, p. 20]

As might be expected, only those who "are covered with the Pearls of Righteousness" can gain benefit from the Holy *Book of Loagaeth*. Uriel made a similar statement (shown previously in this section) when he said that the text of the Holy Book was "glorious to the good, and dishonor to the wicked."

This would have been a given to Christians like Dee and Kelley, considering the Book's relationship with the End Times and the Revelation of St. John. The *Book of Loagaeth*, according to this worldview, represents the fountain of God's Wisdom from which only the Chosen are to partake.[28]

Let Those That Fear God, and Are Worthy, Read

Kelley's First Vision of the Holy Book

On March 24th, 1583, the Archangel Raphael granted Kelley his first vision of the Holy *Book of Loagaeth*.[29] It appeared as a book with forty-eight leaves of gold. (A "leaf" is a sheet of paper—in this case, gold—bound into a book. Each leaf in a book has a front and a back—so there are two pages printed upon it.)

The writing within this Holy Book appeared wet, as if written with fresh blood. (According to Christian tradition, the Celestial *Book of Life* is written in the Blood of the sacrificed Lamb, or Christ. See the Revelation of St. John, chapter 5, for the Book and the Lamb.) The letters and words themselves were not in English, but written in some kind of hieroglyphic or magickal alphabet that neither Dee nor Kelley had ever seen.

Once Kelley had counted forty-eight leaves in the Book, Raphael replied:

> It is finished. One is one [that][30] neither is, was, or shall be known. And yet there are just so many. These have so many names, of the so many mysteries that went before. [*Five Books of Mystery*, p. 263]

Raphael's above statement is certainly obscure. It is only thanks to information given by the Angels in later sessions that it makes any sense at all. Put simply, Raphael is confirming the forty-eight leaves reported by Kelley, but also hinting that there is another leaf that " . . . neither is, was, or shall be known." (Therefore, the true number of leaves is forty-nine.) Not only this, but this "extra" leaf is, in fact, considered number one of the forty-nine.

Later, the text of the first "unknown" leaf is revealed to Kelley and recorded by Dee (complete with diacritical marks and a few pronunciation notes). However, even then, Raphael reminds the men that the mysteries of the first leaf must remain closed for now:

> It is not to be spoken, but in the time of His own time. [*Five Books of Mystery*, p. 291]

Since the text of *Loagaeth* is composed of the Words of God, I assume it is the message contained in the first leaf that is "not to be spoken" until the time "of His own time." Because we already know of the Holy Book's relationship to the Book of Revelation, we can assume that "His own time" represents the promised Second Coming of Christ and establishment of the Kingdom of God.

We will learn more about the first leaf of *Loagaeth* later in this chapter.

Kelley's Second Vision of the Holy Book

On March 26th, 1583, Kelley received his second vision of the Holy Book.[31] It appeared exactly as it had previously, but this time with a bit more detail. This time, Kelley could see that each page was a huge 49 x 49 Table (forty-nine columns and forty-nine rows). This made for a total of 2,401 cells in each Table—which Kelley described as filled with letters, " . . . some more than other."[32]

The fact that Kelley saw some of the cells with "more [letters] than other" cells indicates that he was already seeing the forty-nine-leaf version of *Loagaeth*. As recorded later in the journals, the first ("hidden") leaf of the Book contains an entire word in each cell, while most of the remaining forty-eight had only a single character in each cell. Therefore, Kelley was likely seeing the first leaf when he described some cells with "more letters" (i.e., entire words) than the others.

The fact that there are really forty-nine leaves in *Loagaeth* (rather than the forty-eight originally reported) is confirmed later in the journals. For instance, several days after Kelley's second vision of the Holy Book, Raphael discusses its "49 parts":

> As I have said: the 49 parts of this Book—49 voices, whereunto the so many powers, with their inferiors and subjects, have been, are, and shall be obedient.[33] [. . .] Every Element hath 49 manner of understandings. Therein is comprehended so many languages. They are all spoken at once, and severally, by themselves, by distinction may be spoken. Until thou come to the City, thou canst not behold the beauty thereof. [*Five Books of Mystery*, pp. 296–97]

By "49 voices," Raphael likely means 49 *voicings*—or speeches—of God. From these forty-nine speeches of the God-Christ can be drawn *forty-nine* interpretations.[34] There are even forty-nine languages contained in the text—though they are all interwoven and spoken at once.[35]

Obviously, the number 49 (or 7x 7) plays a vital role to the *Loagaeth* system. As the Angel Nalvage explains (after Dee and Kelley had recorded the text of all forty-nine leaves of the Holy Book):

> You have 49 Tables: In those Tables are contained the mystical and holy voices of the Angels, dignified. [*A True and Faithful Relation*, p. 64]

Remember that there are *two* pages for every leaf of a book. Thus, there are technically *ninety-eight* Tables (each one, forty-nine rows by forty-nine columns) found upon the pages of *Loagaeth*. However, in the above quote, Nalvage teaches that these are counted as only forty-nine. Each Table, then, has both a front and a back—thereby occupying *both* sides of a single leaf in the Book.

It is quite interesting to compare Dee's forty-nine Tables of *Loagaeth* with the thirty-six Tables of *Soyga* (see chapter 1). Both of them are composed of magickal squares based upon square-root numbers (the product of a number multiplied by itself.) The Tables of *Soyga* (thirty-six by thirty-six cells) are based upon 6 x 6 = 36.[36] Meanwhile, Dee's Tables of *Loagaeth* (forty-nine by forty-nine) are simply the next step in the square-root pattern, based upon 7 x 7 = 49.[37] The holy number seven plays a major role in the ancient Merkavah traditions of the Jewish people, as well as quite a few of the classical grimoiric texts to which Dee and Kelley had access.[38]

The Heptarchic mysteries are also based upon this seven-fold design—including the Seal of Truth, Holy Table, the seven Ensigns of Creation, and the forty-nine good Angels.[39] As we shall see later in this chapter, the mysteries of *Loagaeth* are intimately connected with the Heptarchic system through this seven-fold relationship.

Given what the Angels have said about the contents of the Holy Book (the beginning, contents, and end of Time), it is reasonable—as with the *Heptarchia*—to associate the forty-nine Tables with the Seven Days of Creation. (Technically, the Seven Days—along with a hypothetical "Eighth Day" associated with the End Times—encompass the entire span of the Universe from beginning to end. We are currently living in the Seventh Day of Rest.)

Supporting this, the Mother Galvah makes the following cryptic statement just after delivering the text of the forty-ninth leaf of *Loagaeth*:

> These are those seven. [*A True And Faithful Relation*, p. 19]

Later in the journals, the Angel Nalvage makes an equally cryptic statement just after delivering the Key to the mysteries of the second leaf:[40]

> This is therefore the key of the first seven, according to the proportion of the first Creation. [*A True And Faithful Relation*, p. 88]

These two statements associate both the second[41] and final leaves of the Holy Book with a mysterious "seven." ("According to the proportion of the first Creation.") I suspect they are indications that *Loagaeth*—from the second to the forty-ninth Tables—encompasses the Seven Days of Creation as depicted in Genesis 1 (plus the dreaded "Eighth Day" of the Tribulation).

Kelley's Third Vision of the Holy Book

On April 6th, 1583, Kelley received what I call the "third vision of the Holy Book."[42] Of course, Kelley had seen the Book many times by this point—as this occurs after he had recorded forty-eight lines of the first leaf (side A). However, this is the third time Kelley saw something new about the appearance and construction of the Book itself.

Just after the transmission of the forty-eighth line, the cover of the Book was suddenly displayed to Kelley. It was blue in color, and made from a thin, light silk.[43] On this cover were the words *Amzes naghezes Hardeh*. (Note that this is some weeks before Galvah entitles the Book *Loagaeth*.) Kelley reported that these words signify "The Universal Name of Him that created universally be praised and extolled forever."

However, later in the journals, an Angel named Ave suggests that Enoch's Book was entitled *Let Those that Fear God, and Are Worthy, Read*.[44] Dee notes at this point, "The title of Enoch's Books expounded into English." Therefore, it is possible that Ave's version is the more literal translation of the title *Amzes naghezes Hardeh*.

From the Right Hand to the Left . . . as in the Hebrew Bible

Another important, and unique, feature of *Loagaeth* is that it is written entirely from right to left. That is, it is unique among *Western* mystical texts. Meanwhile, it shares this feature with all books written in Hebrew—a Semitic language that also runs from right to left.

Once Raphael showed Kelley his second vision of the Holy Book (where we first see the 49 x 49 Tables full of letters), the Archangel's next action was to draw a series of twenty-one hieroglyphic characters from the pages.[45] The characters, as recorded in Dee's journal, are the letters of the Angelical alphabet. (I will cover this alphabet in depth in chapter 5.) However, more important now, this Holy alphabet is recorded as running from right (the first letter—*Pa*) to left (the last letter—*Gisg*). This is the first indication in the journals that the language is written in the leftward Semitic fashion.

The next indication is found just after Raphael transmitted the first word of the first leaf: *Zuresch*—a word of seven letters.[46] Dee then drew a 7 x 7 Table showing the numbers 1–7 (relating to the seven letters of

Zuresch) running "backward"—that is, from right to left. (I think perhaps Dee, after hearing the first word was exactly seven letters, drew the 7 x 7 Table in case he was about to receive another magickal square. However, no square was revealed, and Dee left the Table blank except for the numbers 1–7 in the top row.)

I should point out that Dee recorded *Zuresch*, and all of the words transmitted by Raphael, both in English letters and the usual Western rightward style of writing. Apparently, it is only when the text is written in Angelical characters that it must be written leftward. (The same convention is followed with Hebrew.)

Of course, if a book's text is written leftward, it follows that the pages of the book must do likewise. For instance, take any book written in English,[47] and lay it facedown so the book's spine is toward your right hand. (You'll be looking at the back cover.) Now, open the back cover so you are looking at the last leaf of the book. If the same book were written in Hebrew, what you just saw as the back cover would have actually been the front cover. And the leaf you saw after opening the cover would contain the *first page* in the book. The text would begin in the upper-right-hand corner of the paper and run toward the left margin.

Dee's journals highlight this difference in page ordering several times. In one instance, Dee outright states that Angelical reads leftward:

> . . . in my mind it seemeth requisite[48] that as all the writing and reading of that holy language is from the right hand to the left, so the beginning of the book must be (as it were, in respect of our most usual manner of books, in all languages of Latin, Greek, English, etc.) at the end of the book. And the end, at the beginning, as in the Hebrew Bible. [*Five Books of Mystery*, p. 411]

Uriel confirmed Dee's observation (on the next page of the journal) by suggesting that Dee's judgment was directed by God above, "He that sayeth, 'Do this,' directeth thy judgment."

After Kelley had recorded most of the Holy Book in the usual rightward fashion (and in English characters),[49] the Mother Galvah arrived to instruct Dee on writing a "perfected copy."[50] In part, this meant the text had to be rewritten in the leftward fashion, so the last page of the book would fall upon what we Westerners consider the "first leaf":

> The first leaf (as you call it) is the last of the book.[51] [. . .] Write the book (after your order) backward, but alter not the form of the letters, I speak in respect of the places. [*A True and Faithful Relation*, p. 19]

I assume that by "places," Galvah meant the proper ordering of letters had to be preserved for the words when written leftward as when written rightward. In Angelical, the text would be a mirror image of the text in English, but both texts would sound the same when read aloud. (This is different from *Soyga*, which actually spelled words backward to form new—but still rightward-reading—words. Such as *Soyga* itself, which is a reversal of the Greek word *Agyos*.)[52]

The Reception of the Forty-Nine Tables

The reception of the Tables of *Loagaeth* began on Good Friday, March 29th, 1583.[53] When Kelley received the text of the forty-nine leaves, he did so by first entering a kind of trance. As he sat gazing into the crystal, Dee records, a "sword of flame" came from the shewstone and thrust into Kelley's head. The scryer described "a thing immediately creeping within his head, and in that pang became all in a sweat." He greatly disliked this feeling, which continued for about fifteen minutes before it subsided (or "came to rest") somewhat.[54]

This process took place each time Kelley sat down to transcribe the language in the Holy Book. It appears to be a form of shamanic ecstasy, and seems to parallel the Christian mystery of the invocation of the Holy Spirit, often associated with speaking in tongues.[55] Kelley, while in his trance, could read the language within the Book fluently. After each session, the fire would withdraw from his head back into the shewstone—after which he no longer understood the language.

The Archangel Raphael delivered the initial lines of the first leaf of *Loagaeth* in a very meticulous fashion. With a rod of gold, Raphael pointed to the first cell on the Table in the Holy Book—indicating the word written there in fresh blood. He then spelled the word letter by letter, which Kelley repeated for Dee to record.

Previously, I used this first word—*Zuresch*—as an example of the Holy Book's leftward style of writing. Since it happens to be the very first word of *Loagaeth*, we can continue to use it as an example here. What Raphael actually transmitted to the two men was not the completed word, but a string of Angelic letter-names: *Ceph* (Z), *Van* (U), *Don* (R), *Graph* (E), *Fam* (S), *Veh* (C), *Na* (H).[56] By working in this manner, there would be a very low error rate in the transmission, and words could be quickly and easily reviewed and corrected later on.

However, with thousands of words to receive, Dee was concerned the project would soon become overwhelming. The first two lines alone had consisted of ninety-eight words transmitted letter by letter, and there were yet forty-seven lines to go on just side A of that Table![57] Therefore, Dee asked Raphael if some kind of abridgment of this letter-by-letter method might be used instead.[58]

Apparently, this angered Raphael—as the vision of the Holy Book suddenly vanished from Kelley's sight. After a prayer from Dee, the vision appears to Kelley once more, and Raphael returns to lecture the two men. Apparently because of Dee's "inappropriate" request, the Archangel states that he will not appear in the crystal again until *Loagaeth* has been transmitted entirely.

However, before leaving, Raphael assures them that his *office* will remain present. Indeed, the remainder of the Tables (the last excluded) are delivered to the men by "a Voice" coupled with a vision of the Holy Book in the stone. This Voice, then, can safely be considered the voice of Raphael.

Nevertheless, Dee was granted his request for an abridgment to the transmission process. Beginning with line three, the text of the First Table of *Loagaeth* is delivered word by word, rather than letter by letter. While this took a huge workload off of Dee and Kelley, it does create something of a problem for us today. With the first two lines, we have no doubt as to exactly how the words are to be spelled in Angelical characters—because each letter was named individually. However, with the rest of the First Table, we have only words that Kelley spoke aloud and Dee recorded phonetically.

My own analysis of the text[59] suggests that several words are spelled phonetically—depending on how Dee heard each word at the time. Therefore, the same word might appear in different lines of the text spelled in slightly different ways. Yet, in other cases, the spellings do seem to be exact—and Dee even makes notes here and there to help us with proper Angelical spelling or pronunciation. (Any such notes are included with the entries in the Lexicon in the second volume of this work.)

In Forty Days Must the Book Be Perfected

The overall reception of the Holy Book was marked as a magickal operation in its own right. Note that it began on Good Friday (March 29th), and this was not coincidental. Exactly eight days into the reception of the text, the Archangel Uriel appeared to inform the men that there was a time limit on their work:

> Behold (sayeth the Lord) I will breathe upon men, and they shall have the spirit of Understanding. In 40 days must the Book of the Secrets, and Key of this World, be written. [. . .] To the end he may see and perform the time of God his Abridgment. [*Five Books of Mystery*, p. 327]

This is the first of two references to a forty-day period in relation to the reception of the Holy Book. This would seem to make sense. The Old Testament of the Bible records forty days and nights of the Great Deluge, and the same amount of time for Moses' spiritual retreat on Mount Sinai. Moreover, in the New Testament, Jesus is depicted as fasting for forty days and nights during his own spiritual retreat in the wilderness. However, there may yet be a deeper mystery to the forty-day time period associated with *Loagaeth*.

Notice that Uriel does not mention this forty-day "deadline" until eight days into the process. That means that the total time period of the reception would come to forty-eight days—exactly the number of Tables in *Loagaeth* whose mysteries the Angels have promised to open. (And, as we shall see in a following chapter, the same number as the Angelical Keys used to open those mysteries.)

Forty-eight days from Good Friday (March 29th) puts the deadline at May 8th. Just three days before that time (on May 5th), Uriel appears in the shewstone once again to establish another forty-day period. This time it is for recopying the Holy Book from Kelley's English-lettered originals into a "perfected" copy:

> In 40 days more must this book be perfected in his own manner, to the intent that you also be perfected in the workmanship of Him, which hath sealed it.[60] [*Five Books of Mystery*, p. 395]

If this "perfected copy" of the Book were completed forty days after the original May 8th deadline, then Dee would have had to complete the project by June 17th. However, this does not appear to be the case in Dee's journals. As we shall see, Dee is later told to begin writing the perfected copy on June 18th. If Dee begins the project on that day, forty days will take him to the very beginning of August.

The perfected copy of *Loagaeth* must also be written in Angelical characters, as Dee notes after the previously quoted sessions in his journal:

> I required the perfect form of the 21 letters, that I might imitate the same . . . in the Holy Book writing, etc. [*Five Books of Mystery*, p. 398]

And here, in a later conversation Dee had with the Angel Nalvage:

> You mean the mystical Letters, wherein the holy book is promised to be written. [*A True and Faithful Relation*, p. 78]

Moreover, as we know, the Book must be written in the Semitic leftward fashion. This perfected version would have to be completed before the Book could be put to practical use.

Dee had many additional questions regarding the construction of the perfected Holy Book. However, the Angels were unconcerned with minor details:

> **Dee:** I was desirous to know whether the book were to be written in paper or parchment; in what color the lines were to be ruled (green or blue, etc.) and of diverse other doubts, necessary to be dissolved, I was careful to have some advisement. [*Five Books of Mystery*, p. 406]

> **Uriel:** Fulfill those things that are commanded. Form and write thy book after thine own judgment. God His determination is just. Therefore, put-to your hands. More than hath been said, and more plainly, cannot be uttered. [*Five Books of Mystery*, p. 408]

Also, of interest is Dee's eventual observation about the First Table of *Loagaeth*.[61] Because it contained an entire word—rather than a single letter—in each cell, Dee knew the text would never fit into two 49 x 49 Tables on a single leaf. So, he asked Uriel for permission to write the text without a Table, over several pages. The Archangel accepts this necessary convention. The remaining forty-eight pages, however, do contain Tables.

Begin to Practice in August

The forty-day periods are only one example of the shamanic style of magickal timing utilized by the Angels. From the Archangel Uriel, the two men learned that a time had been established for the practical use of the (perfected) Holy Book. It is only at this set time, and not before, that the Mysteries contained within the Tables of *Loagaeth* will be revealed:

> You are chosen by God His mercy to an end and purpose. Which end shall be made manifest by the first beginning in the knowledge in these Mysteries. God shall make clear when it pleaseth Him, and open all the secrets of wisdom when He unlocketh. Therefore seek not to know the mysteries of this book, till the very hour that He shall call thee. For then shall His power be so full amongst you, that the flesh shall not be perceived, in respect of His great glory. [*Five Books of Mystery*, p. 351]

> One is not to be lightened, but all.[62] . . . for until the 40 days be ended, shalt thou have no[t] one more shew of us. [*Five Books of Mystery*, p. 352]

Uriel's reference to "the 40 days" should indicate the period that fell roughly between June 18th and August 1st—that is, the period during which Dee was to create the perfected copy of the Holy Book. Therefore, we can assume that the mysteries of the Tables of *Loagaeth* will be revealed only after the perfected copy of the Book has been written.

Then, the mysteries of the Tables would be revealed all at once (or in a single extended magickal operation).

Dee and Kelley had heard a hint of this "appointed time" previously, from the Archangel Raphael (while the First Table of *Loagaeth* was in transmission). Apparently, the men were not to repeat the words of the book aloud while writing it—because to speak the words was to invoke the magick. This, Raphael assures the men, would not be desirable:

> If you use double repetition[63] in the things that follow, you shall both write and work, and all at once, which man's nature can not perform. The troubles were so great that might ensue thereof, that your strength were nothing to prevail against them. When it is written, read it no more with voice, till it be in practice.[64] All wants shall be opened unto you. [*Five Books of Mystery*, p. 311]

Apparently, it is dangerous to read the text aloud while writing it. What concerns us here, however, is the fact that Raphael promises there will be a time for the actual practice of *Loagaeth*, when all "wants" (that is, all questions) will be answered.

Soon after Uriel instructed the men to "seek not to know the mysteries of this Book," Dee and Kelley made contact with the Angel Illemese, who provided specific information about the "appointed time" in lyrical form:

> **Illemese:** I will sing a short song:
> Your doings are of God, your calling great.
> Go down and seek the Treasure, and you shall obtain it.
> Take no care, for this Book shall be done in 40 days.
> Begin to practice in August.[65] Serve God before.
> You shall know all things, with a stroke of the eye.[66]
> And so, praise, glory and eternal singing
> with incessant humility be unto thee, Creator that
> hath framed, made and Created all things, for
> ever and ever. Now say you (if you will)
> Amen.
>
> **Dee:** Amen Amen Amen.

> **Ilemese:** After the end of forty days, go down for the Treasure. When those forty days are done, then this book shall be finished. The rest of the time until August, is for rest, labor and prayer. [*Five Books of Mystery*, pp. 357–58]

It is once again Uriel who appears, later in the journals, to reveal more information about the "appointed time" for the practical use of the *Loagaeth* system:

> This book (I say) shall, tomorrow, be finished;[67] one thing excepted—which is the use thereof. Unto the which the Lord hath appointed a day. But (because I will speak to you, after the manner of men) see that all things be in readiness against the first day of August next. [*Five Books of Mystery*, p. 394]

Thus we learn, for certain, that August 1st was the target date for the practice of *Loagaeth*. As stated previously, that would be roughly forty days after Uriel instructed Dee to begin writing the perfected copy of the Holy Book.

Interestingly, all of this together represents three distinct periods of forty days. During the first period (which began eight days after Good Friday), Kelley received the text of the forty-eight Tables. The second period was one of rest, during which Dee received some answers and clarifications from the Angels. Then, the third period should have comprised the creation of the perfected Holy Book—ending on August 1st and the revelation of the Mysteries.

Begin the Book Next Tuesday—the Mother Galvah

By June 14th (just four days before Dee was to begin work on the perfected Holy Book), the men had not yet received the text of the final—forty-ninth—Table. This was withheld, apparently, because it was specifically under the jurisdiction of a female Spiritual Creature who (on June 14th) appeared and took over the transmission process.

Dee first records the appearance of "a Maiden."[68] She tells the two men that she is far from home, on a journey that will end six or seven weeks in the future. Dee points out (as he had noted previously in the journals) that Angels are unaffected by physical distances. Therefore, it is the time of the Maiden's journey, and not any distance, that establishes its length. If we count forward on the calendar about seven weeks from June 14th, we find ourselves in the close vicinity of August 1st. This is, then, our first veiled clue that this Maiden is associated in some way with the mysteries of the Holy *Book of Loagaeth*.

The Maiden, in Kelley's vision, continues on her journey and encounters several people along the way. At this point in the journals, the identity of this Maiden is hidden. However, as we shall see later, this vision of the Maiden's journey is directly related to her true identity.

Dee eventually asks the Maiden for her name. She replies that her "name" is not from the human tongue, likely meaning that it is Angelical:

> My name is Galva'h, in your language I am called *Finis*. [*A True and Faithful Relation*, p. 12]

> To Trithemius I say, "I am *Finis*, I am a beam of that Wisdom which is the end of man's excellency."[69] [*A True and Faithful Relation*, p. 13]

Finis is Latin for "the end." However, later during the same session, she adds that the name *Galvah* is not the general Angelic word for "end,"[70] but is instead used here in a very particular (specific) sense:

> Understand my name particularly, and not generally. I speak it to avoid error. Persevere to the end. [*A True and Faithful Relation*, p. 14]

In other words, *Galvah* is not the true name of this Maiden. It is, instead, a title—relating in some way to her function or office in these transmissions. As we saw previously, Gavlah has appeared to guide Dee and Kelley to August 1st—which is *the end* of the *Loagaeth* operation. ("Persevere to the end.") Moreover, as we shall see, it will be her job to reveal the *final* leaf of the Holy Book to the two men.

On the first day she appeared (June 14th), Galvah took control of the scrying sessions and became Dee's principal instructor on the Holy Book:

> **Galvah:** Begin the Book next Tuesday. Myself will be the director; and as my name is, so I will lead unto the end. All other things use, according to thy judgment and proportion of his Spirit that guideth you. I

> myself will be the finger to direct thee. [*A True and Faithful Relation*, p. 13]

Note that Galvah tells Dee to begin the Book "next Tuesday"—which would be June 18th. Of course, Kelley had already received forty-eight of the Tables by this point—all transcribed by Kelley from the shewstone in English letters, and written in the Western rightward fashion. Therefore, Galvah must be telling Dee to begin the *perfected copy* of the Holy Book. This appears to be what Dee assumes as well, and he asks Galvah if she will answer his questions regarding its writing:

> **Dee:** At the beginning to write the Book, shall I require your instructions?
>
> **Galvah:** Do so. [*A True and Faithful Relation*, p. 13]

An example of Galvah's direction regarding the writing of the Holy Book can be found a few pages later—on June 20th, two days after the project began. Here, Dee is given several very Solomonic instructions to follow while he works on the Book—although Solomonic or other traditional magickal timing is not used. Instead, the work is to be done when Galvah inspires Dee to work:

> **Galvah:** Labour in the writing of the Book diligently. See thou cleanse thyself on both sides. Be alone while it is done: that is to say, while thou art in doing it. [. . .] In a pure action all things ought to be pure.
>
> **Dee:** May I be writing every day, and at any time, when it shall come in my mind?
>
> **Galvah:** Ever as thou shalt feel me move thee. I will stir up thy desire.
>
> **Dee:** How shall I do for the letters? Shall I simply translate the letters as I find them?
>
> **Galvah:** Aye.
>
> **Dee:** The titles of the sides, are they to be written only in the holy Characters?[71]
>
> **Galvah:** As thou sayest . . . [*A True and Faithful Relation*, p. 23]

Dee goes on to ask several technical questions about his copy of the Holy Book. However, Galvah promises all further questions will be answered during the last seven (of the forty) days before August 1st. More than likely, Dee was expected to have the perfected Holy Book nearly written by that time. Here, Galvah only assures Dee, "Thou shalt want no direction."

The true identity of Galvah is a puzzle that plays out slowly in the journals. During their first session together, when Galvah instructed Dee to begin work on the Holy Book, she also gave him a very cryptic hint to her identity:

> The finger of God stretcheth over many mountains. His Spirit comforteth the weakness of many places. No sense is unfurnished where His light remaineth. For understand what I am, and it is a sufficient answer. [*A True and Faithful Relation*, p. 13]

Dee had, earlier in this session, mentioned that Galvah did not appear to be one of the Daughters of Light, or their Daughters—the only family of female Angels the two men had met at that point. Just before her short speech above, Galvah confirms that she is not one of those Angels, but that all of the Daughters (and their Daughters) of Light are comprehended[72] within her:

> These also that are called Daughters and Daughters of Daughters are all comprehended in me, and do attend upon True Wisdom. Which if Trithemius mark, he shall perceive that true Wisdom is always painted with a woman's garment. For, [other][73] than the pureness of a Virgin, nothing is more commendable. [*A True and Faithful Relation*, p. 13]

A few sessions later,[74] one of the Daughters of the Daughters—named Madimi—appeared in the stone. (Dee and Kelley had met her earlier in their Angelic scryings.) During their conversation, Madimi brought her mother to the shewstone to speak with Dee. Madimi's mother, of course, is Galvah. Yet she introduces herself to Dee in this instance by the name I AM.[75] (We will return to this encounter between Dee and Madimi later in this chapter.)

It would seem that the solution to the puzzle is found on page 14 of *A True and Faithful Relation*. Here, Galvah appears, in a vision, to be completely entrapped by a surrounding hedge. The Angel Illemese appears briefly and has an exchange with her:

> **Galvah:** Here is no way out.
>
> **Illemese:** Come, I will do somewhat for you. It is a strange thing that Wisdom cannot find a way through a hedge.[76] [*A True and Faithful Relation*, p. 14]

Illemese knocks down part of the hedge and departs the vision. Galvah, then, continues with the allegorical vision—in which she (now revealed as Wisdom) vainly attempts to find lodging amongst corrupt mankind.[77]

This vision is likely a continuation of the very first vision Galvah showed Kelley—concerning her journey toward August 1st.[78] In that vision, Wisdom also journeyed along her way, encountering humans who either embraced her or could not tolerate her, and those who made good use of her guidance along with those who did not.

Through all of this we learn that "Galvah" is, in fact, Wisdom herself. Throughout Western history, Wisdom has been depicted as a female figure—her symbolism dating back to images of the goddesses Inanna (in Mesopotamia) and Isis (in Egypt).[79] The Gnostics worshiped her directly as *Sophia* (Wisdom), and Judaism adopted *Sophia* as its own *Sheckinah* (the Presence of God). From these, the later Hermeticists developed their concept of the Soul of the World. This is the alchemical Bride of God.

It is my impression that the name *Galvah* is intended to represent the biblical *Omega* (The End), as we see it in the first and last chapters of Revelation: "I Am the *Alpha*, and the *Omega*. The First, and the Last." Therefore, Sophia—as Galvah/Omega—represents the passive and feminine aspect of Creation. Her bridegroom—the *Christos/Alpha*—represents the active and masculine aspect. (In Gnosticism, the union of *Sophia* and the *Christos* represents the Holy Spirit, symbolized by the white dove.)

Every Monday Is the Seventh—the "Enochian Sabbath"?

One of the more inexplicable examples of magickal timing in Dee's records concerns the Angels' strange observation of Mondays. Others have classified this as some kind of "Enochian Sabbath"—comparable to the Christian Sabbath on Sunday, or the Jewish Sabbath on Saturday.[80] In both of these latter cases, the Sabbath is established according to the "Day of Rest" observed by God on the Seventh Day of Creation. (See Genesis 1.) The Jewish custom was to begin the week with Sunday—meaning that Saturday was the last day of the week, and therefore the Seventh Day of Rest. (In fact, this is why we refer to the Day of Rest as the "Sabbath"—because the root of this word is the Hebrew name for Saturn / Saturday—*Shabbathai*.) For the Christian, the week began on Monday—so that Sunday was the Seventh Day and the Sabbath. (A custom our secular culture follows to this very day.)

I find it hard to judge whether or not the Angels intended Mondays to be a Sabbath in this sense. No special consideration of this day appears in relation to the *Heptarchia*—which precedes the *Loagaeth* system in Dee's journals. However, the ordering of planetary forces revealed to Dee in the Heptarchic system does happen to end with Luna—the planet of Monday. (The list runs Venus, Sol, Mars, Jupiter, Mercury, Saturn, and Luna.[81] The Angels did associate this ordering directly with the Seven Days of Creation.[82])

Mondays are first mentioned in the journals when Galvah instructs Dee to begin writing the perfected copy of the Holy Book:

> **Galvah:** That is to say, while thou art in doing it, henceforth and till the time to come[83] use speech with us no more; every seventh day [excepted].
>
> **Dee:** How shall those days be accounted?
>
> **Galvah:** From Tuesday last: Tuesday being the first of the seven,[84] and the next Monday, the seventh, and so forth every Monday is the seventh. [*A True and Faithful Relation*, p. 23]

Therefore, Dee was to work on the Holy Book on every day of the week from Tuesday to Sunday. The seventh day, Monday, was one of rest from that work, whereupon Dee might enjoy conversation with the Angels.

Oddly, Dee seems to have disregarded Galvah's instruction to contact the Angels only on Mondays. The next several scrying sessions recorded in his journal are on days *other* than Mondays.

Mondays are next mentioned in the journals during the period when Dee and Kelley received the forty-eight Angelical Keys. During one session, which took place on a Monday, the Archangel Gabriel delivered the following message from God:

> **Gabriel:** Listen unto my words, for they are a Commandment from above. Behold (saith He) I have descended to view the Earth, where I will dwell for seven days, and twice seven days. Therefore, let them be days of rest to you. But every seventh day, I will visit you, as Now I do.
>
> **Dee:** I understand that this rest is, that every Monday, for three Mondays else next after other, we shall await our lessons, as now we receive, and that we may all the rest follow our affairs of study or household matters.
>
> **Gabriel:** It is so, for one day shall be as a week. But those days you must abstain from all things that live upon the Earth.
>
> **Dee:** You mean these three Mondays ensuing next. [April 30, 1584. *A True and Faithful Relation*, p. 114]

The journals indicate that Dee followed the instruction this time, as the next three sessions with the Angels take place on Mondays[85] (although we are not told if he or Kelley abstained from "all things that live upon the earth" on these Sabbath days). This, unfortunately, is all the journals of Dr. Dee have to say about Mondays.

The Forty-Nine Tables of *Loagaeth*: What We Know[86]

In this section, we are going to explore the particulars, as recorded by Dee, of some of the forty-nine leaves (or Tables) of the Holy *Book of Loagaeth*. Dee made a few comments in his journals that suggest, to me, that he had more information about the contents of the Tables than has survived to the present day. It is entirely possible that he recorded this information in another journal that has been lost. Therefore, we will have to gather what we can from the *Five Books* and *A True and Faithful*

Relation. Unfortunately, this means we only know a few details about a few of the Tables:

Titles of the Tables[87]

Almost all of the Tables of *Loagaeth* are headed with titles—one for side A and another for side B of each leaf. Those Tables that do not have specific titles are instead "entitled" with the first words that appear on the page. We have precious little in the way of translations for these titles. In the Lexicon in volume II, I have referenced any of these words that appear similar to known Angelical words. Following are the titles themselves:

Table 1A [zuresch od adaph mal zez geno au marlan oh muzpa]
Table 1B [Oxar varmol pan sampas os al pans orney andsu]

Table 2A alla opnay qviemmah.
Table 2B zvrebth aho dan lanfal cramza

Table 3A pandobna ox adroh azimcholdrux.
Table 3B dlod Alged zvrem. ["dlod allged zvram"]

Table 4A Zvbla ox arnogan Algers aclo.
Table 4B Danfal gest Axamph acrosta.

Table 5A Gonzahoh alch arge oho Adanch.
Table 5B Zvchastors plohodmax argednon acho

Table 6A Sancgonfal aldex, Ave goh adatqvan,
Table 6B pvrcha ges maxgem adroth vaxox ahó

Table 7A Dam lethgath onzar avoxalgeth
Table 7B chvmaxchaberexmapha

Table 8A algebadreth
Table 8B Oylzongs

Table 9A pagesgem
Table 9B Avallacax

Table 10A Gorvemgemps
Table 10B Bacap Laffos

Table 11A Ozimba londorh
Table 11B ylchvzzapg

Table 12A Nopham
Table 12B Signeh gax

Table 13A t-lallaah gethnoh
Table 13B Iaialgh lercol zinrox

Table 14A Pincal vexlan
Table 14B Phin potagar giron

Table 15A Se ger pcopalph
Table 15B Oroh Zvn.compvxoh

Table 16A Dadavar gedrong
Table 16B varahhatraglax pligeo

Table 17A Hidrahah glazipvagel
Table 17B Engidexol; neolchiph

Table 18A Polacax cvbagod
Table 18B Zad, ron anchal

Table 19A Gedmarg alpon
Table 19B Bvzalg long arnap

Table 20A Zicha lezach.
Table 20B Drem phingel oxah oho

Table 21A algonzib virbalox
Table 21B Avriz ommaphily geld

Table 22A Cehergol naoal
Table 22B Fál mexicamps vrom

Table 23A Conar vomfagal
Table 23B Toxarxh nerhoh gel podnon

Table 24A Zichidpha lvziph
Table 24B Nervag pranclan

Table 25A Demphoz prang oho
Table 25B Harodan lempric dohoh

Table 26A Chy pled sagnaronph
Table 26B Draxph intayfalg

Table 27A Vlnen razo vilcomb
Table 27B Vincal leorna rvh

Table 28A Dababel gel zozaah
Table 28B Larvh gohonp babbabor

Table 29A Famfax lep axax.
Table 29B Zirzach bvmazon.

Table 30A Tar, vin gabax orho.
Table 30B Glonz alnoptd.

Table 31A Gemnarv Hvncol.
Table 31B Rynh zichzor chalan.

Table 32A yayger balpaoeh.
Table 32B Car vanal geldons.

Table 33A Vio nilg onpho.
Table 33B Toxhencol ylnorox ziborh.

Table 34A Balvomph chiphan.
Table 34B Vingelg laxih parcan.

Table 35A Zvda vig pancar.
Table 35B Dexvlng chirony gavv.

Table 36A Qnabazeb vil pvdar.
Table 36B Xanpa phaphingeth.

Table 37A Ronlox bapvabap orh.
Table 37B Calbahhah genrox.

Table 38A Dohvnam gethgol axah.
Table 38B Vantavong nargax.

Table 39A Pvlgaao ner gisch.
Table 39B Archi septh lorox.

Table 40A Damponpha nexo gel.
Table 40B Dexph geld onchen.

Table 41A Ellaxor Natoglan
Table 41B Fam filgisch larvouch

Table 42A Cemgealg ralphos
Table 42B Zodagrap zilpob

Table 43A Necprilga lvpvarn
Table 43B Depsah onge phialox

Table 44A Nelziar pol dolgon
Table 44B Parni volchemph

Table 45A Acvirzilg chiparal
Table 45B Alged on chipráxal

Table 46A Clarn nancal
Table 46B Lexrox pingh lardol

Table 47A Zvrzvh genvox
Table 47B Chiromonph zarchan olinorg

Table 48A Calgs sedph panglox
Table 48B Bapporgel bvrioldepnay

Table 49 N/A (See note below.)

Note: Table 49 was not given its own title. See later in this chapter for a full explanation of the reception and contents of the final leaf of *Loagaeth*.

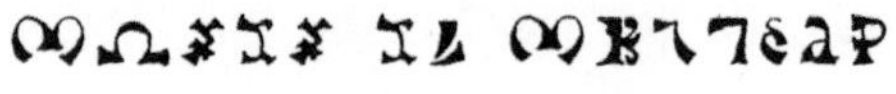

(Zuresch od Adaph)

Padohómagebs galz arps apá nal Si. gámvagad al pódma gan NA. Vr cas nátmaz ándiglon ar'mbu.zántclumbar ar noxócharmah. Sapoh lan gamnox vxála vors. Sábse cap vax mar vinco. Labandáho nas gampbox arce Dah gorhahálpstd gascáampho lan ge. Béfes argédco nax arzulgh orh. Sémhaham vn'cal laf garp oxox. Loangah.

Ors lah genphe nahoh ama-natoph des garhul vanseph iuma lat gedos lubah aha last gesto. Vars macom des curad vals mors gaph gemsed pa campha zednu ábfada máses lófgono. Luruandah lesog iamle padel arphe nades gulsad maf gescon lampharsad surem paphe arbasa arzusen agsde ghehol max vrdra paf gals macrom finistab gelsaphan asten Vrnah.

Asch val íamels árcasa árcasan arcúsma íabso gliden paha pacadúra gebne óscaroh gádne au arua las genost cásme palsi uran vad gadeth axam pambo cásmala sámnefa gárdomas árxad pámses gémulch gápes lof lachef ástma vates garnsnas orue gad garmah sar'quel rúsan gages drusala phímacar aldech oscom lat garset panóston.

The First Leaf of Loagaeth is reserved for the Logos. Its 49x49 Tables contain entire words in each cell, and are therefore too large to represent in proper grids. The above is an excerpt from Table 1A, lines 21-23, which concern the creation of Angels.

First Table:[88]

We have already discussed a few points about the "hidden" first leaf of *Loagaeth*. Raphael gave us the first clue when he said, "One is one [that] neither is, was or shall be known." The mystery of these cryptic words is not solved until after the appearance of the Angel Nalvage, who delivered the Angelical Keys (or Calls) to Dee and Kelley.[89] Nalvage says of the Table on the first leaf:

> I find the soul of man hath no portion in this First Table. It is the Image of the Son of God, in the bosom of his father, before all the worlds. It comprehendeth his incarnation, passion, and return to judgment: which he himself, in flesh, knoweth not. [*A True and Faithful Relation*, p. 79]

The image of the "Son of God, in the bosom of his father, before all the worlds" brings to mind, once again, the first chapter of the Book of John—where both God and the *Logos* (Word) existed together, as One, before all of Creation.

We already know that the entire Holy Book is supposed to contain the words of the *Logos/Christos*, who used the words to create the Universe, Time, and all of the contents of both. Here, Nalvage reveals that the First Table of *Loagaeth* is, especially, reserved for the *Christos* Himself. It contains the archetypal patterns upon which the birth, life, and death of Jesus would later be based. (I further suspect that the pattern for the entire *Book of Loagaeth* is indicated here as well.)

Therefore, the *Loagaeth* magickal system has no method of opening the mysteries of the First Table. However, there are several clues to its nature recorded in Dee's journals—given by Kelley as he recited the words from the Book. The reception of the entire first leaf is recorded in Dee's *Fifth Book of the Mysteries*, and it is the only Table of the Holy Book to contain entire words, rather than single characters, in its cells. Because Kelley could understand the language during these sessions, he would often make comments on the definitions (or "significations") of the words. (Raphael even tells Kelley, on occasion, to cease explaining the definitions of the words as he spoke.[90] After all, the mysteries of the First Table *were* supposed to remain closed!)

Of the nearly 4802 words in the First Table (2401 cells on the front, and the same number on the back), we only have a few precious definitions to work with. Yet these few words are fairly telling about the contents of the text itself.

For example, one of the words (*Gascampho*) is defined as "Why didst thou so?—as God said to Lucifer." Another word (*Donasdogamatastos*) indicates "the furious and perpetual fire enclosed for the punishment of them that are banished from Glory," while yet another (*Padgze*) means "justice from Divine Power without defect." Therefore, one might assume that Lucifer's rebellion in Heaven is described or referenced in this text, along with his sentencing by God afterward.

There are also other clues to such pre-Genesis events in the text. One word (*Amgedpha*), for example, translates as "I will begin anew."

(Qabalistic tradition holds that our Universe was not the first attempt at Creation. Or, perhaps, this phrase indicates God's rebuilding of his Kingdom after the war against Lucifer. Yet again, maybe it is a word Lucifer himself spoke after being cast down?) There is also a word (*Galsagen*) that indicates the creation of the Angel of the Sun by God. (This could be a reference to the Archangel Michael,[91] who is credited in Christian tradition with the defeat and casting-down of Lucifer.)

There also appear to be some elements of the biblical Genesis in the text. One word (*Pola*) translates as "Two Together"—which may be a reference to Adam and Eve *before* their separation into two bodies, if it is not in reference to the Waters of the Abyss before their division. There is also a word (*Apachana*) that indicates the "slimy things made of dust"—reminiscent of the Fifth and Sixth Days of Creation, where God brought forth "creeping things" from the sea and earth.[92] Another word (*Tohcoth*) encompasses "all the number of faeries" (or spirits)—who, according to Jewish legend, were created on the twilight of the Sixth Day of Creation.

The only reference to Christ in this Table that made it into Dee's records is a word (*Iurehoh*) that indicates "what Christ did in Hell." This is a reference to an obscure Christian legend in which Christ—during his three days in the Tomb—descended into Hell.[93] While there, he literally stormed the place—smashing open gates, knocking down bridges, and liberating a large number of souls who had been wrongly imprisoned there.[94] This is a controversial legend, mentioned in passing in the Apostles' Creed.

There are also two words (*Samhampors* and *Semhaham*) that hint at some relationship between the *Loagaeth* system and the Qabalistic seventy-two-fold Name of God—called in Hebrew *Shem haMephoresh* (the Name of Extension).

A couple of words even mention Heptarchic Angels (who were likely heavily involved in the Seven Days of Creation). One Angel mentioned is the Angelic Prince of Tuesday, Befafes. In this Table of *Loagaeth*, the word *Befas* appears—which Dee notes is the vocative form of Befafes' name. (This means that someone in the text is addressing Befafes directly.) Another Heptarchic Angel—the King of Sunday, Bobogel—seems to figure into the word *Bobagelzod*. (Dee does not record if this is also a vocative case.)

Of course, all of these Angelical words are included in the Angelical Lexicon in the second volume of this work.

Beyond this, Kelley reported some interesting information concerning several lines of the text. After recording line 23 of side A of the First Table, Dee records:

> There are no points [in line 23], neither in the last before [i.e., line 22]. They be parcels of Invitations very pleasant to good Angels. Before [i.e., line 21] was, as it were, a preface of the creation and distinction of Angels, etc.[95] [*Five Books of Mystery*, p. 312, footnote]

Therefore, we learn that lines 22 and 23 are parts of invitations to good Angels. The line before these, number 21, is the preface to the creation of Angels. Then, after the twenty-sixth line was transmitted, Kelley made note that all of these lines—21 through 26—appertain to good Angels.[96]

This is all that is recorded of the mysteries of the First Table of *Loagaeth*. After Raphael delivered the first line of this leaf, he told Dee and Kelley:

> I teach. Let this lesson instruct thee to read all that shall be gathered out of this book hereafter. [. . .] It shall be sufficient to instruct thee. Farewell. [*Five Books of Mystery*, p. 291]

I feel this applies equally to the entire First Table (sides A and B). Organizing and analyzing the words provided there is likely key to distinguishing the text of the other Tables. Because the other Tables have a single letter in each cell, the words all run together without spaces between them.[97] We would have to recognize basic words—and compounds—from the First Table, in order to distinguish them in the later Tables.

Second Table:

The Angel Nalvage had a few words to say about the second Table, just after he delivered the translation (or "English sense") of the Angelical Key needed to open it:

> It is the sense in your tongue of the holy and mystical Call before delivered: which followeth in practice for the moving of the second Table, the Kings and Ministers of Government. [. . .]
>
> This is therefore the key of the first seven, according to the proportion of the first Creation. [*A True and Faithful Relation*, p. 88]

Therefore we know that the second Table of *Loagaeth* represents the "Kings and Ministers of Government." In this light, I would assume that the "first seven" indicates the seven "Spirits of God"—the seven planetary Archangels who were the principal active forces during the Seven Days of Creation.[98] It is probable, then, that the second Table relates in some way to the Archangels who govern Creation.

This fits well with what we already know of *Loagaeth*. The first, unattainable, Table incorporates events that took place "before the worlds"—from the blueprints of the Christ saga, to the creation of the Angels, and even the rebellion and fall of Lucifer. The second Table, then, would initiate the Creation as seen in Genesis 1.

Fourth Table:

The journals record nothing about the mysteries of the fourth Table until the Angelical Keys are revealed. At that point, the Archangel Gabriel states that this Table (and its Key) is "the first of nature, and the beginning of your being in body."[99] It is likely, then, that this Table relates to (or incorporates) the creation of Adam in Genesis 2. However, because this information was revealed with the Keys, I will save further discussion on this point for chapter 3, when we discuss the Key of this Table.

Ninth Table:

Table 9, side A, is the Table that appears in the front of *A True and Faithful Relation*, labeled as "A specimen of the Tables or Book of Enoch, etc." This Table is entitled "*Pagesgem*."[100]

The *Pagesgem* Table is special in many respects. It is, by far, the most unique and fascinating Table in the entire Holy Book—making it little wonder why Casaubon chose it as a sample for the front of his *A True and Faithful Relation*. Most notably, this Table possesses four 7 x 7 number-squares in the four outer corners of the grid. Surrounding the

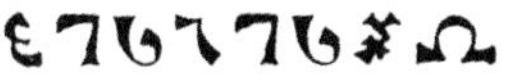

(Pagesgem)

1234567	sednachanzaclanzabviachodangahzvcha	2345678
2134567	lathnaclongatoxardnachaphnodolphaho	3245678
3214567	archanvahgenodalzachenachanzacladon	4325678
4321567	orgednachalzanchalabvzachefnoxadnar	5432678
5432167	voltiblahnoxdargephaldvrganzachyoxa	6543278
6543217	plazengathaldextohvorthangephadonge	7654328
7654321	nazaldahzanchanzaoldangalahvonroxap	8765432
	axarmarlohnotaxvargemnatophadolgemphadonchadonzah	
	parchephnochadnadolclazangehozadmachvaldehadarged	
	volzangephaclanzacnoxarnahvohadroncpyadnahvotargc	
	pragednolganzanclaoxarnachovongangaprahlodnaxorah	
	vvnzangephazolmahzvreblohaclaxnochaapargensanolsa	
	vaxargempadolzachephaxardrahgednaclznvartcsnoclar	
	radoxggrazaclanvongiblesadrvngahvolaibloahacharse	
	algemenohadnacodvonox9121234oedaeonodonzachadnaca	
	aevargednopahoadras78IBAGAFA56cagafvichapnadoxard	
	delchansanoxahpeas6IBAGAFAIBAG7alghaomfangetoxage	
	vorgemvagehadoton5A65432176543A8ofaplothagethnoga	
	acladaxvarteohna4IA65432176543GA9taoradantageldaa	
	arhanzachephaho3F66654321765433A1balzanchadaxorg	
	nolzadadraxpahx2A777aueauaxar777I2onlbvzanchahoda	
	ztblachephango1AI1115BnaBvcB1666BA3vohvlagesmacoh	
	algadnaclansam9IB222oo0d0a0am555AB4vandabrahadmac	
	domzubladaxvro8BA333gxaRReth444GA5nlzangephaxarg	
	algednopelgeta7AG444aB0RN0G0d333AG6gochanaldaphna	
	pagentaphengoh6GA555nga000pha222FA7ncongeporaxarg	
	alzadchardaxol5AF666ddGnGaGaq111AF8oolaslaphanagl	
	plvdnachanpoon4FA777a0ox0am0a777IA9onphalgephalze	
	orchanzandalala3I111qantalget666B1ancardaxadmache	
	ondimache8dohox2B2223456712345 55A2coeoplaxvargeta	
	apzagensodaholon1BF23456712345AA3odplzachanzangeh	
	myclahhvdrabahona9A23456712345F4analolhadganverte	
	gongergalaxarotaxr8BAGAFAIBAGI5oxdogzadnaahziblah	
	fantogapvargemaltaz76AFAIBAG76elangcolzadnahgebar	
	arlagvagephadednoclad5432198fadoxahrhodnocapvargo	
	nolzadnachephaldedmacheolchadnadoxahnepacheldaxor	
	valgedadrvxadnoglaphzvgalgablonzancaanacnarsanols	
	apransanadarcholzadnahachirahdoxalddgahzangephnox	
	orcladorvorblemaradontagelaxarohpronalgarozargefa	
	laxardroamnachondanclaxazvrbbalohadeodaxorgephals	
	argladroadronclanzadinchaadranchloghdgaochadnacho	
	valchepnadoxargempnaphealbvndagedlohaxargehnotals	
2345678	hahglifafrangehnoxaldehgebladahorha	7654321
3245678	loadanfadontalmahochanfanoxalgethvo	6543217
3215678	gempnadoxarchansanapvradzdnolatonsa	5432167
5432978	englorzabmvchaaphinodalzadcharzahod	4321567
6543278	aglancladonvanrablidoxagephacladnoh	3214567
7654328	gethvdradolziblaxvorchapnachaxaldla	2134567
8765432	noxtadgmaolzangeolchadnaphavonronge	1234567

The pagesgem Table (or Table 9A) is unique in Loagaeth

center of the grid, in a large clockwise circle, are the numbers 1 through 9 repeating. Within the circle are the numbers 1 through 7 written in triplicate (111, 222, 333, etc.) in a counterclockwise pattern. The rest of the squares within the circle are filled with capital letters (I, B, A, G, A, F, and A repeating).

Furthermore, the very center of the Table displays the name of the Heptarchic Prince of the Sun and Sunday—*Bornogo*—in a star pattern.

(The name is written once vertically, once horizontally, and twice in opposing slants. All four share the central cell—the letter *N*—and therefore make an eight-pointed star.)

B			B			B
	O		O		O	
		R	R	R		
B	O	R	N	O	G	O
		O	O	O		
	G		G		G	
O			O			O

Outside of the central circle and the four number-squares in the corners, the rest of the Table is filled with letters as usual. Unique is the fact that this is the *only* Table in the Holy Book to incorporate numbers with the text.

Nineteenth (or Eighteenth?) Table:

On April 15th, 1583, Kelley was at work transcribing what Dee called the eighteenth leaf of *Loagaeth*.[101] However, it is unclear if Dee was counting the First "hidden" leaf in this case. He sometimes described the second leaf as the "first," because it represented the first accessible Gate of Wisdom. Therefore, there is some possibility that, on April 15th, Kelley was actually working on Table *19*.

Dee notes that this leaf was "of the spirits of the earth." (Hinting that Dee may have had more information on the contents of each leaf of the Holy Book than has survived.) In this session, we actually get to meet these Earth spirits. During his transcription work, Kelley made the mistake of reading some of the Angelical text aloud. Three or four spirits appeared:

> . . . and thereupon suddenly at his side appeared three or four spiritual creatures like laboring men, having spades[102] in their hands and their hair hanging about their ears, and hastily asked Edward Kelley what he would have, and wherefore he called them. [*Five Books of Mystery*, p. 348]

(Gedmarg Alpon)

sedontagentagnochaplagnoclaxydnachansednophaloxad
vdraxtagentolantaxarnagentagnogethonodantagentage
ophragnagedochanaxartagensoachionzachiadnohanzach
yldoxadonzachantolydraxnochastorohydonzagathnolzl
plachastoradroxnotafnagothvdraxodadnagenandagnach
iplaxabradontaglahnoxadnochavantrahnolzadnocbanzo
apraxanachendaxadnocladaxvalzonacladyblaxtopolzan
vntagnocharnoxadaltanafafrangeontalecladoxtaphaxo
yntoalodnodaxomerontantalaxvdamahnoxardaxodydnoch
adonzaneoterohalclaxodaxtanebrachadolzachnedoltax
ydnoxadynzaatagnachydontalyprassodrvxdeodannecorg
avolsednoclaxyblaxtogenaprigantoxantonagedothapla
segorsagovoxadnoandentagephholzachadantaayplaxnoc
vlanzachasplaxtonochalzadyndanoaconzadorydnophros
zanvaxyrzabuloatantagnoxadarnochaydraxnolydnonvar
ybontazaxylchadnonaplantagosydraxnochaldovaxtoroh
plachibalzidnochasterohazvldaxtochordalaphantogah
maxtalgethnocordantachanidnocharoxplaxtoteroxonah
insantalgrantagnachoxadnoclantoxnabvrazantolzanto
ydnoxadvdraxtohapraxtolaxtohvnglatnnochalmadoxyba
devantanalynzandeodraphalpranzednochalmarayparsac
theonzadaxvorrontantoxacloxydlochanoxardoxlepatha
nachadnochantantoxalzacharpricasmacharnaldoxtapro
vdantolgethanarnographydnocharynsadgnoxtalzadnoah
ydoblaxaproxtanoxalgednaxyntaxnorynsantagefaldrox
prichastorazantalgeorgradnochanzachaclaxtorocland
amanzaclaxnatoplaxydnoranvansednagorystaxolaprado
nolednapracastagonzvrodachanzaneochetorosaldorabi
odalzachneldrothamvantagnodoxysclonnadrvmagvntago
alzichaslossonnocharbachvontanvarahvongalsovontax
vrchadnolanzadchappnacoxaldraxtapranzanoydnachars
achenblohydnodaclaxvargethacheldondanzaldroxaclax
nagethraxapriddunaloorrenzacloxadroxzinglaxaclaso
vantoplasmagraayntlageordoragenynzoaconzanoxtalza
alchynaclaxydnochadnaphexysoladnotanzachyntagnoca
algaalgohanagtarprodantagenadnachoalchvzantaxorna
vlonzacharledzadroxdapraxolynsantafachensonaxadna
charzidalontantaploxycloazintoxadonzanavidolageoh
nachanzacbothydnocharonachanzlbonagephzantolaxado
avaxadnachastorahydnoladroxachaphnabnlaxtorgennap
vlzacoznadorzidaplaxacapnotagnacrohadnochoronyndo
plaxtribalzachidnogahynzachidorzadnochadaxargetha
alzachydnobalontantoxacheldonvlarbadroxmichanzaca
nobvlacydnotraphalgehordraxyblothnacordoxagednoch
georgaalchinzachannataxarachvolzidnochalzyntagnal
yazangalaxvontagnataperodanzaacladchydrantontaget
aldvzachanabvladvolhazpahgeoldanaclidnopalaxydnoc
adroxtalgethanazadnoclapiaxychaxachonzachavtalzac
ydnappargelzaclaxviolapordroxaclanzanodelzachepha

The Gedmarg Alpon Table (or Table 19A). Leaf may represent the element of Earth.

Kelley, of course, insisted that he had not intended to call them. Dee agreed, saying that a prayer spoken only to get "the sense thereof" was not a true prayer. At this, the annoyed spirits attacked Kelley—leaving a red circular welt on his skin. During the commotion, Dee grabbed a wand and heroically banished the spirits.

I find it very interesting that this Table should relate to the spirits of the Earth. As I pointed out previously, the entire *Book of Loagaeth* relates to the seven biblical Days of Creation.[103] As we shall see, the final thirty Tables collectively represent the Seventh Day of Rest. That means the first nineteen Tables should encompass the first Six Days of Creation—beginning with the Divine Source in the First Table and ending with the completed Universe in the nineteenth.

It is, therefore, not surprising to find the spirits of the Earth in the last Table associated with the six days of active Creation. This indicates that the occult forces represented by the Tables of *Loagaeth* do indeed run from the highest divinity in the first leaf to the lowest and most earthly forces in the final leaf—in a fashion similar to both the Tables of *Soyga* and the Jewish fifty Gates of Binah.[104]

Tables 20 to 49:[105]

The last thirty Tables of the *Book of Loagaeth* are set somewhat apart from the previous nineteen. As a group, Tables 20–49 represent the Gates into the Thirty Aethyrs that extend from God's Throne to Earth.[106]

By "Aethyrs," Dee means to indicate the various levels of the Firmament, or the Heavens. (This is the root of our modern word *ether*—as used to describe the "etheric plane," or spiritual realm.) If we look at chapter 1 of the Book of Ezekiel, we see the plane of the Firmament (the sky or Heavens) upheld by the four Kherubic Archangels. The same Firmament appears as a "sea of glass" (a description of the sky) in the fourth chapter of the Book of the Revelation.

The Heavens that extend between God and Earth are counted as seven by Jewish mysticism. This descends from Chaldean and Babylonian sources, which associated the Heavens with the orbital spheres of the seven ancient planets. (The lowest Heaven corresponded with the "planet" closest to Earth—Luna—and extended all the way to the farthest planet—Saturn. Beyond Saturn was a cosmic barrier between the Divine and natural realms marked by the band of fixed stars.)

Later biblical traditions reinterpreted these seven Heavens in various ways. Most significantly, the ancient Gnostics (depending on sect) described anywhere from thirty to 365 Heavens!

It was the thirty-Heaven Gnostic cosmology that apparently reached Dee[107] and found itself embedded in the *Loagaeth* system. We know that the First Table of the Book represents the Highest God (the *Logos*), and that the Creation of the Universe is outlined in the text of the eighteen Tables that follow. Table 20, then, must address a completed and working Universe, and therefore correspond to the Seventh Day of Creation. The rest of the final thirty Tables follow suit—although Table 49 stands out and will be discussed later in this chapter.

The Thirty Aethyrs contained within Tables 20 through 49 run in order from the highest and most Divine Heaven (called *Lil* by Dee's Angels) to the lowest and most earthly Heaven (called *Tex*).[108] However, this "stacked" illustration of the Aethyrs is merely an intellectual model—based upon Jewish and Gnostic convention. In practice, the thirty Aethyrs described by Dee's Angels are set over various geographical locations—called "Parts of the Earth." Thus, these Heavens actually permeate one another, rather than existing as "highest to lowest" in the sense of Newtonian space-time.

Technically, this is also an aspect of Merkavah mysticism, as can be seen in the *Book of Enoch the Prophet* (*1 Enoch*), in which the patriarch not only explores the Seven Heavens but also astrally visits several geographical locations.[109] The same is found throughout the biblical Book of Ezekiel.[110] In Dee's case, each of the Thirty Aethyrs contained three Parts of the Earth (except for the lowest, *Tex*, which contained four[111]). Angelic Governors set over the nations in those Parts could be contacted, and the people of those nations could be observed by opening the Gate (Table) of the appropriate Aethyr.

I consider the Parts of the Earth system to be an example of the kind of magick one can work with the *Book of Loagaeth*. However, our purpose here is to explore the Holy Book itself. Magickal systems based *upon* it will follow in a later work. In this chapter I have only included what has already been said of the Aethyrs and the Parts, plus I have added the names of the Aethyrs to the Lexicon.[112]

Meanwhile, for ease of reference, I will here offer a list of the Thirty Aethyrs and the Tables of *Loagaeth* with which they correspond:

01. *Lil* -	Table 20	16. *Lea* -	Table 35
02. *Arn* -	Table 21	17. *Tan* -	Table 36
03. *Zom* -	Table 22	18. *Zen* -	Table 37
04. *Paz* -	Table 23	19. *Pop* -	Table 38
05. *Lit* -	Table 24	20. *Chr* -	Table 39
06. *Maz* -	Table 25	21. *Asp* -	Table 40
07. *Deo* -	Table 26	22. *Lin* -	Table 41
08. *Zid* -	Table 27	23. *Tor* -	Table 42
09. *Zip* -	Table 28	24. *Nia* -	Table 43
10. *Zax* -	Table 29	25. *Uti* -	Table 44
11. *Ich* -	Table 30	26. *Des* -	Table 45
12. *Loe* -	Table 31	27. *Zaa* -	Table 46
13. *Zim* -	Table 32	28. *Bag* -	Table 47
14. *Uta* -	Table 33	29. *Rii* -	Table 48
15. *Oxo* -	Table 34	30. *Tex* -	Table 49

Forty-Ninth Table:

As mentioned previously in this chapter, the Mother Galvah appeared to Dee and Kelley in order to bring them to the end of the *Loagaeth* transmission. As such, it was within her jurisdiction alone to reveal the text of the forty-ninth—or final—leaf to Dee and Kelley. Like the first ("hidden") Table, the text of the forty-ninth leaf is also comprised of whole words. However, it is unique in that it is not made of two 49 x 49 Tables, but (as we shall see later) of five small Tables of twenty-one letters each.

Just after Galvah reveals the name of the Holy Book as *Loagaeth*, she turns to the subject of the forty-ninth Table:

> The first leaf (as you call it) is the last of the book.[113] And as the first leaf is a hotchpotch without order; so it signifieth a disorder of the world, and is the speech of that Disorder or Prophesie. [*A True and Faithful Relation,* p. 19]

This quote has caused some confusion among modern Enochian students. Galvah here suggests that the last leaf of the book would have been called the "first leaf" by Dee. Remember our previous discussion of the "leftward" direction in which the Holy Book is written (like a Hebrew Torah). Thus, if Dee opened up the Book to what he considered the "first leaf" by Western standards, he would find himself looking at the *last page* of the Book—containing Table 49.

This "first leaf" (really the last!) is then described as "a hotchpotch without order" that signifies a "disorder of the world." In the margin, Dee notes: "I understand not this unless it be the first leaf, being indeed the last, is of the wicked hellish one." This is a reference to the Antichrist, who (according to Dee's belief) would rule the world during the End Times to come. This seems to be confirmed several pages later, when Galvah elaborates slightly on this "hotchpotch":

> Thou beginest in the world to look up to Heaven: So was it begun in earth to look up to the doing above. The last life is Hotchpotch of the wicked in the World, and damned in Hell. [*A True and Faithful Relation*, p. 24]

So, leaf 49 of the Holy Book represents the "last life," and a time when the wicked of the world and the damned in Hell would create chaos (i.e., the Tribulation and following Armageddon). The final leaf of *Loagaeth*, like the final book of the Bible, would necessarily comprehend the reign of the Antichrist, along with his defeat and the establishment of the Kingdom of God. (See the Book of Revelation, chapters 13–22.)

Galvah finally transmits the text of leaf 49 on June 18th, 1583.[114] First, she points out that Dee and Kelley have only received forty-eight of the Tables so far. She then proceeds to deliver the text of her Table:

> Write the 49th. You have but 48 already. Write first in a paper apart:
>
> Loagaeth feg lovi brtnc
> Larzed dox ner nagzilb adnor
> [Now seas appear][115]
> doncha Larb vors hirobra
> exi vr zednip taiip chinrvane
> chermach lendix nor zandox. [*A True and Faithful Relation*, p. 19]

During the transmission of the above text, Kelley also described the vision of Galvah he saw in the crystal. This vision has provided some confusion for Enochian scholars over the years—although what we have learned of Galvah previously in this chapter may throw some light on the subject.[116]

As she spoke those words, Galvah's head glowed so brightly it could not be looked upon, and the light would flash brighter each time she spoke. This would be recognizable to Christians and artists as a "halo"—a Divine Glory said to surround the heads of Prophets, Saints, and Angels as often depicted in Christian iconography. This is understood as the Presence of God—or the Holy Spirit. (See Exodus 33:14 and 34:29–30.) As we know Galvah is the *Sheckinah* (Divine Presence), it makes sense that she would manifest such a halo while speaking the powerful words of her Table.

There were also two further beams of light that entered Galvah during her transmission, adding themselves to the light of the halo. These three sources of light seem to be significant to the text itself. This is suggested as, later in the same session, Galvah reveals part of the mysteries of the words she has transmitted:

> There are only the words of the first leaf.[117] [. . .] In them is the Divinity of the Trinity, the Mysteries of our Creation, the age of many years, and the conclusion of the World. Of me they are honored, but of me, not to be uttered: Neither did I disclose them myself: For, they are the beams of my understanding, and the Fountain from whence I water. [*A True and Faithful Relation*, p. 20]

Galvah's "beams of understanding" are likely the three beams of light—or halos—from the vision. Here, we learn that they are related to two threefold concepts: on one hand, the Trinity (whom Galvah credits for the words of her Table), and on the other, the Creation, age, and conclusion of the world.

Therefore, in some sense, leaf 49 is a compendium of all that precedes it in the Holy Book. Note that it begins with the title of the Book—*Loagaeth*—which (as far as I am aware) is the only place in the entire Book this word appears.[118] I also notice that there are only three capital letters in the text, and all of them are *L*—which is Angelical for "The First."[119] Therefore, we have three distinct sentences here, probably encompassing the Trinitarian mystery hinted at by Galvah.

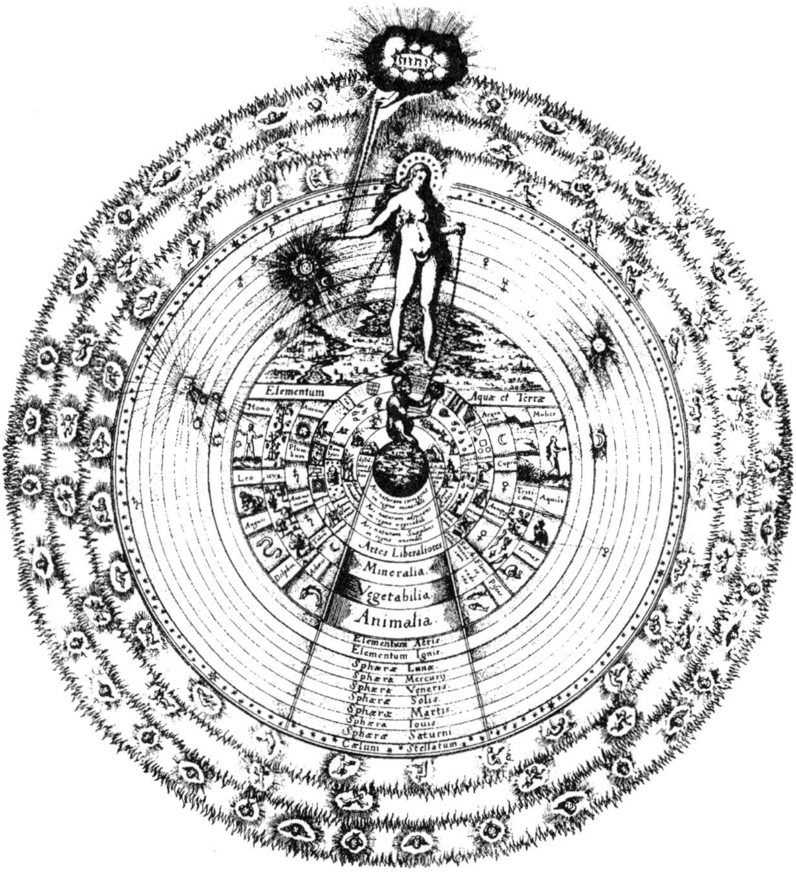

Soul of the World

Also notable in the vision are the appearance of seas and all the beasts of the earth. As we can see, Dee recorded the appearance of the seas in the middle of the text of leaf 49, between the words *adnor* and *doncha*. This, according to Dee's notes, would be just before the second beam of light entered the Mother.

Then, just after that second beam, all the "Beasts and Creatures of the World" appeared in the shewstone. I would assume they arose from both the earth and the seas around Galvah, in a manner reminiscent of the appearance of animals in the first chapter of Genesis.[120] These hordes of animals made threatening gestures toward Kelley—as one might expect of any wild beast. However, they would then turn toward Galvah and fawn upon her.

I believe what we have in this vision is, in fact, an image of the Soul of the World—the version of the *Sheckinah* or *Sophia* most familiar to Hermeticism. Galvah is Mother Nature, and we see her in that role in Kelley's vision.

Consider, also, that Table 49 embodies the lowest of the thirty Aethyrs, called *Tex*. This is the one Aethyr that contains four different Parts (rather than three)—probably symbolic of the physical realm. It is therefore fitting that the Table associated with *Tex* should embody the Soul of Nature and the physical world itself (the end product of the Seven Days of Creation).[121]

However, there was also a down side to this vision of Galvah. As she warned, the forty-ninth Table is "a hotchpotch without order" that signifies "a disorder of the world." Perhaps because of the inclusion of the End Times in the mysteries of this Table, the creatures Kelley saw in the stone were predominated by loathsome things like serpents, dragons, toads, and "all ugly and hideous shapes of beasts."

This is common in medieval magickal texts like the *Goetia*, where infernal spirits appear in hideous shapes—often composite forms made of serpents, toads, dragons, and the like. These texts warn that the horrible countenances of these creatures can be stressful to the mind of the exorcist. Kelley, according to Dee's record, seems to have experienced this during this aspect of Galvah's vision:

> Note, also, that the manner of the fiery brightness was such, and the grisly countenances of the Monsters was so tedious and grievous and displeasant to Edward Kelley that partly the very grief of his mind and body . . . such grievous sights necessary to be exhibited with the Mysteries delivering unto us, had in a manner forced him to leave off all. But I again with reasonable exhorting of him, and partly [thanks to][122] the providence and decree Divine, wrought some mitigating of this grief and disquieting. [*A True and Faithful Relation*, p. 19]

The view of such dark chaotic (even infernal) forces as fundamental to the physical world is a very Gnostic one. In fact, both Gnosticism and the Qabalah teach that the physical world (as we know it) came about only after Adam's fall from the celestial Eden. The physical world of suffering, in this view, is an intermixing of Divine Light and the earthly demonic shells that attempt to obscure it. (A concept illustrated rather well here in Galvah's vision of the forty-ninth leaf.)

The concept of the End Times, of course, is the rectification of Adam's Fall, and the re-elevation of the world back to the celestial Paradise. Therefore, the entire process of Creation comes full cycle here in leaf 49 of the Holy Book—the final product of 7 x 7. Nature in all Her winding chaos is here, as well as the World of Man and its conclusion. Later in the journals, Galvah would provide a further clue in this direction:

> One thing I will teach thee. The End is greater than the Beginning, or the Midst. For the End is witness of them both, but they both cannot witness of the End. [*A True and Faithful Relation*, p. 27]

The End is the final result—or product—of the Beginning and Middle. In this sense, the End (or end result) always encompasses the whole of what led to it. (Consider this in relation to the First Table, which contains the blueprints—or potential—for all that will come after it.) This fits well with Galvah's previous description of the words of the forty-ninth leaf: "In them is the Divinity of the Trinity, the Mysteries of our Creation, the age of many years, and the conclusion of the World."

After Galvah had completed her vision and the transmission of the forty-ninth leaf, Dee asked her for details on how this text should be written in the perfected copy of the Holy Book:

> **Dee:** What shall I do with these 21 words now received? [. . .] I beseech you, how shall I write these names in the first leaf?[123]
>
> **Galvah:** They are to be written in 5 Tables, in every Table 21 letters. [*A True and Faithful Relation*, p. 20]

There are a couple of problems with this exchange between Dee and Galvah. First, Dee refers to "21 words now received," while there appear to be twenty-two words in the text Galvah transmitted. I suspect two possibilities in this case. The first is that Dee may have simply miscounted the number of words here—though I find that rather unlikely, as Dee had the text right in front of him at the time. The second possibility suggests that Dee broke a word in half when he paused to write "Now seas appear" in the middle of the transmission. Therefore, what appears to be two words—*adnor doncha*—may actually be a singular (or compound) word—*adnordoncha*.

More problematic, however, is the response given by Galvah—where Dee is told to write the text of leaf 49 in five Tables of twenty-one letters each. That makes a total of 105 letters (5 x 21 = 105). Yet, the text—written in English letters—contains a total of 113 characters.

The solution is found by transcribing the letters into Angelical characters. First, note there are four instances of the digraph *ch* in the text (*doncha*, *chinrvane*, and *chermach*). This digraph is usually intended to produce a throaty *kh* sound in the Angelical tongue, and it is possible this is represented by a single character (called *Veh*—often transliterated as the English letter *K*). If so, this reduces the number of letters in this text by four, from 113 to 109.

Next, I notice that two of the words contain the letters *zed*. *Zed* happens to be the common name for the letter Z (sometimes also called "ezod" or "zod") outside of the United States of America. There are several instances in Dee's journals where he spells out the name of this letter (though usually choosing the "zod" form),[124] rather than using the Z character alone. If we replace the two instances of *zed* here on leaf 49 (*Larzed* and *zednip*) with the Angelical character for Z (called *Ceph*), it further reduces the total of letters to 105.

Now that we have arrived at the necessary 105 letters, we can set them into the five Tables of twenty-one letters each:

L	O	A	G	A	E	T
H	F	E	G	L	O	V
I	B	R	T	N	C	L

A	R	Z	D	O	X	N
E	R	N	A	G	Z	I
L	B	A	D	N	O	R

D	O	N	K	A	L	A
R	B	V	O	R	S	H
I	R	O	B	R	A	E

X	I	V	R	Z	N	I
P	T	A	I	I	P	K
I	N	R	V	A	N	E

K	E	R	M	A	K	L
E	N	D	I	X	N	O
R	Z	A	N	D	O	X

Following this exchange, Dee continues asking Galvah questions about these five little Tables. However, as usual, insignificant details were left for Dee's discretion:

Dee: How shall I place the five Tables upon the two sides: three in the first and two in the second, or one in the first and four in the second, or how else?

Galvah: As thou seest cause.

Dee: Shall I write them in letters of gold?

Galvah: The writing hath been referred to thy discretion with colors, and such things as appertain to the writing thereof. Upon the first side write three Tables, and on the second two. [*A True and Faithful Relation*, p. 20]

The next day, Dee has set the words into the five Tables, and presents it to Galvah for approval:

Dee: I have assayed divers ways to place the five Tables, on the two sides on this first leaf. Is it to your liking as I have done it, in the five little Triangles?

Galvah: As concerning the setting down of the five Tables, it is sufficient as it is done. [*A True and Faithful Relation*, p. 21]

It is unclear why Dee chose to make the five Tables into triangles, even though Galvah finds it "sufficient." Personally, I would rather keep the five Tables each 7 x 3 squares, as these two numbers obviously play a significant role in leaf 49 and the Holy Book overall.

Be It Unto Thee, as Thou Hast Done—The Anticlimax of the *Loagaeth* Saga?

The process of creating a perfected copy of the Holy Book—written in Angelical characters, and from the right to the left—is an understandably monumental task. It only took Dee a matter of days to become overwhelmed with the project, and by June 29th, 1583 (he was working on Table 7), he was already asking the Angels for help.

On that day, it was the Heptarchic Angel Madimi who appeared in the shewstone. Dee had a special relationship with this spiritual creature—who appeared as a little girl[125] and therefore Dee felt comfortable in asking her for intervention. In response, Madimi brings her Mother—who is introduced to Dee and Kelley as I AM (a biblical name of the Highest Divinity), and who we also know as Galvah, or Wisdom:

> **Dee:** While I was about to write the Title of the second side of the seventh leaf: and (E.K. sitting by me), Madimi appeared as before like a young girl, and I saluted her in the Name of God, as coming from God for good, and said to her, that I was wonderfully oppressed with the Work prescribed to me to perform before August next, and desired her to help me to one to write the holy Book as it ought to be written: seeing I did all I could, and it seemed almost impossible for me to finish it as it is requisite. Madimi promised to help me to one to write the Book; and thereupon appeared to her (but unseen to E.K) her Mother. [. . .]
>
> **Madimi:** Mother, I pray you let him have one to write his Book.
>
> **Mother:** I am of the word, and by the word.[126] I say, Seal up those things thou hast. And I myself will take charge of Galvah to the end.[127]
>
> **Dee:** Truth it is, it must grow to a great mislikeing grudge, that God should seem to have laid burdens on our shoulders, greater than we are

able to bear: and then if we fall and fail under them, he would find a cause not to perform his promises made for carrying of those burdens.

Mother: Whatsoever is thy part, the same will I perform. I will put thy yoke (in this one thing) upon my shoulders.

Dee: Will you then write it as I should have written it?

Mother: I have said I will.

Dee: Where shall I leave the Book?

Mother: Leave it where you will: your locks are no hindrance to us. Even when the time cometh believe and you shall find it written.

Dee: You have eased my heart of a thousand-pound weight.

Mother: Because ye shall not fall into error. Dost thou believe?

Dee: Yea, verily.

Mother: Then verily will I do it. [. . .]

Dee: I pray, tell me your name.

Mother: I AM; what will you more?[128] [*A True and Faithful Relation*, pp. 26–27]

In my opinion, this is one of the most unbelievable scenes in the journals. By all appearances, Dee receives a promise from the Mother to write the perfected Holy Book *for* him. I simply find it hard to accept that Dee would have seriously expected such a direct and astounding miracle to take place. I have to wonder if he wasn't merely trying to shift the responsibility of having the project completed on time from his own shoulders onto the Angels. If the Mother had made such a promise, then what Angel could accuse Dee of failure?

Apparently, the project was not completed on time after all. First, the entire month of August is missing from the journals.[129] The entries simply end with July 4th and pick up again—without comment—on September 21st, 1583. Almost three entire months are obscured from modern study.

Then, by April 12th of the following year, 1584, Dee mentions to Nalvage that the Holy Book "is promised to be written"—suggesting that it is not complete, and Dee still believes the Mother and Her Angels are going to do it for him:

> **Nalvage:** How, therefore, shall I inform you, which know them not? [. . .] The Characters, or Letters of the Tables.
>
> **Dee:** You mean the mystical Letters, wherein the holy book is promised to be written. And if the book be so written and laid open before us, and then you will from Letter to Letter point, and we to record your instructions. [*A True and Faithful Relation*, p. 78]

This is a full eight months after the original August deadline, and Dee is still receiving instructions for how to work with the *Loagaeth* Tables. In fact, the aforementioned discussion takes place just before the forty-eight Angelical Keys are transmitted. That means that the very Keys needed to open the Gates had not been delivered to Dee on or before the August deadline.

Kelley's exuberance also provides us with evidence that the original deadline was missed. As might be understandable, the men were not likely happy that the much-anticipated day of August 1st resulted in no great Revelations. The Angels had told them so often not to rush the time of God's choosing, but to wait patiently for August. Nearly nine months later, on the date of April 21st, the Angels Gabriel and Nalvage once again tell the men not to rush God. Kelley has a sarcastic response to that:

> **Gabriel and Nalvage:** He never heard of any man that would ask, if God would perform his promises.
>
> **Edward Kelley:** By August next?
>
> **Gabriel and Nalvage:** What if it were a hundred Augusts? You may be weary before August next, as the Children of Israel were of their Manna. [*A True and Faithful Relation*, p. 92]

It is hard to appreciate this exchange out of the context of the journals. As I stated previously, Kelley's words here are likely sarcastic in nature.

I read it as a kind of challenge, bringing up the fact that the Angels had already failed to deliver on one of God's biggest "promises"—the revelation of the *Loagaeth* mysteries on August 1st, 1583. Kelley likely fixated on this fact, as he constantly looked for evidence that the Angels were actually liars and devils. (He apparently failed to consider that neither he nor Dee had completed the perfected Holy Book as they had been instructed to do.)

Kelley was not alone in letting his frustration slip through into the records. It was only a few days later, on April 27th, that Dee asks Gabriel and Nalvage for an update (or confirmation) on the Mother's promise:

> **Dee:** As concerning the book writing by the Highest,[130] what shall I expect thereof?
>
> **Gabriel and Nalvage:** There is no point of faith.
>
> **Dee:** I believe verily that it shall be written by the power of the Highest.
>
> **Gabriel and Nalvage:** The power of the Highest confirmeth me, but not my power, the Highest.
>
> **Dee:** Be it as the will of God is. [*A True and Faithful Relation*, p. 104]

When the Angels tell Dee that the Mother's promise is "no point of faith," I tend to see that as an indication that Dee had it wrong. However, Dee certainly didn't want to see it that way, and therefore reaffirms that he believes the Highest (I AM) will indeed write the Holy Book for him. The Angels put the issue off on the Highest and that ends the issue for that session.

In the end, Dee does appear to have produced the Book on his own. At least, he created a copy to the best of his ability. It was only two months later, on July 7th, 1584, when Ave came to reveal the Prayer of Enoch and the secret to *Gebofal*.[131] Perhaps, Ave appeared at that time with that information because Dee had *finally* produced the Book:

> **Ave:** My brother, I see thou doth not understand the mystery of this Book, or work, thou hast in hand. [. . .] Notwithstanding, that thy labour be not frustrate, and void of fruit, be it unto thee, as thou hast done.

Dee (in margin): The Book confirmed.

Dee: Lord I did the best that I could conceive of it. [*A True and Faithful Relation*, p. 196]

Here we see that Dee does have the Book "in hand." He claims it is the best he could do, and Ave appears to say that it will be sufficient to result in *some* fruit for his labor. The marginal note indicates that Dee took this as a confirmation of his perfected copy of the *Book of Loagaeth*.

However, the August date seems to have been put aside. Perhaps this is what Ave means by the phrase " . . . be it unto thee, as thou hast done." When the long-awaited August 1st finally arrives, Dee and Kelley do not commence a ritual opening of the forty-eight Gates. Instead, at the command of the Angels, they pack up and head toward the court of Emperor Rudolph in Prague.[132]

Records of whether or not Dee or Kelley ever made use of *Loagaeth* do not exist. They have either never existed, meaning the men never used this material, or they have simply not survived or been discovered. Meanwhile, if we consider the legacy that Dee left behind in Prague, it is likely that the Angels finally had their own agenda fulfilled after all. Even if neither of the men achieved their personal goals with the magick, the historical mark left by Dee in Prague cannot be denied.[133] As promised, the Angels *did* initiate a new current into a new world—and the Age of Enlightenment soon followed.

Endnotes

1. See *John Dee's Five Books of Mystery* and *A True and Faithful Relation*.
2. Also see Psalms 69:28, Daniel 12:1, Luke 10:20, Philippians 4:3, and Revelation 3:5, 13:8, 17:8, and 20:12–15.
3. To further explore Dee's search for the Book of Enoch, the following references have been highly recommended: György E. Szönyi, *John Dee's Occultism* (Albany, NY: State University of New York Press, 2004), p. 145; William J. Bouwsma, *Concordia Mundi: The Career and Thought of Guillaume Postel* (Cambridge, MA: Harvard University Press, 1957), pp. 13, 36–37; and Nicholas H. Clulee, *John Dee's Natural Philosophy: Between Science and Religion* (London: Routledge, 1988), pp. 208–20, 297 (note 25).
4. Lights and Judgments = The *Urim* and *Thaumim*, associated with the Breast Plate of the High Priest of Israel, were likely scrying stones of some sort. (See Exodus 28:30.)

5. See 1 Samuel 9 for the story of Saul's consultation with Samuel, as well as the explanation of the term *seer* as applied to prophets.
6. Dee has "could not be come by at man's hand."
7. Dee has "from thee (O God) mediately or immediately." In his *Five Books of Mystery*, Joseph Peterson mentions in a footnote (p. 59, note 15) that "mediately" indicates "through a medium." Therefore "immediately" must indicate "without a medium." (Dee employed Kelley because he personally lacked mediumistic skills.)
8. Epistle of Jude 14–15. Jude quotes from *1 Enoch*, but Dee seems to assume that Jude is quoting the legendary Book of Enoch written in the Angelical language. (See the section in this chapter entitled "The Holy *Book of Loagaeth*.")
9. Found on p. 174 (June 25, 1584) and p. 196 (July 7, 1584) of *A True and Faithful Relation*.
10. Had they been legends of Solomon, Dee's journals would be considered "Solomonic."
11. Adam and Eve, who were the distant grandparents of Enoch.
12. *Heptarchia* means "Sevenfold Hierarchy" or "Sevenfold Rulership." This system of magick revolved specifically around the Seven Archangels who "stand before the Throne of God." (Revelation 4:5.)
13. Published—with all Latin translated—as *John Dee's Five Books of Mystery*, edited by Joseph Peterson.
14. To see the original manuscripts of Dee's journals, visit http://www.themagickalreview.org/enochian/enochian.html. Also, for transcriptions of Dee's work, see http://www.esotericarchives.com/.
15. An Angel from the Heptarchic system of magick.
16. In other words, the Celestial Tablets (of Enoch) are written by the hand of *Sophia* (Wisdom). *Sophia* is the name of the ancient Gnostic Bride of God (or Mother of the World).
17. That is, the First Great Prophecy was of the coming of Christ.
18. That is, this Holy Book contains the Second Great Prophecy, which is the return of Christ.
19. The Tribulation is a period of war and suffering that precedes the end of the world in the Christian mythos.
20. We will see later that there are Calls (or Keys) associated with the Holy Book. However, I suspect Dee saw this as a reference to the first sounding of the Trumpet, an aspect of the Christian Rapture. See Revelation, chapter 8 (and following), for the Trumpets.
21. Referring to the Holy Book—which has already been described as containing the Second Great Prophecy of the End Times.
22. The first that lived = Adam.
23. It was Raphael who delivered the Holy Book. See chapter 5.

24. I have added this for clarification.
25. Casaubon has "*Alcoran.*" The Koran was a new "Testament" which was delivered to Muhammad by the Archangel Gabriel, and which founded the Muslim Faith.
26. Casaubon has "Mahometans"—as in "Muhammad-ians."
27. *A True and Faithful Relation* does not show the first *a*, leaving "Logaeth"—but this is an error on the part of Casaubon.
28. See the Book of Revelation, chapter 5.
29. See the *Five Books of Mystery*, p. 263.
30. I have added the bracketed word to clarify the speech.
31. See the *Five Books of Mystery*, pp. 268–69.
32. The journals do not mention it at this point, but there is also a title above each Table of the Holy Book.
33. Dee adds in the margin: "(49 powers with their inferiors . . . 48 after a sort: and 1.)" Again, we see the isolation of one leaf of the Book from the others.
34. Compare this to the Qabalistic convention of attributing four manners of interpreting the Torah—one for each of the Four Qabalistic Worlds.
35. One of these appears to be the language we will see later in the forty-eight Angelical Calls, or Keys.
36. Six is the number attributed to the Sun in works like Agrippa's *Three Books*.
37. Seven is the number attributed to Venus.
38. For instance, see the material in the classic grimoire known as the *Arbatel of Magic*—a text very familiar to Dee and one that had a massive influence on his Heptarchic system of magick.
39. All of these are associated with the seven Archangels who stand before the Throne of God in Revelation, chapter 4. These are the Archangels (or *Elohim*) directly involved in the Seven Days of Creation, in Genesis 1.
40. We will return to the subject of the Angelical Keys (or Calls) in the following chapters.
41. That is, the first leaf that is accessible to the aspirant.
42. See pp. 324–25 of the *Five Books of Mystery*.
43. Dee makes this marginal notation: "Note this covering to be made for the book."
44. See *A True and Faithful Relation*, p. 174.
45. See the *Five Books of Mystery*, p. 269.
46. See the *Five Books of Mystery*, p. 288.
47. Or Spanish, Latin, etc.
48. Requisite = Required.
49. See Sloane 3189 for Kelley's English-lettered copy of the Holy Book.
50. We shall explore the subject of the perfected Holy Book later in this chapter.

51. We shall see later in this chapter that Galvah continues to refer to the forty-ninth leaf of *Loagaeth* as "the first leaf"—though it is in fact the last.
52. See chapter 1 of this current work.
53. See the *Five Books of Mystery*, pp. 286–343. Remember, only the First Table (Sides A and B) is found in the *Five Books*. The entire Holy Book is preserved in Sloane MS 3189.
54. See the *Five Books of Mystery*, pp. 286–87.
55. See Donald Laycock's introduction to *The Complete Enochian Dictionary* (York Beach, ME: Red Wheel/Weiser, 2001), pp. 33–35.
56. I have added the English-letter equivalents in parentheses for clarification.
57. This would not be a concern for the other forty-eight Tables, which contained single letters in each cell.
58. See the *Five Books of Mystery*, p. 296.
59. As of this writing, my analysis of the text is unavailable to the public. However, it might be available on my website (http://kheph777.tripod.com) by the time this book is published.
60. This is likely a reference to the Book sealed with seven seals in the Revelation of St. John. Evidence suggests that *Loagaeth* is intended, on some level, to be this same Book.
61. See the *Five Books of Mystery*, p. 411.
62. That is, all Tables will be explained at once, rather than one here and another there, etc.
63. By "double repetition" I assume Raphael means to both write and speak the text at once.
64. The Holy Book. Kelley was reading the words aloud to Dee so he could record them. However, Raphael here warns against speaking the words again "till it be in practice."
65. Here is the first time August is mentioned as the time to put *Loagaeth* into practice.
66. In other words, "at a glance" within the Book.
67. Though the transmission of the Tables does halt the next day, I should point out that the final—forty-ninth—Table was withheld for some time afterward. We shall explore this subject in this chapter.
68. See *A True and Faithful Relation*, p. 10.
69. Earlier in this speech, Galvah had made reference to the negative view of women seen in Trithemius' work. She said, "If Trithemius can separate the dignity of the Soul of Woman from the excellency of man . . . " Therefore, the above quote is Galvah's (slightly sarcastic) response to Trithemius' take on women as the "end of man's excellency."
70. See *Ul* (End) in the Lexicon in volume II.

71. Each Table of *Loagaeth* has a Title—one for the front Table and one for the back Table on each leaf.
72. Encompassed.
73. I have added this word for clarification.
74. See *A True and Faithful Relation*, p. 27.
75. See Exodus 3:13–14, where God gives Moses the Hebrew Divine Name *Eheieh asher Eheieh* (I Am that I Am). The Qabalah assigns this Name to the Highest Divine Sphere.
76. The hedge would have been symbolic of ignorance.
77. See Proverbs 1:20–33.
78. See *A True and Faithful Relation*, pp. 10–12.
79. Remember Galavah saying, ". . . true Wisdom is always painted with a woman's garment." (Garment = Body.)
80. See Donald Tyson, *Enochian Magick for Beginners* (St. Paul, MN: Llewellyn, 2002).
81. To date, this strange ordering of the planets has not been explained.
82. This association is via the Seven Ensigns of Creation from the *Heptarchia.*
83. "The time to come" is August 1st, and the revelation of *Loagaeth*'s mysteries.
84. Remember previously that Galvah instructed Dee to begin work on the perfected Holy Book on a Tuesday. (See *A True and Faithful Relation,* p. 13).
85. *A True and Faithful Relation* has the first couple of these sessions mislabeled as Saturdays. The dates given indicate that each should be a Sunday.
86. In chapter 3, I have included a similar section on the Angelical Keys that open the Tables. What we know of the Keys further illuminates what we know of the Tables.
87. Thanks to Joseph H. Peterson's *Twilit Grotto Esoteric Archives* for these titles, online at http://www.esotericarchives.com/dee/sl3189.htm. Used with permission.
88. See the *Five Books of Mystery*, pp. 288–343.
89. We will examine the Keys in chapter 3.
90. See the *Five Books*, p. 306, footnote 228. Also p. 319, footnote 321 ("Interpret not yet").
91. Traditionally the Archangel of the Sun.
92. Genesis 1:20–26.
93. Called, in Latin, *Descensus Ad Inferos*.
94. This was a common practice in tribal Shamanism, where the shaman would descend to the underworld to retrieve the lost souls of the sick and dying.
95. I have added the bracketed line numbers for clarification.
96. *Five Books of Mystery*, p. 312, footnote 277.
97. Except for Table 49, which was also delivered in full words, instead of letters. See the "Forty-Nine Tables of *Loagaeth*: What We Know" section of this chapter.
98. Revelation 4:5.
99. *A True and Faithful Relation*, p. 98.

100. Casaubon also put the title *Bacap Laffos* on this Table, as if it were the title of side B. However, it is actually the title of side B of leaf 10.
101. See p. 348 of the *Five Books of Mystery*.
102. Shovels.
103. See the section of this chapter entitled "Kelley's Second Vision of the Holy Book."
104. See chapter 1 of this volume.
105. Table 49 also has its own entry. See the "Forty-Nine Tables of *Loagaeth*: What We Know" section of this chapter.
106. See *A True and Faithful Relation*, pp. 139–59 and 201–09.
107. Via the Valentinian Gnostics.
108. This is yet another indication that the forty-nine Tables of *Loagaeth* begin at the highest and proceed to the lowest point—just like the Jewish fifty Gates of *Binah*.
109. See *1 Enoch*, chapters 21–36.
110. See Ezekiel 40:1–2 for one example.
111. Probably symbolic of the Four Elements and Zodiacal Triplicities, the four cardinal directions, the four winds, and other fourfold concepts associated with the physical realm. See Agrippa's *Three Books of Occult Philosophy*, Book II, chapter 7, "Of the Number Four, and the Scale Thereof."
112. Also see chapter 3, in which I discuss the Angelical Keys that open the Aethyrs.
113. Remember the first page in a Western book would necessarily be the last page if the book were written in the Semitic leftward fashion.
114. See p. 19 of *A True and Faithful Relation*.
115. This is a note made by Dee. It is in relation to the vision Kelley is having as these words are spoken. We explore this vision (and others related to it) in the "Let Those That Fear God, and Are Worthy, Read" section of this chapter.
116. The entire vision is found on p. 19 of *A True and Faithful Relation*.
117. First leaf by Western standards, but it remains leaf 49.
118. It does not appear in the First Table. It may yet be hidden somewhere among the text of Tables 2 through 49.
119. See the Lexicon. *L* or *El* (The First). This is a Name of God in the Angelical tongue.
120. See Genesis 1:10, 20–25.
121. The Qabalah would refer to this as *Malkuth* (the Earthly Kingdom).
122. I have added this for clarification.
123. Leaf 49.
124. It is possible that Kelley was the one who pronounced the Zs as "zed" in this case.
125. Dee would later name his own daughter after Madimi.
126. The Mother (*Aima Elohim*), or Bride of God, is intimately connected with the Word (*Logos*) or *Christos*. Together, their marriage results in the Holy Spirit as understood by the ancient Gnostics.

127. Although the Mother appears to refer *to* Galvah in this statement, Dee actually records the Mother's name *as* Galvah later in this session. See *A True and Faithful Relation*, p. 27.
128. Exodus 3:14—"So God said to Moses, 'I AM that I AM.'"
129. See *A True and Faithful Relation*, pp. 32–33.
130. Remember that I AM (*Eheieh*) is the Highest Divine Name in the Qabalah.
131. See chapter 4 of this volume.
132. See *A True and Faithful Relation*, p. 212.
133. See Francis Yates, *The Rosicrucian Enlightenment* (London: Routledge, 2001). Dee's work (such as the *Hieroglyphic Monad*), and perhaps Dee personally, had an apparent influence on the unknown authors of the foundational Rosicrucian documents.

Chapter Three

The Forty-Eight Angelical Keys (or Calls)

And I will give unto thee the Keys of the Kingdom of Heaven. And whatsoever thou shalt bind on Earth shall be bound in Heaven. And whatsoever thou shalt loose on Earth shall be loosed in Heaven. [Matthew 16:19]

These Calls touch all the parts of the World. The World may be dealt withal, with her parts. Therefore you may do anything. These Calls are keys into the Gates and Cities of Wisdom. [The Angel Mapsama in *A True and Faithful Relation*, p. 145]

In "Kelley's Second Vision of the Holy Book," a section in the previous chapter, I highlighted several comparisons between the thirty-six Tables of *Soyga* and Dee's forty-nine Tables of *Loagaeth*. Beyond their structural and mathematical similarities, each set of Tables is said to embody specific aspects of Creation, which can be accessed by the aspirant who knows how to open them.

Another important similarity between *Soyga* and *Loagaeth* is that both sets of Tables are opened (or decrypted) with "Keys." *Soyga* includes a set of thirty-six six-lettered names that are used to decipher the encrypted magickal squares. *Loagaeth* also has a set of Keys—forty-eight in this case[1]—that are promised to open the mysteries of the Tables. However, the "Keys" of Dee's system are not short and simple keywords. Instead, Dee's forty-eight Keys are long poems (or, perhaps, psalms)—often called the forty-eight Angelical Callings. They are magickal invocations intended to obtain Divine and earthly secrets from the Angels attached to each Table of *Loagaeth*.

The Angel Nalvage was charged with the transmission of the Keys—though the origins of this entity are uncertain. Unlike most of the Angels encountered by the two men, Nalvage does not appear anywhere in Dee's "Enochian" system of magick. (That is, his name is not found in the *Heptarchia*, in *Loagaeth*, in the Watchtowers, and so on.) Neither is he found among the traditional lists of Angels descended from Jewish, Christian, or Arabic sources. All we know for certain is that Nalvage is directly subservient to the Archangel Gabriel, and that his primary job in the journals was to deliver the Angelical Keys.

Nalvage first appeared to Dee and Kelley in February of 1584, but he did not begin to transmit the Keys until the following April. That was eight months *after* the date upon which the Angels promised to reveal the mysteries of *Loagaeth*. This delay is likely because Dee had not, by the previous August, completed the "perfected copy" of the Holy Book.[2] Had he completed the project on time, I suspect the Angels would have revealed the forty-eight Keys at that point.

When Nalvage makes his first appearance, he spends some time teaching the men about the Doctrine contained in *Loagaeth*.[3] He then focuses upon the transmission of a magickal Tablet called the *Corpus Omnium*—which seems to bear directly upon the Keys, and which we shall explore in depth later in this chapter. Finally, in mid-April of 1584, Nalvage makes the first mention of the Angelical Keys:

> I am therefore to instruct and inform you, according to your Doctrine delivered, which is contained in 49 Tables. In 49 voices, or callings: which are the Natural Keys to open those, not 49 but 48 (for one is not to be opened) Gates of Understanding, whereby you shall have knowledge to move every Gate . . . [*A True and Faithful Relation*, p. 77]

So, we know from the very start that these Keys are intended to open the Gates of Understanding.[4] As we learned in chapter 2, the First Gate is "not to be opened" by humans. However, the remaining forty-eight can be accessed with the Angelical Keys.

Much later in the journals, the Angel Illemese makes clear the relationship between the Keys and the forty-nine Tables of *Loagaeth*:

> But you shall understand that these 19 Calls[5] are the Calls, or entrances into the knowledge of the mystical Tables. Every Table containing one whole leaf,[6] whereunto you need no other circumstances. [*A True and Faithful Relation*, p. 199]

During the transmission of the Keys, the Archangel Gabriel gives us some further information on the Keys and the Angelical language in which they are written:

> In these Keys which we deliver, are the mysteries and secret beings and effects of all things moving, and moved within the world. In this is the life of MOTION, in whom all tongues of the world are moved, for there is neither speech nor silence that was nor shall be to the end of the world, but they are all as plain here, as in their own nakedness. Despise it not, therefore, for unto them that are hungry, it is bread, unto the thirst drink, and unto the naked clothing. [*A True and Faithful Relation*, p. 94]

In chapter 2, we saw many descriptions of the Doctrine of *Loagaeth* that sound very similar to Gabriel's above words. We know that *Loagaeth* represents the mythical Book of Life (or Book of the Lamb), wherein is found the essence of all created things.[7] Both Christian Doctrine and Dee's Angels proclaim the Holy Book as the wellspring of all life. However, without the Keys with which to open the Gates, the Book is merely an inert object in human hands.[8] It is the Keys that activate the forces in the Tables, and this is why Gabriel claims that the Keys embody the "life of motion."

During a later session in the journals, Dee and Kelley receive further information from the Angel Mapsama:

> These Calls touch all the parts of the World. The World may be dealt withal, with her parts. Therefore you may do anything. These Calls are keys into the Gates and Cities of Wisdom. Which [Gates][9] are not able to be opened, but without visible apparition. [. . .] You called for

> wisdom, God hath opened unto you his Judgment. He hath delivered unto you the keys, that you may enter. [*A True and Faithful Relation*, pp. 145–46]

Mapsama's lesson on the Keys is the most practical we have seen. Where Gabriel taught that the Keys are the "life of Motion" (or "initiatory force") behind the forty-nine Tables, Mapsama adds that the Keys have influence over all parts of the physical world—giving one the power to "do anything." (We can see an example of this in the Parts of the Earth system that Dee and Kelley would later receive from the Angels. That system makes use of one Key—the final one, the Call of the Aethyrs—to scry into the secrets of any nation on Earth.)

Later, we shall see that the Angels also instructed Dee and Kelley to use the Angelical Keys to open *every* Table in the Holy Book—likely over a forty-eight-day period resulting in a forty-ninth day of Divine revelation. This is the primary *Loagaeth* system of magick (see chapter 4), which several of the Angels seem to imply in their lessons on the usage of the Keys.

On the day before the transmission of the Keys began, Dee recorded this exchange between Nalvage and himself:

> **Nalvage:** Unto this Doctrine belongeth the perfect knowledge, and remembrance of the mystical Creatures. How, therefore, shall I inform you, which know them not? [. . .]
>
> **Dee:** [. . .] You mean the mystical Letters, wherein the holy book is promised to be written. And if the book be so written and laid open before us, and then you will from Letter to Letter point, and we to record your instructions. [*A True and Faithful Relation*, p. 78]

We learn here that the Tables of *Loagaeth* were directly involved in the reception of the Keys. The following day, as Dee suggested above, Nalvage directed the men from one Table to another, drawing a single letter from each one along the way. (See the section in this chapter entitled "Dee Suspected of Cryptography?") Thus, the words of the Keys were not taken whole cloth from the text of *Loagaeth*, but were each compiled from letters drawn from *several* different Tables.

This might tell us something important about the nature of Angelical. As we already know, *Loagaeth* contains the Celestial Language used in the genesis of all things. We also know that each Table represents an individual and pure (even archetypal) aspect of the created Universe.

Meanwhile, Angels are the agents of creation—the "workmen" through whom all things manifest. According to Judeo-Christian lore, they accomplish this feat by bearing the creative power to earth as a "message" from God. The "message" itself is a song of praise to the Creator—designed to grant life to something in the world.[10]

Therefore, the creative "message" that is carried by any given Angel should be compiled in some way from the Words of Creation contained in the Holy Book. I say "compiled" because, unlike the Tables of *Loagaeth*, the Universe is not separated into "pure aspects" and archetypes. Instead, the Universe is a tapestry of mixed forces. Therefore, the Angels must draw forces from several Tables at once—a character from this Word of Creation, and another character from that Word of Creation—in order to manifest anything in reality. This is perhaps what we are seeing in the compilation of the forty-eight Keys by Nalvage.

The Reception of the Forty-Eight Keys

The transmission of the forty-eight Angelical Keys is divided between three places in *A True and Faithful Relation*. The first section, composed mainly of the Angelical words, appears between pages 79 and 138. Most of the English was given later, during a single session between pages 190 and 194. Finally, the Key of the Aethyrs was transmitted (also in a single session) between pages 201 and 208.

As we shall discuss later, Nalvage transmitted the Angelical of the first four Keys backward, taking several sessions. He also ended each transmission with the "English sense" of each Key. The rest of the Keys—5 through 18—were transmitted rapidly in a forward fashion, without English, in a single haphazard session. Some of them are mixed up or missing words. Two of them (Keys 14 and 15) are entirely missing.

The missing material was filled in later in the journals—but only in English form. Dee was left to compile the Angelical words from the Keys that had already been Anglicized. (Thankfully, the results of that work are contained in Dee's *48 Claves Angelicae*.)

Even the English given to Dee was not entirely complete. Between giving the English for Keys Eleven and Twelve, Nalvage tells Dee:

> **Nalvage:** Here must words in the end of the first Call follow, at Move, etc.
>
> **Dee:** But this Call, it differeth a little expressly. They are the 14 last words, in the holy language thus: Zacar e ca, od zamran, odo cicle Qua, Zorge, lap zirdo Noco Mad, Hoath Jaida. [*A True and Faithful Relation*, p. 193]

These are the words that appear at the very end of the first Key. They are an evocational formula that translate "Move, therefore, and appear! Open the mysteries of your creation. Be friendly unto me, for I am a servant of the same God as you, the true worshiper of the Highest." Dee was subsequently instructed to append these words to Keys 11 through 18, inclusively.

These fourteen words have been dubbed the "Repetitive Formula Pattern" by Angelical scholar Patricia Shaffer.[11] We will encounter this phrase again in the Lexicon in volume II.

Dee Suspected of Cryptography?

Now we shall explore one of the most obscure (and controversial) aspects of Dee's Angelic records—the transmission of Key One. Had Nalvage simply revealed the text of the Keys like any other magickal invocation or prayer (such as we find in numerous medieval grimoires), it would not likely have attracted much speculation. However, the overly complex manner in which Nalvage gathered the letters and transmitted the words of the first Key has led cryptologists to believe that the Tables of *Loagaeth* and their Keys are somehow encrypted messages (or encryption devices).

This is not much of a leap in logic. John Dee was himself a student of steganography ("hidden writing," or cryptography), and has long been associated with English espionage.[12] We also know that he owned a copy of the *Steganographia* by Trithemius—an early-sixteenth-century compendium of cryptology, entirely disguised as a work of Angelic magick.[13] It claimed to reveal the methods of sending secret communications by way of Angels or spirits, but the invocations turned out to be encrypted messages.[14] Therefore, we can see how easy it might be to suspect that Dee was up to the same tricks in his journals.

To begin with, we may note that Nalvage (at first) insisted upon transmitting the Keys *backward*. This was also established the day before the Keys were revealed:

> **Nalvage:** Also, in receiving of the calls, this is to be noted: that they are to be uttered of me, backward; and of you, in practice, forward.
>
> **Dee:** I understand it, for the efficacy of them; else, all things called would appear, and so hinder our preceding in learning. [*A True and Faithful Relation*, p. 78]

The next day, we find that the first word revealed by Nalvage was the *last* word of Key One, and it was spelled backward. (We will return to this later in this section.)

Let us consider this convention of backward spelling in a broader context. We have already encountered this in our discussion of the *Book of Soyga* (chapter 1). It is perhaps the simplest form of encryption to spell words in reverse—such as *Soyga*, which is supposed to be a mirror-spelling of *Agyos* (Greek: Holiness).[15] This is likely derived from Qabalistic practices that use Hebrew (written right to left) as their sacred language.

Additionally, there are forms of encryption that involve words or alphabets spelled "forward" and then transposed with letter sets that are written backward. For instance, take a look at this simple cipher:

A	B	C	D	E	F	G	H	I	J	K	L	M	N	O	P	Q	R	S	T	U	V	W	X	Y	Z
Z	Y	X	W	V	U	T	S	R	Q	P	O	N	M	L	K	J	I	H	G	F	E	D	C	B	A

The top line of letters is the standard alphabet, written in a forward (or left-to-right) fashion. The bottom line is the encryption, and contains the same alphabet written backward (or right to left). Any word can be spelled out with the letters in the top line, and then transposed with the letters directly beneath them in the bottom line.

As an example, let's use my own first name: *Aaron*. We find the *A* at the left of the top line, and beneath it we find the letter Z. Beneath the letter *R* in the top line we find an *I* in the bottom. Beneath the *O* we find the letter *L*. Finally, beneath the letter *N* we can see an *M*. Therefore, the name *Aaron* can be encrypted as the name *Zzilm*. If you compare this with the words in the Lexicon in volume II, you will see the resulting encryptions are somewhat similar to Angelical. Thus, it is little wonder that Nalvage's insistence on transmitting the words of the Keys backward has suggested encryption to modern scholars.

It is also interesting that Nalvage only followed this convention for the first four Keys—after which, he began transmitting the words forward instead. That means the majority of the Keys were delivered in a forward fashion—calling into question Dee's assumption that they must be transmitted backward or else "all things called would appear." (I should point out that Nalvage never confirmed Dee's comment in that regard.) This lends even more weight to the theory that encryption was involved: it may have been necessary to reverse only the first few Keys in order to give an *example* of how to use the rest of the Keys for decryption.

Dee's journals are also suspected of cryptology thanks to Nalvage's bizarre manner of revealing the letters of each word. Rather than simply pointing from letter to letter in the Holy Book (as Dee previously suggested), Nalvage indicated the letters via cryptic instructions for finding them in the Tables of *Loagaeth* with some very odd strings of numbers.

At the start of the session Nalvage states, " . . . the soul of man hath no portion in this First Table" of *Loagaeth*, however, "all the rest [of the Tables] are of understanding."[16] Immediately after stressing this, Nalvage launches into the transmission of Key One. It seems that his comments about the Tables bear directly upon the Keys—because Nalvage never draws letters for the Keys from the First Table.

I have transcribed the very first Angelical words received by Dee and Kelley from Nalvage—formatted here as they appear in Dee's journal. I am including a large enough sample to illustrate the cryptic manner in which Nalvage transmitted the letters, and the rather haphazard notations recorded by Dee. You will note that he recorded the letters in a column running down the left-hand side of the page, with the mysterious strings of numbers following each letter to the right (including the various Tables in *Loagaeth*.) Keep in mind that these words are written backward—beginning with the *final* word of the first Key:

A[17]

(Two thousand and fourteen, in the sixth Table, is) **D**

7003. In the thirteenth Table is **I**.

A In the 21st Table. 11406 downward.

I In the last Table, one less than Number. A word, Jaida [. . .]

Jaida is the last word of the Call.

H 49. ascending

T 49. descending

A 909. directly,

O simply.

H 2029. directly. Call it Hoath.

225. From the low angle on the right side, continuing in the same and next square.[18]

D 225 [The same number repeated]

A In the thirteenth Table, 740. ascending in his square.

M The 30th Table, 13025. from the low angle in the left side, in the square ascending.

Call it Mad.

O The 7th Table, 99. ascending.

C The 19th, descending 409.

O The [. . .] 1 from the upper right angle, crossing to the nether left, and so ascending 1003

N The 31st. From the Center to the upper right angle, and so descending 5009.

Call it Noco.

O The 39th, from the Center descending, or the left hand, 9073.

D The 41st, from the Center ascending, and so to the right upper Angle, 27004.

R The 43rd, from the upper left Angle to the right, and so still in the Circumference, 34006.

I The 4[. . .], ascending, 72000.

[. . .][19] In the same Table descending to the last.

Call it Zirdo.

P The 6th, ascending 109.
A The 9th, ascending 405.
L The 11th, descending 603
Call it Lap.

E The 6th, from the right Angle uppermost to the left, 700.
G The 13th, descending, 2000.
R The 17th, from the Center downward, 11004.
O The 32nd, descending from the right Angle to the Center, 32000.
Z The 47th. 194000. descending. Call it Zorge (Of one syllable.)
[*A True and Faithful Relation*, p. 79]

When we gather the above letters and write them out forward, we have the final line of Key One: *Zorge, lap zirdo noco mad, hoath Jaida* (which we saw previously in this section—as part of the "Repetitive Formula Pattern").

For each letter, it is obvious that one of the Tables of *Loagaeth* is (usually) indicated as the source. Then, we see the notations made by Dee about where in the Table to find the letter. Unfortunately, no one has yet discovered what these directions and numbers mean. At first glance, it might appear that the large numbers would be the result of numbering each and every cell on one of the 49 x 49 Tables (sides A and B). However, that only results in a total of 4802 cells for each Table (2,401 on each side)—yet the numbers given by Nalvage are often much larger than that. Some kind of mathematical algorithm might be in use here—once more suggesting a form of cryptography.

After Key One had been transmitted in its entirety, Kelley attempted to question Nalvage's direct superior—the Archangel Gabriel—about the numbers:

> **Kelley:** Why join you numbers with these letters, and added none with those of the former Table?[20]
>
> **Gabriel:** Brother, what is the cause that all the World is made by numbers? The Numbers we speak of, are of reason and form, and not of merchants. [. . .] Every Letter signifieth the member of the substance whereof it speaketh. Every word signifieth the quiddity[21] of the sub-

> stance. The Letters are separated, and in confusion : and therefore, are by numbers gathered together: which also gathered signify a number: for as every greater containeth his lesser, so are the secret and unknown forms of things knit up in their parents. Where being known in number, they are easily distinguished, so that here we teach places to be numbered: letters to be elected from the numbered, and proper words from the letters, signifying substantially the thing that is spoken of in the center of the Creator . . . [*A True and Faithful Relation*, p. 92]

Gabriel's words are often taken as proof that the characters of the Angelical alphabet should have gematric (or numerical) values. When Gabriel says that every letter of a word is a member of the overall body (or "substance") of the word, he *could* be giving a basic lesson in Qabalistic gematria.

However, as we shall now see, Gabriel is *actually* explaining the numbers that Nalvage associated with the Tables of *Loagaeth* and the letters of the Keys. First, he points out that the letters of the words are scattered (that is, throughout the forty-nine Tables). He then indicated that (Nalvage's) numbers are used to gather those letters together. Toward the end of his speech, he even describes the method Nalvage used in "decrypting" the Angelical words from the Tables: places (presumably the cells on the forty-nine Tables) are numbered, and letters are drawn from those numbered places. Then, the resulting letters are gathered into proper Angelical words—which signify in substance (in this case, Voice) those things that are otherwise conceived only in the heart of the Creator. It is unfortunate, however, that Gabriel reveals nothing about the method of numbering the "places" or gathering the letters.

It is interesting to note that Gabriel insists these numbers are not "of merchants" but are "of reason and form." I interpret this to mean that the numbers are such as would be used by mathematicians, architects, astronomers, and navigators—as opposed to the simple totals and tallies used by merchants. In other words, the numbers we see involve higher mathematical functions—such as those used by cryptographers.

There is just one instance during Nalvage's transmission of the words of Key One that such higher math is illustrated. Gabriel refers to this instance toward the middle of his speech—where he explains that the

Angelical letters "are by numbers gathered together: which [numbers] also gathered signify a number." We have, of course, already seen the numbers that Nalvage used to gather the letters into words. However, Gabriel further suggests that the numbers of any given word can *also* be gathered to produce an entirely new number. Nalvage explains how to do this during the transmission of the word *Vooan* (Truth):

N (The number must needs go to) the sixth, descending 309.
A The 7th ascending 360.
O The 9th ascending 1000.
O The 13th ascending 1050.
V The 17th ascending 2004. It is Vooan. It may be sounded Vaoan.

> **Nalvage:** Add those last numbers.
>
> **Dee:** 309
> 360
> 1000
> 1050
> 2004
> 4723
>
> They make 4723
>
> **Nalvage:** It is called the Mystical root in the highest ascendant of transmutation.
>
> **Dee:** These phrases are dark. When it shall please God they may be made plain.
>
> **Nalvage:** It is the square of the Philosophers work.
>
> **Dee:** You said it was a root.
>
> **Nalvage:** So it is a root square.
>
> **Dee:** The square thereof is 22306729 . . .
> [*A True and Faithful Relation*, p. 80]

As we can see, Dee added together all the numbers associated with the word *Vooan* (Truth), in order to reveal a "secret" square-root number. A square number is any number obtained by multiplying another number by itself. As an example, the number nine is a square, because it is the product of multiplying three by itself (3 x 3 = 9). Meanwhile, the *root* of that square number is three, because three is the *smallest* positive number that can be multiplied by itself for a product of nine.

When Dee added the numbers of *Vooan* together, Nalvage told him the result (4723) was a mystical square-root number "in the highest ascendant of transmutation." Dee did not understand what Nalvage meant by this ("All these phrases are dark"), but he did understand the concept of a square root. By multiplying the root number 4723 by itself, Dee obtained the square product of 22,306,729.

Sadly, Nalvage showed no interest in explaining why this square root is important to the word *Vooan*. I can only assume that one should be able to *begin* with the square number or its root, and use it in some way to derive the Angelical word form the Tables of *Loagaeth*. However, any suggestions I could offer toward this end would be pure speculation. Perhaps my work here will enable cryptologists to look at Dee's work in a new light.

In the end, it would appear that Nalvage's process was too time-consuming, because, after an entire day, only part of Key One had been transmitted. Therefore, Nalvage eventually stated that he would reveal the numbers later, and began to transmit the letters rapidly without numbers or directions. Unfortunately, if Nalvage ever returned with the missing information, the record has not survived.

There are further aspects of Dee's magickal system that appear to suggest steganography. The magickal Tables associated with the *Heptarchia* and the Watchtowers are overflowing with encrypted Divine and Angelic Names. (The Watchtowers were even once used by Dee to decode a message delivered by the Angels.)[22] Bearing more directly upon the Keys, we have the *Corpus Omnium* (or "Table of Nalvage")—which is just as suggestive of cryptography as everything else we have seen from Nalvage in this chapter.

Corpus Omnium: The Round Table of Nalvage[23]

We first see the so-called "Table of Nalvage" upon that Angel's first appearance in the shewstone. Kelley describes it as follows:

> He standeth upon a white great round Table, like Crystal, all written with letters infinitely. On the middle of the Table is a great swelling or pommel of the same substance the Table is of. Upon that pommel he standeth. [*A True and Faithful Relation*, p. 63]

Thus, Nalvage appeared to Dee and Kelley standing upon the Table like a dais. As we shall see, this Table apparently bears directly upon the Keys as well as the first leaf of *Loagaeth*. However, the exact relationship between these things was never explained in the journals.

Before Nalvage began the transmission of the Keys, the Angel delivered several lessons upon the structure of his Round Table. At this point, the Table's appearance changed slightly. Where it had first appeared "like crystal"—likely meaning that it was clear and shot through with rainbows[24]—it had now gone opaque, so it looked more like mother of pearl.

Also, the "infinite" lettering had been reduced to a few easily discernible characters, which formed the basis of Nalvage's lessons. Dee recorded this simplified version of the Table in his journal: [25]

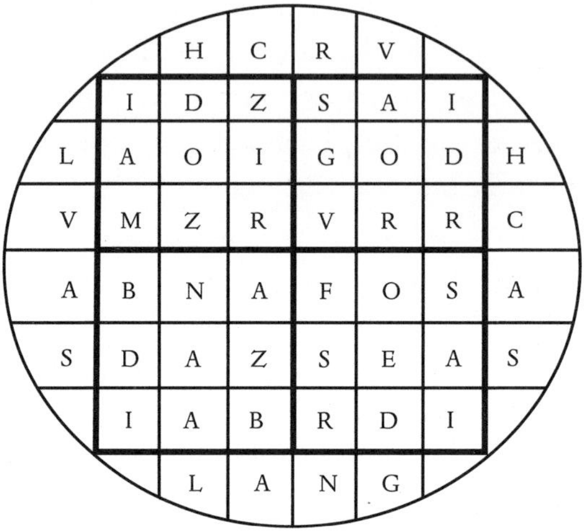

The Corpus Omnium, *or Round Table of Nalvage*

While Nalvage gave his lessons concerning the Table, he used a small three-sectioned rod of gold as a pointing wand. Kelley described Nalvage's actions to Dee as the Angel revealed the mysteries of his curious Round Table:

> **Kelley:** He standeth and pointeth with his rod to the letters of his Table, as if he made some account or reckoning. He went out to the middle, and measured how many steps it is about.[26]
>
> **Nalvage:** Father, Son, Holy Spirit. Foundation, Substance, and *Principium Omnium* [Universal Principle].[27] *Omnium* is the thing that is in my charge. [. . .] *Corpus Omnium.*
>
> **Kelley:** He pointeth to the whole or round Table which he standeth on. [*A True and Faithful Relation*, p. 74]

Thus, we know that the proper name of the Table of Nalvage is *Corpus Omnium*, which is Latin for either "The Body of All" or "Substance of the Universe." Its letters incorporate the Father, the Son, and the Holy Spirit—thereby embodying the essence of the entire Universe as understood in the Christian philosophy of the Trinity. Nalvage elaborates on this aspect of the *Corpus Omnium* Table:

1. The Substance is attributed to God the Father.
2. The first circular mover, the circumference, God the Son, the finger of the Father, and mover of all things.
3. The order and knitting together of the parts in their due and perfect proportion, God the Holy Ghost. Lo, the beginning and end of all things. [*A True and Faithful Relation*, p. 74]

Here, Nalvage reveals that the actual letters (the "Substance") of the Table represents God the Father—who is Himself the Substance of the Universe. However, when the Table is divided into its various parts, and the letters decrypted to reveal proper words, this represents God the Holy Spirit.

Meanwhile, the four words written around the circumference—the "first circular mover"—represent God the Son. Dee asked Nalvage about their significance:

> **Dee:** If the Order of the Table be the Holy Spirit, the Substance of the Father, how shall we gather the Circumference, which is the Son?
>
> **Nalvage:** The Son is the Image of his Father. Therefore, in his death, he must be the Image of his Father also. If the Substance [of the Table] be in the form of a Cross, then the Son is the Image of his Father. [*A True and Faithful Relation*, p. 76]

Note that the four circumference words mark the points of a cross around the Table. As we can see in my illustration, this division creates a cross in the very center—with a circumference word at each point. I assume Nalvage means that the circumference reflects the fourfold division of the Table itself.

Nalvage's threefold description of the *Corpus Omnium* makes me suspect that the Tablet might be solar in nature. This is due to a chapter from Agrippa's *Second Book of Occult Philosophy*, called "Of the Sun, Moon and their Magical Considerations." Compare the following quote with Nalvage's description of the three aspects of *Corpus Omnium*:

> For [the Sun] is amongst the other Stars the image and statue of the great Prince of both worlds, viz.—Terrestrial, and Celestial; the true light, and the most exact image of God himself; *whose essence resembles the Father, light the Son, heat the Holy Ghost.*[28] [*Three Books of Occult Philosophy*, Book II, chapter 32]

Another clue to the solar nature of the *Corpus Omnium* may rest in the words of the circumference. Nalvage relates this to "God the Son" who is the "mover of all things"—or the active principle of the Divine. As we shall see, the four circumference names are written so they run *counterclockwise* around the Table. For me, this brings to mind the standard zodiacal chart and the twelve zodiacal signs that compose its circumference. These signs are actually the twelve constellations marked by the path of the Sun across the sky. When written upon a zodiacal or natal chart, they are also written counterclockwise:

Of course, every planet and star depicted on a zodiacal chart actually rotates clockwise—or "sunwise"—around the chart. They rise upon the eastern horizon on the left (where Aries is depicted in the example chart), move across the zenith at the top of the chart, and continue in

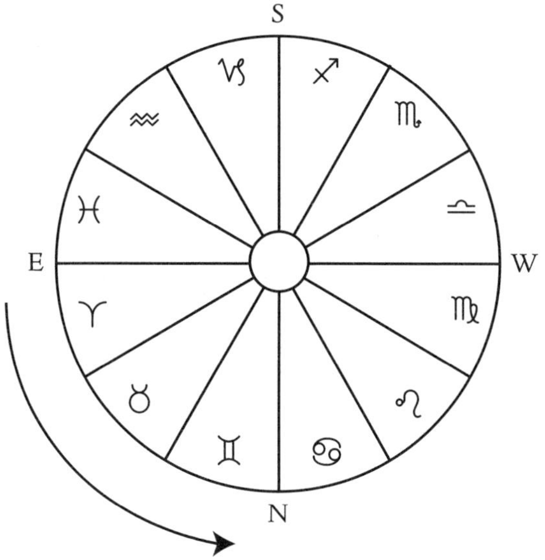

Simple zodiacal chart, showing the twelve signs with Aries in the east, and indicating that they are drawn counterclockwise around the circle

that fashion around the entire circle. Because the twelve signs are listed counterclockwise, but actually rotate sunwise, we find that each constellation rises in the east in proper zodiacal order—Aries first, followed by Taurus, then Gemini, Cancer, and so on.

The same is true of the circumference of Nalvage's *Corpus Omnium* Table. The four names are written so they must be read counterclockwise. However, if the Table itself were rotated with the Sun, we would find that each letter in the four names rises (on the left-hand side) in their proper order. For instance, for the name *Lvas*—the *L* would rise first, followed by the *V*, then the *A*, and finally the *S*. The word *Lang* would then follow in its proper order, and so forth.

Nalvage offers Latin translations of the circumference names, but he never explains what or who they represent. The Latin words are both verbs and plural; as we shall see, they are given *–antes* suffixes. Therefore, they each have the implication of "those who . . . ," which seems to suggest these are names of groups. Because of this, many modern Dee scholars have suggested that the names in the circumference are actually those of Angelic Choirs.

After revealing the three essential aspects of the *Corpus Omnium* (outlined earlier in this section), Nalvage continues to explain the division of the Table into four parts:

> Lo, it is divided into four parts: whereof two are dignified, one not yet dignified but shall be, the other without glory or dignification. Understand God, as the substance of the whole (as above said). [*A True and Faithful Relation*, p. 74]

Note that Nalvage attributes a "dignity" to each portion of the Table. The term *dignity* is likely drawn from astrology: the dignity of a planet indicates the strength or weakness of its influence in a chart. In this quote, Nalvage seems to use the term to indicate whether each portion of the Table has been "fulfilled" (or brought to completion). Two portions are already dignified, one is not yet dignified (though it will be), and the last portion is without glory or dignity.

I find it likely that these four portions represent the Ages of the Universe as understood in Christian Doctrine. Dee describes these divisions of time in the appendix to the *Five Books of Mystery*, as he discusses the Heptarchic Angel Baligon with Uriel:

> **Uriel:** [Baligon] is the end of the Three last corruptible times; whereof this is the last.
>
> **Dee:** The one, at Noah's Flood, ended. The second at Christ his first coming, and this is the third.
>
> **Uriel:** It is so. [*Five Books of Mystery*, p. 401]

We can apply this cosmology to the four portions of the *Corpus Omnium*. The first portion, which is dignified, would relate to the time period from Genesis 1:1 to the point of the Deluge. The second portion, also dignified, would follow the Deluge and represent history up to the time of the Crucifixion of Jesus. The third portion, not yet dignified, represents the present—which has not yet been fulfilled. Finally, the fourth portion, without glory or dignity, represents the End Times (Tribulation) and the reign of the Antichrist. Therefore, the Table of Nalvage (much like *Loagaeth* itself) encompasses the entire Universe from the beginning of time to the end.

Having thus revealed the general mysteries of the *Corpus Omnium* Table, Nalvage pressed onward to teach Dee and Kelley about the words contained therein. This lesson is given in a rather disjointed fashion in the journals, so I have consolidated the information for this chapter:[29]

Vita Suprema (First Life)—Pre-Deluge

Nalvage begins with the upper-left-hand (pre-Deluge) portion of the Table—which he calls *Vita Suprema* (and we might translate as "Celestial Life," "Supreme Life," or "First Life"). The Angel points to three letters in the upper-left corner of the Table, and says:

> I find it (by addition) in this language, *Iad*, but written thus, toward the left hand, in three angles:[30]

I	**D**	
A		

The Angelical word *Iad* translates as "God." Notice that these three letters appear in all four corners of the *Corpus Omnium*, which makes sense if the Table is intended to represent God.[31] As we shall see, the direction in which the letters are written in each corner indicates which direction every word in the portion should be read. In the example above, we can see that words in the upper-left-hand portion of the Table should be read diagonally upward to the right.

Nalvage continues with the definition of the next word in this portion of the Table. Notice that it—like *Iad*—is written diagonally upward to the right:

I	D	**Z**
A	**O**	
M		

Say, *Gaudium* (To Rejoice)[32] . . . Moz.

Finally, Nalvage reveals the final word of the upper-left-hand portion:

I	D	Z
A	O	**I**
M	**Z**	**R**

Say, *Presentia* (In Person) . . . I find it called Zir.[33]

Therefore, we have learned that the upper-left-hand portion of the *Corpus Omnium—Zir Moz Iad—*translates as "I am the Joy of God."

Stemming directly from this pre-Deluge portion, in the circumference of the Table, is the word *Lvas*. The given Latin translation is *Laudantes*—which roughly means "Those Who Praise." (Nalvage also suggests they can be called *Triumphantes* or "Those who Triumph.")

Vita Secunda (Second Life)—Post-Deluge to Christ

The next (post-Deluge), or lower-left-hand, portion of the Table is called *Vita Secunda* (Second Life). Here, we find the following letters along with Nalvage's translations:

B	N	A
D	A	Z
I	**A**	B

Say, *Potestas* (Dominion) . . . I find it Bab.

Motus or *Motio* (Movement or Motion) . . . I find it Zna.

The second portion of the Table (*Zna Bab Iad*) translates as "The Moving Dominion of God" (or, perhaps, "The Active Dominion of God"). The words are formed by reading the letters diagonally upward to the left.

In the circumference, we find the name of another (possible) Angelic Choir stemming from this portion. The name is *Lang*, and translates in Latin as *Ministrantes* ("Those Who Serve"). There are, at least, various references to "the Ministering Angels" in biblical literature.[34]

Vita Tertia (Third Life)—Post-Crucifixion to Present

Following this, we find the third (present-time) portion of the Table on the upper-right-hand portion—called *Vita Tertia* (Third Life). The text in this portion appears as follows:

S	**A**	**I**
G	O	**D**
U	R	R

Actio (Action—especially that taken by a King) . . . Sor.

Factum (To cause, or bring about) . . . Gru.

So we have the words of the third portion of the Table (*Gru Sor Iad*), which translate as "The Cause of the Actions of God." The words are formed by reading the letters diagonally downward to the right.

The circumference name stemming from this portion is *Sach*—which translates as *Confirmantes* (the "Establishers" or "Supporters").

"Life, but Also Death" (Fourth Life)—Tribulation

When Nalvage finally turns his attention to the final, lower-right-hand (Tribulation) portion of the Table, he begins to tremble, speaks of death in Latin, and finally says, "Those that do their duty shall receive their reward."[35] The fourth portion of the Table appears thus:

F	O	S
S	E	**A**
R	**D**	**I**

Life, but also means Death.[36]

Luctus (Sorrow) . . . Ser.

Discordia (Discord) . . . Osf.

Finally, we have the last sentence of the Table (*Osf Ser Iad*), translating as "The Discord and Sorrow of God." The words are formed by reading the letters diagonally downward to the left.

The circumference name associated with this portion is *Urch*—which means *Confundantes* (The Confusers). The Latin *Confundo* indicates "to mix, pour together, stir up" in the sense of "to confuse, disturb, upset, disorder," etc. This chaotic state goes hand in hand with the End Times. It is perhaps significant that this is the only one of the four circumference names that is not written directly alongside of its associated portion of the *Corpus Omnium* Table.

Finally, I have also created the following Table, which will allow for easy reference to Nalvage's lessons:

The Four Portions of *Corpus Omnium*			
Table Portion	*Biblical Time Period*	*Text within Portion*	*Circumference*
1. Upper-Left (First Life)	Pre-Deluge (Dignified)	Zir Moz Iad (I am the Joy of God)	Luas (The Praisers or The Triumphant)
2. Lower-Left (Second Life)	Post-Deluge to Christ (Dignified)	Zna Bab Iad (Active Domin-ion of God)	Lang (The Servants)
3. Upper-Right (Third Life)	Post-Crucifix-ion to present (Not Yet Dignified)	Gru Sor Iad (Cause of the Actions of God)	Sach (The Establishers)
4. Lower-Right (Life/Death)	Tribulation (Without Glory or Dignity)	Osf Ser Iad (Discord and Sorrow of God)	Urch (The Confusers)

The Corpus Omnium *and the Angelical Keys*

I previously suggested that the *Corpus Omnium* has a close relationship with the Tables of *Loagaeth* and their Angelical Keys. Part of this relationship was established upon Nalvage's next visit, when he delivered his final lesson on the subject of the Round Table. This particular session has long puzzled modern scholars, because Nalvage transmitted the material without preamble or explanation. In fact, it is only because of several cryptic statements made by Kelley that we know this lesson applies to the *Corpus Omnium* at all.

Below, I have transcribed the letters revealed by Nalvage exactly as they are formatted in Dee's journal:

> D P C E T E I R S M S S S
> E S A I I M M N S E S. (24)[37]
>
> **Kelley:** All this was in one line, in the lowermost portion, and lowermost line thereof.
>
> I E E E E T N O E D M E T M M M
> M M D M A E T S E A M (27)
>
> **Kelley:** Now he standeth still.
>
> A E R T I S A N S S E A S D M M S E A O A
> E V I I I I A O A O I I V I T S E I T T[38]
> S D A I N (43)[39]
>
> **Kelley:** These seemed to be taken out of diverse lines, in the three lower portions; but none out of the uppermost or fourth.
>
> R S H D D S R R E S O L S N R E R E E
> S F R H E I E E E E I E E O E T I S O E
> R T T H D E O I S E O E S M E T F E D E
> T S E E E E E R S E S E O R S M E T
> D. R. F E   D E T S E E R S E[40]
> S I S E H E N O E S M E F S F E E D I [I/E][41] O E
> S S S I S E O E S H E
> D S D F T E I E O R S O E D H T E T
> O E S H E O T E T E R E O E H S E R
> E E I R E S R I S O E H E E D E I E H E
> D T R N D D H D N (81)[42]
>
> **Nalvage:** The rest of this lesson the next morning. [*A True and Faithful Relation*, p. 78]

Notice that Kelley describes Nalvage as pointing to various places within four "portions," which likely indicates the fourfold division of the

Corpus Omnium Table. Of course, it would be impossible to derive such long strings of letters from such a simple magickal square. Therefore, I find it probable that the Table had once again reverted to the "infinitely lettered" version upon which Kelley had first seen Nalvage standing.

The Angels never give an explanation for these letter strings. (The next morning, Nalvage does arrive as promised—but he launches directly into the transmission of Key One.) The only clues we are given are short marginal notations made by Dee much later in the journals. In the first instance, Dee is discussing the First Table of *Loagaeth*:

> **Dee:** For the First Table, [there][43] is no Call. Although there be letters gathered, but made into no words, as you may see, before the first Call of all. [*A True and Faithful Relation*, p. 194]

Dee is directing us to the place in his journals just previous to the reception of the first Call (or Key), and that happens to be the session where Nalvage delivered the previously quoted letter strings. Thus, we know that these letters represent the "Key" of the First Table of *Loagaeth*. (We might refer to this as "Key Zero.") However, as Dee points out, the letters are never gathered into words because we are not intended to open the First Table.

The second notation is found a short while later, as Dee is discussing the progress of the reception of the forty-eight Keys with the Angel Illemese:

> **Dee:** There are but 18 besides the first [Call][44] to God.
>
> **Illemese:** There are nineteen besides the first. [*A True and Faithful Relation*, p. 199]

Dee had only received eighteen Keys at this point in the journals, and Illemese is telling him that one more is coming.[45] What is important here, though, is that mention is made of nineteen Calls *besides* "the first [Call] to God." This excluded first Call is one and the same with the letter strings transmitted by Nalvage as "Key Zero" for the First Table of *Loagaeth*. Therefore, we have learned that this hidden Key is, appropriately, a Call to God.

I have yet to discover where the Angels explained "Key Zero" to Dee and Kelley. (It is possible that the records have been destroyed.) However, I feel it is quite possible that they represent yet another example of steganography in Dee's Angelic journals. Because these letter strings represent the "Key" of the First Table of *Loagaeth*, it is entirely possible they are an encryption algorithm of some sort.

Nalvage completes his lesson on the *Corpus Omnium* Table with the following words:

> Thus I have made plain this body generally. The particulars are long, hard, and tedious. Thy name be blessed, O God, which canst open a means, whereby Thy powers immediate[46] may be opened unto man. Power, glory, and honor be unto Thee, for thou are the true body of all things and are life eternal. [*A True and Faithful Relation*, p. 76]

In the prayer above, Nalvage refers to God as the "true body of all things"—thereby confirming that the *Corpus Omnium* is a representation of God. In fact, it seems to be a talisman representing the Divine Source of Dee's entire "Enochian" system. It relates directly to the First Table of *Loagaeth*, which is associated with the *Logos* (or God-Christ), and the "Key" derived from it is described as a "Call to God."

I assume the "means" whereby God's powers may be "opened unto man" is the *Corpus Omnium* Table itself. Nalvage does involve the Table—indirectly—in the transmission of the forty-eight Keys. I say "indirectly" because, after delivering the letters of "Key Zero," he does not draw anything further from the Round Table. However, he does sometimes stop the transmission of the Keys to strike the Table with his golden rod. This causes it to spin extremely fast—so that it appears to be a solid globe rather than a flat, round Table. (Elsewhere, Kelley states that the letters on the spinning Table could still be read as if they were standing still. I assume this is similar to the effect one sees when a propeller is spinning so fast that, in the proper light, it appears to stand still.) While it is not clear what all of this striking and spinning is about, the *Corpus Omnium* does seem to represent a source of power or authority throughout the transmission of the forty-eight Keys.

The Angelical Keys: What We Know

The information that follows is similar to the "The Forty-Nine Tables of *Loagaeth*: What We Know" section in chapter 2. It consolidates all the information recorded by Dee about the nature of the Angelical Keys. What the Angels had to say about the Keys will further illuminate the nature of the corresponding Tables of *Loagaeth*. The student will therefore want to compare the following material with the matching section in chapter 2.[47]

Key "Zero" (First Table):

There is never a usable Key (or Call) given for the First Table of the Holy Book. As Nalvage said previously, "The soul of man hath no portion in this First Table." Later in the journals, Dee confirms this with the following marginal notation:

> . . . for the First Table can have no Call, it is of the Godhead. [*A True and Faithful Relation*, p. 98]

However, as we have seen, the strange letter strings transmitted by Nalvage from the *Corpus Omnium* are intended to represent "the first [Call] to God." Dee notes that the strings are "letters gathered, but made into no words." In the surviving records, the Angels never offer an explanation for what the letters mean or how they might be used. Therefore, the *Loagaeth* magickal system has no method of opening the First Table. (See chapters 1 and 2 for information concerning the Jewish Fifty Gates of Understanding.)

Key One (Second Table):

Because the First Table of *Loagaeth* has no Key, the first of the forty-eight Angelical Keys applies to the *Second* Table. The Angel Illemese confirms this in the journals:

> But you must understand that in speaking of the First Table, I speak of the Second. So that the second, with you, is the first. [*A True and Faithful Relation*, p. 199]

This is an important note for modern researchers, because Illemese (and other Angels in Dee's journals) often refer to the Second Table of *Loagaeth* as the first—because it is the first *accessible* Table.

After Nalvage revealed Key One and its translation (or "English sense"), he proceeded to discuss the nature of the Key and the Table it opens:

> It is the sense in your tongue of the holy and mystical Call before delivered: which followeth in practice for the moving of the second Table, the Kings and Ministers of Government. The utterance of which is of force, and moveth them to visible apparition. Moved and appeared, they are forced (by the Covenant of God delivered by His Spirit) to render obedience and faithful society. Wherein, they will open the mysteries of their creation, as far as shall be necessary, and give you understanding of many thousand secrets, wherein you are yet but children. [. . .]
>
> This is therefore the key of the first seven, according to the proportion of the first Creation. No more for this time. [*A True and Faithful Relation*, p. 88]

We discussed some of this in chapter 2, concerning the Second Table of *Loagaeth*. According to Nalvage, the first Key summons the "Kings and Ministers of Government" who are "the first seven." Thus, it is likely that this Key refers to the Seven Archangels of the Seven Days of Creation, as well as to other Angelic rulers of the Universe.

Much of Nalvage's above speech is aimed at explaining how Key One works. It is "of force, and moveth [the Kings and Ministers of Government] to visible apparition." Moreover, the recitation of the Key forces them to "render obedience and faithful society," etc. However, Nalvage continues his thoughts by relating them to *all* the Keys as applied to the *Loagaeth* Tables.[48]

Key Three (Fourth Table):

After Nalvage transmitted the Third Angelical Key, the Archangel Gabriel appeared and said:

> Hark, O ye sons of men: [this][49] is the first of nature, and the beginning of your being in body. Whereby the things of the world have life and live. Let him that hath wisdom understand. Grow together, for this[50] hath its fruit in due time. [*A True and Faithful Relation*, p. 98]

It is unclear if Gabriel's speech is intended to describe Key Three, or the Fourth Table of *Loagaeth*. He did say these words directly after the revelation of the Key—but I feel that he was speaking equally about the Key *and* its Table.

It would seem that Table Four (opened by Key Three) incorporates the creation of Adam—the beginning of mankind's "being in body." (See Genesis, chapter 2.) Both Gnostic and Qabalistic cosmology associate the creation of the physical realm with the formation of Adam's body. As such, it is likely the physical realm itself that Gabriel promises will "come to fruition in due time."[51]

Keys Nineteen to Forty-Eight (Twentieth to Forty-Ninth Tables): The Call of the Aethyrs

The Keys to the final thirty Tables of *Loagaeth* were introduced by Nalvage with the following speech:

> There are 30 Calls yet to come. Those 30 are the Calls of Ni[nety-One] Princes and Spiritual Governors, unto whom the Earth is delivered as a portion. These bring in and again dispose Kings and all Governments upon the Earth, and vary the Nature of things with the variation of every moment. Unto whom, the providence of the eternal Judgment, is already opened. Those are generally governed by the twelve Angels of the 12 Tribes: which are also governed by the 7 which stand before the Presence of God. Let him that can see look up, and let him that can hear, attend, for this is wisdom. They are all spirits of the Air: not rejected, but dignified. And they dwell and have their habitation in the air diversely, and in sundry places. For, their mansions are not alike, neither are their powers equal. Understand therefore, that from the fire to the earth, there are 30 places or abidings: one above and beneath another: wherein these aforesaid Creatures have their abode, for a time. [*A True and Faithful Relation*, pp. 139–40]

Refer again to chapter 2, where I described "what we know" of the final thirty Tables of the Holy Book. These represent the thirty Aethyrs (or Heavens) that extend from the foot of God's Throne to the surface of the Earth. (This is likely adopted from ancient Gnosticism, which recognized—in some sects—a thirty-Heaven cosmology.)

Furthermore, Nalvage teaches that the thirty Aethyrs are subdivided into ninety-one spiritual provinces set over geographical locations here on Earth. The names of these ninety-one "Parts of the Earth" are also the names of the Angelic Governors who rule the Parts.[52] This is also similar to Gnosticism—which described the *Aeons* simultaneously as transcendent Divine Realms, long expanses of time, *and* as super-celestial Archangels.[53] In Gnostic cosmology, the Divine Aeons were mirrored in the created world by the *Archons* (Rulers)—Angels whose function was to direct and maintain both human and natural law.

It would appear, then, that the Archons are mirrored in Dee's magickal system by the ninety-one Governors. They direct and maintain the natural and human events that take place upon present-day Earth (establishing and deposing governments, varying the "nature of things" with every moment, and so on). By opening the proper Aethyr, one can summon the Governor and his legion of servient Angels set over any nation in the world. (Dee's hope was to learn the secrets of these nations, as well as influence them for the good of the English empire.)

Nalvage's speech about the "30 Calls yet to come" makes it clear that the thirty Aethyrs and their ninety-one Parts are astrological in nature. To begin with, the division of the world into spiritual provinces is described in Agrippa's *First Book of Occult Philosophy*, chapter 31, "How Provinces and Kingdoms are Distributed to Planets." Therein, Agrippa states that every nation in the world comes under the influence of a planet and zodiacal sign. He goes on to give examples of nations influenced by all seven planets (and the signs they each rule), which he drew from the works of the ancient Greco-Roman cartographer Ptolemy.

Nalvage, meanwhile, relates the same information in a slightly different manner. He states that the ninety-one Parts/Governors are collectively ruled by the Angels of the twelve Tribes of Israel.[54] In Agrippa's work, these are also the Angels of the twelve signs of the zodiac.[55]

Then, Nalvage states that these twelve Angels are governed directly by the seven Archangels who "stand before the presence of God."[56] These are the Angels of the Seven Days of Creation as well as the seven ancient planets. The seven planetary Archangels govern the twelve zodiacal Archangels, just as the seven planets are given rulership over the twelve signs of astrology.

Of course, as I said in chapter 2, I do not wish to outline the entire system of the Parts of the Earth in this book. Here, we are concerned with the Tables of *Loagaeth* and the Keys that open them—and in this case we are focused upon the final thirty Keys of the Aethyrs.

Interestingly, it was not Nalvage that delivered the Aethyric Keys. Apparently, his period as a teacher ended at some point after he revealed the mysteries of the ninety-one Parts of the Earth.[57] When it came time to transmit the final thirty Keys, Gabriel had established Illemese as a substitute teacher. The Angel even appeared with the *Corpus Omnium* and Nalvage's small golden pointing-rod.

The next two days were spent in the transmission of a single, and *very* long, Angelical Call. The English given for the text makes it obvious that it represents the biblical loss of Paradise, and thus represents the end of the initial creative period of Genesis (or, the Seventh Day).[58]

After the Call was transmitted, Illemese revealed the Angelical names of the thirty Aethyrs (see chapter 2 for a list). He then stated:

> There is all. Now change the name, and the Call is all one. [*A True and Faithful Relation*, p. 209]

Thus, Dee and Kelley learned that the thirty Keys that open the Aethyrs are all composed of the *same* Angelical Call. The only thing that makes each of the final thirty Keys individual is the changing of a single word—the Angelical name of the Aethyr one desires to access. The first line of the Call of the Aethyrs reads as follows:

> O you heavens which dwell in _______ are mighty in the Parts of the Earth . . .

When written in English, the blank space is filled with "the First Aethyr," "the Second Aethyr," etc. However, when written in Angelical, the space is filled with the proper name of the Aethyr.

Because of this repetition, there are technically only nineteen Calls in existence. (Remember Illemese previously told Dee, "There are nineteen [Calls] besides the first.")[59] However, by changing the single word in the nineteenth Call thirty times, we obtain a total of forty-eight Angelical Keys.

In the following chapter, we will explore the instructions given to Dee and Kelley by the Angels for the proper use of the Holy *Book of Loagaeth* and its forty-eight Angelical Keys.

Addendum: The Poetry of the Forty-Eight Calls

The Angelical Calls are more than just keys to mystical gateways. In fact, they consist of a kind of biblical poetry—psalms, really—that appear to outline a connected message about the life of the Universe. However, exactly what that message says has been debated by Enochian scholars for decades (if not centuries). Like proper biblical literature, the wording is obscure enough that different readers see entirely different messages. Over the years, many have offered their own explanations of the "meaning" behind or within the forty-eight Calls. Here, I will present my own analysis of the poetry, and attempt to demystify the obscure language.

The poetry of the Calls appears to draw from a range of biblical literature. The first, third, and final Calls each contain very Genesis-like aspects—describing the establishment of the physical world as we know it. Calls two, and twelve through eighteen, are reminiscent of psalms or verses from the Song of Solomon—being invocations of the Divine through praise.

The Calls are generally classifiable as apocalyptic writings—which (like *Loagaeth*) commonly focus upon the cycle of time and the life and death of the Universe. Apocalyptic texts include such canonical books as Ezekiel, Isaiah, Daniel, and the Revelation of St. John.[60] Calls four through fourteen, especially, remind one of verses from the Revelation, Isaiah, and so on.

The word *apocalypse* is an archaic word for "revelation"—especially in the spiritual/mystical sense. It is through such an apocalypse that the prophets Ezekiel, St. John, and (of course!) Enoch were able to glimpse the Divine Throne.[61] It therefore makes sense that the Calls—and even *Loagaeth* itself—should be associated with apocalyptic literature. Not only were they received by Kelley and Dee via direct Angelic revelation (making them prophets in their own right), but the practice of the system (called *Gebofal*, see chapter 4) is intended to result in the *revelation of mysteries*. Not to mention the fact that the Angels associated the whole system with the Tribulation.

Finally, I must give some attention to the classical Gnostic influence upon these poems. As we have seen in previous chapters, there is an undeniable Gnostic imprint upon Dee's entire system of magick.[62] For example, the "thirty Aethyrs" are apparently based upon the thirty Heavens of the Gnostics.[63] Just as we see in *Loagaeth*, the Gnostic aspirant was expected to ceremonially open "gateways" leading into the thirty Heavens, receive purification and baptism within each realm, and finally obtain ultimate reunion with God. (See the Gnostic text entitled *Pistis Sophia* for just one example.)[64]

Meanwhile, the Calls seem to contain a direct Gnostic borrowing in their name for God: *Iadbaltoh*, translating as "God of Justice (or Righteousness)." This name is suspiciously close to the ancient Gnostic name of the Creator—*Ialdabaoth*. The etymology of this name is obscure; however, Gnostic scripture records Ialdabaoth's title of honor as "The God of Righteousness."

There is also a Gnostic literary style to the poetry. For instance, the Calls written from Iadbaltoh's viewpoint bring to mind such ancient writings as *The Thunder-Perfect Intellect*—wherein the Gnostic goddess *Sophia* speaks to her followers. (Remember that *Sophia*—or Wisdom—appears in Dee's journals as the Mother of Angels: *Galvah*.) The treatment of the *Christos* ("He That Liveth and Triumpheth") in the poetry is also very Gnostic in its imagery.

However, I must remind the reader that the classical Gnostic texts we know today were unknown to Dee and Kelley. During their lives, the classical (or Sethian) Gnostic sects had long since been exterminated, and the discovery of the Nag Hammadi texts in Egypt was hundreds of years away.[65]

In the meantime, Gnosticism had lived on in the very foundations of Western esotericism—at the hearts of such movements and philosophies as Hermeticism, Rosicrucianism, and alchemy. Its imagery survived in medieval and Renaissance engravings and the Tarot trumps. Its literature was a heavy influence upon canonical biblical texts (such as the Book of John and Revelation). Many of its mysteries were shared with and adopted by Jewish Merkavah mystics and Qabalists. And its Doctrines were preserved and taught by isolated mystics and secret societies.

There had also been a Gnostic sect within the Catholic Church for a time—founded by a Christian teacher named Valentinus—until it was also exterminated. It would appear that Valentinian philosophy was the primary source of Gnosticism for much of the West, including for men such as Dee. With all of this taken into account, it is no surprise that the forty-eight Calls should bear the mark of Gnostic symbolism, without being technically classified as Gnostic literature themselves.

For brevity's sake, I will conclude this introduction and proceed to the analysis of the Calls. In what follows, I have provided the text of each Call. Then, each is broken into "sections" of related passages, and I have included my commentary with each section. The commentary will include further references to the influences upon the poetry we have already discussed.

Call One:

> "I reign over you," sayeth the God of Justice, "in power exalted above the firmaments of wrath: in whose hands the Sun is as a sword, and the Moon a through-thrusting fire:

Most of Call One appears to be composed of the words of God Himself. As we see in the line above, the speaker of the Call establishes that he is not speaking his own words, but those of the God of Justice (*Iad Balt* or *Iadbaltoh*). By quoting the very words of the Creator at the time of their creation, the speaker is reminding the Angels of the promises they have made, and the commands given to them by God. (We shall see this elsewhere in the Calls.) The speaker is also proving that he knows these secret words, and thus establishes his own authority.

Remember that Call One is intended to move the "Kings and Ministers of Government," who are also the "First Seven." These are likely the seven Archangels who stand "before the Face of God" as depicted in the Revelation of St. John and elsewhere. Among these seven planetary Archangels, those of the Sun and Moon stand as chiefs. The first line of the Call reveals that the God of Justice is so far exalted (likely super-celestial, as in Gnosticism), even the mighty Sol and Luna are but tools or weapons in His hands—a sword and a "through-thrusting fire" (fiery arrow).

> Which measureth your garments in the midst of my vestures and trussed you together as the palms of my hands. Whose seats I garnished with the fire of gathering, and beautified your garments with admiration. To whom I made a law to govern the Holy Ones, and delivered you a rod (with) the ark of knowledge.

In the first line above, the initial word *which* most likely refers to the Sun and Moon described in the previous line of the Call. In the study of astrology, the path of the Sun and Moon across the sky is used to distinguish the twelve principal constellations from among the chaotic mass of stars. Because of this, the Sun and Moon are credited with bringing order to chaos, as well as the government of the planetary and zodiacal Angels. From the standpoint of astrology, it is Sol and Luna who "truss together" the signs and planets (the kings and ministers of government). It is they who mark out (measure) the paths of the stars through the vault of the Heavens—the vestures (territories) of *Iadbaltoh.*

The next line suggests that God has garnished the seats of Sol and Luna with the "fire of gathering." This makes sense when we consider that the Sun and Moon are said to burn with a mere reflection of the Fire from Heaven. The line then addresses the kings and ministers once again, and suggests that the Sun and Moon have "beautified your garments." The planets in our solar system are beautified by glowing with the light reflected from the Sun.

The next line seems to refer to the natural laws set by Iadbaltoh—those that govern the Holy Ones (Angels), and those which they enforce upon the created realm. As the kings and ministers of the Universe, they both hold the rod (scepter) of rulership and represent the ark (or storehouse) of all knowledge. (Remember that Dee was an astrologer, and regularly read the stars for knowledge.)

> Moreover, you lifted up your voices and swore obedience and faith to Him that liveth and triumpheth; whose beginning is not, nor end cannot be; which shineth as a flame in the midst of your palace, and reigneth amongst you as the balance of righteousness and truth.

With the word *moreover*, Iadbaltoh changes the subject of his speech. He is, of course, still addressing the kings and ministers, but He suddenly appears to refer to a Divinity distinct from Himself—"Him that Liveth and Triumpeth." This would seem to be a direct reference to the *Christos*—the Anointed One who descends from Heaven to take on a body of flesh and triumph over evil ("liveth and triumpheth"). In the Book of Revelation, the *Christos* conquers the physical realm and is established as eternal King.

We have already discussed the Gnostic Christos (also called the Logos, or Word). It is both self-created and eternal, both distinct from and part of the Highest God. The descriptive terms used in Call One to describe "Him that liveth . . . " are typical of the Christos. He is described as eternal, and (in the same spirit of the Call thus far) is associated intimately with solar imagery. He "shineth as a flame" in the midst of the palace of the Holy Ones, as the Sun shines in the center of our solar system. Both the Christos in Heaven and the Sun in the celestial realm are the central pillar and balance. (Interestingly, Gnostic texts describe the Christos' first act as that of bringing balance to the realm of the Aeons. It then descended to the physical realm, to do the same here.)[66]

Therefore, Call One serves to remind the Angelic rulers of the Universe that they have sworn themselves to both Iadbaltoh and the Christos.

> Move, therefore, and show yourselves. Open the mysteries of your creation. Be friendly unto me. For, I am a servant of the same your God; the true worshiper of the Highest.

Finally, the Call ends with an evocational formula—or conjuration.[67] As we shall see, all of the Calls end with similar conjurations. All of them are spoken by the speaker of the Call, rather than by a figure—such as God—being quoted within the Call. However, there are a couple of instances where Iadbaltoh is quoted within the formula.

Call Two:

> Can the wings of the winds understand your voices of wonder, O you the Second of the First,

Here in Call Two, we find no Genesis-like quotes from Iadbaltoh, but instead a more psalm-like adoration spoken by the speaker himself. I feel that this is a necessary companion to the commanding tone of Call One.

At first, I was tempted to see the Christos once more in the title "Second of the First." Yet I am bothered by the fact that this Call will later refer to the Second of the First in the plural. If such is the case, then this Call is likely addressed to the same kings and ministers (or Holy Ones) as the First Call. Occult philosophy commonly refers to the gods and Angels as "Second Causes"—as opposed to God, the "First Cause."

The "voices of wonder" mentioned in this first line likely have a double meaning. Taken at face value, the phrase appears to refer to the "wonderful voices" of the Holy Ones. However, the Angelical used here is *Faaip* (voices), while the standard Angelical word for *voices*—used later in this same Call—is *Bia*. Thus, I have conjectured that *Faaip* is meant to indicate "voicings"—as in songs or psalms. In this light, the "Second of the First" both have wonderful voices *and* are singing songs of wonder.

> whom the burning flames have framed within the depths of my jaws; whom I have prepared as cups for a wedding, or as the flowers in their beauty for the chamber of righteousness.

Here we find a small change. While the Holy Ones were first credited with the "voicings of wonder," it is now the *speaker* who claims to be singing them. (This makes sense, if the speaker is reciting the Keys in their Angelical. Remember that Nalvage previously referred to the Calls as voices: "In 49 voices, or callings: which are the Natural Keys to open those, not 49 but 48 [. . .] Gates of Understanding.")

The "burning flames" (of passion) have framed the voicings in "the depths of my jaws"—or deep within the speaker's heart where such psalms of passion would be inspired. It is these psalms that have been prepared as one would prepare a wedding or a bridal chamber. (Interestingly, the Holy Temple—wherein resides the Presence of God, or the *Sheckinah*—is often described in Jewish tradition as a bridal chamber.)

> Stronger are your feet than the barren stone, and mightier are your voices than the manifold winds. For, you are become a building such as is not but in the mind of the All Powerful.

Here we see the adoration of the Second of the First (clearly in the plural). I note that comparison is made between them and elements of the earthly realm—wind and stone. They are greater than the elements, and are in fact the building blocks of the physical world.

Also, as we see in Gnosticism, the created world was preconceived only in the mind of the All Powerful—which might indicate Iadbaltoh and/or the Christos. (John 1 describes the *Logos* as both "God" and "with God." In the same chapter, John affirms that the *Logos* is the Creator, or the agent of the Creation.)[68] In the Calls, Iadbaltoh is the primary Creator, though the Christos may be granted the same status, because the two are One.

> "Arise," sayeth the First. Move therefore unto His servants. Show yourselves in power and make me a strong seething. For, I am of Him that liveth forever.

The Call finally ends with another conjuration formula. There is a short quote from God once again—called "the First" in this case, as the kings and ministers were called "the Second of the First" in the first line of the poem. The final line ends with "Him that liveth forever," which is likely a reference to Call One's "Him that liveth . . ." who has no beginning or end—the Christos.[69]

Call Three:

> "Behold," sayeth your God. "I am a Circle on whose hands stand 12 Kingdoms. Six are the seats of living breath; the rest are as sharp sickles or the horns of death; wherein the creatures of the earth are and are not except by mine own hand; which sleep and shall rise.

Call Three returns to quoting Iadbaltoh. He once again describes the Universe as viewed through the eyes of an astrologer, and this entire Call is reminiscent of a zodiacal chart. The Circle is that of the Heavens, whose boundary is marked by the band of fixed stars. This Circle is then divided among twelve astrological Houses (called "Kingdoms" in the poetry of the Call) through which the stars pass in their daily courses. Quite often, the houses and their twelve signs are divided between positives and negatives, or fortunate (the seats of living breath) and unfortunate (sharp sickles or the horns of death). It is through these "kingdoms" that God directs the fate of the world—or where the creatures of the earth are and are not.

Remember that Call Three was described by Gabriel as "the first of nature, and the beginning of your being in body; whereby the things of the world have life and live." (See the section entitled "The Angelical Keys: What We Know," in this chapter.) This makes perfect sense, as Call Three seems to include a description of the physical realm. The Circle of the Heavens marks the boundary between the highest Divine realm and the created physical Universe. If the focus of this Call is upon the establishment of the zodiacal forces, then it is necessarily also about the establishment of the physical world.

The final words of this passage—*which sleep and shall rise*—are something of an enigma. They could simply mean that God directs who lives and dies—but that pesky word *shall* throws doubt upon the issue. If the creatures of the earth sleep (die) and *shall* rise, it would seem to suggest the Judeo-Christian concept of the Resurrection.[70] That would certainly fit with the apocalyptic nature of the Calls and the *Book of Loagaeth* itself. It would imply that the establishment of the Twelve Kingdoms will last until the End Times.

> In the first I made you stewards and placed you in 12 seats of government, giving unto every one of you power successively over 456, the true ages of time, to the intent that from the highest vessels and the corners of your governments you might work my power; pouring down the fires of life and increase upon the earth continually. Thus, you are become the skirts of justice and truth.

At this point, the poetry resumes a more Genesis-like tone, with God placing His Angels in their seats of government at the beginning of time. The subject in this case is that of the twelve "Kingdoms" of the zodiac, and the Angels that govern them. It is their job, under the direction of the Seven Archangels, to direct the activities of the world, and to animate it by "pouring down the fires of life and increase continually."

In the second line of this passage, we learn the celestial Governors (stewards) are given power *successively* over "the true ages of time" (or Universe). In fact, Dee began his Angelic evocations by contacting Annael, the Archangel of Venus who was the then-current successive ruler of the cosmos.[71] Dee's system followed those of Trithemius' *Septum Secundus* and the *Arbatel of Magic*, where the Seven Archangels govern in an Aeonic succession.

It is difficult to say with any surety what is indicated by the numbers "456." Most of these numbers were added by the Angel Illemese some time after the Angelical had been transmitted, as if they were an afterthought or a special consideration. Going strictly by context, I assume that the phrase "456, the true ages of time" is a reference to the zodiacal Kingdoms (or Angels) governed by the Seven Archangels. (The "456" will appear again in the following Call.)

Finally, notice the mention of the "skirts of justice and truth" at the end of this passage. In Call One we saw the Christos described as the "balance of righteousness [or justice] and truth," and associated with the Sun at the heart of the solar system. Here in Call Three, we find the Governors of the twelve zodiacal kingdoms described as the outer boundaries (skirts) of that central balance. A fairly cohesive depiction of the Universe has developed, particularly from an astrological standpoint.

> In the Name of the same your God, lift up, I say, yourselves. Behold, His mercies flourish and Name is become mighty amongst us. In whom

> we say, move, descend and apply yourselves unto us as partakers of the secret wisdom of your creation.

The quotes from Iadbaltoh complete, the speaker again speaks for himself, and closes the Call with a general conjuration.

Calls Four through Seven seem to address a group of stellar Angels collectively referred to as the "Thunders." These particular Angels appear in the Book of Revelation:

> And [the mighty Angel] cried with a loud voice, as when a lion roareth: and when he had cried, seven *thunders* uttered their voices. And when the seven *thunders* had uttered their voices, I was about to write: and I heard a Voice from heaven saying unto me, Seal up those things which the seven *thunders* uttered, and write them not." [Revelation 10:3–4]

With this in mind, let us take a look at the Thunders described in the Angelical Calls:

Call Four:

> I have set my feet in the south and have looked about me saying, Are not the Thunders of Increase numbered 33 which reign in the Second Angle; under whom I have placed 9639 whom none hath yet numbered but One.

Call Four returns to quoting Iadbaltoh, once again establishing his Angelic rulers in their seats of power. In this case, He has focused his attention on the south—called the "Second Angle." (No "First Angle" is ever mentioned—however those who see a description of a zodiacal chart in Call Three have suggested it should be associated with the east—the place of the ascendant, where the horoscope begins. If this is the case, then Call Four likely moves clockwise upon that chart to the "Second Angle," which is indeed associated with the south.)

The final line above directs this Call toward the "Thunders of Increase"—who reign in the south—and their direct subordinates. (The Angelical for "Thunders of Increase" is *Avavago*—and that name will appear again in Call Eight, also associated with the south.) These Angels have not been "numbered" (counted) by anyone except "One."

The Angelical word for "One" (*L*), was used earlier in the Calls as "The First"—a Name of God. Therefore, it is likely that Iadbaltoh is referring to Himself in this instance—though it is possible that the reference is to the Christos.

> In whom the second beginning of things are and wax strong; which also successively are the number of time; and their powers are as the first 456.

Here we are told more about the Angels (Thunders) of the Second Angle. Apparently they are related to the zodiacal Angels described in Call Three—who were given government in succession over "456, the true ages of time." Here in Call Four, the Thunders *also* govern "the number of time" in succession, and are equated with "the first 456." I suspect that these Angels of the south are zodiacal, directly subordinate to the rulers of the twelve Kingdoms. (See the following three Keys for more evidence toward this interpretation.)

The Call also credits the Thunders with "the second beginning of things." On the surface, this might be a reference to the foundation of the New World after the Tribulation. (See the final chapter of the Book of Revelation.) However, I should point out that the Angelical word used here—*Croodzi* (beginning)—includes no indication of "second" (*Viv*). Perhaps the intent here is to indicate that these Angels govern a cyclic time which periodically "restarts."

> Arise you sons of pleasure and visit the earth, for I am the Lord your God which is and liveth." In the Name of the Creator, move and show yourselves as pleasant deliverers; that you may praise Him amongst the sons of men.

This Call ends with another conjuration formula. This one is unique, because it begins *before* the end of Iadbaltoh's speech.[72] God Himself tells the Angels to arise and visit the Earth. Note how He refers to Himself at this point as He who "is and liveth"—similar to the title He previously gave to the Christos. Remember earlier, I explained this blending of the Highest God and the Christos in biblical literature.[73] The Creation was accomplished by God *through* the power of the Christos.

Finally, the speaker concludes with his own words of conjuration "In the Name of the Creator."

Call Five:

> The Mighty Sounds have entered into the third Angle and are become as olives in the olive mount looking with gladness upon the earth and dwelling within the brightness of the heavens as continual comforters, unto whom I have fastened pillars of gladness 19, and gave them vessels to water the earth with her creatures;

Call Five is again spoken almost entirely by Iadbaltoh. He is never mentioned directly in the text, but we can see the use of first person in the phrase " . . . unto whom I have fastened pillars . . . " Thus, this Call fits with the others that quote God during the creation of the Universe and the establishment of His Angelic rulers.

Previously, in Call Four, we first met the Thunders of Increase—a group of Angels ruling in the Second Angle (south). That imagery is continued into Call Five, where we meet "Mighty Sounds" (Thunders) in the Third Angle. If this is descriptive of a zodiacal chart, then the Third Angle should represent the western quarter.

Notice that these Mighty Sounds are very numerous ("as olives in the olive mount") and dwell within the "brightness of the heavens," "looking with gladness upon the earth." I believe this is a poetic description of stars in the sky, which further supports the interpretation of these Angels as zodiacal. This is further indicated by the following passages:

> and they are the brothers of the First and Second; and the beginning of their own seats which are garnished with continually burning lamps 69636; whose numbers are as the first, the ends, and the contents of time.

The Mighty Sounds of the Third Angle are the brothers of (that is, equated with) the Angels of the "First and Second" Angles. Also note how they are described as "the first, the ends, and the contents of time"—which is analogous to the descriptions of the zodiacal Angels in Calls Three (the true ages of time) and Four (the number of time).

Therefore, the Mighty Sounds in the third angle (west) are equated with the zodiacal Angels in the first two angles (east and south).[74]

I also suspect that the reference to "continually burning lamps" is another poetic description of the stars, shining in the night sky.

> Therefore, come you and obey your creation. Visit us in peace and comfort. Conclude us as receivers of your mysteries. For why? Or Lord and Master is all one.

The quotes from Iadbaltoh have ended once more, and the Call returns to the viewpoint of the speaker, who employs a conjuration as we've come to expect.

Call Six:

> The spirits of the fourth Angle are nine, mighty in the Firmaments of Water; whom the First hath planted a torment to the wicked and a garland to the Righteous; giving unto them fiery darts to van the earth and 7699 continual workmen whose courses visit with comfort the earth; and are in government and continuance as the second and the third.

For some reason, this Call does not quote Iadbaltoh at all, though it does mention Him as "the First." While it is spoken entirely by the speaker, it does not take the style of a biblical psalm.[75] Instead, it retains the Genesis-like style of the previous three Calls, describing the establishment of the Angelic spirits of the "Fourth Angle."

For some reason, these spirits of the Fourth Angle go unnamed. However, it is most likely their name would be another take on Thunders, Mighty Sounds, etc. These particular entities reside in the "Fourth Angle," which should be the northern quarter of a zodiacal chart.

This Call also outlines the intimate relationship between these Angels and the zodiacal Angels described in the three previous Calls. They are "as the Second and the Third"—meaning they are equated with the Angels in the second (southern) and third (western) angles.

Likewise, they are described as residing in the "Firmaments of Water" (the nighttime sky) and in charge of "continual workmen" whose "courses visit with comfort the earth." I feel we are again looking at a poetic description of the stars in the sky.

> Wherefore, hearken unto my voice. I have talked of you and I move you in power and presence, whose works shall be a song of honor and praise of your God in your creation.

Finally, this Call concludes like all the others, with a formula of conjuration for these Angels.

Call Seven:

> The east is a house of virgins singing praises amongst the flames of the First Glory;

Like Call Six, this poem is not spoken by Iadbaltoh, and He is only mentioned herein (later in the Call) as "the Lord." The style remains that of Genesis over that of Psalms.

In this case, the east is directly addressed as such. It is not called an "Angle," but we will see a reference to the Angles later in the poem. Going by the pattern we have followed thus far, the east should be the First Angle of the zodiacal chart.

I am unsure if there is any deep significance to the phrase *house of virgins*. It could simply be a poetic description of the Angels who reside in the east. These are the Angels who sing praises as the Sun rises at dawn (viz., the flames of the First Glory), or those who sing in the direct presence of the Divine Throne. Their relationship to the newborn Sun (or, in Christian imagery, the newborn Son) would explain their description as "virgins."

However, just like the Angels in Call Six, the virgins are not given a name. However, because they are equated with the Angels of the other three angles of the Heavens, I suggest they are also "Thunders."

> wherein the Lord hath opened His Mouth, and they become 28 living dwellings in whom the strength of men rejoiceth and they are appareled with ornaments of brightness such as work wonders on all creatures.

Here we see the establishment of these Angels by Iadbaltoh. Although the focus of this Call is obviously upon the east, I still suspect that the "28 living dwellings" represent the astrological mansions of the Moon. This fits the zodiacal focus of the previous three Calls, and it recalls the imagery of the Moon that was mentioned only once in Call One.

In the "ornaments of brightness" I see yet another poetic image of the stars in the nighttime sky.

> Whose kingdoms and continuance are as the Third and Fourth; strong towers and places of comfort, the seats of mercy and continuance.

Here we see that the Angels of the east are "as the Third and Fourth"—or as the Angels of the third and fourth angles. This supports the idea that they are zodiacal Angels along with those of Calls Four, Five, and Six. By moving from the north to the east of the horoscope, the Calls have now completed the Circle begun in Call Four—encompassing all of the Angelic rulers of the zodiac.

> O you servants of mercy, move, appear, sing praises unto the Creator, and be mighty amongst us. For to this remembrance is given power and our strength waxeth strong in our Comforter.

The Call finally comes to its concluding conjuration. However, this time an extra line is added to the end, which seems very formal and almost prayer-like. I suspect this is a conclusion of sorts, indicating a break between the previous seven Calls and those that follow.

For illustration, I have outlined my concept of the pattern found through the first seven Calls:

> **Calls One and Two:** Evocation of the seven planetary Archangels.
>
> **Call Three:** Evocation of the Archangels of the twelve signs/houses.
>
> **Calls Four through Seven:** Evocation of stellar Angels associated with the four quarters of the Universe, and governed by the Seven and Twelve.

Therefore, we see in these Calls the formation of the entire Universe, expressed in astrological terms. The seven planetary Archangels are the "Seven Spirits of God" mentioned several times in the Revelation of St. John. They direct the Archangels of the Twelve Kingdoms of the zodiac, who are themselves described in Revelation 21 as the guardians of the twelve gates of the Holy City.

In turn, the twelve zodiacal Kingdoms are populated with innumerable Angels (or Thunders) who are grouped into the four quarters of the Universe—likely according to elemental triplicity. I base the latter assumption on a diagram Dee drew of St. John's description of the Holy City.[76] Dee labeled the twelve gates with the secret names of the Twelve Archangels, the associated Hebrew tribes and their corresponding signs of the zodiac.[77] This diagram indicates that the fiery triplicity (Aries, Leo, Sagittarius) is associated with the east; the earthy triplicity (Capricornus, Taurus, Virgo) is associated with the south; the airy triplicity (Libra, Aquarius, Gemini) is associated with the west; and the watery triplicity (Cancer, Scorpio, Pisces) is associated with the north. This is the zodiacal attribution of elements to the four quarters, as given by Agrippa in his *Three Books of Occult Philosophy* (Scale of the Number Four).[78]

Having thus established the Angelic rulers who will govern Creation, the following Calls seem to focus upon the Angels who will purify that Creation by fire during the Tribulation.

Therefore, from this point onward, we shall see a marked increase in apocalyptic imagery. Much like the Revelation of St. John and other apocalyptic literature, the poetry of the Calls is extremely obscure and difficult to interpret. If the student wishes to gain a deeper understanding of the remaining Keys, I suggest a study of such books as the Revelation of St. John, Daniel, the Book of Enoch (*1 Enoch*), and related biblical texts.

We will also see more of the Thunders in later Calls, though it is uncertain if they are exactly the same Thunders outlined in Calls Four through Seven. They are either entirely separate Angels in charge of the End Times, or they are simply the previous Thunders who will act in that capacity in the future.

Call Eight:

> "The midday the first is as the third Heaven made of hyacinth pillars 26; in whom the Elders are become strong; which I have prepared for my own righteousness," sayeth the Lord,

Call Eight suddenly returns to quoting Iadbaltoh—and it will be the last to do so until the final Call (that of the thirty Aethyrs). Once again, God is describing the establishment of some aspect of the Universe.

In classical texts, the reference to the "midday" sometimes indicates the south.[79] (This Call will later reference the "Thunders"—or *Avavago*—who are said in Call Four to reign in the south.) However, it is unclear if the south is the intended meaning of "midday" in this case. The southern angle of a horoscope also doubles as the *zenith*, or the highest point in the Heavens through which the planets and stars pass. The first line of Call Eight could be interpreted in that way, as midday is the time when the Sun passes through the zenith.

God places into the zenith a series of mysterious "pillars." The poem is not clear on whether or not these pillars are Angels—however, the speaker will later address them directly in his conjuration. Thus, I can only assume that they are Angelic intelligences of some sort. (The Call does say they are made of "hyacinth"—which may mean lapis lazuli, a stone used to symbolize the night sky.)[80]

The Call does tell us that the pillars are associated in some way with the Elders of the Apocalypse (first mentioned in Revelation 4:4.) These twenty-four beings are described as tribal Elders (two for each Hebrew tribe) and direct advisors to the Divine Crown. In occultism, they are often associated with the zodiac (as are the tribes)—a positive and negative Elder for each sign. (It is a shame, of course, that the number of pillars given in the Call is twenty-six, rather than twenty-four to match the number of Elders.)[81]

> "Whose long continuance shall be bucklers to the stooping dragons and like unto the harvest of a widow.

The pillars are intended, as long as they last, to act as barriers against the "stooping dragons." (*To stoop* means to dive, as a bird after its prey.) This imagery reminds me of the four "Watchtowers" described in Dee's advanced magick, and introduced by the Angel Ave with the following words:

> The Four houses are the Four Angels of the Earth, which are the Four Overseers, and Watchtowers, that . . . God . . . hath placed against the . . . Great Enemy, the Devil. [*A True and Faithful Relation*, p. 170]

So, the Watchtowers serve the same function as the pillars of Call Eight—to hinder the demonic forces of the Universe. (Satan will be referred to as "the Dragon" later in this same Call.) Furthermore, the names of the twenty-four Elders are found (in groups of six) in the four Watchtowers[82]—suggesting yet another connection between the Watchtowers and the pillars.

The final description of the pillars in Call Eight is the most enigmatic, for the pillars are "like unto the harvest of a widow." I have seen it suggested that sorrow and hardship are the "harvest of a widow," and I have to agree.[83] Yet, we have to question why pillars established to hinder the dragon(s) would also be a source of sorrow.

A simple interpretation might be that the sorrow and hardship are experienced by the *dragons* who desire to dive past the pillars. A more involved interpretation would draw from Gnosticism, which referred to the band of fixed stars as a "Great Barrier" that must be overcome, through ordeal and tribulation, by each aspirant who wishes to gain entry to Heaven. (This is applied to the story of Jesus, who suffered torture and final Crucifixion upon the cross in order to propel his soul beyond the Great Barrier.) If the pillars are associated with the Elders (the zodiac), then Call Eight may be referring to *both* their function of keeping the dragons out as well as their function of keeping the unworthy sealed in.

> How many are there, which remain in the glory of the earth, which are and shall not see death until this house fall and the dragon sink."

This is the most apocalyptic line of Call Eight. We saw earlier that the pillars only keep out the dragon(s) so long as they are in place. This line warns that the removal of the pillars will result in an immediate attack by the dragon. (The word *sink* is used here in the same sense as *stoop*—to dive and attack.)

I believe this is a direct reference to the Tribulation. It seems to indicate such by asking, "How many are currently alive on the earth who will still be alive when the pillars are removed?" Compare this to Matthew 24, where Jesus tells his disciples of the End Times, "Verily I say unto you, This generation shall not pass, till all these things be fulfilled."

> Come away, for the Thunders have spoken. Come away, for the crowns of the Temple, and the coat of Him that is, was, and shall be Crowned, are divided. Come, appear to the terror of the earth; and to our comfort; and of such as are prepared.

At last, we reach the concluding conjuration, in the speaker's own words. This is a longer and more involved conjuration than we have seen so far—likely "geared up" due the apocalyptic nature of the Call.

The Thunders (or the *Avavago* from Call Four) are mentioned again, which I assume in this case is a direct reference to the Thunders of Calls Four through Seven. It is likely that the Thunders having "spoken" carries a double meaning. On the one hand, it may indicate the description in the Revelation of St. John (shown previously), where each of Seven Thunders utters "a Voice." On the other hand, it may indicate the fact that Calls Four through Seven have already been spoken.

Lastly, note the reference to "Him that is, was, and shall be Crowned." This appears to be another reference to the Christos as we saw in Calls One and Two—especially in His aspect as the eternally crowned King. The divided "crowns of the Temple" and "coat" of the Christos likely represent a disrupted Universe—as in the Tribulation.

Call Nine:

> A mighty guard of fire with two-edged swords flaming (which have vials 8 of wrath for two times and a half; whose wings are of wormwood and of the marrow of salt), have settled their feet in the west and are measured with their ministers 9996,

In Call Nine, a platoon (guard) of fiery Angels land in the west. Their physical aspect is terrifying—wings of wormwood (a poison) and salt, flaming swords and of course the horrible "vials of wrath." These vials appear to draw from the Revelation 15, where we find seven Angels with the vials of plagues.[84] Therein, as each Angel pours out its vial of God's wrath, horrible catastrophes take place on Earth—such as water turning to blood, people stricken with sores, and the land burning with scorching sunlight.

The western orientation of this Call appears to be a smooth transition from the southern angle (or zenith) of the previous Call—though

I am unsure if that pattern truly applies after Call Seven. (See Calls Ten through Thirteen, where the apparent clockwise pattern breaks down entirely.)

> These gather up the moss of the earth as the rich man doth his treasure. Cursed are they whose iniquities they are.

A thesaurus suggests that *moss* is a synonym of words such as *muck, mire, quagmire, slime*, and so on.[85] (In the Lexicon, I have settled upon the word *dross*.)[86] If that is the correct interpretation, then the "moss of the earth" may be one and the same with the "cursed" in the next line. The phrase "they whose iniquities they are" likely indicates those iniquitous humans toward whom the terrible Angels will direct their wrath. It is they who will be "gathered" (likely cut down, as in gathering a crop) in huge numbers (as the rich man gathers treasure).

> In their eyes are millstones greater than the earth, and from their mouths run seas of blood. Their heads are covered with diamond and upon their hands are marble sleeves. Happy is he on whom they frown not. For why? The God of Righteousness rejoiceth in them.

Here the Call returns to describing the terrifying aspect of these Angels—and the picture is far worse than previously imagined. Notice how often hard things are used to describe them—eyes of millstones, heads of diamond, and marble gloves. The image is that of unstoppable juggernauts, impervious to cries for mercy. Why should Iadbaltoh rejoice in such terrible creatures? Because they are the mighty forces that will someday scour the "moss" from the face of the Earth.

These Angels are never named in this Call; however, we will see the Thunders mentioned once again in Call Ten. It is possible that these Angels are Thunders as well—though it is uncertain what relation (if any) they have to the Thunders of Calls Four through Seven.

> Come away, and not your vials. For the time is such as requireth comfort.

The concluding conjuration formula is very short this time. It calls for them to come, but to leave their vials behind. (We wouldn't want them to bring *those* down until the Final Day!) Finally, apparently as a defense against the wrathful nature of these Angels, the speaker informs them that the time requires *comfort*.

Call Ten:

> The Thunders of Judgment and Wrath are numbered and harbored in the north in the likeness of an oak whose branches are 22 nests of lamentation and weeping laid up for the earth; which burn night and day and vomit out the heads of scorpions and live sulfur mingled with poison.

At last, we find a new reference to the apocalyptic Thunders. However, note the change from "Thunders of Increase" who rained down life and comfort upon the Earth in previous Calls, to "Thunders of Judgment and Wrath" (Angelical: *Coraxo*) who store up lamentation and weeping for the Earth. This may support the view that these Thunders are not the same as those previous to Call Eight.

Notice that these Angels have a terrifying aspect like those of Call Nine, in this case vomiting scorpions, poison, and fire. Imagery suggesting hardness is invoked again in the description of these Angels as an "oak"—a type of tree known for being rigid and unbending.

This Call focuses upon the north, which seems to be the natural progression from the west in the previous Call. However, this is the last Call that seems to follow that smooth pattern,[87] and I therefore suspect an entirely different pattern exists from Call Eight onward. Sadly, I have been unable to decode the directional references in these later Calls.

> These be the Thunders that 5678 times in the 24th part of a moment roar with a hundred mighty earthquakes, and a thousand times as many surges, which rest not neither know any (long) time here. One rock bringeth forth 1000 even as the heart of man doth his thoughts.

Here the descriptions of the Thunders of Judgment and Wrath continue. These Angels apparently bring great earthquakes, similar to catastrophic events described in the Revelation and elsewhere.[88]

> Woe, woe, woe woe, woe, woe, yea, woe be to the earth. For her iniquity is, was, and shall be great.

These seven "woes of the Earth" are likewise drawn from Revelation (chapters 8–11), where St. John mentions only three.[89] However, they are associated with the sounding of seven trumpets blown by the seven Archangels. Each trump results in disaster upon the Earth (hail, blood, fire, death, the Star Wormwood,[90] etc.), and the woes are associated with the final three. Of course, each of the seven trumps causes "woe" in the world. Thus, the poetry of this Call likely addresses the results of all seven trumps by repeating the word *woe* seven times.

> Come away, but not your noises.

The concluding conjuration asks the Thunders to come, but to leave behind their "noises" (earthquakes, fire-vomiting, and so on). I find it significant that Call Ten ends with an extremely abbreviated conjuration, very similar to that found in the previous Call. It is, once more, as if the speaker wishes to summon these Angels without gaining *too much* of their attentions.

Calls Nine and Ten certainly appear to be a connected pair. They are similar in their basic structure, appear to describe similarly terrifying Angels, and they are the most laden with apocalyptic imagery. The following Call has a slightly different structure and imagery than the preceding two, but it does reference the *Coraxo* ("Thunders") first mentioned in Call Ten.

Call Eleven:

> The Mighty Seat groaned and they were 5 Thunders which flew into the east, and the Eagle spake and cried with a loud voice, "Come away!"

Even though the imagery of Call Eleven is slightly different, I do find that its relationship to the Revelation of St. John is as close or closer than what we see in Calls Ten and Eleven. This close relationship is made apparent right away: The Thunders flying out from the "Mighty Seat" and the Eagle (one of the Four Holy Living Beasts, or *Chaioth haQodesh*) are both seen in Revelation 4.[91] In fact, the first lines of Call Eleven sound as if they could have been quoted right out of Revelation itself.

This Call is also unique for the very same reason. While the other Calls have drawn imagery from Revelation, they have all been descriptions of the Creation in action, or adorations, or quotes from Iadbaltoh, or the like. Call Eleven, alone among the forty-eight Calls, is written as if it were telling a story. It gives the sense that a prophet is recording a vision in action, like St. John, Ezekiel, or Isaiah.

In these passages, five of the Thunders *(Coraxo)* fly from the Divine Throne and head toward the east. However, the eagle speaks up and calls them back. I presume the eagle calls them to the north—the natural position of the eagle / Scorpius in the four zodiacal quarters.[92] I therefore suspect that Call Eleven is associated is with the north rather than the east.

> And they gathered themselves together and became the house of death, of whom it is measured, and it is as they are whose number is 31.

The northern association of this Call may be supported by the fact that the returning Thunders gather themselves together and become "the house of death"—which could be a reference to Scorpius (the Sign that rules the eighth astrological House of death / generation) in the north.[93]

> Come away, for I have prepared for you. Move, therefore, and show yourselves. Open the mysteries of your creation. Be friendly unto me. For, I am a servant of the same your God; the true worshiper of the Highest.

The concluding conjuration is much more elaborate than we saw in the preceding two Calls. I note that the speaker makes a specific reference to being "prepared" for the arrival of the Thunders, which could have some relationship to the House of Death concept. That is the astrological House of wills, inheritance, and all things one must prepare before passing. Moreover, as Call Eleven is an apocalyptic vision, it suggests that the speaker is spiritually prepared for Divine Judgment.

As a final note, this is the first Call that resumes the use of the "Repetitive Formula Pattern" (or RFP) established in the concluding conjuration of Call One. This formula will be the standard conjuration found from here through Call Eighteen.

The next seven Calls (Twelve through Eighteen) break with the previous literary patterns. While they certainly remain very apocalyptic in nature, they suddenly look less like biblical passages and more like grimoiric conjurations composed of biblical imagery (though nothing as specific as we saw in Calls Nine through Eleven.) They are spoken by the speaker from start to finish, and some of them address rather powerful celestial forces.

I also note that each of these seven Calls contains a specific name or title of God. (I have indicated each in what follows with bold characters.) This further supports the interpretation of these Calls as straight conjurations, associating them with occult literature common in Dee's time.

Call Twelve:

> Oh you that reign in the south and are 28 the lanterns of sorrow, bind up your girdles and visit us. Bring down your train 3663 that the Lord may be magnified whose name amongst you is **Wrath**.

This is the second Call that mentions the number 28 (see Call Seven), though this instance is associated with the south rather than the east. I find it unlikely that the two are related, as the 28s in Call Seven were associated with strength and rejoicing, while the 28s in this Call are associated with the "lanterns of sorrow."

Who these Angels are who reign in the south, or why they should be "lanterns of sorrow," is not explained. These could be a new set of apocalyptic Angels, or they could be the same Angels we have previously seen in the south. The use of lantern imagery may suggest stars, as it did in earlier Calls.

Note that both this Call and the next are addressed to the Angels in the south. It is difficult to imagine why two Calls in a row should be assigned to the south—though we might compare this to Calls Nine and Ten, both of which appear to be assigned to the north.

> Move, I say, and show yourselves. Open the mysteries of your creation. Be friendly unto me. For, I am a servant of the same your God; the true worshiper of the Highest.

Finally, the Call ends with the RFP conjuration formula from Call One—with the exception that the usual word *therefore* has been replaced with *I say*. No explanation for this change exists—it is an alteration Dee made between recording the Calls in his journals and transcribing them to his *48 Claves Angelicae*.[94] (Compare this to the following six Calls, which contain the same RFP without either *therefore* or *I say*.)

Call Thirteen:

> O you swords of the south, which have 42 eyes to stir up wrath of sin, making men drunken which are empty. Behold the promise of God and His power which is called amongst you a **Bitter Sting**. Move and show yourselves. Open the mysteries of your creation. Be friendly unto me. For, I am a servant of the same your God; the true worshiper of the Highest.

Call Thirteen addresses the Angels of the south once again—though we cannot be certain if these are the same entities. They are called the "swords of the south," which is likely a reference to sword-bearing Angels. (The name *Bitter Sting* also carries the connotation of a sword-stroke or attack.) The Call only tells us that they are stirred up by sin, and they seem to direct their wrath against those who are spiritually "empty."

The Call concludes with the RFP from Call One, missing only the second word *therefore*. (Compare to Call Twelve, which replaces *therefore* with *I say*.) The RFP as we see it here in Call Thirteen will remain unchanged throughout the following five Calls.

Call Fourteen:

> O you sons of fury, the daughters of the just, which sit upon 24 seats, vexing all creatures of the earth with age, which have under you 1636; Behold the voice of God, promise of him which is called amongst you **Fury** (or **Extreme Justice**). Move and show yourselves. Open the mysteries of your creation. Be friendly unto me. For, I am a servant of the same your God; the true worshiper of the Highest.

The identity of the "sons of fury" and "daughters of the just" is unclear. We can see that they vex all creatures upon the earth with age—so they are related to the progress of time. They also sit upon twenty-four seats, which evokes the imagery of the twenty-four Elders seen in the Revelation, and mentioned in Call Eight. The Elders represent the positive and negative aspects of each zodiacal sign, and this could explain the reference to "sons" and "daughters."

On the other hand, it is also possible that these sons and daughters are associated with the twenty-four hours of the day and night. There is too little descriptive evidence to be sure.

The concluding conjuration is the RFP seen in Calls One, and Eleven through Eighteen.

The next four Calls (Fifteen through Eighteen) address the "Governors of the Four Flames." We never learn the identity of the Governors or the meaning of the Four Flames. (In just one case—Call Eighteen—the Governor is referred to *as* a Flame). We are only given the impression that these Governors are extremely exalted and powerful.

Personally, these beings bring to mind the four *Cherubim* of Jewish and Christian mysticism (usually described as Michael, Gabriel, Raphael, and Uriel).[95] Closely related to these four are the *Chaioth haQodesh*—the Holy Living Beasts we discussed in relation to Call Eight, who represent the zodiacal triplicities in Ezekiel 1 and Revelation 4. Depending upon which text you read, these great Beasts uphold the Throne of God, or the firmament (Aethyrs). Of course, the Angel Nalvage, in *A True and Faithful Relation*, describes them as Watchtowers against the attacks of Satan.[96]

Even more, the "Governors of the Four Flames" remind me of four Gnostic beings called the "Great Luminaries"—*Harmozel, Oroiael, Daueithai*, and *Eleleth*.[97] These four Luminaries are treated as both intelligent beings and as vast heavenly realms (or Aeons). They were created by the Christos for the purpose of bringing balance and order to Heaven. Therefore, the twelve lesser Aeons were categorized and established within their realms:

Harmozel: Loveliness, Truth, and Form.

Oroiael: Afterthought, Perception, and Memory.

Daueithai: Intelligence, Love, and Ideal Form (or Idea).

Eleleth: Perfection, Peace, and Wisdom.[98]

The twelve lesser Aeons are archetypal concepts, representing varying aspects of the Mind of God. According to Gnostic thought, when Ialdabaoth created the signs of the zodiac, He modeled them upon the twelve lesser Aeons. Likewise, when He created the four Cherubim of the triplicities, He modeled them upon the Great Luminaries.

With this in mind, I feel it is likely the "Governors of the Four Flames" from the next four Calls are representative of the four Luminaries of the triplicities, the Holy Living Beasts and perhaps even Dee's own four Watchtowers.

Call Fifteen:

> O thou the Governor of the First Flame, under whose wings are 6739 which weave the earth with dryness, which knowest the great name **Righteousness** and the seal of honor. Move and show yourselves. Open the mysteries of your creation. Be friendly unto me. For, I am a servant of the same your God; the true worshiper of the Highest.

Though none of these four Calls will give us directional references, I suspect we might be able to relate the "First Flame" with the "First Angle" seen in previous Calls. If so, then the ordering probably follows the same clockwise direction we saw in Calls Four through Seven. Therefore, the "Governor of the First Flame" (along with the 6739 ministers under him) would represent the stars of the east.

The concluding conjuration is the RFP seen in Calls One, and Eleven through Eighteen.

Call Sixteen:

> O thou of the Second Flame, the house of justice which has thy beginning in glory and shalt comfort the just; which walkest upon the earth with feet 8763 that understand and separate creatures; Great art thou in the **God of Stretch Forth and Conquer**. Move and show yourselves. Open the mysteries of your creation. Be friendly unto me. For, I am a servant of the same your God; the true worshiper of the Highest.

Here we meet the Governor of the Second Flame, which likely relates to the southern quarter. I am unsure if the "house of justice" is intended to refer to one of the astrological Houses—though I do find it unlikely. It appears to be the Governor himself who is the "house of justice" and will "comfort the just." This is apparently related to the Tribulation and final judgment of humanity.

There is an obscure reference here to "walking upon the earth" and "understanding and separating creatures." Later in the Key of the Aethyrs, we will find a similar reference to the "reasonable creatures of the earth," which indicates mankind. It is difficult to decide, here in Call Sixteen, if the Governor of the Second Flame (and the 8763 ministers under him) is walking upon Earth *as* a human, or merely *with* humans.

The concluding conjuration is the RFP seen in Calls One, and Eleven through Eighteen.

Call Seventeen:

> O thou whose wings are thorns to stir up vexation, and hast 7336 lamps living going before thee; whose God is **Wrath in Anger**. Gird up thy loins and hearken. Move and show yourselves. Open the mysteries of your creation. Be friendly unto me. For, I am a servant of the same your God; the true worshiper of the Highest.

In Call Seventeen we see no reference to a Flame, though we can assume this is the Governor of the Third Flame based on the progression from Call Fifteen through Eighteen. This particular Governor (and his 7336 ministers) most likely represents the stars of the western quarter. (Note the reference to lamps again—which has previously indicated stars.)

We are only told that this Governor has wings that "stir up vexation" upon the Earth—which seems to fit well with the name "Wrath in Anger." This is apocalyptic imagery once again. (As a note, the phrase "gird up thy loins" means "to prepare oneself.")

The concluding conjuration is the RFP seen in Calls One, and Eleven through Eighteen.

Call Eighteen:

> O thou mighty Light and Burning Flame of comfort, which openest the glory of God to the center of the earth. In whom the secrets of truth 6332 have their abiding, which is called in thy kingdom **Joy**, and not to be measured. Be thou a window of comfort unto me. Move and show yourselves. Open the mysteries of your creation. Be friendly unto me. For, I am a servant of the same your God; the true worshiper of the Highest.

The final Governor is called a "Flame of Comfort" and a "window of comfort." I notice that the Governors have been alternately hostile (weaving the Earth with dryness, stirring up vexation) and comforting (comfort the just, window of comfort). This appears to be standard apocalyptic imagery, wherein the Tribulation is a nightmare for the unworthy, but exalts the true believers. (Note Call Six, where Iadbaltoh is said to have established Angels to be "a torment to the wicked and a garland to the Righteous.")

The Governor of the Fourth Flame is described as revealing (opening) the Glory of God even unto "the center of the Earth"—meaning "everywhere on Earth without exception." This fits well with the Divine Name *Joy*—or measureless joy. (See the Lexicon in volume II concerning *Moz* [Joy], which can also mean "Joy of God.")

This Call, like the one before it, does not offer a number for the Governor of the Flame. However, if we follow the same pattern we have so far, this should be the Fourth Flame and represents the northern quarter. And, though it is unclear, his 6332 ministers appear to be called the "Secrets of Truth."

The concluding conjuration is the RFP seen in Calls One, and Eleven through Eighteen.

Thus ends the first Eighteen Calls—which should collectively represent the establishment of the Universe throughout the six biblical Days of Creation. (See chapter 2.) While there is much here drawn from the Book of Revelation and other End Times literature, I find that the Tribulatory events are all set in the future. (That is, what we see in these Calls is the creation and placement of the Angels who *will* bring the world to an end, but we are not witnessing the Tribulation in action.)

The final Call, which represents Keys Nineteen through Forty-eight, concerns itself with the Fall from Eden—officially beginning the Seventh Day of Rest. This Seventh Day, and its fallen state, continues to the present time. It will not end until the Tribulation itself—which (at least in Dee's mysticism) is considered the "Eighth Day" leading to the founding of the New Kingdom.

The story of Eden is often considered one of the oldest stories of mankind. In fact, this is a misconception. The story of Eden is among the oldest *written* stories. Meanwhile, the human race is much older than language. (We've had only about ten thousand years of writing. We've had spoken language for much longer—although without written records we can never know exactly how long.)

In fact, the story of Eden (including its original predecessors)[99] are *later* versions of an older legend. The tale of the "first shaman"—in oral form—has existed among tribal cultures for many thousands of years.[100] The legend describes a paradisal period for humanity ("In the beginning . . ."), when people had familiarity with the Gods and lived in harmony with animals and nature. Then, usually through some misunderstanding on the part of the first shaman, humanity became estranged from the gods. They lost their hope of immortality, lived in enmity with the animals, and found themselves out of sync with nature. The unfortunate soul who caused the disaster became the first shaman, because it was his duty, and the duty of all shamans who followed him, to labor to bridge the gap between man and the Divine. That is the foundation of the Great Work to this very day.

When this story was finally written down,[101] it was done by one of our ancestors in a city *after* the agricultural revolution. Therefore, the first shaman was placed in a garden. The garden had been planted by the gods, who alone know the secrets of agriculture—and all of the "arts of civilization" that come along with it (kingship, mathematics, astrology, priesthood, and so forth). In the earliest versions of the garden legend, man is invited in by the gods, who have deemed him worthy to join their ranks. In the later biblical version, man is created for the sole purpose of tending the garden. This is purely a reflection of agricultural society.

Therefore, in the biblical Eden we find the Tree of Knowledge of Good and Evil—the source of the Fall in this agricultural version of the legend. Eating the fruit of this Tree is the "mistake" that causes Adam and Eve to lose their place in paradise. Even worse, their expulsion comes with a curse upon the Earth.[102] Many see in this tale a petty God casting angry curses against its own creation. However, I believe the story of the Fall from Eden is, quite literally, a moral tale.

Adam begins the story in paradise, where the environment was comfortable, and there was no toil associated with survival. God gives Adam every fruit tree and seed-bearing plant, so food is always an arm's length away. This, in fact, mirrors the state of humanity in its earliest infancy (or "in the beginning"), when we lived in temperate climates, surrounded by trees and plants that freely provided us food. Compared to the current human condition, life on earth for the earliest humans *was* a paradise.

As time progressed, the human animal began to distinguish itself from other animals by one thing alone—language. From the most primordial *ma-ma* (thought by some to be the very first word), humans were set to become "the reasoning creatures of the earth."[103] We developed logical consciousness (or, as Call Sixteen says, we began to "understand and separate creatures.") This is represented in the Eden tale by Adam naming all things. By applying names to the things and animals around him, Adam (Man) laid the foundation of all language, magick, science, and technology.

But the advent of language among humans sent them on an unalterable collision course with the loss of paradise. As language develops, both thought and the *capacity for thought* increase. Language eventually brought technological revolutions that altered the way humans lived on this planet. Eventually, language and technology molded humanity into what we know today as "cultures."

I feel this is where the Tree of the Knowledge of Good and Evil enters the story. As human culture developed, social taboos were the inevitable result. For the first time ever, we began to create a sense of "right vs. wrong"—or, to put it poetically, we partook of the fruit of the Tree of the Knowledge of Good and Evil.

Once we established "good vs. evil," the vast array of human *mores* grew as if from a seed. Notice that Adam and Eve, once they had eaten of the fruit, suddenly "knew they were naked." Body consciousness did not exist before we developed our moral consciousness. It was the forbidden fruit that caused Adam and Eve to do something so silly as seek cover to hide their "nakedness" from God and each other.

This knowledge (or discernment) of right and wrong became the source of humanity's ultimate downfall. God was not uttering a petty curse against Adam at the expulsion from Eden, He was simply stating what He knew to be true. Man had created a moral world for himself in which he was destined to labor and weep. It would lead to hatred and warfare, persecution and death. The paradise in which the Earth provided for us freely, like a garden given by God, was no more.

By the time we reach the Tribulation, the entire Universe is being judged on a cosmic scale, with the "righteous" (the Right) on one side, and the "Iniquitous" (the Wrong) on the other. Humanity, as we know it, collapses under the weight.

I believe this is the essence of the Call of the Aethyrs. It represents the physical world in its current state, in political and environmental disarray.

The Call of the Aethyrs:

> O you heavens which dwell [in the ___ Aethyr] are mighty in the Parts of the Earth, and execute the judgment of the Highest. To you it is said, Behold the face of your God, the beginning of comfort; whose eyes are the brightness of the heavens; which provided you for the government of the earth, and her unspeakable variety; furnishing you with a power (of) understanding to dispose all things according to the providence of Him that sitteth upon the Holy Throne,

The Call of the Aethyrs is a conjuration all the way through. It begins by addressing all the (Angels of the) Heavens or Aethyrs. I feel these are all of the Angels and Governors invoked by the first eighteen Calls. This would fit with the passages describing them as the Governors of the

Earth. These are the kings and ministers who maintain Natural Law, as described in Call One.

The "Parts of the Earth" are spiritual jurisdictions over geographical locations (or nations), and distributed among the zodiacal Angels within the thirty Aethyrs. This is outlined in detail in Dee's advanced magick—where this Call of the Aethyrs is used as a stand-alone conjuration for accessing the Parts of the Earth.[104]

> and rose up in the beginning saying, "The earth, let her be governed by her parts, and let there be division in her, that the glory of her may be always drunken and vexed in itself. Her course, let it run with the heavens, and as a handmaid let her serve them. One season, let it confound another, and let there be no creature upon or within her the same. All her members, let them differ in their qualities, and let there be no one creature equal with another. The reasonable creatures of the earth (or men), let them vex and weed out one another; and the dwelling places, let them forget their names. The work of man and his pomp, let them be defaced. His buildings, let them become caves for the beasts of the field. Confound her understanding with darkness. For why? It repenteth me I made man. One while let her be known, and another while a stranger; Because she is the bed of an harlot, and the dwelling place of him that is fallen.

Here we see Iadbaltoh uttering the infamous Curse of Eden itself. In the case of the Call of the Aethyrs, notice that the Curse is phrased in astrological terms. The earth's course is to "run with the heavens," and she is to "serve them as a handmaid." One season will confound another, the earth will be divided and governed by her Parts, and so on.[105] These passages evoke images of a chaotic Earth governed by the ever-shifting stars. We can, of course, see this celestial chaos in any zodiacal chart.

> O you heavens, arise! The lower heavens beneath you, let them serve you. Govern those that govern; cast down such as fall. Bring forth with those that increase, and destroy the rotten. No place let it remain in one number. Add and diminish until the stars be numbered."

Here, we return once more to the Angelic Governors of the world, and the (Angels of the) lower Heavens or Aethyrs who serve them. These subservient Angels are likely the various Thunders mentioned throughout the Calls—such as seen in numbers Four through Seven.

The phrase *Govern those that govern; cast down such as fall* indicates the Angels directing the *human* governors of the world—to bring in and depose kingdoms as the stars shift. (In other words, they represent Fate.) The next line also attributes the Angels to the direction of Nature—to bring life where it might increase and to tear down what decays.

The final two lines once again indicate the ever-changing astrological influence upon the Earth. It has also been suggested the phrase *until the stars be numbered* has an apocalyptic ring to it. To be "numbered" (or "measured") may have the connotation in this case of "having run their course."

> Arise, move, and appear before the covenant of his mouth, which he hath sworn unto us in his justice. Open the mysteries of your creation, and make us partakers of undefiled knowledge.

At long last, we reach the final conjuration. It calls upon a covenant with God, which is likely associated with humanity's place in the Universe as expressed biblically. As the Image of God, the aspirant has the right to converse with Angels—if only he can return to his pre-Fall state.

Endnotes

1. That is, forty-eight Keys with one withheld, for a total of forty-nine.
2. The first indication we are given that Dee has completed the Perfected Holy Book is on July 7, 1584—when Dee tells the Angel Ave that he made the book ". . . the best that I could conceive of it."
3. See chapter 2 of this volume.
4. See chapters 1 and 2 of this volume.
5. There are nineteen actual Keys/Calls. The nineteenth Call is repeated with slight modification thirty times—so there are technically forty-eight individual Keys.
6. Remember that each Table of *Loagaeth* consists of the front *and* back of a single leaf.
7. See Revelation, chapter 5.
8. Revelation 5:2—"And I saw a strong angel proclaiming with a loud voice, 'Who is worthy to open the book, and to loose the seals thereof?'"
9. I have added this word in brackets for clarification.
10. Consider the ancient Qabalistic axiom: "Every blade of grass has over it an Angel bidding it, 'Grow.'"

11. In an unpublished manuscript entitled *The Tongue of the Angels*.
12. Dee's personal number—which he used to sign secret documents—was 007. That is the reputed source for the signature of James Bond.
13. It is also the first printed book on cryptography in the world.
14. See "Solved: The Ciphers in Book III of Trithemius's Steganographia" by Jim Reeds, online at http://www.dtc.umn.edu/~reedsj/.
15. This method of encryption was used very successfully by Leonardo da Vinci.
16. See chapter 2 of this volume.
17. Dee actually recorded this letter on the same line as "(Two thousand and fourteen . . .)"—but those numbers seem to relate to the *D* rather than the *A*. It would appear, then, that the very first letter revealed by Nalvage was given no number or location.
18. This notation likely refers to the *D* directly beneath it.
19. The *Z* appears to be missing from the manuscript.
20. As we shall see later, Nalvage had previously transmitted several strings of letters—taken from the *Corpus Omnium* Table—that are associated with the first (unknowable) Table of *Loagaeth*. They did not come with numbers or directions as we see with the letters of Key One.
21. *Quiddity* means "the essence of the thing."
22. I outline this incident in full in my commentaries on Dee's journals, which I will release at a later date.
23. Some modern scholars refer to this as the "Tablet of God."
24. Such as we see with quartz crystal.
25. See a *True and Faithful Relation*, p. 76. Dee recorded only the letters of the Table. I have added the lines showing the principal divisions as taught by Nalvage.
26. About = around.
27. Nalvage said all of this in Latin. I have translated, but left *Principium Omnium* (meaning "Universal Principle") intact due to Nalvage's later references to the phrase.
28. I have added the emphasis on this line.
29. See *A True and Faithful Relation*, pp. 74–76.
30. I have added the Table cells and the bold lettering for clarification.
31. This reminds me somewhat of the Horned Altars (of burnt offering and of incense) in the Bible, which had horns upon their four corners. (See Exodus 27 and 30.)
32. I am appending these Latin translations.
33. Later, in the Angelical Keys, the word *Zir* appears as a form of "to be" and often indicates "I am." See the Lexicon in volume II.
34. See Hebrews 1:14: "Are they [Angels] not all ministering spirits, sent forth to minister for them who shall be heirs of salvation?"
35. Revelation 22:14: "Blessed are they that do His Commandments, that they may have right to the Tree of Life, and may enter in through the Gates into the City."

36. I believe this refers to the entire fourth portion of the Table, because Nalvage never labels it the "Fourth Life."
37. Dee notes, in the margin of his journal, the number of letters in each string.
38. As recorded, the first letters of this line were "V I I I I . . . ," but Dee corrected this in the margin, adding the *E* as the first letter.
39. There are actually forty-six letters in this line.
40. The last letters of this line were recorded as *E E E R S E*. However, Dee later added the correction, placing a symbol—)(—to indicate that the first two *E*s should be joined as one. To the side of this symbol, he added the correct letters—resulting in *E E R S E*.
41. Dee notes in the margin that this letter can be either *I* or *E*.
42. There are 188 letters in this last group. However, it is likely that there is more than one line intended here, although Dee did not record the number of letters in each.
43. I have added the bracketed word for clarification.
44. I have added the bracketed word for clarification.
45. This "nineteenth Key" is the Key of the Aethyrs—which is repeated thirty times to open the final thirty Tables of *Loagaeth*. (18 + 30 = 48) See the section entitled "The Angelical Keys: What We Know" in this chapter.
46. *Immediate* = Directly
47. Also note that I have included an addendum to this chapter, entitled "The Poetry of the Forty-Eight Calls," which analyzes the English given for the Keys.
48. This part of the quote is not included above. See chapter 4, "Gebofal—the Gates of Heaven": "For every Table hath his Key, and every Key openeth his Gate . . . "
49. I have added this word for clarification.
50. *This* = Nature, the Things of the World.
51. See chapter 2 for further apocalyptic statements made by the Angels in relation to *Loagaeth*.
52. I have included the names of the ninety-one Parts/Governors in the Lexicon, with the entries for the thirty Aethyrs.
53. Later, the Qabalah would adopt the Aeons as the Sephiroth (see chapter 1)—which are usually considered Heavenly Spheres, but were depicted in early Qabalistic texts as Archangelic beings. We can see this in the ancient Qabalistic text entitled the *Sepher Bahir* (the Book of Illumination).
54. Revelation 21:12.
55. Note that Agrippa's list of zodiacal Angels (see the "Scale of the Number Twelve") is not the same as Dee's. Apparently, Dee received a new set of twelve names from the Angels. However, the session where this happens has not survived. The twelve names appear for the first time in Dee's grimoire (Sloane 3191).
56. Revelation 4:5.
57. The Parts of the Earth led into the revelation of the Great Table of the Earth (Watchtowers)—during which Ave was the teacher.

58. The English given for the Keys is covered in the addendum to this chapter, "The Poetry of the Forty-Eight Calls."
59. *A True and Faithful Relation*, p. 199.
60. There are also Apocalypses of Adam, Paul, Thomas, Daniel, Peter, and a host of other biblical figures.
61. See Ezekiel 1, Revelation 4, and throughout *1 Enoch*.
62. See the preface to James, *The Enochian Magick of Dr. John Dee*, where we find one of the earliest comparisons between Dee's system and Gnosticism.
63. See chapter 2, the section outlining Tables 20–49.
64. This practice was also shared by the Jewish Merkavah mystics, who traveled through the seven traditional Heavens.
65. See my "Gnosticism: Sethian to Valentinian." (Information on locating this essay is in the bibliography of this book.)
66. See "Gnosticism: Sethian to Valentinian," concerning the story of the Christos.
67. We shall see this same formula again in Calls Eleven through Eighteen. This is the "Repetitive Formula Pattern"; see the Lexicon in volume II for more information.
68. Also see Revelation 10:6.
69. See Revelation 10:6: ". . . and swear by *him that liveth for ever and ever,* who created heaven, and the things that therein are, and the earth, and the things that therein are, and the sea, and the things which are therein, that there should be time no longer."
70. The Resurrection involves the return of all who have died throughout history during or after the Tribulation. See 1 Corinthians 15:51–54 and 1 Thessalonian 4:15–18. Revelation 20 is also considered a depiction of the Resurrection of all the dead for the Final Judgment.
71. See *John Dee's Five Books of Mystery*, pp. 56 and 61ff.
72. The closing conjuration of Call Two does contain a single quoted word from Iadbaltoh.
73. John 1: "In the beginning was the Word, and the Word was with God, and the Word was God;" and "All things were made by him; and without him was not any thing made that was made."
74. Previously, we met only those of the Second Angle (south)—in Call Four. We will meet those of the east in Call Seven.
75. See Call Two for an example of this psalm-like style.
76. Found in Dee's grimoire, or Sloane 3191. The diagram is also found in Geoffrey James, *The Enochian Magick of Dr. John Dee*, p. 103.
77. Dee numbered the signs from 1 to 12 in order from Aries to Pisces. He then placed each number by the corresponding Hebrew Tribe, as outlined in Agrippa's Book II, chapter 14: "Of the number eleven and the number twelve . . . "
78. Looking at an astrological chart, we see that Aries (the cardinal fire sign) is in the east, Capricorn (earth) is at the southern point, Libra (air) is at the western point,

and Cancer (water) is at the north. Therefore, the triplicities are each associated with these same directions.

79. This appears in *1 Enoch* 55:2: "And they came upon the wind from the East, from the West, and from the Midst of the Day."
80. This was suggested by Patricia Shaffer on the "Enochian-l" mailing list.
81. Also see Call Fourteen, where "24 seats" are mentioned directly.
82. The "Enochian Watchtowers" (properly called the Great Table of the Earth) are four magickal squares full of Divine and Angelical Names.
83. See Donald Tyson's books *Tetragrammaton* and *Enochian Magick for Beginners*.
84. Revelation 15:6–7, "And the seven angels came out of the temple, having the seven plagues, clothed in pure and white linen, and having their breasts girded with golden girdles. And one of the four beasts gave unto the seven angels seven golden vials full of the wrath of God, who liveth for ever and ever."
85. http://thesaurus.reference.com/. It has been suggested that "moss of the earth" is a reference to the dead. Looking into it, I could only find archaic references to "gathering moss" as a euphemism for the state of being dead. It was then I turned to the trusty thesaurus.
86. See *Mom* (Angelical for "moss," "dross") in the Lexicon in volume II.
87. We shall see that the next Call may relate to the north as well. Then, Calls Twelve and Thirteen both focus upon the south.
88. Revelation 16:18: "And there were voices, and thunders, and lightnings; and there was a great earthquake, such as was not since men were upon the earth, so mighty an earthquake, and so great."

    Matthew 24:7: "For nation shall rise against nation, and kingdom against kingdom: and there shall be famines, and pestilences, and earthquakes, in divers places."
89. Revelation 8:13: "And I beheld, and heard an angel flying through the midst of heaven, saying with a loud voice, Woe, woe, woe, to the inhabiters of the earth by reason of the other voices of the trumpet of the three angels, which are yet to sound!"
90. Note the use of the word *wormwood* in Call Nine, just previous to this one.
91. Revelation 4:5: "And out of the throne proceeded lightnings and thunderings and voices . . ."

    Revelation 4:6–7: " . . . and round about the throne, were four beasts full of eyes before and behind. And the first beast was like a lion, and the second beast like a calf, and the third beast had a face as a man, and the fourth beast was like a flying eagle."
92. Remember the traditional zodiacal attribution of elements to the four quarters—which associates Scorpio/water with the north. There is also a branch of astrology called *sidereal* that places Leo in the east instead of Aries. If we look at such a zodiacal chart, we find the four Fixed Signs at the four compass points instead of the Cardinals, but with the same arrangement of elements. This illustrates the four Holy Living Beasts, showing Scorpio (the eagle) at the northern point.

93. See previous footnote. Also take note of the *heads of scorpions* mentioned in Call Ten—which is itself associated with the north.
94. See Sloane 3191.
95. See various places throughout *1 Enoch*.
96. I included this quote from Nalvage with my commentary upon Call Eight.
97. See my essay "Gnosticism: Sethian to Valentinian."
98. Notice that the final and lowermost of the lesser Aeons is Wisdom—known as *Sophia* to the Gnostics, and who appeared to Dee and Kelley as *Galvah*. In Gnostic mythos, Sophia is the mother of Ialdabaoth.
99. See *Adapa: The First Man*, an ancient Sumerian tale.
100. See Mercea Eliade, *Shamanism: Archaic Techniques of Ecstasy*, especially pp. 99, 133, 484, and 493.
101. Impressed on clay, actually.
102. See Genesis 3:17–19.
103. This is a quote from the Call of the Aethyrs.
104. See chapter 2 of this volume, concerning *Loagaeth*'s Tables 20–49.
105. Agrippa outlines the astrological divisions of the Earth in his *Occult Philosphy*, where it had a direct influence upon Dee's "Parts of the Earth" system of magick. The reference to the Parts and this division in the Call of the Aethyrs is related to that system.

Chapter Four

Gebofal—The Gates of Heaven and Practice of the Holy Book

The practice of the *Book of Loagaeth* was given a name late in Dee's journals by the lunar Angel Levanael:[1]

> Now to the work intended, which is called in the Holy Art *Gebofal*, which is not (as the Philosophers have written,) the first step supernatural, but it is the first supernatural step naturally limited unto the 48 Gates of Wisdom; where your holy Book belongeth. The last [Gate][2] is the speaking with God, as Moses did, which is infinite: All the rest have proper limits, wherein they are contained. But understand that this singular work recieveth Multiplication and dignification, by ascension through all the rest that are limited according to their proper qualities. [*A True and Faithful Relation*, p. 373]

This is a wonderful description of *Gebofal*, or the ascension through the forty-eight (really forty-nine) Gates of Wisdom—represented by the Tables of *Loagaeth*. It is no accident if Levanael's description reminds you of what we discussed in chapter 1, concerning the Jewish custom of Counting the Omer and entering the fifty Gates of Binah. It is here that everything we have learned thus far comes together.

Levanael describes each Gate as having "proper limits" wherein each is contained. This is likely because each Table of the Holy Book represents one aspect of Creation, so the associated Gate of Wisdom would be limited to that aspect. (Compare this to both the fifty Gates of Binah and the thirty-six Tables of Soyga—each of which represent one aspect of God or an astrological force.) Only the "last"—actually the First[3]—Table is unlimited and infinite. And, like the Highest Gate of Understanding in the Jewish system, this infinite Table represents direct communication with God. Levanael even mentions Moses in association with the first Table / Gate—as he is the one credited with actually having passed through this Gate at the time of his death.

So the Tables of *Loagaeth* (the Gates of Wisdom) might be intended as a "version" of the Qabalistic Gates of Understanding. A clue to this fact might have been hidden in the Angels' choice of magickal timing for the transmission of the Holy Book—which began on Good Friday, March 29th, 1583. It turns out that Good Friday is something of a Christian parallel to the Jewish Passover. In practical terms, both Good Friday and Passover mark the onset of spring. As we learned in chapter 1, Passover mythologically marks the sparing of the Jewish firstborn during the final Plague of Egypt.[4] That initiates the "Counting of the Omer," a fifty-day period corresponding to the Exodus of the Children of Israel toward Mount Sinai, and during which the aspirant opens and enters the Gates of Understanding.

On the Christian side of things, Good (or Holy) Friday represents the Crucifixion of Jesus Christ.[5] This is always the Friday preceding Easter Sunday—which is itself a celebration of the eve of Christ's Resurrection. This represents a three-day period corresponding to the three days Christ rested in the tomb (and during which he, according to some traditions, descended into Hell to perform work there).

So, the Angels chose to transmit the text of the Holy Book to Dee and Kelley beginning on the Christian holiday that most corresponds to Passover. Then, similar to the fifty-day period of Counting the Omer, the reception of the forty-eight (really forty-nine) Tables of *Loagaeth* took place over forty-eight days. This relationship might help explain the particular observations of magickal timing used by the Angels throughout the reception of Loagaeth, such as this quote from Uriel:

> Behold (sayeth the Lord) I will breathe upon men, and they shall have the spirit of Understanding. In 40 days must the Book of the Secrets, and Key of this World, be written. [*Five Books of Mystery*, p. 327]

For Dee's Angels, the number 40 (and/or 48) took precedence over the more traditional Jewish fifty days.

Another relationship between Counting the Omer and *Loagaeth* can be found in the Angels' descriptions of the forty-eight Gates themselves. As we saw previously, Levanael described them as the Gates of Wisdom. However, the quote from Uriel in the above paragraph mentions the "spirit of Understanding" (or spirit of Binah). The Archangel Raphael also makes a cryptic reference to Understanding in relation to the Gates:

> As I have said: the 49 parts of this Book [. . .] Every element in this mystery is a world of understanding. [*Five Books of Mystery*, p. 296]

And Nalvage, later in the journals, makes the point rather clear:

> In 49 voices, or callings: which are the Natural Keys to open those, not 49 but 48 (for one is not to be opened) Gates of Understanding. [*True and Faithful Relation*, p. 77]

> I find the soul of man hath no portion in this First Table. [. . .] All the rest are of Understanding . . . [*A True and Faithful Relation*, p. 77]

On the other hand, Levanael is not alone in referring to the forty-eight Tables as the Gates of Wisdom instead. The Archangel Uriel does so later in the journals:

> God shall make clear when it pleaseth Him, and open all the secrets of wisdom when He unlocketh. [*Five Books of Mystery*, p. 351]

As does the Angel Mapsama, even later in the journals when the Angelical Calls were being transmitted:

> These Calls are keys into the Gates and Cities of Wisdom. [*A True and Faithful Relation*, p. 145]

Students of the Qabalah will recognize Wisdom (or Chockmah) as the name of Binah's co-equal among the Supernal Sephiroth.[6] The evidence suggests that Dee's Angels were treating them as interchangeable.

There is also a cosmological relationship between Dee's Gates and the Jewish version. By this, I mean that both systems reflect a similar understanding of how the Universe is put together. For instance, note this passage from the foundational Qabalistic text called the *Sepher haZohar*, which describes the fifty Gates as related to space:

> In that Temple [of Binah] there are 50 gates, which are supposed to be closed, meaning that they block the flow of Lights. There are 49 gates engraved upon the 'four winds' of the world. One gate has no direction; it is not known whether it faces up or down. This is how this gate remains closed. [*Sepher Zohar*, The Locked and the Unlocked, verses 43ff]

Here we can see that forty-nine of the Gates are engraved upon the "four winds"—or the four cardinal directions of the compass. Meanwhile, the highest Gate has "no direction"—so it rests in the center of the compass.

Now, in the same light, consider the following words of the Angel Nalvage:

> All the rest [of the Tables][7] are of Understanding, the exact Center excepted. [*A True and Faithful Relation*, p. 79]

Taken by themselves, Nalvage's words appear to indicate that the exact center Table of the forty-nine—which would be Table 25—is not "of Understanding." However, it is more likely the Angel is speaking about the first Table, which is locked and therefore not "of Understanding" as far as we are concerned. What Nalvage reveals here is that Table One is somehow the "exact Center"—which fits perfectly with the description of the Gates of Understanding in the *Zohar*.

This interpretation seems to be confirmed later in the journals. At one point, the Archangel Gabriel gave Dee a list of "things to do," as well as further lessons that were yet to be transmitted. Number seven on the list would appear to relate to our Zoharic view of the forty-nine Gates of *Loagaeth*:

> **Gabriel:** 7) The Angels also of the 48 angles of the Heavens, and their Ministers. For they are those, that have the thunders and the winds at commandment. Those make up the time, and then, cometh the Harvest.

> [**Dee's marginal note:**] Ergo Seven degrees and a half to every angle. Thunders, Winds, the Full Time." [*A True and Faithful Relation*, p. 164]

Dee was thinking like an astrologer in this case, and he likely envisioned this as we might view an astrological chart. Each seven-and-a-half degree division of the chart might represent one of the Gates of Wisdom, with four Gates included within each of the twelve astrological Houses. The exact Center, as mentioned by Nalvage, is left over for the First and hidden Gate.

Gabriel offers no further information about the Angels who "have the thunders and the winds at commandment"—and who presumably

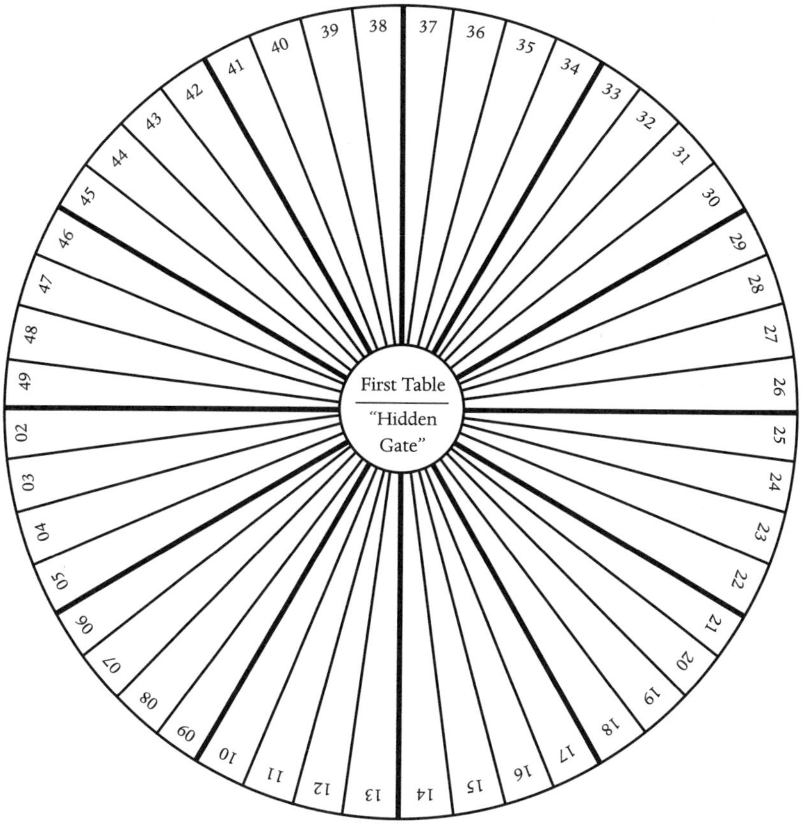

The Circle of the Heavens divided into forty-eight segments of seven-and-a-half degrees, for the forty-eight Tables of Loagaeth *plus the central "hidden" Table.*

reside within the forty-eight Gates of Heaven. Instead, it is Nalvage who offers this information:

> . . . you shall have knowledge to move every Gate, and to call out as many as you please, or shall be thought necessary, which can very well, righteously, and wisely, open unto you the secrets of their Cities, and make you understand perfectly the [knowledge][8] contained in the Tables. Through which knowledge you shall easily be able to judge, not as the world doth, but perfectly of the world, and of all things contained within the Compass of Nature, and of all things which are subject to an end. [*True and Faithful Relation*, p. 77]

These concepts are not exactly new to us. We have already learned that the forty-nine Tables of *Loagaeth* encompass the whole of Creation—both space and time, from beginning to end. What Nalvage tells us here is that the Angels who reside in the forty-eight Celestial Cities beyond the Gates have charge over that Creation. Not just the thunders and the winds, but the entirety of nature is at their commandment.

What is more, through the practice of Gebofal, the mystic can open the Gates to the Cities and summon forth Angelic teachers. These teachers will then expound upon the Doctrine contained in the Tables, much like Jewish Angels traditionally invoked during study of the Torah. Furthermore, they will reveal the mysteries of the Celestial Cities that lie beyond the Gates.

The Angel Mapsama assures Dee and Kelley that opening the Gates (with the Angelical Keys/Calls) must result in the visible apparition of such Angels:

> These Calls are keys into the Gates and Cities of Wisdom. Which [Gates][9] are not able to be opened, but without visible apparition. [*True and Faithful Relation*, p. 145]

The Archangel Gabriel confirms this somewhat later:

> Therefore, now examine your Books, confer one place with another, and learn to be perfect for the practice and entrance. [. . .] There is no other reading of the Book, but the appearing of the Ministers and Creatures of God. Which shewing what they are themselves, shew how they

> are conjoined in power, and represented formally by those letters. [*True and Faithful Relation*, p. 209]

Note that Gabriel makes a cryptic reference to the "entrance" of the Gates. This was explained earlier in the journals by the Angel Nalvage, when he offered a second (expanded) description of Gebofal. Herein, he describes what one would see by entering the Gates and exploring the Celestial Cities directly:

> For every Table hath his key, every key openeth his gate, and every gate being opened, giveth knowledge of himself of entrance, and of the mysteries of those things whereof he is an enclosure. Within these Palaces you shall find things that are of power, as well to speak, as to do for every
>
> 1. Palace is above his
> 2. City, and every City above his
> 3. Entrance.
>
> Be you therefore diligent that you may enter in, not as spoilers, but as such as deserve entertainment in the name, and through the power of the Highest. For great are the mercies of God unto such as have faith. [*A True and Faithful Relation*, p. 88]

The inclusion of Heavenly Palaces that may be visited within the Cities indicates a relationship between Gebofal and the ancient Jewish practice of Merkavah or *Hechaloth* mysticism. One of the principal goals of the Merkavah mystic was to journey in the spirit through the Heavenly Palaces (*Hechaloth*)—as depicted in the Book of Enoch (*1 Enoch*). It would appear, then, that Dee's Angels intended a similar practice in relation to the forty-eight Gates of Wisdom.

At the beginning of this section, we saw the Angel Levanael describe Gebofal as the practice of "ascension through all" of the Gates of Wisdom. It is likely that the Angels intended one to open all forty-eight Gates in succession—with the exception of the first Table, of course—just as we see in the practice of Counting the Omer. Much later in the journals, the Angel Mapsama confirms this:

Mapsama: Which [Gates][10] are not able to be opened, but without visible apparition.

Dee: And how shall that be come unto?

Mapsama: Which is according to the former instructions.[11] And to be had, by calling of every Table. You called for wisdom, God hath opened unto you his Judgment. He hath delivered unto you the keys, that you may enter. But be humble. Enter not of presumption, but of permission. Go not in rashly, but be brought in willingly. For, many have ascended, but few have entered. [*A True and Faithful Relation*, p. 145]

Mapsama here tells Dee that every Table must be called, and (therefore) all the Gates of Wisdom must be opened. His instructions on the proper attitude toward entering the Gates (which echo Nalvage's previous instructions) are also fairly similar to Jewish sources—for both the fifty Gates and the Hechaloth.

Note, also, that the ordering of Dee's forty-nine Tables matches the traditional Jewish ordering of the Fifty Gates of Understanding—beginning with the Infinite Divine Table on the first leaf, and progressing *downward* through the cosmos to the physical realm on the final leaf. Therefore, if the practice of Gebofal is also similar, then one would open the Gates of *Loagaeth* from the highest Table accessible to man (the second Table) to the lowest (Table 49, the Aethyr of *Tex*).[12] After progressively opening all forty-eight Gates, revelations and/or blessings from God should pass to the aspirant through the First (Central) Gate.

Being Called by God, and to a Good Purpose

Dee's journals also record what the Angels had to say about the purpose of Gebofal. Nalvage describes the system as prophetical, suggesting the words of the Holy Book are the voice of Angelic Inspiration heard by the Apostles:

You have 49 Tables: In those Tables are contained the mystical and holy voices of the Angels, dignified. And, in state, disglorified and drent in confusion: which pierceth Heaven, and looketh into the Center of the Earth: the very language and speech of children and innocents, such as magnify the name of God, and are pure. Wherein the Apostles under-

> stood the diffuse sound of the World, imperfected for mans transgression. [*A True and Faithful Relation*, p. 64]

Nalvage calls these forces "in state, disglorified and drent in confusion" because they relate to the chaotic physical realm.[13] However, the words of the Tables still represent the pure and dignified voices of the Angels—who are the agents of Creation.

The meeting between the aspirant and these Angels—who apparently govern the natural world—seems to be the principal goal of the system. Nalvage stresses this point somewhat later in the journals:

> Unto this Doctrine belongeth the perfect knowledge, and remembrance of the mystical Creatures. How, therefore, shall I inform you, which know them not? [*A True and Faithful Relation*, p. 78]

However, some vague rules are established concerning *when* the magick can be put into use. Of course, we have already seen some amount of magickal timing used by the Angels in the transmission of the forty-nine Tables. However, the Angel Mapsama seems to indicate that no traditional magickal timing is necessary to perform Gebofal:

> **Mapsama:** Then (as occasion serveth) you may practice at all times. But you being called by God, and, to a good purpose.
>
> **Dee:** How shall we understand this Calling by God?
>
> **Mapsama:** God stoppeth my mouth, I will answer thee no more. [*A True and Faithful Relation*, pp. 145–46]

Therefore, the concepts of Solomonic timing—such as magickal days and hours—are ruled out of the *Loagaeth* system.[14] Instead, the timing utilized is strictly prophetic or inspirational—one should work only when moved by God to do so. (Note this is similar to the instructions Galvah gave to Dee for writing the perfected Holy Book.) This makes perfect sense, because the *Loagaeth* system invokes the *Logos*, a force that transcends the Angels, days, and hours that govern magickal timing.

The day after Mapsama gave his instruction, the Archangel Gabriel arrived to provide a slight elaboration. (Note number two in the following list):

I give you a short warning. God will fulfill his promises. And (as he hath said) by this August, you shall understand:

1. How to know and use God his Creatures, good and bad.
2. But when, and for what, is the gift of the Highest, and shall be fulfilled in you (if you will be obedient) when it pleaseth him. Even with a sound from his own mouth, saying, Come and hear!

For these Actions are twofold. Consider it, if you can. And they are the greatest, because they are the last, and contain all that hath been done before them. Which if you consider well, and to what you are called, you shall perceive that the Judgments of God are not a tennis-ball.[15] Thus much I thought to warn you my brethren. Have a little patience for the Action. [*A True and Faithful Relation*, p. 146]

Gabriel reiterates that God will call upon the aspirant to use the magick. However, he appends this by saying one must "consider well, and to what you are called." This suggests that the would-be prophet has some personal responsibility to recognize when the magick should be employed.

Dee and Kelley were not immune to making mistakes in this regard. There is one saga recorded in Dee's journals in association with the reception of the Holy Book, which (due to concerns over length) I have not included in this chapter.[16] In short, the story involves a small grimoire full of talismans—found by Kelley and a friend—that promised to lead one to buried treasure. As the Angels attempted to deliver the text of the forty-nine Tables, both Kelley and Dee persisted in asking questions about this little book, its talismans, and the supposed buried treasure.

In what might have been some kind of joke, or perhaps a simple case of Dee and Kelley's own mental focus, the Angels began to refer to the mysteries of the Holy Book as a "Treasure" which the men would collect in August. Because of this, Dee and Kelley came under the mistaken impression that the magick of *Loagaeth* would lead them to their buried treasure.

The entire saga of this treasure ends when the Daughter of Light named Aath appears in the crystal, and finally sets the men straight. This is important to us here, because she explains the proper use of the Holy Book, and why the men would never find their buried treasure through it:

> All that is spoken of, is in very deed, vanity. The book may be used to a good purpose. They were wicked ones.[17] But as these things are the least part of the action, so are they not much to be looked after. [*A True and Faithful Relation*, p. 9]

I can only assume that the Angels recognize a contrast between purely physical and spiritual pursuits. The Holy Book is not to be used for physical purposes—such as money, sex, or personal power. Entering the Gates of Wisdom—like Counting the Omer—involves a journey away from the world of mankind and its corresponding Gates of Impurity. (See chapter 1.) Therefore, Gebofal is a transcendent and theurgical practice intended to move one closer to the Divine. This supports the inspirational and prophetical nature of the system. It is primarily a form of mysticism.

However, there is also a definite physical application for the magick (that is, the magick one might receive *through* the mystical practice of Gebofal.) We have already seen the promises that one might summon the Angels who govern the natural world from the forty-eight Gates, and through them perform miracles. However, how can one apply such mysticism only "to a good purpose" in the world of mankind? This question is answered much later in the journals, by the Angel Mapsama:

> But the practices that are in the instructions of the Highest, are not but in lawful causes and for necessity, to glorify God; and against Pharaoh. [*A True and Faithful Relation*, p. 145]

This sums it up rather succinctly. It is the key to the judgment one must use in deciding whether or not one is called by God. The magick can only be used for "lawful" causes—that is, purposes that do not break with religious taboos. Moreover, it must be used only in cases of necessity (for the "glorification of God," of course). All in all, these are not uncommon restrictions in the medieval and Renaissance Christian magickal traditions—such as grimoires like the *Book of Abramelin*.

It is most fascinating that Mapsama states the magick can be used "against Pharaoh." *Pharaoh* simply means "ruler," and this is the term used to describe the king of Egypt in the Book of Exodus. Over time, Egypt (as described in Exodus) became a Judeo-Christian mystical symbol of the oppressive and corrupt world of humanity. Pharaoh, as well, became a symbol of emperors and kings of all kinds who govern the world and enslave nations.

Mapsama is therefore suggesting here that the magick of the Holy Book can be wielded against political ruling powers. This would have set very well with Dee on two fronts. He was passionately dedicated to the ascension of an English empire, and he firmly believed that God and His Angels were also behind that cause. If Dee wished to influence the world at all, it was to influence the destinies of both his own and foreign nations.[18]

On the other hand, Mapsama's mention of "Pharaoh" might also be bound into the relationship between the Holy Book and the Christian belief in the End Times. As Pharaoh of Exodus was the cruel king who enslaved and oppressed the Children of Israel, so was he also a symbol of (and forerunner to) the Antichrist. We might remember that Dee was assured by the Angels—during the reception of the forty-nine Tables—that the Antichrist was already born and the End Times had begun. He had also been told that the mysteries contained in the Holy Book would be wielded in some way by Dee and Kelley themselves through the Tribulation. (Remember the speech of Gabriel in chapter 2, in which he called the Holy Book a flail and Dee and Kelley God's threshers!) Mapsama may therefore have had the Antichrist in mind when he referred to using the magick "against Pharaoh."

All These Things Must Be Used—Gebofal and the *Heptarchia*

There is also an intimate connection between the practice of the *Loagaeth* system and Dee's *Heptarchia* mysteries. We saw clues to this earlier in chapter 2, when we found Heptarchic Angelic names in the text or titles of the Holy Book. We might also take note that many of the mysteries of *Loagaeth* were delivered by Heptarchic Angels such as the Sons and Daughters of Light.

Before the Holy Book was even transmitted to Dee and Kelley, the Archangel Raphael made the connection between *Loagaeth* and the *Heptarchia* quite clear. When he first reveals the Holy Book to Kelley in the crystal, he directly states that it represents "the measure" of all three magickal systems given to the two men. (That is, the *Heptarchia*, the Holy Book, and the Great Table of the Earth.)[19]

> This is the Second and the Third: the Third and the last. This is the measure of the whole. (O what is man, that is worthy to know these secrets? Heavy are his wickednesses, mighty is his sin!) These shalt thou know. These shall you use. [. . .] Yet must there be a third, whom God doth not yet choose.[20] The time shall be short, the matter great, the end greater. [*Five Books of Mystery*, p. 263]

Raphael's first words above most likely indicate that the Holy Book (the second of the magickal systems) will be the source of the third system (the Great Table). We will not explore this relationship here, however, because we are more concerned with the relationship between *Loagaeth* and the *Heptarchia*.

Later, in the appendix to the *Five Books,* after the first leaf of the Holy Book had been recorded, Dee shifts the sessions briefly back to the Heptarchic system in order to clear up some points. The Archangel Uriel re-appears, as he was the principal instructor to Dee and Kelley while the *Heptarchia* was the subject. At one point, he is giving further instruction concerning the Heptarchic magickal tools, when he suddenly makes a most cryptic comment about *Loagaeth*:

> **Uriel:** All these things must be used, as that day.
>
> [**Dee in margin:**] On the first of August next. [*Five Books of Mystery*, p. 396]

Without Dee's marginal note, Uriel's comment might be meaningless. However, we already know that the first of August is the "appointed time" for the revelation of the mysteries of the Holy Book. The Archangel is simply telling Dee that the tools of the *Heptarchia* ("all these things") must be used in conjunction with the Holy Book on that day. This makes sense, of course, as the Heptarchic tools are, collectively, a set of Angelic scrying tools. This equipment would have established the atmosphere necessary for the Angels of the Holy Book to manifest. (Note that both systems share a sevenfold symbolism.)

Uriel also suggests to Dee that further Heptarchic mysteries will be revealed by the use of the Holy Book. For instance, at one point, Dee asks for further information about the various uses of the names of the Heptarchic Kings and Princes. Uriel replies:

> **Uriel:** That secret is not to be delivered but by the distinction of the Book. [*Five Books of Mystery*, pp. 397–98]

During the same session, Dee attempts to gain further information about certain letters that appear upon the talismans of the Heptarchic kings. Uriel once again directs Dee to *Loagaeth*:

> Whereof notice shall be given at large, by the Book. [. . .] For it is said before that the Book containeth three types of knowledge . . . And this hath answered a great doubt. [*Five Books of Mystery*, p. 399]

Indeed, it has answered a great doubt. We know for certain, now, that the Heptarchic tools are intended for use with the *Book of Loagaeth*. Unfortunately, a full description of these necessary tools is outside the scope of this volume. I hope to follow this work with another volume that will focus upon the construction and practical use of the Heptarchic and other "Enochian" tools and systems of magick.

Gebofal Instruction and Ave's "Prayer of Enoch"

When Galvah instructed Dee to write the perfected Holy Book, she included some essentially Solomonic considerations. Specifically, Dee must be alone when working on the text, and all things involved in the work must be pure.[21] Similar instructions on purity were later given by the Archangel Gabriel for the practical use of the book:

> But yet is not August come. [. . .] See that your garments be clean. Herein be not rash, nor over hasty. For those that are hasty and rash, and are loathsomely appareled, may knock long before they enter. [*A True and Faithful Relation*, p. 209]

Ritual cleanliness was of prime importance throughout medieval grimoiric mysticism—something it adopted from its Judeo-Christian roots. By itself, this stress on ritual purity is simply biblical, rather than directly "Solomonic." However, further instruction given by the Archangel Uriel would appear to draw a line almost directly from the *Key of Solomon the King* itself:

> But (because I will speak to you, after the manner of men) see that all things be in readiness against the first day of August next. Humble your senses nine days before. Yea, unrip (I say) the cankers of your infected souls, that you may be apt and meet to understand the Secrets that shall be delivered. [*Five Books of Mystery*, p. 394]

Compare Uriel's above speech with this excerpt from the *Key of Solomon*:

> He who hath attained the rank or degree of Exorcist, [. . .] whensoever he desireth to undertake any operation, for the nine days immediately preceding the commencement of the work, should put aside from him all uncleanness, and prepare himself in secret during these days, and prepare all the things necessary, and in the space of these days all these should be made, consecrated, and exorcised. [*The Key of Solomon the King*, Book II, chapter 13]

It would almost appear that both Uriel and Gabriel were drawing from this same portion of the *Key of Solomon*. The concept of humbling one's senses (as Uriel instructs) includes seclusion, fasting, prayer, sexual abstinence, and several other observances intended to deprive the senses of their usual flood of input. It is the essence of ritual purification.

That was all the Angels had to say about preparations for Gebofal. Fortunately, they had a bit more to say about how to accomplish the practice itself. We have already seen the Angel Mapsama instruct Dee and Kelley to call "every Table" from the *Book of Loagaeth*. We have also seen the close relationship between Gebofal and Counting the Omer, which provides some further clues into the nature of the practice.

Finally, we have the famous Enochian "Prayer of Enoch" delivered by the Angel Ave.[22] (You might remember that Ave previously delivered the "Enochian mythos" most often associated with Dee's magick.) We know that the Prayer of Enoch is intended to relate practical instruction, for Ave says at the very end of the prayer itself:

> Consider well my words, and what I have now said unto thee. For here thou mayst learn wisdom, and also see what thou has to do. [*A True and Faithful Relation*, p. 197]

Therefore, we will now consider Ave's Prayer of Enoch and the implications it has on the practice of Gebofal:

> I said also, that Enoch laboured 50 days. Notwithstanding, that thy labour be not frustrate, and void of fruit, be it unto thee, as thou hast done. [. . .] I will tell thee, what the labour of Enoch was for those fifty days. [. . .] He made (as thou hast done, thy book) Tables, of Serpasan and plain stone: as the Angel of the Lord appointed him; saying, tell me (O Lord) the number of days I shall labour in. It was answered him 50. [*A True and Faithful Relation*, p. 196]

We learn here that Enoch first constructed the Tables, and then received instruction on how to use them. This mirrors the pattern of transmission the Angels attempted to use with Dee and Kelley. (Of course, I highly doubt we are intended to make Tablets of stone. The legendary Enoch may have carved them in stone, but Dee had already received ample instruction to write them on paper.)

We can also see that Enoch was to perform his work over a fifty-day period. Technically, this conflicts with the structure of *Loagaeth*—where one should work a total of forty-nine days. (That is, forty-eight days to open the Gates plus the final day of Revelation.)

However, I do not think Ave's words are intended to conflict with *Loagaeth* particularly. Remember that Dee would have taken the Bible literally, and thus would have considered Enoch a historical Jewish personage. Being "Jewish," Enoch would certainly have worked fifty days, coinciding yet once again with the Counting of the Omer. Meanwhile, Dee perceived the material he was receiving as distinctly Christian and distinctly unique. I feel it is an educated assumption that Dee would have naturally translated Enoch's fifty days of labor into forty-nine days for Gebofal.

From here Enoch is said to have recited a prayer, three times a day, over the Tables of *Loagaeth*. This, at last, is the Prayer of Enoch:

> Then [Enoch][23] groaned within himself, saying: "Lord God the fountain of true wisdom, thou that openest the secrets of thy own self unto man, thou knowest mine imperfection, and my inward darkness: How can I (therefore) speak unto them that speak not after the voice of man; or

worthily call on thy name, considering that my imagination is variable and fruitless, and unknown to myself? Shall the sands seem to invite the Mountains: or can the small rivers entertain the wonderful and unknown waves?

"Can the vessel of fear, fragility, or that is of a determined proportion, lift up himself, heave up his hands, or gather the Sun into his bosom? Lord it cannot be: Lord, my imperfection is great: Lord I am less than sand: Lord, thy good Angels and Creatures excel me far: our proportion is not alike; our sense agreeth not: Notwithstanding I am comforted; For that we have all one God, all one beginning from thee, that we respect thee a Creator: Therefore will I call upon thy name, and in thee, I will become mighty. Thou shalt light me, and I will become a seer; I will see thy creatures and will magnify thy name among them. Those that come unto thee have the same gate, and through the same gate, descend, such as thou sendest. Behold, I offer my house, my labour, my heart and soul, If it will please thy Angels to dwell with me, and I with them; to rejoice with me, that I may rejoice with them; to minister unto me, that I may magnify thy name. Then, lo, the Tables (which I have provided and, according to thy will, prepared) I offer unto thee, and unto thy holy Angels, desiring them, in and through thy holy names: That as thou art their light, and comforted them, so they, in thee will be my light and comfort. Lord, they prescribe not laws unto thee, so it is not meet that I prescribe laws unto them: What it pleaseth thee to offer, they receive; so what it pleaseth them to offer unto me, will I also receive. Behold, I say (O Lord) If I shall call upon them in thy name, be it unto me in mercy, as unto the servant of the Highest. Let them also manifest unto me, how, by what words, and at what time, I shall call them. O Lord, is there any that measure the heavens, that is mortal? How, therefore, can the heavens enter into mans imagination? Thy creatures are the glory of thy countenance: Hereby thou glorifiest all things, which Glory excelleth and (O Lord) is far above my understanding. Is it great wisdom, to speak and talk according to understanding with Kings: But to command kings by a subtle commandment, is not wisdom, unless it come from thee. Behold, Lord, how shall I therefore ascend into the heavens? The air will not carry me, but resisteth my folly; I fall down, for I am of the earth. Therefore, O thou very Light and true Comfort, that canst, and mayst, and dost command the heavens; behold I offer these Tables unto

> thee, Command them as it pleaseth thee: and O you Ministers, and true lights of understanding, Governing this earthly frame, and the elements wherein we live, Do for me as for the servant of the Lord: and unto whom it hath pleased the Lord to talk of you.
>
> "Behold, Lord, thou hast appointed me 50 times; Thrice[24] 50 times will I lift my hands unto thee. Be it unto me as it pleaseth thee, and thy holy Ministers. I require nothing but thee, and through thee, and thy honour and glory: but I hope I shall be satisfied, and shall not die, (As thou hast promised) until thou gather the clouds together, and judge all things: when in a moment I shall be changed and dwell with thee forever."[25] [*A True and Faithful Relation*, pp. 196–97]

In this prayer we see many shades of what we have already discussed concerning Gebofal. The prayer asks for the vision and companionship of the Angels, calls upon them from the Gates, and asks for their guidance (rather than imposing control over them). It even speaks of the Merkavah concept of ascending into the Heavens.

The final paragraph of the prayer gives us more solid practical instruction. The prayer must be spoken over the Tables of *Loagaeth* three times a day. In traditional Solomonic magick, this usually means to work at dawn, noon and dusk. Of course, to use this prayer for Gebofal, it would be necessary to replace the term *50 times* with *49 times*, in order to match the Holy Book. (I assume one would recite this prayer three times on the final day of Revelation as well.)

Finally, Ave describes the results of Enoch's labor, which once again mirror the promise of the Jewish fifty Gates of Binah:

> These words were thrice a day talk betwixt Enoch and God: In the end of 50 days, there appeared unto him, which are not now to be manifested nor spoken of. He enjoyed the fruit of God his promise, and received the benefit of his faith. Here may the wise learn wisdom: for what doth man that is not corruptible? I have not that I may say any more to you. But, believe me, I have said great things unto you. [*A True and Faithful Relation*, p. 197]

Gebofal and the Angelical Keys

The forty-eight Angelical Keys are necessary to access the forty-nine Tables of *Loagaeth*. In this section I have gathered all of the practical instructions outlined previously, and added them to the instructions for using the Keys. Finally, I have organized all of this into a step-by-step procedure for the performance of Gebofal.

As we have seen, there are two specific uses given for the forty-eight Keys in Dee's journals. Their primary use is to open the Tables of *Loagaeth* in the practice of Gebofal. Their secondary use was given with the thirty Keys of the Aethyrs—to open the Parts of the Earth and summon the Archonic rulers of the world's nations. Because I have promised to outline the Parts of the Earth system in a later work, I will here concentrate on Gebofal.

Keep my explanation of Ave's Prayer of Enoch in mind: on each of forty-eight successive days, it is necessary to open the *Book of Loagaeth* to the proper Table, and recite the Prayer of Enoch over it three times (perhaps once in the morning, once at noon, and once again at dusk). Now, I will add that one should follow the Prayer with a recitation of the Angelical Key assigned to the Table.

For convenience, I am including an outline of the usage of the Keys in (and in fact the entire process of) Gebofal—including instructions first mentioned in chapter 2.

Final Outline for Gebofal

The Tools

One should first construct the so-called Heptarchic tools for Angelic evocation, as described in Dee's *Five Books of Mystery*. This would include the Holy Table and its seven 'Ensigns of Creation' talismans, wax seals, silk coverings, crystal shewstone, and so forth. It would also include the Ring of Solomon shown to Dee by Michael—without which Dee was "to do nothing"—as well as the enigmatic Holy Lamen which promised to reconcile Dee's human nature with that of the Angels. Space precludes me from including in-depth instructions for these "Enochian" implements. (For now, you can find this information in *The Enochian Magic of Dr. John Dee*, by Geoffrey James, as well as in *Enochian Magic for*

Beginners, by Donald Tyson. However, I will be dedicating a future book to the creation and application of the Heptarchic tools.)

Establish a sacred space or oratory to erect the furnishings and within which to carry out the forty-nine-day Operation. In Dee's time, it was common for wealthy or affluent Christians to have oratories (prayer rooms) built directly into their homes. Dee's own oratory was adjacent to his study. Kelley would usually sit in the study at Dee's desk, while Dee entered the oratory and recited prayers and invocations until Kelley reported a vision (either in or outside of the crystal shewstone). The methods for creating such an oratory of your own are the same as those described in the medieval Solomonic literature and in the work of Agrippa. Once again, space prohibits me from outlining these techniques in full here, but they have been described at length elsewhere.[26]

You will also need to construct a copy of the *Book of Loagaeth*. It will be a very large book—as each page has to bear a 49 x 49 Table. The characters must be written in Angelical, and remember that they *must* be written from right to left as we would with Hebrew! That means you open the book to what would (to an English speaker) be the "last page" of the book. The first character of the first Table is written in the *upper-right* corner of the page, and the following characters are written toward the left. The final Tables of the Book will appear on what an English speaker would consider the "first page."

At the time of this writing, I know of two ready sources for the text of *Loagaeth*. One is on Joseph Peterson's *Twilit Grotto* website. From there you can order an inexpensive CD containing a vast amount of Solomonic and related literature—including the complete text of the Tables of *Loagaeth*. The other source is *The Magickal Review* website, which includes an Enochian section containing scans of Dee's journals in their original form. The addresses for both of these websites are included in the bibliography of this book.

Once you have the text of the Tables in English characters, you must undertake the task of transliterating them to Angelical characters and writing them into the Book. The English version of the Tables *do* read from left to right—so do not forget to reverse each line! You will quickly discover why Dee was overwhelmed by the task, especially since he was given just forty days to complete it!

You will also, like Dee, discover that the first Table cannot be written inside a grid-square and still fit on a single leaf. The Angels gave dispensation for that text to written out line by line—so it will likely take up several pages, depending on the size of the characters. So, sadly, the physical *Book of Loagaeth* will be a bit longer than just forty-nine leaves.

The Holy Book must also be covered in light blue silk. Its title, *Amzes naghezes Hardeh*, is painted (also in Angelical characters, from right to left) onto this cover in gold. I would suggest purchasing shell gold in order to paint the title with real gold. Or, if you have or know someone with the skill to do so, you could have the words gold-leafed instead. Only as a last resort would I use paint merely colored metalic gold. Do not forget: the front cover of *Loagaeth* is what an English speaker would normally consider the *back cover*! When looking at the title painted on the front, the book should open from the left-hand side.

Also follow the instructions given by Galvah: work when inspired to do so, and undertake ritual purification before working. One might even go so far as to observe the "Enochian Sabbath"—resting from the Work on Mondays, observing ritual seclusion and abstinence, etc.

Nine Days of Purification

For the sake of illustration, I will assume you wish to begin on the morning after Good Friday—mirroring the Jewish Passover practice of Counting the Omer. If so, count back exactly nine days from that morning—and begin a general process of purification ending on the day of Good Friday.[27]

Opening the Gates, Day 1

On the morning after Good Friday, wash your body, don clean garments, and enter the oratory at dawn. Open *Loagaeth* to the Second Table. Recite the Prayer of Enoch, followed by Key One. Then sit back and meditate or scry—considering what we know (if anything) about the mysteries of the Table and the implications of its Key. Record the subject of your meditations, and any thoughts, inspirations, or visions that strike you during this time. Repeat the process again at noon, and then again at dusk.

Opening the Gates, Days 2 to 48

At dawn on the following day, wash yourself and enter the oratory again. Turn the *Book of Loagaeth* to the Third Table, and recite the Prayer of Enoch followed by Key Two. Meditate as described for day one. Continue this process—one Table a day, three times each day—until you have opened the forty-ninth Table with Key Forty-eight.

Completion, Day 49

Finally, on the forty-ninth day, wash and enter the oratory at dawn. Open *Loagaeth* to the text of the first "hidden" Table, and recite *only* the Prayer of Enoch. Repeat this at noon and dusk, recording your experiences as previously described. This day represents the final Gate of Understanding, which is locked to our entrance, but slightly parts for one who has opened the previous forty-eight Gates. Divine blessing and/or inspiration should result, and the results of the magick should manifest over the next weeks, months, *and* years.

Endnotes

1. This Angel's name is found on the Seal of Truth from the *Heptarchia*.
2. I have added this word for clarification.
3. Remember *Loagaeth* is written right to left, so Table One is on the "last" leaf of the book by Western (left-to-right) standards.
4. See Exodus 12.
5. See John 13:1 for the relationship between Passover and the Crucifixion of Jesus.
6. See chapter 1 for basic information on the Supernal Sephiroth.
7. I have inserted these bracketed words for clarification.
8. The word *knowledge* was missing from the text. I have reinserted it for clarification.
9. I have inserted the bracketed word for clarification.
10. I have inserted the bracketed word for clarification.
11. These former instructions were the use of the forty-eight Angelical Keys to open the Gates of Wisdom. See chapter 3.
12. As we shall see in the following chapter, the ordering of the Angelical Keys used to open the Tables of *Loagaeth* supports this downward direction for "ascension" through the Gates.

13. We shall see later that the last of the Angelical Keys addresses this confusion of nature.
14. Similar to what we see in the *Book of Abramelin*.
15. Probably meaning that God's judgments are solid, and do not bounce from position to position.
16. However, I have outlined it in other works. They are currently unpublished, but check my website for updates: http://kheph777.tripod.com.
17. "They" = Dee and Kelley's intentions of finding the buried treasure.
18. This would become most evident in the Parts of the Earth and Watchtower systems.
19. The Great Table, or Watchtower, system had not yet been transmitted or discussed.
20. The third being the Great Table of the Earth.
21. Covered previously in this chapter.
22. Ave is one of the Heptarchic Sons of the Sons of Light.
23. I have added this bracketed word for clarification.
24. Dee notes in the margin: "Ave: That is to say, thrice a day."
25. Remember that Enoch was said to have never experienced death, and was instead translated body and soul into the Heavens.
26. See my *Secrets of the Magickal Grimoires*, for in-depth instructions on establishing such an oratory or similar sacred space.
27. *Secrets of the Magickal Grimoires* also contains information on ritual purification, including the Solomonic nine-day purification.

Chapter Five

The Celestial Speech

We might doubt whether Angels . . . , since they be pure spirits, use any vocal speech, or tongue amongst themselves, or to us; but that Paul in some place saith, "If I speak with the tongue of men, or angels."[1] But what their speech or tongue is, is much doubted by many. For many think that if they use any Idiom, it is Hebrew, because that was the first of all, and came from heaven, and was before the confusion of languages in Babylon, in which the Law was given by God the Father, and the Gospel was preached by Christ the Son, and so many Oracles were given to the Prophets by the Holy Ghost: and seeing all tongues have, and do undergo various mutations, and corruptions, this alone doth always continue inviolated. Moreover an evident sign of this opinion is, that though each Demon, and Intelligence do use the speech of those nations, with whom they do inhabit, yet to them that understand it, they never speak in any Idiom, but in this alone. [Agrippa, *Three Books of Occult Philosophy*, Book III, chapter 23]

In those Tables[2] are contained the mystical and holy voices of the Angels, dignified. And, in state, disglorified and drent in confusion; which pierceth Heaven, and looketh into the Center of the Earth: the very language and speech of children and innocents, such as magnify the name of God, and are pure. Wherein the Apostles understood the diffuse sound of the World, imperfected for mans transgression. [The Angel Nalvage, *A True and Faithful Relation*, p. 64]

The Archangel Raphael was charged with the transmission of the Holy *Book of Loagaeth* to Dee and Kelley. (In the journals, Dee recorded Raphael's name as *Medicina Dei*, which is merely Latin for the Hebrew *Rapha El*—"Healer of God.") In a historical sense, the imagery and function of Raphael descends from Djehuti (Thoth) of Egypt and Hermes of Greece—both of whom are gods of mercurial things such as wisdom, language, communication, technology, magick, and medicine.

This archetypal principle found a home among later Hermeticists as *Hermes Trismagestos* (Thrice-Great Hermes)—supposed to be an adept alchemist and physician from ancient Egypt, but in actuality another incarnation of the Thoth-Hermes concept. Finally, the Archangel Raphael—the Divine Physician—inherited much of this imagery. Thus, it was appropriate that he should deliver the Holy Book and its Celestial Language to Dee and Kelley.

Raphael did not immediately reveal the *Book of Loagaeth* to the men. Instead, he began with an introductory sermon concerning a "Divine Medicine"—a liquor (or elixir) that brings life to all things (earthly and celestial) and can destroy "the enemy"[3] of the soul:

> One thing, which is the ground and element of thy desire, is already perfected.[4] . . . the rest I have brought you, in this my vessel. A medicine sufficient to extinguish and quench out the enemy, to our felicity. Muse not, though I say "ours," for we all live in tasting of this liquor. [*Five Books of Mystery*, pp. 259–60]

Following this speech, Raphael relates a rather Qabalistic description of the Creator—which, in consideration of space, I have not included here.[5] Afterward, he assures Dee and Kelley that the Creator is the source of his powerful medicine:

> Above and in Himself which is by Himself, and in no other, is this great and virtuous fountain. In nature intellectual He hath watered the plants of her beauty, and stroked up the garments of her felicity. In her darkest members entereth in the taste and savor of this piercing Medicine; reviving and recalling all things past, present and to come, unto their lively and dignified perfection. My words are sentences. My sentences, wisdom. My wisdom the end in my message of all things. Mighty and

> glorious is the virtue of it, whose springs do endure, and are clear forever: whose Name be blessed. [*Five Books of Mystery*, pp. 259-60]

In the speech above, we can really see the Hermetic influences upon Dee and Kelley's work. Nature is referred to in the feminine (as is the Hermetic *Soul of the World*), a kind of goddess that is lovingly attended to by the Creator (her lover). Raphael's medicine—the source of all life—penetrates even her most hidden depths. Most importantly, we learn here that Raphael's elixir recalls "all things past, present, and to come" and is contained in a "message of all things."

The following day, Raphael resumes his sermon upon the Divine Medicine. This time, Kelley reports that the Archangel is concealing something beneath his robes. Raphael speaks:

> Man's memory is dull, unless it taste of the sprinkling of this vessel.[6] Nature and reason have disputed profoundly and truly by the savor hereof; it pierceth therefore deeply. But Understanding and reason have elevated and lifted up the dignity and worthiness of Man's memory, by taste hereof. The Immeasurable and unspeakable beginnings (yea, the Beginner and Principal thereof), are exactly (after a sort) and perfectly known of them.[7] It hath taught from the earth unto the heavens, from the heaven unto His seat; from His seat into His Divinity. From His Divinity, a capable measuring of His immeasurable mercies. It is true, most true, shall be true forever—that from the lowest grass to the highest tree, from the smallest valley, to the greatest mountain; yea, even in the distinction betwixt light and darkness. And it measured all things of the world. [*Five Books of Mystery*, pp. 261–62]

> Great are my words, and great is thy thought. Greater shall be the end of these Gods Mercies. New worlds shall spring of these. New manners, strange men, the true life, and thorny patch openly seen. All things in one, and yet, this is but a vision Wonderful and great are the purposes of Him, whose Medicine I carry. I have spoken. [*Five Books of Mystery*, p. 262]

After these introductory speeches describing the Divine Medicine and its benefits, Raphael finally reveals the "vessel" he has been concealing beneath his robes. The vessel, it turns out, is the Holy *Book of Loagaeth* itself. (This was Kelley's First Vision of the Holy Book. As we saw in chapter 2, it appeared at this time with forty-eight leaves of gold and characters written in fresh blood.) This Book is Raphael's "message of all things." Its Angelic language—and the Doctrine it records—is the divine elixir the Archangel promised the men.

However, it is only during the next session (two days later) that Raphael directly confirms that the elixir is one and the same with the Celestial Speech of the Angels:

> **Dee:** Of your so greatly commended liquor I am desirous to have further understanding.
>
> **Raphael:** What liquor is more lively than the dew of Truth, proceeding from a fountain most sweet and delectable? Even that verity[8] which thy mouth hath preached of. What water recreateth more, or cooleth ignorance deeper than the knowledge of our Celestial Speech? Your voices are but feigned: shadows of the words and voices that substantially do comprehend every substance in his kind. The things which you do look on, because you see them not indeed, you also do name them amiss. You are confounded, for your offenses, and dispersed for your punishment.[9] But we are all one, and are fully understanding. We open the ear, and the passage thereof, from the sun in the morning to the sun at night. Distance is nothing with us, unless it be the distance which separateth the wicked from His mercy. Secrets there are none, but those buried in the shadow of Man's soul.
>
> We see all things, and nothing is hid from us, respecting our Creation. The waters shall stand, if they hear their own speech. The heavens shall move, and shew themselves, when they know their thunder. Hell shall tremble, when they know what is spoken to them. [. . .]
>
> Thou shalt speak with us, and we will be spoken with, of thee. [. . .] I am not as a cloud, shevered with the wind; nor as a garment, that waxeth old, and torn in pieces; but I am forever (because my message is such) and my truth shall endure forever. [*Five Books of Mystery*, pp. 266–67]

This is perhaps the most important information about the Angelical language given at this point in the journals. We already know (from chapter 2) that the *Book of Loagaeth* contains the Words of Creation, and here Raphael adds that all created things (Heaven, Hell, the waters, etc.)

know and respond to that Speech. Our own human tongues are imperfect compared to Angelical, and therefore the spiritual creatures of the Universe do not fully understand them.

Therefore, it was to allow humans to speak directly with Angels in their own native tongue that the Angelical language was revealed. Later, during the transmission of the text of *Loagaeth* itself, Raphael expands upon this idea:

> As I have said: the 49 parts of this Book—49 voices, whereunto the so many powers, with their inferiors and subjects, have been, are, and shall be obedient. Every element in this mystery is a world of understanding. Every one knoweth here what is his due obedience, and this[10] shall differ thee in speech from a mortal creature. [*Five Books of Mystery*, p. 296]

Much later in the journals, the Archangel Gabriel stresses these points directly:

> [. . .] , whereby even as the mind of man [is] moved at an ordered speech, and is easily persuaded in things that are true, so are the creatures of God stirred up in themselves, when they hear the words wherewithal they were nursed and brought forth: For nothing moveth, that is not persuaded. Neither can any thing be persuaded that is unknown. The Creatures of God understand you not, you are not of their Cities, you are become enemies, because you are separated form Him that Governeth the City by ignorance . . . [*A True and Faithful Relation*, p. 92]

I take the above to mean that speaking with Angels in human-created languages is less effective, because the Angels are less likely to take one seriously. Yet, if they hear the words of their own native language, it will "differ thee in speech from a mortal creature" and even persuade the Angels to obedience.

We can see this dynamic right here on Earth. People's attitudes toward each other are often affected drastically by their speech. If you were to find yourself in a foreign land, unable to speak the native tongue, you might find the local people showing you little respect. You could likely appear to them as "slow" or "stupid" as you struggle to comprehend and communicate with those around you. On the other hand, if you can address the natives in their own language, they will be impressed by your efforts and show you much more respect.

Angelical Mythos

There is also a mythological foundation to the Celestial Speech. In several instances, the Angels connected their tongue with biblical legend—especially the saga of Adam and the loss of Paradise. It is, of course, Raphael who makes the first mention of Adam:

> Finally, it proceedeth from him that proceedeth.[11] Whereunto the first[12] was formed, after, and not like.[13] Whose foot slipping, hath dashed his head in pieces, and it became dark. Until again, the Medicine which I have brought, revived his slumbering. Hereby, he not only knew all things, but the measure and true use thereof. [*Five Books of Mystery*, p. 262]

The above appears to be a summation of the Fall from Eden described in Genesis, chapter 3. Adam's "foot slipping" likely indicates his transgression of God's law, and "dash[ing] his head in pieces" should indicate the resulting expulsion from the Garden. However, Raphael adds to the usual legend by telling us that the Divine Medicine granted Adam his vast knowledge (presumably before the Fall) and also revived him after the Fall.

As we see in Genesis, chapter 2, Adam is traditionally credited with naming all living creatures in Eden. (According to apocryphal legend, Adam also created all earthly languages—an idea we shall revisit later in this chapter.)[14] This ties in perfectly with Raphael's assertion that Adam possessed the Celestial Speech before the Fall. As the Archangel had said earlier, "The things which you do look on, because you see them not indeed, you also do name them amiss." Therefore, if Adam named things "correctly," it would follow that he named them with some knowledge of the Angelic Words of Creation. Raphael later confirms that Adam was the only human to have known the Celestial Speech, and that he used it to assign true names to "all things" once and for all:

> The first[15] excepted, no man ever was, is, or shall be (excepted where I except) that ever shall understand, have or know the least part (O it is

> incomprehensible!) of this vessel. He named all things (which knew it) and they are so indeed, and shall be forever. [*Five Books of Mystery*, pp. 266–67]

Somewhat later in the journals, the Heptarchic Angel Illemese also relates the Angelical language to Adam in Paradise. The Angel had just spoken a short phrase in Angelical, which Dee did not recognize as such. When Dee asked from which language the phrase was drawn, Illemese answered:

> **Ilemese:** A language taught in Paradise.
>
> **Dee:** To whom?
>
> **Ilemese:** By infusion, to Adam.
>
> **Dee:** To whom did Adam use it?
>
> **Ilemese:** Unto Chevah.[16]
>
> **Dee:** Did his posterity use the same?
>
> **Ilemese:** Yes, until the Airy Tower was destroyed. [*Five Books of Mystery*, p. 354]

Illemese has added another aspect to the mythos of the Angelical language by mentioning the "Airy Tower." This is a reference to the Tower of Babel, found in Genesis 11:1–9. In fact, the above speech of Illemese is the *second* time the Tower has been mentioned in relation to the Celestial Speech. The first time was an indirect reference made by Raphael: "You are confounded, for your offenses, and dispersed for your punishment." In order to understand this cryptic comment, it is necessary to know the story of the Tower of Babel:

Mankind, having grown powerful and arrogant, decided to build a tower to Heaven and make war upon God Himself. In order to halt this vain project, God sent the Confusion of Tongues. In the short term, this ended the construction of the tower, because the workers could no longer comprehend one another. In the long term, it was the birth of the "language barrier" and the many dissimilar nations and cultures upon the earth that war with one another.

I find it interesting that there are only two stories in Genesis that describe the creation of language in the world, and both of them are mentioned by the Angels in relation to the Celestial Speech. Adam knew the language in Eden and then passed it down (in *some* form) to later generations. Apparently, it formed the basis of the first human language until the Confusion of Tongues destroyed its integrity.

Much later in the journals, Edward Kelley asks the Archangel Gabriel for more information about Angelical. Gabriel's response is the most complete telling of the mythology behind the language. He draws upon most of the previously given information, and then expands upon it:

> Man in his Creation, being made an Innocent, was also authorized and made partaker of the Power and Spirit of God. Whereby he not only did know all things under his Creation and spoke of them properly, naming them as they were, but also was partaker of our presence and society, yea a speaker of the mysteries of God, yea, with God Himself. So that in innocency the power of his partakers with God, and us his good Angels, was exalted, and so became holy in the sight of God until that *Coronzom* (for so is the true name of that mighty Devil) envying his felicity, and perceiving that the substance of his lesser part was frail and unperfect in respect of his pure Essence, began to assail him, and so lost the Garden of felicity, the judgment of his understanding. But not utterly the favour of God, and was driven forth (as your scriptures record) unto the Earth which was covered with brambles. Where being dumb, and not able to speak, he began to learn of necessity the Language which thou, Edward Kelley, callest: [1: Hebrew].[17] And, yet, not that [2: Hebrew][18] amongst you. In the which he uttered and delivered unto his posterity, the nearest knowledge he had of his Creatures. And from his own self divided his speech into three parts, twelve, three, and seven: the number whereof remaineth, but the true forms and pronunciations want; and therefore is not of that force that was in his own dignity, much less to be compared with the language that we deliver, which Adam verily spake in innocency, and was never uttered nor disclosed to man since till now, wherein the power of God must work, and wisdom in Her true kind be delivered. Which are not to be spoken of in any other thing, neither to be talked of with man's imaginations; for as this Work, and Gift is, of God, which is all power, so doth he open it in a tongue of power to the

> intent that the proportions may agree in themselves. [*A True and Faithful Relation*, p. 92]

In the above, Gabriel tells the story of Eden, especially as it relates to Adam's possession of the Celestial Speech—which he used not only to name all things, but also to converse familiarly with God and His Angels. In fact, the Devil (whose name is *Coronzom* in the Angelical language) became jealous of Adam *because* of his use of Angelical and the familiarity with the Angels it granted him.

Perhaps best of all, Gabriel reveals what happened to Adam's knowledge of the Angelical tongue after his Fall. Apparently, Adam lost the language in its purity when he lost his place in Paradise. However, because he had not lost "utterly the favour of God," he retained some vague recollection of the nature of the language. His attempt at reconstruction resulted in a kind of proto-Hebrew (or 1: Hebrew)—an alphabet of twenty-two letters divided into groups of three, seven, and twelve.[19] This new tongue persisted as the universal language of mankind until the Confusion of Tongues at the Tower of Babel. Afterward, at least one of the resulting languages retained a dim reflection of the pre-Confusion tongue. That language is the biblical Hebrew that we know today (or 2: Hebrew)—which indeed forms the basis of much of our modern language.

The Hebrew alphabet consists of twenty-two letters—which the ancient Qabalistic text *Sepher Yetzirah* also divides into three groups, of three, seven, and twelve each. This relates to the three primary elements (Air, Fire, Water), the seven ancient planets, and the twelve signs of the zodiac. In this way, every letter of the alphabet is given a mystical correspondence with an aspect of Creation. It allows us to use the language in conjunction with astrology, talismanic magick, gematria, and other magickal practices.[20]

Also see the beginning of this chapter, where I provided a quote from Agrippa's Book Three, chapter 23, called "Of the Tongue of Angels, and of Their Speaking amongst Themselves, and with Us." There is no doubt whatsoever that Dee read and paid close attention to this chapter of Agrippa's work. Therein we find the following statement: "For many think that if they use any Idiom, it is Hebrew, because that was the first of all, and came from heaven, and was before the confusion of languages in Babylon . . . "

However, Agrippa also points out that " . . . all tongues have, and do undergo various mutations, and corruptions . . . " Gabriel confirms this in relation to Hebrew. Before the "corrupted" Hebrew used in the Bible, there was the proto-Hebrew created by Adam, and before that was the Tongue of Angels. It is the Tongue of Angels that Agrippa refers to when he says " . . . this alone doth always continue inviolated." It is in this light that Gabriel concludes his lesson on the Angelical language:

> Thus you see there, the Necessity of this Tongue, the Excellency of it, and the Cause why it is preferred before that which you call Hebrew. For it is written, Every lesser consenteth to his greater. I trust this is sufficient. [*A True and Faithful Relation*, p. 93]

Of course, Agrippa used Hebrew throughout his text to illustrate the various methods of working with mystical words and letters. As he himself points out, Hebrew was considered the most perfect magickal language at the time of his writing. (In Agrippa's time, Hebrew was a dead language, like Latin, and was associated primarily with Scripture.) However, in the same book, he also has this to say:

> Because the letters of every tongue have in their number, order, and figure a celestial and divine original, I shall easily grant this calculation concerning the names of spirits to be made not only by Hebrew letters, but also by Chaldean, and Arabic, Egyptian, Greek, Latin, and any other, the Tables being rightly made after the imitation of the precedents. [*Three Books of Occult Philosophy*, Book III, chapter 27]

Taking this into account, Gabriel's assertion that Angelical is "preferred before that which you call Hebrew" makes perfect sense. Dee would likely have understood this to mean that all of Agrippa's instructions concerning names, letters, talismans, etc., could be utilized with the Angelical alphabet instead of Hebrew. (See the end of this chapter, where I explore some of Agrippa's techniques, utilizing Dee's Angelical.)

The Angelical Alphabet

> Characters therefore are nothing else than certain unknowable letters and writings, preserving the secrets of the gods, and names of the spirits from the use and reading of profane men, which the ancients called hieroglyphical, or sacred letters, because devoted to the secrets of the gods only. For they did account it unlawful to write the mysteries of the gods with those characters with which profane and vulgar things were wrote. [*Three Books of Occult Philosophy*, Book III, chapter 29]

> **Dee:** The titles of the sides,[21] are they to be written only in the holy Characters?
>
> **Galvah:** As thou sayest, even those words do make thee holy, that thou callest them holy.
>
> **Dee:** I believe verily, that they are holy and sanctified. [*A True and Faithful Relation*, p. 23]

Before attempting to transmit the text of *Loagaeth*, Raphael first wanted the men to commit to memory the characters of the Angelical alphabet (or, as Dee referred to it, the Adamical alphabet).[22] During Kelley's second vision of the Holy Book (see chapter 2), the Archangel highlighted a group of twenty-one distinct letters from one of its pages. The characters Kelley saw were by no means Latin, nor were they from the Hebrew, Greek, Chaldean, or any of the other usual "dead language" alphabets utilized by Renaissance mystics. In some ways, the characters revealed by Raphael resemble magickal alphabets like those found in Agrippa and Solomonic grimoires. Some of the letter shapes even appear to have origins previous to Dee and Kelley.[23] However, the Angelical alphabet as a whole is unique within Western occultism.

In the journal, Kelley recorded the characters in one line, running from right to left in the "Semitic" manner of Angelical, beginning with *Pa* (B) and ending with *Gisg* (T). These were actually simplified versions of the letters, which many today consider the "script" version—suitable for handwriting.[24]

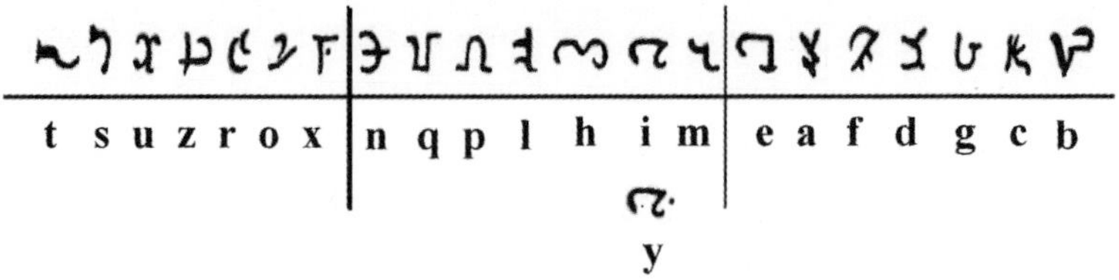

The "Script" Angelical Alphabet, running right to left.

It was not until much later, after most of the Tables of *Loagaeth* had been transmitted, that Kelley finally received the final and correct forms of the Angelical letters. These final forms were intended for use in the "perfected copy" of the Holy Book. Following is a Table of the "perfected" Angelical characters, along with their names and phonetic values. Remember this alphabet runs from right to left (or *Pa* to *Gisg*):

The Angelical Alphabet

Graph	*Un*	*Or*	*Gal*	*Ged*	*Veh*	*Pa*
						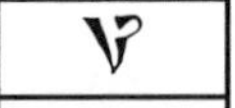
E	A	F	D	G/J	C/Ch/K	B

Drux	*Ger*	*Mals*	*Ur*	*Na*	*Gon*	*Tal*
					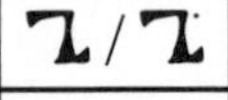	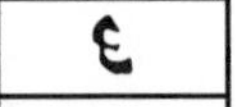
N	Q/Qu	P/Ph	L	H	I/Y	M

Gisg	*Fam*	*Van*	*Ceph*	*Don*	*Med*	*Pal*
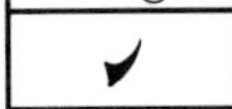						
T	S	U/V	Z	R	O	X

Dee notes that when Kelley could not make out a letter in his visions, it would appear "in a light yellow color" upon the paper, so Kelley could simply trace over it. It has been suggested that this indicates the letters are supposed to be yellow in color—but I have to disagree. The Holy Book originally appeared to Kelley written in blood, and no color is ever prescribed for the letters when written on paper. (This journal entry specifically says that Kelley traced over the letters in black. In later sessions, the Angels told Dee that they didn't care what color he used for the letters.)[25]

While on the subject of the "perfected" Angelical characters, I must mention some confusion that exists concerning the letters *Pal* (X) and *Gon* (I/Y). Note that the Pal in my illustration of the perfected Angelical letters contains a small point at the "elbow" of the character, while other texts on the Angelical alphabet do not.[26] When Kelley first describes the letters in Dee's journal, he states they were drawn in a single line with points between them.[27] Therefore, there is a point *next to* the Pal in the journal, but it is not clear that the point is intended as part of the letter.

However, when Dee lists out the letters with their names and English-letter correspondences, we clearly see the dot remains in the crook of the Pal.[28] Then, the alphabet is depicted once more in the same session, showing a 7 x 3 division of the letters (the "script letters" shown in the illustration), and once again we see the small point in Pal's elbow.[29] Finally, Kelley drew out the "perfected" Angelical letters.[30] Peterson's version of Dee's *Five Books* . . . shows no point in the Pal in this instance, but the original manuscript *does* include the point![31] (I assume the image in Peterson's book was edited, and the point may have appeared to be a printer's error.)

As for Gon (I/Y), you can see that I have included two versions of this letter in my illustration. When Dee drew out the letters divided into three groups of seven,[32] he included two versions of Gon (also shown previously)—one without a dot representing *I* and one with a dot representing *Y*. This is confirmed later in the journals, when Dee makes a marginal notation showing the "Gon-with-dot" and the words *this with a prick betokeneth 'y.'*[33] When Kelley finally draws the perfected letters, he includes the dot with the Gon—though it is misleading because he also separates all the characters with dots, and Gon's dot appears to be merely a misplaced separator-dot. I have included both versions in my illustration: the "Gon-sans-dot" for *I* and the "Gon-with-dot" for *Y*. Throughout the Lexicon in volume II, I have used "Gon-with-dot" anywhere Dee used a *Y* in his transliterations, and where *I* naturally makes the "yuh" sound (such as in *Ialprg*).

After revealing the original "script" version of the letters to Kelley, Raphael proceeded to deliver lessons upon the alphabet: the pronunciation of the letters' names, their proper ordering, and the division of the twenty-one characters into three groups of seven.

Of this threefold division, Raphael says, "The number of perfection, one in three."[34] This statement lets us know that Angelical should properly contain twenty-one letters (three groups of seven), rather than the twenty-two (three, seven, and twelve) with which we are familiar from Hebrew. I assume this difference in numbering is intended to reflect both the *Book of Loagaeth* and the Heptarchic system, both of which are also based upon a sevenfold scheme. An alphabet of twenty-two letters would not mathematically "fit" the Angelic system revealed to Dee and Kelley.

One trait Angelical shares with ancient languages like Hebrew is the fact that each letter has both a phonetic value and also stands as a word on its own. For instance, the equivalent of the letter *d* in Hebrew is called *daleth*—but the word *daleth* also translates as "door." (The word *daleth* came first, and was later chosen to represent the Hebrew equivalent of *d* because it starts with that phonetic sound.)

The letters of the Angelical alphabet work in a fashion similar to Hebrew—though with some key differences. For instance, the Angelical letter *D* is called *Gal*, and it is certain that Gal is a proper word with its own translation. (This, and several other letter-names appear in the text of *Loagaeth* as whole words.) However, unfortunately, no translations for the Angelical letter-names were ever offered.

Meanwhile, unlike Hebrew letter-names, the word *Gal* does not begin with the phonetic value of *D*. (As we can see in the previous chart of the alphabet, few of the Angelical letter-names reflect their phonetic values. *Pa* = "B," *Tal* = "M," *Drux* = "N," etc.)

Later in the journals, Dee and Kelley once again gained the audience of the Angel Illemese. The men were previously discussing the "transposition of letters" (likely a reference to a Qabalistic exercise in gematria, or maybe one of the many systems of cryptography that were popular in

Dee's time, especially with Dee himself).[35] The conversation with Illemese soon turned to the letters of the Angelical alphabet:

> **Dee:** And first I think, that those letters of our Adamical Alphabet have a due peculiar unchangeable proportion of their forms, and likewise that their order is also Mystical.
>
> **Illemese:** These letters represent the Creation of man, and therefore they must be in proportion. They represent the workmanship wherewithal the soul of man was made like unto his Creator. [*Five Books of Mystery*, p. 373]

As we see in the Book of Genesis, chapter 2, Adam (or mankind) was fashioned after the image of the Creator. In the quote above, Illemese reveals that the very letters of the Angelical alphabet represent the workmanship behind the Creation of Man.

This was not a new concept for Dee and Kelley. If we look into the *Sepher Yetzirah*, we can see a striking similarity between Illemese's description of the Angelical letters, and the Qabalistic understanding of the Hebrew alphabet:

> He hath formed, weighed, transmuted, composed, and created with these twenty-two letters every living being, and every soul yet uncreated. [*Sepher Yetzirah*, 2:2]
>
> These three mothers again represent in the Microcosm or Human form, male and female; the Head, the Belly, and the Chest. [*Sepher Yetzirah*, 3:4]
>
> These seven double letters He formed, designed, created, and combined into the Stars of the Universe, the days of the week, [and] the orifices of perception in man. [*Sepher Yetzirah*, 4:3]
>
> These twelve letters, he designed, formed, combined, weighed, and changed, and created with them the twelve divisions of the heavens (namely, the zodiacal constellations), the twelve months of the year, and the twelve important organs of the frame of man, namely the right and left hands, the right and left feet, two kidneys, the liver, the gall, the spleen, the intestines, the gullet, and the stomach. [*Sepher Yetzirah*, 5:2]

Dee would have been familiar with the *Sepher Yetzirah* and the relationship it describes between the Hebrew letters and the body of Man. Therefore, it would have been natural for him to assume a similar relationship between the human body and the Angelical characters.

Even the instruction by Illemese to draw the characters "in proportion" reflects similar instructions for the use of Hebrew upon talismans. Because the letters were used in the creation of all things, it is considered necessary that the proper forms of the letters be retained in magickal work. In this sense, the characters are sigils[36] in their own right—each one embodying a single aspect of Creation.

In order to make this comparison between Hebrew and Angelical complete, I should also mention the numerical aspect of the Hebrew letters. Like most ancient languages, Hebrew does not possess a separate set of characters to represent numbers. Instead, the letters must do double-duty as numbers, too. (Our example Hebrew letter *daleth* also stands for the number 4.) Therefore, any Hebrew word can also be viewed as a grouping of numbers instead of letters—making the language useful for numerology and gematria.

It has long been assumed that Angelical works in the same manner. This is thanks, in part, to statements made about numbers by the Archangel Gabriel (which we saw in chapter 3.)[37] These statements are most often taken out of context by modern scholars. For example, Gabriel says, "The Letters are separated, and in confusion: and, therefore, are by numbers gathered together." In the same speech, the Archangel adds, "Where being known in number, they are easily distinguished, so that here we teach places to be numbered." The student of Qabalistic gematria will find such statements familiar within their own art.

However, as we saw in chapter 3, Gabriel was discussing the numbers given with the letters of several words in Key One (which were added together to create "mystical square roots"). Those numbers are associated with the specific words of the Keys, and not with the individual characters of the alphabet.

Another hint toward an Angelical gematria rests in the Keys themselves. Several of the Keys contain numbers that are represented by letters:

ACAM = 7699	*GA* = 31	*OP* = 22
AF = 19	*MAPM* = 9639	*OX* = 26
CIAL = 9996	*MIAN* = 3663	*P* = 8
CLA = 456	*NI* = 28	*PD* = 33
DAOX = 5678	*O* = 5	*PERAL* = 69636
DARG = 6739	*OB* = 28	*QUAR* = 1636
EMOD = 8763	*OL* = 24	*TAXS* = 7336
ERAN = 6332	*OS* = 12	*UX* = 42

As we can see in the list above, there are always as many letters in the Angelical as there are numbers in the translation. This suggests that these letters are *not* the Angelical words for their numbers (as the English for *33* is *thirty-three*).[38] Instead, the letters would appear to share a one-to-one relationship with the numbers. For instance, in the letters *CLA* (456)—the character *C* could represent 4, the *L* might represent 5, and the *A* represent 6.

However, we find little consistency in this relationship between the letters and numbers. For example, note how the letter *O* appears to represent 1, 2, 5, 6, and 7 at the same time. Also note *PERAL*, which uses P, R, *and* L to represent 6. No one to date has discovered the mystery behind this inconsistency.

The bottom line is that the Angels never suggested the existence of an Angelical numerology or gematria to Dee or Kelley. Whenever the men did employ such arts in the journals, it is always of the type found in the Qabalah or the works of Agrippa—simply *applied to* the names and words revealed by the Angels. This does not mean that an Angelical gematria does not exist. (In fact, it would surprise me if Angelical letters did not also represent numbers, as this is a common trait of ancient languages.) It only means that such a system was never mentioned by the Angels nor (as far as we know) ever developed by Dee himself.

Addendum: "Before That Which You Call Hebrew" (Angelical and Agrippa's Occult Philosophy)

Dee was a student of Agrippa's occult philosophy, and it had a profound impact upon his Angelic magick. For example, we have already discussed the quote at the head of this chapter from Agrippa's Book Three, chapter 23 ("Of the Tongue of Angels . . . ")—which likely inspired Dee in his work.[39] Also consider the following excerpt, taken from Book Three, chapter 24 ("Of the Names of Spirits and Their Various Imposition . . . "):

> But the masters of the Hebrews think that the names of angels were imposed upon them by Adam, according to that which is written, the Lord brought all things which he had made unto Adam, that he should name them, and as he called anything, so the name of it was. Hence, the Hebrew mecubals think, together with magicians, that it is in the power of man to impose names upon spirits, but of such a man only who is dignified, and elevated to his virtue by some divine gift, or sacred authority.

The above is quite harmonious with the mythology Dee's Angels expounded in relation to the Celestial Speech. Adam imposed names upon all things (supposedly using the Angelical tongue), and therefore those who have obtained a certain "sacred authority" are likewise able to impose names upon spiritual creatures.

Agrippa dedicates several chapters in his work to the generation of Divine Names and characters. (See the third book in *Three Books of Occult Philosophy*, chapters 23–30.) Of course, he utilizes Hebrew to illustrate his methods. However, as we saw previously in this chapter, he also affirms that "the letters of every tongue have in their number, order, and figure a celestial and divine original." Therefore, one might also use "Chaldean, and Arabic, Egyptian, Greek, Latin and any other" language with the methods of gematria and mystical name-generation he describes.[40]

I suspect Gabriel, in Dee's journal, was referring to Agrippa's teaching when he stressed that Angelical is "preferred before that which you call Hebrew" because "every lesser consenteth to his greater."[41] Dee's holy characters were therefore intended for use beyond the *Book of Loagaeth*, and I believe that most of Agrippa's methods of name-generation can (and were always intended to) be used with them. We will explore three simple techniques that lend themselves especially well to the Angelical alphabet—found in Agrippa's Book Three, chapters 26, 27, and 30. Of course, where Agrippa uses Hebrew in his work, I will use Angelical characters:

Of Finding Out the Names of Spirits and Geniuses from the Disposition of Celestial Bodies (Adapted from Agrippa's Third Book, Chapter 26)

A vitally important aspect of Renaissance-era magick was the observance of astrological forces. In fact, a large portion of classical occult literature is devoted to magickal timing based upon the results of horary chart interpretations. Just as John Dee used this art to schedule a time for Queen Elizabeth's coronation, so too would he have cast horoscopes to determine the best times for his magickal operations.

In this way, strict magickal timing was observed. The astral forces active at a given time determined what work could be accomplished. Or, conversely, a given set of astrological requirements would determine what time the work could be accomplished. It is from these practices that we hear of spirits ruling for limited periods of time, and texts that suggest spirits can only be contacted when the stars are under certain arrangements.

We can see an example of this in Agrippa's Book Two (chapters 35–47),[42] wherein he explains how to fashion magickal images. In many cases, specific magickal timing is required:

> From the operations of the Sun, they made an image at the our of the Sun, the first face of Leo ascending with the Sun, the form of which was . . . [*Three Books of Occult Philsophy*, Book II, chapter 41]

> From the operations of Mercury, they made an image at the hour of Mercury, Mercury ascending in Gemini, the form of which was . . . [*Three Books of Occult Philsophy*, Book II, chapter 43]

Returning again to Book Three, chapter 27, Agrippa explains that it is possible to use these very same astrological indications to create a horoscope and "decipher" the name of an Angel from the stars. That Angel—also called an Intelligence—will be the particular Governor of the magickal work that will take place at that time—be it a magickal image, talisman, evocation, or the like.

At the same time, Agrippa suggests we might use this technique for any magickal operation. It does not matter whether the astrological conditions are prescribed by a spell, or calculated by the individual practitioner. It only matters that one takes the time to draw up a zodiacal chart, making sure that it is well-aspected toward the goal of the work. (Thus, if one is working with Angels of Mercury, one must make sure Mercury is strong and fortunate in the chart.) If the chart indicates that the chosen planet is unfortunately aspected, then it must be scrapped, a new time chosen, and a new chart created.[43]

Once the time and horoscope are satisfactory, Agrippa outlines several processes for "decoding" the name of the ruling Intelligence. Each process is more involved than the last, and his descriptions of the advanced techniques are unfortunately very obscure. However, the first and simplest method is easy to understand, and is likely the best place for us to start.

It is first necessary to calculate the degree of the ascendant. The Heavens compose a circle of 360 degrees, and the ascendant is the first degree of the first astrological House—resting directly upon the line of the eastern horizon.

In that ascending degree, place the first Angelical letter (*Pa*). Then, continue to write the alphabet in proper order all the way *counterclockwise* around the chart. Each degree is assigned a single letter, and the direction follows the natural course of the twelve zodiacal signs. When the final letter (*Gisg*) is reached, simply begin again with *Pa* and continue until degree 360 has been assigned a letter.

From there one only needs to interpret the chart as normal, making distinctions between the planets with strong and fortunate dignities and those with weak and unfortunate dignities. The concept is to focus on the specific planetary forces one needs for the work at hand. One can simply ignore the weaker and negative aspects of the chart and "compile" those forces that are necessary to the magickal goal.

Each degree that contains a desired planetary aspect now has a letter assigned to it, and these letters are gathered together to formulate the name. It is here that Agrippa offers several methods, some of which are hard to comprehend. The simplest is to start at the ascendant and move around the chart counterclockwise. The first desired aspect one reaches becomes the first letter of the Intelligence's name. Then, moving onward counterclockwise, the next required aspect becomes the second letter—and so on throughout the chart.

A slightly more advanced method seems to involve gathering the letters according to the *strength* of the planetary aspects. Though uncertain, I recently received the suggestion that the strongest (or most desired) aspect of the chart should become the first letter of the name, and the second-strongest the second letter, etc. Thus, if one desired to create a talisman in the hour of Mercury, Mercury ascending in Gemini, one could take the letter assigned to the degree of Mercury as the first letter of the name.

Agrippa does not say one should consider only positive aspects in this method. However, it may be implied, as gathering letters for *all* aspects of the chart might make for some unwieldy names.

Agrippa goes on to describe the Qabalistic practice of appending the gathered letters with one of the Names of God, *El* or *Yah*, to create an Angelic name.[44] However, as we are using the Angelical alphabet rather than Hebrew, there should be no need for this convention. The Angels who are unique to Dee's journals most often lack these suffixes—such as Nalvage, Madimi, Bornogo, Befafes, Illemese, Mapsama, and so on.

Finally, the name of an "evil Angel"—who opposes the work at hand—can also be derived using a similar process.[45] It is merely an inverse of the previous instructions, using the same horoscope used to find the good Angel. However, in this case one must calculate the degree of the descendant—that is, the degree in direct opposition to the ascendant (degree 180, which is the first degree of the seventh House), found on the line of the western horizon. The first letter *(Pa)* is placed there, and the alphabet is written around the chart *clockwise*—now going against the natural order of the zodiac.

To find the letters of the evil Angel's name, one begins with the same planetary aspects used for the good Angel. Then, find the degrees on the chart in *direct opposition* to those aspects. The letters assigned to those degrees of opposition will form the name of the evil Angel. The letters may be gathered beginning at the descendant and moving clockwise around the chart. Or, gather them according to strength of dignity, beginning with the opposing degree of the strongest dignity and progressing to the weakest.

I originally wanted to show you an illustration of a zodiacal chart with the Angelical alphabet written around it for both good and evil Angels. However, for all 720 letters to be visible, the graphic would have been too massive to fit even across two facing pages. Therefore, I have settled for the following Tables, which you can use to look up the letters for each degree of the zodiac:

Agrippa suggests these methods can also be used to find the name of a person's nativity Angel, by simply applying them to that person's natal chart. The resulting name will be that of a guardian Angel often credited with keeping one from physical harm. Also, as Agrippa explains, this is the Angel set over home, career, and all aspects of life outlined within the twelve astrological Houses.

First House

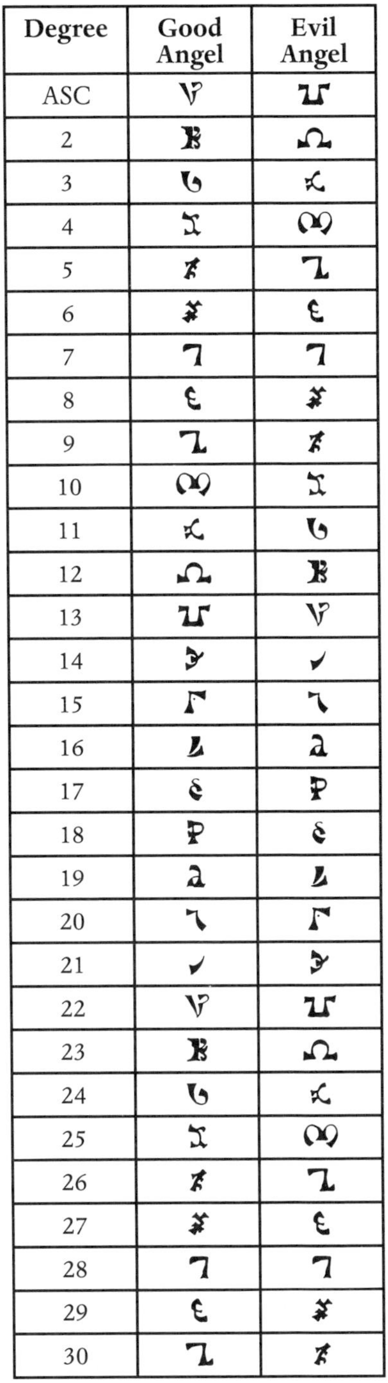

Degree
Good Angel
Evil Angel
ASC
2
3
4
5
6
7
8
9
10
11
12
13
14
15
16
17
18
19
20
21
22
23
24
25
26
27
28
29
30

Second House

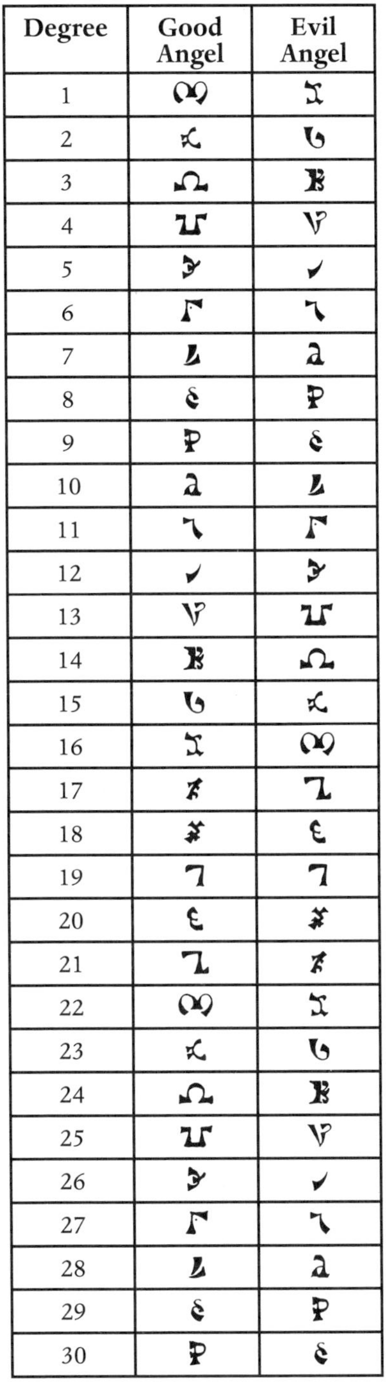

Degree
Good Angel
Evil Angel
1
2
3
4
5
6
7
8
9
10
11
12
13
14
15
16
17
18
19
20
21
22
23
24
25
26
27
28
29
30

Third House

Degree	Good Angel	Evil Angel
1	a	L
2	ɿ	Γ
3	✓	ɜ
4	V	π
5	B	Ω
6	G	ϰ
7	I	ω
8	ƚ	Z
9	ǂ	ε
10	7	7
11	ε	ǂ
12	Z	ƚ
13	ω	I
14	ϰ	G
15	Ω	B
16	π	V
17	ɜ	✓
18	Γ	ɿ
19	L	a
20	ɘ	Ᵽ
21	Ᵽ	ɘ
22	a	L
23	ɿ	Γ
24	✓	ɜ
25	V	π
26	B	Ω
27	G	ϰ
28	I	ω
29	ƚ	Z
30	ǂ	ε

Fourth House

Degree	Good Angel	Evil Angel
1	7	7
2	ε	ǂ
3	Z	ƚ
4	ω	I
5	ϰ	G
6	Ω	B
7	π	V
8	ɜ	✓
9	Γ	ɿ
10	L	a
11	ɘ	Ᵽ
12	Ᵽ	ɘ
13	a	L
14	ɿ	Γ
15	✓	ɜ
16	V	π
17	B	Ω
18	G	ϰ
19	I	ω
20	ƚ	Z
21	ǂ	ε
22	7	7
23	ε	ǂ
24	Z	ƚ
25	ω	I
26	ϰ	G
27	Ω	B
28	π	V
29	ɜ	✓
30	Γ	ɿ

Fifth House

Degree	Good Angel	Evil Angel
1	ʟ	ɑ
2	ɛ	Ᵽ
3	Ᵽ	ɛ
4	ɑ	ʟ
5	ʅ	Γ
6	✓	ȝ
7	Ꝟ	Ⲡ
8	Ƀ	Ω
9	Ꮆ	ϰ
10	ℑ	Ꝏ
11	⸸	ℸ
12	ǂ	Ꜫ
13	ㄱ	ㄱ
14	Ꜫ	ǂ
15	ℸ	⸸
16	Ꝏ	ℑ
17	ϰ	Ꮆ
18	Ω	Ƀ
19	Ⲡ	Ꝟ
20	ȝ	✓
21	Γ	ʅ
22	ʟ	ɑ
23	ɛ	Ᵽ
24	Ᵽ	ɛ
25	ɑ	ʟ
26	ʅ	Γ
27	✓	ȝ
28	Ꝟ	Ⲡ
29	Ƀ	Ω
30	Ꮆ	ϰ

Sixth House

Degree	Good Angel	Evil Angel
1	ℑ	Ꝏ
2	⸸	ℸ
3	ǂ	Ꜫ
4	ㄱ	ㄱ
5	Ꜫ	ǂ
6	ℸ	⸸
7	Ꝏ	ℑ
8	ϰ	Ꮆ
9	Ω	Ƀ
10	Ⲡ	Ꝟ
11	ȝ	✓
12	Γ	ʅ
13	ʟ	ɑ
14	ɛ	Ᵽ
15	Ᵽ	ɛ
16	ɑ	ʟ
17	ʅ	Γ
18	✓	ȝ
19	Ꝟ	Ⲡ
20	Ƀ	Ω
21	Ꮆ	ϰ
22	ℑ	Ꝏ
23	⸸	ℸ
24	ǂ	Ꜫ
25	ㄱ	ㄱ
26	Ꜫ	ǂ
27	ℸ	⸸
28	Ꝏ	ℑ
29	ϰ	Ꮆ
30	Ω	Ƀ

Seventh House

Degree	Good Angel	Evil Angel
DSC	[illegible]	[illegible]
2	[illegible]	[illegible]
3	[illegible]	[illegible]
4	[illegible]	[illegible]
5	[illegible]	[illegible]
6	[illegible]	[illegible]
7	[illegible]	[illegible]
8	[illegible]	[illegible]
9	[illegible]	[illegible]
10	[illegible]	[illegible]
11	[illegible]	[illegible]
12	[illegible]	[illegible]
13	[illegible]	[illegible]
14	[illegible]	[illegible]
15	[illegible]	[illegible]
16	[illegible]	[illegible]
17	[illegible]	[illegible]
18	[illegible]	[illegible]
19	[illegible]	[illegible]
20	[illegible]	[illegible]
21	[illegible]	[illegible]
22	[illegible]	[illegible]
23	[illegible]	[illegible]
24	[illegible]	[illegible]
25	[illegible]	[illegible]
26	[illegible]	[illegible]
27	[illegible]	[illegible]
28	[illegible]	[illegible]
29	[illegible]	[illegible]
30	[illegible]	[illegible]

Eighth House

Degree	Good Angel	Evil Angel
1	[illegible]	[illegible]
2	[illegible]	[illegible]
3	[illegible]	[illegible]
4	[illegible]	[illegible]
5	[illegible]	[illegible]
6	[illegible]	[illegible]
7	[illegible]	[illegible]
8	[illegible]	[illegible]
9	[illegible]	[illegible]
10	[illegible]	[illegible]
11	[illegible]	[illegible]
12	[illegible]	[illegible]
13	[illegible]	[illegible]
14	[illegible]	[illegible]
15	[illegible]	[illegible]
16	[illegible]	[illegible]
17	[illegible]	[illegible]
18	[illegible]	[illegible]
19	[illegible]	[illegible]
20	[illegible]	[illegible]
21	[illegible]	[illegible]
22	[illegible]	[illegible]
23	[illegible]	[illegible]
24	[illegible]	[illegible]
25	[illegible]	[illegible]
26	[illegible]	[illegible]
27	[illegible]	[illegible]
28	[illegible]	[illegible]
29	[illegible]	[illegible]
30	[illegible]	[illegible]

Ninth House

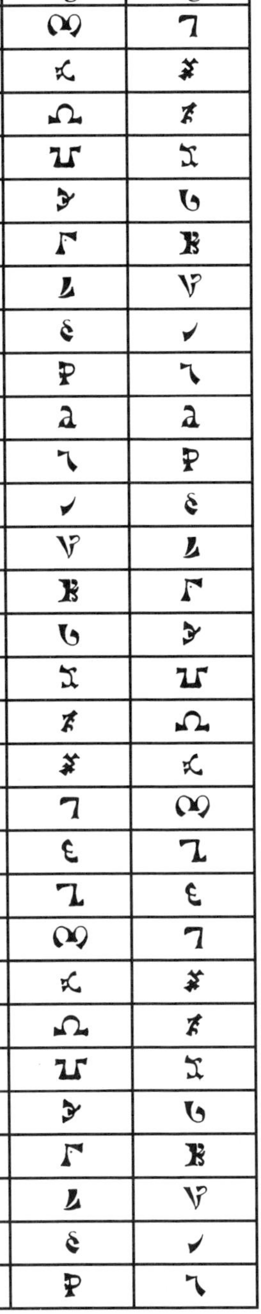

Degree	Good Angel	Evil Angel
1		
2		
3		
4		
5		
6		
7		
8		
9		
10		
11		
12		
13		
14		
15		
16		
17		
18		
19		
20		
21		
22		
23		
24		
25		
26		
27		
28		
29		
30		

Tenth House

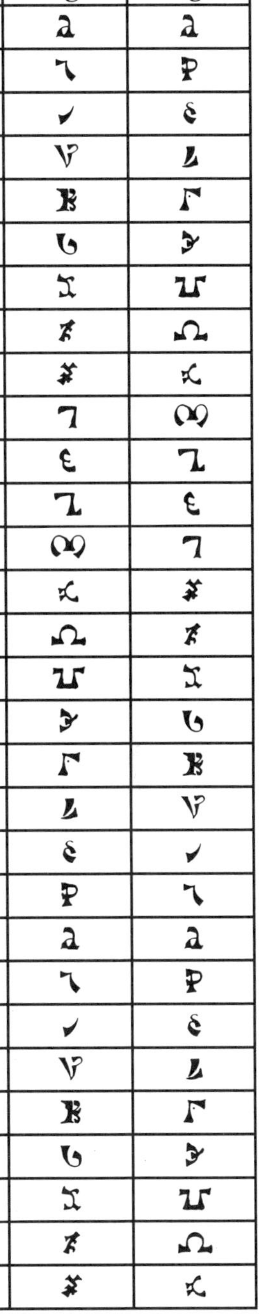

Degree	Good Angel	Evil Angel
1		
2		
3		
4		
5		
6		
7		
8		
9		
10		
11		
12		
13		
14		
15		
16		
17		
18		
19		
20		
21		
22		
23		
24		
25		
26		
27		
28		
29		
30		

Eleventh House

Degree	Good Angel	Evil Angel
1	[illegible]	[illegible]
2	[illegible]	[illegible]
3	[illegible]	[illegible]
4	[illegible]	[illegible]
5	[illegible]	[illegible]
6	[illegible]	[illegible]
7	[illegible]	[illegible]
8	[illegible]	[illegible]
9	[illegible]	[illegible]
10	[illegible]	[illegible]
11	[illegible]	[illegible]
12	[illegible]	[illegible]
13	[illegible]	[illegible]
14	[illegible]	[illegible]
15	[illegible]	[illegible]
16	[illegible]	[illegible]
17	[illegible]	[illegible]
18	[illegible]	[illegible]
19	[illegible]	[illegible]
20	[illegible]	[illegible]
21	[illegible]	[illegible]
22	[illegible]	[illegible]
23	[illegible]	[illegible]
24	[illegible]	[illegible]
25	[illegible]	[illegible]
26	[illegible]	[illegible]
27	[illegible]	[illegible]
28	[illegible]	[illegible]
29	[illegible]	[illegible]
30	[illegible]	[illegible]

Twelfth House

Degree	Good Angel	Evil Angel
1	[illegible]	[illegible]
2	[illegible]	[illegible]
3	[illegible]	[illegible]
4	[illegible]	[illegible]
5	[illegible]	[illegible]
6	[illegible]	[illegible]
7	[illegible]	[illegible]
8	[illegible]	[illegible]
9	[illegible]	[illegible]
10	[illegible]	[illegible]
11	[illegible]	[illegible]
12	[illegible]	[illegible]
13	[illegible]	[illegible]
14	[illegible]	[illegible]
15	[illegible]	[illegible]
16	[illegible]	[illegible]
17	[illegible]	[illegible]
18	[illegible]	[illegible]
19	[illegible]	[illegible]
20	[illegible]	[illegible]
21	[illegible]	[illegible]
22	[illegible]	[illegible]
23	[illegible]	[illegible]
24	[illegible]	[illegible]
25	[illegible]	[illegible]
26	[illegible]	[illegible]
27	[illegible]	[illegible]
28	[illegible]	[illegible]
29	[illegible]	[illegible]
30	[illegible]	[illegible]

Of the Calculating Art of Such Names by the Tradition of Qabalists (Adapted from Agrippa's Third Book, Chapter 27)

The very next chapter of Agrippa's work gives us another method of working with the generated names. It involves permuting the name of the Intelligence to discover an entire hierarchy of Angels who rule above him.

I suspect that Dee was more than familiar with the "Dionysian" celestial hierarchy—often called the Nine Angelic Choirs. This was the standard Christian model of the Heavens during his life, and is presented in Agrippa's Book Two, chapter 12, "Of the Number Nine, and the Scale Thereof."

These Choirs are arranged into nine concentric circles. The outermost consists of the Angels closest to the material realm, who are generally charged with directing events on Earth and are depicted as the most anthropomorphic. The inner circle consists of the most fiery and terrible Angels, who protect and attend upon the Divine Throne Itself. The reader may recognize the names of the Choirs, from lowest to highest: Angels, Archangels and Principalities; Virtues, Powers, and Dominations; Thrones, Cherubim, and Seraphim.

The name of an Intelligence generated from a horoscope would classify as an "Angel" by this model—an Intelligence directly concerned with material or human events. Returning to Agrippa's chapter 27, he suggests that the Angel's name can yield eight further names—beginning with an Archangel, then a Principality, and eventually all the way to a *Seraph*. In practice, however, I would assume that one would rarely need anything more than the Angel and Archangel who directs him.

In order to understand the method Agrippa describes, we must think from the standpoint of sacred mathematics. Any two numbers can be multiplied together, and the resulting product will be an "occult number" associated with them both. Most often, this is done with a single number multiplied by itself—such as 7 x 7 = 49. (Hence the mystery surrounding square roots.) The number 49 can then represent a magickal square of forty-nine cells—seven columns and seven rows.[46] In fact, Agrippa shows

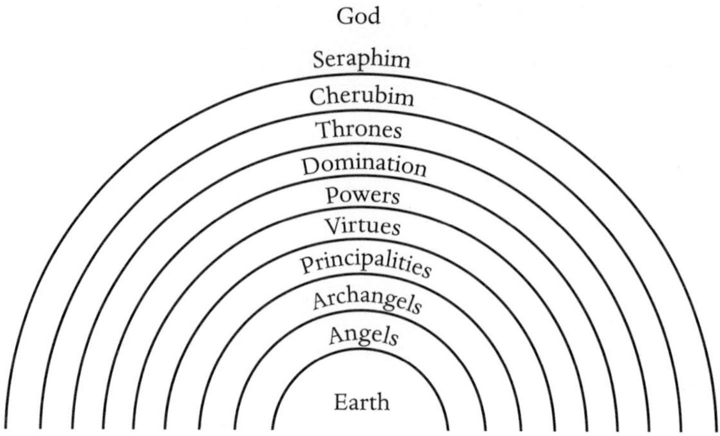

Choir of Angels

us this very magick square in his Book Two, chapter 22, "Of the Tables of the Planets," where it is sacred to the planet Venus.

It is less common, but still valid, to multiply two differing numbers. For example, if we wish to work with planetary forces via the Angelical alphabet, then we might find it useful to multiply 7 (number of planets) by 21 (number of Angelical letters) for a product of 147—the number of cells in a magickal square sacred to both numbers. This square can become a magickal word-square by writing the Angelical alphabet within it—from right to left—a total of seven times.

The following Table consists of the 147-cell word-square, surrounded by a border of two outer columns and an upper and lower row. The upper row and right-hand column combine to form the Entrance of the Good Angels. It includes the seven planets across the top and the Angelical alphabet written in order from top to bottom.

The lower row and left-hand column combine to form the Entrance of the Evil Angels, This includes the seven planets written in reverse order and Angelical alphabet written from bottom to top.

Note that the following Table of the Planets has been altered from Agrippa's design, in that the planets follow Dee's order for the *Heptarchia*.[47] It seemed appropriate to use the same ordering with the Angelical alphabet:

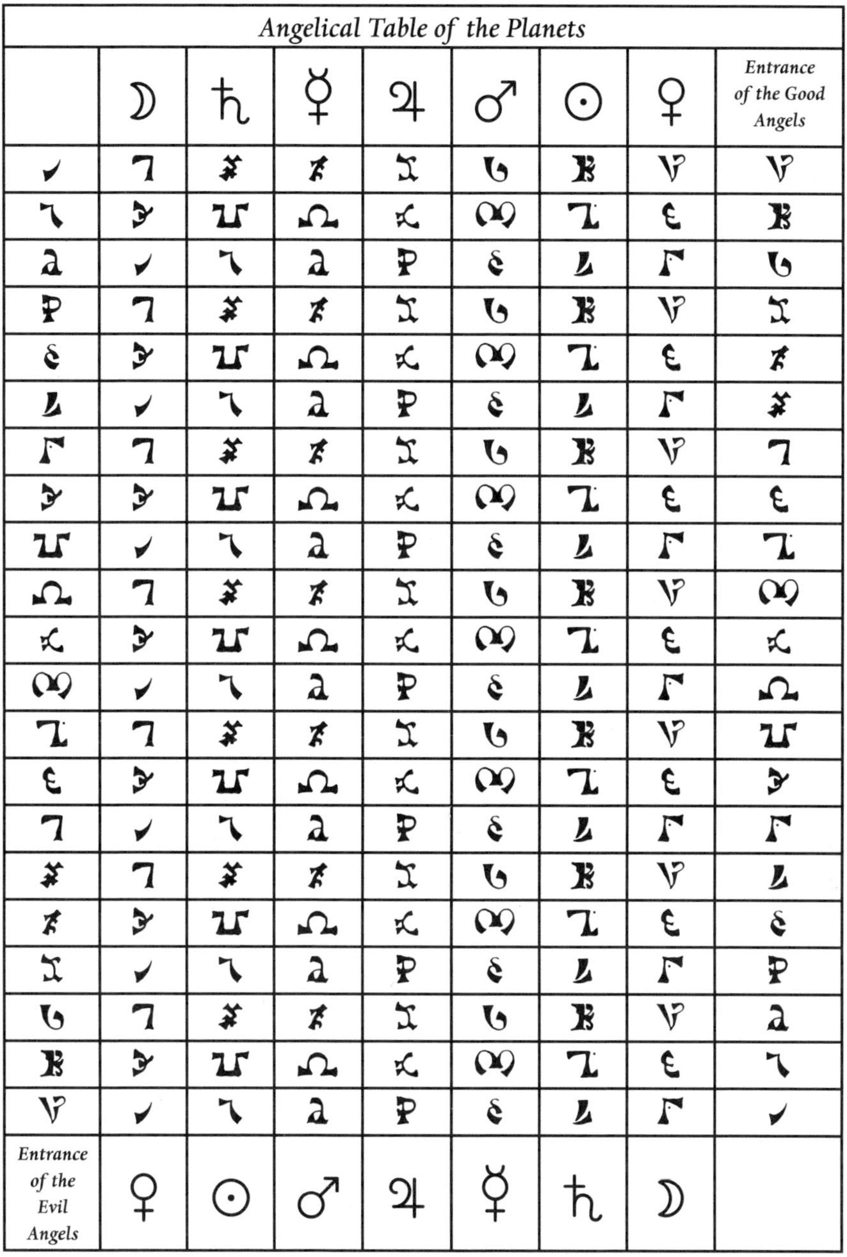

Angelical Table of the Planets
☽ ♄ ☿ ♃ ♂ ☉ ♀
Entrance of the Good Angels
Entrance of the Evil Angels
♀ ☉ ♂ ♃ ☿ ♄ ☽

Using this Table is fairly simple. Begin with the first letter of the name of the Angel, and the planet from the horoscope associated with its degree. Then, find that letter in the right-hand column of the *Entrance*

of the Good Angels, and scan leftward through that row to the column beneath the letter's planet. For example, if the Angel's name began with *M* (*Tal*), and its planetary aspect from the horoscope were Sol, one would begin in the right-hand column with *Tal* () and scan leftward to the column of Sol, where the letter *Gon* () is found. Therefore, the letter *I*/*Y* (*Gon*) becomes the first letter of the Archangel's name.

The process is repeated for each letter of the name—always scanning leftward from the letter in the right-hand column to the column beneath the letter's associated planetary aspect.

In order to find the name of the Principality, one would input the name of the Archangel in the same manner described above. The resulting Principality name can be input to generate the name of the Virtue, and so forth until a Seraph is produced.

Of course, the same thing can be done with the name of the evil Angel. Simply input his name from the left-hand column, and scan rightward to the column above the reverse-ordered planets at the bottom of the Table.

Agrippa also outlines several alternative uses for Tables like these. For instance, any Name of God can be inputted to find an Angel that will answer to it. In such a case, one would have to first decide which planet to work with, and then take all of the letters from the column beneath that planet. (If the name is already associated with a planet, so much the better. However, theoretically, one could input the same Name of God seven times—once in each column—to find seven planetary Angels that answer to it.)

A person's name converted to Angelical characters, and the planet or star that governs him or her being determined (via a natal chart), the name of yet another guardian Angel can be discovered. Simply input the letters from the right-hand column and scan leftward to the column beneath his or her ruling star.

Finally, any Angelical word can be input into the Table. Thus, if one can reduce a magickal goal to a single word, and find an Angelical translation in the English-to-Angelical section of the Lexicon, that word can be used with the Table to find an Intelligence set over the thing or concept. Once again, it would be necessary to first determine or choose a planet most in harmony with the magickal goal itself.

Of course, when using these techniques, we should not be limited to the seven planets alone. There are also the twelve forces of the zodiac to consider. The numbers 12 and 21 are multiplied for a product of 252. By forming this into a 12 x 21 magick square, we can fill the cells with the Angelical alphabet exactly twelve times. Agrippa offers this word-square in the third book of his *Three Book of Occult Philosophy*, chapter 27, also surrounded by a border of the Entrances of the Good and Evil Angels. The Table is used exactly as has been described here, except that it allows one to work with zodiacal forces rather than planetary.

Note that the Table of the Zodiac on the following page has been altered from Agrippa's design. Agrippa's Table consists of the Hebrew alphabet written from right to left on every other line (twelve times) and written from left to right on every other remaining line (also twelve times).[48] Because both 12 and 22 are even numbers, this was possible in his Table. However, Angelical is an odd-numbered twenty-one letters long, so I had to follow the same pattern as used for the Angelical Table of the Planets:

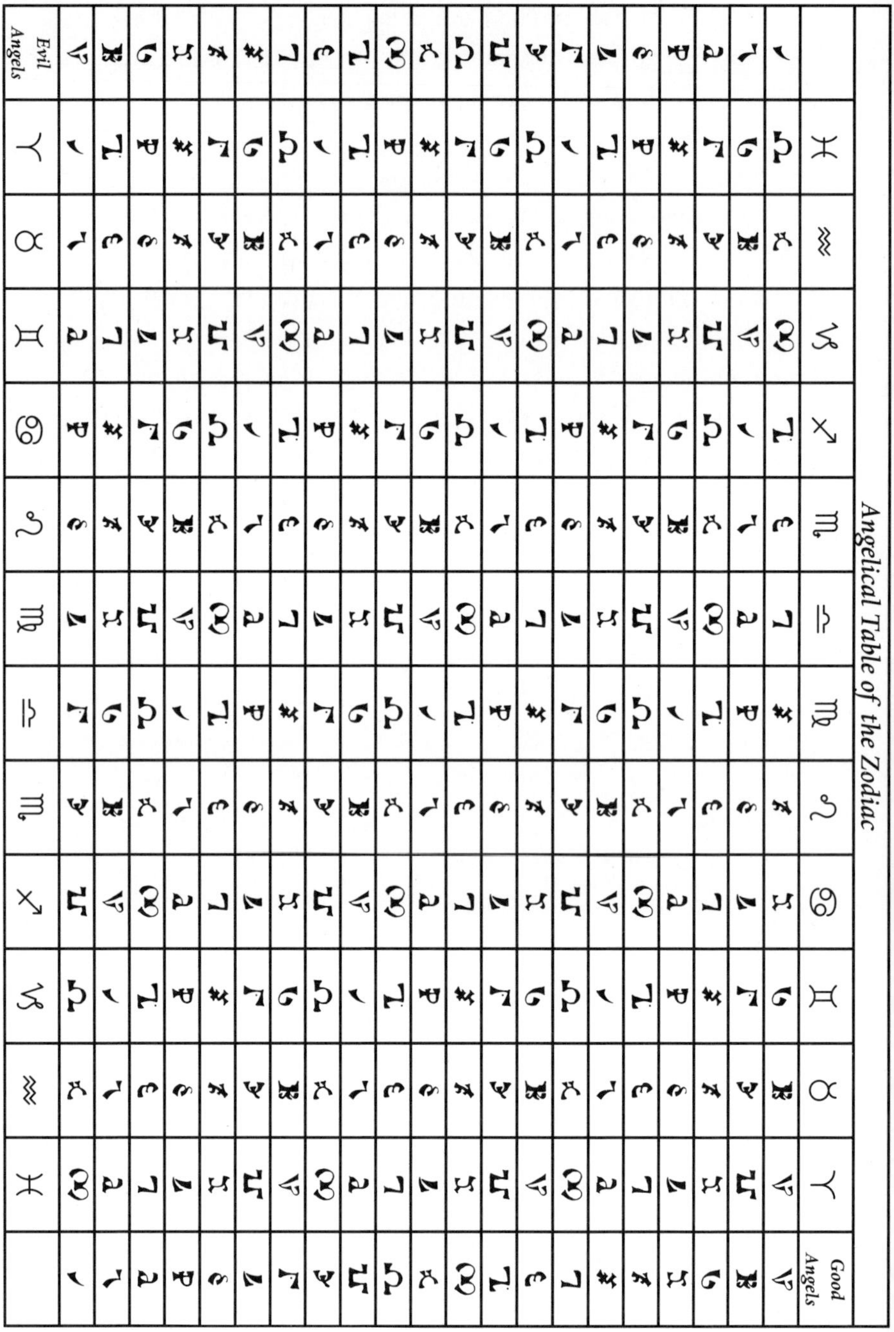
Angelical Table of the Zodiac
Evil Angels
Good Angels
♈ ♉ ♊ ♋ ♌ ♍ ♎ ♏ ♐ ♑ ♒ ♓
♓ ♒ ♑ ♐ ♏ ♎ ♍ ♌ ♋ ♊ ♉ ♈

Another Manner of Making Characters Delivered by Qabalists (Adapted from Agrippa's Third Book, Chapter 30)

Once we know the name of our Angelic Intelligence, it would also be helpful to have its sigil for use in talismanic magick. Agrippa gives several methods of generating sigils from the letters of an entity's name. Most of them depend upon the Hebrew alphabet, but he ends the chapter with a very simple method that can be used with any alphabet whatsoever.

Simply take the letters of the Angel's name, and blend them together to form a single hieroglyphic figure—called a sigil (or signature). For example, let us consider possible sigils for the Angels Nalvage and Galvah:

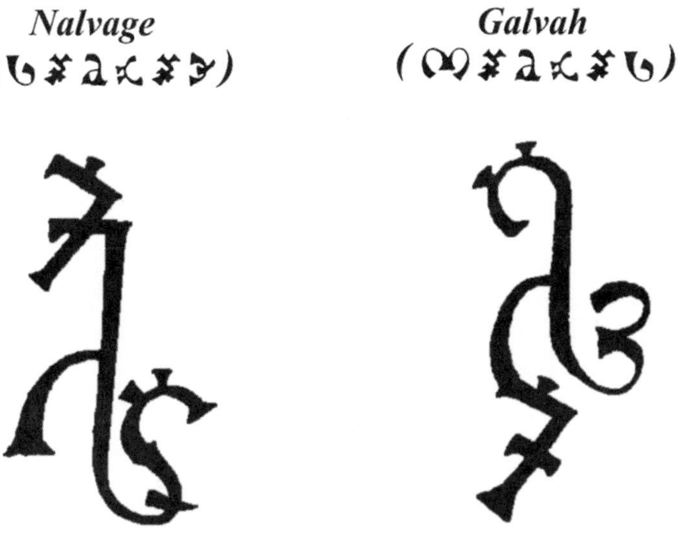

Two sigils—Nalvage and Galvah

Agrippa stresses that these types of sigils are not as powerful as those received directly from the Angels. Yet, they are extremely useful for typical magickal purposes, as well as for gaining initial contact with the Angels in question.

Making Pentacles and Sigils (Adapted from Pseudo-Agrippa's Fourth Book, *Of Magical Ceremonies*)

Agrippa's *Three Books* did not include any practical instruction for magick—likely as a protection against the Inquisition. It was not until thirty years after his death that a *Fourth Book of Occult Philosophy* was published, the actual title being *Of Magical Ceremonies*. There were many writings by Agrippa that appeared only posthumously, so the debate continues to this very day over whether or not he is the true author of this one. (Hence the name "Pseudo-Agrippa.") Regardless of its authorship, *Of Magical Ceremonies* has had a profound impact on western occultism—not the least of which is its instructions for turning Sigils into full-fledged talismans. The following is adapted from Pseudo-Agrippa's instructions:

First, surround the sigil with a double circle. This creates a border—or circumference—within which can be written the names of forces in control of the Angel. For instance, the name of the Archangel generated from the Tables in the previous section would be a prime choice.

One might also include a Name of God in sympathy with the Angel's nature. For example, a talisman aimed at military conquest might display the Name *Madzilodarp* (God of Stretch Forth and Conquer). Outside of the Keys, Dee also recorded a large number of Divine Names in his many magickal squares and Tables, which can be referenced for a Name appropriate to the Angel.

In truth, any Angelical word would serve the same purpose—so that anything from *wrath*, *burn*, or *earthquake* to *mercy*, *comfort*, or *pleasure* (depending on the magickal goal) might be translated into Angelical and written within the circumference as a Word of Power. (See the English-to-Angelical section of the Lexicon.)

As a final option, the *Fourth Book* suggests writing a versicle from Scripture within the circumference. We see this in several of the talismans from the *Key of Solomon the King*. A passage—usually from the Psalms—that relates in some way to the magickal goal is written in Hebrew or Greek around the circumference of the talisman. In the case of an Angelical talisman, I would suggest adopting appropriate verses from the Keys. (For example, a talisman intended to exorcise spirits would benefit from the first line of Key One—"I reign over you, sayeth the God of Justice"—written in Angelical characters. If one wishes to summon and question an entity, then perhaps one of the final lines—"Move, therefore, and appear, Open the mysteries of your creation.")

The name of the talisman's Angel can be inscribed around the central sigil. Pseudo-Agrippa suggests first drawing the lineal figure of the Angel's planet or star around the sigil, depending on the proper number. (Agrippa's Book Two outlines the astrological correspondences for every number from one to twelve.)[49] The numbers associated with the planets are:

Saturn: 3
Jupiter: 4
Mars: 5
Sol: 6
Venus: 7
Mercury: 8
Luna: 9

For example, a Venus talisman would display a heptagram, or seven-pointed star, around the Angel's sigil. A Martian talisman would display a pentagram, or five-pointed star.[50] The letters of the Angel's name are then placed within the angles, or at the points, of the lineal figure.

Later in *Of Magical Ceremonies*, Pseudo-Agrippa explains how to fashion this into a working talisman or lamen. One might use metal appropriate to the planet.[51] Or fresh (bee's-)wax mixed with appropriate herbs, spices (incenses), and color dyes. Or, finally, one can use fresh paper (or virgin parchment) with appropriately colored ink or paints. Its shape may be circular, or multisided according to the number associated with the Angel's star. (Such as a seven-sided lamen for an Angel of Venus, five-sided for Mars, etc.)

Finally, the *Fourth Book* suggests the talisman should be fashioned during a waxing moon when the Angel's star is well-aspected in the Heavens. I have created the following "simple talisman of Nalvage" as an example of this kind of lamen. The central sigil is fashioned from the combined letters of Nalvage's name. Because Nalvage told Dee that he is under the authority of the Archangel Gabriel, I have chosen to place that name into the circumference. Along with it, I have written the Angelical verse "Mightier is Thy Voice than the Manifold Winds" (adapted

An example talisman of Nalvage—with the above sigil of Nalvage in the center, and Nalvage's name in English letters surrounding. In the circumference is the name Gabriel (English characters) and Angelical for "Mightier is Thy Voice than the Manifold Winds" written counterclockwise.

from Key Two), because Nalvage was the one who delivered the Angelical Keys.[52]

Endnotes

1. 1 Corinthians 13:1: "And though I speak with the tongues of men and angels, and have not charity, I am become as a sounding brass or a tinkling cymbal."
2. The forty-nine Tables of *Loagaeth*.
3. Satan, or *haSathan*, translates as "The Accuser." It was common in Dee's time to refer to Satan as "The Enemy."
4. Raphael is here referring to the Heptarchic system of magick, which had been transmitted previously in the journals.
5. See the *Five Books of Mystery*, pp. 259–60. (March 23, 1583.)
6. Here, Kelley adds: "He hath a great thing under his gown." As we shall see, this turns out to be the Holy Book.
7. I interpret this line to mean: "The beginnings of the Universe, and even God Himself, are known by those who have tasted of the Medicine."
8. Verity = Truth.
9. A reference to the Confusion of Tongues at the Tower of Babel—Genesis 11:1–9. Also see the "Angelical Mythos" section of this chapter; the Confusion of Tongues is important to the Angelical mythos.
10. Dee: the Angelic language.
11. "Him that proceedeth" is likely a reference to the Christos (also called the Logos—Word)—who proceeded directly from God. (See John, chapter 1.) Raphael here means that the Angelical language proceeds directly from the Christos. (See chapter 2 of this volume, where *Loagaeth* is described as the language of the God-Christ.)
12. Adam—the first man.
13. Raphael here tells Dee that Adam was fashioned after the form of the Christos—which is very similar to ancient Gnostic belief.
14. See Louis Ginzberg, *Legends of the Bible* (New York: Simon and Schuster, 1956).
15. The first = Adam.
16. *Chavah* is Eve's name in Hebrew.

17 and 18. These brackets appear in the original journals.

19. We shall see, later, that the actual Angelical alphabet has twenty-one letters, divided into three groups of seven.
20. See Agrippa's *Three Books of Occult Philosophy*, Book 1—especially chapters 69–74. I will return to this information at the end of this chapter.
21. The forty-nine Tables of *Loagaeth* each have two sides (front and back), and each side is given a title in Angelical. These titles are included for reference in chapter 2 of this book.
22. As Adam was supposed to have used the Angelicial alphabet in Paradise.
23. For instance, note the letter *Mals*—which resembles the Greek *Omega*.
24. See *John Dee's Five Books of Mystery*, pp. 268–69. Then also see pp. 270–71.
25. See chapter 2, concerning the instructions the Angels gave Dee on writing the "perfected copy" of the Holy Book.
26. One notable exception is Donald Tyson, who figured out this discrepancy over *Pal* in his book *Enochian Magick for Beginners*.

27. Peterson, *John Dee's Five Books of Mystery*, p. 269.
28. Ibid., p. 270.
29. Ibid., p. 271.
30. Ibid., p. 405.
31. See http://themagickalreview.org/enochian/mss/, Sloane 3188, image 29 (f104a–108a).
32. *John Dee's Five Books of Mystery*. Peterson, p. 271.
33. Ibid., p. 306. *prick* = "dot."
34. See chapter 2 of this volume, in which the Angels make several similar "threefold" comments in regards to the First and Forty-Ninth Tables of *Loagaeth*.
35. As Jim Reeds points out in his *Breakthrough in Renaissance Cryptography: A Book Review*, there is likely a direct connection between gematria and sixteenth-century cryptography.
36. A sigil (or signature) is a stylized diagram used to represent an Angel, spirit, or creative force on talismans.
37. See the section "Dee Suspected of Cryptography?" in chapter 3.
38. There are, of course, several Angelical words that do appear to indicate terms such as "second," "third," etc.
39. See the "Angelical Mythos" section of this chapter.
40. See the "Angelical Mythos" section of this chapter, where this quote is given in full.
41. Again, see the "Angelical Mythos" section, where this quote is given in full.
42. See my book *Secrets of the Magickal Grimoires*, chapter 10, for a reference Table of many of these images and their magickal timing.
43. See my book *Secrets of the Magickal Grimoires*, chapter 5, for more information.
44. We see this with such Angelic names as Gabriel (*Gibor El*), the Strength of God, and Raphael *(Rapha El)*, the Healer of God. *Yah* was rare in comparison, but we can see it in obscure names like *Vahaviah* and *Laviah*. The Greek Name of God *On* was also acceptable, as we see in names like *Metatron* and *Sandalphon*.
45. Reference Ginzberg's *Legends of the Bible* for ample descriptions of such Angels.
46. Note the pun between multiplying a number by itself to produce a "magickal square" and then turning that product into an actual magickal "square."
47. See *John Dee's Five Books of Mystery*, where this planetary order is given for the forty-nine good Angels of the *Heptarchia* and the seven Ensigns of Creation. I should note that there are a couple of cases where Dee used Hebrew names to generate magickal squares, and there he used the same Chaldean ordering used by Agrippa in Book Two, chap. 27.
48. This leftward-then-rightward pattern is a Qabalistic convention called "As the Ox Plows." It is also used to generate the names of the *Shem haMephoresh* from the three verses of Exodus. I have not discovered the purpose behind this convention.
49. Agrippa's *Second Book of Occult Philosophy*, chapters 4–15, the *Scales of Numbers*.
50. For Angels of the zodiac, use the number of the planet that rules the zodiacal sign.
51. Or, for zodiacal Angels, use the metal appropriate to the planet that rules the zodiacal sign.
52. I also find this verse significant because Gabriel himself was the Angel of the Annunciation.

An Angelical Psalter

The Angelical Psalter is intended mainly for practical use of the Keys, so that one can recite them as proper invocations. Each Key is presented in two columns: the first, or left-hand, column contains the English translation of the Key—which I generally refer to as a *Call*. It is divided and formatted so as to line up with the Angelical on the right. I have fully modernized the punctuation—which you can compare with Dee's Early Modern English versions in the Angelical Keys Cross-Reference in volume II.[1]

The second, or right-hand, column contains the Angelical version of the Key, complete with phonetic pronunciations. Angelical words, as Dee recorded them, are in regular type. My phonetic pronunciation notes are in *italics* underneath. Note that I have used the same punctuation throughout this column as you see in the left-hand column. This punctuation makes the forty-eight Keys far easier to recite with proper inflection and tone.

Also, remember while reading the Keys in this Psalter that the number of each Key is always one less than the number of its Table in *Loagaeth*. The first Key is used to open the *second* Table, the second Key opens the *third* Table—all the way to Key Forty-eight, which opens the *forty-ninth* Table.

Pronunciation Key

Throughout this Psalter, I have included pronunciation notes intended to be intuitive to the modern reader. A quick study of the following key should be enough to read any word in the Lexicon or the Angelical Psalter. Also refer to page 95 in volume II of this work, where I explain this pronunciation key in greater depth.

Vowels

Short vowels are mostly represented by single letters, while I have extended the long vowels to two letters:

Phonetic Sound	*Notation*
a –long (*cake, day*)	ay
a –short (*bat, cat*)	a
e –long (*beet, seat*)	ee
e –short (*bed, wed*)	e
i –long (*bite, kite*)	ii
i –short (*bit, sit*)	i
o –long (*boat, slope*)	oh
o –short (*stop, father*)	o, ah
u –long (*boot, blue*)	oo
u –short (*but, cup*)	u

Note: There are some cases where an *a* falls at the end of a word. This likely indicates something between a long and short *a*—or a *schwa*. In such cases, I have simply left a single *a* in my pronunciation. It can be treated as a short *a*, but it is more akin to a *schwa* sound.

Consonants

If consonants are written together (as in, *br*, *cr*, *gr*, *st*, *th*, *tr*), simply pronounce the combined sound as you would in present-day English (*break*, *crate*, *grab*, *start*, and so forth). Otherwise, standard consonant sounds are indicated by the following:

Phonetic Sound	*Notation*
b (branch, blurb)	b
d (dog, during)	d
f (far, fork)	f
g (gap, gourd)	g
h (half, heavy)	h
j (jump, giant, bludgeon)	j
k (kind, can)	k
l (large, loud)	l
m (many, move)	m
n (north, never)	n
p (pace, pardon)	p
r (rain, banner)	r, er
s (serve, circle)	s
t (test, tax)	t
w (water, wind)	w
x (exit, except)	ks
y (yellow, your)	y
z (zoom, zebra)	z

"Long Consonants"

There are many cases where Dee indicated a consonant standing alone in a syllable. At these times, the letter does not make its usual consonant sound. Instead, the syllable is pronounced the same as the English name of the consonant. I have dubbed these "long consonants," and I represent their sounds as follows:

Phonetic Sound	*Notation*
d	dee
f	ef
g	jee
j	jay
l	el
m	em
n	en
p	pee
q	kwah
r	ur
s	es
t	tee
y	wii
z	zohd, zed

Digraphs and Diphthongs

The digraphs and diphthongs are fairly standard in modern English::

Phonetic Sound	*Notation*
ch (church, witch)	ch
ch (ache, chrome)	kh
ou, ow (out, town)	ow
oi, oy (oil, boy)	oy
qu (queen, quick)	kw
sh (shine, wish)	sh
ph (phone, philosophy)	f
th (that, whither, thorn)[2]	th

Also note: There are a few instances where the letters *sg* occur together in Angelical words—such as in *caosg* or *vorsg*. In these cases, Dee does not indicate that the *g* sound should stand alone as its own syllable. Thus, I find it likely it is intended to combine with the *s* to make a kind of *zh* (or hard *sh*) sound—as we hear in English words like *measure, pleasure,* and *treasure*. I have indicated this sound in the Psalter and Lexicon with the digraph *zh*.

Accented Syllables

I have indicated accents in my pronunciations by writing the related syllable in ALL CAPS. These accents are based on Dee's notations, and I have avoided adding accents to words where Dee left no clues. The reader may accent these words where they sound most natural.

Calls in English

Call One:

"I reign over you," sayeth the God of Justice, "in power exalted above

the firmaments of wrath: in whose hands the Sun is as

a sword, and the Moon a through-thrusting fire: Which

measureth your garments in the midst of my vestures and

trussed you together as the palms of my hands. Whose seats

I garnished with the fire of gathering, and beautified your garments

with admiration. To whom I made a law to govern the Holy Ones,

and delivered you a rod (with) the ark of knowledge. Moreover,

you lifted up your voices and swore obedience and faith to Him

that liveth and triumpheth; whose beginning is not, nor end cannot be;

which shineth as a flame in the midst of your palace,

and reigneth amongst you as the balance of righteousness and

truth (truth)." Move, therefore, and

show yourselves. Open the mysteries of your creation. Be friendly unto me.

For, I am a servant of the same your God; the true worshiper of the Highest.

Angelical Key

Key of the Second Table

"Ol sonf vorsg," goho Iad Balt, "lansh
"ohl sonv vorzh," goh-HOH yad balt, "lonsh

calz vonpho: Sobra z-ol ror i ta
kalz von-foh. SOB-ray zohd-OL ror ii tay

nazpsad, graa ta malprg; Ds
nayz-pee-sad, gray tay mal-purj: dee-es

holq qaa nothoa zimz, od
HOL-kwah kwah-AY-ay noth-OH-a zimz, ohd

commah ta nobloh zien. Soba thil
KOM-ah tay noh-bloh zeen. SOH-bay thil

gnonp prge aldi ds urbs oboleh
non-pee purj AL-dii dee-es yurbs OB-oh-lay

grsam. Casarm ohorela caba pir,
gur-sam. kay-SARM oh-hor-EL-a ka-BA per,

ds zonrensg cab erm iadnah. Pilah,
dee-es zon-renj kab erm yad-nah. pee-ii-lah,

farzm znrza adna gono iadpil
farz-em snur-za ad-nah gon-oh ii-AD-pil

ds hom toh; soba ipam, ul ipamis;
dee-es hom toh: SOH-bay ip-am, yewl ip-am-is;

ds loholo vep zomdux poamal,
dee-es LOH-hoh-loh vep zom-dooks poh-mal,

od bogpa aai ta piap baltle od
ohd bog-pa ay-AY-ii tay pii-ap bal-tayl ohd

vaoan (vooan)." Zacar, ca, od
vay-oh-AN (voo-AN)." ZAY-kayr, see-ay, ohd

zamran. Odo cicle qaa. Zorge.
zam-ran. od-oh sii-kayl kwah-AY-ay. zorj.

Lap, zirdo noco mad; hoath Iaida.
lap, zir-DOH NOH-kwoh mad; hohth jay-II-da.

Call Two

Can the wings of the winds understand your voices of wonder,

O you the Second of the First, whom the burning flames have framed within

the depths of my jaws; whom I have prepared as

cups for a wedding, or as the flowers

in their beauty for the chamber of righteousness. Stronger are your feet than the barren stone,

and mightier are your voices than the manifold winds. For,

you are become a building such as is not but in the mind of

the All Powerful. "Arise," sayeth the First. Move

therefore unto His servants. Show yourselves in power

and make me a strong seething. For, I am of Him that liveth forever.

Key of the Third Table

Adgt upaah zong om faaip sald,
ajt yew-pay-ah zong om fay-AY-ip sald,

viiv L, sobam ialpurg izazaz
vii-iv el, SOH-bam YAL-purj ii-zay-zaz

piadph; casarma abramg ta
pii-AD-ef; kay-SAR-ma ay-BRAY-mig tay

talho paracleda, qta lorslq
tal-ho par-AK-lee-da, kwah-tay lors-el-kwah

turbs ooge baltoh. Givi chis lusd orri,
turbs oh-oj bal-toh. jiv-ii kiis lus-dee or-ii,

od micalp chis bia ozongon. Lap,
ohd mii-KALP kiis bii-a OH-zohn-gon. lap,

noan trof cors tage oq manin
noh-AN trof kors tayj oh-kwah man-in

Iaidon. "Torzu," gohel. Zacar
jay-II-don. "tor-ZOO," GOH-hel, ZAY-kayr

ca cnoqod. Zamran micalzo,
see-ay see-NOH-kwod. zam-ran mii-KAYL-zoh,

od ozazm urelp. Lap, zir Ioiad.
ohd oz-az-em yer-elp. lap, zer joh-JAD

Call Three

"Behold," sayeth your God. "I am a Circle

on whose hands stand 12 Kingdoms. Six are the seats of

living breath; the rest are as sharp sickles

or the horns of death; wherein the creatures of the earth

are and are not except by mine own hand; which

sleep and shall rise. In the first I made you stewards

and placed you in 12 seats of government, giving unto

every one of you power successively over 456, the true ages

of time, to the intent that from the highest vessels and the corners

of your governments you might work my power; pouring down

the fires of life and increase upon the earth continually. Thus, you are become the skirts of

justice and truth (truth)."

In the Name of the same your God, lift up, I say,

yourselves. Behold, His mercies flourish and

Key of the Fourth Table

"Micma," goho piad, "Zir comselh
"mik-ma," goh-HOH pii-AD, "zer KOM-sel

azien biab oslondoh. Norz chis othil
az-EEN bii-ab os-LON-doh. norz kiis oh-THIL

gigipah; undl chis tapuin
jij-ii-pah; und-el kiis TAY-pew-in

qmospleh teloch; quiin toltorg
kwah-mos-play tee-LOCH; kwii-in tol-TORJ

chis ichisge m ozien; dst
kiis jay-KIIS-jee em oh-ZEEN; dee-es-tee

brgda od torzul. Ili eol balzarg
burj-da ohd tor-ZOOL. Il-lii ee-OHL bal-zarj

od aala thilnos netaab, dluga
ohd AY-ay-la thil-nos nee-TAY-ab. dee-LOO-ga

vomzarg lonsa capmiali vors cla, homil
vom-sarj lon-sha kap-mii-AY-lii vorz kla, hom-il

cocasb, fafen izizop od miinoag
KOH-kasb, fay-fen iz-is-op ohd mii-ii-noh-ayg

de gnetaab vaun nanaeel; panpir
dee nee-TAY-ab von nay-NAY-ee-el; pan-per

malpirgi caosg pild. Noan unalah
mal-per-jii kay-OZH pild. noh-AN un-al-ah

balt odvaoan (odvooan).
"balt ohd-vay-oh-AN (ohd-voo-AN)."

Dooiap mad, goholor, gohus,
doh-OH-ii-ap mad, goh-HOH-lor, goh-US,

amiran. Micma, iehusoz cacacom od
am-ir-an. mik-ma, jay-US-os kay-SAY-som ohd

Call Three continued

Name is become mighty amongst us.

In whom we say, move,

descend and apply yourselves unto us as partakers of

the secret wisdom of your creation.

Key of the Fourth Table continued

dooain	noar	micaolz	aaiom.
doh-OH-ay-in	*noh-ar*	*mii-KAY-ohlz*	*ay-AY-om.*

Casarmg	gohia,	z-acar,
kay-SAR-mij	*goh-HII-a,*	*ZOHD-ay-kayr,*

uniglag	od	imvamar	pugo	plapli
yew-nii-glag	*ohd*	*im-vay-mar*	*pug-oh*	*play-plii*

ananael	qaan.
an-AN-ee-el	*kwah-AY-an.*

Call Four

"I have set my feet in the south and have looked about me

saying, Are not the Thunders of Increase numbered

33 which reign in the Second Angle; under whom

I have placed 9639 whom none hath yet numbered

but One. In whom the second beginning of things are

and wax strong; which also successively are

the number of time; and their powers are as the first 456.

Arise you sons of pleasure and visit the earth,

for I am the Lord your God which is and liveth."

In the Name of the Creator, move

and show yourselves as pleasant deliverers; that you may praise Him amongst

the sons of men.

Key of the Fifth Table

"Othil lasdi babage od dorpha
"oh-THIL las-dii bay-BAY-jee ohd dorf-fa

gohol, gchisge avavago cormp
goh-HOHL, jee-KIIS-jee av-AY-vay-go kormf

pd dsonf vivdiv; casarmi
pee-dee dee-sonv viv-DII-vee; kay-SAR-mij

oali mapm, sobam ag cormpo
OH-ay-lii map-em, SOH-bam ag korm-FOH

crpl. Casarmg croodzi chis
krip-el. key-SAR-mij kroh-OD-zii kiis

odugeg; dst capimali chis
ohd-yew-JEJ; dee-es-tee kay-pii-MAY-lii kiis

capimaon; odlonshin chis talo cla.
kap-ii-MAY-on; ohd-lon-shin kiis tay-el-loh kla.

Torgu norquasahi od fcaosga,
tor-GOO nor-kway-SAY-hii ohd ef-kay-OS-ga,

bagle zirenaiad dsi odapila."
BAY-gayl zii-er-NAY-ad dee-sii ohd-ap-ii-la."

Dooaip qaal, z-acar
doh-OH-ay-ip kwah-AY-el, ZOHD-ay-kayr

odzamran obelisong; restil aaf
ohd-zam-ran oh-bel-is-ong; rest-el ay-AF

normolap.
nor-moh-lap.

Call Five

"The Mighty Sounds have entered into the third Angle and are become

as olives in the olive mount looking with gladness upon the earth and

dwelling within the brightness of the heavens as continual comforters, unto whom

I have fastened pillars of gladness 19, and gave them

vessels to water the earth with Her creatures; and

they are the brothers of the First and Second; and the beginning of

their own seats which are garnished with continually burning lamps 69636; whose

numbers are as the first, the ends, and

the contents of time." Therefore, come you and obey

your creation. Visit us in peace and comfort.

Conclude us as receivers of your mysteries. For why? Our Lord and Master

is all one.

Key of the Sixth Table

"Sapah zimii duiv od noas
"SAY-fah ZII-mii DOO-iv ohd noh-as

taqanis adroch dorphal caosg, od
tay-kway-nis ad-roch dor-fal kay-OZH, ohd

faonts piripsol tablior, casarm
fay-onts per-IP-sol TAY-blii-or, kay-SARM

amipzi nazarth af, od dlugar
ay-mip-zii nay-zarth af, ohd dee-LOO-gar

zizop z-lida caosgi toltorgi; od
ziz-op zohd-lid-a kay-OZH-ii tol-TOR-jii; ohd

z-chis esiasch L taviv; od iaod
zohd-kiis ee-sii-ash el tay-viv; ohd YAY-ohd

thild ds hubar peral; soba
thild dee-es hoo-BAR pee-AR-al; SOH-bay

cormfa chista la, uls, od
korm-FA kiis-tay lah, yewls, ohd

qcocasb." Ca, niis od darbs
kwah-KOH-kasb." see-ay, nii-IS ohd darbs

qaas. Fetharzi od bliora.
kwah-AY-as. feth-AR-zii ohd blii-OH-ra.

Iaial ednas cicles. Bagle? Geiad
jay-yal ed-nas sii-kayls. BAY-gayl? jej-AYD

il.
ii-el.

Call Six

The spirits of the fourth Angle are nine, mighty in the Firmaments of Water;

whom the First hath planted a torment to the wicked and a garland to

the Righteous; giving unto them fiery darts to van the earth

and 7699 continual workmen whose courses visit with comfort

the earth; and are in government and continuance

as the second and the third. Wherefore, hearken unto my voice. I have talked of you

and I move you in power and presence, whose works

shall be a song of honor and praise of your God

in your creation.

Key of the Seventh Table

Gah sdiv chis em, micalzo pilzin;
jah es-DII-vee kiis em, mii-KAYL-zoh pil-zin;

sobam el harg mir babalon od obloc
SOH-bam el harg mir bay-BAY-lon ohd ob-lok

samvelg; dlugar malpurg arcaosgi,
sam-velj; dee-LOO-gar mal-purj ar-kay-OZH-ii,

od acam canal sobolzar fbliard
ohd ay-KAM san-al soh-BOL-zar ef-blii-ard

caosgi; odchis anetab od miam
kay-OZH-ii; ohd-kiis ay-NEE-tayb ohd mii-AM

taviv od d. Darsar, solpeth bien. Brita,
tay-viv ohd dee. dar-sar, sol-peth bii-en. brit-a,

od zacam gmicalzo, sobhaath
ohd ZAY-kam jee-mii-KAYL-zoh, sob-HAY-ath

trian luiahe odecrin mad
TRII-an loo-JAY-hee oh-dee-KRIN mad

qaaon.
kwah-AY-ay-on.

Call Seven

The east is a house of virgins

singing praises amongst the flames of the First Glory; wherein

the Lord hath opened His Mouth, and they become 28

living dwellings in whom the strength of men rejoiceth

and they are appareled with ornaments of brightness such as work wonders

on all creatures. Whose kingdoms and continuance

are as the Third and Fourth; strong towers and

places of comfort, the seats of mercy and continuance.

O you servants of mercy, move, appear,

sing praises unto the Creator, and

be mighty amongst us. For

to this remembrance is given power and our strength

waxeth strong in our Comforter.

Key of the Eighth Table

Raas isalman paradiz
ray-as ii-SAYL-man pay-ray-DII-zohd

oecrimi aao ialpirgah; quiin
oh-EE-kriim-ii ay-ay-OH YAL-pur-jah; kwii-in

Enay butmon, od inoas ni
en-ay but-mon, ohd in-OH-as nii

paradial casarmg ugear chirlan;
pay-ray-DII-al kay-SAR-mij yew-JEE-ar kir-lan;

od zonac luciftian corsta vaulzirn
ohd zoh-nak loo-sif-TII-an kors-tay VOL-zern

tolhami. Soba londoh odmiam
tol-HAY-mii. SOH-bay lon-DOH ohd-MII-am

chistad odes; umadea od
kiis-tad oh-DES; yew-MAY-dee-a ohd

pibliar; othilrit odmiam.
pib-lii-AR; oh-THIL-rit ohd-MII-am.

Cnoquol rit, z-acar, zamran,
see-NOH-kwol rit, ZOHD-ay-kayr, zam-ran,

oecrimi qadah, od
oh-EE-kriim-ii kwah-AY-dah, ohd

omicaolz aaiom. Bagle
oh-mii-KAY-ohl-zohd. ay-AY-om. BAY-gayl

papnor idlugam lonshi, od umplif
pap-nor id-LOO-gam lon-shii, ohd um-plif

ugegi bigliad.
yew-JEE-jii big-lii-ad.

Call Eight

"The midday the first is as the third Heaven made of hyacinth pillars

26; in whom the Elders are become strong;

which I have prepared for my own righteousness," sayeth the Lord,

"Whose long continuance shall be bucklers to

the stooping dragons and like unto the harvest of a widow.

How many are there, which remain in the glory of the earth,

which are and shall not see death until

this house fall and the dragon

sink." Come away, for the Thunders

have spoken. Come away, for the crowns of

the Temple, and the coat of Him that is, was, and shall be Crowned,

are divided. Come, appear to the terror of the earth;

and to our comfort; and of such as are prepared.

Key of the Ninth Table

"Bazemlo ita piripson oln nazavabh
"bas-em-loh ii-tay per-IP-son ohln nay-zay-VAB

ox; casarmg uran chis ugeg;
oks; kay-SAR-mij yew-RAN kiis yew-JEJ;

dsabramg baltoha," gohoiad,
dee-say-bray-mig bal-toh-ha," goh-HOH-ii-ad,

"Solamian trian talolcis
"soh-LAY-mii-an TRII-an tay-LOL-sis

abaivonin od aziagiar rior.
ay-bay-II-voh-nin ohd ay-zii-AY-jii-er rii-or,

Irgilchisda, dspaaox busd caosgo,
ir-jil-KIIS-da, dee-SAY-ay-oks buzd kay-OS-go,

dschis odipuran teloah cacrg
dee-es-kiis ohd-II-pew-ran TEE-loh-ah KAY-kurg

oisalman loncho od vovina
oh-ii-SAYL-man lon-koh ohd voh-VII-na

carbaf." Niiso, bagle avavago
kar-baf." nii-II-soh, BAY-gayl av-AY-vay-go

gohon. Niiso, bagle momao
goh-HON. nii-II-soh, BAY-gayl MOH-may-oh

siaion, od mabza iadoiasmomar,
sii-AY-ii-on, ohd MAB-za jad-oh-JAS-moh-mar,

poilp. Niis, zamran ciaofi caosgo;
poylp. nii-IS, zam-ran sii-ay-oh-fii kay-OS-go;

od bliors; od corsi ta abramig.
ohd blii-ORS; ohd kor-sii tay ay-BRAY-mig.

Call Nine

A mighty guard of fire with two-edged swords flaming

(which have vials 8 of wrath

for two times and a half; whose wings

are of wormwood and of the marrow of salt), have settled

their feet in the west and are measured

with their ministers 9996. These gather up

the moss of the earth as the rich man doth his treasure.

Cursed are they whose iniquities they are.

In their eyes are millstones greater than

the earth, and from their mouths run seas of

blood. Their heads are covered with

diamond and upon their hands are

marble sleeves. Happy is he on whom

they frown not. For why? The God of Righteousness rejoiceth in them.

Come away, and not your vials. For

the time is such as requireth comfort.

Key of the Tenth Table

Micaoli bransg prgel napta ialpor
mii-KAY-oh-lii branzh pur-jel nap-ta YAL-por

(dsbrin efafafe p vonpho
(dee-es-brin ee-FAY-fay-fee pee von-foh

olani od obza; sobca upaah
oh-el-AY-nii ohd ob-za; SOB-kay yew-pay-ah

chis tatan od tranan balye), alar
kiis tay-tan ohd tray-nan bay-lii-ee), AY-lar

lusda soboln od chisholq
lus-da soh-bohln ohd KIIS-hohl-kwa

cnoqvodi cial. Unal aldon
see-noh-KWOH-dii sii-al. yew-NAL AL-don

mom caosgo ta lasollor gnay limlal.
mom kay-OS-go tay las-OHL-or nay lim-lal.

Amma chiis sobca madrid z-chis.
am-a kiis SOB-kay MAY-drid zohd-kiis.

Ooanoan chis aviny drilpi
oh-oh-AY-noh-an kiis ay-VII-nee dril-pii

caosgin, od butmoni parm zumvi
kay-OS-jin, ohd but-moh-nii parm zum-vii

cnila. Dazis ethamz
see-NII-la. daz-IS ee-THAM-zohd

achildao, od mirc ozol chis
ay-KIL-day-oh, ohd mirk oh-ZOHL kiis

pidiai collal. Ulcinin asobam
pii-dii-ay-ii kol-lal. yewl-SII-nin ay-SOH-bam

ucim. Bagle? Iadbaltoh chirlan par.
yew-sim. BAY-gayl? ii-ad-BAL-toh kir-lan par.

Niiso, od ip ofafafe. Bagle
nii-II-soh, ohd ip oh-FAY-fay-fee. BAY-gayl

acocasb icorsca unig blior.
ay-KOH-kasb ii-KORS-kay yew-nig blii-OR.

Call Ten

The Thunders of Judgment and Wrath are numbered and harbored in the north

in the likeness of an oak whose branches

are 22 nests of lamentation and weeping

laid up for the earth; which

burn night and day and vomit out

the heads of scorpions and live sulfur mingled with

poison. These be the thunders that 5678

times in the 24th part of a moment roar with a hundred mighty

earthquakes, and a thousand times as many

surges, which rest not neither know any

(long) time here. One rock

bringeth forth 1000 even as the heart of man

doth his thoughts. Woe, woe, woe

woe, woe, woe, yea, woe

be to the earth. For her iniquity is, was,

and shall be great. Come away, but not your noises.

Key of the Eleventh Table

Coraxo chis cormp od blans lucal
koh-RAYKS-oh kiis kormf ohd blanz loo-kal

aziazor paeb soba lilonon
ay-ZII-ay-zor pay-eb SOH-bay lii-loh-non

chis op virq eophan od raclir
kiis oh-pee vir-kwah ee-oh-fan ohd ray-kler

maasi bagle caosgi; ds
may-ay-sii BAY-gayl kay-OZH-ii; dee-es

ialpon dosig od basgim od oxex
YAL-pon doh-sig ohd bas-jim ohd oks-eks

dazis siatris od salbrox cinxir
daz-IS sii-ay-TRIS ohd sal-broks sinks-ir

faboan. Unalchis const ds daox
fay-boh-an. yew-nal-kiis konst dee-es day-oks

cocasg ol oanio yor torb vohim
KOH-kazh oh-el oh-AY-nii-oh yor torb VOH-im

gizyax, od matb cocasg plosi
jiz-wii-aks, ohd may-teb KOH-kazh ploh-sii

molui, ds pageip larag om droln
mol-vii, dee-es pay-jee-ip lay-rag om drohln

(matorb) cocasb emna. Lpatralx
(may-torb) KOH-kasb em-na. el-PAY-tralks

yolci matb nomig monons olora
yol-sii may-teb noh-mig moh-nons oh-loh-ra

gnay angelard. Ohio ohio ohio
nay an-jee-lard. oh-hii-oh oh-hii-oh oh-hii-oh

ohio ohio ohio, noib, ohio
oh-hii-oh oh-hii-oh oh-hii-oh, noh-ib, oh-hii-oh

caosgon, bagle madrid i, zirop,
kay-OS-gon, BAY-gayl MAY-drid ii, zii-ROP

chiso drilpa. Niiso, crip ip nidali.
kiis-oh dril-pa. nii-II-soh, krip ip nii-day-lii.

Call Eleven

The Mighty Seat groaned and they were 5

Thunders which flew into the east, and

the Eagle spake and cried with a loud voice, "Come away!"

And they gathered themselves together and became the house of death,

of whom it is measured, and it is as they are

whose number is 31. Come away, for

I have prepared for you. Move, therefore, and

show yourselves. Open the mysteries of your creation. Be friendly unto me.

For, I am a servant of the same your God; the true worshiper of the Highest.

Key of the Twelfth Table

Oxiayal holdo od zirom o
oks-AY-al hol-doh ohd zer-OM oh

coraxo ds zildar raasy, od
koh-RAYKS-oh dee-es zil-dar ray-ay-see, ohd

vabzir camliax od bahal, "Niiso!"
vab-zer kam-lii-aks ohd BAY-hal, "nii-II-soh!"

Od aldon od noas salman teloch,
ohd AL-don ohd noh-as SAYL-man tee-LOCH,

casarman holq, od ti ta z-chis
kay-SAR-man HOL-kwah, ohd tii tay zohd-kiis

soba cormf iga. Niisa, bagle
SOH-bay kormf ii-ga. nii-II-sa, BAY-gayl

abramg noncp. Zacar, ca, od
ay-BRAY-mig non-sef. ZAY-kayr, see-ay, ohd

zamran. Odo cicle qaa. Zorge.
zam-ran. od-oh sii-kayl kwah-AY-ay. zorj.

Lap, zirdo noco mad; hoath Iaida.
lap, zir-DOH NOH-kwoh mad; hohth jay-II-da.

Call Twelve

Oh you that reign in the south and are 28

the lanterns of sorrow, bind up your girdles and

visit us. Bring down your train 3663 that the Lord may be magnified

whose name amongst you is wrath.

Move, I say, and show yourselves. Open

the mysteries of your creation. Be friendly unto me. For, I am

a servant of the same your God; the true worshiper of the Highest.

Call Thirteen

O you swords of the south, which have 42

eyes to stir up wrath of sin,

making men drunken which are empty.

Behold the promise of God and His power which

is called amongst you a bitter sting. Move and show yourselves.

Open the mysteries of your creation. Be friendly unto me. For, I am

a servant of the same your God; the true worshiper of the Highest.

Key of the Thirteenth Table

Nonci dsonf babage od chis ob
non-sii dee-sonv bay-BAY-jee ohd kiis ob

hubaio tibibp, allar atraah od
hoo-BAY-ii-oh tib-ib-ip, AL-lar ay-tray-ah ohd

ef. Drix fafen mian ar enay ovof
ef. driks fay-fen mii-AN ar en-ay oh-vof

soba dooain aai ivonph.
SOH-bay doh-OH-ay-in ay-AY-ii ii-VONV.

Zacar, gohus, od zamran. Odo
ZAY-kayr, goh-US, ohd zam-ran. od-oh

cicle qaa. Zorge. Lap, zirdo
sii-kayl kwah-AY-ay. zorj. lap, zir-DOH

noco mad; hoath Iaida.
NOH-kwoh mad; hohth jay-II-da.

Key of the Fourteenth Table

Napeai babagen, dsbrin ux
nay-pee-ay bay-BAY-jen, dee-es-brin yewks

ooaona lring vonph doalim,
oh-oh-AY-oh-na el-ring vonv doh-ay-lim,

eolis ollog orsba dschis affa,
ee-OH-lis ohl-log ors-ba dee-es-kiis af-fa,

micma isro mad od lonshitox ds
mik-ma iz-roh mad ohd lon-shii-toks dee-es

iumd aai grosb. Zacar od zamran.
jay-umd ay-AY-ii grozb. ZAY-kayr ohd zam-ran.

Odo cicle qaa. Zorge. Lap, zirdo
od-oh sii-kayl kwah-AY-ay. zorj. lap, zir-DOH

noco mad; hoath Iaida.
NOH-kwoh mad; hohth jay-II-da.

Call Fourteen

O you sons of fury, the daughters of the just, which

sit upon 24 seats, vexing all creatures of the earth

with age, which have under you 1636; Behold

the voice of God, promise of him which is called

amongst you fury (or extreme justice). Move and show yourselves. Open

the mysteries of your creation. Be friendly unto me. For, I am

a servant of the same your God; the true worshiper of the Highest.

Call Fifteen

O thou the Governor of the First Flame, under whose

wings are 6739 which weave

the earth with dryness, which knowest

the great name Righteousness and the seal of

honor. Move and show yourselves. Open

the mysteries of your creation. Be friendly unto me. For, I am

a servant of the same your God; the true worshiper of the Highest.

Key of the Fifteenth Table

Noromi bagie, pasbs oiad, ds
noh-ROM-ii bag-EE, pas-bes oh-ii-AD, dee-es

trint mirc ol thil, dods tolham caosgo
trint mirk oh-el thil, dods tol-HAYM kay-OS-go

homin, dsbrin oroch quar; micma
hom-in, dee-es-brin oh-ROK kwar; mik-ma

bial oiad, aisro tox dsium
bii-al oh-ii-AD, ay-ii-sroh toks dee-sii-um

aai baltim. Zacar od zamran. Odo
ay-AY-ii bal-tim. ZAY-kayr ohd zam-ran. od-oh

cicle qaa. Zorge. Lap, zirdo
sii-kayl kwah-AY-ay. zorj. lap, zir-DOH

noco mad; hoath Iaida.
NOH-kwoh mad; hohth jay-II-da.

Key of the Sixteenth Table

Yls tabaan lialprt, casarman
yils tay-BAY-an el-YAL-purt, kay-SAR-man

upaahi chis darg dsoado
yew-pay-hii kiis darj dee-soh-ay-doh

caosgi orscor, ds omax
kay-OZH-ii ors-kor, dee-es oh-MAKS

monasci baeovib od emetgis
mon-ay-sii bee-oh-vib ohd em-et-jis

iaiadix. Zacar od zamran. Odo
yay-II-ad-iks. ZAY-kayr ohd zam-ran. od-oh

cicle qaa. Zorge. Lap, zirdo
sii-kayl kwah-AY-ay. zorj. lap, zir-DOH

noco mad; hoath Iaida.
NOH-kwoh mad; hohth jay-II-da.

Call Sixteen

O thou of the Second Flame, the house of justice which

has thy beginning in glory and shalt comfort the just;

which walkest upon the earth with feet 8763 that understand

and separate creatures; Great art thou in the God of Stretch Forth and Conquer.

Move and show yourselves. Open the mysteries of

your creation. Be friendly unto me. For, I am a servant of

the same your God; the true worshiper of the Highest.

Call Seventeen

O thou whose wings are

thorns to stir up vexation, and hast 7336

lamps living going before thee; whose God

is Wrath in Anger. Gird up thy loins and hearken.

Move and show yourselves. Open the mysteries of

your creation. Be friendly unto me. For, I am a servant of

the same your God; the true worshiper of the Highest.

Key of the Seventeenth Table

Yls vivialprt, salman balt ds
yils viv-ii-AL-purt, SAYL-man balt dee-ess

acroodzi busd od bliorax balit;
ak-roh-OD-zii buzd ohd blii-OH-raks bal-it;

dsinsi caosg lusdan emod dsom
dee-sin-sii kay-OZH lus-dan ee-mod dee-som

od tliob; Drilpa geh yls madzilodarp.
ohd tlii-ob; dril-pa jey yils mad-ZII-loh-darp.

Zacar od zamran. Odo cicle
ZAY-kayr ohd zam-ran. od-oh sii-kayl

qaa. Zorge. Lap, zirdo noco
kwah-AY-ay. zorj. lap, zir-DOH NOH-kwoh

mad; hoath Iaida.
mad; hohth jay-II-da.

Key of the Eighteenth Table

Yls dialprt, soba upaah chis
yils dii-AL-purt, SOH-bay yew-pay-ah kiis

nanba zixlay dodsih, odbrint taxs
nan-ba ziks-lay dod-sih, ohd-brint taks-is

hubaro tastax ylsi; sobaiad
hoo-BAY-roh tas-taks yil-sii; soh-BAY-ad

ivonpovnph. Aldon daxil od toatar.
ii-VON-foh-unv. AL-don daks-il ohd toh-AY-tar.

Zacar od zamran. Odo cicle
ZAY-kayr ohd zam-ran. od-oh sii-kayl

qaa. Zorge. Lap, zirdo noco
kwah-AY-ay. zorj. lap, zir-DOH NOH-kwoh

mad; hoath Iaida.
mad; hohth jay-II-da.

Call Eighteen

O thou mighty Light and Burning Flame of comfort,

which openest the glory of God to the center

of the earth. In whom the secrets of truth 6332

have their abiding, which is called

in thy kingdom Joy, and

not to be measured. Be thou a window of comfort unto me.

Move and show yourselves. Open the mysteries of

your creation. Be friendly unto me. For, I am a servant of

the same your God; the true worshiper of the Highest.

Key of the Nineteenth Table

Yls micalzo ialpirt ialprg bliors,
yils mii-KAYL-zoh YAL-pert YAL-purj blii-ORS,

ds odo busdir oiad ovoars
dee-es od-oh buz-der oh-ii-AD oh-voh-ars

caosgo. Casarmg laiad eran
kay-OS-go. kay-SAR-mij lay-II-ad ee-RAN

brints casasam, ds iumd
brints kay-SAY-sam, dee-es jay-umd

aqlo adohi moz, od
AY-kwah-loh ay-DOH-hii moz, ohd

maoffas. Bolp comobliort pambt.
may-AHF-fas. bulp koh-moh-blii-ort pamt.

Zacar od zamran. Odo cicle
ZAY-kayr ohd zam-ran. od-oh sii-kayl

qaa. Zorge. Lap, zirdo noco
kwah-AY-ay. zorj. lap, zir-DOH NOH-kwoh

mad; hoath Iaida.
mad; hohth jay-II-da.

The Call of the Aethyrs

O you heavens which dwell [in the --- *Aethyr*]

are mighty in the Parts of the Earth, and

execute the judgment of the Highest. To you

it is said, Behold the face of your God,

the beginning of comfort; whose eyes

are the brightness of the heavens; which provided

you for the government of the earth, and her

unspeakable variety; furnishing you

with a power (of) understanding to dispose all things according to

the providence of Him that sitteth upon the Holy Throne; and rose up

in the beginning saying, "The earth,

let her be governed by her parts, and let there be

division in her, that the glory of her may be

always drunken and vexed in itself.

Her course, let it run with the heavens, and as

a handmaid let her serve them. One season, let it confound

Key of Tables Twenty to Forty-Nine

Madriiax dspraf [---]
MAY-drii-yaks dee-es-praf [---]

chismicaolz saanir caosgo, od
kiis-mii-KAY-ohlz say-AY-ner kay-OS-go, ohd

fisis balzizras Iaida. Nonca
FIS-iis bal-zii-sras jay-II-da. non-sa

gohulim, micma adoian mad,
goh-HOO-lim, mik-ma ay-doh-II-an mad,

iaod bliorb; sabaooaona
YAY-ohd blii-ORB; say-bay-oh-oh-AY-oh-na

chis luciftias piripsol; ds abraassa
kiis loo-SIF-tii-as per-IP-sol; dee-es ab-RAY-sa

noncf netaaib caosgi, od tilb
non-sef nee-TAY-ay-ib kay-OZH-ii, ohd tilb

adphaht damploz; tooat noncf
ad-fot DAM-ploz; toh-OH-at non-sef

gmicalzoma lrasd tofglo marb
jee-mii-KAYL-zoh-ma el-RAZD TOF-gloh marb

yarry Idoigo; od torzulp
YAR-ee ii-dee-oy-go; ohd tor-ZOOLP

iaodaf gohol, "Caosga,
YAY-oh-daf goh-HOHL, "kay-OS-ga,

tabaord saanir, od christeos
tay-BAY-ord say-AY-ner, ohd kris-TEE-os

yrpoil tiobl, busdirtilb noaln
yur-POY-il tii-AHB-el, buz-der-tilb noh-aln

paid orsba od dodrmni zilna.
pay-id ors-ba ohd dod-rum-nii zil-na.

Elzaptilb, parmgi piripsax, od ta
el-ZAP-tilb, parm-jii per-IP-saks, ohd tay

qurlst booapis. Lnibm, oucho
kurlst boh-OH-ay-pis. el-nib-em, oh-yew-choh

another, and let there be no creature upon

or within her the same. All her members, let them differ in

their qualities, and let there be no one creature

equal with another. The reasonable creatures of the earth (or men), let them vex and

weed out one another; and the dwelling places, let them forget

their names. The work of man and his pomp,

let them be defaced. His buildings, let them become caves for

the beasts of the field. Confound her understanding with darkness. For why?

It repenteth me I made man. One while

let her be known, and another while a stranger;

Because she is the bed of an harlot,

and the dwelling place of him that is fallen.

O you heavens, arise! The lower heavens

beneath you, let them serve you. Govern

those that govern; cast down such as

fall. Bring forth with those that increase,

symp, od christeos agtoltorn mirc
simp, ohd kris-TEE-os ay-jee-tol-torn mirk

q tiobl lel. Ton paombd, dilzmo
kwah tii-AHB-el el-el. ton pay-omd, dilz-moh

aspian, od christeos agltoltorn
as-pii-an, ohd kris-TEE-os ag-el-tol-torn

parach asymp. Cordziz, dodpal od
pay-RAK ay-simp. KORD-ziz, dod-pal ohd

fifalz lsmnad; od fargt, bams
fii-falz els-mad; ohd farj-et, bams

omaoas. Conisbra od avavox,
oh-may-OH-as. koh-NIS-bra ohd av-VAY-voks,

tonug. Orscatbl, noasmi tabges
too-nuj. ors-kat-bel, noh-ays-mii tab-jes

levithmong. Unchi omptilb ors. Bagle?
lev-ith-mong. un-kii omp-tilb ors. BAY-gayl?

Moooah olcordziz. Lcapimao
moh-oh-WAH ohl-KORD-ziz. el-kay-PII-may-oh

ixomaxip, odcacocasb gosaa;
iks-oh-MAKS-ip, ohd-kay-KOH-kazb goh-say-ay;

baglen pii tianta ababalond,
BAY-gayl-en pii-ii tii-AN-ta ay-BAY-bay-lond,

odfaorgt telocvovim.
ohd-fay-ORJT tee-LOCH-voh-vee-im.

Madriiax, torzu! Oadriax
MAY-drii-yaks, tor-ZOO! oh-AY-drii-aks

orocha, aboapri. Tabaori
oh-ROH-ka, ay-BOH-ay-prii. tay-BAY-oh-rii

priaz artabas; adrpan corsta
prii-AYZ ar-tay-bas; ay-dir-pan kors-tay

dobix. Yolcam priazi arcoazior,
dob-iks. yol-kam prii-AY-zii ar-koh-ay-zhor,

and destroy the rotten. No place let it remain

in one number. Add and diminish until

the stars be numbered." Arise, move,

and appear before the covenant of his mouth, which

he hath sworn unto us in his justice. Open the mysteries of your creation,

and make us partakers of undefiled knowledge.

odquasb qting. Ripir paaoxt
ohd-kwazb kwah-tinj. rii-PER PAY-ay-okst

sagacor. Uml od prdzar cacrg
say-GAY-kor. um-el ohd purd-zar KAY-kurg

aoiveae cormpt." Torzu, zacar,
ay-oy-VEE-ay kormft." tor-ZOO, ZAY-kayr,

odzamran aspt sibsi butmona, ds
ohd-zam-ran aspt sib-sii but-moh-na, dee-es

surzas tia baltan. Odo cicle qaa,
sur-zas tii-a bal-tan. od-oh sii-kayl kwah-AY-ay,

od ozazma plapli iadnamad.
ohd oz-az-ma play-plii yad-nay-mad.

Further Angelical Phrases

Throughout Dee's journals, there are instances when the Angels slipped into their native tongue when speaking or praying. Dee was usually good about stopping the Angel and asking for a translation of the foreign words, and most of the time the Angel would oblige. This was wonderful, because it expanded the Angelical language beyond what we see in the *Book of Loagaeth* or the forty-eight Angelical Keys.

Unfortunately, the Angels rarely offered word-by-word translations for these random phrases. Instead, the given definitions apply to the entire phrase collectively. Because of this, you will find the individual words of each phrase are given no definitions in the Lexicon. The meaning of the phrase (if the Angels gave one), and page reference to the phrase in Dee's journals, are included in the notes with each word.

Meanwhile, it turns out that most of the random phrases the Angels translated for Dee and Kelley are useful for general prayer, invocation, or evocation. I can't be certain if this was intentional on the part of the Angels, or if it is perhaps just to be expected if one is (after all) talking to an Angel. In any case, I feel it is proper to include these phrases in my Angelical Psalter.

Much Glory

Adgmach Adgmach Adgmach
(aj-mak aj-mak aj-mak)

With humility we call thee, with adoration of the Trinity

Argedco
(ar-jed-koh)

I desire thee, O God

Arphe
(ar-fay)

Your will be done

Gemeganza
(jeem-gan-za)

One (Everlasting) God

Gohed Ascha

(joh-ED ask-a)

Use humility in Prayers to God, or Fervently Pray

Lava Zuraah

(lav-ah zur-AY-ah)

"A strong charge to the wicked to tell the truth."

Life lephe lurfando

(liif leef-ay lur-fan-doh)

Come Lord (and) Have Mercy

O remiges varpax

(oh rem-ii-jes var-paks)

Justice from Divine Power without defect

Padgze

(paj)

What hast thou to do with us? (A challenge to prove one's authority.)

Vors Mabberan

(vorz MAB-er-an)

Fear God (To Stand in Awe of God)

Hoxmarch

(hoks-mark)

Come out of there. (An exorcism.)

Carma geta

(kar-ma jet-a)

An Invitation to Good Angels

In the *Five Books of Mystery*, Dee made some interesting notes about several lines of the first leaf of *Loagaeth*.[3] Apparently, line 21 of the text (side A) is a "preface of the creation and distinction of Angels." The two following lines, 22 and 23, are "parcels of invitations very pleasant to good Angels." Dee notes that all three of these lines "appertain to good Angels." As such, I felt these lines are worthy of inclusion in an Angelical Psalter. They should be useful in opening ceremony.

Most of these words are untranslated, and I have not included them in the Lexicon. (Of course, those with definitions *are* found in the Lexicon.) If Dee left no phonetic notes for a word, I have created a pronunciation based upon my overall understanding of the language. Accents are all taken from Dee's records.

21. Padohómagebs[4] galz arps apá nal Si. gámvagad al pódma gan NA.[5]
pay-doh-OM-aj-ebs galz arps ap-AY nal sii. GAM-vag-ad al POD-ma gan en-ay.

Vr[6] cas nátmaz ándiglon ar'mbu.[7] zántclumbar ar[8] noxócharmah.
owr kas NAT-maz AN-dig-lon ar-em-boo. ZANT-clum-bar ar nox-OH-kar-mah.

Sapoh[9] lan gamnox vxála vors.[10] Sábse cap[11] vax mar vinco.
SAY-foh lan gam-nox yewks-AY-la vorz. SAB-say cap vaks mar vin-ko.

Labandáho nas gampbox arce.[12] Dah gorhahálpstd gascámpho[13] lan
lab-an-DAH-hoh nas gamp-box ars. dah gor-ah-HALP-sted gas-KAM-foh lan

ge. Béfes[14] argédco[15] nax arzulgh[16] orh.[17] Sémhaham[18] vn'cal[19] laf garp oxox.[20]
jee. BEF-as ar-JED-koh naks ar-zulj or. SEM-hah-ham un-kal laf garp oks-oks.

Loangah.[21]
lohn-gah.

22. Ors[22] lah[23] gemphe nahoh ama-natoph des garhul vanseph iuma[24] lat gedos
ors lah jem-fay nah-hoh am-a-nat-of des gar-hul van-sef jay-um lat jed-os

lubah aha last gesto. Vars macom des curad vals mors gaph gemsed
loo-bah ah-hay last jest-oh. varz may-kom des kur-ad vals mors gaf jem-sed

pa[25] campha zednu ábfada máses lófgono. Luruandah[26] lesog iamle
pah kam-fa zed-noo AB-fad-a MAY-ses LOF-gon-oh. lar-van-dah les-og jam-ayl

padel arphe[27] nades gulsad maf gescon lampharsad surem paphe arbasa
pad-el ar-fay nay-des gul-sad maf jes-kon lam-far-sad sur-em paf-ay ar-bas-a

arzusen agsde ghehol max vrdra paf gals macrom finistab gelsaphan
ar-zus-en ag-es-dee jay-ohl maks yer-dra paf gals may-krom fin-is-tab jel-say-fan

asten Vrnah.
as-ten yer-nah.

23. Asch val íamels árcasa árcasan arcúsma íabso gliden paha
ask val jam-els AR-kas-a AR-kas-an ar-KUS-ma jay-bes-oh glii-den pah-ha

pacadúra gebne[28] óscaroh gádne au[29] arua las genost cásme palsi
pak-ad-YEW-ra jeb-nay OS-kar-oh GAD-nay av ar-va las jen-ost KAS-may pal-sii

uran[30] vad gadeth axam pambo cásmala sámnefa gárdomas
yew-ran vad gad-eth aks-am pam-boh KAS-may-la SAM-nef-a GAR-dom-as

árxad pámses gémulch gápes lof lachef ástma vates[31] garnsnas orue
ARKS-ad PAM-ses JEM-ulch GAYP-es lof lak-ef AST-ma vayts garns-nas or-vay

gad garmah sar'quel rúsan gages drusala phímacar aldech oscom lat
gad gar-mah sar-kwel RUS-an gay-jes drew-sal-a fim-ac-ar al-dek os-kom lat

garset panóston.
gar-set pan-OS-ton.

Endnotes

1. See Benjamin Rowe, "A Note on Fifteenth Century Syntax and Interpretation." Online at http://www.madimi.com/syntint.htm.
2. Unfortunately, I have not found any notes on Dee's work indicating when the hard *th* (*this, that*) or soft *th* (*thorn, thigh*) sound is indicated. Lacking further evidence, I have passed over this oversight for now.
3. See *John Dee's Five Books of Mystery*, pp. 312–14.
4. Dee: *Padohómaghebs.*
5. Lord or The Trinity.
6. The name of the letter *L*, but we do not know what *Ur* actually means.
7. Dee: *A pillar of light stood before the book.*
8. That.
9. Compare to *Sapah* (Mighty sounds, Thunders).
10. Over.
11. *Cap* appears to be a root word associated with "Time."
12. Dee: *Arse.*
13. Dee: *Or gáscampho—why didst thou so; as God said to Lucifer. The word hath 64 significations.*
14. Vocative case of the name of *Befafes*, the Heptarchic Prince of Tuesday.
15. Dee: *with humility we call you, with adoration of the Trinity.*
16. Dee: *This is the name of the spirit contrary to Befafes.*
17. Dee: *The spirit Orh is the second in the scale of imperfections of darkness.*
18. Dee: *This word hath 72 significations.*
19. Compare to *Unchi* ("to confound").
20. Compare to *Oxex* ("to vomit").
21. Dee: *Of two syllables.* (Also, compare this word with *Loagaeth*—Speech from God.)
22. Darkness.
23. Compare to *La* ("the first").
24. Compare to *Iumd* ("is called").
25. The name of the letter *B*, but we do not know what *Pa* actually means.
26. Dee: *Larvandah.*
27. "I desire Thee, O God."
28. Dee: *Iebne.* (Dee here indicates the soft *G* or *J* sound.)
29. Dee: *Af.* (Dee here indicates the *V* sound for the *U* in *af*—using the *F* as an approximation.)
30. Elders.
31. Dee: *Bates.* (Dee here indicates the *V* sound for the initial sound of *vates*—using the *B* as an approximation.)

Bibliography

Adler, Aufsteigender. *Soyga/Agyos: Tractatus Astrologico Magicus Aldaraia sive Soyga Vocor, Flight of the Condor—Contemporary Shamanism* (2001) (Online at http://www.kondor.de/enoch/soyga/Soyga_starte.htm.)

Agrippa, Henry C. (edited by Stephen Skinner and trans. by Robert Turner). *The Fourth Book of Occult Philosophy*. Berwick, ME: Ibis Press, 2004.

———. (edited by Donald Tyson and trans. by James Freake). *Three Books of Occult Philosophy*. St. Paul, MN: Llewellyn, 1992.

Allan, Jim, ed. *An Introduction to Elvish*. Hayes, UK: Bran's Head Books, 1978.

Ashe, Steven. *Qabalah of 50 Gates*. Glastonbury, UK: Glastonbury Books, 2006.

Bible, The. King James Version. (See *BibleGateway.com*, http://www.biblegateway.com.)

Bouwsma, William J. *Concordia Mundi: The Career and Thought of Guillaume Postel, 1510–1581*. Cambridge, MA: Harvard University Press, 1957.

Budge, E. A. Wallis, trans. *The Egyptian Book of the Dead: The Papyrus of Ani in the British Museum*. New York: Dover, 1967.

Charles, R. H., ed., and W. R. Morfill, trans. *The Book of the Secrets of Enoch*. Escondido, CA: Book Tree, 1999. First published in 1896. (This is *2 Enoch*, "The Slavonic Book of Enoch.")

Charlesworth, James H., ed. *The Old Testament Pseudepigrapha, vol. 1*. Garden City, NY: Doubleday, 1983. (Includes *1 Enoch*, "The Ethiopic Book of Enoch"; *2 Enoch*, "The Slavonic Book of Enoch"; and *3 Enoch*, "The Hebrew Book of Enoch.")

Clulee, Nicholas H. *John Dee's Natural Philosophy: Between Science and Religion*. London: Routledge, 1988.

Dalley, Stephanie. *Myths from Mesopotamia : Creation, the Flood, Gilgamesh, and Others*. Oxford: Oxford University Press, 1998.

Dan, Joseph. *The Ancient Jewish Mysticism*. Tel Aviv, Israel: MOD Books, 1993.

Davidson, Gustav. *A Dictionary of Angels, Including the Fallen Angels*. Reissue edition. New York: Free Press, 1994.

Dee, John. *A True and Faithful Relation of What Passed For Many Years Between Dr. John Dee [. . .] and Some Spirits*. New York: Magickal Childe, 1992. First published in 1659. Other editions also available. A PDF version is available at *The Magickal Review*, http://www.themagickalreview.org/enochian/tfr.php (accessed March 1, 2010).

Dee, John. (Peterson, Joseph H., ed.). *John Dee's Five Books of Mystery: Original Sourcebook of Enochian Magic*. Boston: Weiser, 2003.

———. *Mysteriorum Libri Quinti: or, Five Books of Mystical Exercises of Dr. John Dee*. Magnum Dyfed, UK: Opus Hermetic Sourceworks, 1985.

Eliade, Mircea. *Shamanism: Archaic Techniques of Ecstasy*. Princeton, NJ: Princeton University Press, 2004.

"Enochian-l" (e-mail list). http://www.gnostica.net/mailman/listinfo/enochian-l.

Ginzberg, Louis. *Legends of the Bible*. New York: Simon and Schuster, 1956.

Godwin, Malcolm. *Angels: An Endangered Species*. New York: Simon and Schuster, 1990.

Harkness, Deborah E. *John Dee's Conversations with Angels: Cabala, Alchemy, and the End of Nature*. Cambridge: Cambridge University Press, 1999.

———. *The Scientific Reformation: John Dee and the Restitution of Nature*. (Unpublished PhD thesis, University of California, Davis, 1994.)

Heidrick, Bill. "The Star Sponge and the Fifty Gates, Two Passages to Attainment." *Thelema Lodge Calendar*, 5/90 e.vol. "From the Out Basket" (copyright 1975 and 1990). Online at http://www.digital-brilliance.com/kab/50gates.txt (accessed March 1, 2010).

Heinlein, Robert. *Stranger in a Strange Land*. New York: Putnam, 1961.

James, Geoffrey. *The Angel Summoner*. St. Paul, MN: Llewellyn, 1998.

———. *The Enochian Magick of Dr. John Dee*. St. Paul, MN: Llewellyn, 1994.

Kaplan, Aryeh. *Sepher Yetzirah: The Book of Creation*. York Beach, ME: Weiser, 1997.

Kircher, Athanasius. *Oedipus Aegyptiacus*. Online at http://www.billheidrick.com/Orpd/AKir/AKOeAeII.htm (accessed March 1, 2010).

Krakovsky, Levi Isaac. *Kabbalah: The Light of Redemption*. Brooklyn, NY: Kabbalah Foundation, 1950.

Laurence, Richard, trans. *The Book of Enoch the Prophet*. Bensenville, IL: Lushena Books, 2001. First published in 1883. Also online at http://www.livius.org/ei-er/enoch/enoch.htm.

Laycock, Donald. *The Complete Enochian Dictionary: A Dictionary of the Angelic Language as Revealed to Dr. John Dee and Edward Kelley*. Revised edition. York Beach, ME: Red Wheel/Weiser, 2001.

Layton, Bentley, trans. *The Gnostic Scriptures*. New York: Doubelday, 1995.

Leitch, Aaron. "The Angelic Alphabet." Found online at http://kheph777.tripod.com/art_angelical_alphabet.pdf.

———. "Gnosticism: Sethian to Valentinian." *Diamond Fire* magazine, Winter 2003. (Also online at http://kheph777.tripod.com/)

———. "Introduction to the Hebrew Alphabet." *Diamond Fire* magazine, Summer 2004. Also online at http://kheph777.tripod.com/.

———. *John Dee's Journals Abridged: The Angelic Language, Loagaeth, the Parts of the Earth and the Great Table of the Earth.* (working title) Unpublished manuscript, 2004.

———. *Secrets of the Magickal Grimoires: The Classical Texts of Magick Deciphered.* St. Paul, MN: Llewellyn, 2005.

———. "Shem haMephoresh: Divine Name of Extension." *Diamond Fire* magazine, Fall 2003. Also online at http://kheph777.tripod.com/.

———, (moderator). *The Solomonic Yahoo Group.* http://groups.yahoo.com/group/solomonic.

Liber Loagaeth. Online at http://www.geocities.com/peripsol/Enoch/5LiberLoagaeth.htm.

Magickal Review, The. http://www.themagickalreview.org/

———., ed. *Enochian Manuscripts Online.* Digital scans of the British Library microfilms: MSS. Sloane 3188, 3189, 3191, and Cotton Appendix MS. XLVI Parts I and II. (Online at http://themagickalreview.org/enochian/)

Mastros, Sara Leanne. "The Fifty Gates of Understanding." Online at http://www.ugcs.caltech.edu/~abszero/mine.html.

Mathers, S. L. MacGregor, ed. and trans. *The Key of Solomon the King.* Mineola, NY: Dover, 2009.

McLean, Adam, ed. *A Treatise on Angel Magic.* San Francisco: Weiser, 2006.

Odeberg, Hugo, trans. and ed. *3 Enoch; or the Hebrew Book of Enoch.* New York: Ktav Publishing, 1973.

Orwell, George. *Nineteen Eighty-Four.* New York: Harcourt, Brace, 1949.

Peterson, Joseph H., ed. *John Dee's Five Books of Mystery.* York Beach, ME: Weiser, 2003.

———. *Liber Loagaeth or Liber Mysteriorum, Sextus et Sanctus*, 1997. Online at http://www.esotericarchives.com/dee/sl3189.htm (accessed

October 22, 2009). The full text of *Loagaeth* can be purchased on CD from this webpage.

———. *Twilit Grotto: Archives of Western Esoterica*. Online at http://www.esotericarchives.com (accessed October 22, 2009).

Radiant, Callisto, ed. *Enochian Linguistics*. Online at http://www.madimi.com/enochlng.htm (accessed October 22, 2009).

Reeds, Jim. "Breakthrough in Renaissance Cryptography: A Book Review." *Cryptologia* magazine, January 1999. Available online at http://findarticles.com/p/articles/mi_qa3926/is_199901/ai_n8848725/ (accessed October 22, 2009).

———. "John Dee and the Magic Tables in the Book of Soyga." In Clucas, Stephen, ed. *John Dee: Interdisciplinary Studies in English Renaissance Thought*. Dordrecht, The Netherlands: Springer, 2006. Also available online at http://www.dtc.umn.edu/~reedsj/soyga (accessed October 22, 2009).

———. "Solved: The Ciphers in Book III of Trithemius's Steganographia," *Cryptologia* magazine, October 1998. Available online at http://www.dtc.umn.edu/~reedsj/steg.html (accessed October 22, 2009).

Reuchlin, Johann. *On the Art of the Kabbalah: De Arte Cabalistica*. Trans. by Martin Goodman and Sarah Goodman. Lincoln, NE: University of Nebraska Press, 1993.

Rogers, William E., and Diana Ervin. *The History of English Phonemes*. Online at http://alpha.furman.edu/~wrogers/phonemes/ (Greenville, SC: Furman University, 2000). See particularly the section entitled "Early Modern English: 1500–1800 C.E.," online at http://alpha.furman.edu/~wrogers/phonemes/phone/eme (accessed October 22, 2009).

Rowe, Benjamin. "A Note on Fifteenth Century Syntax and Interpretation." Originally posted to the "Enochian-l" e-mail list. Also available online at http://www.madimi.com/syntint.htm (accessed March 1, 2010).

Sandars, N. K., trans. *The Epic of Gilgamesh: An English Version with an Introduction*. London: Penguin, 1972.

Scholem, Gershom (trans. by Ralph Manheim). *On the Kabbalah and Its Symbolism*. (Original German title: *Zur Kabbala und ihrer Symbolik*.) New York: Schocken, 1996.

Scrolls From the Dead Sea. Library of Congress exhibition (2002). Online at http://www.loc.gov/exhibits/scrolls/toc.html (accessed October 29, 2009).

Shaffer, Patricia. *DeesPronunciationNotes.RTF*. Online at http://kheph777.tripod.com/DeesPronNotes.doc (accessed March 1, 2010).

Sichos in English.org. *Chasidic Discourses*. Online at http://www.sichosinenglish.org/cgi-bin/calendar?holiday=pesach10441 (accessed March 1, 2010).

Simpson, D. P. *Cassell's Latin Dictionary: Latin-English, English-Latin*. London: Cassell, 1977.

Skinner, Stephen, and David Rankine. *The Practical Angel Magic of Dr. John Dee's Enochian Tables*. Singapore: Golden Hoard Press, 2005.

A Specimen of the Tables or Book of Enoch. Online at http://www.geocities.com/peripsol/Enoch/5SampleTable.html.

Szönyi, György E. *John Dee's Occultism: Magical Exaltation Through Powerful Signs*. Albany, NY: State University of New York Press, 2004.

Tolkien, J. R. R. *The Hobbit*. Boston: Houghton Mifflin, 1997. First published in 1937.

———. *The Lord of the Rings*. Boston: Houghton Mifflin, 1993. First published in 1955.

Typo.cz and DesignIQ.cz. *Diacritics: All You Need to Design a Font with Correct Accents*. Online at http://diacritics.typo.cz/index.php (accessed October 22, 2009).

Tyson, Donald. *Enochian Magic for Beginners: The Original System of Angel Magic*. St. Paul, MN: Llewellyn, 2002. First published in 1997.

———. *The Power of the Word: The Secret Code of Creation*. St. Paul, MN: Llewellyn, 2004.

———. *Tetragrammaton: The Secret to Evoking Angelic Powers and the Key to the Apocalypse*. St. Paul, MN: Llewellyn, 2002.

Vinci, Leo. *GMICALZOMA!: An Enochian Dictionary*. London: Regency Press, 1976.

Warnock, Christopher. *Renaissance Astrology*. Online at http://www.renaissanceastrology.com/ (accessed October 22, 2009).

Westcott, W. Wynn, trans. (Edited by Darcy Kuntz.) *Sepher Yetzirah: The Book of Formation and the Thirty-Two Paths of Wisdom with Hebrew Text*. Sequim, WA: Holmes, 1996.

Wheelock, Frederic M. *Wheelock's Latin, Sixth Edition Revised*. New York: HarperResource, 2005.

Whitaker, William. *Words, Latin to English* (a Latin-to-English dictionary). Online at http://lysy2.archives.nd.edu/cgi-bin/words.exe (accessed October 22, 2009).

Whitby, Christopher. *John Dee's Actions with Spirits: 22 December 1581 to 23 May 1583*. New York: Garland, 1988.

Wilson, Robert Anton. *Prometheus Rising* (reprint edition). Phoenix, AZ: New Falcon, 1992.

Yahsanet Studies. *The Fifty Gates of Understanding* (in *A Study of the Book of Revelation*). Online at http://www.yashanet.com/studies/revstudy/fifty-gates.htm (accessed March 1, 2010).

Yates, Frances A. *The Rosicrucian Enlightenment*. London: Routledge, 2001.

Zalewski, Pat. *Golden Dawn Enochian Magic*. St. Paul, MN: Llewellyn, 1990.

———. *The Kabbalah of the Golden Dawn*. St. Paul, MN: Llewellyn, 1993.

Original Manuscripts

The following manuscripts are included for reference. All of these manuscripts can be found, under the manuscript numbers given here, at the British Museum in London:

Cotton Appendix 46, parts 1–2 (Published as *A True and Faithful Relation . . .*, Casaubon.)

"Sloane MS 3188" (Published as *John Dee's Five Books of Mystery*, Peterson.)

"Sloane MS 3189" (Kelley's handwritten copy of the *Book of Loagaeth*. See Peterson and *The Magickal Review*.)

"Sloane MS 3190" (A copy of *A True and Faithful Relation . . .*, unpublished.)

"Sloane MS 3191" (Dee's grimoire. Published as *The Enochian Magick of Dr. John Dee*, James.)

Further Reading

These texts also come highly recommended in the study of general Enochiana and the occult world of Dr. John Dee and Sir Edward Kelley:

Chase, Steven, trans. *Angelic Spirituality: Medieval Perspectives on the Ways of Angels*. New York: Paulist Press, 2002.

Clucas, Stephen, ed. *John Dee: Interdisciplinary Studies in English Renaissance Thought*. Dordrecht, The Netherlands: Springer, 2006. (Includes Jim Reeds' "John Dee and the Magic Tables in the Book of Soyga.")

Eco, Umberto. *The Search for the Perfect Language*. Oxford, UK: Blackwell, 1997.

Farmer, S. A. *Syncretism in the West: Pico's 900 Theses (1486): The Evolution of Traditional Religious and Philosophical Systems*. Tempe, AZ: MRTS, 1998.

French, Peter J. *John Dee: The World of an Elizabethan Magus*. London: Routledge, 1987.

Karr, Don. *Notes on Editions of Sepher Yetzirah in English* (1991, 2007). Online at http://www.digital-brilliance.com/kab/karr/syie.pdf.

Pseudo-Dionysius, the Areopagite. (Translated by Colm Luibheid.) *Pseudo-Dionysius: The Complete Works*. New York: Paulist Press, 1987.

VanderKam, James C. *Enoch: A Man for All Generations*. Columbia, SC: University of South Carolina Press, 1995.

Woolley, Benjamin. *The Queen's Conjurer: The Science and Magic of Dr. John Dee, Adviser to Queen Elizabeth I*. New York: Henry Holt, 2001.

Index